PSALMS 1–59

PSALMS 1–59

HANS-JOACHIM
KRAUS

PSALMS 1–59

A Continental Commentary

Translated by

Hilton C. Oswald

FORTRESS PRESS
MINNEAPOLIS

PSALMS 1–59
A Continental Commentary

First Fortress Press edition 1993

Translated from the 5th edition of *Psalmen*, 1. Teilband, *Psalmen 1–59*, published by Neukirchener Verlag, Neukirchen-Vluyn, in 1978 in the Biblischer Kommentar series.

Library of Congress Cataloging-in-Publication Data

Kraus, Hans-Joachim.
   [Psalmen. Teilbd. 1. English]
   Psalms 1–59 : a continental commentary / Hans-Joachim Kraus ;
translated by Hilton C. Oswald. — 1st Fortress Press ed.
     p. cm.
   Originally published: Minneapolis : Augsburg Pub. House, 1988.
   Includes bibliographical references and indexes.
   ISBN 0-8006-9503-8 :
   1. Bible. O.T. Psalms I–LIX—Commentaries. I. Title.
[BS1430.3.K713 1993]
223'.2077—dc20
                                          93-26900
                                             CIP

Manufactured in the U.S.A.   AF 1-9503

97   96   95   94   93   1   2   3   4   5   6   7   8   9   10

In Memory of
my wife
Ingrid
née Kossmann
born April 7, 1921   died January 11, 1978

Contents

Translator's Preface

The reader and student of the Hans-Joachim Kraus commentary on the Psalms is surely impressed with the penetrating and wide-ranging scholarship of the author, but the translator is from page one obsessed with the fear that many of Dr. Kraus's observations and interpretations can be stated adequately only in German. Only little by little does he find English words and phrases and combinations of ideas that can contain and transmit the full thought and flavor of Dr. Kraus's discourses. The present work is offered in the hope that this great commentary will now be accessible to a far wider circle of readers.

The English biblical text of the Psalms commented on represents a rather literal translation of Dr. Kraus's own scholarly translation of the Hebrew text, in which he too strives for a rather literal rendering of the text as emended. This prepares the way for the commentary.

Citations of biblical texts other than the specific psalm under discussion are usually from the Revised Standard Version of the Bible, copyright 1946, 1952, and 1971 by the Division of Christian Education of the National Council of Churches. A few quotations go back to the King James Version to incorporate that version's special emphasis.

The frequent citations from the Latin commentary on the Psalms by John Calvin are for convenience and consistency quoted from the English translation by James Anderson (Eerdmans, 1949). Although somewhat Victorian in punctuation and literary style, this translation nicely transmits Calvin's thought and emphasis. All other English translations of quotations (e.g., of Augustine, Luther, Melanchthon, Delitzsch) are the translator's own.

HILTON C. OSWALD
St. Louis, Missouri

9

Introduction

§1. The Name of the Book and Its Place in the Canon

1. Among the Hebrew- or Aramaic-speaking Jews the "Psalter," containing 150 psalms, appears under the title תהלים "Songs of Praise," "Songs of Adoration," "Hymns." In addition to this designation, we also find the titles ספר תהלים, תלים, תלין, or ספר תלין. These names are also attested by the church fathers (C. Steuernagel, *Einleitung in das Alte Testament*, §152, 1). The preferred title, תהלים, is a peculiar special formation from תהלה, the technical term for psalms of the hymn-type (cf. §4, No. 7, and §6). For the masculine plural form, cf. Ges-K §87n,o. "Compared with the otherwise usual form, תהלות," this form very likely would "express a special meaning of the word that is to be reserved for the title of the book" (R. Kittel). Accordingly, תהלים is an exclusive name for the "Song Collection," for the "Hymnal" of the 150 psalms.

However, the concept תהלים is not at all suitable to serve as a general title that is exhaustive and at all adequate for the contents of the 150 psalms. The title probably originated in a time when the Psalter was used and understood primarily as the "hymnal of the Jewish community." It is interesting to note, however, that in earlier times the title תפלות = "prayers" was preferred (cf. Ps. 72:20). For תפלה, cf. §4, 8. This title takes into consideration especially the songs and prayers of lament which make up the real basic stock of the Psalter. In earlier times, therefore, the Psalter was primarily thought of as a collection of prayers. But even then, if we should adopt the two names תהלים and תפלות as cotitles, the complex contents of the Psalter would not be comprehended. We have only to think of the didactic sections that would in no way be represented by either of the titles.

Finally, in the promotion of the chief designations to form a title, we must not overlook the term מזמר. It is witnessed 57 times in psalm headings and obviously must have been a preferred name for the individual psalm (cf. §4, 2).

11

2. The Greek textual tradition in the codexes of the Septuagint presents the following picture concerning the titles. The earliest designation that can be documented is ψαλμοί in Codex B and in Luke 24:44. At the same time, in Codex B as well as in Luke 20:42 and Acts 1:20 we find the title βίβλος ψαλμῶν ("Book of Psalms"). Which Hebrew word was translated with ψαλμός? That question has been raised again and again. An examination of correspondences shows that the translation מזמר = ψαλμός is documented most frequently. It follows that Gk took the term מזמר—which occurs 57 times as a title of individual psalms in the Hebrew text—as a characteristic possibility for designating the entire collection.

Another title is preferred by Gk^A. The collection of 150 psalms is called ψαλτήριον (τῷ Δαυίδ, Gk^R). But ψαλτήριον obviously corresponds to the Hebrew term נבל, which denotes a musical instrument. We could understand ψαλτήριον to be the name of a collection of songs with stringed accompaniment. The current term "Psalter" has its origin in the titles of Gk^A.

3. The position of the Psalter in the Hebrew canon presents a perplexing picture in the various areas of text tradition. The familiar printed editions in most cases place the Psalter at the head of the Kethubim (the third, final section of the Hebrew Bible) and thus follow the tradition of the Jews of central Europe. The order varies between Psalms-Job-Proverbs and Psalms-Proverbs-Job. But if we go back to the earliest time in the canon tradition that is still recognizable today, we find that the order is extraordinarily various. In the Palestinian text tradition, Chronicles seems to have stood at the head of the Kethubim. Witnesses are Codex L, Michael ben 'Uzziel, and the manuscripts of the Masora of Palestine. The Spanish Jews follow this tradition, that is, in which the Psalter appears in the second place in the Kethubim. Still other principles of arrangement were operative among the Jews of the Eastern Dispersion. From the Talmud (B. Bat. 14b) we learn that also the book of Ruth, among others, was placed directly before the Psalter. Obviously the ancestry of the psalmist David was especially to be emphasized.

4. In the canon of the MT the books Psalms, Job, and Proverbs form a characteristic group within the Kethubim. A peculiar accent system is used exclusively in these books. The special characteristic of this system is that in addition to the 'atnah we also find the 'ōlēh wĕyōrēd. While the 'atnah appears as the divider between verses only in shorter sentences, the 'ōlēh wĕyōrēd serves as the chief divider in longer sentence structure.

The 150 psalms of the Psalter have different numbers in Gk than in MT. A table will show the differences:

MT	Gk	MT	Gk
Psalms 1-8	= Psalms 1-8	Ps. 116:10-19	= Psalm 115
Psalms 9-10	= Psalm 9	Psalms 117-146	= Psalms 116-145
Psalms 11-113	= Psalms 10-112	Ps. 147:1-11	= Psalm 146
Psalms 114-115	= Psalm 113	Ps. 147:12-20	= Psalm 147
Ps. 116:1-9	= Psalm 114	Psalms 148-150	= Psalms 148-150

Accordingly, Gk contracts Psalms 9 and 10, and later also Psalms 114 and 115, into one psalm each. In addition, at the end Gk also preserves an additional Psalm 151, in which 1 Sam. 16:1-14 and 1 Sam. 17 are freely used. But already in the oldest tradition this additional product is consistently labeled as ἔξωθεν ἀριθμοῦ ("supernumerary"). Psalm 151 is an example of the later offshoots of psalm writing as we see it in the noncanonical collections of the

Thanksgiving Hymns from Qumran, the "Psalms of Solomon," and the "Odes of Solomon."

For the variations in the order and numeration of the psalm manuscripts found in Qumran, cf. *RB* 63 (1956) 59. Also cf. J. A. Sanders, "Psalm 151 in 11 QPSS*," *ZAW* 75 (1963) 73-85.

§2. The Masoretic Text and the Ancient Translations

1. In contrast to the commentaries of B. Duhm and H. Gunkel, who in their treatment of the Masoretic text (MT) have gone beyond the extreme boundaries of criticism (J. J. Stamm, *ThR* NF 3 [1955] 16), the present commentary has a good deal of confidence in MT and tries to explore the text-critical possibilities of the transmission of the Hebrew Bible to their fullest extent. The treatment of the text approaches that of the commentary by H. Schmidt, but it is not able to follow the conservative procedure as it appears, for instance, in the translations of A. Weiser and F. Nötscher. The reasons will be given later. For the present, a survey will indicate the special position of the text-critical procedure adopted in this commentary. Indeed, it is striking especially in the commentaries of the Psalter how drastically the basic positions and methods of treating the text differ from one another. Whereas B. Duhm and H. Gunkel show us the extreme limits of critical text research, we must list as the opposite extreme the strictly conservative position of B. D. Eerdmans, W. E. Barnes, and A. Cohen. Eerdmans everywhere grants preeminence to MT—even at the risk of unintelligible malformations. Modern views of metrical structure are rejected. As a result the reconstruction of the original Hebrew text can take place unburdened by every pressure of form. Cf. B. D. Eerdmans, "Essays on Masoretic Psalms," *OTS* 1 (1942) 105-300; "The Hebrew Book of Psalms," *OTS* 4 (1947). But A. Cohen sets up this procedure in his foreword: "The commentary is invariably based on the received Hebrew text. When this presents difficulties, the most probable translation and interpretation are suggested, without resort to textual emendation" (A. Cohen, *The Psalms,* vol. 5).

Between the two extremes exemplified on the one side by B. Duhm and H. Gunkel, and on the other side by B. D. Eerdmans, W. E. Barnes, and A. Cohen, the newer commentaries, among which A. Weiser and F. Nötscher lean toward the conservative view, have various tendencies. A. Schulz develops an independent method in his preference for the Masoretic tradition ("Kritisches zum Psalter," *ATA* 12.1 [1932]; "Psalmen-Fragen," *ATA* 14.1 [1940]). Also I. Engnell, in his article "Psaltaren," *Svenskt Bibliskt Uppslagsverk* (1952, cols. 787ff.), expresses himself as very negative over against all text-critical ventures in the Psalter. In connection with his understanding of tradition, he recommends extreme reticence.

But now the unlimited confidence in MT, and therefore also the conservative position over against the Hebrew text, has been subjected to question from various quarters. The problematic nature of MT was first recognized in connection with observations about psalms with multiple transmission. The following correspondences are involved:

Psalm 18	= 2 Sam. 22
Psalm 14	= Psalm 53
Psalm 70	= Ps. 40:12-16
Psalm 108	= Ps. 57:7-11 and Ps. 60:5-12

In the numerous divergences and variations of these double texts it was first recognized how unreliable the Hebrew text tradition is in the area of the Psalms. Already in the year 1633 J. Morinus, in his *Exercitiones biblicae de hebraei graecique textus sinceritate,* developed two theses: (*a*) the original Hebrew text is so much interpolated and so shot through with mistakes that it can no longer serve as source and norm of biblical study; (*b*) only the Septuagint transmits the reliable material for an approximate reconstruction of the "original text" (*Urtext*), which is basically inaccessible. It is interesting to discover that H. Herkenne in his *Psalmenkommentar* (1936) expounds almost the same theses. In more recent times, he champions a critical departure from MT and a preference for Gk. He says: "The Masoretic Text (MT) in its form after the rise of Christianity swarms with countless unfortunate distortions" (20). "Accordingly, for the emendation of the text of the Psalter we are dependent mainly on the old translations, which are based on a textual form older than the Masoretic. Here the Septuagint (Gk) is the first to be considered" (21). This tendency to prefer Gk may also be observed in the commentaries of W. O. E. Oesterly, E. Podechard, and E. J. Kissane—although with greater restraint.

To be sure, it is correct clearly to expose the manifold injuries of the Hebrew text of the Masora. But we certainly should consider many other ways of restoring the hypothetical original text before we yield the superiority to one of the old translations or, with the help of the old translations and free conjectures, undertake strong assaults on the transmitted text.

2. The mistakes in MT that come again and again are well known (cf. the large collection of materials by F. Delitzsch, *Die Lese- und Schreibfehler im Alten Testament* [1920]). There are, among other things, exchanges of letters, transpositions of letters, departures from the *plene* style, haplography, dittography, and copyists' errors that entail greater complications. All these mistakes and injuries of the transmission of the text in MT are constantly observable also in the Psalter. Additionally, there are glosses and supplements that have been added to the text as explanations or extensions. Also variant readings, above the line or below it, that copyists inadvertently entered as part of the text can be pointed out. A complete confusion of the verse sequence is observable in Psalm 87. We cannot here deal with the method of treating these textual errors (cf. M. Noth, *The OT World* [1966] 349-363; E. Würthwein, *Der Text des Alten Testaments* [1973[4]]). We should, however, discuss the special text-critical considerations and possibilities of modern interpretation of the psalms. But before these questions can be dealt with, we must raise and at least in outline answer the constantly restated question of the extent to which laws of prosody entitle us to make corrections *metri causa* (in view of the meter). The metrical questions are dealt with in §5. We need here merely refer to the extensive treatment of the pertinent facts provided there. But in any case we must now already establish the following: (a) According to the rules of the rhythmic system that can serve as an appropriate explanation of psalm composition, the shortest metrical unit has two accents, the longest four. Thus, texual criticism has an obligation to investigate the correctness of parts of verses that go beyond this necessary limit or fall short of it. (b) If in the arrangement of verses a certain meter (e.g., 3 + 3) should turn out to be dominant, then those verses that do not conform to the dominating meter are to be investigated critically and to be made to conform to the dominant pattern, if possible. (c) But under all circumstances, we must avoid carrying through a particular metrical principle or scheme by whatever means. Elasticity and accommodation to the constantly new data of the individual songs must be the governing attitudes.

3. Once we have fully made use of all the traditional methods of text criticism respecting the Masoretic text and its variants, we must bring to bear several points of view which in more recent times have merited constantly increasing attention. Form criticism has recognized the characteristic stylistic patterns and forms of expression of the language of the Psalms. A wealth of traditionally shaped, conventional formulations was identified and lucidly presented (cf., above all, H. Gunkel and J. Begrich, *EinlPs*). Some advances have been made toward developing a thematic structure of the language of the Psalms. Now it would be appropriate further to develop and critically to apply this thematic structure of psalm language. Considering the type (*Gattung*) of a given psalm (cf. §6) and considering both the context and the *parallelismus membrorum,* words and half-verses misshapen in the Hebrew text tradition can be conjectured on the basis of the thematic structure of the expected and appropriate conventional psalm language (cf., e.g., the comment on Ps. 4:3). The possibilities of a text-critical thematic structure, especially in the Psalter, have not as yet been disclosed or exhausted by a long way. Naturally, here too we must guard against every rule of thumb and all rigidity. There will always have to be room for a new and unexpected formulation—also in the obscure and hitherto inexplicable passages. Besides, "the thematic structure of the language of the Psalms" would also have to include the ancient Near Eastern psalm literature, or at least take cognizance of it. It could well happen that a unique, heretofore inexplicable formulation or expression of thought would find in the ancient Near Eastern literature a clarifying explanation that restores the meaning. Especially the texts from Ras Shamra, ancient Ugarit, are giving many new impulses for conjecture. Sometimes difficult or rare Hebrew words can be interpreted from Ugaritic poetry (cf., above all, Psalm 68). But even here criticism has its limits. W. F. Albright goes too far in drawing Psalm 68 into the world of Old Canaanite lyrics, gauging it with foreign measuring sticks (cf. W. F. Albright, "A Catalogue of Early Hebrew Lyric Poems: Psalm 68," *HUCA* 23, 1 [1950/51] 1-39). We must be very careful to test whether new possibilities of understanding are disclosed for individual words and formulations from the Ugaritic area. We must always hear the psalm in its entirety to see whether and how the new interpretation finds a place in its formal structure and in its contextual flow.

4. In the text-critical process also the old translations naturally find their proper place. But we must reject the preference on principle of Gk, for instance, over against MT and reject in general a premature resort to the old translations. In the area of Hebrew and ancient Near Eastern traditions, every other way and path ought to be pursued before we take ship to the opposite shore and so from a new perspective allow ourselves to draw conclusions a posteriori regarding the probable "original text" involved. Textual criticism shows that especially the Septuagint (Gk) deserves strong recognition in the process of reconstructing the hypothetical original text. In *Psalmi cum Odis,* volume 10, published in 1931, A. Rahlfs collated the manuscripts and convincingly localized the three great forms of the text: those of Lower Egypt, Upper Egypt, and the West (cf. 21ff.). J. W. Wevers reports concerning newly found fragments (cf. *ThR* 22 [1954] 131ff., 135ff.). In the present commentary the variants in Gk that depart from MT are given consideration even when priority was conceded to MT. But we have hardly begun to deal with the problem of extracting the characteristic features of the statements of the Septuagint respecting its particular content and its peculiar way of expressing itself. Such an investigation would be of the

highest importance for the surprisingly frequent citation of the Psalms in the NT. Closest to Gk in text-critical value are the fragments from Aquila (α'), Symmachus (σ'), and Theodotion (θ'), as well as, among the daughter translations of Gk, the Old Latin, the earliest traces of which are to be sought in Northern Africa. The text-critical value of the Peshitta (S) is disputed. The basic discussions of L. Haefeli, "Die Peschitta des Alten Testaments," ATA 11.1 (1927) 35-40, have been extended notably by A. Vogel (cf. A. Vogel, "Studien zum Pešitta-Psalter," *Biblica 32* [1951] 32-56, 198-231, 336-363, 481-502). Vogel pays special attention to the "extra-Masoretic correspondences" between Gk and S. He comes to the conclusion that the Syriac text proves to be "in a general way reliable over against the Hebrew original and independent of Gk." It is true that S is no longer extant in the original form in a number of passages; also cf. F. Zimmermann, "The Text of Psalms in the Peshitta," *JTS* 41 (1940) 44-46. The Aramaic Targum of the Psalter (Targ) proves to be not without worth in textual criticism. Even though paraphrasing expansion and the elaboration in the manner of the haggadah produce an obscuring effect, the Hebrew original twinkles through in individual passages.

But finally, the *Psalterium* of Jerome (Hier), translated from the Hebrew (*iuxta hebraicam veritatem*), deserves special recognition. Originating ca. A.D. 391, this ancient translation is close to MT. Still, Jerome did not disengage himself from the Old Latin, and on the other hand also contacts with θ' and σ' are demonstrable (cf. J. H. Marks, *Der textkritische Wert des Psalterium Hieronymi iuxta Hebraeos* [1956].

5. Beside many corrections and a number of conjectures, obscure and inexplicable passages will remain. That is unavoidable. In this matter the limits of our momentary ability to comprehend must not be concealed.

§3. The Psalter as a Collection

1. The Hebrew Psalter is divided into five books. The extent of these books we can ascertain exactly, for each book always closes with a doxological formulation. An overview of the five books and their doxological closing formulations yields the following picture:

Book I (Psalms 1-41)

Ps. 41:13   ברוך יהוה אלהי ישראל מעולם ועד העולם
אמן אמן

Book II (Psalms 42-72)

Ps. 72:19   ברוך יהוה [אלהים] אלהי ישראל עשה נפלאות לבדו
וברוך שם כבודו לעולם וימלא כבודו את־כל־הארץ
אמן אמן

Book III (Psalms 73-89)

Ps. 89:51   ברוך יהוה לעולם
אמן אמן

Book IV (Psalms 90-106)

Ps. 106:48   ברוך יהוה אלהי ישראל מן־העולם ועד העולם
ואמר כל־העם אמן

Book V (Psalms 107-150)

Ps. 150:6   כל הנשמה תהלל יה

If we compare these doxological closing formulas, we notice that Ps. 150:6 seems entirely out of place. We could ask whether the canonical collection of the five books really closed with Psalm 150 at one time. This question suggests itself when we read the last verse of Psalm 135, which sounds like a doxological closing formula:

ברוך יהוה מציון שכן ירושלם

But even this "closing formula" (if we may consider it such at all) does not entirely correspond to the closing formulas of Pss. 41:41; 72:19; 89:51; 106:48. In the last section of the Psalter difficulties are to be noted that will reappear also in another connection. However, skepticism about the significance of the doxologies as closing acts of praise, as C. T. Niemeyer expresses it in his dissertation, is not well-founded (cf. C. T. Niemeyer, "Het probleem van de rangschikking der psalmen," Diss. Groningen [1950]).

But what significance does the division of the Psalter into five books have? Again and again we encounter the explanation that in the process of canonization a counterpart to the Pentateuch (תורה) was fashioned. This statement certainly can refer only to the formal division and the technical process of canonization. If we were to construe an analogy in substance between the books of the Pentateuch and those of the Psalter, the results would show a series of absurd correspondences (contrary to J. Dahse, *Das Rätsel des Psalters gelöst* [1927]). But if we now go back beyond the formal division of the Psalter into five books and search for points of view governing the formation and arrangement of the collection of the Psalter, we shall be faced with complicated problems that have to be dealt with while disregarding the division into five books. Partial compilations can be discerned that in no way coincide with those of the five books.

2. Among these partial compilations, the so-called "Elohistic Psalter" undoubtedly occupies a leading position. In Psalms 42-83 the consistent use of אלהים as the name for God is striking. This extensive partial compilation overlaps the division into books and must be viewed without regard to the closing doxology in Ps. 72:19. The division into books definitely proves to be secondary, also in other connections. If we think of the "Elohistic Psalter" as a separate component, a partial compilation within the chief collection of the Psalter, then it becomes apparent: (a) that the "Elohistic Psalter" is put together from three sources; and (b) that it was the compiler of the Elohistic part of the Psalter who undertook the consistent use of אלהים as the name of God. For one thing, as far as the sources of the "Elohistic Psalter" are concerned, the following groups (discernible from the titles), presented according to a well-planned arrangement, can be identified:

A. Psalms of the sons of Korah, לבני־קרח   (Psalms 42-49):

Psalms 42-45	משכיל
Psalm 46	שיר
Psalms 47-49	מזמור

Only partially were psalms from the לבני־קרח source incorporated in the "Elohistic Psalter." From the hymnal of the Korahites also Psalms 84-88 are derived. Or is a second "Korahite source" involved there? For the Korahites, see Ezra 2:41 and Neh. 7:44. Are these postexilic groups of singers and transmitters of Old Israelite psalms the descendants of the preexilic cultic prophets (S. Mowinckel, *Psalmenstudien III: Kultprophetie und kultprophetische Psalmen* [1923])? This question is to be dealt with later. Also cf. H. Gese, *Zur Geschichte der Kultsänger am zweiten Tempel: Abraham unser Vater;*

17

Festschrift für O. Michel (1963) 222-234 = "Vom Sinai zum Zion," *BEvTh* 64 (1974) 147-158.

B. Psalms of David, לדוד	(Psalms 51-65;	67; 68-71):
	Psalms 52-55	משכיל
	Psalms 56-60	מכתם
	Psalms 62-65	מזמור
	67-68	
	Psalms 69-71	without precise classification
	Psalm 72	לשלמה (appendix)

A closing formula that brings to a close the group of Psalms of David collected by the "Elohistic compiler" is found in Ps. 72:20, כלו תפלות דוד בן־ישי. For other psalms of David not in the "Elohistic Psalter," see below.

C. Psalms of Asaph, לאסף (Psalms 73-83):

Also Psalm 50 is a psalm לאסף. Very likely this psalm assumed its present place at or after the completion of the entire Psalter.

Concerning the dating: ". . . the Elohistic redaction of Psalms 42-83, which already presupposes the existence of individual collections such as Psalms 42-50; 51-72; 73-83 and their coalescence, must still belong to the time of the origin of the Chronicler's work, for group A psalms, *libne qorah*, occur as an appendix in Psalms 84f.; 87; 88, and only Psalm 88 reflects group B, and Psalm 89 Group C2. Thereby we have achieved a highly desirable limit for dating the time of origin of the psalms in Books II and III" (H. Gese, *Zur Geschichte der Kultsänger am zweiten Tempel: Abraham unser Vater; Festschrift für O. Michel* [1963] 234 = "Vom Sinai zum Zion," *BEvTh* 64 [1974], 158; on the dating of the individual stages, cf. H. Gese).

Since the "Elohistic Psalter" emerges clearly from its context in the middle of the entire Psalter as the largest partial compilation, we must now investigate Psalms 1-41 and Psalms 84-150 to see whether here, too, compilations of groups of hymns and prayers are demonstrable. First, a conspicuous position is occupied by a group of psalms of David, Psalms 3-41, which are to be distinguished from the לדוד Psalms in the "Elohistic Psalter." Obviously, we are here dealing with a source that was not available to the Elohistic compiler or one that he did not draw on. We must note that, in contrast to the psalms of David in the "Elohistic Psalter," Psalms 3-41 lack a systematic arrangement. Accordingly, the grouping that we observed in the "Elohistic Psalter" (see above) is the work of the Elohistic compiler. Psalm 33, the only one of Psalms 3-41 that has no heading, may have intruded into the compilation. On the other hand, we might ask whether Psalm 2, which has been transmitted without a heading, should not be counted among the psalms of David. But Psalm 1 has the character of a proem. The conditions of the transmission of Psalms 84-150 are difficult to fathom. Though individual groups are demonstrable, definite characterization (except in the case of Psalms 120-134) is lacking. An attempt to produce an overview would yield the following picture:

A. Appendix to the "Elohistic Psalter" (Psalms 84-89):

Psalms 84; 85; 87; 88	לבני־קרח
Psalm 86	לדוד
Psalm 89	לאיתם

These psalms did not undergo a change of the name of God. Perhaps also Psalms 90 and 91 belong to this appendix.

B. Collection of hymns in which Yahweh is praised as the king and judge of the world (Psalms 93-99). This collection is above all characterized by the hymnic exclamation יהוה מלך in Psalms 93; 96; 97; 99.

C. "Alleluia Psalms" (Psalms 104-106; 111-117; 135; 146-150). Here we are dealing with psalms that either begin with the exclamation of praise הללו־יה (Psalms 111; 112) or close with it (Psalms 104; 105; 114-116; 135) or even open and close with it (Psalms 106; 113; 117; 146-150).

D. Hymns that have as their heading either שיר המעלות or שיר למעלות (Psalms 120-134). For the meaning of שיר המעלות cf. §4, 3.

E. Additional psalms of David (Psalms 101; 103; 108-110; 138-145).

It is difficult to discern the perspective according to which these groups were collected. Also, some psalms that lie between the collections or entered through intrusion remain unexplained. Finally, it will hardly be possible to trace the process by which the partial compilations gradually came together. In this matter research encounters definite limits. We will have to content ourselves with listing the partial compilations and with as precise a description as possible of the coordination of the individual groups in the Psalter as a whole.

3. C. Westermann has approached the theme of "The Compilation of the Psalter." He has proceeded from the observation that at least two compilations are discernible and that these have been compiled from the viewpoint of their individual types: the laments, whose form and "Sitz im Leben" reflect a uniform viewpoint (cf. H.-J. Kraus, BK XX, 8ff.), and the collection of *hodayoth,* which contains psalms of praise. Cf. C. Westermann, "Zur Sammlung des Psalters," *Forschung am Alten Testament,* ThB 24 (1964) 336f. Moreover, since we can with certainty recognize in the Psalter a similar, once independent, and uniformly cast collection in Psalms 120-134 (*ma'alot* psalms), the question arises whether similar combinations can be discerned in the fabric of the psalms of David (Psalms 3-41), the "Elohistic Psalter," etc. Westermann arrives at the following conclusions, and they are to be viewed and understood in the framework of Gunkel's classification of types or possibly Westermann's own observations: "the lament of the individual, the most frequent type occurring in the Psalter, is concentrated entirely in the first half of the book of Psalms, namely in the two large collections, Psalms 3-41 and 51-72; to this also the small collection, Psalms 140-143, is later added" (341f.). "Larger groups of psalms of praise we meet only in the second half of the Psalter; except for Psalms 120-134 and 140-143, all collections after Psalm 90 contain psalms of praise" (342). "In the smaller collections, the psalms of praise often function as the conclusion of a collection; thus the doxologies at the end of the five books of psalms (Pss. 14:14; 72:19; 89:4, 106:48; 150), thus Psalm 134 (the collection 120-134), 117 (111-118), 100 (93-99), 145 (?)(140-143)" (342). "The royal psalms . . . occur only as additions throughout the Psalter" (342). Without question, these observations and conclusions carry a great deal of weight. But the determination of form groups (*Gattungen*) must certainly be modified (cf. §6).

C. Barth has investigated the principle that is determinative in the arrangement of the Psalter; he has studied the "concatenation" of the psalms, especially in Book I (Psalms 1-41). Cf. C. Barth, "Concatenatio im ersten Buch des Psalters," *Wort und Wirklichkeit: Festschrift für E. L. Rapp* (1976) 30-40.

4. When did the Psalter as a collection come into existence? To what time are we to assign the completion of the entire canonical book? There are three considerations for determining the terminus ad quem: (a) The pseudepigraphal Psalms of Solomon originated between 63 and 30 B.C. (cf. Eissfeldt,

Introduction [1965] 612). This apocryphal collection of psalms presupposes the completion of the Psalter. (b) In 1 Macc. 7:17 (about 100 B.C.) Ps. 79:2-3 is quoted. (c) The Prologue of Sirach already takes a three-part OT canon for granted: We read, literally: Πολλῶν καὶ μεγάλων ἡμῖν διὰ τοῦ νόμου καὶ τῶν προφητῶν καὶ τῶν ἄλλων τῶν κατ' αὐτοὺς ἠκολουθηκότων δεδομένων . . . ("Whereas many great things [RSV, teachings] have been given to us through the law and the prophets and the others that followed them . . ."). That the third part of the canon here mentioned included the collection of the psalms can hardly be doubted. Accordingly, we could set the time of origin at about 190 B.C. Thus the destination point of the development would have to be about 200 B.C. (cf. also H. Gunkel and J. Begrich, *EinlPs* 438). With this conclusion the dating of the composition of the Psalms in the time of the Maccabees, as represented above all by B. Duhm, is excluded (cf. also §7). It is more difficult to determine the terminus a quo of the collection and the canonization of the Psalter. Very likely a rather long period of time has to be assumed. Already in the sixth and fifth centuries B.C. the first partial collections may have originated. The "Elohistic" collector seems to have affinity with the circles of the Priestly source. There are many evidences that the entire Psalter was complete and available as early as 300 B.C. For an attempt to provide a more exact dating, cf. H. Gese, *Zur Geschichte der Kultsänger am zweiten Tempel: Abraham unser Vater; FS O. Michel* (1963) 222-234. Problematic is the attempt to derive from the attaining of a more clear picture of the Korahites significant results concerning their traditions, theology, and datable poetry (against G. Wanke, *Die Zionstheologie der Korachiten,* BZAW 97 [1966]).

     5. Again and again the question has been asked: For what purpose was the Psalter collected? This question is not stated quite correctly. In the first place we have to make it clear to ourselves that the transmission and collection of individual psalms exercised a certain pressure toward bringing together and arranging all the partial collections and groups of songs. The formation of a canon is not primarily determined by the customary tendency authoritatively to standardize and circumscribe. It is above all a compulsion that arises from tradition itself that strives to combine to a unified whole the profusion of treasures transmitted in disparate partial collections. It is a natural assumption that a central place of collection and a transmission group acting jointly may be presupposed. Such presuppositions are given in the postexilic temple in Jerusalem. Here the treasury of older hymns and prayers of Israel must have impressed itself anew on the worshiping congregation. The designations תהלים and תפלות (cf. §1) indicate that the collected psalms played a leading role both in the singing in corporate worship and also in private prayers. The Psalter could therefore be called "the hymnal and prayer book of the postexilic congregation." Of course, here we have to take into consideration that this postexilic congregation in some cases carried on a highly independent adoption of the older hymns and prayers. Thus, for instance, Psalm 30, originally a hymn of thanksgiving "by an individual," now was intoned as a hymn of public worship at the festival of the dedication of the temple. Psalm 92 was sung on the Sabbath, and Psalm 29 (according to the LXX) on the last day of the Feast of Tabernacles. Cf. further: the LXX of Psalms 24 (23); 48 (47); 94 (93); and 93 (92).

     We still cannot observe clearly to what extent the Psalter was also drawn on for lections in the worship of the Jewish community. N. H. Snaith ("The Triennial Cycle and the Psalter," *ZAW* [1933] 302-307) and A. Guilding ("Some Obscured Rubrics and Lectionary in the Psalter," *JTS* Ns 3 [1952]

41-55) take a three-year cycle for granted. But C. T. Niemeyer, with rather cogent arguments, has objected (*Het probleem van de rangschikking der psalmen,* 79ff.). A new approach to the problem was made by A. Arens, "Hat der Psalter seinen 'Sitz im Leben' in der synagogalen Leseordnung des Pentateuch?" (*Le Psautier,* ed. R. de Langhe [1962] 107-132). Arens refers to Jewish research on the synagogue worship that has definitely made it possible to discern a three-year Torah cycle (I. Elbogen, *Der jüdische Gottesdienst in seiner geschichtlichen Entwicklung* [1931] 159ff.). Here again, we have a new suggestion for the relation of the collection of the Psalms to these Torah readings: "Also the total number of the 150 hymns of the Psalter can be explained on the basis of their assignment to the three-year cycle of Pentateuch readings. If we disregard the occasional fifth Sabbath in a month, a three-year term showed 144 Sabbaths (12 times 4 times 3). If we add the Sabbaths of the 'second Adar,' we get 148. This number exactly corresponds to the number of independent hymns of the Psalter, since Psalm 1 is to be considered a preface and Psalm 150 a closing doxology for the entire collection" (115). Plausible though this may be, open questions remain (cf. Niemeyer).

§4. The Titles of the Psalms

The individual psalms of the canonical collection of the Psalter have titles. It will be the purpose of this section to explain the various Hebrew terms and, as far as possible, to ascertain the meaning of these headings. The difficulties involved are in most cases formidable. It is hardly possible to clarify the sense and meaning of certain technical terms. The context of the Hebrew Bible is not sufficiently extensive to gain a clear picture. Problematic are all attempts to engage in an etymological investigation of roots and in the course of such research to provide possible explanations on the basis of Semitic linguistics. Neither do the explanations of the Midrashic literature provide satisfactory elucidation. Cf. H. D. Preuss, "Die Psalmenüberschriften in Targum und Midrasch," *ZAW* 71 (1959) 44-55; B. S. Childs, "Psalm Titles and Midrashic Exegesis," *JST* 16 (1971) 137-150. Many things in the following interpretation must therefore remain hypothetical.

No. 1: שיר in the Psalms denotes the song, the cultic song. This term is often used together with מזמור (cf. No. 2) in the headings of Psalms 30; 48; 65; 66; 67; 68; 75; 76; 83; 87; 88; 92; 108. The particular differentiation between שיר and מזמור is not discernible. The "song" (שיר) is most often accompanied by musical instruments. These instruments are called כלי־שיר (Amos 6:5; 1 Chron. 15:16; 16:42; 2 Chron. 5:13; 23:13, 18; 34:12). There may be an attempt to express the "soughing" or "undulating" of hymns: המון־שיר in Amos 5:23; Ezek. 26:13. Revealing are the combinations in which שיר can appear in the Psalms. In Psalms 120-134 we meet the characteristic title שיר המעלות (cf. No. 3). We should also note the combinations שיר ציון (Ps. 137:3) and שיר בית יהוה in 1 Chron. 6:16; 25:6. שיר therefore always appears in connection with the temple worship on Zion and could be a specific designation for the cultic song and temple song in which Yahweh and the place of his presence are praised. Chronicles tells us of groups of singers that perform their ministries in the area of worship; they present their songs with an accompaniment of musical instruments (cf. 1 Chron. 6:16f.; 25:6f.; 2 Chron. 5:13; 23:18). It is therefore by no means unequivocally true that the concept שיר denotes a vocal presentation exclusively (against O. Kaiser, *Introduction to the Old Testament*) [1975] 352). But in any case we could state that שיר probably originally and preponderantly was the term for vocal song, or cantillating presentation.

No. 2: מזמור (like שיר, cf. No. 1) has the meaning "song," "psalm." The LXX translates the Hebrew term most often with ψαλμός (psalmos). A differentiation between שיר and מזמור could be stated only in this way, that שיר probably originally and preponderantly denoted the vocal, cantillating presentation of a psalm, whereas מזמור primarily referred to singing accompanied instrumentally. Cf. S. Mowinckel, *Psalmenstudien* IV (1923); L. Delekat, "Probleme der Psalmenüberschriften," *ZAW* 76 (1964) 280ff.; J. J. Glueck, "Some Remarks on the Introductory Notes of the Psalms," *Studies on the Psalms* (1963) 30-39.

We should note the fact that מזמור occurs 57 times as a technical term in the titles of the Psalms; in other words, it has achieved a specific, characteristic meaning in this apparatus. And yet, what thought content is to be elicited from the Hebrew word? Formerly, in the explanation of this concept there was time and again a reference to the root meaning of the *piel* זמר. This זמר may mean "to dress a grapevine" (cf. Lev. 25:3f. and Isa. 5:6 *ni*). Thus we got over to the basic meaning "pluck" (*carpere*), which—if transferred to the instrument—would find an application in the idea of "plucking a stringed instrument." But already in Akkadian, *zamāru* only means "to sing," and *zammeru* is "the singer." Also in the OT זמר first and foremost has the meaning "to sing," "to play," "to praise." To be sure, the reference is primarily to the singing that is accompanied by musical instruments (cf. Pss. 33:2; 71:22; 98:5; 147:7; 149:3). Whereas שיר most often points to the act of worship or to the holy place and suggests the meaning "cultic (temple) song," it is a striking fact that זמר, used with לְ, always refers to Yahweh, to whom the song (מזמור) is addressed.

Altogether, מזמור is applied to a psalm לדוד 35 times in the connection מזמור לדוד or לדוד מזמור. The interpretation of this לְ has at all times caused special difficulties. לְ can mean "for," "about," or "by." Already early on, the fact that in 13 cases we are told at what occasion David sang or composed the psalm in question led to our interpreting this לְ as a לְ *auctoris* (denoting the author). Thereby the author of the song would be named in the headings. Such a notice would be in keeping with the tradition of Chronicles that David is the initiator and creator of the cultic institutions and ceremonies (cf. 1 Chron. 22:2—29:5). Accordingly, we would have to assume a postexilic view which—unquestionably of older origin—is pervasive in the titles. This view and interpretation has been contradicted by T. K. Cheyne (*Origin of the Psalter* [1889]). Cheyne separates לדוד from the additions that refer to historical occurrences and interprets the use of the name in the sense of "belonging to the collection of David's psalms." Thus this would refer to a registry notice corresponding to notices of the series of Akkadian psalm compositions. The headings of the clay tablet texts of Ras Shamra (*lb'l—l'qht—lkrt*) could be understood as "registry notices" (e.g., "belonging to the Baal cycle"). But still it is questionable whether this view is correct. In the headings of Psalms 3; 7; 18; 34; 51; 52; 54; 56; 57; 59; 60; 63; and 142 the connection between לדוד and the description of the situation that follows immediately is so close that it is impossible to construe the ל in לדוד as anything else than the ל *auctoris* (Ges-K §129c). Even if we should construe the "historicizing comment" to be an addition to the older לדוד and so declare the historical notes to be a later commentary of the Jewish community added to an older registry note, it would be important to observe that this same Jewish community already understood the heading לדוד as a statement regarding the author. And how else could it receive the statement, seeing that in various places of the OT the old tradition persists that David is the author of individual psalms (1 Sam. 16:17ff.; 2 Sam. 1:17ff.; 22:1f.; 23:1f.; Amos 6:5)? This tradition then finds special expression in Chronicles. Here the OT differs from the Akkadian and the Ugaritic transmission of psalms. From ancient times it is part of David's story that he was a poet and a singer.

And so also another explanation is eliminated, one that is variously reported in connection with the Ugaritic headings. *lb'l*, *l'qht*, and *lkrt* are understood to be a reference to the chief character of the transmitted poetry. In the Psalms such an interpretation leads to a curious mythicizing or dynastic generalization of "David." "David" becomes a phenomenon of the "divine king." Regarding him and about him the psalm with the heading לדוד reports. In light of the distinctive OT situation, this conception is hardly correct. The same skepticism must be expressed when we consider the attempts of I. Engnell and S. Mowinckel to extend the designation לדוד to all the kings of the lineage of David. Engnell considers לדוד (in connection with the designation *dawidum*, familiar from the Mari texts, but of which the meaning "commander," "leader," has, however, proved to be erroneous) a technical, appellative expression which is supposed to have had the general meaning of "for the king." Cf. I. Engnell, *Studies in Divine Kingship in the Ancient Near East* (1943) 176f. And Mowinckel is of the opinion that the psalm with the heading לדוד was intended "for David," that is, however, "for a king of the lineage of David" (cf. S. Mowinckel, *Offersang og sangoffer* [1951] 87ff.). Finally, A. Weiser assumes a development in the conception and the understanding of לדוד.

All these attempts break down as they encounter the facts established above, which suggest the concept of the ל *auctoris* (denoting the author). So also Eissfeldt, *Introduction* (1965) 452.

No. 3: שיר המעלות (or שיר למעלות, in Psalm 121) is an expression the translation and meaning of which are sharply disputed. A whole series of explanations have been offered, five of which we must consider. These five views divide into three groups, of which the first relates to the literary-poetical possibility of interpreting the characteristic group of psalms (Psalms 120-134), the second relates to the historical possibility, and the third to the cultic possibility. (a) The first conception simply considers שיר המעלות a designation for this connected sequence of psalms. According to that, the title would have the meaning "Songs in a Sequence," "Songs in a Series." But this interpretation is much too formal. It is not able to interpret the term מעלות. (b) The second conception is more noteworthy, for it considers the poetic art-form of the group of psalms (Psalms 120-134). It calls attention to the so-called anadiplosis, whereby the closing word of a verse or section is repeated at the beginning of the verse or section immediately following (cf., e.g., "to live" in Pss. 120:2-3, 6-7; 121:1-2, 3-4, 4-5, and often). But this artistic device is not at all peculiar to the collection of Psalms 120–134; it occurs also in Psalms 93; 96; 103; and 118 (cf. R. Kittel, 388). Besides, the term מעלות as applied to the anadiplosis does not have an adequate explanation. (c) The third conception refers to the history of Israel. Referring to Ezra 2:1; 7:9, this conception assumes that שיר מעלות points to a group of songs that belong to the context of the Jews' "going back up" after the Exile and are understood as "wayfaring songs" of the people returning home. מעלות is interpreted as related to מעלה (Ezra 7:9) or העלים משבי הגולה (Ezra 2:1). This conception seems to be expressed already in α´, σ´, θ´

23

(ἀναβάσεων "having gone up"). But it is questionable whether such a historical interpretation can do justice to the characteristics of the songs brought together in Psalms 120-134. (d) Here the cultic conceptions begin. מעלה may be the word used for the step of a throne, an anteroom, or an altar (cf. 1 Kings 10:19f.; 2 Chron. 9:18f.; Ezek. 40:6, 22, 26, 31, 34, 37, 49; Exod. 20:26; Ezek. 43:17). Accordingly, מעלות would be the "steps," and the psalms gathered under the title שיר המעלות would be "songs of the steps." Therefore what we would be dealing with is the cultic station from which the psalms in question were presented. From the Mishnah tractate *Middôth* we learn that the Levites performed their songs on the 15 steps at the Nicanor Gate. Accordingly, מעלות would have denoted the station, or the cultic *Sitz*[1] (cf. Jerome, *canticum graduum*). But this localized interpretation produces a certain inflexibility. One thinks of choirs that are drawn up in tiered arrangements. This conception can hardly be adequate. (e) Thus the fifth conception is still the most reasonable. From מעלות one will have to go back to the characteristic verb עלה. This is the technical term for pilgrimage (cf. Pss. 24:2; 122:4; Mark 10:33; Luke 2:42; and often). But עלה also denotes the final act of the pilgrimage, namely, the procession to the shrine (cf. 2 Sam. 6; 1 Kings 12:32f.; 2 Kings 23:1f.; H.-J. Kraus, *Die Königsherrschaft Gottes im Alten Testament,* 48). Thus שיר המעלות could be understood to mean "pilgrimage song" or "processional song." But we do have to consider that in the group Psalms 120-134 only Psalm 122 is to be applied to a pilgrimage, and only Psalm 132 to a procession. Therefore we will have to assume that שיר המעלות denoted a collection of psalms which one could call "songbook for pilgrimages," but in which also other prayers and songs have been collected.

A combination of the fourth and fifth conceptions becomes possible if we consider that מעלות also denoted "the steps" that led up to the City of David (cf. Neh. 3:15; 12:37). According to that, שיר המעלות would be the "song of steps" that was intoned during the act of procession up to the City of David. But this explanation is in any case perhaps too exclusive. We would have to consider the entire proceedings of the pilgrimage (cf. the comment on Ps. 122:4).

No. 4: מכתם. This is present in the headings of Psalms 16; 56; 57; 58; 59; and 60; cf. also the conjecture in Ps. 38:8. S. Mowinckel (*Offersang og Sangoffer,* 492) makes an attempt to interpret it with a reference to the Akkadian verb *katâmu,* which carries the meaning "to cover." Mowinckel conjectures that there is a reference to "atonement" and suggests the translation "atonement psalm" (*PsStud* IV, 4f.). But this attempt at an interpretation is just as problematic as that of R. Tournay, to interpret מכתם as "secret prayer"; cf. R. Tournay, "Sur quelques rubriques des Psaumes," *Mélanges Bibliques rédigés en l'honneur de A. Robert* (1957) 205-213. The conception espoused by Tournay is already present in the commentary on the Psalms by F. Hitzig. There the meaning "conceal" is assigned to the root כתם. Accordingly, מכתם would be the poem that has not yet been made public, the poem that has been kept secret.

In his translation, *gülden Kleinod* (golden jewel), Luther goes back to Ibn Esra (מכתם from כֶּ.תם = "gold"). This derivation is hardly possible.

---

1. Probably following the expression *canticum graduum* ["song of steps"], the term customary in the Latin tradition, Luther is of the opinion that a number of "superior Levites," or such as happened to be in charge of the temple service, sang the psalms so designated—and did so the way he who sings the mass or preaches the sermon "among us" stands in an elevated place so that he can be seen by all (WA 40[III], 12).

But the translations of מכתם in Gk and Targ, στηλογραφία ("pillar inscription"), or גליפא תריצא, merit some consideration. Here the conception of an inscription in stone is basic. Could this interpretation perhaps provide insight for the term מכתם? The root כתם occurs only a single time in the OT—in Jer. 2:22. This hapax legomenon is most frequently translated "remain soiled." This translation has been derived from the context (and from the Aramaic). But could not נכתם in Jer. 2:22 also have the meaning "be indelible"? From this root meaning we could arrive at a new possibility in interpreting מכתם, for now מכתם would be the poem or song that indelibly retains things that have happened (cf. Job 19:23). In that case, Gk would appropriately have chosen the designation στηλογραφία. In this connection it would be possible to refer to presentations of offerings that are witnessed to on stelae inscriptions of Asia Minor. And to these presentations is immediately added the inference "that in Israel, too, a written report concerning the activities of the petitioner and of Yahweh's dealing with him was publicly displayed in the temple. 'In the roll of the book it is written of me' (Ps. 40:8) then means: In the scrolls of Scripture it is recorded what I have done, what I have suffered, and how Yahweh rescued me. But this is nothing but the written form of the song of praise which was otherwise presented orally in the sanctuary—which was in this case probably done as well" (H. J. Hermisson, *Sprache und Ritus im altisraelitischen Kult,* WMANT 19 [1965] 45. Cf. the comment on Ps. 40:8). Viewed in this context, מכתם could be understood to be an expression for a "stelographic publication." But this explanation, too, can be understood only as a hypothetical attempt at elucidation. מכתם is and remains an obscure term.

No. 5: משכיל, in view of the hiphil השכיל, is most often thought of as a poem that is intellectually and artistically conceived or that produces an intellectual or artistic effect, in other words, an "artistic song" or "didactic song." The concept is found in the headings of Psalms 32; 42; 44; 45; 52-55; 74; 78; 88; 89; 142, and in Ps. 47:7. Most of the interpreters then assume that the thought of wisdom and teaching impresses itself on משכיל either in the element of "meditation" (Briggs), or in the "maxim" (V. Maag, "Zur Übersetzung von *maskil* in Amos 5:13; Ps. 47:7 und in den Überschriften einiger Psalmen," *Schweiz. Theol. Umschau* [1943] 108-115), or even in "discipline and admonition" (for the last position, cf. H. S. Nyberg, "Smärtornas man," *SEÅ* 7 [1942] 43). But, in his commentary, E. J. Kissane rightly calls attention to the fact that didactic elements actually do not at all occur in the psalms that bear the heading משכיל; Psalm 32 (אשכילך in v. 8) and Psalm 78 would of course have to be excepted. But it is advisable to pursue the other possibilities of interpretation too (משכיל = "the artistically devised song," "the art song"). This interpretation would apply above all to Ps. 47:7). Here there is undoubtedly no thought of a "didactic poem." On the contrary, a passage like 2 Chron. 30:22, where the Levites are called המשכילים שכל־טוב ליהוה, shows that the idea of presenting songs and poems in a skilled, intelligent, and artistic way has something to do with the explanation of משכיל. משכיל would be the "artistically molded song," which has been created in accordance with the principles of "wisdom" (חכמה). Such an "art song" searches for the fitting, uplifting, mighty word that is suitable for the object to be sung about and to be praised. The bent toward such an artistic, wise organization is expressed in Ps. 49:3: פי ידבר חכמות. In any case, such an interpretation would be more appropriate than a conception that refers to didactic elements. This conception is also supported by L. Delekat, who sees the real meaning of משכיל revealed in Ps. 47:6f. and adds: "The closest approach to our passage is the phrase 'sing to Yahweh a new song!' (Ps. 96:1, and often). The interpretation must begin there'' (L. Delekat, "Probleme der Psalmenüberschriften," *ZAW* 76 [1964] 282f.). But the new song is the song inspired by Yahweh's רוח (spirit), the artistic new form of which would have to be understood charismatically. Still, in this passage too, sense and meaning of the concept can only be groped for.

Completely unsupported is the view of G. W. Ahlström that משכיל denotes a psalm that expresses the lament of the king. This opinion is indebted to I. Engnell (cf. G. W. Ahlström, *Psalm 89—Eine Liturgie aus dem Ritual des leidenden Königs* [1925] 25).

No. 6: שגיון (*shiggaion*) in the heading of Psalm 7 (Hab. 3:1?) probably is related to the Akkadian concept *šegû* = "lamentation." Thus the meaning "agitated lament" is thought of. For the explanation of the concept, also cf. F. Gössmann, "Der *šiggājōn*," *Augustinianum* 8 (1968) 367-381. Gössmann points to the Arabic *šg'* = "to be moved."

No. 7: תהלה appears in the heading of Psalm 145, but also in Pss. 22:25; 33:1; 34:1; 40:3; 48:10; 65:1; 71:8; 100:4; 106:12, 47; 119:171; 147:1; 148:14; 149:1. תהלה designates "song of praise," "hymn" (from הלל II). We should notice that תהלה can be a synonym for תודא ("thanksgiving," cf. Ps. 100:4). The grateful song of praise of an individual is called תהלה (cf. Pss. 22:25; 65:1; 71:8; 119:171). But also the hymn of the congregation is covered by the word (Ps. 100:4). The combination שיר תהלה is found Neh. 12:46. Parallel to שיר חדש we have תהלה in Ps. 40:3 and Ps. 149:1. In these two passages the "new song" corresponds to the new action of God that brings about a radical change (cf. Isa. 42:9; 48:6). For שיר, cf. No. 1.

Finally, a double reference is necessary: first, a reference to §1, 1 (תהלים as the designation for the collection of the Psalter); second, the announcement that in the determination of the form groups (*Gattungen*) the term תהלה will play a decisive role (cf. §6, 1).

No. 8: תפלה in the Psalter is a word for the prayer of lament and the bidding prayer. The word is documented in the headings of Psalms 17; 86; 90; 102; 142 (Hab. 3:1). The headings of Psalms 17; 86; and 142 are considered תפלה לדוד. The concluding formula in Ps. 72:20 forms the close of a collection of תפלות לדוד. In Ps. 90:1 the תפלה is applied to Moses. The meaning of the concept, derived from פלל II, is clear in the OT. Under the chastisements of Yahweh, in dire tribulation, the תפלה of the sufferer is heard (cf. 1 Kings 8:38; Pss. 4:1; 102:1, and often). Also the people's prayer of lament and bidding prayer is called תפלה (Ps. 80:4). The תפלה is intoned in mourning clothes and with fasting (Ps. 35:13). Like an offering, it ascends to Yahweh (Ps. 141:2). Also the prayer for others, the intercession, can be called תפלה (Ps. 109:4). But significant is the heading of Psalm 102: תפלה לעני כי־יעטף. As a generalized designation of the Psalms (Ps. 72:20) the term תפלה encompasses the basic character of the overwhelming majority of the songs collected in the Psalter; they are prayers. In §6, 2 the designation תפלה will be used to name the classification "songs of prayer" in order to replace type definitions that were determinative ever since the work of Gunkel but have now become problematic.

No. 9: בנגינות is found in the headings of Psalms 4; 6; 54; 55; 61 (corr.); 67; 76. נגינה (cf. נגן) is "stringed music." נגן means "to run over the strings." Stringed music comes in for mention in various places in the OT. David intones his songs to the accompaniment of strings before Saul (1 Sam. 16:16ff.; 18:10; 19:9). Elisha summons a string player so that he might go into ecstasy at the sound of the instrument (2 Kings 3:15). Also the song of thanksgiving sung by an individual is heard at the sound of strings (Isa. 38:20). At a procession, singers, string players, and maidens with timbrels make their appearance (Ps. 68:25). And also at the singing of the choir hymn, while trumpets sound, stringed instruments are played (Ps. 33:2). Is בנגינות to elucidate the sense of למנצח (cf. L. Delekat, "Probleme der Psalmenüberschriften," *ZAW* 76 [1964] 286)? For למנצח, cf. No. 17.

For the interpretation of the term, cf. also J. J. Glueck, "Some Remarks on the Introductory Notes of the Psalms," *Studies on the Psalms* (1963) 31ff.

No. 10: אל־הנחילות in the heading of Psalm 5 is difficult. A number of exegetes assume that this is a reference to the tune according to which the psalm is to be intoned. In this connection reference is made to the root נחל, or to נחלה ("according to 'The Inheritance' "). But we must give attention to the connection of the word to חלל II (1 Kings 1:40) and to חליל. In 1 Sam. 10:5 חליל, along with תף, נבל, and כנור, is a musical instrument used by a band of prophets to achieve the state of ecstasy. One obviously thinks of a "flute" or a "shawm." Also in Isa. 30:29 and 1 Kings 1:40 one could assume that there is mention of flute playing to accompany the worshiping congregation on its journey or procession in a pilgrimage. The preposition אם in the heading of Psalm 5 is probably to be understood as על in the heading of Psalm 61. Accordingly, we could provisionally translate אל־הנחילות as "for flute accompaniment."

No. 11: על־מחלת in the headings of Psalms 53 and 88 can hardly yet be interpreted. Gk simply transliterates, ὑπὲρ μαελεθ. The supposition has been that this might have to do with a melody. In the process of interpreting the term, the root חלה, in the sense of "in melancholy manner," was used as the base; this interpretation was to reflect the content of Psalms 53 and 88. α', σ', θ' thought of the cultic round dance (מחול) and understood the heading as a reference to a roundelay (cf. also No. 14). But on the basis of Ethiopian one could also think of "singing" and "playing," perhaps even "flute playing" (חליל, cf. No. 10).

No. 12: הגיון is to be interpreted as derived from הגה, which denotes the growling of the lion (Isa. 31:4), the cooing of the dove (Isa. 38:4), the groaning of a human being (Isa. 16:7), and the muttering of one who reads to oneself (Ps. 1:2). Finally, also—abstractly—"thinking" and "reflecting" are covered by the verb. In this sense we have הגיון in Lam. 3:62 and Ps. 19:14. But in Ps. 92:3 the thought is of the sound, the resounding of the stringed instrument (עלי הגיון בכנור). In Ps. 9:16 הגיון immediately precedes סלה (cf. No. 13) and could call either for a pause for reflection or for an instrumental interlude. In view of Ps. 92:3 the latter assumption is more immediate (cf. Gk: ᾠδή).

No. 13: סלה greets the reader all told 71 times (Gk 92 times) in 39 psalms, and confronts the interpreter with a multitude of problems. Of course, this is not a matter of a "title"; still, the term is to be introduced here in the series of explanations of technical expressions of the Psalter.

The best and most suggestive approach probably begins with the observation that α' and Jerome render the term in the sense of "always" (Jerome: *semper*). This translation is very likely a signal that סלה in a certain area of tradition was vocalized and read like נֶצַח (B. D. Eerdmans). The meaning of the word could then be that it is a reference to a doxology (cf. *per omnia saecula saeculorum* in the liturgy). This view would correspond to the translation in Gk (διάψαλμα), which obviously refers to an interlude by instruments. But the original meaning of סלה remains unexplained. How is this term to be derived etymologically? From among the wealth of conjectures let us especially point to two noteworthy explanations.

One appeals to the root סלל. This yields two possible interpretations. "The lifting up" either of the voice or of the eye may be meant. סלל, it has often been supposed, is a summons to sound a higher pitch. E. König understands סלה to be a loud interruption: "Up!" A "rousing performance" is to follow. R. Stieb thinks of "lifting up the eyes" when he explains: "He who prays or leads in prayer is to let his eyes soar upward so that he may repeat the verses in question. סלה is a repeat sign" (cf. R. Stieb, "Die Versdubletten des Psalters," *ZAW* 57 [1939] 104, and *ZAW* 58 [1940/41] 317f.). This interpretation of סלה as a repeat sign has been defended (also independently of the reference to סלל) by a number of researchers (סב למעלה השר). R. Stieb, in *Deutsches Pfarrerblatt* 54 (1954), changed his view and agreed that the direction "da capo" is the proper interpretation of סלה.

An altogether different etymological derivation is suggested by B. D. Eerdmans. He considers the Aramaic root *sl* ("to bow," "to pray") and finds in סלה a summons to bow in prayer. In Arabic, *salāt* is the prayer spoken while bowing (cf. also Akkadian *salû* and *salâlu*). In this connection we probably should also call attention to the very significant fact that Sumerian cult poetry contains certain types that are composed of ten main sections. These chapters are called *kirugu* = "bowing," and this name probably refers to the custom of kneeling and bowing at the conclusion of each chapter (cf. A. Falkenstein and W. von Soden, *Sumerische und akkadische Hymnen und Gebete,* 21).

Around these three basic interpretations—doxological interlude, repetition, and bowing—are grouped the most varied conceptions that see in סלה a reference to incidents in cultic presentation, recitation, or lection. Thus R. Gyllenberg takes the view that סלה is a directive for choral singing. While the psalm otherwise is performed by a precentor, סלה indicates communal singing; cf. R. Gyllenberg, "Die Bedeutung des Wortes Sela," *ZAW* 58 (1940/41) 153-156. N. H. Snaith thinks otherwise. Following the Mishnah tractate *Taanith,* he proceeds from a distinctive view of the Psalm lections and declares: "The word Selah therefore is a relic of the days when psalms were sung in three sections"; cf. N. H. Smith, "Selah," *VT* 2 (1952) 43-56.

An overview of all these attempts at interpretation reveals the problems of interpreting the term. Basically, the concept סלה remains unclarified. Of course, the question arises whether one would not have to give special attention to a passage like Ps. 9:16. Here the Hebrew text reads: הגיון סלה. Gk translates, ῳδὴ διαψάλματος, and accordingly has understood the Hebrew as a construct connection. הגיון means either "thinking"[2] or "sounding forth." According to Ps. 92:3, it seems obvious to think of the sound of a stringed instrument (cf. No. 12). Gk, however, thinks of the "singing," or "sounding," of the "interlude." MT and Gk in Ps. 9:16 point to an instrumental or also vocal "intermezzo" which could be understood as a doxology (α', Jerome) or also as an ovation (S. Mowinckel, *Offersang og Sangoffer,* 494f.). If, then, it is really possible to revert to the root סלל, the interpretation of A. König ("Up!"—"rousing

---

2. The translation הגיון = "thinking," "contemplating" in Ps. 9:16 corresponds to Luther's explanation of סלה: "Selah, that little word, whenever it occurs in the Psalms, ordinarily is a sign that we are to think more deeply and at greater length what the words to which it is attached mean to say" (Luther, WA 31,1; 31, 25 f.; cf. *LW* 13:37, but contrast *LW* 19:142).

music'') would also etymologically present a clue.

In any case, we have again been reminded that סלה in a number of cases could have the meaning "pause," "interruption." Cf. Z. Malachi, "Zur Erklärung des Wortes 'Selah' in der Bibel," *Bet Miqra'* 11 (1965/66), fascicle 3 (27) 104-110.

I am indebted to the work on the Psalms done in Scheyern Abbey for a summary of the occurrence of סלה in the Psalms. With gratitude to the compilers, I should like to share this summary at this point, so that the corrigenda of textual criticism may not be overburdened: Pss. 2:2 only in Gk; 3:2, 4 (8 missing in Gk); 4:2, 4; 7:5; 9:16, 20; 20:3; 21:2; 24:6 (10 missing in Gk); 32:4 missing in Gk, 5 missing in Vg, 7; 34:10 only in Gk; 39:5, 11; 44:8; 46:3, 7 (11 missing in Gk); 45:4 Lat; 48:8 Lat; 49:13 Lat, 15; 50:6 Lat (15 only in Gk); 52:3, 5 Lat; 54:2; 55:2 Lat, 18?; 59:5, 13 Lat; 60:4; 61:4; 62:4, 8; 66:4, 7, 15; 67:1, 4; 68:7, 19, 31 (14 only in Gk); 75:3; 76:3, 9; 77:3, 9, 15; 80:7 only in Gk^sa; 81:7; 82:2; 83:9; 84:4, 8; 85:2, 8; 87:3, 6; 88:7 (10 missing in Gk); 89:4, 37, 45, 48; 94:15 only in Gk; 140:3, 95 (8 missing in Gk); 143:6.

No. 14: לתודה in Ps. 100:1 is a worship direction: "for a thank offering." Concerning the תודה, cf. Lev. 7:12; Amos 4:5; Jer. 17:26; 33:11; 2 Chron. 29:31; Pss. 50:14, 23; 102:22; 116:17. Details in §6, 2a γ.

No. 15: לענות in the heading of Psalm 88 is a construct infinitive *piel* of ענה and probably has the meaning "to sing" or "to play." The combination על־מחלת לענות will need attention. Is על־מחלת the name of the tune? Or is this a matter of a "round dance"? Or are we to look for a connection with חליל = "flute"? Cf. No. 11. It is a significant fact that קול ענות in Exod. 32:18 denotes the cultic song that is intoned for the round dance (cf. also 1 Sam. 21:12; 29:15). But we could also think of the "flute song" that is used in a lament.

No. 16: להזכיר in the headings of Psalms 38 and 70 could literally mean "to bring to remembrance." But Targ thinks of the word as a denominative from אַזְכָּרָה. According to Lev. 2:2, 9, 16; 5:12; 6:8; Num. 5:16, אזכרה is that part of the cereal offering which, with the addition of frankincense, is to be burned. We are therefore to think of an act of worship. In Isa. 66:3 מזכיר לבנה has the meaning "to make an offering of frankincense." We could therefore easily think of להזכיר as a reference to the "offering of frankincense."

No. 17: למנצח in 55 psalm headings and Hab. 3:19 is basically still unexplained. The application of the concept in the Chronicler's history provides a clue for two possible explanations. In Ezra 3:8; 1 Chron. 23:4; and 2 Chron. 2:1, נצח has the meaning "to excel," "to lead," "to be at the head," "to direct." Thus we might think of the "director of music" or "choirmaster" for למנצח. But what is the force of the ל? Are the messages of the heading intended "for" the choirmaster? That leads to difficulties. But also the other possible explanation, based on 1 Chron. 15:21, does not take us appreciably further. נצח here probably means "to make music." Accordingly, למנצח would have to be translated "for the musical performance." But the *piel* participle of נצח is rendered better by the first explanation. The translation of למנצח in Gk, εἰς τὸ τέλος, is completely enigmatic. Occasionally, completely new derivations are attempted. S. Mowinckel concentrates on the meaning "render graciously disposed" ("for making the face to shine") and wants to recognize a stated time of worship in למנצח (S. Mowinckel, *Offersang og Sangoffer*, 495f.). But also the "ideology of the king" makes its presence felt. One could begin with the idea that למנצח should be translated "from him who excels." In that case, was למנצח perhaps a standing title of David or perhaps of the king generally? Cf. C. Lindhagen, *The Servant Motiv* (1950) 282; K. H. Bernhardt, *VTS* 7 (1961) 12,

n. 4; A. Bentzen, *Introduction to the Old Testament* (1952) 28; L. E. F. le Mat, *Textual Criticism and Exegesis of Psalm 36* (1957) 45. But even if the translation of למנצח = "from him who excels" were to be correct, we should in the first place have to think of poetic qualities and not of regal gifts and outstanding capacities (L. Delekat, "Probleme der Psalmenüberschriften" *ZAW* 76 [1964] 288). Accordingly, if we could take an "ל-*auctoris*" (cf. No. 2: לדוד) as our starting point, then our understanding would have to be sought in the meaning "from him who excels (as poet and singer)."

No. 18: לידותון in the title of Psalm 39 and על-ידותון in the titles of Psalms 62 and 77 probably refer to the proper noun Jeduthun. This is the name of a musicmaster of David's (cf. 1 Chron. 9:16; 16:38, 41; 25:1, 3, 6; 2 Chron. 5:12). Accordingly, לידותון means "by Jeduthun" or "for Jeduthun," whereas על-ידותון is to be translated: "after Jeduthun" ("after the manner of Jeduthun's music making").

No. 19: על-יונת אלם רחקים (in the title of Psalm 56) is the name of a melody. MT would have to be translated, "a dove of silence among the distant ones." But perhaps we ought to read אלים instead of אֵלֶם (F. Baethgen). We have to dispense with a survey of other translations here. We shall here refer only to the possibility of finding *nomina gentilicia* in the titles of the Psalms (cf. H. Gunkel and J. Begrich, *EinlPs*, 457). Also cf. J. E. Viana, "Indicaciones musicales en los titulos de los Salmos," *Misc. bibl. Ubach.*, Montserrat (1953) 185-200.

The meaning of the headings construed with על has been studied by L. Delekat. He departs from the view that has been standard since Gunkel-Begrich, that is, to interpret the statements construed with על as uniformly as possible. In this process especially two possible explanations emerge: (1) By means of על a melody might be indicated (as interpretations have it time and again). But it has been emphasized correctly that the term "melody" is misleading. In any case, we are to think of psalm tones, in other words, of recitative with fixed (initial and) closing cadences (cf. E. Werner, *New Oxford History of Music*, 1:316-320; D. Wohlenberg, "Kultmusik in Israel," diss. Hamburg [1967]). (2) The statements construed with על could in a few cases also contain special directions for the accompanying instruments.

No. 20: על-אילת השחר is (like No. 19) a name of a melody which is to be translated "hind of the dawn." Gk, σ', and Targ read אֱיָלֻת = "strength." For the meaning of על-אילת השחר, A. Jirku has pointed to the Ugaritic deity *šhr* and at the same time called attention to the fact that H. Bessert in Anatolia found the image of a deer that represented a sun deity. Of course, whether from the two words of the title of Psalm 22 such far-reaching conclusions may be drawn is certainly very doubtful. Cf. A. Jirku, "'*Ajjelet haš-Šahar* (Ps. 22, 1)," *ZAW* 65 (1953) 85f.

No. 21: על-ששנים (Psalms 45 and 69) and על-שושן עדות (Psalms 60 and 80) are (like Nos. 19 and 20) names of melodies. שושן probably is the "lily" (1 Kings 7:26; 2 Chron. 4:5; Song of Sol. 2:1f., 16). It is very difficult to grasp the catchwords of the headings correctly. Whether also a derivation from the Akkadian word *šuššu* = "a shock of" is in question must remain unresolved. In that case, the heading would have to be translated, "the six-stringed one."

No. 22: אל-תשחת in the headings of Psalms 57, 58, 59, and 75 remains inexplicable. This could also be a reference to a tune for singing ("Let It Not

Ruin . . . , cf. Isa. 65:8).

No. 23: על־הגתית in the headings of Psalms 8, 81, and 84 probably refers to a melody: "According to the Githitic (tune)." Since Gk in its translation recalls that גת = "winepress," a slight possibility of reference to a "Song of the Winepress" exists. Or could there be a family name involved? But cf. also the explanation of L. Delekat, "Probleme der Psalterüberschriften," *ZAW* 76 (1964) 293 f.

No. 24: על־מות (in the title of Psalm 9 and in Ps. 48:14) and עלמות (in the title of Psalm 46 and in 1 Chron. 15:20) are references to the manner of musical presentation that can hardly be elucidated any longer. Perhaps the title of Psalm 9 and Ps. 48:14 should be read as in the title of Psalm 46, עלמות. On the problem, cf. also S. Jellicoe, "A Note on '*al mut*, Ps. 48:14," *JTS* 49 (1948) 52f.; R. de Vaux, *Ancient Israel: Its Life and Institutions* (1961) 383.

No. 25: על־השמינית in the titles of Psalms 6 and 12 probably means, "on the 8-stringed (instrument)." On the basis of 1 Chron. 15:21, scholars are trying to conclude that there is a high-pitched range (עלמות, "in maidenly manner") and a low-pitched one. In that case, the title of Psalms 6 and 12 would have the meaning, "on the eighth string." But all these attempts at interpretation are uncertain.

1. The compilation of technical terms of the psalm titles assembled under Nos. 1-25 is arranged according to the following viewpoints: Nos. 1-8, terms for collections; Nos. 9-13, musical technical terms; Nos. 14-18, cultic-liturgical directions; Nos. 19-25, melodies and tunes. If we examine the psalm titles to see whether a definite scheme in the arrangement of technical, musical, and cultic-liturgical terms is observable, we could establish the following basic pattern: למנצח—preposition (above all: על and אל)—noun (mostly with the feminine ending ת)—author. If למנצח may be translated "to the choirmaster," it is clear that the basic order thinks of the titles as references to and directions for the musical performance.

In the overview (Nos. 1-25) the notes regarding the historical situations are not taken into consideration. These declarations are in most cases appended immediately to לדוד. Cf., e.g., Psalm 3: "A Psalm of David, when he fled from Absalom his son." For these notes regarding historical situations, cf. §7.

A few psalms have no headings at all. Gk, Targ, and Jerome have taken the psalm headings over from the Hebrew original. Here we must establish the fact that Gk occasionally transmits headings where MT gives no indication of them. Syr has omitted the musical directions and has replaced the notes regarding historical situations with others. For this, cf. J. M. Vosté, "Sur les titres des psaumes dans la pešitta surtout d'après la recension orientale," *Biblica* 25 (1944) 210-235.

2. The question now arises what the importance and the worth of the headings of the Psalms are for the understanding of the individual song and poem. Is there reliable guidance for comprehension of the content? Historical-critical research since the end of the 18th century has discovered more and more that the instructions above the psalms do not provide an adequate introduction for understanding the songs. These titles have been looked upon as late additions of Jewish tradition and as untrustworthy distortions. Above all, the study of types originated by H. Gunkel has completely ignored the titles of the Psalms in order to develop new viewpoints regarding the organization and arrangement from what the form itself of the Psalms has to say (cf. §6). In more recent times, however, there is an apparent tendency to give greater attention to the titles. In

taking a look at these efforts, we must of course in the first place call attention to an erroneous development. The Scandinavian direction of research of the so-called "Uppsala school" largely overrides the principles of the study of types in order to understand all the psalms from the viewpoint of a general theory of worship. In this connection new possibilities of interpreting the psalm titles are discovered. It will be sufficient to point to I. Engnell's interpretation of לדוד (*Studies in Divine Kingship in the Ancient Near East,* 176f.) and to G. W. Ahlström's explanation of משׂכיל (*Psalm 89—Eine Liturgie aus dem Ritual des leidenden Königs,* 21ff.). If these interpretations are to be apostrophized as an erroneous development, we ought on the other hand to ask whether it is time to concede to the titles an appropriate position within the framework of a history of the transmission and collection of the Psalms (cf. §8). Certainly, tremendous difficulties present themselves here. For the most part, we are no longer in a position to ascertain the meanings of the technical expressions. But the attempt would at least have to be made to determine the "setting" of the headings. In this attempt it is clear from the start that terms like מכתם, שׁיר המעלות, מזמור, or משׂכיל are not designations of "types" (*Gattungen*). What, for instance, have Psalms 32; 45; 78; and 89 in common, all of which have the title משׂכיל? Basically, nothing. Therefore משׂכיל must designate a collection and not a type. The same applies to שׁיר, שׁיר המעלות, and the other terms under Nos. 1-8.

3. Concerning the origin of the titles, we shall for the present cautiously put forth only a few tentative considerations. A comparison between the titles of the Psalms and the cultic-liturgical traditions of the Chronicler's history has again and again revealed a surprising agreement. There can be no doubt that there are here connecting traditions. But of what kind are these connections? The Levitical circle of transmitters that stands behind the Chronicler's history presents itself as the priesthood responsible for the vocal and instrumental performance of the Psalms in the postexilic temple community. The providing of explanatory headings, the collecting, and the canonization of the Psalms was unquestionably promoted, if not even carried out, by this Levitical circle, to a large degree. Thus one could say: In the formation of the titles the responsible cultic agents of transmission, the Levites who stood behind the Chronicler's history, were involved to an eminent degree. But that does not yet solve the problem by a long way. Those Levites must have gone back to their own traditions, to the cultic traditions of the Jerusalem temple of preexilic times, and to extant groups of psalms and collections of psalms. The lack of uniformity of the titles is rooted in the manifold stratification of the psalm tradition. It is entirely possible that individual technical terms and references go back to the earliest times. The interest in David as the founder of the temple and the organized worship is not merely a trend in Chronicles but a turn to the basic Jerusalem psalm tradition. Many an ancient technical term could have emerged again in these circles. The postexilic circle of worshipers very probably did not understand the older terms at all anymore and used original designations of type as names of collections. This ignorance reveals itself also in the Gk, where a certain acquaintance with postexilic worship should be taken for granted. But these explanations are a first attempt. We shall have to come back to these problems again somewhat later (cf. §8).

§5. The Poetic Form of the Psalms

1. Already very early a conspicuous feature of Hebrew poetry was observed: parallelism of lines (*parallelismus membrorum*). Detailed investigations of this

poetic feature were begun by the English Bishop Robert Lowth in his *De sacra poesi Hebraeorum* (1753). It was recognized more and more clearly that two (occasionally also three) ''stichs'' (lines) make up a verse, the parts of which lie parallel as to form and content. The stichs were also called ''members'' or ''half-verses.'' Close examination of *parallelismus membrorum* has shown that four different types occur: (*a*) Synonymous parallelism recasts the content of the first line with new words in the parallel member of the verse. We have an example in Psalm 114 (cf., e.g., v. 6: ההרים תרקדו כאלים גבעות כבני־צאן). (*b*) Antithetic parallelism in its second (parallel) member of the verse contains a statement that is the opposite of the first stich. As an example we might choose Ps. 20:8. (*c*) Synthetic parallelism in the second stich carries forward and supplements the thought expressed in the first member. Cf., e.g., Ps. 126:1. (*d*) In climactic parallelism the second stich repeats a word from the preceding one. The two characteristic examples are found in Ps. 29:1 and Ps. 93:1.

For Israel, the parallelism of members was the most basic poetic form of expression. The poet felt moved to express in two lines of verse, but also from two aspects, however constituted, whatever needed to be said at any given point. Vast possibilities for a wealth of variation and poetic adaptability were thus opened up, even though ancient Near Eastern poetry did not have at its disposal every imaginable, extravagant kind of creativity for free and easy use. The scope of the poet's activity was circumscribed by conventionalized forms and traditional directives (cf. §6). And yet it is not difficult to realize that, especially in the smallest poetic construction—the *parallelismus membrorum*—inexhaustible possibilities were opened up. But the parallelism of members was not unique to the OT. Ever so many ancient Near Eastern texts have convinced us that the poetic form, the parallelism of members, was spread abroad not only in Israel but throughout the surrounding world. On Egyptian poetry, cf. A. Erman and H. Ranke, *Ägypten* (1923) 468-474. On Sumerian-Akkadian poetry, cf. A. Falkenstein and W. von Soden, *Sumerian and Akkadian Hymns and Prayers* (1953) 30ff., 40ff. On Canaanite-Syrian poetry, cf. J. H. Patton, *Canaanite Parallels in the Book of Psalms* (1944). In more recent times the fragmentary psalm manuscripts from Qumran Cave 4 have shown that parallelism was indicated in the sacred scrolls by means of space between the half-verses (P. W. Skehan, *RB* 63 [1956] 59). What we have before us, therefore, is a basic poetic form that is an unmistakable criterion for distinguishing prose from poetry. Of course, there are problems of precise demarcation. ''Synthetic parallelism'' is a disputed structure. Where does poetry begin and prose end? Although the climactic parallelism with its repetition contains a mark of poetic structure, all criteria in synthetic parallelism may become blurred. Psalm 2 is an example of such problems. Above all, in the case of ''mixed meters'' (see below) it becomes difficult precisely to determine the analogy between the two members. Yet, in psalm poetry a continuous effort will have to be made to discover the parallelism. Another difficulty is presented by the line that stands alone. Again and again we meet in the Psalms isolated individual lines that are given no parallel completion. Psalms 111 and 112 even represent the exceptional case in which only individual members are strung together; a parallelism of members cannot be established. However, these two psalms display another art form: they follow the alphabet as they begin each new stich. ''The learned poet wanted to show that he could manage the difficult alphabetical form even with the shortest entities, the half-sentences'' (S. Mowinckel, ''Marginalien zur hebräischen Metrik,'' *ZAW* 68 [1956] 101).

This is not the place to take up the question of the existence of so-called short verses, a question dealing with that gray area where it is not easy to demonstrate parallelism of members (cf. G. Fohrer, ZAW 66 [1954] 199ff.). We can only indicate that the Psalms present no occasion for the reconstruction of short verses.

2. Once we admit the existence of the *parallelismus membrorum,* we face considerable difficulties in dealing with the question whether meter can be proved to exist in Hebrew poetry and how the principles of this meter are to be established. A number of scholars deny the presence of metrics within the OT altogether. Others again, while considering it possible that there were once in ancient times metrical laws, dismiss the possibility of reconstructing them. Actually, four viewpoints must in any case be considered: (*a*) It is hardly conceivable that psalmody, carried on during almost a millenium of Israel's history .(cf. §8), could always have been subject to the same metrical principles. In this time frame we would have to reckon with recasts, new directions, foreign influences, and other factors. (*b*) Problems of pronunciation of the Hebrew language complicate the access to the "original form" of a psalm. Here, too, changes have taken place that can no longer be detected (cf. P. Kahle, "Die überlieferte Aussprache des Hebräischen und die Punktation der Masoreten," ZAW 39 [1921] 230-239). (*c*) The transmission of the Hebrew text has brought with it mistakes and distortions, amplifications and transpositions. Today the "original text" can be restored only approximately. (*d*) The vocalization of the Hebrew consonantal text inaugurated a new phase of recasting, which in turn has affected the nuances of possible metrical patterns.

All of these factors make the restoration of metrical laws and norms difficult. And even if it would be too rash to consider the reconstruction of meters altogether impossible, it is nonetheless true that we still lack firm bases for ascertaining meter. All our efforts regarding meter are mere experiments. At the present time the presuppositions for working out the meter have again become shaky, and we must forge our way through a jungle of hypotheses and observations.

For the first, we must emphasize the fact that a metrical organization of poetic texts has been shown to exist also in the environs of Israel. Besides the observations on Egyptian poetry (A. Erman and H. Ranke, *Ägypten,* 468ff.) and Akkadian verse (B. Meissner, *Babylonia and Assyria,* 2:64f.; A. Falkenstein and W. von Soden, 40f.), there are also important findings on the metrical form of Old Canaanite poetry (H. L. Ginsberg, "The Rebellion and Death of Ba'lu," *Orientalia* NS 5 [1936] 180; F. M. Cross, "Notes on a Canaanite Psalm in the Old Testament," *BASOR* 117 [1950] 19-21). Searching for a metrical system in Hebrew poetry is therefore indispensable. The only question is according to which system our search ought to proceed. For our discussion there are two possibilities to begin with: (a) The alternating system was developed by Bickel and Hölscher and at present has experienced new currency through S. Mowinckel and F. Horst. Bickel and Hölscher extracted this system basically from the Syrian system to achieve an alternating system that is based on trochaic and iambic (dissyllabic) feet. Cf. G. W. Bickel, *Carmina Veteris Testamenti metrice* (1882); G. Hölscher, *Elemente arabischer, syrischer und hebräischer Metrik,* BZAW 34 (1920) 93-101. In more recent times, S. Mowinckel has called attention especially to the "meter of the sense" within the alternating system (S. Mowinckel, "Zum Problem der hebräischen Metrik," *Bartholet-Festschrift* [1950] 379-394; idem, *Offersang og Sangoffer* [1951] 418-435; idem, "Margi-

nalien zur hebräischen Metrik," *ZAW* 68 [1956] 97-123). F. Horst has called attention to the appearance of the "prosodic revolution" (F. Horst, "Die Kennzeichen der hebräischen Poesie," *ThR* 21 [1954] 54-85). A particular development is described by S. Segert in his "Vorarbeiten zur hebräischen Metrik,"*Archiv Orientální* 21 (1953) 481-542.

(b) The accenting system assumes that the basic unit of the Hebrew verse consists of quaternary measures that carry an anapestic accent. This system was developed by Ley, Budde, and Sievers (cf. J. Ley, *Grundzüge des Rhythmus, des Vers- und Strophenbaus in der hebräischen Poesie* [1875]; K. Budde, "Das hebräische Klagelied," *ZAW* 2 [1882] 1-52; D. Sievers, *Metrische Studien* I [1901], II [1904-1905], III [1907]). This system conveys three important perceptions: (1) Hebrew rhythm is essentially accentual; (2) verse accent and word accent, metrical and grammatical accent, coincide; (3) the verse has an anapestic character. But difficulties arose early on in the accenting system because of the question how the number of unaccented syllables was to be determined. At first it was considered more or less immaterial how many unaccented syllables ought to be posited. But E. Sievers believed that he could prove that the rhythm was made up of basically quaternary measures. Consistent application of this principle, however, came up against considerable difficulties. One can probably not escape pointing out the "weak side" of the accenting system here; compare also J. Begrich, "Zur Hebräischen Metrik," *ThR* (1932) 67-89. Still, this system, fortified convincingly in its foundations by E. Sievers, has so many advantages that it prevails in the present commentary as the more suitable one. But we should repeat that only an attempt at metrical apprehension can be submitted.

Following E. Sievers, we will in the first place have to distinguish the following verses: the duple (2), the triple (3), and the quadruple (4) as simple series (without parallel amplification); further, as parallelisms: the double duple (2 + 2), the double triple (3 + 3), the double quadruple (4 + 4), the septuple (4 + 3 or 3 + 4), the quintuple (3 + 2, less frequently 2 + 3), and the sextuple (2 + 2 + 2). In addition, mention must be made of the three-member verses (*tricola*), which may have symmetrical forms (3 + 3 + 3 and 4 + 4 + 4) or asymmetrical ones (3 + 3 + 2, 3 + 2 + 3, 4 + 4 + 3, etc.). But how are these periods structured in the individual psalms? What is their relation to one another? Is it possible for mixed meters to appear in irregular succession in one and the same psalm? Here unforeseeable problems arise. In connection with H. Gressmann, J. Begrich made the point: "The recognition of the mixed meter, however, carries with it undeniable dangers. What assurance do we have that a text which according to analysis shows a mixed meter was actually meant that way originally and was not somehow expanded?" ("Zur Hebräischen Metrik" 83). On the other hand, we ought to ask to what extent principles of meter justify corrections for the sake of the meter. Concerning textual criticism (corrections *metri causa*), a number of viewpoints were presented already in §2,2. Here we should state once more that text-critical encroachments for the purpose of restoring the meter are objectively justified only if a line (stich) falls short of the metrical possibilities (2 to 4 accents) or goes beyond them or if within a psalm a certain meter proves to be absolutely dominant. In individual cases we must study the special situation presented by the psalm. Certain limits are set when we consider the text-critical possibilities, but regarding the mixed meter we lack all authoritative orientation. In the metrical study of a psalm interlaced with mixed meters one might ask, According to what pattern do the various meters alternate? Are there definite series that belong together? But in many cases there are no answers to these questions and no clues to any clarification. May we expect definite symmetry in the first place? Are those who try to clarify perhaps still too much under the influence of classicism's harmonious laws of form? Comparisons with Old Canaanite and Ugaritic poetry have shown that mixed meters are to be presupposed everywhere in early poetry. Only very few clues for determining a definite arrangement are given. Cf. F. M. Cross, "Notes on a Canaanite Psalm in the Old Testament," *BASOR* 117 (1950) 19ff. It will therefore be uncommonly difficult to find authoritative fundamental principles. Moreover, the psalms are too various. If a metrical peculiarity turns up once in a psalm, it is sometimes only a brief phase that comes to light. Most often the thread of metrical orientation is broken again in the very same psalm. Let us here list some noteworthy characteristics of the most ancient poetry:

In Psalms 24; 29; 68; and 93 three metrical types may be observed: (a) double duple, arranged in pairs (2 + 2/2 + 2); (b) asymmetrical tricola (2 + 2 + 3); (c) symmetrical tricola (3 + 3 + 3). These give the impression that the oldest structural elements of Hebrew poetry are here involved. Of course, these elements make their appearance in various mixtures (cf., among others, Psalm 110).

(a) Double duple arranged in pairs: Ps. 29:1f.:

בני אלים	הבו ליהוה	2 + 2
כבוד ועז	הבו ליהוה	2 + 2
כבוד שמו	הבו ליהוה	2 + 2

Ps. 93:1:

גאות לבש	יהוה מלך	2 + 2
עז התאזר	לבש יהוה	2 + 2

(b) Asymmetrical tricola: Ps. 68:1, 4:

וינוסו מפניו	יפוצו אויביו	יקום אלהים	2 + 2 + 3
סלו לרכב בערבות	זמרו שמו	שירו לאלהים	2 + 2 + 3

(Also cf. Ps. 29:3-6)

(c) Symmetrical tricola: Ps. 24:7, 8:

שׂאו שערים ראשיכם
והנשׂאו פתחי עולם
ויבוא מלך הכבוד   3 + 3 + 3

מי זה מלך הכבוד
יהוה עזוז וגבור
יהוה גבור מלחמה   3 + 3 + 3

(Also cf. Ps. 93:3-5.)

Particularly in these oldest double verses and tricola, fitfully following upon one another, is the accentual system demonstrated best of all. Also the basic forms of the double triple verse and the quintuple verse (characteristic of the *qinah*) are still most appropriately to be understood according to the viewpoints outlined by E. Sievers. Example of the double triple verse: Ps. 18:5, 6:

חבלי שאול סבבוני	קדמוני מוקשי מות	3 + 3

3 + 3   בצר־לי אקרא יהוה   ואל־אלהי אשוע

Example of the quintuple verse: Ps. 27:9f.:

3 + 2   אל־תט־באף עבדך   עזרתי היית
3 + 2   אל־תטשני ואל־תעזבני אלהי ישעי
3 + 2   כי־אבי ואמי עזבוני   ויהוה יאספני

For details of the metrical system, cf. J. Begrich, "Zur Hebräischen Metrik," *ThR* NF4(1932) 67ff., and the bibliography assembled there.

Comprehensive particulars concerning the methods and problems of the metrical system are found in S. Mowinckel, *The Psalms in Israel's Worship* II (1962). New metrical principles are listed by M. Dahood, "A New Metrical Pattern in Biblical Poetry," *CBQ* 29 (1967) 574-599.

    3. Turning to the question whether stanzas may be recognized in Hebrew poetry, we are confronted with such a jumble of opinions and suppositions in the relevant literature that it can hardly be taken in at a glance. Cf. K. Fullerton, "The Strophe in Hebrew Poetry and Psalm 29," *JBL* 48 (1929) 274-290; H. Möller, "Der Strophenbau der Psalmen," *ZAW* 50 (1932) 240-256; A. Condamin, *Poèmes de la Bible: Avec une introducion sur la strophique hébraïque* (1933); C. F. Kraft, *The Strophic Structure of Hebrew Poetry as Illustrated in the First Book of the Psalter* (1938). J. A. Montgomery, "Stanza-Formation in Hebrew Poetry," *JBL* 64 (1945) 379-384, should be taken into consideration here, also the discussion of E. J. Kissane in his commentary on the Psalms (XXXVf.). In addition: J. Schildenberger, "Bemerkungen zum Strophenbau der Psalmen," *Estudios Eclesiaticos* 34 (1960), Miscelánea Andrés Fernandez, 673-687; E. Beaucamp, "Structure strophique des Psaumes," *RSR* 56 (1968) 199-224. Against all arbitrary or unfounded claims regarding a "strophe," we must call attention to the basic definition of E. Sievers: "Strophe is a rhythmic concept." In this sense O. Eissfeldt defines: "The strophe is a metrical unit which may be recognized where the same number and type of verses, two or more in number, are repeated two or more times, in such a way that the first verse of the second and subsequent groups is metrically exactly equal to the first verse of the first group, the second verse in the one corresponds to the second verse in the others, and so on. . . . Existence of such strophes has not yet been certainly demonstrated" (Eissfeldt, *Introduction* [1965] 62).

    In a wider sense the concept "strophe" then came to denote combinations of a like or approximately corresponding number of verses to form larger sections. With proper reservations, the term "strophe" can presumably also be used to describe the sections of Psalms 42/43; 46 (cf. the supplement); 80; and 107, circumscribed as they are by a refrain, or also Psalm 119 with its sections in alphabetical arrangement. Unfortunately, clear parallels from the world of the ancient Near East that could be adduced to explain the formation of strophes in the OT psalms are not available. For the formation of strophes in Sumerian poetry, cf. S. Falkenstein and W. von Soden, *Sumerische und akkadische Hymnen und Gebete* (1953) 26f.

    4. Finally, as a technique of poetic style and arrangement, we must mention acrostic. Cf. Psalms 9/10; 25; 34; 111; 112; 119; 145; Prov. 31:10ff.; Lam. 1-4; (Nah. 1:2ff.). In these songs the alphabetical sequence is entirely or partly determinative for the form, in that the first letter of the first word of each

verse or section (cf. Psalm 119) corresponds to the alphabetical sequence. The meaning of this unique way of determining form has so far not been completely clear. Among other things, even magical implications have been assumed. But today it is a well-known fact that the alphabet is recorded very early as a means of education. Cf. W. F. Albright, "Alphabetic Origins and the Idrimi Statue," *BASOR* 118 (1950) 11ff.; idem, "The Origin of the Alphabet and the Ugaritic ABC Again," *BASOR* 119 (1950) 23ff.; E. A. Speiser, "A Note on Alphabetic Origins," *BASOR* 121 (1952) 17ff.; G. R. Driver, "Semitic Writing," *Schweich Lectures* (1954[2]). We may assume that the alphabetic arrangement was an aid to the memory and also served pedagogical purposes. It certainly carries with it a strong effect on form as well as a decisive technique for schematic structure. Very likely the tendency toward acrostic originated in the period immediately preceding the exile or in the exilic period of OT psalm writing. But we should note that already a thousand years before Christ there originated in Akkadian hymn writing the formal artistic device of the acrostic, "which made its appeal more to the eye of the learned reader than to the ear of the hearer." "In such hymns every strophe, or even every verse of every strophe, begins with a determinant syllable sign." "When set up over against each other, these syllable signs yield a religious formula or a king's name with attributes that characterize the king's piety. Hymns of this kind remind us of the so-called alphabetical psalms of the Old Testament (e.g., Psalm 119), in which one may read the Hebrew alphabet from the first letters of verse and strophes" (A. Falkenstein and W. von Soden, *Sumerische und akkadische Hymnen und Gebete*, 42f.).

§6. The Categories and Their "Sitz im Leben"

The investigation of types (*Gattungsforschung*) introduced into the scholarly work on the Psalms by H. Gunkel may rightly be called a decisive event in the history of biblical interpretation. Even though there had been efforts before H. Gunkel to arrange the Psalms in groups according to contents, it was finally the form-critical method introduced by him that led the way to a systematic and categorized differentiation. Gunkel's basic demand was that "literary material must first of all be classified according to laws of its own type, in other words, according to laws taken from literary history" (H. Gunkel and J. Begrich, *Einl-Ps* 9). "The scholar is to strive to feel his way into the native and natural structure of this poetic genre" (*Einl-Ps* 10). This leads to the identification of definite "types" (*Gattungen*). Thereby the presuppositions for comprehensive classification are precisely fixed, for we can speak of a "type" only when very definite and strictly applied conditions are maintained. Three presuppositions and conditions are mentioned by Gunkel: (a) Only such poems may constitute a type as belong entirely to a specific occasion in worship or at least have emerged from this occasion. The cultic stimulus must be grasped as precisely as possible—in constant correspondence to the form and content of the songs that belong to it. (b) "Furthermore, such songs as belong naturally together must show a common treasury of thoughts and moods, such as were given precisely by their Sitz im Leben or easily could be linked with it. It will be up to us to point out also this common ground of the individual types" (*Einl-Ps* 22f.). (c) "A third, absolutely essential characteristic of the type is that all individual pieces belonging to it—of course, more or less clearly—are united by their common literary form (*Formensprache*). This is the area in which the scholar can hardly get along without an aesthetic consideration" (*Einl-Ps* 22f.). These basic principles for setting up literary types are indispensable positions for appropriate scholarly work on the Psalms.

In dealing with the question of the types of OT psalms, we must of course meticulously investigate not only the state of affairs obtaining in the OT; Gunkel has emphasized that we must adduce and investigate ancient Near Eastern parallels. In this connection Gunkel heartily welcomed F. Stummer's book *Sumerisch-akkadische Parallelen zum Aufbau alttestamentlicher Psalmen* (1922), even though he allowed himself the criticism that "the study's chief weakness is that it brings in the comparison of the Babylonian and the biblical too soon, before even the forms of the two literary traditions have been more or less completely investigated" (*Einl-Ps* 19 A.1). We now have substantial help concerning the problems of Sumerian and Akkadian types in the introductions by A. Falkenstein and W. von Soden, in *Sumerische und akkadische Hymnen und Gebete* (1953). But great difficulties concerning the investigation of types are occasioned by the oft-cited Ugaritic poetry. Important basic questions are not yet decided (are they mythical poetry or cultic rituals?). Therefore we have to be very reticent about bringing the Ugaritic material into the area of the investigation of types. Yet it is generally acknowledged that because of the expansion of the ancient Near Eastern field of vision in the last decades we now have a better understanding of many problems involved in psalms research than was possible for Gunkel in his time. This is in the nature of things. Of course, in a few points—apart from this observation concerning the history of research—we must raise criticisms regarding Gunkel's methods: (a) the dominating principle of formal-aesthetical classification often introduces judgments in the history of literature that are not to the point. Thus, e.g., Gunkel has concluded that the short psalm that is also pure in type is a most ancient element of tradition, whereas the poem that is extensive and mixed in type is thought of as "late." (b) The continuous influence of formal and aesthetic judgments on the interpretation of the "piety" of a psalmist reveals a dubious overestimation of form-critical methods. (c) Problematical above all in the expositions of Gunkel is the relation of psalm and cult. Uncertainties reveal themselves in the perception of the so-called liturgies. G. Wahlström rightly states that "the types are not ready-made patterns that were strictly followed, but the psalms in every case sprang from the actual situations for which they were intended. For that reason a psalm with what Gunkel calls a rather mixed form cannot a priori be called irregular" (*Psalm 89—Eine Liturgie aus dem Ritual des leidenden Königs,* 9). But the conclusion that Ahlström draws from his critical observation (see below) is indeed doubtful.

But this criticism of the methods of Gunkel is incomplete. In the last decades it has become more and more clear that the investigation of types as Gunkel and Begrich presented it is in need of considerable correction—and, in part, of basic reorganization. The first four German editions of this commentary were essentially still determined and influenced by Gunkel's investigation of types. But now, in this new edition, it has proved to be indispensable to restudy the principles and presuppositions, but especially the basic concepts, of Gunkel's and Begrich's form-critical research. We thus, first, make the following critical observations, which go beyond the criticisms of Gunkel's methods already stated above.

1. Gunkel identified as one of the most important conditions for the categorical determination of a "type" the "common literary forms" (*gemeinsame Formensprache*) of the psalms under consideration (*Einl-Ps* 22f.). But now, in so significant a "type" as that of the "royal psalms," it appears that

such a "common literary form" can be neither determined nor presupposed. The unifying principle, according to Gunkel, would then be a "common treasury of thoughts and moods" (*Einl-Ps* 22). But this formulation of a norm is so vague and lyrical and indefinite that it could describe everything as well as nothing. Here a new definition, one that actually catches hold of the contents of a group of psalms, is absolutely necessary. We must overcome the formalism of the school of form criticism and more precisely define the criteria of the psalms that belong together.

2. As is well known, according to Gunkel a majority of the psalms is to be listed under the type "laments of the individual." Let us take this "type" as an example to illustrate how inadequate are the categorical designation and its application. (a) Who is the "individual" who "laments"? According to Gunkel, he is a personality, an individual. It is therefore only consistent that among Gunkel's followers the name "individual lament" was able to prevail. But later research has shown more and more clearly that there are absolutely no cases of unmitigated isolation present in these songs, but that the one who prays participates in the prayer language of the community (cf. especially E. Gerstenberger, "Der bittende Mensch," diss., Heidelberg). This is where the problem begins. (b) Is the designation "lament" adequate? In no way does it correspond to the intent of most of the psalms listed under this title. There is no lamenting. Rather, we could speak of two foci that are determinative in given cases, namely, a description of distress, or cry of distress, and a cry for help. (c) Is the designation "lament of the individual" able to cover all the psalms subsumed by Gunkel under this title? Wherever more accurate investigations have been made, we discover that the categorical designation is not adequate. Take as an example W. Beyerlin, *Die Rettung der Bedrängten in den Feindpsalmen der Einzelnen auf institutionelle Zusammenhänge untersucht*, FRLANT 99 (1970). Beyerlin has convincingly proved that the so-called "enemies of the individual" psalms can no longer be accommodated by Gunkel's definition of type. The deficiency of the type designations and the classifications is becoming more obvious right along.

3. According to Gunkel, common Sitz im Leben is an important ingredient of a type. But we must here simply state that the extensive and careful studies of worship in the last decade have provided new insights into the cultic occasions and acts of Israelite worship. Above all, we have succeeded in learning to recognize liturgies in the way they are practiced and put together, and in forming suitable conclusions for naming and classifying these psalms. Cf., e.g., Jörg Jeremias, *Kultprophetie und Gerichtsverkündigung in der späteren Königszeit*, WMANT 35 (1970). The question arises of which new ways can be found and followed. At this point we can only briefly sketch what must later be set forth systematically and assembled as a summary of the commentary on the individual psalms.

The "new ways" which we shall follow in this commentary in the area of literary-historical research begin with a consideration of the most characteristic designations in the Hebrew Psalter. In order not to employ in our groupings foreign categories and designations that introduce modern aspects, it is advisable to introduce terms such as תהלה, תפלה, שיר ציון, etc. and to take them into account as the first and the principal designations of the psalm groups in question. In other words, we would have to begin with general designations such as "songs of prayer," "songs of praise," "songs of Zion," and so on—with designations that correspond to the basic Hebrew concepts. Altogether six groups can be established and set up together: "songs of praise" (תהלה), "songs of prayer" (תפלה), "royal psalms" (מעשי למלך, Ps. 45:1), "songs of Zion" (שיר ציון, Ps. 137:3), "didactic (wisdom) poems" (cf. the Hebrew terms in Ps. 49:3f.), and "liturgies," or "festival psalms." In the general groups thus set up, the first requirement is form-critical analysis and classification, as far as the texts permit. This analysis, for instance, in the area of the "songs of prayer," would lead to a distinction between "songs of prayer of individuals," "community songs of prayer" (תפלת עם, Ps. 80:4), and "thanksgiving songs of individuals" (תודה). But this cannot be a matter of isolating form criticism and form analysis. A thematic grouping, corresponding to this and freshly arranged, will have to be undertaken. In this procedure the term "theme," which M. Noth introduced into OT scholarship (M. Noth, *A History of Pentateuchal Traditions* [1981] §7), ought finally to replace the vague inquiry after a "common treasury of thoughts and moods" (Gunkel and Begrich, *Einl-Ps* 22). Determining the theme, for instance, in the general group of "songs of prayer," and in the "songs of prayer of individuals" as isolated by form-critical analysis, would lead to designations such as "song of prayer of one who is ill," "song of prayer of one who is accused and persecuted," "song of prayer of a sinner," etc. These designations that derive from considerations of themes and contents are not appendices but necessary, appropriate qualifications of what may henceforth be called a "theme-oriented form group." Such cooperation and correlation between form criticism and theme orientation are indispensable if studies in the Psalms are not to deteriorate into a criticism of formulas and formalism or disintegrate into generalizing "types."

M. Noth bids us ponder the following: "There is great danger now that our interest no longer turns toward 'forms' but toward 'formulas'—in other words, that 'form criticism' becomes 'formula criticism' and that, adopting the tacit presupposition that a 'formula' once coined always stays the same, 'formula criticism' (*Formelgeschichte*) becomes 'formula uncriticism' (*Formel-Ungeschichte*)" (M. Noth, "Tendenzen theologischer Forschung in Deutschland," *Ges-StudzAT* II [1969] 120).

Finally, it would be our task to set forth the principles that govern the relation between "theme-oriented form groups" and worship life in Israel. At present, two extreme opinions confront each other. On the one side, the interpretation gives precedence to the formal-literary shape of the psalms, in which case the cultic occasion recedes completely into the background. On the other side, an all-embracing act of worship, a decisive cultic festival, is presupposed, to which (disregarding all formal-literary properties) the most disparate psalms are then attached. The latter procedure originated with S. Mowinckel's "discovery" of the festival of Yahweh's enthronement (*PsStud* II). Later, Mowinckel displayed a more reserved attitude and strove toward a more generous differentiation of textual relations—even though the "Salmer til tronstiningsfest" (enthronement psalms) still occupied a dominating position (*Offersang og Sangoffer*, 118-192). In the so-called Uppsala school the dominant cult principle has enjoyed a lively development. There is danger of succumbing to a threatening short circuit. This is revealed by G. W. Ahlström, who, generally following I. Engnell, gives the following explanation of Gunkel's study of types: "His system, it seems to me, is due for a thorough revision. The starting-point for a division into various types would have to be the Psalter's own designations, משכיל, למנעה, לדוד, etc. This method is, after all, employed also in the Akkadian and Ugaritic psalm material. That is to say, one may proceed from the view that the titles of the Psalms are intended to designate either the nature of the psalm in question or its place in the ritual'' (*Psalm 89—Eine Liturgie aus dem Ritual des leidenden Königs,* 10f). This explanation is very problematic. It is of course correct to say that in Sumerian and Akkadian psalm writing, for instance, the manner of musical performance represents a principle of classification (cf. A. Falkenstein and W. von Soden, 19). But especially we must keep in mind that the titles of the OT Psalms not only are still now mostly inexplicable but also without doubt introduce most disparate poems (cf. §4). It is very dubious to introduce ritual groupings from unexplained psalm headings with questionable translations on the basis of a dominating cultic theory. And when the still basically unexplained headings of Ugaritic poetry also are added to this experiment, it becomes patent that we are going around in a vicious circle.

In spite of all reservations about the results that Gunkel has brought to light with regard to the cultic "Sitz im Leben" of the Psalms, we must acknowledge the fact that in his *Einleitung in die Psalmen* he shows the way to a careful correlation between the formal-literary shape of the Psalms and the cultus that may possibly underlie them. The effort to do justice to this interrelation is a distinguishing feature of the commentaries of H. Schmidt and A. Weiser, even if one is unable to follow the postulate of the "festival of Yahweh's enthronement" in the former work and the affirmation of a "covenant cult" in the latter. Here too there is the danger that an all-encompassing cultic act becomes a fascinating principle of explanation. By contrast, the present commentary in the explanation of each psalm is concerned first with a precise investigation of the formal data. The literary form is then also pursued and defined—even in its ramifications—whenever there could be danger that the entire psalm disintegrate and split apart. Only this consistent form-critical work can call a halt to arbitrary cultic hypotheses. Under the subhead "Setting" in the commentary of the individual psalm, the opportunity will then always be afforded to inquire about an underlying "situation" that unites and illuminates the individual parts. But also in this explanatory section ("Setting") our commentary strives for as much openness and lack of prejudice as possible. It will never take for granted that all psalms occupy a cultic Sitz im Leben. Even where cultic data undeniably shine through, we will look for sharp differentiating and nuancing. The wholesale effort to lock the Psalms into preconceived cultic situations is apostrophized again and again. Unfortunately, we still know altogether too little about the worship of Israel. Ancient Near Eastern worship can be a dominating principle of exegesis only in those scholarly circles in which people elevate themselves above the historical and theological character of the OT with the help of determinant Old Testament and ancient Near Eastern schemata ("patterns"), or cultic-mythical principles.

With all these preliminary explanations the path, or at least the direction of the path, is given. Now we must follow through with the consequences of the sketched plan and present them in summary fashion. In so doing we will from the very beginning keep this thought in mind: "Even the best and most complete system will fail to include a considerable number of psalms, which it is either impossible to fit into any category, or which can be included only by a forced interpretation" (C. Barth, *Introduction to the Psalms* [1966]. Thus also the following statements may be thought of only as an attempt to arrange the Psalms according to inner (formal and thematically by content) principles of disposition in order by this means to create a practical presupposition for a context-oriented interpretation. To keep the presentation from going out of bounds, we must therefore dispense with a detailed consideration of the psalms outside the Psalter. In individual cases, associations and explanatory relations will be pointed out.

1. Songs of Praise (תהלה)

We have to proceed from the general designation of a group of psalms with the Hebrew term תהלה = "song of praise." Setting aside every form-critical differentiation, we may state that the following belong to the group "songs of praise": Psalms 8; 19A; 29; 33; 47; 65; 66A; 68; 93; 96; 97; 98; 99; 100; 104; 105; 106; 111; 113; 114; 117; 134; 135; 136; 145; 146; 147; 148; 149; 150. At times also the terms מזמור, זמרה, שיר, or שירה may appear as the Hebrew designation for a "song of praise." For the meaning of זמר, cf. C. Barth, *ThWAT* II, 603-612.

Since the time when Gunkel investigated the literary form and structural form of the hymn and described it in detail (*Einl-Ps* §2), especially two investigations have thoroughly sifted the relations in this psalm group and have come to understand them anew. In the process it has been shown that the hymn type can by no means be registered in one uniform categorical schema but that a more differentiated research must rather highlight the form-types that are present in the general range of a hymn. Thus C. Westermann distinguished between two basic types, the narrative and the descriptive psalm of praise. Cf. C. Westermann, *The Praise of God in the Psalms* (1965). But especially F. Crüsemann has placed the study of the hymns on completely new foundations and presuppositions. Cf. F. Crüsemann, *Studien zur Formgeschichte von Hymnus und Danklied in Israel*, WMANT 32 (1969). The essential differentiations are indicated by three terms: "imperative hymn," "hymnic participles," and "hymn of an individual."

From now on, the studies of Crüsemann will have to be dealt with wherever a form-critical analysis and closer definition of the psalms collected under the general term תהלה begins. Nevertheless, the cardinal question has at the same time to be asked: To what extent and with what consequences can research exclusively oriented to form criticism actually do justice to the subject at hand? The overemphasis on the formal element that has come about through the form-critical method needs a critical supplement that avoids diluting and blurring of the methodical approach.

A. Alt very lucidly described the study of types as follows: "It is based on the insight that in every single type of literature, as long as it leads its own life, certain contents are intimately combined with certain forms of expression, and that these characteristic combinations are not merely impressed on the materials subsequently and arbitrarily by writers. It is the case, rather, that from time immemorial, and therefore also in the early ages of folk and oral formation and tradition, before all literature, they belonged together essentially because they corresponded to the regularly recurring events and needs of life, from which the types, each by itself, emerged . . ." (*KlSchr* I, 284).

Three facts must be addressed clearly: (1) "Certain contents are intimately combined with certain forms of expression"—contents. Without persistent inquiry about these contents, and that means themes that are expressed in these forms, we shall never be able to reach the goal of achieving a practical comprehension. (2) We must emphasize the condition formulated by Alt: "As long as it leads its own life," a literary type is to be dealt with in the sense indicated and with corresponding methods. What does "as long as it leads its own life" mean, and to what extent is it applicable? History-of-tradition research has definitely demonstrated *that* and *how* transmitted items in the various relations of space and time have been altered, superseded, recast, supplemented, and expanded. Form criticism cannot presume to be able to distill a "pure case" (*actus purus*) from the materials at hand and to elevate it to a criterion for all type alterations. Caution and care, elasticity and readiness to be corrected—these necessary accompaniments of any hypothesis, cannot be stated too explicitly and too often in connection with research in the Psalms. (3) We will have to point a finger at "the regularly recurring events and needs of life." What do we actually know about these things? It is not merely a matter of arranging the local and historical gradations of worship as the (original) "Sitz im Leben"; we must also deal with the revival of a psalm in new cultic—and possibly also group-activity related—connections. The questions that arise are more numerous and more weighty than the answers that have been found.

Therefore it is prudent and appropriate to begin with a careful general designation of the psalm groups ("types"), then to institute a number of form-critical determinations, and finally to take up thematically oriented groupings. In this process we need to strive to answer the question about the "Sitz im Leben" of the theme-oriented psalm groups.

Concerning the question about the "Sitz im Leben," we need to recall H. Gunkel's statements about research: "Every ancient literary type originally has its setting in the communal life of Israel in a very specific place. As even today the sermon belongs to the pulpit, but fairy tales are told to children, so in ancient Israel maidens greeted the returning army with the song of victory; the funerary hymn is intoned by the hired female mourner at the bier of the deceased; the priest proclaims the Torah to the layman at the sanctuary; the legal precedent . . . is quoted before the court by the judge to support his decision; the prophet probably pronounces his saying in the temple court; the wisdom saying is enjoyed by the ancients at the city gate; and so on. One who wants to understand the type must in each case define the whole situation and ask, Who is speaking? Who are the hearers? What is the mood of the situation? What is the effect desired?" (H. Gunkel, *Reden und Aufsätze* [1913], 33). On the form-critical method and the investigation of types, cf. K. Koch, *The Growth of the Biblical Tradition* (1969).

A. We must now present the form-critical differentiation. We propose to do this with reference to the studies of F. Crüsemann.

α The imperative hymn (song of praise) is a basic form of hymn in Israel. We must begin with the "basic model" of Exod. 15:21 (Crüsemann 19ff.). In the Psalter the imperative form is most clearly expressed in Psalm 117. Crüsemann deals in detail with the "carrying out" of the song of praise (32ff.) following upon the imperatives and mostly introduced by כִּי and with the development of the imperative hymn in the Psalms (65ff.). Examples are Psalms 96; 98; 100; and 136. The originally independent basic form of imperative hymn was of course in time combined (in part without showing a seam) with other hymnic forms. Examples are Psalms 113; 135; 147. Still quite general in nature, but approaching more definite conclusions, is the statement about the imperative hymn: "Its situation (*Sitz*) is the regular cultus, its original content the experience of Yahweh's historical treatment of Israel" (308).

β The participial hymn is the other basic form of the hymn in Israel (81ff.). Ancient Near Eastern, especially Babylonian, parallels indicate the importance of this form also in Israel's surrounding world. In the OT the hymnic participles are traceable above all in the prophecy of "Deutero-Isaiah" (Isaiah 40–55) (86ff.). It remains generally to be established that "the hymnic form element of participial predication, derived from the surrounding world, is alive in Israel in formula-like expressions . . ." (308).

γ Finally, the hymn of the individual is a basic form of the hymn of Israel. This form-type must be distinguished clearly from the *todah*, the thanksgiving song of the individual, which objectively belongs to another connection (cf. p. 51 below). As examples of the hymn of the individual we should mention Psalms 8 and 104. For the diversity of the form, cf. Crüsemann, 294ff.

B.   Following the form-critical assessment, we must take up the thematically oriented grouping. Five thematically oriented groups of psalms are to be distinguished.

α   The praise of the Creator resounds in Psalms 8; 19A; 33; 104; (136). We may note that Psalm 19A lies ''entirely outside the regular literary form of the hymn'' (Crüsemann, 306, n. 1), in other words, that we can speak in this case of a hymn of praise only ''in a wider sense.'' It is improper to speak of this group of psalms as ''psalms of nature''; even the designation ''psalms of creation'' is unsuitable, for praise is given not to creation but to the Creator, Yahweh. In addition, we must be careful to observe that the term ''creation'' as a noun is foreign to the Hebrew OT; this designation as a noun first comes into use in Judaism.

The Sitz im Leben of the hymns of praise to Yahweh the Creator is not clear. They unquestionably were connected with the visualization of the creation story in word and symbol to be used in worship. According to very ancient custom, God was in Jerusalem honored as אל עליון קנה שמים וארץ (Gen. 14:19). This occurred, for instance, at the cultic act of proskynesis (prostration) (Pss. 95:6; 99:5; 100:4). But Psalm 8 points to a hymn of praise sung at night (cf. also Ps. 134:1; Isa. 30:29; 1 Chron. 9:33).

β   The hymns of Yahweh as king are clearly identified by the theme of Yahweh's kingship, by which the group is held together: Psalms 47; 93; 96; 97; 98; 99. The question as to where and when these hymns of Yahweh as king were first sung has again and again been answered unequivocally in terms of S. Mowinckel's reconstruction of a festival of the enthronement of Yahweh, referring precisely to a cult of the enthronement of God (S. Mowinckel, *PsStud* II). The acceptance and modification of Mowinckel's hypothesis we may disregard here, for the doubts that arise about accepting a cultic enthronement of Yahweh are heavy and suggest eliminating this hypothesis. Cf. H.-J. Kraus, *Worship in Israel,* see below §9, 3. The Sitz im Leben of the psalms of Yahweh as king is clearly seen in Pss. 24; 95:6; 99:5; 100:4. These psalms were sung at the proskynesis of the worshiping congregation before ''King'' Yahweh.

The hymns of Yahweh as king belong to the context of the proskynesis before the *deus praesens.* They glorify the enthroned God-King and speak of his universal might. The affirmation of an ''enthronement of Yahweh'' must proceed from the assumption that Yahweh is subject to the cyclical turns of the wheel of fortune, dying and arising again. ''To become king'' or ''to be enthroned'' can happen only to him who was not king before or who has temporarily lost his kingship (corresponding to the cultic-mythical drama). No one who affirms an ''enthronement of Yahweh'' can avoid this implication. Such a one bears the burden of proof to show from the OT that Yahweh for a time lost or gave up his kingship. It will hardly be possible to adduce this proof. But if one affirms an Israelite reception of an OT modification of the enthronement festival, then one must make clear which basic idea the term ''enthronement'' contains, after the Israelite borrowing and before. In many circles the view that Yahweh solemnly mounted the throne in a cultic act in Jerusalem is associated with the ark, the throne of God. But where in the OT is there a declaration that Yahweh mounts the throne of the ark only in the sanctuary? According to Ps. 24:8ff., Yahweh Sebaoth sits enthroned above the ark as he makes his entrance into the temple. Cf. also Ps. 132:8. Accordingly, when thinking of the bringing in of the ark, we should speak of an "entrance of the enthroned King" and not of an "enthronement." The psalms of Yahweh as king all originate from the presupposition:

> Thy throne is established from of old;
> thou art from everlasting, O God!
>
> (Ps. 93:2)

But if Yahweh is eternal king, why do we speak of an "enthronement"?

I freely admit here that in my book *Die Königsherrschaft Gottes im Alten Testament* (1951) I was wrong when I interpreted the cry יהוה מלך as an "enthronement formula" (*Inthronisationsformel*). But even then I was convinced that it was impossible to apply the "enthronement psalms" to a cultic-mythical act. Following the suggestions of Gunkel (*EinlPs* 110ff.), I at that time carried out the interpretation of the "enthronement psalms" as a cultic-hymnic proclamation of the historical upheaval inaugurated by the message of Deutero-Isaiah. Since then I have corrected some misconceptions and have recognized, first, the great antiquity of the cultic tradition of the "God-King," and, second, the probably correct translation of the cry יהוה מלך: "Yahweh is King" (cf. the comment on Psalm 93). The correction of that interpretation is to be put on record clearly here. For the problems, cf. §10, 1b.

γ The assumption of "harvest songs" in the worship of Israel in Psalms 65; (145) is only weakly supported. Still, basic considerations prompt us to assume that the cultic festivals designed as harvest festivals in the calendar of festivals found expression in corresponding hymns of praise to the "Lord of the Harvest" (Matt. 9:38; cf. Isa. 9:2).

δ In the historical hymns the song of praise of Yahweh's activity in history is sung: Psalms 105; (106); 114; 135; (136). Without question, such hymns of praise corresponded to the narrations and representations in the worship of Israel of the great acts of Yahweh; they were themselves a proclamation in the celebration. Of course, it is a long and hardly traceable way that leads from Exod. 15:21 up to a psalm like Psalm 78. Psalm 78 belongs to the group of didactic poems (§6, 5) and documents the complete integration of historical tradition into the genre of reflection and didactic proclamation.

ε As entrance hymns we should list Psalms 24; 95; and 100. The cultic situation is to be recognized in connection with festival processions. Cf. §6, 6.

For the OT hymns there are parallel "types" in Israel's surroundings. From the Sumerian poetry we should mention above all the hymns of the gods (*adab*) and the drum songs (*tigi*). These are types in which the high gods, and then also the rulers, are praised. In addition, we should also mention the "long song" (*shirgidda*), which was sung by a single singer; cf. A. Falkenstein and W. von Soden, *Sumerische und akkadische Hymnen und Gebete*, 20f. Among the Akkadian poems the "song of celebration" (*zamar tanitti*) is closest to the hymn type. The praise of the god or goddess is here entirely in the foreground. There are also various special forms of the hymn; so, for instance, the "self-hymn," which is borrowed from the Sumerian tradition. Hymnic elements further extend to the psalms of lament and of repentance, "so that we can speak of a hymn associated with a prayer of lament or repentance" (A. Falkenstein and W. von Soden, 45). From a hymn of Ashurbanipal addressed to Anshar we can see that Akkadian poetry too knows the typical forms of predication (hymnic relative clause, hymnic participles):

Mighty, great ruler of the gods, who knows all things,
most worthy Enlil of the gods, exalted above all, who determines destinies;
Anshar, mighty and great Lord, who knows all things,

most worthy Enlil of the gods, who determines destinies!
[I will] extol great and mighty Anshar, the ruler of the gods, the lord of the lands,
[I will glorify] his mighty deeds, his renown praise again and again!
Anshar's name I will glorify, extol on high his name;
the renown of him [who] lives in Ehursanggalkurkurra will I praise again and again!

(Cf. A. Falkenstein and W. von Soden, 254)

For the Babylonian parallels, cf. above all F. Crüsemann, 135ff.

The Egyptian hymns also are above all songs of praise concerning the gods. The elements of structure of this type correspond conspicuously to those of the OT psalms. "They begin with the name of the one who is praised, which is sometimes preceded also by an acclamation such as 'praise be to you!' or 'glory to you!' Then there follows, actually as descriptive appellations of this name, a series of adjectives, nouns, participles, and relative clauses that depict the characteristics of the one who is praised or call his deeds to remembrance" (A. Erman, *Literatur der Ägypter*, 13). We cite an Osiris hymn as an example:

Praise be to you, Osiris, son of Nut,
you who bear the horns and lean against a high pillar;
to whom the crown was given and joy before the new gods,
whose might Atum created in the hearts of men, of gods, and of the transfigured;
to whom the lordship was given in Heliopolis;
great in being in Busiris, feared in both holy places;
great in power in Rosetta, a ruler over the might in Enas, a ruler over the power in Tenent;
dearly beloved on earth, in fond remembrance in God's palace;
of whom the great powers were afraid;
before whom the great arose on their mats;
for whom Shu stirred up fear, and whose power Tefnet created;
to whom Upper and Lower Egypt approach bowing,
for their fear of him is so great and his might so powerful.

(Cf. A Erman, *Ägypt. Rel.*[2] 61)

2. Songs of Prayer (תפלה)

A.   By far the largest number of psalms collected in the Psalter belong to the songs of prayer. The general term תפלה includes prayer songs of the individual, community prayer songs (תפלת עם Ps. 80:4), and thanksgiving songs (תודה). For an understanding of the basic Hebrew term תפלה, cf. §4, No. 8, and K. Heinen, "Das Nomen *tᵉfillā* als Gattungsbezeichnung," *BZ* NF 16 (1972) 103-105. The three subgroups named can be differentiated form-critically (cf. below). For the present we need only to state in a general way that the prayer songs of the individual are clearly recognizable by the "I" that speaks and sings (cf. E. Balla, *Das Ich der Psalmen*, 1912). But concerning this "I" some greater detail will be given. Correspondingly, in regard to the prayer songs of the cult and the community we need to state that in them the "we" of the speaking and singing assembly clearly emerges. But according to the criteria of content and in view of the Sitz im Leben (see below), the song of thanksgiving (תודה) without question belongs to the context of the prayer song of the individual. We refer to the studies of F. Crüsemann, in which we read: The *todah* stands "in a clear and unequivocal relation to the lament of the individual" (F. Crüsemann, *Studien zur Formgeschichte von Hymnus und Danklied in Israel*, WMANT 32 [1969], 309).

With this first general grasp of the group of prayer songs, the designations introduced by H. Gunkel are eliminated (cf. Gunkel and Begrich, *EinlPs* §6: "laments of the individual"; §4: "community laments"). For the problems, see above, §6. But, as noted above, in the arrangement of the psalms that belong together we shall have to go somewhat further. The psalms listed under the general designation תפלה will in the first phase have to bearranged form-critically and in the second phase according to the perspective of the contents (thematically).

α The prayer songs of the individual are in the first place to be analyzed form-critically, i.e., according to structure and organization. Cf. Gunkel and Begrich, *EinlPs* §6, and C. Westermann, "Struktur und Geschichte der Klage im Alten Testament," *ZAW* 66 (1954) 44-80 = *Forschung am Alten Testament,* ThB 24 (1964) 266-305; J. W. Wevers, "A Study in the Form Criticism of Individual Complaint Psalms," *VT* 6 (1956) 80ff.

A. Introduction:

a. In the first words of the prayer song, the invocation of the name of Yahweh (in the vocative case) occurs. Usually the invocation reads יהוה or אלהי.

b. The invocation is immediately accompanied by a cry for help, which is most often in the imperative mood.

c. The invocation may be repeated in ever-new arrangements. In this repetition the petitioner declares what Yahweh means to him. Illustrations and comparisons underscore God's power to save and his goodness, in which the petitioner takes refuge.

d. Following the invocation there is sometimes a self-description by the afflicted petitioner. He describes himself as "distressed and poor" and with a few indications portrays his present condition.

e. Elements of the body may already be suggested in the introduction, especially: distress, plea, and request (jussive).

B. Body:

a. The petitioner and singer declares that he will pour out his נפש ("soul") before Yahweh. This immediate transition to the presentation or depiction of the complaint may be thought of as the first element of the body.

b. But the essential ingredient of the body is the narrative, or the portrayal of the distress experienced and now still present. This may have to do with sickness, a legal problem (indictment), persecution by enemies, being abandoned to forces of destruction (שאול), being forsaken by God, or guilt. The portrayals of the situation most often point to the present state of affairs, to the petitioner's present position, or to manners of conduct.

c. The prayer song is laced with questions and surrounded by them: "Why?" "How long?" These are the pleas to Yahweh which at times come very close to the borderline of accusation.

d. The plea stands in immediate connection with the depiction of the distress. The petitioner pleads and prays for Yahweh's gracious intervention, a turn for the better in the misfortune that has befallen the afflicted in a given case. The pleas most often are uttered as cries for help in the imperative mood.

e. Beside the pleas, or in the place of the imperatives, requests may be used in the jussive mood of the third person.

f. When the requests have to do with turning back or overcoming enemies, they may take the form of imprecations or maledictions. Above the pleas and requests the basic tone of trust is often heard, which may also make its presence felt already in the introduction. Expressions of this kind of trust dominate in Psalms 16; 23; and 62. On these expressions of trust in the prayer hymn, see P. Vonck, *L'expression de confiance dans le Psautier: Message and Mission,* Publications de l'université Lovanium de Kishana (1969).

g. Inducements for an effectual intervention are presented and suggested to Yahweh. These inducements may be variously motivated. The appeal is to Yahweh's favor, Yahweh's honor and faithfulness over against the elect. Also the enormous magnitude of the distress and the צדקה ("righteousness") of the petitioner may be held up to Yahweh.

h. In this connection the declarations of innocence deserve special attention. Especially in hymns in which people who have been persecuted and accused raise their voice, can this motive turn up (cf., e.g., Ps. 7:3ff.).

i. A special element of the body that we could also label "closing section" is the vow. The person who complains and prays vows that he will present an offering of thanksgiving to Yahweh and praise and proclaim his name. This "vow of thanksgiving" has not always been recognized clearly. Cf. D. Michel, *Tempora und Satzstellung in the Psalmen* (1960).

j. It can happen that the petitioner looks forward to the occasion of the great turning point. He looks forward to and awaits the intervention of Yahweh that takes place in the "oracle of healing" or in the "theophany." The assurance of being heard asserts itself. He who cries from depths of woe already thinks of himself as one who is giving thanks. Expressions of certainty lead and show the way to the *todah* (see below).

That it is out of place and irrelevant to associate the concept of an "individual," unshared "complaint" with the prayer songs of individuals was emphasized already at the beginning of this section. The "I" of the petitioner is not a single person who may possibly also perhaps be understood to be the skilled writer of the psalm. Here we must bid an unremitting farewell to the conceptions and interpretations of the Gunkel school (cf. §8, 1). Moving towards a new orientation, G. von Rad had already stated that the modern reader "constantly comes up against formulations of incomparable personal fervour and earnestness: but form-criticism long ago showed that, as far as phraseology goes, even the wholly personal prayers of lamentation move with few exceptions in an obviously completely conventionalized body of formulae. In spite of the entirely personal form of style in these prayers, the exegete will hardly ever succeed in discerning anything like an individual or biographically contoured fate behind the details given by the suppliant. Rather, the suppliants express their sufferings in a few typical and often very faded concepts" (G. von Rad, *Theol OT*, 1:398-399). E. Gerstenberger has delineated the prayer and lament rituals of the songs of prayer in even sharper definition. Cf. E. Gerstenberger, "Der bittende Mensch: Bittritual und Klagelied des Einzelnen im Alten Testament" (diss., Heidelberg, n.d.). The only question is whether Gerstenberger, with his strict reference to the Babylonian (and other ancient Near Eastern) prayer rituals, has not exaggerated his attack. Does the Psalter really contain "rituals"? Should we not try rather carefully to develop the concept "conventionalized body of formulas," as used by G. von Rad, by speaking of evidences in the prayer language of Israel that were present in the temple area in the form of liturgies and formularies? Without being misunderstood as proposing a kind of vitalism, we can say that in Israel's songs of prayer there is life and testimonial power, emotion, and a wealth of relevance, while it is precisely the Babylonian rituals that present a noticeably stiff, formalistic, and monotonous impression. The language of the תפלה is a living language, open to manifold possibilities of application (cf. §8, 1). The speaking and singing "I" of the Psalms participates in this prayer language of Israel. And this process of participation is not simply a matter of coming in and taking over rigid, stanza-bound ritual formulations, but participation in the history of Israel's language of prayer:

Yet you are enthroned as the Holy One,
    you Praise of Israel!
In you our fathers trusted,
    they trusted, and you delivered them.

> To you they cried and were saved,
>   in you they trusted and were not disappointed!
>
> (Ps. 22:3-5)

The history of Yahweh with the fathers and the history of the fathers with the God of Israel—these are the shaping forces of the prayer language of the Psalms, a language that cannot just simply be patched into the category of ancient Near Eastern ritual and thereby be leveled down to the unhistorical area of a schematized encounter with the gods.

In the prayer songs of the individual we must ascertain case by case whether and to what degree the language of prayer represents living and intensely relevant liturgy, generalized formulary, or the literature of prayer. Those prayer songs are to be understood as intensely relevant liturgy which clearly—or at least roughly so in their contours—display the relation to the concrete vicissitudes of life that are at issue in the cultus (cf. below). In the generalized formulary the concrete cultic relations, but also the contours of the vicissitudes of life, have faded away; they appear only in standardized form. The possibilities of participation by an individual have therefore become more abundant and more relevant by the expanded language. Finally, we must refer to the literature of prayer. Here we have relatively late, artificial structures—for instance, in the form of the acrostic. For this form of prayer literature, new attention will still be due. Its late form gathers the "conventionalized body of formulas" of the prayer tradition and brings together prayer psalms. Cf. L. Ruppert, "Psalm 25 und die Grenze der kult-orientierten Psalmenexegese," *ZAW* 84 (1922) 576-582.

β In Ps. 80:4, the community prayer song is referred to with the term תפלה עם, which characterizes the group. Characteristic is the "we" of the speaking and singing community. While the prayer songs of the individual are regularly to be listed in the thematically determined categories (cf. below), we should list as prayer songs of the cult and of the community Psalms 44; 60; 74; 77; 79; 80; 83; 85; 90; 94; 123; 126; 129; and 137. The classification and designation community thanksgiving songs and songs of trust, used in the first four editions of this work, is now abandoned. On the elimination of the "community songs of thanksgiving" cf. F. Crüsemann, *Studien zur Form-geschichte von Hymnus und Danklied in Israel,* WMANT 32 (1969) 3-9. On "the community song of prayer," cf. Gunkel and Begrich, *EinlPs* §4; H. W. Wolff, "Der Aufruf zur Volksklage," *ZAW* 76 (1964) 48-56 = *GesStudzAT,* ThB 22 (1973²) 392-401.

Like the prayer songs of the individual, the community prayer songs in most instances begin with an invocation of Yahweh. Conspicuous after that is the historical overview, which considers Yahweh's work of salvation in earlier times and culminates in an appeal for the confirming of the saving faithfulness of the God of Israel (cf. Pss. 44:1ff.; 126:2ff.). Depiction of the distress, cries for help, reflections, and questions determine the main thrust of the prayer (cf. Psalms 44 and 83). Statements of trust occur again and again (Pss. 44:4ff.; 46; 125; 126). In Psalm 123 the motives of the prayer song of the individual and of the community intertwine. Obviously, an individual could emerge as the speaker for the community. We may not preclude that the king was this individual (cf. 1 Kings 8:29). But here the prayer liturgy comes into consideration. By its refrains Psalm 80 is clearly marked as a liturgical prayer. Liturgical endings cast their shadows also in Psalms 77 and 85. Psalm 137 participates in the language of the "songs of Zion" (§6, 4). Wisdom traditions show through in Psalms 90 and 94;

and with this characteristic these psalms move close to "didactic poetry" (§6, 5).

In each of the community prayer songs we must ask anew about the situation of distress that has given rise to the prayer liturgy in the holy place. Among the situations in which a community prayer song needed to be spoken were those mentioned in 1 Kings 8:33-40. In any case, it was a custom in Israel to "proclaim a fast" in times of great distress (cf. H. W. Wolff, *ZAW* 76 [1964] 48ff.) and to repent in the sanctuary with ceremonies and rites. We should remember that in the time after the destruction of Solomon's temple regular services of repentance and fasting took place in Jerusalem (Jer. 41:5ff.; Zech. 7:1ff.; 8:18ff.). On these cultic observances, see H. E. von Waldow, "Anlass und Hintergrund der Verkündigung Deuterojesaias" (diss. Bonn, 1953); H.-J. Kraus, BK XX (1968³) 8ff. The prayer songs of the cult and of the community looked for an answer from Yahweh transmitted in the form of a "priestly oracle of salvation" or a cultic-prophetic statement. Cf. J. Begrich, "Das priesterliche Heilsorakel," *ZAW* 52 (1934) 81-92; S. Mowinckel, *Offersang og Sangoffer*, 305ff.

γ The thanksgiving song of the individual (תודה) is very closely related to the prayer song of individuals, as we have already shown. A presupposition in every case is the turn of events, the rescue from the depth of distress. How can this turn of events be designated? First and foremost by means of a reference to the occurrence of the deliverance. But then also in the light of "fortune-changing interventions" as they have taken place in the "priestly oracle of salvation," in a cultic-prophetic saying, in the judgment of God, through signs (interpreted by priests), or through theophanic visions. In the psalms of thanksgiving we shall have to examine each case in turn to see which occurrence brought about the change of events. The *todah* shows a correspondence (often clearly indicated) to the vow of thanks which the petitioner had made in his prayer in distress. The thanksgiving song of the individual in the Psalter has a clearly recognizable intention and theme. To the group תודה belong Psalms 18; 30; 31; 32; 40A; 52; 66B; 92; 116; 118; 120: In the songs mentioned the form is not always clear and unambiguous. For the form-critical analysis and determination see F. Crüsemann, *Studien zur Formgeschichte von Hymnus und Danklied in Israel*, WMANT 32 (1969) 210ff. For the hymn of thanksgiving of the individual, also cf. W. Beyerlin, "Kontinuität beim 'berichtenden' Lobpreis des Einzelnen," in *Wort und Geschichte: Festschrift für K. Elliger*, AOAT 18 (1973) 17-24.

The confluence of several elements of form is, for example, clearly observable in Psalm 92. Above all, the *todah* has the tendency to combine didactic messages with the retrospective descriptions of the distress and the occurrence of the turn of events (cf. §6, 5). The Sitz im Leben of the songs of thanksgiving then carries with it the idea that the act of giving thanks (thankoffering, song of thanks) is thought of as taking place in the great cultic context of the entrance into the temple (Psalm 118) or in a liturgical situation (Psalm 52). On Psalm 52, cf. Jörg Jeremias, *Kultprophetie und Gerichtsverkündigung in der späteren Königszeit*, WMANT 35 (1970) 120. But the תודה can also be brought into relation to a "royal psalm" (§6, 3) so that the description "royal song of thanksgiving" (Psalm 18) would be in place (F. Crüsemann, 256).

Of the essence is the question about the cultic Sitz im Leben of the songs of thanksgiving. An answer is provided by a description of a situation as it is demonstrable also in other songs of thanksgiving:

> I will announce your name to my brothers,
>> will praise you in the midst of the congregation.
> To you I am indebted for praise in the great congregation;
>> my vows I will pay before those who fear him.
>
> (Ps. 22:22, 25)

During the great worship festivals of Israel one who was rescued from distress and suffering had opportunity to present his thankoffering in the circle of family members, friends, and other witnesses, to report concerning distress and deliverance, and to sing praises. His thanksgiving is a תהלה (Ps. 22:25). And yet, the song of thanksgiving of an individual does not belong to the group of "songs of praise" (§6, 1), but to the association of the תפלה that is characterized thematically and through the "Sitz im Leben." For in the act of thanksgiving the תפלה was recapitulated from the depths of the distress. At the festival of thanksgiving, prayer songs were communicated (cf. §8, 1) that had originated far from the place of worship (Ps. 42:6). Worth noting in this connection is a custom that has become known through stelae from Asia Minor. The report of the distress and the occurrence of the rescue were published in written form. Thus Ps. 40:39f. probably refers to the practice of reporting on a written scroll concerning suffering and rescue. Cf. H. J. Hermisson, *Sprache und Ritus im altisraelitischen Kult,* WMANT 19 (1965) 43ff.

In connection with the songs of thanksgiving of an individual we shall have to remind ourselves of the differentiation made above. There is a context-rich thanksgiving liturgy in which the cult relationship is clearly noticeable in the corresponding manners of presentation (Psalms 40A; 116; 118). Of a different kind are the formularies, in which several elements of form can also come together (Psalm 92); the cultic contours have faded, and elements of didactic poetry have been added (cf. §6, 5). Finally, the form of the song of thanksgiving has also been transferred to the literature of prayer; it has found expression in the artificial, constructed form of an acrostic (Psalm 9/10).

In its report on distress, the song of thanksgiving of the individual only rarely permits recognition of the concrete suffering and distress to which the petitioner was exposed. In any case, it will be necessary to investigate more thoroughly the תפלה of an individual, or the indications that turn up in the song of thanksgiving of an individual, with special emphasis on the concrete condition of distress. Here a study that deals with the theme and the content and a corresponding grouping of the prayer songs is necessary.

B. The inquiry about the theme, or about the specific occasion of distress of the petitioners, leads to the following grouping, which is indispensable for the more exact investigation of the prayer songs of the individual (see above): (*a*) the prayer song of the sick; (*b*) the prayer song of the persecuted and the accused; (*c*) the prayer song of a sinner; in addition we must consider (*d*) the "summons to give thanks," and (*e*) the prayer literature. In the following sections the comprehensive enumeration of the prayer songs of the individual are reviewed in such a way that psalms belonging to the general group are named in their specific thematic definition.

α According to the arrangement of K. Seybold, what are here designated as prayer songs of a sick person belong to the psalms of sickness and healing:

—certainly: Psalms 38; 41; 88;

—relatively certainly: Psalms 30; 39; 69; 102; 103;

—probably: Psalms 6; 13; (31); 32; (35); 51; (71); 77; 91.

Still, not only the degree of certainty but also the assignment to the form groups will have to be modified in individual cases. In any case, we will have to assign to the theme-oriented group Psalms 6; 13; 22; (31); 38; 41; 69; 71; 88; 102; and 103. On these prayer songs of a sick person, cf. R. Martin-Achard, "Approche des Psaumes," *Cahiers Théologiques* 60 (1969) 49-55; K. Seybold, "Krankheit und Heilung: Soziale Aspekte in den Psalmen," *BiKi* 20 (1971) 107-111; K. Seybold, *Das Gebet des Kranken im Alten Testament: Untersuchungen zur Bestimmung und Zuordnung der Krankheits- und Heilungspsalmen*, BWANT V, 19 (1973). In Psalm 102 the Hebrew title of such a psalm is תפלה לעני. The specific sickness of the petitioner emerges in the report with varying emphasis and with changing clarity. The petitioner finds himself near death and therefore already in the sphere of death (Psalm 88). Psalms 38; 41; and 69 speak clearly about the afflictions of the sickness. That the petitioner of Psalm 69 must endure heavy afflictions is clearly expressed in vv. 27 and 30. In vv. 20ff. we then hear of the abuse and the accusations of the enemies. This fact could move us to think of classifying the psalm in B, β. But we will have to consider that the sick and suffering person was exposed to the question: "Who sinned, this man or his parents . . . ?" (John 9:2). The possibility of an accusation and of a hostile position is inherent in this logic of causality; at the same time, so is the tendency of the prayer songs of the sick toward the expressions of prayer of those who, weighed down with guilt and sin, speak a prayer of repentance (B, γ). We will have to make allowances for this overlapping, especially since not a few of the prayer songs of a sick person have the character of a formulary (cf. especially Psalm 103). In extreme distress the sick person utters the vow of thanksgiving, with which he combines the hope and the assurance that he will praise Yahweh at the festival of thanksgiving. In every case, however, we will have to assume that the prayer songs of the sick were sung when the sufferings—now overcome—were recapitulated at the festival of thanksgiving in the report on the distress. The sick person was not allowed to come to the temple until he was healed. Rites of expiation and cleansing were required before the restored could again take part in the celebration of the congregation and offer his תודה (cf. A, γ). For the individual phases: K. Seybold, BWANT V, 19 (1973).

β   The prayer songs of the accused and persecuted first came into clear view with the studies of H. Schmidt. There was never any doubt that in numerous psalms the theme "accusation and persecution" played a large role, that enemies who lie in wait and protestations of innocence were expressed; yet it was H. Schmidt who first described that group of prayer songs of individuals which he called "the prayer of the accused." Cf. H. Schmidt, *Das Gebet der Angeklagten im Alten Testament*, BZAW 49 (1928). With this study the institution of divine jurisdiction in the sanctuary came into view. In 1 Kings 8:31f., in Solomon's prayer at the dedication of the temple, we read: "If a man sins against his neighbor and is made to take an oath, and comes and swears his oath before thine altar in this house, then hear thou in heaven, and act, and judge thy servants, condemning the guilty by bringing his conduct upon his own head, and vindicating the righteous by rewarding him according to his righteousness." Similarly also those cases in local jurisprudence that gave the impression of being "too difficult," for instance, because no witnesses could be supplied, were remanded to the sanctuary (cf. Deut. 17:8ff.). The institution of divine jurisdiction here under discussion and to be presupposed as the "Sitz im Leben" for numerous psalms has been investigated more closely, especially by W. Beyerlin. Cf. W. Beyerlin, *Die Rettung der Bedrängten in den Feindpsalmen der Einzelnen auf institutionelle Zusammenhänge untersucht,* FRLANT 99 (1970). Under the title "prayer songs of the accused and persecuted" the coordination of the respective psalms can be undertaken in the way Beyerlin does it. According to this, the psalms with statements of rescue that are related to the institution are Psalms 3; 4; 5; 7; 11; 17; 23; 26; 27; 57; and 63. As psalms in which the relation to the institution is only weakly discernible we count Psalms 9/10; 12; 25; 42/43; 54; 55; 56; 57; 59; 62; 64; 70; 86; 94; 109; 140; 142; and 143. But what can we ascertain on the subject of the institution of divine jurisprudence and deduce especially from the psalms listed? Beyerlin, with critical scrutiny, has built on the studies of H. Schmidt (see above) and the papers of L. Delekat. Cf. L. Delekat, "Katoche, Hierodulie und Adoptionsfreilassung," *Münchener Beiträge zur Papyrusforschung und antiken Rechtsgeschichte* 47 (1964); L. Delekat, *Asilie und Schutzorakel am Zionheiligtum: Eine Untersuchung zu den privaten Feindpsalmen* (1967). After all that has been learned from the study of the institution of divine jurisdiction, the following phases and acts in the basic structure can be discerned:

1. "To thee do I flee"; "with thee do I take refuge": looking to the protection of the temple area in the need for justice for the accused and persecuted person.

2. Preliminary investigation of the subject of admittance to the temple: Ps. 5:5-7; the accused and persecuted individual may enter the temple—for proskynesis.

3. He hides in the "shadow of the wings" of Yahweh (Pss. 17:8; 27:5; 57:1; and often): expressions of trust manifest the security in the protection of God (for the wings of the cherubim, see H.-J. Kraus, "Archäologische und topographische Probleme Jerusalems im Lichte der Psalmenexegese," *ZDPV* 75 [1959] 125-140).

4. Oath of purification and self-malediction as ritual acts that the accused person takes up (cf. 1 Kings 8:31; Ps. 7:3f.; on this, see J. Pedersen, *Der Eid bei den Semiten* [1914] 6, 82f., 103f., 112ff.; and M. Noth, BK IX/1 186).

5. "Judge me, Yahweh!" "Vindicate me!" These petitions aim at the rendition of the divine judgment that is given "in the morning." But before that the accused, lying in the temple at night, exposes himself to examination and testing by the *Deus praesens* (Ps. 17:3; 139ff.). With the sacrifice of the early morning and a last appeal, the petitioner submits to divine judgment.

6. It can happen that those who accuse the petitioner and the persecuting enemies will not acknowledge nor accept the judgment of God (cf. Ps. 4:1ff.). But the cultic process is not complete until the enemies agree with the divine judgment and "come to shame" with their persecuting accusation.

7. Once the rescuing acquittal has been spoken, he who has been saved from the distress of judgment engages in the תודה (thanksgiving) (A, γ), in which not infrequently the occasion of defeating the accusation and putting a stop to the persecution is envisioned. In the festival of thanksgiving the communion meal "in the presence of my enemies," who were present at the place of worship and are still present, is prepared (Ps. 23:5).

Here, too, we should again point out that the degree of belonging and proximity of the "prayer songs of the accused and persecuted" to the institution of divine justice can be extremely various. The scale extends from the intensively attached institutional agenda over the formulary that lies close to the institution and is yet detached from it all the way to the prayer literature that reworks the older tradition anew.

But wherever the cultic relation is clear or still recognizable, there mostly the worship of the temple of Zion (of the preexilic time) is involved.

γ   The existence of special prayer songs of a sinner is disputed. Not infrequently psalms that are characterized by the theme "guilt," or the distress of sin and the petitioner's readiness to repent, are connected with prayer songs of a sick person (which see). Just the same, especially Psalms 51 and 130 are to be thought of as "prayer songs of a sinner." The heading explanation in Psalm 51 makes an unambiguous assertion in this respect and provides a clear reference. But also Psalms 13 and 40B probably are to be added, while Psalm 32 from the viewpoint of the תודה praises the turn away from the burden of the guilt to forgiveness as the liberating event. Rites of purification probably accompanied the entreaty of the prayer (Ps. 51:2, 7). But the תודה appears under the banner of forgiveness that has been pronounced and applied as sure (Psalm 32).

δ   With the vow of thanksgiving already mentioned, which can turn up in the various prayer songs of an individual, and with the summons to give thanks (Psalm 107) we must once more consider the bridge from a prayer song seeking release from distress to the תודה. In the depth of distress the petitioner vows praise and thanksgiving in the תודה. In the festival worship of Israel, at the appointed time, the summons to pay the vows and to present this תודה resounds.

ε   Finally let us once more refer to the prayer literature, that is, to that late artistic undertaking to fashion comprehensive compositions (e.g., characterized by the form of the acrostic) in which a wealth of conventionalized prayer formulas and prayer traditions was used. For prayer literature, see L. Ruppert, "Psalm 25 und die Grenze der kultorientierten Psalmenexegese," ZAW 84 (1932) 576-582.

Even though the concept of the "private" is not without its own problems, reference can be made to the following explanation of G. von Rad: "The power of the compulsion of style can hardly be overestimated in these poems. Types can also leave their 'Sitz im Leben,' that is, people learn to express themselves in poetry also outside the hallowed institutions, in other words, at home. Thus types wander off into the private sector, but— and this is the interesting point—the type with all its characteristics of form, with all its traditional topicality, is preserved, even where the compulsion of style resident in the 'Sitz im Leben' has vanished. The conventional form can hardly be destroyed. Naturally, there are possibilities of variations that are especially interesting precisely in consideration of the omnipotence of the compulsion of style. Styles can, as Gunkel already liked to say, finally also be sung to pieces" (G. von Rad, *God at Work in Israel* [1980], 212). Still, the expression "wander off into the private sector" has not really encompassed the process that was described in this section—apart from the problem of the concept of the "private."

For the OT prayer songs of individual suppliants, there are many instructive parallels, especially in the Akkadian literature. Cf. F. Stummer, *Sumerisch-akkadische Parallelen zum Aufbau alttestamentlicher Psalmen* (1922); J. Begrich, "Die Vertrauensäusserungen im Israelitischen Klagelied des Einzelnen und in seinem babylonischen Gegenstück," ZAW 46 (1928) 221-260; G. Widengren, *The Akkadian and Hebrew Psalms of Lamentation as Religious Documents* (1936); G. D. Castellino, *Le lamentazioni individuali e gli inni in Babylonia e in Israele* (1939). As an example of Akkadian composition of songs of lamentation we here quote a single psalm from an inscription of Ashurbanipal:

To God and man, to the dead and the living have I done what is good.
Why (in spite of that) are sickness, heartbreak, consumption, ruin attached to me?
In the country discord and at home wild quarreling never leaves my side;
Sedition and evil talk are constantly plotted against me.
Great affliction and bodily suffering have bent my figure low;
In woe and lamentation have I passed my days.
On the day of the city's god, at the monthly festival, I am troubled;
Death holds me in its grasp, I get into (bitter) distress.
In agony of heart and wretchedness I lament day and night,
Have become so worn out: 'O God, give (this) to him who is not
   godfearing; but may I see your light!
How long will you inflict this on me, O God?
I am treated like one who does not fear gods and goddesses!
                                        (A. Falkenstein and W. von Soden, 269f.)

From this lament a number of basic forms that stand out also in the OT lament (see above) are discernible. Of course, most of the Akkadian laments are characterized by elements of form that very substantially depart from the OT psalms. The hymnic element in the introduction to the lament plays an important role in the Akkadian prayer literature. The object is to make the godhead invoked propitious and gain its good will through doxologies. Also adjurations and magical exorcisms constantly find a place in the Akkadian song.

3. Royal Psalms (מעשי למלך Ps. 45:1)

The following psalms of the Psalter are to be listed in the group that is thematically characterized as royal psalms: Psalms 2; (18); 20; 21; 45; 72; 89; 101; 110; 132; 141:1-11. "The songs referred to have their inner unity in the fact that they all deal with kings" (H. Gunkel and J. Begrich, *EinlPs* 140). This preliminary explanation will have to suffice as we begin to deal with this group of psalms. But the definition does set certain limits. Under no circumstances will it be possible to expand the concept "royal psalms" to include also texts that contain no "royal themes" at all or only weak echoes of the same but are characterized by the heading לדוד (of David), which refers to a king.

We shall do well to begin this section with the question about the "Sitz im Leben" of the royal psalms listed above. At what kind of occasion are "royal psalms" presented? Is it possible to infer from these songs that they deal with a definite ritual act? Psalm 110 affords a first insight. Obviously we have there a song that contains descriptions and messages that have to do with the festival of the enthronement of a king of Jerusalem. The age-old privileges of the (Jebusite) city-king of Jerusalem are conveyed to the ruler that has issued from the dynasty of David. The solemn rites of initiation and the oracular pronouncements clearly indicate that a king is being enthroned. We could also describe Psalms 2; 72; and 101 as "royal psalms" that have to do with the enthronement of the ruler. But the question persists whether there was not an annual "king-and-temple festival" corresponding to the basic process of enthronement which, in a solemn opening ceremony at the annual chief festival, portrayed for the pilgrims coming to the festival the basic foundations of the Jerusalem rite, the election of David and the election of Zion. It was H. Gunkel who first pointed to this "annual festival" (H. Gunkel and J. Begrich, *EinlPs* 141). In this connection Psalm 132 plays a decisive role (cf. the commentary on Psalm 132). This psalm lets us witness a cultic act which, with the solemn procession of the ark of the covenant up to Zion, celebrates the "election of Jerusalem" (Ps. 132:13) and with the recitation of 2 Samuel 7 solemnizes the "election of David and his dynasty" (Ps. 132:11f.). Psalms 2; 72; and 101 could possibly be connected with this "royal festival of Zion" that took place annually and was the opening feature of the Feast of Tabernacles. Cf. H.-J. Kraus, *Die Königsherrschaft Gottes im Alten Testament* (1951) 50ff.; H.-J. Kraus, *Worship in Israel* (1966). In addition to the "festival of enthronement" and the annual "festival of the king and the sanctuary," we would then also have to refer to the wedding of the ruler. Psalm 45 glorifies the king in his splendor and very clearly refers to a wedding celebration. Finally, we must mention serious times of distress that have caused the ruler to call upon Yahweh before all the people in a service of lamentation, or to intone a song of thanksgiving in the sanctuary after a miraculous deliverance (cf. Psalms 18 and 20).

After these references to the "Sitz im Leben" of the "royal psalms," let us enumerate the chief elements of the literary forms. First there is the "oracle"—the (cultic-prophetic) address to the ruler (cf. Pss. 2:7ff.; 21:8-12; 110:1, 3, 4; 89:19ff.; 132:11f.). In connection with the pronouncement of God that lays the foundation of the dynasty, at festal occasions good fortune is predicted for the king. Ancient Near Eastern parallels to this solemn address may be found in J. B. Pritchard, *ANET* 449f. (also cf. A. Falkenstein and W. von Soden, *Sumerische und akkadische Hymnen und Gebete,* 229f., 393f.). G. von Rad has called attention to the Egyptian parallels: "Das judäische Königsritual," *ThLZ* 72 (1947) 211-216 = *GesStud:* ThB 8 (1971) 205-213. Another typical element of the royal psalms is intercession. Priests or prophets intercede for the king before Yahweh (Pss. 20:1-5; 72:1; 132:1f., 10). In Psalm 72 this intercession finds characteristic expression in benedictions that are addressed to the ruler as a word of power with immediate efficacy. Unique in the OT is the style of the song of praise that is in evidence in Psalm 45. In hymnic style an ode is sung to the king (למלך Ps. 45:1). The elements of form of a תפלה originating from distress, or perhaps of thanksgiving, have arisen from special occasions. In Ps. 89:38ff. a prayer is intoned for deliverance from the distress represented by the decline experienced by the dynasty of David. The style of a song of thanksgiving is decisive in Pss. 18; 20:6; 21:1ff.; 144:1ff. Still another unique element of form ought to be mentioned, one that can be explained on the basis of definite ritualistic presuppositions: in Psalm 101 the king makes a declaration of loyalty and takes a vow.

In addition to the psalms that are clearly designated as "royal psalms," the intercessions for the king appearing in a number of songs of prayer and of thanksgiving ought to be mentioned: Pss. 61:6ff.; 63:11; 80:17ff.; 84:9.

But all royal psalms have reference to the time in which the monarchy existed in Israel; they are in origin preexilic—even though we cannot rule out later shaping. On the strength of the data in the Psalter, we may in addition state that all decisive references are to the monarchy in Jerusalem. Even in the places where north-Israelite traditions have been suspected (Psalm 45), it is more plausible to think of Jerusalem.

On the royal psalms, cf., among others, Keith R. Crim, *The Royal Psalms* (1962); W. H. Schmidt, *Alttestamentlicher Glaube in seiner Geschichte* (1975) 180ff. (additional bibliography there); S. S. Patro, "Royal Psalms in Modern Scholarship," diss. Kiel (1976).

4. Songs of Zion (שִׁיר צִיוֹן)

The designation of this group of psalms as שִׁיר צִיוֹן is based on Ps. 137:3. From this passage it follows that in exile this clearly defined group of hymns, songs, and artistic psalms existed among the Jews and that they were known even to strangers as ''songs of Zion.'' What we have here is psalms that glorify Zion. The holy mountain of Jerusalem is the place where Yahweh is present (Ps. 46:5). To this type belong Psalms (46); 48; 76; 84; 87; 122; (132). The situation and the context of these psalms can well be ascertained from a number of revealing verses. Thus (according to Pss. 84:2f.; 122:2) Zion was celebrated in song as one entered the holy place. At this occasion the psalmists look back upon their pilgrimage (Ps. 122:1) but then turn toward the wonders of the city of God. Elements of the pilgrims' song (שִׁיר הַמַּעֲלוֹת §4, No. 3) belong among the songs of Zion. A special theme then is the ''choosing of Zion'' (cf. Pss. 132:13; 87:1ff.). Associations with the great cultic ceremony of entrance, with the ark of the covenant as the focal point, are here discernible; cf. the commentary on Psalm 46. In the glorification of Zion, reference is made to the age-old cultic traditions of the Jebusite sanctuary. We can imagine that these songs of praise had a connection with that festal activity which has found its literary expression in Psalm 132. But it is also conceivable that solemn processions round about the temple area were organized during the great annual festivals (Ps. 48:2ff.).

In a study on the theme ''the Ark and Zion,'' Jörg Jeremias has brought together Psalms 46; 48; 76; and (87) and in the first place stated: ''Regarding the Zion psalms, in my opinion, the observation carries great weight that not only are they organized very similarly but also they make use of the same three syntactical constructions for the chief assertions of the psalms'' (cf. Jörg Jeremias, ''Lade und Zion: Probleme biblischer Theologie,'' in *Festschrift für G. von Rad* [1971] 183-198; 189f.). The form-analytical investigations arrive at the following observations:

1. At the beginning stand confessionallike static expressions, emphatic and similar headings, almost always in the form of predicate nominatives in sentences that describe God as resident and protector of Zion, or Zion as a fortress splendidly furnished and fortified by God.

2. These static statements are then factually supported by sentences with verbs in the perfect tense: the Lord and protector of Zion is Yahweh, because he has averted the assaults of the nations.

3. At the conclusion, detailed consequences are sometimes given to the hearers in imperative sentences, preceded in Psalms 48 and 76 by jussive forms and enjoining people to acknowledge Yahweh (Ps. 46:8a, 10), to join in the festal procession (Ps. 48:12ff.) or in the song of thanksgiving, and to perform their vows (Ps. 76:10f.).

For variations in the middle sections of these psalms, cf. J. Jeremias, 190.

Most of the songs of Zion probably originated in preexilic times. But their materials were handed down in most diverse ways and in later times adapted.

5. Didactic Poetry

As a clue for an appropriate Hebrew designation for didactic poems or also didactic songs, we could mention the terms חָכְמוֹת (''wisdom,'' pl.) and תְּבוּנוֹת (''understanding,'' pl.) from Ps. 49:3. About the origin, transmission, and shaping of the wisdom tradition in Israel we cannot report here. We shall refer only to the effect of חכמה on the writing of psalms. We shall do this, first, by means of an overview; later we shall deal with the themes systematically. Finally we shall also summarize some form-critical observations.

Wherever in the Psalms there are approaches to a didactic presentation of materials poetically conceived, there חכמה also appears as a cooperating principle of organization. It is conspicuous, for instance, how the "song of thanksgiving of an individual," wherever it takes on didactic characteristics, is shaped by wisdom poetry in both form and content (cf., e.g., Psalm 34). Also the "historical psalm" has the rhythm of חכמה pulse through it to the extent that it presumes to address the worshiping congregation in a teaching capacity (cf. Psalm 78). The "Torah psalms," which must be dated as relatively late, likewise assimilate "wisdom's" ideas (cf. Psalms 1 and 119). Psalm 1 shows the right way of צדקה ("righteousness") and teaches both the blessedness of the צדיק ("righteous person") and also the wretchedness of the רשע ("wicked person"). Psalms 37 and 73 report and teach concerning "Yahweh's righteous ways." Here again חכמה enters in, to enable adequate discussion of the basic theological problems. And yet, actually the proper form of wisdom poetry is the proverb (cf. Proverbs). In Psalms 127 and 133 חכמה asserts itself in the Psalter in its proverb form, and maxims also make their appearance in Psalms 112 and 128.

A larger group of psalms with a wisdom slant is characterized by the theme תורה *(torah)* and are therefore appropriately called Torah psalms. To this thematically classified group of Torah psalms belong Psalms 1; 19B; and 119, but in a wider sense also Psalms 34; 37; 49; 111; 112; 127; 128; and 139. Cf. G. von Rad, *Wisdom in Israel* (1972) 48f. Reflection inspired by wisdom has laid hold of the old Torah tradition, and in the altered situation, in which "the congregation of the righteous" (Ps. 1:5) no longer is identified with "all Israel," it has in such a way made that (Torah) tradition a didactic lecture that could mold decisions and analyses. Of unique character is Psalm 119, which surely must be thought of as a collection of expressions of Torah piety in postexilic times. The psalm developed from elements of scripture study, from the cultic Torah instruction of individuals, and from stimuli of wisdom instruction. Within the circle of this theme we are to see and understand also those psalms which we have listed in addition to Psalms 1; 19B; and 119.

A group that shows special characteristics comes to our attention in the problem poetry. Psalms 37, 49, 73, and 139 are involved. In Egyptology the term "discussion literature" has been introduced. Cf. E. Otto, *Der Vorwurf an Gott: Zur Entstehung der ägyptischen Auseinandersetzungsliteratur,* Vorträge der orientalischen Tagung in Marburg, Fachgruppe Ägyptologie (1950 [1951]). In this stream of tradition, known already in ancient Egypt, also the OT psalms named are to be thought of; and yet these psalms always deal with themes that are to be elaborated in connection with the tradition of Israel (cf. the interpretation of the psalms mentioned). Above all, the borderline between them and the Torah psalms is fluid.

As reflection on wisdom has found its way into the most dissimilar materials and traditions, so also it has penetrated to the historical psalms (cf. §6, 1, B. δ). Historical events have become an example for instruction and for the raising of puzzling relationships of life: Psalm 78.

In most cases, however, the diverse themes and traditions in which wisdom reflection and sapiential teaching are expressed should not be understood systematically. Especially in the תפלה and in the תודה has the didactic poetry of wisdom left its tracks. Behind the establishment of wisdom character "there remains much that is still obscure, for one cannot speak of a particular *Gattung* of didactic prayers, only of a common language and motif" (G. von Rad, *Wisdom in Israel* [1972] 47f.). Also cf. S. Mowinckel, *Psalms and Wisdom*, VTSuppl 3 (1955); R. E. Murphy, *A Consideration of the Classification "Wisdom Psalms,"* VTSuppl 9 (1963) 156-167; P. W. Skehan, *Studies in Israelite Poetry and Wisdom, CBQ* Monograph Series 1 (1971).

From the area of proverbial wisdom especially three themes are traceable: the transitoriness of life in time (Psalm 90); house building, protection of the city, and the toils of labor (Psalm 127); and the common life of brothers (Psalm 133).

A remarkable element of wisdom poetry is autobiographical stylization. It is traceable, for instance, in Psalm 73. A fictitious experience or suffering of life pervades the teaching and strives for the effect of typification, in which an autobiographically charming fate materializes. For autobiographical typification in the wisdom tradition, see G. von Rad, *Wisdom in Israel* (1972) 36f. Parallel texts for visualization of the process: Prov. 24:30-34; Sir. 33:16-19; 51:13-16.

Form criticism is able to trace only a few characteristic formulas and ways of formulating in didactic wisdom poetry, as, for instance, the instructor's opening call in Pss. 49:1 and 78:1 (also cf. Prov. 7:24; Isa. 28:23; Deut. 32:1). For the beginning of the proverbs of Amen-em-ope, cf. *AOT* 39 and *ANET* 421; in the Babylonian wisdom: *AOT* 290 and *ANET* 440. Basic information on the "instructor's opening call": H. W. Wolff, BK XIV/1 (1976) 122f.

Also the macarism is a characteristic element introducing wisdom teaching: Pss. 1:1; 32:1; 33:12; 34:8; 40:4; 41:1; and often. Cf. W. Janzen, "'*Ašrê* in the Old Testament," *HTR* 58 (1965) 215-226; Elipiński, "Macarismes et Psaumes de congratulation," *RB* 75 (1968) 321-367; K. Koch, *The Growth of the Biblical Tradition* (1969) 20-22; M. Soeb, אשׁר, *THAT* I 257ff.

Finally, the acrostic appears to have been a favorite artistic form of sapiential didactic poetry (details at Psalm 9/10, "Form").

6. Festival Psalms and Liturgies

In view of the numerous hypotheses and speculations that have crept into the study of the Psalms in connection with questions about worship and liturgy, we must first deal with basic methodological considerations and a critical discussion. In this process we will have to begin by simply stating this fact: In the OT Psalter there is no ritual transmitted anywhere. While we know ancient Near Eastern texts that very precisely regulate the entire course of the worship and even provide individual directions for managing it, the Psalter in this matter leaves us without a satisfactory clarification. The Psalms have basically a fragmentary, incomplete character if we consider them from the viewpoint of a closed ritual. This shortcoming has become the point of attack for many theories about worship. The principles of ancient Near Eastern ritual were adduced for the purpose of "filling out" and "completing" the fragmentary OT worship traditions. Surreptitiously, what was "filled in" and "completed" then became the governing principle of interpretation. From S. Mowinckel all the way to I. Engnell the Psalter was placed into the framework of ancient Near Eastern ritual of the renewal of life at the turn of the year. A. Weiser adduces the hypothesis of the covenant renewal festival; he places the Psalms into the fictitious framework of the ritual of an OT covenant cult. The mistake in method always begins at the place where cultic arrangements are already taken up (with disregard for the types) before a careful form-critical analysis of the Psalms has been done. This commentary, in contrast to the investigations and interpretations that begin with great cultic rituals, attempts to work out the possible cultic backgrounds case by case. The form-critical analysis is in every case the new point of departure. Against this procedure the charge may be made that it has the effect of dissecting and dismembering things. We have to put up with this accusation if we want to lay hold of the nuances and to escape the tendency to standardize things. Also, occasionally there will be open questions concerning the cultic situation of a psalm, or many possibilities for it will be discussed. The commentary is not afraid frequently to acknowledge the limits of understanding clearly, and it considers the question mark a more appropriate bet than the introduction of an unlimited cult theory.

The term "liturgy" is just as doubtful and questionable as the term "ritual." Are individual psalms really based on "liturgies"? Is a closed course involved? Are we dealing with "fragments of liturgy" (A. Weiser 22)? These questions cannot be answered with a single sentence. Not infrequently one has the impression that in the Psalms individual elements have been brought together from a "liturgy" by the singers and poets quite arbitrarily or with a very definite bias. A unique "selection" was possibly struck, for example, in Psalm 132 or Psalm 110. Also the "gate liturgies" (Psalms 15 and 24) are "excerpts." Thus the interpreter receives notice to exercise the greatest restraint. In what follows, therefore, we can only make a careful attempt to put together a few observations under the theme "festival psalms and liturgies."

We should first point out the three great festival psalms in the Psalter: Psalms 50; 81; and 95. J. Jeremias correctly states that these great festival psalms are in the Psalter "an entity in their own right" (Jörg Jeremias, *Kultprophetie und Gerichtsverkündigung in der späten Königszeit Israels*, WMANT 35 [1970], 125). The setting of the cultic festival is definitely indicated in Ps. 81:1-4. The other two psalms are parallel in content and structure. Characteristic is the description of the theophany in Psalm 50, which points to a "type" for which precisely the Psalter must have a special interest. For the theme "theophany," cf. J. Jeremias, *Theophanie: Die Geschichte einer alttestamentlichen Gattung,* WMANT 10 [1965]. Furthermore, the festival psalms inform us that the proclamation of the commandments and admonitions attached to this proclamation took place in the cultus. However, it is very difficult to describe the cultic setting in detail. But see the excursus on Psalm 50.

An extract from the ritual of the entrance to the temple is contained in those psalms that have been characterized as entrance liturgies, liturgies at admittance to the temple, gate liturgies, and Torah liturgies: Psalms 15 and 24. Cf. K. Koch, *Tempeleinlassliturgien und Dekaloge: Studien zur Theologie der alttestamentlichen Überlieferung* (1961) 45-60. The entrance liturgies are intimately connected with the songs of Zion (§6,4). Also Psalm 118 with its exclamations, exhortations, and responsories reminds us of the liturgical ritual of being admitted to the temple. For details, see the comments on Psalm 24. A contrast to the entrance is the ceremony of dismissal at leaving the temple. Psalm 121 points to this situation. The psalm contains a liturgical dialog comparable to that of Psalm 24. But this may be a matter of a secondary stylization, and yet one that clearly has reference to the cultic-liturgical act of the recessional from the temple.

Lately the cultic-prophetic lamentation liturgy has come into prominence. Cf. J. Jeremias, *Kultprophetie und Gerichtsverkündigung in der späten Königszeit Israels,* WMANT 35 (1970). To this context belong Psalms 12; 14 (=53); 52; 75; 82. In Psalm 52 we might have an imitation of a lamentation liturgy. For the details of the structure of the psalms and the course of the liturgy, cf. J. Jeremias, or see our commentary on the psalms named. At this point we should only still call attention to the relation of the psalms mentioned to Habakkuk 1 and 3.

In the interpretation of Psalm 107 commentators have again and again come to think of a liturgy for a festival of thanksgiving that was presented at the occasion of a "crowded festival of thanksgiving." From the viewpoint of form criticism this interpretation would be appropriate: "From an expansion of the summons of groups by name in an imperative hymn the basic structure of Psalm 107 is to be understood" (F. Crüsemann, *Studien zur Formgeschichte von Hymnus und Danklied in Israel,* WMANT 32 [1969], 73). But in fact it is probable that a liturgical summons to a תודה (thanksgiving) is to be thought of as the "Sitz im Leben" for the psalm.

Psalm 115 might be called a liturgical temple song. Its development permits us to think of a course of liturgical acts: vv. 1-2, prayer song of the assembled congregation; 3-8, confession in hymnic style; 9-11, admonition; 12-15, blessing; 16-18, statements in hymnic style.

Also Psalm 67, a curious "psalm of blessing" expressed in the form of request and prayer, could point to a cultic-liturgical situation. But this is where the difficulties begin to arise. Individual psalms that lead us by their structure to think that they suggest a liturgical situation have no way of proving it. A secondary combination of various elements taken from disparate events might be involved. There might even be literary compositions present that forbid every kind of conclusion a posteriori.

Therefore we shall once more refer to the methodological considerations and critical discussions with which this section began. We still know altogether too little about the festivals of Israel and their celebration to be able to give clear information. We know liturgies only in snatches or combinations of a selection. All interpretations bear the signature of a hypothesis.

§7. The Relation of the Psalms to the History of Israel

1. When we approach the Psalms with questions about history, we are met by a multitude of difficulties. The study of types (*Gattungsforschung*) prompts us to let questions of history recede into the background as secondary. The area of worship, it was thought, is entirely a stranger to history. But in more recent times it has been demonstrated that the absolute preeminence of the cultic discussion has led to many a wrong interpretation and to many a distortion. If the dimension of history is overlooked, mythical and ideological categories of interpretation force their way into the exposition of the Psalms. It is therefore a necessary requirement constantly to investigate the relation of the Psalms to the history of Israel. This can of course be done today only if the reality of worship in its full extent is presupposed and taken into account. An unbroken correlation between the Psalms and a corresponding "historical situation" can no longer be claimed. The three factors "psalm writing—worship—history" are to be investigated as to their interior and exterior correlation. And therefore the heading of this section is not "The Historical Situation of the Psalms" but, carefully stated, "The Relation of the Psalms to the History of Israel." To which areas could this investigation that integrates worship extend? (*a*) Questions could be asked about

the age of the Psalms with special reference to their language and style; certain themes, concept groups, and manners of expression might also provide clues for dating them. (*b*) We could try to stake out the period to which a psalm belongs. The cultus, too, has its history. The history of the cultus makes possible deductions concerning the period to which the worship song in question should be assigned. (*c*) Many psalms make reference to older historical events. The study of the history of tradition has the responsibility to investigate the nature of this adaptation, recitation, or even brief mention of historical or salvation-historical traditions. (*d*) In individual cases the reference of the Psalms to the history of Israel is direct. Above all, the "community prayer songs" that emerge from a definite time of distress refer directly to a historical situation.

In most cases, however, it is impossible to establish a relation to history. Particularly the prayer songs of the individual and the songs of praise usually elude every attempt at historical coordination. Even if today we are inclined to assign most of the psalms of these two types to the preexilic period, we still lack unequivocal and unquestioned proof. Here two factors that make for difficulty are involved, factors which in more recent times have come to be recognized more and more clearly: the conventional form of speech and conception, which from generation to generation can assert itself without change, and the history of tradition of each psalm that has introduced transformation and concretization into the hymns (cf. §8). Both factors essentially belong to the cultus, which fosters the conventionalized form of speech but under certain circumstances also actualizes the new formation of transmitted formularies and poems (cf. §8).

2. The oldest psalms in the Psalter may be recognized by their archaic language and by the unpolished style formations and images that point back to the Canaanite world. Naturally, we cannot precisely determine the time of the actual adoption of Canaanite language and ideas, and yet the immediacy of ideas and conceptions in Psalms 29; 68; and 18 is especially noticeable. One is inclined to call Psalm 29 the oldest psalm and to place it in the time before the monarchy. If the observations in the commentary are correct, also Psalms 68 and 18 would have to be dated to the 12th and 11th centuries B.C., respectively. On Psalm 18 cf. F. M. Cross and D. N. Freedman, "A Royal Song of Thanksgiving," *JBL* 72 (1953) 16; on Psalm 68 cf. W. F. Albright, "A Catalogue of Early Hebrew Poems: Psalm 68," *HUCA* 23, 1 (1950/51) 1-39.

3. The basic history-of-salvation traditions of Israel (patriarchal tradition, exodus from Egypt, revelation at Sinai, sojourn in the desert, entry into the land of Canaan) are very frequently in evidence in the psalms in brief mention or in extensive recitation. Cf. M. Noth, *A History of Pentateuchal Traditions* [1981] 47ff., 51, 58. The two chief complexes of the tradition, the exodus from Egypt and the revelation at Sinai, whose traditional foundations were first recognized by G. von Rad, are present in Psalms 78; 105; 106; and 136, and also with a cultic-poetic stamp in Psalms 50 and 81; cf. G. von Rad, *The Problem of the Hexateuch and Other Essays* (1966) 8ff. = *GesStud:* ThB 8 (1971) 16ff., 31f. The basic salvation-history traditions of Israel were actualized in worship. In these traditions also the act of crossing the Jordan or entering the promised land is included (cf. Psalms 66 and 114).

But we must now be very strict about our distinction between this reference of the psalms to basic historical traditions and the actual formation of these psalms. We will have to probe from case to case to see the implications for dating provided by the form-critical analysis. It is quite possible that cultic poetry of a relatively late period takes historical events (according to canonical patterns of tradition) and reproduces them. It is also not out of the question that individual historical psalms or references to history already refer to the Pentateuch in written form. On these questions, cf. A. Lauha, *Die Geschichtsmotive in den alttestamentlichen Psalmen* (1945); S. du Toit, *The Psalms and History: Studies on the Psalms, Papers Read at the 6th Meeting of Die O.T. Werkgemeenskap in Suid-Afrika* (1963) 18-29; C. Westermann, "Die Geschichtsbezogenheit menschlicher Rede von Gott im Alten Testament," *Weltgespräch* 1 (1967); F. N. Jasper, "Early Israelite Traditions and the Psalter," *VT* 17 (1967) 50-59.

4. The time of David is a frequently occurring theme in the psalms that are rooted mainly in the temple cultus of Jerusalem. Special historical interest is riveted on the cult founder and the father of a dynasty of leaders of the temple. We can say that the time of David in the Psalter is among the fundamental historical events to which reference is made again and again. That David brought the ark of the covenant, that sacral focus of the confederacy of the twelve tribes of Israel, to Jerusalem and thus declared Zion the cultic center—this deed was retained in memory (cf. Psalm 132 and the excursus on that psalm). If we overlook this reference to the history of the Jerusalem cultus and monarchy, then the ideological-mythical categories of explanation of the ancient Near Eastern environment will make their inroads into the psalms at this very point. In the Psalms we must clearly recognize that the foundations of the cultus and the monarchy lie in the time of David. But the cultic proclamation and actualization of these basic traditions from the time of David is a problem by itself. We will always have to ask when and how the traditions were represented (on this question, also cf. the excursus on Psalm 132).

Alongside the traditions about David the cult founder and David the father of a dynasty, we must now also consider the traditions that describe David as a poet and singer (cf. §4, No. 2). Without doubt the report that David wrote psalms and sang them goes back to historical fact. But the transmitters and collectors have obviously made rather liberal use of the notice "A Psalm of David." They evidently found that the historical fact of David's having written psalms was not adequately brought to light and therefore provided mostly the historically imprecise prayer songs of an individual with the heading לדוד. At times, even precise indications of situations from the life of David were added. These secondary additions let us recognize the effort of the transmitters and collectors to solidify the historical reference of the psalms by anchoring them in the time of David. The situations indicated in the titles are historically untenable; but they reveal an interest, a tendency, that must by all means be taken into consideration. The transmitters and collectors wanted to see to it that the psalm thus provided with a title and a reference to a situation be understood as being related to the indicated events in the life of David. We could refer to this as "the oldest commentary." We could in any case think of Psalm 18 as a "true psalm of David," although here too we must allow for further development on the basis of the history of tradition.

5. The fact that a considerable number of OT psalms belong to the time of the history of Israel's monarchy has rightly been emphasized again and again. In the first place, we are of course to think of the history of the Judean monarchy. The period of research that dated the type "royal psalms" to the time of the Maccabees has conclusively been refuted. Today there is no longer doubt that Psalms 2; 20; 21; 45; 72; 89; 101; and 110 belong to the historical epoch of the time of the kings. But the deep roots these psalms have in the Jerusalem cultus (cf. §6, 3) hardly enable a more precise dating. We could only indicate that very likely Psalm 110 is to be dated in the earliest time of the kings and Psalm 89 in the latest. To the time of the kings in the broadest sense also those psalms belong

that (for instance, in a prayer of intercession) allude to the ruler (cf., e.g., Psalms 28; 84; and others). We might in general date also the "songs of Zion" to the time of the kings; especially in those cases when the most ancient (pre-Israelite) traditions glorify the city of God (cf. Psalms 46; 48; 76, and the excursus on Psalm 46).

Difficulties are still encountered in connection with the historical understanding of Psalm 80. It is perhaps permissible to think of the time of Josiah (cf. the commentary on the psalm). Otherwise, only few clues for dating can be found; yet the mention of "Assyria" in Ps. 83:8 might provide a hint.

It can more frequently be stated as probable that the majority of "prayer songs of individuals" and "songs of praise" are preexilic.

6. The destruction of Jerusalem and the rule-in-exile of the Judeans is a historical episode that is reflected also in the Psalms. The "prayer songs of the community" in most cases refer to this upsetting event. Psalm 60 could have scenes of the year 587 B.C. in mind. Also Psalms 44; 74; and 79 are best understood with reference to the exile. In exilic and immediately postexilic times continual great festivals of lamentation would have brought before Yahweh the destruction of Jerusalem (cf. Zech. 7:3). The remembrance of the cruel event could not be erased.

Psalm 137 refers to the Babylonian captivity. The dispersion of the Jews henceforth is an important theme that allows us to recognize the exilic or postexilic setting of a psalm (cf., e.g., Psalm 87). But also the change of fortune represented by the return home is heard in a number of psalms and is a clue for dating (cf. especially Psalms 85 and 126).

But from case to case we must investigate how close the psalms in question stand to the events named and to what degree, for instance, the message of Deutero-Isaiah influenced them (cf., e.g., the commentary on Psalms 96 and 98).

7. For the rest, the psalms of the late exilic and postexilic period are not always easy to recognize. We can point to three views that can be effective in dating them: (*a*) Wisdom poetry asserts itself more vigorously and, with its widely ranging, pensive themes, as well as with its aphoristic forms that find their way into psalm poetry, influences individual psalms (cf. §6, 9). Naturally, we do not mean to maintain here that the creative powers of חכמה (wisdom) are generally postexilic. We are merely referring to the noticeable influence of content and formal factors on the psalm types. (*b*) A well-developed Torah piety is the mark of late poetry (cf. the commentary on Psalm 119). (*c*) Aramaisms show that a psalm is "postexilic" (cf. Psalms 116 and 124).

Of course, these three viewpoints cannot be applied mechanically. Moreover, the Torah theme is not unconditionally late. And Aramaisms can also be very ancient. We mean to point out the noticeable prevalence of the themes and elements in the cases referred to. On §7 cf. G. Sauer, "Erwägungen zum Alter der Psalmdichtung in Israel," *ThZ* 22 (1966) 81-95.

§ 8. Concerning the Origin of the Psalms and Their Tradition History

1. In §4, 2 and §7, 4 we have pointed out that לדוד ("of David") is not a reliable reference to the writer of a psalm. This critical judgment applies also for those psalms which according to the information in the title are to be credited to Solomon, Moses, Asaph, the Korahites, Heman, or Ethan. Originally all of the psalm poetry was transmitted anonymously. It could be possible that only the

psalms personally composed by David carried a corresponding notice. In any case, we cannot determine authentic naming of poets in the Psalter. This fact raises for psalm research the question whom we should take to be the poets of the Psalms. For a time, two views stood in stark contrast to each other. One group declared that the Psalter was an exclusively cultic-priestly book; others thought of it as a collection of "private poems." These alternatives could well be thought of as obsolete today; cf. S. Mowinckel, *Offersang og Sangoffer,* 353ff. We should have to start with the assumption that the vast majority of the psalms were the work of the priests and temple singers, who drew up the liturgies and formularies. In the case of the prayer songs and thanksgiving songs of individuals, we shall have to assume that priests and temple singers derived the psalms from the reports of those who had been in distress and had recovered but in the process generally made use of the conventionalized formulations. Only so can we account for the fact that Psalms 42/43 with their distinctive references could be handed down to us. In every case priests and temple singers were the transmitting agencies. They not only collected the descriptions of distress and the first expressions of thanks, but they also led in reciting the liturgies and formularies when an individual—in relation to various fortunes (cf. §6, 2b)—presented the תפלה and the תודה. We have to assume that those who prayed in most cases sang and prayed such psalms as were available as liturgies and formularies in the sanctuary and such texts as were familiar to the priests and to the temple singers (like hymns in a hymnal). Still we ought also to take note of what has become known through stelae of Asia Minor. An Israelite who has been rescued from distress might let the story of his distress and his expression of thanks be transposed to a prayer song through the services of the priests and temple singers and have them inscribed on a stele or scroll. The following might be a reference to one such inscribing:

> Then I said, "Lo, I come;
>> in the roll of the book it is written of me."
>>> (Ps. 40:7)

But the context in Psalm 40 invites us to differentiate. While according to ancient ritual the liturgies and formularies uttered by proxy (cantillated) by the priest or temple singer were spoken at the offering, the dedication of a psalm to the *deus praesens* and to the assembled congregation obviously displays the character of a statement by the one who is bringing the offering, a statement that was presented in offertory formulas such as Ps. 19:14. The "records" collected by the priests and temple singers—in other words, the stories on the basis of which prayer songs and songs of thanksgiving were fashioned in accordance with the poetic rules and traditional variations of formulas familiar to the worship personnel—will have become a part of the temple archives. This explanation of the origin of prayer songs and songs of thanksgiving of an individual stands distinctively between the extremes of the assumption of a ritual and the assumption of a "private composition." Rituals, as they are familiar especially from the Babylonian worship forms, would be stark, patterned exhibits—without the living, suffering, and experiencing present in the OT prayer songs and songs of thanksgiving, without participation in history. "Private compositions," on the other hand, would be exceptional creations which could be projected into ancient Israel and its cultus only as anachronisms. In such an attempt at explanation the cultural situation of the ancient world is totally misunderstood. Reading, writing, and composing were simply the private preserve of the priests and temple singers, which corresponded to the privilege of the "scribes" (ספרים), that is, the officials and secretaries at the court of the king. Thus, since according to everything that is known about the origin, history, and tradition of wisdom in Israel the "scribes" were also the keepers and transmitters of חכמה, it makes good sense to explain wisdom's influence on psalm writing on the basis of an increasing "correspondence" among the traditions, gifts, and capacities present in the Jerusalem temple and in the area of the royal court.

We shall do well to summarize at this point what we are told in the OT regarding the activity of the priests (and temple singers) alluded to. The most interesting sequence is found in Deut. 31:19, 22. Here three activities of the priest are expressed in these concepts: כתב את־השירה ("write this song"), למד ("teach it"), and שים בפי ("put [it] in [their] mouth"). Concerning the wish that a prayer song that depicts the distress be written down, see Job 19:23f. In view of Yahweh's saving deeds, we read in Ps. 102:18: תכתב זאת לדור אחרון ("Let this be recorded for a generation to come"). On the service of the singers in the area of the sanctuary, see 1 Chron. 9:33; 15:16ff.; 2 Chron. 20:21ff.; 23:13; 29:25ff.; Neh. 12:28ff. Naturally, the passages cited are given from a historical perspective. But we may certainly assume that the temple singers in preexilic times cooperated with the priests and performed the tasks noted in Deut. 31:19, 22.

Also for the origin and the history of the formation of the other groups ("types") of psalms a similar process as the one assumed for the prayer songs and songs of thanksgiving will have to be presupposed. In the group of songs of Zion, Psalms 84 and 122 give us opportunity to recognize the outlines of a pilgrimage narrative adopted by the worship personnel, while Psalms 46; 48; and 76 may have been composed by priests. This may well explain the strict adherence to form in the three last-named psalms (cf. §6, 4).

Psalms intended for the whole worship community probably originated exclusively in the circle of priests and temple singers. To this group belong the songs of praise and the prayer songs of the community. It is hardly conceivable that these "types" were composed outside the sanctuary area. Also the "historical psalms" are a characteristic opus of priestly origin. We could think of the type "Levitical sermon" (cf. the comment on Psalm 78), which is basic to this worship poetry.

A special problem in the history of the origins of psalms is presented in the "royal psalms." Who is the author of these psalms? In Psalms 2 and 10 the king himself is the speaker. Is he also the composer? That possibility is not to be dismissed offhand; but we might also think of a specially gifted person among the worship leaders who composed the song for the king. Psalm 45 is the song of praise of a prophetically inspired singer from the royal environment. But how are Psalms 110 and 132 to be interpreted? In both cases we have not a compact ritual but a recital of definite messages of a festival, descriptions of situations, and episodes of a solemn course of events. Who composed these poems? Did a cult prophet try most of all to retain his own inspirations (cf. Psalm 110), or have parts of the ritual, especially the basic oracles, been put on record by a charismatic singer? The same question could also be asked in connection with Psalms 50; 81; and 95, which are of a different kind. In these we have in the first place prophetic messages that were announced at a festival of the assembled cultic community. The framework of a cultic sequence is discernible. But the chief subject is the prophetic message. Did the prophet himself retain the message? Did the prophet's disciples fixate the event?

Why were the "liturgies of the gate" (Psalms 15 and 24) preserved and transmitted? The interest in ritual is insignificant within the Psalter. Was it the תורה that was to be transmitted?

Again we should emphasize that we can here only make an attempt to shed light on occurrences lying in the darkness of the distant past. Finally, that the comments in this section in part present an incisively new approach in comparison with earlier editions of this commentary should be stated emphatically.

2. The history of tradition of the OT psalms can hardly be viewed in a too highly adventurous or diversified manner. In view of the abundance of the psalm material encountered, a strict selection must have been made very early. Many psalms must continuously have remained in use as formulas. A number of them surely belonged to a treasury of psalms that was memorized and well known everywhere. Certain formulations and expressions were indelibly inculcated. In the course of time the poems found their way to the temple archives. The manuscripts were sorted and collected. Already early, smaller partial collections must have been made. Accession notes, such as we know from the Akkadian cultic poetry, were helpful when the first organization was undertaken. This entire process of collecting and shaping individual "song scrolls" we are no longer able to unravel.

But it is worth asking about the extent to which the priests who did the transmitting and collecting influenced the traditional materials left in their charge. Two examples may illustrate the problem. Psalm 68 is probably the only psalm that can be derived from the realm of the north-Israelite cultus (cf. the comment on Psalm 68). Unless we are totally mistaken, this psalm has its "Sitz im Leben" in the early history of Israel on Mount Tabor; also cf. H.-J. Kraus, "Die Kulttradition des Berges Tabor," Festschrift für W. Freytag, BASILEIA (1959) 177-184; H.-J. Kraus, *Worship in Israel* (1966) 165ff. But, as we learn from Ps. 68:29, the older song was adopted and expanded in Jerusalem. In other words, a poem from northern Israel was later taken up and recast. Something similar is to be observed in Psalm 107. Here we have a liturgy for a festival of thanksgiving that originally probably was a liturgical introduction to the various תודות. In later (postexilic) times the psalm was recast and applied with reference to the thanksgiving of the returning exiles (Ps. 107:3, 33-43). From these two examples we can observe that adaptations, extensions, and contemporizings were accomplished. The psalm titles are an extension of these tendencies, which, after a time, could no longer apply to the received text but only to its introduction. The gradually forming partial collections and smaller scrolls of psalms, referred to above, probably around 300 B.C. coalesced into the canon, the rise of which cannot be explained in greater detail (cf. §3, 3). Thus the Psalter contains poetry from almost a thousand years (cf. §7, 2). The center of this history of origin, transmission, and collection was the temple of Jerusalem.

§ 9. On the Theology of the Psalms

1. If we approach the OT Psalms with the question where one should look for and find the God of Israel whom the hymns and songs of thanksgiving glorify, on whom the laments call, and whom all the songs and poems involve, the unanimous, never doubted, and ceaselessly expressed answer is: Yahweh Sebaoth is present in the sanctuary in Jerusalem. Zion is the place of God's presence. The name of the abode of the divine presence (*deus praesens*) varies. Beside the name "Jerusalem" (Pss. 122:2ff.; 128:5; 137:5; 147:2) and the more

frequent "Zion" (Pss. 2:6; 9:11; 15:7; 20:2; 48:2ff.; 50:2; 74:2; 99:2; and often), mention may also be made of the "holy hill" (Pss. 2:6; 48:1; 87:1; 99:9), of the "(holy) temple" (היכל, Pss. 5:7; 11:4; 27:4; 48:9; 65:4; 138:2; and often), or of the "house (of Yahweh)" (בית יהוה, Pss. 5:7; 23:6; 26:8; 27:4; 36:8; 52:8; 65:4; 69:9; and often). Jerusalem is considered the "central sanctuary" of Israel, to which the tribes make their pilgrimage (Ps. 122:4). There Yahweh Sebaoth "dwells" or "is enthroned" (Pss. 9:11; 74:2). Though all the lands are full of his glorious presence (Ps. 8:1), still when one wants to meet the God of Israel, one turns only to Zion. Only from the site of Yahweh's presence are help and salvation to be expected (Ps. 14:7). Accordingly, the members of the OT people of God set out annually to make a pilgrimage to the sanctuary for the great festivals (Ps. 122:1). Those who must linger at a distance are full of sadness at the thought of the days of pilgrimage (Ps. 42:4). The call בית יהוה נלך (Ps. 122:1) is the beginning of all joy and all salvation. The longing for the place of the presence of God carries the pilgrims along (Ps. 84:2). They shoulder the burdens of the journey and with growing strength approach the wonderful goal (Ps. 84:6f.). The moment of arrival at the gates of the holy city provides a sense of fulfillment and greatest ecstasy (Pss. 122:2; 84:2), for now the pilgrim may be near Yahweh in the midst of the exulting congregation. It is not the immanent holiness or the magic saturation with the numinous that these prayerful people seek. They enter into a meeting with the majestic person of Yahweh. The mystery of the city of God is this wonderful occasion: "Yahweh is in the midst of her" (Ps. 46:5). Therefore Zion is a "fountain of life" (Ps. 36:9). The אל־חי ("living God," Ps. 84:2) provides the good fortune of a "new world" that transcends time and space (Ps. 84:10). The sanctuary lies in an eternal radiance. Here שלום reigns according to the fullness of the word (Ps. 122:8). Under "the shadow of the wings of Yahweh," under the outspread wings of cherubim, there is an untouchable place of shelter.

The miracle of the presence of God on Zion is every year demonstratively portrayed for the festival congregation before their very eyes by means of a sacred act at the beginning of the celebration. The holy ark, that throne of the invisibly present God and central shrine of ancient Israel, is brought into the temple in a liturgical procession (Psalms 24B and 132). This ceremony is not (as many scholars think) the "enthronement of Yahweh," but a cultic act which—corresponding to the foundational cult legend of 2 Samuel 6—proclaims to the festival congregation the "election of Jerusalem" as the *verbum visibile:* Ps. 132:13f. Above the throne of God the מלך הכבוד, Yahweh Sebaoth, is present when the ark is brought through the gates of the sanctuary (Ps. 24:7-10). Remembrance is made of the first historical events: It was David who liberated the ark from its "emergency quarters," Kiriath-jearim (Ps. 132:6), and brought it to Jerusalem. Reminiscences of the late great central sanctuary of pre-Davidic times, of Shiloh, are heard when the cultic name יהוה צבאות is pronounced. Thus the entry of the ark recalls the basic event; it brings home to the present the cultic legend of Jerusalem that is attached to the central shrine of the ark. At that time Yahweh "chose" Zion as his "habitation" (מושב, Ps. 132:13) and as his "resting place" (Ps. 132:14). This basic event is the foundation and the center of the present worship.

With the ark the worshiping congregation enters the sanctuary. Jubilation and thanksgiving accompany the solemn act (Pss. 95:2; 100:4). An entrance is made through the "gates of righteousness" (שערי־צדק, Ps. 118:19). And at this point the question is asked, "Who may ascend the hill of Yahweh, and who may stand in his holy place?'' (Pss. 24:3; 15:1). Yahweh is a God of justice and righteousness. Worship in the OT is not a natural and magical renewal of life, no dramatically engineered importation of power, but an encounter with the Lord of all of life. The cult participant does not enter a sphere of ecstasy, but is asked about his everyday behavior, about his obedience to Yahweh's instructions. A ''declaration of loyalty to Jahweh's sense of justice'' (G. von Rad, *OT Theology*, 1:379) is demanded of every individual. An assortment of commandments is called to remembrance (Pss. 15:2ff.; 24:4ff.). Like a confessional looking glass the statements of the תורה are held up before him. Only the פעל־צדק (Ps. 15:2) may enter through the שערי־צדק (Ps. 118:19). The festival joy of those entering the sanctuary may abruptly be interrupted by the message of a prophet who with a voice of warning may enjoin the worshiping congregation not to harden their hearts but to lead a life of obedience to Yahweh (Ps. 95:8ff.). He who enters the place of the presence of Yahweh confronts the Lord of all life.

But in the domain of the sanctuary the pilgrim is surrounded by the indescribable glory of Zion that is celebrated in hymns and poems. ''Like the high heavens'' (Ps. 78:69) is the sanctuary built. ''The perfection of beauty'' (Ps. 50:2), it is ''the joy of all the earth'' (Ps. 48:2). Marvelous streams provide the city of God with life and joy (Ps. 46:4). It is built with indestructible solidity (Ps. 48:3, 13). Neither natural catastrophes (Ps. 46:2ff.) nor uprisings of the nations (Pss. 46:6ff.; 48:4ff.; 76:2ff.) can touch the holy city. ''Yahweh is in the midst of her'' (Ps. 46:5). That is the secret and the wonder. Pre-Israelite cultic traditions have been adopted by the singers to glorify the unearthly splendor and inviolability of Zion.

2. Praise and glorification are in the last analysis always applied to Yahweh himself. On Zion the festival congregation pays homage to the *deus praesens*. On him, the highest God, the King, the Creator, and the Judge of the world, is the honor bestowed. But before we deal with the most important predicates and divine names, we ask the question, How does God on Zion manifest his presence? Many psalms declare that he ''appears,'' he ''shines forth'' in his splendor and glory (cf. Pss. 50:2; 97:3ff.; 18:9ff.). The theophany of Yahweh is attested. In powerful descriptions the phenomenon of a consuming fire announces his appearance. Lightning and thunder accompany the radiant advance of God. His ''face'' (פנים) flashes up. The worshiping congregation prays: ''Shine forth!'' (Pss. 80:1; 94:1). They plead: ''Let thy face shine'' (Ps. 80:3). And also the individual at prayer, calling out: ''Arise!'' ''Awake!'' (Pss. 7:6; 9:19; 10:12; 17:13; 35:23; 44:23; 57:8; and often), awaits an overpowering self-manifestation of the God of Israel.

The question has been raised again and again: How are these descriptions of theophany in the Psalms to be imagined? Did people at one time dramatically and visibly represent the phenomena of the appearance of God in worship by means of a manipulation of scenes? But such actions would be inconsistent with OT faith, for it everywhere emphasizes the invisibility and the lack of a representative image of God, and it strictly rejects, above all, human control over the appearance of God. One easily thinks of charismatic announcements and proclamations in worship on the part of active prophets who draw on the unfathomable coincidence of tradition and vision. The elements of tradition are the old Israelite stories of the theophany at Sinai and the conceptions of the appearance of the God of the thunderstorm adopted from the surrounding Canaanite world (cf. the comment on Psalm 29). But the actuality of the experience of revelation is communicated in vision (cf. Isaiah 6). The element in

the cultus corresponding to Yahweh's freedom is the charisma. A congregation
that has to ask for Yahweh's appearance (Pss. 80:1; 94:1) does not control the
theophany. The fact that Yahweh does appear and does turn toward the people
is made known in the charismatic proclamation. The cultic formulas יהוה בהיכל
קדשו (Ps. 11:4) and יהוה בהיכל קדשו הס מפניו כל־הארץ (Hab. 2:20) must
probably be explained as the determinative announcements of the appearance and
presence of Yahweh. The festival congregation is called upon to prostrate itself
in adoration and obeisance before the *deus praesens* (Psalm 29). This is not a
matter of mass suggestion dramatically staged but a prophetic proclamation. As
a result of this also the individual member of the worshiping community that has
prayed for Yahweh's appearance in power and for his intervention in a matter of
personal distress can experience assurance by means of vision. But basically
theophany and prophecy belong together most intimately. Yahweh is not a silent
numen, not a phenomenon that naturally breaks forth or is even available to
religious manipulations. Yahweh comes and does not keep silence (Ps. 50:3); the
appearance is essentially an announcement of a message. The theophany is a
disclosure of the קול־יהוה (Ps. 29:3ff.). Yahweh ''speaks'' (דבר) and ''summons'' (קרא), Ps. 50:1, and manifests his presence by appearing for the
transmission of his word. Israel is to be spoken to. The prophet takes up the
message of God and calls out: שמעה עמי ואדברה (Pss. 50:7ff.; 81:8ff.). Thus the
God of Israel reveals himself in Jerusalem.

Before the *deus praesens* the festival congregation prostrates itself. The
proskynesis before the presence of God is the high point of the procession into
the sacred area (Pss. 95:6; 96:9; 99:5, 9; 132:7; 138:2). It was probably at this
cultic act of homage that the hymns were sung. The praise of God breaks out.
The glorification knows no bounds. Also the heavenly powers join in the praise
of Yahweh (Pss. 29:1; 103:20f.; 149:1ff.). All creatures, the whole creation,
chime in (Psalms 96 and 98). At this act of homage sacrifices were probably
presented, although in Ps. 50:8ff. we learn that the prophetic office keeps strict
watch over the presentation of offerings. Only sacrifices that manifest thanksgiving and homage may be brought before Yahweh (cf. the comment on Ps.
50:8ff.); sacrifices are not a means of influencing God.

The hymns honor the God of Israel as highest God, King, Creator, and
Judge of the world. The predicates and appellations applied to Yahweh in the
doxology are of pre-Israelite origin (cf. §10, 1); they have been transferred to the
God of Israel. These predicates and titles bespeak majestic greatness and
universal perfection of power. Yahweh is עליון (אל), ''God Most High.'' He is
exalted above all gods (Ps. 97:9). The powers have been stripped of their might.
They have lost all their might. Yahweh alone is עליון על־כל־הארץ, ''Most high
over all the earth'' (Pss. 83:18; 97:9). From the heavens his voice resounds (Ps.
18:13). From Ps. 47:2 and Psalm 97 we learn that the appellation מלך (''King'')
corresponds to the name of deity אל עליון. As עליון, Yahweh is מלך גדול על־
כל־הארץ (Ps. 47:2). In his כבוד this ''great king over all the earth'' is enthroned
on Zion (Pss. 24:7ff.; 48:2; 99:2). His throne is established from eternity (Ps.
93:2). Therefore the God of Israel has no need of an enthronement that takes
place periodically or of a renewal of power, as do the dying and rising deities of
the environs of the ancient Near East. The worshiping congregation pays homage
to him with the shout יהוה מלך = ''Yahweh is King'' (Pss. 93:1; 96:10; 97:1;
99:1) and acknowledges the universal power of the God-king whose splendor
fills the whole world. But the one who is God Most High and king is at the same
time the creator: Pss. 24:1; 93:1; 95:3ff.; 96:5, 10. He has overcome the powers

of chaos (Pss. 24:13ff.; 89:9ff.), to the earth he has given stability (Pss. 93:1; 96:10), and with wondrous order and conformity to law he has permeated all of creation (Psalm 104). Also the heavenly sphere and the constellations are the work of his hands (Psalms 8 and 19A). The act of creation is the basis of God's world dominion (Pss. 24:1f.; 47:2ff.; 97:9). The כבוד of the king and creator goes into all the lands (Ps. 8:1; Isa. 6:3). The peoples are subjected to him (Pss. 47:3, 8; 99:2).

But finally, the king and creator is also the judge (Pss. 96:10; 99:6). He is enthroned בעדת־אל (Ps. 82:1) in heavenly height above the peoples (Ps. 7:7) and "judges" the nations (Pss. 7:8; 9:8; 96:10).

In all these perfections of power, so clearly expressed by the predicates, the worshiping community in its cultic act of homage glorifies the God of Israel enthroned on Zion.

In view of the theological facts here presented, the difficult question about the relation of revelation and worship arises. Two views are diametrically opposed to each other. In his essay "Kultus und Offenbarung" (*Festschrift für S. Mowinckel*, 1955), R. Gyllenberg writes: "the cultus signifies that God and the world meet: the God who ordinarily is distant and unapproachable comes near and lets his face shine on the assembled congregation, the *deus absconditus* becomes the *deus revelatus*. Thus worship is the framework of experiencing God, meeting God, and the self-impartation of the deity . . ." (76). While revelation is here almost completely integrated with worship, G. von Rad calls the Psalms essentially "Israel's response" (*OT Theol* 1:355). Both interpretations raise doubts. Gyllenberg proceeds too much from a general phenomenon of cultic performance. There is not enough regard for the mystery of the independence of Yahweh, which is attested everywhere in the Psalms.

Certainly we must remember that worship is always in danger of falling into the trap of religious ceremonies, of becoming a law unto itself. Security leads to stabilization and presupposes inviolable data. For this problem, cf. the comment on Psalm 46 (Purpose and Thrust). But we will have to consider that in the Psalter a great deal of pleading, wailing, and questioning is heard. For Yahweh is obviously not the one at our disposal, he who grants "renewal of life" in processes that repeat periodically. He is an independent, sovereign Lord. This fact will have to be regarded whenever the theme "worship and revelation" is discussed. On the other hand, it is too little to speak of the "Israel's response" when we consider the Psalms. Many psalms witness to an act of revelation that is immediately present. Also in this respect, therefore, we shall have to make a correction.

3. On Zion, the chosen site of the presence of Yahweh, the Davidic king, as lord of the temple, is a central figure of cultic life. For his office and influence the prophecy of Nathan (2 Samuel 7) is the decisive foundation. At that time Yahweh had "chosen" and installed David and his dynasty by means of prophetic address. He had made a "covenant" with David (cf. Pss. 89:3ff.; 132:12). In keeping with this basic arrangement, all rulers from the dynasty of David were called "Yahweh's kings" (Pss. 2:6; 18:50). At their enthronement, and probably also at a cultic ceremony repeated annually (cf. the comment on Psalm 132), the Davidites were elevated by Yahweh himself (Ps. 110:1) and promoted to a unique position by means of a cultic-prophetic declaration. Inviolable stands the declaration of God: "I myself have consecrated my king on Zion, my holy hill" (Ps. 2:6). "At the right hand of Yahweh" (Ps. 110:1), in wondrous nearness to God, the ruler stands as משיח, as the unimpeachable anointed of the God of Israel (Pss. 2:2; 18:50; 20:6; 89:51; 132:10). He serves Yahweh in the honored position of עבד, servant (Ps. 89:50). Yahweh stands in אמונה, unshakable faithfulness, to this "covenant" (Ps. 89:19ff.). And only in

complete helplessness in times of the ruin of the dynasty can the complaints and questions of Psalm 89 be expressed.

In the worship of Jerusalem the eminent position of the king is obvious. A Davidite is installed at his enthronement as a priest (after the order of Melchizedek)—as we see from Ps. 110:4. The prerogative of free request belongs to the king (Pss. 2:8; 21:2, 4). He lives in a unique kind of well-being (Ps. 21:2, 6) that has prompted many praying individuals to adopt the conventional formulations of royal prerogatives for their own petitions and songs (cf. the comment on Psalm 3).

The "royal psalms" are full of ancient Near Eastern conceptions of the ideal ruler. Elements of court style and royal ideology were adopted in Jerusalem and were in remarkable manner freshly accommodated. The mystery of nearness to God is expressed in the form of the proclamation of adoption (cf. the comment on Pss. 2:7; 110:3). In an authoritative word of a prophet the ruler is declared to be the "son of God." The mythical elements of the *hieros gamos* and the divine birth have largely been sloughed off, even though they still seem to glimmer through in Psalm 110. The earthly king in his beaming beauty and in the splendor of his courtly dress is the "reflection of the glory of God" (Psalm 45). The song of praise at the celebration of his wedding is able to call him אלהים, a god (Ps. 45:6) and thereby go far beyond all limits observed scrupulously otherwise. The Davidite is the viceroy of God—representative of the royal rule of Yahweh. Thus the rule of the world is transferred to him (cf. the excursus on Psalm 2). Peoples and kings are subdued under him. And if foreign powers revolt, Yahweh himself immediately takes up the cause of his anointed one and by means of the arm of his viceroy beats down the rebelling foes (Pss. 2:8ff.; 110:5). In the protective power of the divine שם (name) the king lives (Ps. 20:6). Yahweh is at his right hand (Ps. 110:5) and strides down from heaven when his servant gets into difficulties (Pss. 72:1; 122:5). From his rule the poor hope for justice and help (Ps. 72:4). And the produce of the land is increased in wondrous ways (Pss. 72:3, 6ff.; 132:15). But the festival congregation makes intercession for the king (Ps. 84:9). It knows that all of life is dependent on the ruler's statement of loyalty (Psalm 101) and on the preservation of the covenant of David.

Thus the chosen king of the lineage of David occupies a key position in the worship of Jerusalem. As lord of the temple and as the anointed one he assumes a mediating function. He is the instrument of Yahweh's rule and judgment, of his help and salvation. If the ruler resists, the gate from which the blessings of God issue is closed. Therefore the congregation surrounds him with petitions and wishes. And yet, even though the Psalms know about the humanity and the fallibility of the king, the psalms—mostly in prophetic address—still heap profuse expressions of glory on the anointed of Yahweh. Even the insignificance of a nation that is ever more shrinking does not keep the singers from proclaiming indefatigably the worldwide rule and saving power of the Davidite. The source of all this glorification is the promise that rests on David and his lineage. And wherever incomprehensible expressions of perfection are expressed, there is basically no exaggeration on the basis of an ancient Near Eastern ideal of a king, but a correspondence to Yahweh's own rule and activity is sought in the government and operation of the ruler. Expressions that strike us as frenzy and as enthusiasm removed from reality are in the last analysis charismatic references to a glory still hidden but—because of Yahweh's promise—capable of breaking out in full splendor any moment (cf. also G. von Rad, "Erwägungen zu den Königspsalmen," *ZAW* 58 [1940/41], 219f.). The kings of Jerusalem are not simply to be listed under the mythical rubric of "divine rulers." They are Yahweh's kings. They were chosen and installed in a particular hour of Israel's history. Their existence stands and falls with the basic word of the covenant with David. Their office and rule is to be understood from the viewpoint of the mystery and wonder of their position as viceroys.

4. It goes without saying that in psalms that almost without exception have originated in Jerusalem, or were transmitted and collected in Jerusalem, traditions and institutions of Zion should be predominant. But this does not mean that in any place or time the older Israelitic traditions would have retreated into the background. The God present in Jerusalem bears the name "Yahweh Sebaoth." This name points back to the time before the kings, when the association of the 12 tribes gathered at Shiloh (§10, 1). The *deus praesens* of Zion is the "God of Israel," or the "God of Jacob" (Pss. 72:18; 106:48; 46:7, 11; and often). Above all, the ark with its traditions is the guarantee of continuity with the early history (cf. M. Noth, "Jerusalem und die israelitische Tradition," *OTS* 8 [1950], 28-46 = *GesStud:* ThB 6 [1966], 172-187). Accordingly, there are continually in the Psalms countless remembrances and allusions to the life, the institutions, and traditions of the old 12-tribe confederacy. The basic transmissions of salvation history are the foundation of the people of God gathered in Jerusalem. Without ceasing, the "wonders" and "deeds" that the God of Israel manifested to his people are in everybody's mouth. The great cycles of tradition, "the patriarchal narratives," "the exodus from Egypt," "guidance in the wilderness," "revelation at Sinai," "gift of the promised land," find characteristic expression in the Psalms. If we consider, for example, the historical psalms (Psalms 78; 105; 106; 136), we should observe that in them a view of salvation history is reflected that probably had canonical standing already very early and that is present in its primitive form in Deut. 26:5ff. (cf. G. von Rad, *OT Theol* 1:357). Very likely the cultic-poetical recital and the "almost unconnected enumeration of the bare facts of creation and of the saving history" (G. von Rad), as this is observable in Psalm 136, was the older form of cultic contemporizing of the authoritative original history. Psalms 78 and 106 then show a more recent form of the poetical presentation, in which the theological theme "Yahweh's grace and Israel's guilt" (*Jahwes Huld und Israels Schuld*) is the determining factor of history. The proclamation and the teaching of history was brought home to the festival congregation.

Turning to the individual cycles of tradition in their cultic-poetic form, we must first rivet our attention on the adoption of "patriarchal narratives" in the Psalms. Only Psalm 105 deals in detail with the "covenant" that Yahweh made with Abraham. The content of this covenant and of the assurance under oath given to the patriarch is the promise of land (Ps. 105:9ff.). The psalmist relates the experiences of the patriarch, who wandered about as a "stranger" (Ps. 105:12) but in all situations was the inviolable "anointed" and "prophet" (Ps. 105:15). The psalm especially emphasizes the covenant faithfulness of the God of Abraham. God remembered his pledge and gave the promised land to Israel (Ps. 105:42). These deeds of Yahweh apply directly to Israel, the "songs of Abraham" and of Jacob, the "chosen ones of Yahweh" (Ps. 105:6). The cultic community at Jerusalem is "the people of the God of Abraham" (Ps. 47:9). The traditional identification, "Israel" = "Jacob," also appears in the Psalms (Pss. 14:7; 53:6; 59:13; 85:1; 135:4; 147:19; and often).

The theme of the exodus from Egypt is in evidence in the Psalms even more prominently than the tradition of the patriarchs. In Ps. 105:23 the connection between the prehistory of the patriarchal period and the experiences of the Israelites in Egypt is preserved. Concerning the "wonders in Egypt" (Ps. 78:12), especially concerning the killing of the firstborn, the record is presented in Pss. 78:43ff.; 135:8f.; 136:10. In these events Yahweh demonstrated his power over the great kingdom of Pharaoh and gave his people the way to freedom. But the miracle at the Sea of Reeds (Red Sea) stands out especially in the depictions. We have reports in Pss. 78:13 and 136:13f. of the wondrous "parting" of the sea. Mythological conceptions of the victory over the chaotic primal sea had an influence, especially when it says in Ps. 106:9f. that Yahweh parted the Red Sea with his rebuke. Theophany traditions are decisive in Psalm 114: the sea "flees" before Yahweh's powerful appearance. The amazing exodus from Egypt is thought of as a fundamental bestowal of grace by the God of Israel. He has plucked up his people from Egypt like a grapevine and brought them to Canaan (Ps. 80:5ff.). The tradition of bringing out the people is the basic tradition of election (Ps. 114:1f.).

The theme "guidance in the wilderness" has a secure place in the historical psalms (Psalms 78; 105; 106; 136). In wondrous ways Yahweh led his people through the barren land (Pss. 78:52; 136:16). God furnished water in the desert (Pss. 78:15; 105:41) and fed the people (Ps. 78:19). But the revolt and the murmuring of the people is the expression of a guilt deeply rooted in Israel. The people did not want to entrust themselves to the miraculous guidance of Yahweh. Wantonness (Pss. 78:18; 106:14) and hardening of the heart (Ps. 95:8) triumph. Particularly in the didactic psalms, which want to reveal the guilt of Israel, is the theme "murmuring in the wilderness" an important ingredient.

A noticeably small role in the historical psalms is given to the theme "revelation and lawgiving at Sinai." It is true, there is a reminder in Ps. 78:5f. that Yahweh at that time gave the determinative instruction; still this reference points to the disclosure, "They did not keep the covenant" (Ps. 78:10). Psalm 106 mentions only the signal failure that (at Sinai) a molten image of a calf was made (v. 19). But special importance must be assigned to Psalms 50; 81; and also 68. The first two inform us that the events at Sinai were recreated in a cultic festival. By sacrifice in worship at Jerusalem the "covenant was made" (Ps. 50:5). Ps. 81:9f. contains a direct restatement of the First Commandment. From Psalms 50 and 81—together with other OT passages—we could infer "a covenant renewal festival" (cf. A. Alt, *KlSchr* I, 328f.; G. von Rad, *The Problem of the Hexateuch and Other Essays* (1966) 20ff. = *GesStud:* ThB 8 [1971], 28ff.). We would of course be well advised not to assign the dominant position to this festival that A. Weiser presupposes. In this connection cf. the comment on Psalm 50. A problem arising from altogether different circumstances is posed by Psalm 68. If this psalm is to be assigned originally to the cultic tradition of Mount Tabor (cf. the commentary on Psalm 68), then the unique adoption of appearance theology is to be considered. Whereas on Zion the theophany of Yahweh is an integral ingredient of the cultic place-tradition (Ps. 50:2) and stands in strong tension with "the idea of inhabitation" of the temple, the conviction of Ps. 68:8, 17 is that the God of Israel is enthroned on Mount Sinai and there "comes" and "appears" for worship (cf. the commentary on Psalm 68).

Finally, let us call attention to the theme "gift of the promised land" in the Psalms. The gift of the land is the fulfillment of the covenant made with Abraham (Ps. 105:11). Yahweh has driven out nations and presented to his people a territory that is a basic blessing of salvation (Pss. 44:2; 78:55f.; 80:8ff.;

105:44). This land is the chosen נחלה ("heritage," Ps. 47:4), where Israel may forever experience and taste the life-giving, sustaining goodness of Yahweh.

5. The festival congregation comes together before Yahweh not only for praise and jubilant homage, for adoration and for meeting the manifestation and the word of the God of Israel that proclaims Yahweh's great deeds of the past and of the present; in time of great afflictions it also enters the holy place with prayers and petitions in sackcloth and ashes. The "prayer songs of the people" are witnesses to this cultic act. The affliction is unspeakably grievous. Yahweh has "rejected" his people (Ps. 60:1ff.). On this account, not only has the history of salvation become problematic in its very fundamentals, but even the foundations of the earth have begun to totter (Ps. 60:2ff.). Is the God of Israel really the lord of history? Is he the Creator and king of the universe? The complaining congregation looks back. It sets before Yahweh the great events and miracles of calling, liberating, and bestowing of land (Pss. 44:1ff.; 80:8ff.); it recalls the ברית ("covenant," Ps. 44:17) in which the "servants of Yahweh" (Ps. 79:2) lived. Has all of this now become ineffective? Hymnic interludes recall the royal power of the Creator who conquered the primal sea (Ps. 74:12-17).

How are we to explain the great catastrophe? Why has the wrath of Yahweh been kindled? These questions break out with elemental force. Are the sons bearing the iniquities of their fathers (Ps. 79:8)? How is Yahweh's conduct to be understood? Psalm 44 expresses the conviction most clearly: God's people are suffering for Yahweh's sake. Because of its ties to Yahweh, Israel is assailed by insult and enmity. Not self-righteous impenitence but a profound understanding of the mystery of "Israel" comes to light in Psalm 44. The ברית assigns all questions and afflictions to a lower stratum than the causality of guilt and punishment. God's honor is in the balance (Ps. 74:18f.). The nations have mocked Yahweh (Ps. 79:12). With a challenge they watch to see whether Yahweh will really let his promise of salvation to Israel come true (Ps. 79:10). The sufferings of the people of God are no passing political crises; they are imponderable afflictions that arise in view of the foundation of the history of salvation and Yahweh's universal power over history. For that reason pleas are raised that Yahweh step forth from seclusion and "shine forth" (Ps. 80:1ff.), that Yahweh let his wrath turn and "restore" Israel (Pss. 80:3; 85:4). In this connection the frightful call for judgment uttered by those who lament and pray is not simply to be explained as a "wild outburst of a fiendish spirit of vengeance." The cruel words of Ps. 83:9-18 are to be viewed from the background of the all-encompassing question: Is Yahweh lord of history? Will Yahweh display his might in the midst of this world? Will God counteract the devastation of his people with a sign that will manifest Yahweh's control of history among the nations? It would be a serious mistake to apply as a critical measuring stick to the OT the docetism of the 19th century, which believed that it recognized the "ideas" of the world's course, and then at the same time, with the help of psychologisms, to point to unwholesome emotions in its moral reprehensibility. The greatest restraint is imperative here. The prayer songs of Israel evince the unfathomable mystery that the nations, who do not know Yahweh (Ps. 79:6) and yet hate him (Ps. 83:2), rise up against the witness of God's saving and ruling will in order to destroy him.

6. As we have pointed out in §6, 2, the prayer songs and thanksgiving songs of individuals occupy the most space in the Psalter. But these songs are simply unintelligible if they are not considered from the viewpoint both of the fundamental traditions of the history of salvation and of the cultus and also of the

reality of the OT congregation assembled in Jerusalem. There is no "private piety" in the Psalter. The singers of the psalms of prayer and thanksgiving always arise from the worship of the congregation of Israel. The formulas and formulations have evolved from the world of the cultus. Also, the conviction of being heard, the very heart of songs of lament and petition, lives on the unshakable reality that the God of Israel showed grace to the fathers who turned to him, and he helped them (Ps. 22:4f.). Accordingly, also the deliverance experienced by individual members of the people of God does not remain "private knowledge" but is communicated and witnessed to the "great congregation" (קהל רב, Ps. 22:25). Prayer and thanksgiving of the individual are encompassed by the reality of the congregation.

Those who lament come before Yahweh with characteristic self-identifications. As in the heading תפלה לעני (Psalm 102), so the afflicted singers of psalms often call themselves דל, אביון, ענו, ענו, עני ("poor," cf. §10, 3). These concepts do not—as was supposed for a long time—refer to a designation of a group, an order, or a party. The "poor" are those who need help, those who lay claim to the saving privilege of the cultic center. This "privilege" is, so to say, implicit in the charter of the founding of Jerusalem: "The Lord has founded Zion, and in her the afflicted of his people find refuge" (Isa. 14:32). The עניים have a legitimate claim to Yahweh's help. For the purpose of helping them the God of Israel is present in Jerusalem. Whoever, therefore, calls himself עני lays claim to the "sacral right of the poor." This explains the עניים-piety outlined in the Psalms. But alongside the self-reference עני (or the other expressions for "poor") there is the designation צדיק ("righteous") that is more frequently found in the prayer songs (Pss. 7:9; 31:18; 34:17; 55:22; and frequently). Only the צדיק has access to Yahweh (cf. Ps. 15:1ff.); he who is רשע or רע ("evil") cannot stand before him (Ps. 5:4). But the צדיק is the socially faithful person who lives in accordance with the covenant. When he becomes עני, needy, his צדקה is in doubt (see below); but that is precisely the subject of the prayer songs of an individual: the צדקה of the צדיק is established and again newly proved through Yahweh's helpful intervention. Among the self-designations we also find the word חסיד ("pious," RSV: "saints," Pss. 30:4; 31:23; 37:28), by means of which the condition of loving, gracious devotion is characterized. Finally, there is the term עבד ("servant," Pss. 27:9; 69:17; 86:2; 116:16; 143:2). The one who is praying or pleading calls himself "God's servant."

Which ailments, cares, and afflictions can we recognize in the prayer songs of individuals? We could very cautiously refer first to sickness (Pss. 6:2; 22:14ff.; and frequently), legal problems (Psalms 7; 17; and frequently), and guilt (Psalms 32 and 51). But these afflictions are interconnected in many ways. The ever-present knowledge of impending threat makes the sick person immediately ask about his guilt. The legal problem immediately arises if those around the sick person set about to assign the reason for the affliction to a concrete offense and to bring forth an accusation. This reciprocal relation, this complexity of distress causes all clear contours of the experience of specific misfortune to become blurred. Comprehensive terms and metaphors that transcend the individual signalize the affliction. In the language of prayer already very early standing idioms and images were coined that in part came from the ancient Near Eastern surroundings and were adopted by Israel. The afflicted person is surrounded by the chaotic forces of שאול (Sheol) that reach into the area of life. The waters and waves of the world of the dead encompass him (Ps. 18:4ff.). He sinks into the mire of an area that is far from God (Pss. 69:2ff.; 88:7) and approaches the world of the departed. Every impairment of life, every diminution of vital strength (נפש) is considered an attack by שאול. The underworld that lies in the depths is the hostile force that reaches up into the area of life and devours the נפש. But it is also distant from the cult, and infinitely far removed from God (Pss. 6:5; 88:10). Whoever comes under its spell stands far from Yahweh (Ps. 10:1). The essence of all that is frightening is to be forsaken by God, and that is what is being suffered in this sphere of death (Ps. 22:1). In the prayer songs of individuals we observe again and again how far the conventional elements of image and conception which the man at prayer has adopted transcend all concrete conditions of distress. The singers speak of their affliction in standard metaphors that go beyond what is individual. They know all about the primal distress of being forsaken by God and of being abandoned to שאול, which is manifested in all situations of distress. The torment is incalculable, since all suffering before Yahweh becomes truly distressful and bitter. The depths of torment are fathomed more than ever by him who knows the Holy One who is enthroned high above Israel's hymns of praise (Ps. 22:3). "Affliction" (*Anfechtung*) in the Psalms is not an easily defined phenomenon of being abandoned to Sheol, but a distress that finds its full weight of endlessness only in relation to Yahweh. The hyperboles give the impression of glossolalia, which expresses the unfathomable in code. It is the צדיק ("righteous"), the "servant of God," who suffers what is frightful. From an incomparable abyss emerge the shrill cries and questions: "How long?" "Why?"

All these torments are intensified by the appearance of the enemies (cf. §10, 4). At the sight of a sick person, the logic of the "enemy" says: God has afflicted him because of his guilt! The accusation is added to the physical suffering. Sinister forces arise, even among friends and relatives, and they want to separate the servant of God from Yahweh by means of accusations and persecution. The verdict of condemnation is to be pronounced over the צדיק. Curses pursue him. Magical imprecations are to ruin him. In scorn the question is heard: "Where is now your God?" Godforsakenness must lead to a definitive separation from God—that is the endeavor of these enemies.

A theme that is frequently to be noted—independent of the situation of sickness—is slander and persecution, the false accusations that assail the צדיקים. Many prayer songs of individuals are prayers of the accused (H. Schmidt). Hunted like a wild animal by its pursuers, and surrounded by enemies that are as numerous as an army—so the innocent seek refuge with Yahweh. The sanctuary is the asylum, the place of refuge for those accused and persecuted, who as ענוים take advantage of the "sacred right of the poor" (see above) and invoke the privilege of legal assistance and of the help of Yahweh. On Zion Yahweh is enthroned as "judge of the nations" (cf. §9, 2). To him the accused now appeals in his need (cf. especially Ps. 7:6ff.). He lays bare his innermost being before the omniscient God (Pss. 7:9; 17:3; 139:1ff.) and entrusts himself "for better or for worse" to the judgment of God. Rituals of cleansing, oaths, and maledictions of self (for the case of proved guilt) are heard in the holy place. As the sick prays, "Heal me!" (Ps. 6:20), and the guilty desires to have a "clean heart" (Ps. 51:8), so the accused pleads: "Judge me!" (Pss. 7:8; 43:1). May Yahweh intervene, grant real proof of power and help, and overcome the enemy—this is the action, this the turn of fortune that those who lament pray for. They "call," "cry," "weep," and "plead." They appeal to Yahweh's "justice" and "grace," to his faithfulness, to his help and promises. They remind Yahweh of the wonderful works that have been experienced and witnessed. They address Yahweh on the basis of his honor. And in all their lamenting and pleading these petitioners unceasingly manifest hope, confidence, and the conviction that they will be heard.

But how are the tables now turned? How does the helpful intervention of Yahweh come about? The singers await Yahweh's "word" (Ps. 130:5). Here we will have to think of the priestly oracle of deliverance which is also cited in a number of psalms. God's word can heal the sick (Ps. 107:20); it is the inviolable sign of his healing favor. With that word there is certainty: "You have answered me" (Pss. 22:21 [MT]; 118:21; 138:3). The "change of attitude" that may be observed in a number of prayer songs is probably to be attributed to the "oracle of healing" (Psalms 6; 28; 56; 69).

In the case of an accusation the oracle assumes the character of a divine judgment. But in various ways it becomes apparent that those lamenting are praying for a theophany (Pss. 3:17; 7:6; 9:19; 17:13; and frequently). It is difficult to detect whether this petition aims at experiencing a vision (in connection with the theophany before the cultic community) or whether the proof of the appearance of God is seen in the occurrence of an actual change of fortune (and the overcoming of the enemies). In Ps. 18:7ff. a theophany is described that brings about the occurrence of deliverance. But always the יְשׁוּעָה (deliverance) carried out is fully this-worldly. The sufferer is plucked out of שְׁאוֹל (Sheol, Pss. 9:13; 18:16f.; 30:1, 3; and frequently). The צְדָקָה of the צַדִּיק is proved. The condemnation expressed by the enemies falls apart. Certainty triumphs: "Who shall bring any charge against God's elect? It is God who justifies; who is to condemn?" (Rom. 8:33f.). The enemies are overcome. The desire for judgment on the part of the afflicted, a desire which occasionally expresses itself in a wish to curse and to avenge, awaits God's demonstrable act. Here all the psychological judgments and moral indignation of the interpreters fail. The salvation of God in the OT is no spiritual or ideal phenomenon of change but an event that intervenes in the world. The Jews' demand for signs, of which Paul speaks (1 Cor. 1:22), steers toward *securitas;* but the plea of the afflicted, which grows out of too large a measure of suffering, begs for *certitudo.* Granted that in the NT a new *certitudo* becomes apparent in Christ crucified, but this event must not become the occasion for criticizing inferior thoughts of revenge on the basis of a gospel ideology of love. The question of God's power in history remains also in the NT; it extends even to the exalted Lord (Rev. 6:10). Here a limit is set for premature religious value judgments.

Once Yahweh has intervened and made an end of the distress of the sufferers, then the תּוֹדָה ("thanksgiving") comes into being. In the thanksgiving song the singer tells of the days of torment and of the wondrous deliverance. The entire community is to be a witness to Yahweh's saving act (Ps. 22:22ff.). And yet, the emphasis in the narration and the testimonial is not on the "personal experience" but on the proclamation of the "name of Yahweh" (Ps. 22:30). Again, manners of expression and metaphors that go beyond the individual come into prominence. It looks as if all those who pray belong to a single context of events that transcends their own lives but still in a wonderful way determines and upholds them directly. The תּוֹדָה-offerings are signs of thanksgiving and homage (Ps. 27:6). Along with relatives and friends, the "poor" and those in search of help who had not yet experienced the saving power of Yahweh were probably also invited to the communal meal of the festival (Ps. 22:26). The cup of salvation is lifted up (Ps. 116:13). Rites of thanksgiving accompany the singing and playing (Ps. 43:4), which is at the same time a confession. In Hebrew, תּוֹדָה

has a double connotation, "thanksgiving" and "confession." The experiences of an individual are to provide helpful guidance for others (Psalm 34). People are to learn to trust Yahweh completely and to expect help from him alone.

Finally we should point to the expression of confidence. The trust and assurance of being heard that already pulses through the lament now finds full expression. The felicity of communion with Yahweh is extolled in exuberant phrases. With the God of Israel the man of prayer knows that he is well sheltered (Pss. 16:9; 23:6), and toward him his soul waits in silence (Ps. 62:1). No harm will assail him who trusts (Ps. 23:1, 4). He now knows that he is at all times protected and led by Yahweh (Ps. 23:3).

7. Among the great variety of suffering about which the songs of prayer and thanksgiving in the Psalter speak, difficult existential questions loom like a steep wall. The great problems of life are roused. Why must I suffer? Why am I thrust into the depths of שְׁאוֹל? This is the tenor of the psalms of lament. With such questions those who pray approach the thought-world of חכמה ("wisdom"), in which the attempt is made to comprehend and to master the problems of life. But it would be a mistake to identify the intellectual accomplishments of חכמה with the idealistic categories of "theory." The trend of "wisdom" taken over by Israel from the surrounding world of the ancient Near East, with its fixed forms and themes, is deeply rooted in existence. The thinker does not dissociate himself; he does not "contemplate." Basically, he does not "reflect" either. Aspects of life are directly dealt with in the proverbs and love of חכמה. Orientation and questions of goals here are deposited. The problem of the אחרית, the good and wholesome conclusion of all things, is discussed with immediate existential empathy. In the OT the "fear of Yahweh," the elemental awareness concerning the reality of God that upholds and controls all of life, plays a dominating role in חכמה. A critical theme is "life in the presence of Yahweh." It is in this sense that "wisdom" is adopted in the laments and thanksgivings.

Why do I suffer? The answer may be: Yahweh has "chastised" me to bring me to "salvation" (Pss. 66:10; 118:18; 119:67, 71); he has worked toward a good purpose and has let the sufferers "taste" his goodness anew (Ps. 34:8). The abasement had as its goal a wondrous exaltation (Ps. 118:22). A new witness for the living, beneficial intervention of Yahweh has been brought back from the domain of death into the world of life (Ps. 118:17). Especially the songs of thanksgiving come to this liberating knowledge. In the joy over God's saving intervention the time of lamentation shrinks and vanishes (Ps. 30:5). But this cheering knowledge does not win the day everywhere. A number of psalms speak of an excess of suffering in which the sufferer looks for orientation. Persisting torments summon all the powers of the spirit. He who is praying penetrates the riddle of his situation. He becomes aware of the transitory and nonessential nature of his life. Like a "vapor," thin and fragile, evanescent and disintegrating, is existence (Pss. 39:4; 62:9; 78:39; 144:4); it has no value and no weight by itself. Psalm 90 shows how this existence in view of the eternity of God only arrives at its final abyss. God's time is different from that of humans. He is the preexistent, the permanent. The human being is dust and ashes; a perishing, guilty creature. Futile is all "ostentation" (Ps. 90:10), hollow and deceptive are all possessions (Psalm 49). These things are not "thoughts," but final experiences in life, expressed in words. In the domain of death the צדיק inquires about Yahweh's saving faithfulness. Will the God of Israel let his servant perish? This question appears in all its bitterness especially when the צדיק contemplates the distribution of the fortunes of life. The רשע ("wicked"), who has dissociated himself from Yahweh in his way of life, experiences good fortune and the joys of existence. His life follows a pattern of blessing and fulfillment. But the צדיק must suffer. He lies in the domains of שׁאול and bears the stigma of rejection and exclusion from salvation. In Psalms 37 and 73 this problem is unfolded. But we must of course consider the fact that these two psalms do not present theoretical doctrinal essays about "retribution," "theodicy," or "the moral world order." Rather, we have here a narrative and a report, showing how a צדיק has become disillusioned about Yahweh's perfection and saving faithfulness. In utter loneliness he finds himself confronted with difficult questions. Will God give an answer? He who prays in Psalm 73 reports further how he took refuge at the place where God is present, at the sanctuary, and how the final truth was revealed to him there. "Remaining with Yahweh" (Ps. 73:23) and the assurance of removal to glory (cf. the commentary on Ps. 73:24) then are the basis of the faith in an indestructible life of communion with Yahweh. But the well-being of the רשׁעים, in light of the final revelation, will be unmasked as a fool's paradise (Ps. 73:17ff.). Beyond the fulfillment in this world, Yahweh's saving faithfulness is here revealed as a last act reaching out into the "eschaton." The lamenting and questioning psalms all look toward the reestablishment of communion with God. They expect the new assurance in most cases in the present world (Psalm 37). In Psalm 73 a last barrier is broken. Only in the NT, through the death and resurrection of Jesus Christ, is the fulfillment of God's saving faithfulness disclosed. At the same time, however, God conceals himself in this last event in the depth of suffering and shame.

How are the problems of life solved, the questions that buffet and assail the person living before God, not only in times of suffering but every day? חכמה ("wisdom") teaches that all human exertion is for nothing (Ps. 127:1ff.). "The fear of Yahweh is the beginning of wisdom" (Ps. 111:10). However, remaining and being rooted unshakably in the תורה (Torah), the gracious revelation of God's will, lends salvation and stability to life (Psalm 1). This is the only way that is practicable in this world (cf. the commentary on Psalm 1). The way of the רשׁע leads to destruction (Ps. 1:6)—no matter how successfully it may go along at first. In the joy and desire to do God's will, life finds meaning, shape, and purpose (Psalm 119). If all ways are committed to Yahweh (Ps. 37:5), he who is obedient and trusting will not waver and go astray.

§10. Excursuses

1. The Cultic Traditions of Jerusalem

S. Mowinckel, *Psalmenstudien II: Das Thronbesteigungsfest Jahwäs und der Ursprung der Eschatologie* (1922); H. Schmidt, *Die Thronfahrt Jahwes* (1927); B. N. Wambacq, *L'épithète divine Jahwé Sebaoth* (1947); S. Mowinckel, *Offersang og Sangoffer* (1951); J. Gray, "Canaanite Kingship in Theory and Practice," *VT* 2 (1952) 193-220; A. Alt, "Gedanken über das Königtum Jahwes," *KlSchr* I (1953) 345-357; H. Schmid, "Jahwe und die Kulttraditionen von Jerusalem," *ZAW* 67 (1955) 168-197; D. Michel, "Studien zu den sog. Thronbesteigungspsalmen," *VT* 6 (1956) 40ff.; H. Gross, "Lässt sich aus den Psalmen ein 'Thronbesteigungsfest Jahwes' nachweisen?" *TTZ* 65 (1956) 24-40; J. Gray, "The Hebrew Conception of the Kingship of God," *VT* 6 (1956) 268-285; S. H. Hooke, *Myth, Ritual, and Kingship* (1958); R. Mayer, "Der Gottesname Jahwe im Lichte der neuesten Forschung," *BZ* (1958) 26-53; H.-J. Kraus, *Worship in Israel* (1966); J. D. W. Watts, "Yahweh Málak Psalms," *ThZ* 21 (1965) 341-348; W. H. Schmidt, *Königtum Gottes in Ugarit und Israel* (1966), additional bibliography there; A. Albright, *Yahweh and the Gods of Canaan* (1968); H. Gese, *Die Religionen Altsyriens* (1970); F. M. Cross, *Canaanite Myth and Hebrew Epic* (1973).

a. The Names of Yahweh

In Ps. 24:7, 10 Yahweh is called מלך הכבוד. This appellation is an occasion for providing a summary overview and a preliminary explanation of the names of Yahweh used in the cultic tradition of Jerusalem. To which complex of traditions does Yahweh's particular name of מלך belong? Which data in the history of religion and cultic history do we need to consider?

In his book *Das Königtum Gottes* (1932), M. Buber still supported the conception that the epithet מלך had been applied to the God of Israel already at Sinai. The covenant at Sinai is called a "royal covenant" by Buber. A passage like Deut. 33:5 takes center stage in this interpretation. But this interpretation of the kingship of God came increasingly to be rejected as inapplicable. The thought prevailed "that the conception of the kingship of Yahweh does not seem to have formed a constitutive element in the original components of the Israelite religion" (A. Alt, "Gedanken über das Königtum Jahwes," *KlSchr* I, 348). Attention was more intensely focused on Yahweh's entrance into the world of Canaanite religion (G. von Rad, *OT Theol*, 1:25). Thus the history-of-religions question about pre-Israelite cultic traditions gained a remarkable priority (H. Schmid, "Jahwe und die Kulttradition von Jerusalem," *ZAW* 67 [1955], 168-197). The results of the excavations in the Syrian-Canaanite area contributed to letting the religious and cultic traditions of the original inhabitants of the country come more clearly into prominence. Thus the problem arose: Which Canaanite elements gained entrance into the world of Israel's worship? Which cultic traditions did Israel find in the sanctuaries of the Palestine that it took over? And how were such traditions adopted? These questions have become very important especially as applied to the central shrine, Jerusalem.

It turned out that, for instance, the Yahweh name מלך belongs to a religious-cultic complex of conceptions that played an important role in the Canaanite-Syrian area. מלך as an epithet applied to God belongs to the cycle of cultic venerations of the "Most High God." Individual prominent local numina of the old world were elevated to god-kings during the move toward a hierarchy of the pantheon of gods. This process in most cases reflected the political-dynastic constellation of the leading power of a particular city-state. Thus—to call attention first to the situation outside the Canaanite-Syrian area—with the claim to leadership of the city-state Babylon in southern Mesopotamia, the city god Marduk gained the rank in the pantheon of "king of the gods," "most honored among the great gods" (*AOT*[2], 116, 117, 121, 122, 124). Egypt also was familiar with religious reverence of the "king of the gods" (K. Sethe, "Amun und die acht Urgötter von Hermopolis," *Abh. d. preuss. Akad. d. Wiss., phil.-hist. Kl.* [1929], 128; H. Kees, *Der Götterglaube im alten Ägypten* [1941], 468). But the cultic and religious circumstances of Canaan and Syria have been illumined by the Amarna letters and the Ras Shamra texts. Thus the monarchical hierarchy in the world of the gods, for instance, is mentioned already in a letter of the Amarna correspondence, in which the moon god is called *ilani ša ilani* ("the gods of the gods," i.e., "the highest God") (cf. W. Eichrodt, *Theology of the OT*, 1:185). And in other letters a *ba'alu ina šamê* stands out, a "Baal of Heaven," one of highest rank (cf. W. Eichrodt, *Theology of the OT*, 1:201, n.2). Through the Ras Shamra texts the religious mystery of the chief deity has become especially clear. The בעל שמם, which had already become identified through the inscription of Jehimilk of Byblos as a prominent figure of the Syrian world of gods (R. Dussaud, *Syria* 11 [1930], 306), takes on sharper contours-through these texts (O. Eissfeldt, *"Ba'alšamen* und Jahwe," *ZAW* 57, 1939, 1-31 = *KlSchr* II [1963], 171-198). The figure highly venerated in old Ugarit, *Al'iyān Ba'al,* is, among other things, once called "prince, the lord of the earth" (I AB III 8-9, 20-21; cf. G. Widengren, *Sakrales Königtum im Alten Testament und im Judentum* [1955], 69). As Virolleaud declares, *al'iyu* very likely contains the meaning "to get the upper hand" (cf. W. F. Albright, *From Stone Age to Christianity* [1946], 176). In another connection, in the Ras Shamra texts *'el* is said to mean "king" and "judge" (cf. H. Bauer, *ZAW* 51 [1933], 82f.; O. Eissfeldt, *EL im ugaritischen Pantheon,* Berichte über die Verhandlungen d. Sachs. Akad. der Wiss., phil.-hist. Kl 98, 4 [1951]. All these examples—and they could easily be multiplied—show that in the ancient Near East, particularly in the Canaanite-Syrian world, there was this type of "highest God" who, as "king," "lord of heaven," "prince of the earth," and "judge," enjoyed preeminence over all other powers and spiritual forces. This religious and cultic view of the "highest God" of the community, which had achieved the position of being the leading political power, doubtlessly involved a tendency toward universal claim. The holy place at which this deity was venerated is now the "center of the world" (cf. §10, 2).

For pre-Israelite Jerusalem, the old Jebusite city, the religious and cultic conceptions of the "highest God" here sketched are to be presupposed. The names of Yahweh that occur especially in the Psalter, such as אל עליון (*'el 'elyon*), אדון כל־הארץ ("Lord of all the earth"), מלך ("king"), and שופט ("judge"), are in all likelihood derived from the cultic tradition of the old Jebusite city. For the terms עליון (אל) and מלך, clues for such an origin of the designations of Yahweh in terms of the history-of-religions and cultic history are at hand. Thus in Gen. 14:18 the city god of שלם (Salem) (and the reference here is surely to Jerusalem; cf. Psalm 110) is called אל עליון. And the presence of a מלך-cult in the area of the original population of Jerusalem may be deduced from Lev. 18:21; 20:2f.; 2 Kings 23:10; Mic. 6:7; Ezek. 20:25f.; as well as Jer. 7:18 and 44:17. In the Canaanite fertility cult a מלכת השמים ("queen of heaven") was added to the אל עליון and the מלך. As the cited passages indicate, the inhabitants of Jerusalem in the time of Israel were constantly tempted to forsake Yahweh and to engage in the ancient cults of the deity of nature—as far as the horrible practice of sacrificing a son to the "god-king." In the worship of Israel these demands of the heathen deity were strictly rejected. The titles אל עליון, מלך, and אדון כל־הארץ fit only Yahweh. The appellations and their universalizing intention are transferred to the God of Israel. He is the "highest God." The Canaanite pantheon, which in the conception of Psalm 82 was still in evidence also in connection with Yahweh, now sinks away to the idea of בני־האלהים ("sons of God") that surround Yahweh as "ministering spirits" (Ps. 103:19ff.; Isa. 6:1ff.; 1 Kings 22:19; Job. 1:6ff.). The entry of Yahweh into the world of the Canaanite religion brings with it a tremendous enlargement of the horizon in the history of OT worship. Already in the central holy places of ancient Israel—Shechem, Shiloh, Gilgal, and Bethel—Canaanite cultic traditions were instrumental in first displaying the comprehensive sphere of influence of Yahweh and in seeing new relations. But no other holy place of the Canaanite world presented Israel with the problem of such far-reaching adoptions as the old Jebusite city that was endowed with highest divine testimonies and cultic traditions. The prophet Jeremiah sees this business of adopting foreign cultural and cultic aspects in that the priests of Israel, indeed, the entire congregation, are charged in a foreign land constantly to become certain of the presence and power of Yahweh anew with the question איה יהוה ("Where is the Lord?" Jer. 2:6, 8). In the titles and concepts connected with Yahweh in the Psalms, the struggle for a right reception and integration of the pre-Israelite cultic traditions into the Yahweh faith is everywhere apparent. Here we must be clear that the "universalism" in the theology of the OT Psalms is not the late product of a process of religious development within the history of Israel but rather an element of the Canaanite world that already existed in the example of the veneration of the "highest God." If we examine statements in the Psalms concerning Yahweh the אדון, מלך, אל עליון, and שופט, it will immediately become clear on the basis of the background of data from the history-of-religions and from cultic history that we are here dealing with a very closely knit complex.

Yahweh is the עליון (אל) *('el 'elyon)*. With this name of God the following conceptions are associated: As עליון Yahweh is enthroned on heights of clouds (Isa. 14:14) above all other gods (Ps. 97:9). According to Gen. 14:19, the אל־עליון is the creator (קנה) of heaven and earth. Here the creative power of the "Most High God" is attested in a very old passage. To this tradition the statements about Yahweh, the עליון על־כל־הארץ, are attached (Pss. 83:18; 97:9). According to Ps. 47:2, the עליון is מלך גדול על־כל־הארץ: "great king over all the earth." He assigns to the nations their territories (Deut. 32:8) and is exalted in the hymn of praise by the congregation of Israel (Pss. 7:17; 9:12; 92:1). From the heavens his voice resounds (Ps. 18:13).

As Pss. 47:2 and 97:9 reveal, the conceptions of Yahweh the אל עליון and מלך coincide. Yahweh's title מלך belongs to the complex of theologoumena about "God Most High." This relationship of content will immediately become clear if we parallel the עליון concepts with the statements about Yahweh as מלך. The oldest element, still very closely connected to the archaic Canaanite conceptions of the "king of heaven," is probably to be found in Ps. 29:9ff. As מלך הכבוד (Ps. 24:7, 10) Yahweh is enthroned above the heavenly "ocean" (מבול, Ps. 29:9ff.). Also in Pss. 99:1 and 97:2 perceptions concerning the abode of the "king of heaven" in the home of the clouds glimmer through. But the sanctuary of this "Most High God" and "king" is located on Zion (Pss. 97:8; 99:2; Isa. 6:5), which the cultic tradition of Jerusalem calls the "hill of God in the north" (Ps. 48:2; cf. §10, 2). As in the ancient Babylonian myths and epics, the highest God and King is the creator of the world (Pss. 24:1; 93:1; 95:3ff.; 96:5, 10; cf. Gen. 14:19). His act of creation is the foundation of world dominion (Pss. 24:1, 2; 47:2, 7; 97:9). The מלך ("king") Yahweh is "Lord of all the earth" (Pss. 97:5; 24:1; 50:12; 74:16; 89:11; 115:16). His כבוד ("glory") goes out to all lands (Ps. 8:1; Isa. 6:3). The nations are subject to him (Pss. 47:3, 8; 99:2), as all gods too are subdued under him (Pss. 96:4ff.; 97:7). Proskynesis before Yahweh, the "king of the world," is demanded in the Psalms as the cultic act on Zion (Pss. 95:6; 96:9; 99:5, 9).

Yahweh the עליון, מלך, and אדון, the Creator and Lord of the world, is at the same time the שופט ("judge"; Pss. 96:10, 13; 99:8). Also in this conception we could first refer to an archaic tradition which thinks of the אל עליון as a judging God, בעדת־אל, or בקרב אלהים (Ps. 82:1). God is enthroned in "heights of heaven" above the world of people (Ps. 7:7) and judges the nations (Pss. 7:8; 9:8, 19; 96:10). About the God enthroned on Zion, Ps. 9:8 tells us: ישפט־תבל—ידין לאמים ("he judges the world and the peoples"). So Yahweh is the "judge of the world" (Pss. 58:11; 76:8ff.; 94:2ff.).

Apparently the ancient Israelite tradition that Yahweh judges Israel was derived from this universal picture of judgment which is to be attributed to the cultic tradition of the "highest God." We would, of course, have to think of the references to judgment over Israel as more closely connected to the announcement of God's judgment from Sinai (cf. the comment on Ps. 50:4). But the judgment over the nations, as it proceeds from Mount Zion, for instance, in Amos 1:2ff., belongs to the complex of the עליון-tradition, which of course was probably imbued with the justice of God already very early (Isa. 2:2-5).

While the divine name מלך הכבוד ("king of glory") in Ps. 24:7, 10 is to be understood in connection with the history-of-religions type of "highest God," the other prominent names of Yahweh in Ps. 24:8, 10 now oblige us to outline the corresponding explanation from cultic history. If Yahweh in v. 8 is called עזוז וגבור ("strong and mighty") and גבור מלחמה ("mighty in battle"), the derivation of this title is easily perceived. The concepts refer to the institution of the "holy war," in which Yahweh as the *deus praesens*, as "war God" and hero, substituted for Israel (cf. Exod. 15:3; Josh. 6:17; 2 Sam. 5:10; G. von Rad, *Der Heilige Krieg im alten Israel*, ATANT 29 [1951], 82). Concerning גבור as a name for Yahweh, cf. Deut. 10:17; Jer. 32:18. The palladium of the "holy war" in the time of the Judges was the ark of the covenant. Above this cultic object, יהוה צבאות was present as ישב הכרבים ("enthroned on cherubim") in war (1 Sam. 4:4). But that immediately brings us to the next designation of Yahweh in Ps. 24:10. The God of Israel is called יהוה צבאות. There should be no doubt that the divine name יהוה צבאות in Ps. 24:10 has an undeniable connection with the ark as the ancient war palladium. The conceptions to which the term יהוה צבאות refers are those of the "holy war." Thus in 1 Sam. 17:45 the צבאות are declared to be the "lines of battle." Also in 1 Sam. 4:4 and in Ps. 24:8-10 the term יהוה צבאות is conspicuous in its relation to Yahweh as the "God of war." But does the term צבאות originally really mean the armies of war? Even syntactically the combination יהוה צבאות presents difficulties. We cannot simply assume a construct state to be in operation here. That is proved by the simplifying and interpretative phrase יהוה אלהי צבאות, which occurs 18 times in the OT, but could hardly have been original. Except for the OT interpretation given in 1 Sam. 17:45, some, in view of "hosts of angels" (Ps. 103:21), have been persuaded to interpret צבאות as "stars" (Isa. 40:26) or as "the essence of all earthly and heavenly existence" (Gen. 2:1). Opposed to that interpretation is the fact that in the OT only the singular, צבא, regularly denotes the hosts of angels, stars, and so on. And, above all, the distinctive construct combination remains unexplained. O. Eissfeldt has struck out on a new interpretive path by recognizing an "intensive abstract plural" in צבאות, with the meaning "might," and by construing the phrase in the attributive sense (O. Eissfeldt, "Jahwä Zebaoth," *Miscellanea academica Berolinensia* [1950], 128-150 = *KlSchr* III [1966], 103-123). But this interpretation, too, remains problematic, because in it the concept צבאות loses its distinctive richness and is generalized. G. von Rad correctly asks whether it is right to make "an element of cultic epiclesis as old as this is in all circumstances capable of rational explanation" (*OT Theol*, 1:19). Perhaps צבאות originally refered to secret mythical potencies of natural religion (cf. V. Maag, *Jahwäs Heerscharen: Festschrift für L. Köhler* [1950], 27-52). There may be relatively certain agreement that the name יהוה צבאות had its origin at Shiloh and that it, together with the ark as the old war palladium of Israel and in view of "Yahweh's armed forces,'' was demythologized. According to this—apparently prevailing—view, יהוה צבאות was the cultic name of Yahweh in Shiloh (1 Sam. 1:3, 11; 4:4) and was later transferred to Zion together with the long story of the fate of the ark (cf. L. Rost, *Die Überlieferung von der Thronnachfolge Davids,* BWANT III, 6 [1920], 4ff. = *Das kleine Credo und andere Studien zum Alten Testament* [1965], 119-253).

b. Did Jerusalem Celebrate a "Festival of Yahweh's Enthronement?"

There are a number of psalms that celebrate Yahweh the king with special emphasis: Psalms 24:7ff.: 47; 93; 96; 98; 99. These Yahweh-as-king psalms in OT research have been the subject of the most diverse interpretation. Once the historical interpretation had proved to be inadequate and also the eschatological understanding had left many questions unanswered, the cultic interpretation of S. Mowinckel prevailed and found wide recognition. For the history of the exegesis of the psalms of Yahweh-as-king psalms, cf. H.-J. Kraus, *Die Königsherrschaft Gottes im Alten Testament,* BHT 13 (1951) 15-20. In his cultic interpretation Mowinckel took the history-of-religions discoveries in Mesopotamia as a guide and set up an OT parallel to the enthronement festival of Marduk. (On the Babylonian festival, cf. H. Zimmern, *Das babylonische Neujahrsfest* [1926]; *Zum babylonischen Neujahrsfest* [1928].) P. Volz had already called attention to this parallel (P. Volz, *Das Neujahrsfest Jahwes* [1912]). At the center of the Israelite enthronement festival Mowinckel saw the enthronement cry יהוה מלך (''Yahweh has become king!'') and the depiction of the cultic-mystic event (*PsStud* II). At the beginning of the year, according to Mowinckel, Yahweh was newly enthroned and celebrated as king and creator. With a number of reservations, H. Gunkel concurred in this cultic interpretation, although he understood the cultic-mystic elements of the Yahweh-as-king psalms primarily in an eschatological sense (*EinlPs,* 94ff.). In more recent years, however, a number of critical voices have been raised and have challenged the entire cultic conception (cf. J. J. Stamm, ''Ein Vierteljahrhundert Psalmenforschung,'' *ThR* 23/1, 46ff.).

Every interpretation of the Yahweh-as-king psalms is critically dependent on the way the central formula יהוה מלך is translated and understood. It had been considered a settled matter for a long time that יהוה מלך was an ''enthronement cry'' (''Yahweh has become king!''), but today this interpretation faces serious doubts. According to lexicographical findings, the verb מלך has two meanings: ''to be king'' and ''to become king.'' The translation ''to be king'' (with עַל, בְּ, or לְ) is unequivocally demonstrable in Gen. 36:31; Josh. 13:12, 21; Judg. 4:2; 9:8; 2 Sam. 16:8; 1 Kings 14:20; and often. The meaning ''to become king,'' on the other hand, is to be presumed in the ''enthronement cry'' heard to the accompaniment of trumpet flourishes in 2 Sam. 15:10 (1 Kings 1:11); 2 Kings 9:13. But here the word order מלך אדניהו is important. The verbal sentence (*Verbalsatz*)—plainly indicated as an exclamation—announces an act that has just been concluded. Accordingly, we could vacillate in the translation and prefer to emphasize either the act (''Adonijah has become king'') or the resulting state or condition (''Adonijah is king''). But the syntactical problem is cleared up by the fact that in 1 Kings 1:18 the resulting state or condition is described with the word order ועתה הנה אדניה מלך (''And now, behold, Adonijah is king''). If we consider, for instance, that the cry מלך אבשלום ''Absalom is king!'' 2 Sam. 15:10), accompanied by trumpet flourishes, suggests the immediate nearness of becoming king, or of having become king (in other words, of the enthronement, cf. also 2 Kings 9:13), we feel induced to translate the two-member verbal sentence that begins with מלך: ". . . has become king." By the same token, the reverse word order describes a state or condition in which the king involved simply continues: " . . . is king." The subject in preceding position already points to a sentence expressing a state or condition, in which the ambiguous verb functions in the sense "to be king." On the basis of these syntactical observations and determinations, we must conclude regarding the psalms of Yahweh-as-king that יהוה מלך in Pss. 93:1; 96:10; 97:1; 99:1 must be translated, "Yahweh is king!" A proclamation of an enthronement close to its actual occurrence would then be involved only in Ps. 47:8 in the verbal sentence מלך אלהים (cf. also Isa. 52:7). On the problem of the translation and the syntactical understanding of the formula יהוה מלך, cf. L. Köhler, "Jahwä mālāk," *VT* 3 (1953) 188f.; J. Ridderbos, "JAWÄH MALAK," *VT* 4 (1954) 87-89; D. Michel, "Studien zu den sogenannten Thronbesteigungspsalmen," *VT* 6, 1 (1956) 40-68.

Added to the arguments which in the verbal sentence of condition יהוה מלך wipe out the idea of an act of enthronement, there are three basic considerations that make it seem impossible that a cultic enthronement of Yahweh could have been enacted in OT worship. (1) How could an enthronement of Yahweh in Israel have been carried out in the first place? There is here no divine image that could have been lifted up to a throne, nor is any cultic symbol familiar to us that might have represented Yahweh (cf. D. Michel, *VT* 6, 1. 47). The Babylonian "parallels," which today recede farther and farther from the horizon of the Jerusalem cultus, have their own presuppositions in the massive ritualistic furnishings of the statue of the god and its elevation to the throne of the temple in which he appears. (2) Again, we should have to ask further what the theological connection of an "enthronement of Yahweh" might actually be. H. Schmidt (following S. Mowinckel) comes to the conclusion that Yahweh "for a time actually loses" his rule in the rhythm of the seasonal myth of nature; he declares: "This is a myth similar to that of the temporary descent of the gods to the underworld and their rising again" (on Psalm 47 in his commentary on the Psalms). This presuming of a mythicization of Yahweh lacks all foundation in the Yahweh-as-king psalms—and beyond that in the whole OT. (3) Against all "mythicizations" that are necessarily associated with the idea of an enthronement, we will much more have to take note of the emphasis of the psalms of Yahweh-as-king on both the unchangeable kingship of Yahweh that is superior to all divine power and also his continuous tenure as king. This is done most clearly in that psalm which up to now has been considered most clearly tied to the nature myth of the renewal of creation—in Ps. 93:2: נכון כסאך מאז מעולם אתה ("Thy throne is established from of old; thou art from everlasting"). Thus, also for practical reasons an enthronement of Yahweh is hardly acceptable.

But against that stands the fact that Psalm 47 contains the "enthronement formula" מלך אלהים as well as all the marks of an enthronement procedure (v. 5, עלה אלהים בתרועה). Against it as well could be the fact that the ark of Yahweh is at characteristic places in the OT called the "throne of Yahweh" (Jer. 3:16, 17; 17:12; 1 Sam. 4:4; M. Dibelius, *Die Lade Yahwehs,* 1906) and was obviously brought into the temple in a cultic act (2 Samuel 6; 1 Kings 8; Psalm 132). Such an entrance of King Yahweh may be noted in Ps. 24:7ff. and in Ps. 68:24 too. Therefore, must we not—against all the critical arguments enumerated above—still speak of a cultic enthronement of Yahweh? We shall probably do well to set aside Psalm 47 for the time being in consideration of the factual reasons that speak against a festival of the enthronement of Yahweh. We should pay special attention to the other texts that reveal a cultic installation of the ark in the temple or give notice of an entrance of King Yahweh: 2 Samuel 6; 1 Kings 8; Pss. 132; 24:7ff.; 68:25. Cf. H.-J. Kraus, *Die Königsherrschaft Gottes im Alten Testament,* 23ff., and W. Eichrodt, *Theol. OT.* But the question immediately arises whether after considering these connections we can still speak of a "festival of the enthronement of Yahweh" (thus W. Eichrodt). Yahweh does not actually ascend a throne at all, but enters the temple together with the throne of God, being present above the ark. It would be more correct to speak of an installation of the throne of God (namely the ark) and consider that the Yahweh-as-king tradition is a remnant of cultic tradition from the old Jebusite sanctuary that has been added to the conception of the ark as a throne, which is already recognizable in 1 Sam. 4:4. The glorification of Yahweh as king was combined with a festival of entrance, the roots of which are present in 2 Samuel 6; 1 Kings 8; and Psalm 132. The meaning of this entrance festival, which very likely took place on the first day of the Feast of Tabernacles, is not that of an enthronement of Yahweh but of a celebration of the election of Jerusalem and of David (cf. the commentary on Psalm 132). Psalm 24:7ff. and Ps. 68:25 make reference to this entrance festival of King Yahweh—according to the old Jerusalem tradition. The installation of the ark achieves its climax in the proskynesis before "King" Yahweh, who, according to cultic transmissions given in this excursus under §a is described as "creator," "Lord of the world," and "judge" (Pss. 95:3-6; 96:9ff.; 99:9; 100:4).

But with this explanation there remains Psalm 47 (and Isa. 52:7). If in view of the interpretation so far given we may begin with the presupposition that a festival of the enthronement of Yahweh is unthinkable in the OT on the basis of fundamental theological considerations, and if we further have recognized that the descriptions of the entrance of the ark in 2 Samuel 6; 1 Kings 8; and Psalm 132 have a different meaning than that of an enthronement of Yahweh, it will be up to us to provide a pertinent interpretation. Three different possible interpretations may be considered: (1) It could be possible that in the cultic tradition of pre-Israelite Jerusalem an enthronement festival of the kingly divinity was celebrated—a festival that left behind its sacred traditions and conceptual forms. (2) It could be that the political dependence of Jerusalem on Assyria and Babylon, which involved new cultic orientations, brought to Jerusalem the idea and custom of an enthronement of the divinity. In that case we should have to consider whether perhaps in the time of the exile of the Southern Kingdom an enthronement festival was introduced in Jerusalem (thus H. Gunkel, *EinlPs* 94ff.)—or that the festival of installation of the throne was understood as an enthronement. (3) We could ask whether O. Eissfeldt has not hit upon the correct solution when he declares that the psalmsinger of Psalm 47 "means that Yahweh *is* king, but describes how he becomes king because he can best depict the importance of the situation by describing the splendor of the act" (O. Eissfeldt, "Jahwe als König," *ZAW* 46 [1928], 102 = *KlSchr* I [1962], 190f.). According to this, we would in this psalm have a figurative presentation that has been taken from the model of the enthronement of a human king. (4) Would it be reasonable to suppose that Psalm 47 has reference to the cultic situation in Jerusalem as changed by the exile? The message of Deutero-Isaiah (Isaiah 40–55) informs us that the time in which the dynasty of David stood at the center of the people of God has come to an end. Now Yahweh himself is king of Israel. He ascends the throne (Isa. 52:7: מלך אלהים). Already W. Baudissin correctly showed that not until Deutero-Isaiah did the naming of Yahweh as king emerge in prophetic proclamation (*KYRIOS* III [1929] 235f.). This no doubt is associated with the fact that the unknown prophet looks back to the Yahweh-as-king tradition of the Jerusalem cult. But these traditions now enter the proclamation of an eschatological upheaval. The kingship of Yahweh leaves the area of cultic-hymnic glorification and becomes historically influential in an eschatological sense. It could be that Psalm 47 is connected to such a message. In any case, we should be clear on the fact that Psalm 47 is the only one of the Yahweh-as-king hymns in the Psalter that transparently presents an act of enthronement. We shall not be able to pass off to this single psalm the entire weight of an "enthronement of Yahweh" with all its cultic and theological consequences. But the parallel of the Babylonian New Year's festival that influences the interpretation takes us beyond the area of the Jerusalem cultus. In particular, all phenomenological generalizations of the OT worship based on the assumption of an ancient Near Eastern cultic pattern are to be rejected.

2. The Glorification of the City of God

W. F. Albright, "Baal Zaphon," *Bertholet-Festschrift* (1950) 2ff.; H. Schmid, "Jahwe und die Kulttraditionen von Jerusalem," *ZAW* 67 (1955) 168-197; E. Rohland, "Die Bedeutung der Erwählungstraditionen Israels für die Eschatologie der alttestamentlichen Propheten," diss. Heidelberg (1956); A. Alt, "Jerusalems Aufstieg," *KlSchr* III (1959) 243-257; J. Schreiner, *Sion-Jerusalem: Jahwes Königssitz* (1963); M. Noth, "Jerusalem und die israelitische Tradition," *GesStudAt* (1966) 172-187; G. Wanke, *Die Zionstheologie der Korachiten* (1966); H. Schmidt, "Israel, Zion und die Völker," diss. Zurich (1966); H. M. Lutz, *Jahwe, Jerusalem und die Völker* (1968); M. Metzger, "Himmlische und irdische Wohnstatt Jahwes," *Ugarit-Forshungen* 2 (1970) 139-158; J. Jeremias, "Lade und Zion: Zur Entstehung der Ziontradition," *Probleme biblischer Theologie: G. von Rad zum 70. Geburtstag* (1971) 183-198; O. H. Steck, *Friedensvorstellungen im alten Jerusalem*, ThSt Zurich III (1972); R. J. Clifford, *The Cosmic Mountain in Canaan and the Old Testament* (1972); J. J. M. Roberts, "The Davidic Origin of the Zion Tradition," *JBL* 92 (1972) 329-344; W. H. Schmidt, *Alttestamentlicher Glaube in seiner Geschichte* (1975) 206ff., additional bibliography there.

In striking fashion, Psalm 46 contains conceptions and descriptions which, according to all topographical and geographical data, do not originally belong to Jerusalem but were only secondarily transferred to the holy city of God. H. Gunkel thought of these foreign elements as "eschatological," but it has become more and more obvious that we here have to do with very ancient cultic traditions that for the most part already in pre-Israelite times experienced a "history of tradition" in the Syrian-Canaanite area, a history that can hardly be penetrated any longer.

In Ps. 48:2 the following description of the "situation" is given: הר־ ציון ירכתי צפון. Of what significance is the fact that Mount Zion is called the "mount in the far north"? A step in the right direction in the OT for the first is the passage Isa. 14:13-14 (in bold presumption a satirical song about the king of Babylon echoes the haughty words of the foreign ruler): "I will ascend to heaven; above the stars of God I will set my throne on high; I will sit on the mount of assembly [of the gods] in the far north; I will ascend above heights of the clouds. I will make myself like the Most High!" According to this, Mount צפון (entirely independent of Jerusalem) is a heavenly Olympus—above clouds and stars, the throne of עליון (Most High), and the assembly place of the pantheon of the gods. Not only in the OT, however, but also in the Phoenician-Syrian world is there mention of this Mount צפון. Texts that have been unearthed have proved more and more clearly that this hill of the gods lay north of ancient

Ugarit. Involved is the Jebel el 'Aqra (Mount Casius), on which, according to Old Syrian transmission, *b'l spn* (Baal Zaphon) was enthroned as "God Most High." This mountain of the gods—capable of precise topographical determination—was the prototype of Olympus in the Syrian-Canaanite area. Together with the conception of "God Most High" (cf. §10, 1) the traditional image of the mountain of the gods "in the far north" migrated and was thus transferred also to the holy Mount Zion—very likely already in pre-Israelite times by the Jebusites. In this manner universal top billing could be ascribed to a mountain sanctuary (for the conception, cf. also Isa. 2:2ff.). Cf. O. Eissfeldt, "Baal Zaphon, Zeus Kasios und der Durchzug der Israeliten durchs Meer," *Beiträge zur Religions-geschichte des Altertums* I (1932) 14ff.; W. F. Albright, "Baal Zaphon," *Bertholet-Festschrift* (1950) 2ff.

As the seat of the gods and throne of "God Most High," the "mountain in the north" is the center of the earth; it is משׂושׂ כל־הארץ (Ps. 48:2). Everywhere there is a report of the beauty and delight of the mountain of the gods (Lam. 2:15). Conceptions of a paradisiacal locality are associated with Mount צפון and lead into a deeper tier of mythology. Also these conceptions were applied to Jerusalem.

In Ps. 46:4, in the description of the city of God, Jerusalem, there is reference to streams that "make glad" the holy city. It is self-evident that נהר פלגיו cannot be meant to refer to the Gihon Spring that gushed forth at the foot of the hill of the old city. Also Ps. 65:9 and Isa. 33:21 speak of streams in Jerusalem. A spring that flows forth from the temple of Yahweh and lavishly bestows fertility and salvation is attested in Joel 3:18; Ezekiel 47; Zech. 14:8. H. Gunkel and H. Gressmann were the first to recognize that mythical conceptions of the paradisiacal garden of God were here transferred to the city Jerusalem (H. Gunkel, *Das Märchen im Alten Testament: Religionsgeschichtliche Bücher* II, 23/26 [1921], 48ff.; H. Gressmann, *Der Messias* [1929], 179f.). The "primeval" garden of God is described in the OT in Genesis 2 and Ezekiel 47. On the basis of a primeval-time/end-time schema, H. Gunkel, considering Ps. 46:4, was able to conclude that "eschatological" conceptions were involved. But now texts from Ras Shamra (Ugarit) have demonstrated that the picture of a well-watered garden of God may not be considered in isolation but belongs together with the conceptions of the mountain of the gods and the seat of "God Most High." The protological or eschatological relation thereby drops away. In ancient Ugarit people saw *El* sitting "at the source of the (two) rivers, in the midst of the fountains of the two deeps" (cf. G. E. Wright, *Biblical Archaeology* [1957] 106). The godhead therefore dwells in a place where the subterranean primeval stream (*nhrm*) emerges and in controlled form (פלג) waters the land and makes it fruitful (very likely also אד in Gen. 2:6 is to be understood in this sense). These conceptions have been transferred to Jerusalem. The "molten sea" (1 Kings 7:23-26) and the "fountain from the house of the Lord" (Joel 3:18; Ezekiel 47; Zech. 14:8) attest the transmission of a Syrian-Canaanite *yammu* or *naharu* conception that belonged to the mythology of the seat of the gods. Very likely also these cultic traditions and institutions were adopted from the Jebusite sanctuary as the home of the אל־עליון in pre-Israelite times. For details, cf. H. Schmid, "Jahwe und die Kulttraditionen von Jerusalem," *ZAW* 68, 187ff.; E. Rohland, *Die Bedeutung der Erwählungstraditionen Israels für die Eschatologie der alttestamentlichen Propheten,* 127ff.; concerning the meaning of the "molten sea," cf. W. F. Albright.

In Ps. 46:3 violent, chaotic waters, agitated by an earthquake, tumble against the hills. In Ps. 46:6 the chaotic, destructive forces appear in "histori-cized" form: "nations rage, kingdoms totter." The city of God is threatened round about by hostile armies (cf. Pss. 2:2; 48:4ff.), which, like the "waves," roar and break (cf. Isa. 17:12; Jer. 6:23). The myth of the raging of the chaotic forces of the primeval flood has here been applied to Jerusalem in historicized form. The city of God in its paradisiacal beauty is not left untouched. A revolt of the powers hostile to God, a revolt bent on destroying the order of creation, is in the offing. Here we must think not so much of a battle staged in the cultic presentation (thus S. Mowinckel, *PsStud* II, 128) but rather of primeval cultic traditions that continued to flourish in narrative and song on Zion.

The city of God is invincible: Ps. 46:6ff. In the cultic tradition of Jerusalem we hear more often of the city that cannot be taken by storm (cf. 2 Sam. 5:6; Pss. 87:5; 125:1f.; Isa. 26:1). The assailing enemies are driven back and annihilated (Pss. 76:3ff.; 48:5, 6; Isa. 17:13ff.; 24:21; 29:8). Yahweh himself shatters the foreign forces with his thunder (Ps. 46:6), his rebuke (Ps. 76:6; Isa. 17:13), and with the "terror of God" (Ps. 46:8; Isa. 17:14). He breaks the weapons (Pss. 46:9; 76:3ff.). Closely allied to the conceptions of the lofty, impregnable mountain of God are these motifs of the attack and annihilation of the enemies' armies. Yahweh confronts them as אֵל־עֶלְיוֹן, the thundering "king of heaven" (cf. §10, 1 and the comments on Psalm 29) and the rebuking "Creator God." It is possible that also this complex of conceptions that deals with the storming attack of the enemies, the invincibility of Zion, and God's frightening power of intervention was transferred to the Jebusite city of Jerusalem in pre-Israelite times (cf. 2 Sam. 5:6).

In sum, we can see that in Psalm 46 a very remarkable cultic tradition of Jerusalem emerges, one that very probably goes back to pre-Israelite times and one that has conveyed a series of mythological, ancient Canaanite or Syrian conceptions to Mount Zion. But this cultic tradition is traceable not only in the Psalms (e.g., Psalms 48 and 76) but above all in Isaiah, the Jerusalem prophet, or in the prophecy related to Isaiah (cf. Isa. 17:12ff.; 24:21; 26:1; 33:20f.).

After all these observations, however, the relation between cultic tradition and prophecy must certainly be determined in such a way that the cultic traditions are primary and prophecies transmuted to eschatological statements are secondary. In other words, the prophets have drawn the expressions and images of their message from the cultic tradition of Jerusalem. Beside Isaiah and the non-Isaianic prophecies in Isaiah 1–39, we should mention especially also Micah and Jeremiah (but also Ezekiel, Zephaniah, and Deutero-Isaiah). E. Rohland has correctly evaluated the relation of the Jerusalem cultic tradition to prophecy and eschatology (E. Rohland, *Die Bedeutung der Erwählungstradition Israels für die Eschatologie der alttestamentlichen Propheten,* 145ff.). But Rohland is incorrect in labeling these cultic transmissions "election traditions." We must distinguish strictly between the (pre-Israelite) cultic traditions, as they were set forth above in this excursus, and the genuinely Israelitic act of the "election of Zion" (cf. the comment on Psalm 132). It cannot escape notice that in the cultic traditions that were pre-Israelite and deeply rooted in myth the ark is never mentioned. On the other hand, for instance, in Psalm 132 we expressly hear of the bringing in of the ark and of the election of Zion. Therefore we must classify the statements made in this excursus under the theme "Cultic Traditions for the Glorification of Zion."

Objection to the interpretation of the Zion tradition as here presented has been raised by G. Wanke, *Die Zionstradition der Korachiten in ihrem tradi-*

tionsgeschichtlichen Zusammenhang (1966). Wanke wanted to say and prove that "not only the Korahites and the collection of psalms ascribed to them but also the theology expressed in a part of the collected Psalter . . . belong to the postexilic period" (108). The motif of the battle of the nations takes on a separate meaning in Wanke's exposition (70ff.). In this process the obviously correct observation and assertion that there is no parallel for this motif in extra-Israelite literature is emphasized very strongly and advanced as an important argument. The possibility of deducing this motif from the battle of chaos is challenged and disallowed (77). All of the provisional decisions thereby fall into place and are settled in such a way as to have far-reaching consequences. Because the Psalms do not present sufficient possibilities for dating and assessing, the texts Zechariah 14; 12; Joel 3; and Micah 4:11ff. are adduced; from these texts the battle of the nations is claimed as an "eschatological motif." The origin of this motif (in its eschatological relevance) is found in Jeremiah, or in the late preexilic period. In connection with this exposition—in contrast to the conception presented above—the relation of cultic tradition and prophecy is reversed. The motif of the battle of the nations is developed only in late prophecy and then first introduced into the psalms (for which late dates are to be supplied) by the "theology of the Korahites" (Psalms 46 and 48). Against this argumentation, of course, are texts like Isa. 17:12ff. but they are without hesitation dated as postexilic and in this way are no longer a hindrance (116f.). More annoying, however, than all these expedients is the complete disregard for the archaic traditions in Psalms 46 and 48 (but also in Psalm 76 and in numerous passages that may be cited in other psalms). In the process essential aspects of work in the history-of-religions and the history-of-traditions are from the beginning excluded. Here a methodological analysis and discussion would shed light on the individual procedures and critically address them. For a critical debate with Wanke, cf. H. M. Lutz, *Jahwe, Jerusalem und die Völker*, WMANT 27 (1968) 213ff. We can refer only briefly to the seven points that Lutz makes in his criticism and debate: (1) The prophetic texts from Zechariah and Joel, only briefly treated by Wanke, may not summarily and with arbitrary dating be claimed as proofs for the motif of the battle of the nations. (2) The conception of the "foe from the north" has no original connection with any of the three basic conceptions of the theme "Yahweh, Jerusalem, and the nations." (3) Ezekiel 38f. can only conditionally be dovetailed into a prehistory of the motif of the raging of the nations as Wanke projects it. (4) Wanke quickly rids himself of the "uncomfortable" texts Isa. 8:9f. and 17:12ff. in order to be able to assign the songs of Zion, Psalms 46; 48; and 76, to a late time. (5) The conciseness and uniformity with which the motif of the raging of the nations appears in the OT must lead to the conclusion that this tradition must have gained its full stature before Isaiah, but at its latest during his time. (6) Not the frequency with which a motif or concept occurs in the OT decides the question of its age, but the weight with which a motif or concept asserts its position in its early days. (7) Therefore we will have to continue to reckon with the assumption "that there was a Jerusalem cultic tradition"—a tradition such as we have presented in this excursus.

3. The Poor

A. Rahlfs, *'Anī und 'Anāw in den Psalmen* (1892); A. Causse, *Les "pauvres" d'Israël* (1922); H. Birkeland, *'Anī und 'Anāw in den Psalmen*, SNVAO II Hist-Filos.Kl. (1933); P. A. Munch, "Einige Bemerkungen zu den *'anijjim* und den *reša'im* in den Psalmen,"

Le Monde Oriental 30 (1936) 13-26; A. Causse, *Du groupe ethnique à la communauté religieuse* (1937); A. Kuschke, "Arm und reich im Alten Testament," *ZAW* 57 (1939) 31-57; J. J. Stamm, *Die Leiden des Unschuldigen in Babylon und Israel* (1946); J. Van der Ploeg, "Les pauvres d'Israël et leur piété," *OTS* 7 (1950) 236-270; H. Brunner, "Die religiöse Wertung der Armut im alten Ägypten," *Saeculum* 31 (1961) 319-344; P. Van der Berghe, "Ani et Anaw dans les psaumes," *Le Psautier*, ed. R. DeLanghe (1962) 273-298; R. Martin-Achard, "Yahwe et les Anawim," *ThZ* 21 (1965) 349-357; L. E. Keck, "The Poor among the Saints in Jewish Christianity and Qumran," *ZNW* 57 (1966) 54-78; O. Bächli, "Die Erwählung der Geringen im Alten Testament," *ThZ* 22 (1966) 385-395; J. M. Liaño, "Los pobres en el A.T.," *EstB* (1966) 117-167.

It is our intention here to gather and sort the statements of the OT Psalms concerning the poor and the destitute and to provide a preliminary discussion of them. We shall concentrate especially on the following terms, which serve as the designation or self-designation of people close to Yahweh: עני (Pss. 9:18; 10:2, 9; 14:6; 18:27; 68:10; 72:2; 74:19; and often), ענו (Pss. 9:12; 10:17; 22:26; 25:9; 34:2; 37:11; 69:32; 147:6; 149:4), אביון (Pss. 40:17; 70:5; 72:4; 86:1; 109:22), דל (Pss. 41:1; 72:13; 82:3f.), חלכה (Ps. 10:8, 10, 14). The impetus toward a detailed consideration of these concepts of the Psalter was provided by the study of A. Rahlfs, *'Anî und 'Anāw in den Psalmen* (1892). Since then the problem has been the subject of continuous thorough discussions and explanations. Rahlfs thought of the "poor" as a party within the OT people of God—the group of determined followers of Yahweh. This interpretation continued in effect with Duhm, Kittel, Staerk, and Gunkel, among others. It was modified by A. Causse, *Les "pauvres" d'Israël* (1922). Causse interpreted the "poor" to be "a spiritual family and brotherhood" whose members "knew the lowly meekness of the union of souls, union in the cult and in inspiration" (105). Opposition to this concept of a party or group in the OT picture of the "poor" came especially from H. A. Brongers and J. Van der Ploeg (bibliography and review in J. J. Stamm, "Ein Vierteljahrhundert Psalmenforschung," *ThR* NF 23 [1955], 1-68). S. Mowinckel approached the question about the statements concerning the "poor" from another angle. The interpretation that the "poor" referred to a party is denied. Mowinckel sees constant opposition between the "enemies" and the "poor." Thus interpretation (in connection with his conception of the enemies— cf. §10, 4) concluded that the "poor" were originally victims of the magic influence of their enemies; S. Mowinckel, *PsStud* I, 113f. VI, 61. H. Birkeland, in his book *'Anî und 'Anāw in den Psalmen* (1933), shows that he is dependent on Mowinckel. He, too, refuses to see a party in the "poor"; they are rather those who "actually suffer"—although it remains a completely open question how the "actuality" of suffering is in each case to be described and imagined.

In their approach the investigations of Mowinckel no doubt show us the right way: in the Psalms the "poor" are not a party but the victims of the "enemies." A detailed investigation of the occurrence of the terms shows that the "poor" person is the persecuted and disfranchised one, who seeks refuge against his powerful enemies (cf. §10, 4) with Yahweh and entrusts his lost cause to God as the righteous judge. The "poor" person therefore is he who is dependent on God's legal aid: Pss. 9:18; 10:2, 8, 9, 10, 14; 18:27; 35:10; 74:19. The terms listed above almost universally have the meaning "helpless," "miserable," "oppressed," "lowly," "weak," "poor." In their need the "poor" take refuge in the temple area and plead with Yahweh for his intervention and defeat of the enemies. A noteworthy parallel from the Egyptian religion is the prayer to Amon: "Amon, lend your ear to one who stands alone in the judgment, who is poor and whose opponent is powerful. Judgment oppresses him: 'Silver and gold for the scribes! And raiment for the servants!' But he finds that Amon transforms himself into the vizier so that the poor may go free" (A. Erman, *Die Religion der Ägypter* [1934], 40). In this connection we also refer to the study of H. Brunner, "Die religiöse Wertung der Armut im alten Ägypten," *Saeculum* 31 (1961) 319-344.

The enemies' persecution that is to be presupposed can take a great variety of forms: slander, cheating, banishment—or (as Mowinckel particularly emphasizes) it may take the form of a magically effective curse, although we may not emphasize this point in a one-sided way.

The "poor" are the most intensive frequenters of Zion. They can be called יודעי שמך (Ps. 9:10, "those who know thy name"), because they stand in familiar association and intimate communion with the God who is present in his שם. Above all, however, the עני experiences the wonder of God's turning to him to provide his salvation with the kind of strength that can turn his fate and renew his life. Thus the "poor" become the outstanding recipients of the ישועה ("deliverance"). They are the witnesses of the effectual gracious presence of God and the legal aid of him who is enthroned on Zion, אל־עליון: Pss. 9:18; 10:17; 18:27; 22:26; 25:9; 37:11; 69:32; 147:6; 149:4. Thus we can say that the "poor" on Zion enjoy unexampled privileges that have their basis in this alone, that Yahweh is the God of the helpless.

This singular manner in which the Psalms speak of the "poor and helpless" as a group of people is not to be traced back to any organized party but to the privileges of salvation which the עני receives on Zion. With the praise of God's demonstration of deliverance with respect to the "lowly" and with the confession to Yahweh, the legal helper of the "poor," the song of thanksgiving of the individual has developed privileges and legal claims that are valid for all those who look for help. Only so are we to understand it that hereafter the most diverse petitioners claim the privileges of the "poor" when they call to Yahweh: Pss. 40:17; 70:5; 86:1; 109:22. In the interpretation of such passages we will have to be careful to avoid two false interpretations: the "poor" as a group neither represent a party in the organizational sense nor do they in a spiritualized way portray a type of people whose brand of piety would have been elevated into a symbol. Rather, all those who join the ranks of the group of the "poor" (i.e., those who without reservation seek refuge with Yahweh) receive the right to a legal claim to Yahweh's help: Isa. 14:32, "Yahweh has founded Zion, and in her the afflicted [poor] of his people find refuge." This privilege, formulated in experience and confession, marks the entire group, and their intensive participation in the salvation of Yahweh would be influential even in prophetic eschatology (Zeph. 3:12).

Even if it is unmistakable that the poor in the Psalms represent that group of people who not only find themselves in acute legal need (persecution, indictment) but in general are without legal standing and without influence (Ps. 82:3f.), like widows and orphans, we should not overlook the fact that "the poor" is in his social station reduced to inferior status, "underprivileged": he is the person lacking bread (Ps. 132:15), the despoiled (Isa. 3:14), the one without land and property, the outcast, the alien. The extent of the socioeconomic need is recognized when prophecy and wisdom literature are consulted. The poor are those who are underprivileged and helpless in the struggle for existence. No one helps them. For that very reason they find not only recognition and aid but also a change in their fortune with Yahweh—this is the certainty that pervades the Psalms. Not only Yahweh, however, but also the king, the "anointed of

Yahweh," assumes the role of representative and savior of the poor: "May he defend the cause of the poor of the people, give deliverance to the needy, and crush the oppressor!" (Ps. 72:4). As in the ancient Near East, so also and above all in Israel, the king is the legal aid of the poor. The OT here emphasizes the corresponding case for the legal help of Yahweh. "The conviction that those whose legal standing was weak and who were less privileged in the struggle of life were the objects of Jahweh's particular interest reaches far back into the history of the people of Jahweh. This conception of the poor practically contains a legal claim upon Jahweh; and it was precisely this which later made it a self-designation of the pious before Jahweh" (G. von Rad, *OT Theol*, 1:400). But "pious" in this connection can only mean: "cast" entirely on Yahweh (Ps. 22:10), completely dependent on him and on him alone. In the OT we cannot separate socioeconomic and spiritual "poverty," indeed we cannot even distinguish between them. Poverty (in all its forms of expression) is indigence of life, and that can only be understood as life before Yahweh.

4. The Enemies

H. Schmid, *Das Gebet des Angeklagten im Alten Testament*, BZAW 49 (1928); H. Birkeland, *Die Feinde des Individuums in der israelitischen Psalmenliteratur* (1933); P. A. Munch, "Einige Bemerkungen zu den ʿanijjim und den rešaʿim in den Psalmen," *Le Monde Oriental* 30 (1936) 13-26; H. Birkeland, *The Evildoers in the Book of Psalms* (1955); K. Schwarzwäller, "Die Feinde des Individuums in den Psalmen," diss. Hamburg (1963); G. W. Anderson, "Enemies and Evildoers in the Book of Psalms," *BJRL* 48 (1965) 16-29; L. Delekat, *Asylie und Schutzorakel am Zionheiligtum* (1967); O. Keel, *Feinde und Gottesleugner. Studien zum Image der Widersacher in den Individualpsalmen*, SBM 7 (1969); W. Beyerlin, *Die Rettung der Bedrängten in den Feindpsalmen der Einzelnen auf institutionelle Zusammenhänge untersucht*, FRLANT 99 (1970); L. Ruppert, *Der leidende Gerechte und seine Feinde* (1973).

Particularly the songs of prayer and the songs of thanksgiving by individuals provide occasion for us to ask basic questions concerning the nature, role, and significance of the enemies of individuals. If we pointedly inquire in this way about the enemies of the individual, we will from the very beginning have to make a strict distinction. In the communal prayer songs dealt with in §6, 2aβ, as well as in the royal psalms, the enemies involved (צרים; אויבים) are without doubt foreign forces that threaten the people of God and its chosen king (Pss. 44:10; 74:3ff.; 78:42ff.; 89:22; 106:10). In the final and decisive sense these are the enemies of God ("your enemies," Pss. 21:8; 66:3; 83:2; 89:10, 51; 92:9; 110:1, 2; "his enemies," Pss. 18, title; 89:42; 132:18).

The "enemies of individuals," on the other hand, are mentioned in the prayer songs and songs of thanksgiving of individuals. They are predominantly referred to with the terms צר, רשׁע, אויב, or also (to name a much disputed term) with the construct combination פעלי און. They appear as "pursuers" (Pss. 7:1; 142:6) and are "slanderers" (Pss. 5:8; 27:11; 54:5; 56:2; 59:10) and "haters" (Pss. 35:19; 38:19; 41:7; 69:4; 86:17), deal "insolently" (Pss. 54:3; 86:14) and "ruthlessly" (Pss. 54:3;86:14) and lie in wait for individuals with fraud and falsehood. Three series of images illustrate the dangerous activity of these enemies: (1) the image of an attacking and besieging army (Pss. 3:6; 27:3; 55:18; 56:1; 59:4; 62:3; and often); (2) the image of a hunter or fisherman who tries to catch his prey (Pss. 7:15; 9:15; 31:4; 35:7-8; 57:6; 59:7; 64:3; 140:5); (3) the image of wild animals that pursue their prey (Pss. 7:2; 22:12-13; 27:2; 35:21). Who are these enemies of the individual? First, we note that our distinction between foreign enemies and foes of the "individual" is set aside by those scholars (principally Scandinavians) who also include the prayer songs and songs of thanksgiving of the individual in the large group, royal psalms. This conception, originating with S. Mowinckel, has particularly influenced the research of H. Birkeland (*Die Feinde des Individuums in der israelitischen Psalmenliteratur* [1933]). The enemies are all identified as non-Israelites. The enmity carried out in the Psalms would therefore be determined as primarily national in character and would reflect contests which in more ancient times a king or his army general but in later times the high priest had to deal with. Accordingly, the individual petitioner would always have to be sought among the high officials of the people. This conception receives a distinctive aspect if the "royal ideology" of "individual songs of lament" is additionally embedded in the domain of a mythical enthronement festival. Then (especially according to S. Mowinckel, *PsStud* II) we would have to consider points of view according to which originally mythical forces of chaos enter the picture in the most varied psalms in "historicized" form. In short, in this explanatory conception the enemies are entities that originally in part were historicized from myth, and in part emerged from the national struggle with foreign forces. But Mowinckel represents the view that these psalms later were transferred to the individual: "Psalms were also presented at cultic acts for the use of the individual—originally perhaps only for the upper class" (*Religion und Kultus* [1953], 119). The Scandinavians like to speak of a "democratization" of songs of lament and psalms that originally belonged to the "royal ideology." But with this explanation the strict distinction given above between the enemies of the people and those of the individual would be eliminated. It is questionable, however, whether it is appropriate and right to break down this distinction. But first we will certainly admit that above and beyond the demarcation between the enemies of the people and those of the individual an interchange has taken place respecting the metaphors. Thus when an individual, for instance, speaks of armies that pursue and surround him, reference here in the prayer of an individual has unquestionably been had to the conceptions of the king's world (cf. especially Psalm 3). And also in the series of images in which the enemies pursue the petitioner like wild animals, a conception has gained entrance that is occasionally colored with a mythical-demonic hue and that originates from a series of conceptions that transcend the life and suffering of the individual. Here motifs and metaphors from the area of the royal psalms are poured into the "individual laments and thanksgivings." But because of this explanation the Scandinavians' process of "democratization" of psalms that originally belonged to the royal cultic drama already becomes at least problematic. Again, we should ask whether one can establish a "royal ideology" in the prayer songs and songs of thanksgiving of individuals. In most of these psalms often not even a trace of the supposed royal cultic drama can be recognized. Rather, the case by case interpretation of the prayer songs and thanksgiving songs shows again and again that we here have to do with a single member of the OT people of God (one who is not distinguished by any dignity, often very poor and without influence). And of course, if this observation of the Scandinavian scholars is also embodied in a mythical sacral act of the royal cult (the king as "penitent" who resigns his rights), then the vicious circle of the supposed sacral royal ideology has been completely closed (cf. M. Noth, "Gott, König, Volk im Alten Testament," *GesStudzAT*, 188-229).

If we agree to the explanation already stated by Gunkel that motifs and metaphors from the domain of kingship found their way into the prayer songs and songs of thanksgiving of the individual, and if with this explanation we recognize a trace of relative correctness in the Scandinavian dispositions of the "sacral royal ideology" and their "democratization," we should have to ask anew who the enemies of the individual really are. Before we attempt to answer this question, it would be worthwhile to present an overview of the various explanations so far given:

1. The views of Mowinckel and of those who followed in his footsteps we have already outlined, but not fully developed. Even if the "royal ideology" tends to obliterate the boundary between external enemies and the enemies of the individual, since also in the prayer songs and the songs of thanksgiving of individuals the very same "royal ideology" is determinative, still we cannot overlook the fact that in the image of the "external enemies" mythological characteristics have been drawn in. The enemies are mythical forces of death that transcend the aspect of a "national enemy" and see the king as exposed to anti-Godly forces and sinister dangers.

2. H. Schmidt saw in the enemies of the individual in the first place the accusers and persecutors who, because of the sickness of the righteous and pious ("poor") person, raise suspicions against him and put him in judgment. This conception—in respect to the institution of God's jurisdiction—has been defined exactly by W. Beyerlin, *Die Rettung der Bedrängten in den Feindpsalmen der Einzelnen auf institutionelle Zusammenhänge untersucht*, FRLANT 99 (1970). The enemies are by Beyerlin more clearly interpreted as the accusers and persecutors who wanted to appear in the sacral judgment of God and provoke a verdict of guilty, a judgment of God.

3. With special emphasis on the term פעלי און (*po'aley awen*), H. Birkeland expressed the opinion that the "enemies" were originally magicians (Pss. 7:12ff.; 10:7ff.), who wanted to conjure up the ruin of the "poor" with magic manipulations. This explanation was able to refer to the fact that in the Mesopotamian world, pictures of enemies were projected in which the depiction of the magical and the demonic predominated.

4. A conception that today is hardly considered or discussed any longer was promoted by B. Duhm in his commentary. In his view the enemies of the pious were "partisans friendly to Greeks" who lay in wait for the backward-looking חסידים. This manner of explanation is consistent with the dating of the Psalms by Duhm, who thought that most of the Psalms were written in the time of the Maccabees.

5. To be noted in addition is a richly varied understanding of "enemies," one that is characterized by strong realism. The enemy is the extortioner of the poor, the oppressor of those without legal rights and of the helpless, the tormentor of the socially disadvantaged. Or the enemy is the avenger of blood, the bloodthirsty persecutor of him who is threatened and who flees to asylum in the sanctuary. On "right of asylum," cf. L. Delekat, *Asylie und Schutzorakel am Zionheiligtum* (1967).

6. The prayer songs of individuals—according to Keel—by no means offer factual descriptions. Rather, the fear of the oppressed person is objectified in both language and metaphor. The images of the enemies may be understood as "projections." The "enemy" is the nonentity that shows up in the form of death and experiences a concrete incarnation in a hostile human being; cf. O. Keel, *Feinde und Gottesleugner* (1969).

In view of all these attempts at explanation and with the question that remains about the textual foundation and the rightness of the conceptions advanced, we advance the following. Especially in the prayer songs and songs of thanksgiving of individuals the "poor person," the "persecuted" or oppressed, identifies his adversaries—no matter how they may appear—mostly with the term "my enemies" (Pss. 3:7; 6:10; 9:3; 17:9; 25:11; 27:6; 30:1; 31:15; 35:19; 41:5; and often). We may well begin with the two instances of suffering and distress that turn up again and again in the prayer songs of individuals, problems that the petitioner has to bear. They are serious illness and gross injustice (cf. H. Schmidt, *Die Psalmen* [1934], Einl. p.6). It is worth noting that the "enemies" of the suffering individual always turn up in these connections. They declare the sick person to be visibly "forsaken by God," they ferret out the cause of his affliction and find it in an "offense" on his part and deride him as one undergoing "just punishment." The real depth of enmity lies in this, that the צדיק is to be separated from Yahweh by these assertions, accusations, and judgments of the enemies. These enemies are motivated by a "crass cause-and-effect piety," and the wickedness of these foes of the צדיק who clings to Yahweh is immeasurable; it opens up perspectives in which the enemies take for granted the demonic appearance of one who simply turns away from God. Here the reason for borrowing from the domain of the mythic-demonic metaphor lies at hand.

A still sharper profile is assumed by the figure of the enemy in the prayer songs of the one who is denied justice. In this connection we will have to give special attention to two endeavors of the enemies: defamation and persecution. In difficult legal cases in which delicate situations are involved, OT law requires that the case be remanded to the central sanctuary (Deut. 17:8-13). Here the case is then settled by the "verdict of God" as transmitted by the priest. The enemies also enter the sanctuary; even then they often still attempt to bring up new schemes and slander if the verdict of God has turned out to be in favor of the oppressed person (Psalm 4). But the one who laments pleads with Yahweh for his rights; he declares that he is innocent (Psalm 7), and he takes refuge in the saving verdict of God. Beyond that, we may not disregard the asylum function of the sanctuary. The helpless victim of persecution flees to the temple area and waits for Yahweh's verdict concerning the justice and injustice of those who are lying in wait for him. All these connections need to be kept in mind as we account for the enemies of the individual. And always there are final actions that separate from God which the lamenting petitioner recognizes in the enterprise of his enemies. Cf. the comment on Psalm 4 ("Purpose and Thrust").

We may summarize these observations by pointing to three aspects of the image of the enemy in the psalms.

1. The enemies of the individual are beyond all doubt people. They think, speak, and act like (wicked) people, like "malefactors." As such they are also called to account, are judged and condemned (cf. Pss. 7:12ff.; 9:15; 35:7f.; 141:10; and often).

2. Still, this enemy image that resembles the human being is regularly transcendentalized: "It is obvious that the psalms are describing not a reality that faced righteous men at any particular time, but—apparently—present a picture of the utmost degree of godlessness and violent evil, a picture that already existed for them in the tradition they received" (C. Barth, *Introduction to the Psalms* [1966] 46). The "exaggerated colors and dimensions" mark the enemy as the "archetype," as the "primal image" of all that is evil, all that ruins human beings, all that corrupts creation, and all that separates from Yahweh. The components of this image of the enemy were taken from the most varied areas of

the surrounding world and Israel's own experience of life and suffering.

3. In the psalms the original image of the enemy has been developed and worked out to develop into an ever clearer and growing contrast as the counterimage of the primal "poor" and "righteous" person. The "violent" person is the "negative counterpart" of the עני. Cf. G. von Rad, *OT Theol,* 1:401.

Finally, we should take a stand on Mowinckel's (and Birkeland's) interpretation of the term פעלי און (cf. *PsStud* I, 1-58). Mowinckel is of the opinion that און is the magic spell that issues from the "enemies." Accordingly, the enemies would be "magic sorcerers." J. Pedersen, too, interprets און as "the magic power" (*Israel I-II* [1926], 431). And actually, the term in the OT does describe something "sinister, weird, and obscurantist" (Gunkel-Begrich, *EinlPs* 201). The פעלי און (expressed cautiously for the first) would therefore be "practitioners of all that is weird." The magic and bewitching sense of און in the Psalms can be recognized now only in a few passages in faded traces. Thus, for instance, we recognize from Ps. 19:9 that the פעלי און adopt the secret power of the curse to ruin a person (cf. also Ps. 59:12). With the conception of an effective curse we may in some passages be permitted to explain the designation of the enemies as פעלי און. They impose on the צדיק a magical incantation that separates him from Yahweh and his blessing. But the distress of the individual thereby receives an additional and especially sinister background.

§11. Literature

1. Commentaries: E. W. Hengstenberg, *Kommentar zu den Psalmen,* 4 vols. (1849-1852[2]). J. Olshausen, *Die Psalmen* (1853). W. M. L. DeWette, *Commentar zu den Psalmen* (1856[5]). P. Schegg, *Die Psalmen,* 3 vols. (1857[2]). F. Hitzig, *Die Psalmen,* 2 vols. (1863-1865). H. Ewald, *Die Dichter des Alten Bundes* I, 2 (1866[3]). H. Graetz, *Kritischer Commentar zu den Psalmen,* 2 vols. (1882/83). H. Hupfeld, *Die Psalmen,* 2 vols. (1888[3]). H. Lesêtre, *Le Livre des Psaumes* (1886). F. Delitzsch, *Biblischer Kommentar über die Psalmen* (1894[5]). J. Wellhausen, *The Book of Psalms* (1898). H. Kessler, *Die Psalmen* (1899[2]). F. Baethgen, *Die Psalmen,* Gött. Handkommentar z. AT (1904[3]). T. K. Cheyne, *The Book of Psalms* (1904). A. B. Ehrlich, *Die Psalmen* (1905). J. K. Zenner and H. Weismann, *Die Psalmen nach dem Urtext* I (1906). Ch. A. Briggs, *A Critical and Exegetical Commentary on the Book of Psalms* I-II (1906/07). N. Schlögl, *Die Psalmen hebraisch und deutsch* (1911). S. R. Hirsch, *Die Psalmen* (1914[3]). K. Budde, *Die schönsten Psalmen* (1915). W. Staerk, *Lyrik,* SAT (1920[2]). B. Duhm, *Die Psalmen* (1922[2]). S. Landersdorfer, *Die Psalmen lateinisch und deutsch* (1922). K. Leimbach, *Die Psalmen erklärt* (1922[4]). A Bertholet, *Das Buch der Psalmen,* Die Heil. Schr. d. ATs II (1923[4]). H. Gunkel, *Die Psalmen,* Göttinger Handkommentar z. AT (1926[4]; 1968[5]). P. Boylan, *The Psalms,* 2 vols. (1926–31[2]). E. König, *Die Psalmen* (1927). R. Kittel, *Die Psalmen,* (1929[5 6]). N. Peters, *Das Buch der Psalmen* (1930). W. E. Barnes, *The Psalms* I-II (1931). J. Knabenhauer, *Commentarius in Psalmos* (1930[2]). G. R. Berry, *The Book of Psalms* (1934). J. de Groot, *De Psalmen* (1932). H. Schmidt, *Die Psalmen,* Handbuch z. AT, ed. O. Eissfeldt (1934). E. Kalt, *Die Psalmen,* Herders Bibelkommentar z. AT (1935). J. Calès, *Le livre des Psaumes,* 2 vols. (1936). H. Herkenne, *Das Buch der Psalmen,* Die Heil. Schr. d. ATs (1936). M. Buttenwieser, *The Psalms—Chronologically Treated with a New Translation* (1938). S. B. Freehof, *The Book of Psalms: A Commentary* (1938). F. James, *Thirty Psalmists* (1938). R. Abramowski, *Das Buch des* *betenden Volkes: Psalmen I* (1938); *Das Buch des betenden Gottesknechts: Psalmen II* (1939). W. O. E. Oesterley, *The Psalms* (1939, 1953). A. Bentzen, *Fortolkning til de gammeltestamentlige salmer* (1939). Ch. J. Callan, *The Psalms* (1944). F. M. Th. DeLiagre Böhl and B. Gemser, *De Psalmen: Tekst en Uitleg* (1946-49). F. Nötscher, *Die Psalmen,* Die Heil. Schr. in deutscher Übersetzung, Die Echter-Bibel (1947). B. D. Eerdmans, *The Hebrew Book of Psalms,* OTS IV (1947). E. A. Leslie, *The Psalms* (1949). W. G. Scroggie, *The Psalms* (1948-51). B. Bonkamp, *Die Psalmen nach dem hebräischen Grundtext* (1949). E. Podechard, *Le Psautier* (1949). R. J. Tournay, *Les Psaumes: Bible de Jérusalem* (1950). A. Cohen, *The Psalms,* Soncino (1945). A. Clamer, *Les Psaumes,* La Sainte Bible Tome V (1950). E. G. Briggs, *A Critical and Exegetical Commentary on the Book of Psalms* (1951/53; cf. Ch. A. Briggs, 1906/07). F. M. Th. DeLiagre Böhl, *De Psalmen,* Commentar op de Heilige Schrift (1952). E. J. Kissane, *The Book of Psalms,* 2 vols. (I 1953; II 1954). T. Piatti, *Il Libro dei Salmi* (1954). W. S. McCullough, W. R. Taylor, et al. *Psalms* IB 4 (1955). A Chouraqui, *Psaumes, Trad. et présentés* (1956). P. Gouichou, *Les Psaumes commentés par la Bible* I and II (1958). P. Drijvers, *Les Psaumes: Genres littéraires et thèmes doctrinaux* (1958). J. Ridderbos, *De Psalmen* II (1958). H. Lamparter, *Das Buch der Psalmen übers. und ausgelegt* (I 1958, II 1959). E. Osy, *Les Psaumes* (1960). A. Bileham, *El primer libro de los Salmos (Ps 1-41). Commentario mesiánico-escatológico sacerdotal* (1965). A. C. Gaebelein, *The Book of Psalms: A Devotional and Prophetic Commentary* (1965). A. Maillot and A. Lelièvre, *Les Psaumes: Traduction nouvelle et commentaire* (1966). A. Weiser, *The Psalms* (1962). J. H. Eaton, *Psalms: Introduction and Commentary,* Torch Bible Commentary (1967). C. Westermann, *The Psalms* (1980). M. Mannati and E. de Solms, *Les Psaumes* I (1966), II (1967), III (1967, IV (1968). E. A. Leslie, *The Psalms: Translated and Interpreted in the Light of Hebrew Life and Worship* (1968). H. Gunkel, *Die Psalmen* (1968[5]). A. Deissler, *Die Psalmen* I (1966[3]), II (1967[2]), III (1969[2]). M. Buttenwieser, *The Psalms,* Prolegomenon by N. M. Sarna (1969). S. Bullough, *The Psalms* (1969). R. E. Murphy, *The Psalms,* Jerome Biblical Commentary (1970). J. P. M. van der Ploeg, *Psalmen* (1971). A. A. Anderson, *The Book of Psalms* (1972). L. Jacquet, *Les Psaumes, 1-41* (1975).

 2. Text and Canon: J. V. Ortenberg, *Zur Textkritik der Psalmen* (1861). E. Nestle, *Psalterium Tetraglottum* (1879). Ch. Bruston, *Le texte primitif des Psaumes* (1873). P. de Lagarde, *Psalterium juxta Hebraeos Hieronymi* (1874). F. Baethgen, "Der textkritische Wert der alten Ubersetzungen zu den Psalmen," *JPTh* 8 (1882) 405ff., 593ff. J. Wellhausen, *Bemerkungen zu den Psalmen: Skizzen und Vorarbeiten* VI (1899). F. Perles, *Analekten zur Textkritik des Alten Testaments* (1895). E. König, *Stilistik, Rhetorik, Poetik in bezug auf die biblische Literatur* (1900). J. Halévy, *Recherches bibliques* III (1905). G. Müller, *Studien zum Text der Psalmen* (1910). A. B. Ehrlich, *Randglossen zur hebräischen Bibel* VI (1913). J. Joüon, *Mélanges de la faculté orientale à Beyrouth* VI 184ff. (1913). Ch. D. Ginsburg, *Liber Psalmorum* (1913). K. Budde, "Zum Text der Psalmen," *ZAW* 35 (1915) 175ff. F. Delitzsch, *Die Lese- und Schreibfehler im Alten Testament* (1920). F. Wutz, *Die Psalmen textkritisch untersucht* (1925). F. Buhl, *Liber Psalmorum* (1930[8]). A. Rahlfs, *Psalmi cum Odis:* Septuaginta Soc. Scient. Gotting. auct. X (1931). A. Schulz, *Kritisches zum Psalter,* AT Abh XII, 1 (1932). W. A. Irwin, "Critical Notes on 5 Psalms," *AJSL* 49 (1932) 9ff. N. Peters, "Senkrechte Doppelschreibung als Fehlerquelle in den Psalmen," *BZ* 22 (1934) 1-12. N.

Pigoulewsky, "Fragments syro-palestiniens des psaumes," RB 43 (1934) 519-527. G. R. Driver, "Textual and Linguistic Problems of the Book of Psalms," *HTR* 29 (1936) 171-195. Idem, "Problems in Job and Psalms Reconsidered," *JTS* 40 (1939) 391-394. Idem, "Notes on the Psalms," *JTS* 36 (1935) 147-156; 43 (1942) 149-160; 44 (1943) 12-23. Idem, "Hebrew Notes," *VT* 1 (1951) 241-250. F. Zimmermann, "The Text of Psalms in the Peshitta," *JTS* 41 (1940) 44-46. R. Rowlands, "Inner-Syriac Corruptions in the Book of Psalms," *JTS* 42 (1941). A. Guillaume, "Notes on the Psalms II," *JTS* 45 (1944) 14f. A. Closen, "Gedanken zur Textkritik von Ps. 2:11b-12a," *Bibl* 21 (1940) 288-309. H. Junker, "Einige Rätsel im Urtext der Psalmen," *Bibl* 30 (1949) 197-212. H. Ginsberg, "Some Emendations in Psalms," *HUCA* 23, 1 (1950/51) 97-104. C. Th. Niemeyer, *Het probleem van de rangschikking der Psalmen* (1950). A. Bruno, *Die Psalmen: Eine rhythmische und textkritische Untersuchung* (1954). J. H. Marks, *Der textkritische Wert des Psalterium Hieronymi juxta Hebraeos* (1956). J. T. Milik, "Deux documents inédits du désert de Juda," *Biblica* 38 (1957) 245-268. J. W. B. Barns and G. D. Kilpatrick, "A New Psalms Fragment," PBA 43 (1957) 229ff. A. Bea, *El Nuevo Salterio Latino* (1957). D. W. Gooding, "The Text of the Psalms in Two Durham Bibles," *Scriptorum* 12 (1958) 94-96. G. Mercati, *Psalterii Hexapli reliquiae cura et studio . . .*, Sacra Civ. Vatic. (1958). L. Bieler, "Notes on the Durham Copies of the Psalterium juxta Hebraeos," *Scriptorum* 12 (1958) 282f. T. Ayuso Marazuela, "Un Salterio 'juxta Hebraeos' y un Salterio Romano en un Códice tardio del Escorial," *EstB* 17 (1958) 5-46. M. Allony and A. Diez Macho, "Dos manuscritos 'palestinenses' más de la Geniza del Cairo," *EstB* 17 (1958) 83-100. G. Bertram, "Zur Prägung der bibl. Gottesvorstellung in der griech. Übersetzung des AT," WO 2, 5 (1959) 502-513. P. Salmon, *Les 'tituli Psalmorum' des manuscrits latins* (1959). J. Gribomont and A. Thibaut, *Méthode et esprit des transductions du Psautier grec,* Coll. Bibl. Lat. 13 (1959) 51-105. D. Michel, "Tempora und Satzstellung in den Psalmen," Abh. z. Ev. Theol., vol. 1 (1960). A. R. Hulst, *Old Testament Translation Problems* (1960) 92-114. H. D. Preuss, "Die Psalmenüberschriften in Targum und Midrasch," ZAW 71 (1959) 44-54. C. Westermann, "The Formation of the Psalter," *Praise and Lament in the Psalms* (1981) 250-258. G. C. Mercati, *Psalterii hexapli reliquiae: Pars prima "Osservationi," Commento critico al testo dei frammenti esaplari* (1965). J. A. Sanders, "Variorum in the Psalms Scroll (11 QPsa)," *HTR* 59 (1966) 83-94. Y. Yadin, "Another Fragment (E) of the Psalms Scroll from Qumran Cave 11 (11 QPsa)," *Textus* 5 (1966) 1-10. J. Van der Pleog, "Fragments d'un manuscrit de Psaumes de Qumran (11 QPsb)," *RB* 74 (1967) 408-412. J. Quellete, "Variantes qumrâniennes du Livre des Psaumes," *RQ* 7, 1 (1969) 105-123. H. Bardtke, *Liber Psalmorum: Biblica Hebraica Stuttgartensia 11* (1969). J. D. Barthélemy, "Le Psautier grec et le papyrus Bodmer XXIV," *RThPh* III, 19 (1969) 106-110. B. S. Childs, "Psalm Titles and Midrashic Exegesis," *JSt* 16 (1971) 137-150. J. Leveen, "Textual Problems in the Psalms," *VT* 21 (1971) 48-58. C. Barth, "Concatenatio im ersten Buch des Psalters," *Wort und Wirklichkeit: Festschrift für E. L. Rapp* (1976) 30-40.

   3. On poetic form (rhythm and meter): G. Bickell, *Carmina Veteris Testamenti metrice* (1882). J. Ley, *Leitfaden der Metrik der hebräischen Poesie* (1887). E. Sievers, *Studien zur hebräischen Metrik* I, 2 (1901). H. Grimme, *Psalmenprobleme* (1902). D. H. Müller, "Strophenbau und Responsion," *BiblStud* III, IV (1907, 1908). W. R. Arnold, "The Rhythmus of the Ancient Hebrews," *OT and Semitic Studies in Memory of W. R. Harper* I (1908)

165-204. J. W. Rothstein, *Grundzüge des hebräischen Rhythmus* (1909). E. König, *Hebräische Rhythmik* (1914). G. B. Gray, *The Forms of Hebrew Poetry* (1915). G. Hölscher, *Elemente arabischer, syrischer und hebräischer Metrik,* BZAW 34 (1920) 93-101. K. Fullerton, "The Strophe in Hebrew Poetry and Psalm 29," *JBL* 48 (1929) 274-290. J. Gabor, *Der Urrhythmus im Alten Testament,* BZAW 52 (1929). A. Bruno, *Der Rhythmus der alttestamentlichen Dichtung—Eine Untersuchung über die Psalmen 1-72* (1930). J. Begrich, "Zur hebräischen Metrik," *ThR* NF 4 (1932) 67-89. W. E. Barnes, "Hebrew Metre and the Text of the Psalms," *JTS* 33 (1932) 374-382. A. Condamin, *Poèmes de la Bible: Avec une introduction sur la strophique hébraique* (1933). H. W. Lund, "Chiasmus in the Psalms," *AJSL* (1933) 281-312. L. Desnoyers, *Les Psaumes. Traduction rhythmée d'après l'hébreu* (1935). T. H. Robinson, "Some Principles of Hebrew Metrics," *ZAW* 54 (1936) 28-43. Ch. F. Kraft, "The Stophic of Hebrew Poetry as Illustrated in the First Book of the Psalter," diss. Chicago (1938). T. H. Robinson, "Basic Principles of Hebrew Poetic Form," *Bertholet Festschrift* (1950) 438-450. Idem, *Hebrew Poetic Form,* VTSuppl I (1953) 128-149. S. Mowinckel, "Zum Problem der hebräischen Metrik," *Bertholet Festschrift* (1950) 379-394. Idem, *Offersang og sangoffer* (1951) 418-435. Idem, "Metrischer Aufbau und Textkritik an Ps 8 illustriert," *Stud. Or. Ioanni Pedersen* (1953) 250-262. F. Horst, "Die Kennzeichen der hebräischen Poesie," *ThR* NF 21 (1953) 97-121. S. Segert, "Vorarbeiten zur hebräischen Metrik," *Archiv Orientalni* 21 (1953) 481-542. J. Muilenburg, *A Study in Hebrew Rhetoric: Repetition and Style,* VTSuppl I (1953) 97-111. S. Mowinckel, "Real and Apparent Tricola in Hebrew Psalms Poetry," Avh. Norsk. Akad. I (1957). R. G. Bowling, " 'Synonymous' Parallelism in the Psalms," *JSS* 5 (1960) 221-255. D. N. Freedman, "Archaic Forms in Early Hebrew Poetry," *ZAW* 72 (1960) 101-107. S. Mowinckel, *The Psalms in Israel's Worship* II (1962). M. Dahood, "A New Metrical Pattern in Biblical Poetry," *CBQ* 29 (1967) 574-579. E. Beaucamp, "Structure Strophique des Psaumes," *RSR* 56 (1968) 199-224. S. Segert, *Versbau und Sprachbau in der althebräischen Poesie,* MIO 15 (1969) 312-321. G. B. Gray, *The Forms of Hebrew Poetry* (1972). J. Schildenberger, "Bemerkungen zum Strophenbau der Psalmen," *Estudios Eclesiaticos* 34 (1960) 673-687.

4. On literary-criticism and historical questions: F. Giesebrecht, "Über die Abfassungszeit des Psalters," *ZAW* 1 (1881) 276ff. W. Staerk, "Zur Kritik der Psalmenüberschriften," *ZAW* 12 (1892) 91ff. J. Köberle, *Die Tempelsänger im Alten Testament* (1899). A Büchler, "Zur Geschichte der Tempelmusik und der Tempelpsalmen," *ZAW* 19 (1899) 96ff., 329ff.; 20 (1900) 97ff. R. H. Kenneth, "The Historical Background of the Psalms," *OT Essays* (1928) 119ff. A. Schulz, *Kritisches zum Psalter* (1932). N. H. Snaith, *Studies in the Psalter* (1934). W. O. E. Oesterley, *A Fresh Approach to the Psalms* (1937). H. L. Jansen, *Die spät-jüdische Psalmendichtung—ihr Entstehungskreis und ihr "Sitz im Leben,"* SNVAO II Hist.-Filos. Kl. (1937). M. Buttenwieser, *The Psalms Chronologically Treated* (1938). F. H. Cosgrave, "Recent Studies on the Psalms," Bull. Canad. Soc. Bibl. Stud. 5 (1939) 3-15. A. Schulz, *Psalmen-Fragen* (1940). B. D. Eerdmans, *Essays on Masoretic Psalms,* OTS I, 2/3 (1942) 105-300. J. Lindblom, "Bemerkungen zu den Psalmen I," *ZAW* 59 (1942/43) 1-13. A. Lauha, *Die Geschichtsmotive in den alttestamentlichen Psalmen* (1945). C. H. L. Feinberg, "The Date of the Psalms," *BS* 104 (1947) 426-440. A. G. Clarke, *Analytical Studies in the Psalms* (1949). E. Baumann, "Struktur-Untersuchungen im Psalter," *ZAW* 61 (1949) 114-176; 62 (1950)

115-152. N. H. Tur-Sinai, "The Literary Character of the Book of Psalms," *OTS* 8 (1950) 263-281. P. R. Ackroyd, "Criteria for the Maccabean Dating of Old Testament Literature," *VT* 3 (1953) 113-132. M. Tsevat, *A Study of the Language of the Biblical Psalms* (1955). P. Descamps, "Pour un classement litteŕraire des Psaumes," *Mél. A. Robert* (1957) 187-204. R. Tournay, "Recherches sur la chronologie des Psaumes," *RB* 65 (1958) 321-357; 66 (1959) 161-190. A. v. Selms, "Historiese en geografiese name in die boeck van die Psalmen," *Hervormde Teologiese Studies* 14 (1958) 1-12. G. Pidoux, *Du portique à l'autel: Introduction aux Psaumes* (1959). N. H. Ridderbos, "De huidige stand van het onderzoek der Psalmen," *Gereform. Theol. Tijdschr.* 60 (1960) 8-14. C. Westermann, "Vergegenwärtigung der Geschichte in den Psalmen," *Forschung am Alten Testament* (1964) 306-335. A. S. Kapelrud, "Die skandinavische Einleitungswissenschaft zu den Psalmen," *VF* 11 (1966) 62-93. G. Sauer, "Erwägungen zum Alter der Psalmendichtungen in Israel," *ThZ* 22 (1966) 81-95. J. Coppens, "La date des Psaumes de l'Intronisation et de la Royauté de Yahvé," *Misc. Bibl.* 43: *EThL* 43 (1967) 192-197. D. J. A. Clines, "Psalm Research since 1955," *Tyndale Bulletin* 18 (1967) 103-126; 20 (1969) 105-125.

5. On the history of form and tradition: H. Gunkel, *Die Psalmen: Reden und Aufsätze* (1913) 92-125. Idem, *Die alttestamentliche Literaturgeschichte und die Ansetzung der Psalmen,* ThBl 7 (1928) 85ff. H. Gunkel and J. Begrich, *Einleitung in die Psalmen* (1933; 1975[9]). H. Jahnow, *Das hebräische Leichenlied im Rahmen der Völkerdichtung,* BZAW 36 (1923). A. Causse, "L'ancienne poésie culturelle d'Israël et les origines du Psautier," *RHPhR* 6 (1926) 1-37. H. Schmidt, *Das Gebet der Angeklagten im Alten Testament,* BZAW 49 (1928). Idem, "Grüsse und Glückwünsche im Psalter," *ThStKr* 103 (1931) 141-150. K. Galling, "Der Beichtspiegel: Eine gattungsgeschichtliche Studie," *ZAW* 54 (1929) 125-130. J. Begrich, "Das priesterliche Heilsorakel," *ZAW* 52 (1934) 81-92 = *GesStud* ThB 21 (1964) 217-291. G. von Rad, "Das jüdische Königsritual" *ThLZ* 72 (1947) 211-218 = *GesStud* ThB 8 (1971[4]) 205-213. M. Noth, *Überlieferungsgeschichte des Pentateuch* (1948). Idem, "Jerusalem und die israelitische Tradition," OTS 8 (1950) 28-46 = *GesStud* ThB 6 (1966[3]) 172-187. A. R. Johnson, *The Psalms,* OTMSt (1951) 162-209. H.-J. Kraus, *Die Königsherrschaft Gottes im Alten Testament* (1951). H. Bückers, "Zur Verwertung der Sinaitraditionen in den Psalmen," *Biblica* 32 (1951) 401-422. A Feuillet, "Les Psaumes eschatologiques du règne de JHWH," *NRTh* 73 (1951) 244-260, 352-363. S. Mowinckel, *Offersang og sangoffer* (1951) 50ff. C. Westermann, *The Praise of God in the Psalms* (1965). A. Robert, "L'exégèse des Psaumes selon les méthodes de la 'Formgeschichte,' " *Misc. bibl. Ubach.* (1953) 211-225. C. Westermann, "Struktur und Geschichte der Klage im Alten Testament," *ZAW* 66 (1954) 44-80 = *Forschung am Alten Testament,* ThB 24 (1964) 266-305. J. W. Wevers, "A Study of the Form Criticism of Individual Complaint Psalms," *VT* 6 (1956) 80-96. R. Tournay, "En marge d'une traduction des Psaumes," *RB* 63 (1956) 496-512. A. Gelin, "Genres littéraires dans la Bible," *Diction. de Theol. Cathol.* Tabl. 8 (1959) 1790-1794. K. H. Bernhardt, *Die gattungsgeschichtliche Forschung am AT als exegetische Methode* (1959). R. E. Murphy, "A New Classification of Literary Forms in the Psalms," *CBQ* 21 (1959) 83-87. F. Mand, "Die Eigenständigkeit der Danklieder des Psalters als Bekenntnislieder," *ZAW* 70 (1958). W. Beyerlin, *Herkunft und Geschichte der ältesten Sinaitraditionen* (1961). H. W. Wolff, "Der Aufruf zur Volksklage," *ZAW* 76 (1964) 48-65 =

GesStud ThB 22 (1973[2]) 392-401. F. Luke, "The Songs of Zion as a Literary Category of the Psalter," *Indian Journal of Theology* 14 (1965) 72-90. P. Drijvers, *The Psalms: Their Structure and Meaning* (1965). J. Van der Ploeg, "Réflexions sur les genres littéraires, des Psaumes," *Studia biblica et semitica Th. C. Vriezen dedicata* (1966) 265-277. G. v. Rad, *The Problem of the Hexateuch and Other Essays* (1966). H. Kosmala, "Form and Structure in Ancient Hebrew Poetry," *VT* 16 (1966) 153-180. F. N. Jasper, "Early Israelite Traditions and the Psalter," *VT* 17 (1967) 50-59. E. Lipiński, "Les psaumes de supplication individuelle," *Revue Ecclésiastique de Liège* 53 (1967) 129-138. R. C. Culley, *Oral Formulaic Language in the Biblical Psalms,* Middle and Near East Series 4 (1967). W. Beyerlin, "Die *tôdā* der Heilsverkündigung in den Klageliedern des Einzelnen," *ZAW* 79 (1967) 208-224. L. T. Whitelocke, *The* rib-*Pattern and the Concept of Judgment in the Book of Psalms* (1968). R. Martin-Achard, "La prière des malades dans le psautier d'Israël," *LV*(B) 86 (1968) 25-43. E. Lipiński, "Les psaumes d'action de grâces individuelle," *Revue Ecclésiastique de Liège* 53 (1967) 346-366. F. Crüsemann, *Studien zur Formgeschichte von Hymnus und Danklied in Israel,* WMANT 32 (1969). W. Beyerlin, *Die Rettung der Bedrängten in den Feindpsalmen der Einzelnen* (1970). E. Gerstenberger, "Der bittende Mensch. Bittritual und Klagelied des Einzelnen im Alten Testament," diss., Heidelberg. E. Gerstenberger, "Der klagende Mensch," *Probleme biblischer Theologie: G. von Rad zum 70. Geburtstag* (1971) 64-72. K. Heinen, "Das Nomen *tefillā* als Gattungsbezeichnung," *BZ* NF 16 (1972) 103-105. W. Beyerlin, "Kontinuität beim 'berichtenden' Lobpreis des Einzelnen," *Wort und Geschichte: Festschrift für K. Elliger* (1973) 17-24. K. Koch, *Was ist Formgeschichte? Methoden der Bibelexegese* (1974). E. Gerstenberger, *Psalms: Old Testament Form Criticism,* ed. J. H. Hayes (1974) 179-223. S. S. Patro, "Royal Psalms in Modern Scholarship," diss., Kiel (1976).

6. On Old Testament worship: S. Mowinckel, "Tronstigningssalmerne og Jahves tronstigningsfest," *Norsk teologi til reformationsjubileet* (1917) 13ff. Idem, *Psalmenstudien: vol. 2, Das Thronbesteigungsfest Jahwäs und der Ursprung der Eschatologie* (1922); Vol. 3, *Kultusprophetie und prophetische Psalmen* (1923); vol. 5, *Segen und Fluch in Israels Kult und Psalmdichtung* (1924). Idem, "Det kultiske, synspunkt som forskningsprinsipp i den gammeltestamentlige videnskap," *NTT* (1924) 1ff. Idem, *Le Décalogue* (1927). Idem, "A quel moment le culte de Jahwé à Jerusalem ist-il officiellement devenu un culte d'images?" *RHPhR* 9 (1929) 197ff. Idem, *Offersang og sangoffer* (1951). Idem, *Zum israelitischen Neujahr und zur Deutung der Thronbesteigungspsalmen,* ANVAO II Hist.-Filos. Kl. (1952). Idem, *Religion und Kultus* (1953). J. B. Peters, *The Psalms as Liturgies,* Paddock Lectures (1922). W. O. E. Oesterley, *The Sacred Dance* (1923). P. Volz, *Das Neujahrsfest Jahwes* (1924). G. Quell, *Das kultische Problem der Psalmen,* BWANT NF 11 (1926). H. Schmidt, *Die Thronfahrt Jahwes* (1927). L. Aubert, "Les Psaumes dans le culte d'Israel," *RThPh* NS XV (1927). A. Lods, "Eléments anciens et éléments modernes dans le rituel du sacrifice israélite," PHPhR (1928) 399ff. I. Elbogen, *Der jüdische Gottesdienst in seiner geschichtlichen Entwicklung* (1931[3]). L. I. Pap, *Das israelitische Neujahrsfest* (1933). S. H. Hooke, *Myth and Ritual: Essays on the Myth and Ritual of the Hebrew in Relation to the Cultic Pattern of the Ancient East* (1933). Idem, *The Labyrinth: Further Studies in the Relation between Myth and Ritual in the Ancient World* (1935). Idem, *The Origins of Early Semitic Ritual* (1938). Idem, *Myth, Ritual and Kingship* (1958). R. Press,

"Das Ordal im alten Israel," *ZAW* 51 (1933) 121ff., 227ff. J. Pedersen, "Passahfest und Passahlegende," *ZAW* 52 (1934) 161ff. A. R. Johnson, "The Role of the King in the Jerusalem Cultus," *The Labyrinth* (1935) 71ff. Idem, *The Cultic Prophet in Ancient Israel* (1944). P. Humbert, *La terou'a: Analyse d'un rite Biblique* (1946). N. H. Snaith, *The Jewish New Year Festival, Its Origins and Development* (1947). Idem, *Hymns of the Temple* (1951). E. Kolari, *Musikinstrumente und ihre Verwendung im Alten Testament* (1947). A. Bentzen, "The Cultic Use of the Story of the Ark of Samuel," *JBL* 67 (1948) 37ff. T. H. Gaster, *Passover: Its History and Traditions* (1958). M. Noth, "Gott—König—Volk im Alten Testament," *ZThK* 47 (1950) 157-191 = *GesStud* ThB 6 (1960) 188-229. N. H. Ridderbos, *Psalmen en Cultus* (1950). A. Weiser, "Zur Frage nach den Beziehungen der Psalmen zum Kult," *Bertholet Festschrift* (1950) 513ff. H.-J. Kraus, "Gilgal: Ein Beitrag zur Kultusgeschichte Israels," *VT* 1 (1951) 181-199. Idem, *Worship in Israel* (1966). Idem, "Zur Geschichte des Passah-Massot-Festes im Alten Testament," *EvTh* 18 (1958) 47-67. E. Werner, "The Origin of Psalmody," *HUCA* 25 (1954) 327-345. H. Schmid, "Jahwe und die Kulttraditionen von Jerusalem," *ZAW* 67 (1955) 168ff. E. Kutsch, "Das Herbstfest in Israel," diss., Mainz (1955). D. Michel, "Studien zu den sog. Thronbesteigungspsalmen," *VT* 6 (1956) 40ff. R. Rendtorff, "Der Kultus im alten Israel," *Jahrbuch für Liturgik und Hymnologie* (1956) 1-21. Idem, "Kult, Mythos und Geschichte im alten Israel," *Festschrift für H. Rendtorff* (1957) 121-129. M. Bič, "Das erste Buch des Psalters: eine Thronbesteigungsfestliturgie," *Atti dell' VIII Congr. Intern. di Storia delle Religioni* (1956). K. Roubos, "Profetie en cultus in Israel," diss., Utrecht (1956). H. Gross, "Lässt sich in den Psalmen ein 'Thronbesteigungsfest Jahwes' nachweisen?" *TTZ* 65, 1 (1956) 24-40. W. S. McCullough, "The 'Enthronement of Yahweh Psalms,' " *Papers W. A. Irwin* (1956). W. G. Williams, "Liturgical Problems in Enthronement Psalms," *JBR* 25 (1957) 118-122. E. Kutsch, "Erwägungen zur Geschichte der Passafeier und des Massotfestes," *ZThK* 55 (1958) 1-35. E. Auerbach, "Die Feste im Alten Testament," *VT* 8 (1958) 1-18. C. E. B. Cranfield, "Divine and Human Action: The Biblical Concept of Worship," *Interpr.* 12 (1958) 387-398. E. Auersbach, "Neujahrs- und Versöhnungsfest in den bibl. Quellen," *VT 8* (1958) 337-343. A. S. Herbert, *Worship in Ancient Israel* (1959). A. G. Hebert, "The Idea of Kingship in the OT," *RTR* 18 (1959) 34-45. C. Hauret, "L'interprétation de Psaumes selon l'école 'Myth and Ritual,' " *RSR* 33 (1959) 321-346; 34 (1960) 1-34. E. Ehrlich, *Die Kultsymbolik im AT und im nachbibl. Judentum* (1959). J. L. McKenzie, "Myth and the OT," *CBQ* 21 (1959) 265-282. M. Haran, "The Uses of Incense in the Ancient Israel Rituals," *VT* 10, 2 (1960) 113-129. R. DeVaux, *Ancient Israel,* vol. 2: *Religious Institutions* (1965). Th. C. Vriezen, *De godsdienst van Israël* (1963). H. Zirker, *Die kultische Vergegenwärtigung der Vergangenheit in den Psalmen* (1964). M. J. Buss, "The Meaning of 'Cult' and the Intepretation of the Old Testament," *JBR* 32 (1964) 317-325. D. Wohlenberg, "Kultmusik in Israel: Eine forschungsgeschichtliche Untersuchung," diss. Hamburg (1967). H. H. Rowley, *Worship in Ancient Israel: Its Forms and Meaning* (1967). R. Rendtorff, *Studien zur Geschichte des Opfers im alten Israel,* WMANT 24 (1967). A. Arens, *Die Psalmen im Gottesdienst des alten Bundes* (1968). E. Lipiński, *La liturgie pénitentielle dans la Bible* (1969). P. Welten, "Kulthöhe und Jahwetempel," *ZDPV* 88 (1972) 19-32. F. Stolz, *Strukturen und Figuren im Kult von Jerusalem,* BZAW 118 (1970). J. Jeremias, "Lade und Zion: Zur Entstehung der Ziontradition," *Probleme biblischer Theologie: G. von Rad zum 70. Geburtstag* (1971)

183-198. E. Beaucamp, "Liturgia e Salmi nelle grandi tappe della storia d'Israele," *BeO* 13 (1971) 9-25. C. J. de Moor, *New Year with Canaanites and Israelites I-II* (1972). B. A. Levine, *In the Presence of the Lord* (1974).

7. Ancient Near Eastern parallels: H. Zimmern, "Babylonische Hymnen und Gebete in Auswahl," *AO* 7, 3 (1905); *AO* 13, 1 (1911). Idem, "Das babylonische Neujahrsfest," *AO* 25, 3 (1926). H. Gunkel, "Ägyptische Parallelen zum Alten Testament," *Reden und Aufsätze* (1913) 131-141. Idem, "Ägyptische Danklieder," *Reden und Aufsätze* (1913) 141-149. Idem, *Schöpfung und Chaos in Urzeit und Endzeit* (1921²). R. Dussaud, *Les origines cananéennes du sacrifice Israelite* (1921). F. Stummer, *Sumerisch-akkadische Parallelen zum Aufbau alttestamentlicher Psalmen* (1922). Idem, "Die Psalmengattungen im Lichte der altorientalischen Hymnen-literatur," *JSOR* 8 (1924) 123ff. A. J. Wensinck, "The Semitic New Year and the Origin of Eschatology," *AcOr* (1922) 158ff. Idem, *The Arabic New Year and the Feast of Tabernacles* (1925). H. Gressmann, ed., *Altorientalische Texte zum Alten Testament* (1926²). G. R. Driver, "The Psalms in the Light of Babylonian Research," *The Psalmists*, ed. Simpson (1926) 109ff. (cf. also the other essays in this collection). F. M. Th. de Liagre Böhl, *Nieuwjaarsfeest en koningsdag in Babylon en in Israel* (1927). Idem, "Hymnisches und Rhythmisches in den Amarnabriefen aus Kanaan," *ThLBl* (1914) 137ff. (also cf. OPERA MINORA, 1953). J. Begrich, "Die Vertrauensäusserungen im israelitischen Klagelied des Einzelnen und in seinem babylonischen Gegenstück," *ZAW* 46 (1928) 221-260 = *GesStud*, ThB 21 (1964) 168-216. K. Sethe, *Dramatische Texte zu altägyptischen Mysterienspielen* (1928). L. Dürr, *Psalm 110 im Lichte der neueren altorientalischen Forschungen* (1929). A. Jeremias, *Das Alte Testament im Lichte des Alten Orients* (1930⁴). T. E. Peet, *Comparative Study in the Literatures of Egypt, Palestine and Mesopotamia*, Schweich Lecture 21 (1931). H. Bauer, "Die Gottheiten von Ras Schamra," *ZAW* 51 (1933) 81-101; 53 (1935) 54-57. S. H. Hooke, *Myth and Ritual: Essays on the Myth and Ritual of the Hebrew in Relation to the Cultic Pattern of the Ancient East* (1933). Idem, *The Labyrinth: Further Studies in the Relation between Myth and Ritual in the Ancient World* (1935). Idem, *Myth, Ritual and Kingship* (1958). A. Jirku, "Kanaanäische Psalmenfragmente in der vorisraelitischen Zeit Palästinas und Syriens," *JBL* 52 (1933) 108ff. Ch. G. Cumming, *The Assyrian and the Hebrew Hymns of Praise*, Columbia Univ. Orient. Studies 12 (1934). H. L. Ginsberg, "A Phoenician Hymn in the Psalter," *Atti del XIX. Congr. Intern. d. Orient* (1935) 472ff. Idem, "Psalms and Inscriptions of Petitions and Acknowledgement," *L. Ginsberg Jubilee Volume* (145) 159ff. M. Witzel, "Tamuz-Liturgien und Verwandtes," *AnOr* 10 (1935). G. Widengren, "The Accadian and Hebrew Psalms of Lamentation as Religious Documents: A Comparative Study," diss. Uppsala (1936). Idem, "Det sakrala kungadömet bland öst- och västsemiter," *RoB* 2 (1943) 49ff. K. F. Müller, *Das assyrische Ritual I: Texte zum assyrischen Königsritual*, Mitteilungen d. vorderasiat.-ägypt. Ges. XLI, 3 (1937). K. Grzegorzewski, "Elemente vorderasiatischen Hofstils auf kanaanäischem Boden," diss., Königsberg (1937). R. G. Castellino, *Le lamentazioni individuali e gli inni in Babilonia e in Israele* (1939). J. Pedersen, "Canaanite and Israelite Cultus," *AcOr* 18 (1940) 1ff. W. Baumgartner, "Ras Schamra und das Alte Testament," *ThR* NF 12 (1940) 163-188; NF 13 (1941) 1-20, 85-102, 157-183. Idem, "Ugaritische Probleme in ihrer Tragweite für das Alte Testament," *ThZ* 3 (1947) 81ff. A Kapelrud, "Jahves tronstigningsfest og funnene i Ras Sjamra," *NTT* (1940) 38ff. I. Engnell, *Studies in Divine Kingship in the Ancient Near East*

(1943). J. H. Patton, *Canaanite Parallels to the Book of Psalms* (1944). A. Bentzen, *Det sakrale kongedomme* (1945). Al Halder, *Associations of Cult Prophets among the Ancient Semites* (1945). R. de Langhe, *Les Textes de Ras Shamra-Ugarit et leurs Rapport avec le Milieu Biblique de l'Ancient Testament* I-II (1945). J. Coppens, "Les Paralleles du Psautier avec les Textes de Ras-Shamra-Ougarit," *Bulletin d'hist. et exeg. de AT* (1946) 113-142. J. J. Stamm, *Die Leiden des Unschuldigen in Babylon und Israel* (1946) Ch. L. Feinberg, "Parallels to the Psalms in Near Eastern Literature," *BiblS* 104 (1947) 290-321. H. Frankfort, *Kingship and the Gods: A Study of Near Eastern Religion as the Integration of Society and Nature* (1948). Idem, *The Problem of Similarity in Ancient Eastern Religions* (1951). C. J. Gadd, *Ideas of Divine Rule in the Ancient Near East* (1948). F. M. Cross, "Notes on a Canaanite Psalm in the Old Testament," *BASOR* 117 (1950) 19-21. Th. Gaster, *Thespis: Ritual, Myth and Drama in the Ancient Near East* (1950). J. Gray, "Canaanite Kingship in Theory and Practice," *VT* 2 (1952) 193-220. T. Worden, "The Literary Influence of the Ugaritic Fertility Myth on the Old Testament," *VT* 3 (1953) 273-297. R. T. O'Callaghan, "Echoes of Canaanite Literature in the Psalms," *VT* 4 (1954) 164-176. A Falkenstein and W. von Soden, *Sumerische und akkadische Hymnen und Gebete* (1953). J. B. Pritchard, *The Ancient Near East in Pictures* (1954). Idem, *Ancient Near Eastern Texts Relating to the Old Testament* (1955[2]). M. H. Pope, *El in the Ugarit Texts* (1955). H. G. Jefferson, "Canaanite Literature and the Psalms," *The Personalist* 39,4 (1958) 202-211. W. Röllig, "El als Gottesbezeichnung im Phönikischen," *Festschr. J. Friedrich* (1959) 403-416. C. H. Gordon, "Ugaritic Manual," *AnOr* 35 (1955). H. Cazelles, E. Dhorne, et al., *La Bible et l'Orient* (1955). G. R. Driver, *Canaanite Myths and Legends* (1956). R. Tournay, "En marge d'une traduction des Psaumes," *RB* 63 (1956) 161-181. J. de Savignac, "Theologie Pharaonique et Messianisme d'Israel," *VT* 7 (1957) 82-90. A. Kuschke, "Altbabylonische Texte zum Thema 'Der leidende Gerechte,' " *ThLZ* 81 (1956) 69-76. G. Roeder, *Kulte, Orakel und Naturverehrung im alten Ägypten* (1960). K. H. Bernhardt, *Das Problem de altorientalischen Königsideologie im Alten Testament*, VTSuppl. 8 (1961). J. Aistleitner, *Die mythologischen und kultischen Texte aus Ras Schamra* (1959). A. S. Kapelrud, *The Ras Shamra Discoveries and the Old Testament* (1965). J. A. Taylor, *The Signification of Mythological Motifs of Death and Netherworld in the Psalms* (1967). H. Donner, "Ugaritismen in der Psalmenforschung," *ZAW* 79 (1967) 322-350. A. Albright, *Yahweh and the Gods of Canaan* (1968). M. H. Pope and W. Röllig, "Die Mythologie der Ugariter und Phönizier," *Wörterbuch der Mythologie* I, ed. H. W. Haussig (1965) 217-312. M. J. Mulder, *Kanaänitische Goden in het Oude Testament* (1965). W. H. Schmidt, *Königtum Gottes in Ugarit und Israel* (1966[2]). H. Gese, "Die Religionen Altsyriens," *Die Religionen der Menschheit* X, 2 (1970) 1-232. H. H. Schmid, *Šālōm: 'Frieden' im alten Orient und im Alten Tesament*, SBS 51 (1971). R. J. Clifford, *The Cosmic Mountain in Canaan and the Old Testament* (1972). F. M. Cross, *Canaanite Myth and Hebrew Epic* (1973). M. Wakeman, *God's Battle with the Monster* (1973).

8. Problems of detail; theology of the Psalms: B. Stade, "Die messianische Hoffnung im Psalter," *ZThK* 2 (1892) 369ff. R. Smend, "Über das Ich der Psalmen," *ZAW* 8 (1888) 49-147. A. Rahlfs, *'Ani und 'anaw in den Psalmen* (1892). G. Beer, *Individual- und Gemeindepsalmen* (1894). E. Balla, *Das Ich der Psalmen*, FRLANT 16 (1912). H. Gunkel, "Die Endhoffnung der Psalmisten," *Reden und Aufsätze* (1913) 123-130. Idem, "Die Frömmigkeit der

Psalmen," *Chr. Welt* (1922) 2ff., 18ff., 78ff., 94ff., 105ff. S. Mowinckel, *Psalmenstudien I: 'Awän und die individuellen Klagepsalmen* (1921). Idem, *Urmensch und "Königsideologie,"* StudTheol 2 (1948) 71-89. J. Hempel, *Gebet und Frömmigkeit im Alten Testament* (1922). E. König, *Theologie der Psalmen* (1923). E. L. Dietrich, *"Šub šebut,"* BZAW 40 (1925). L Dürr, *Ursprung und Ausbau der israelitisch-jüdischen Heilandserwartung* (1925). J. Hempel, "Die israelitischen Anschauungen von Segen und Fluch im Lichte altorientalischer Parallelen," *ZDMG* 79 (1925) 20-110. Idem, *Gott und Mensch im Alten Testament* (1936²). A. C. Welch, *The Psalter in Life: Worship and History* (1926). D. S. Simpson, ed., *The Psalmists* (1926). H. Schmidt, *Gott und das Leid im Alten Testament* (1926). N. Nicolsky, *Spuren magischer Formeln in den Psalmen,* BZAW 46 (1927). C. C. Keet, *Liturgical Study of the Psalter* (1928). O. Eissfeldt, "Jahwe als König," *ZAW* 46 (1928) 81-100 = *KlSchr* I (1962)·172-193. Idem, " 'Mein Gott' im Alten Testament," *ZAW* 61 (1945/48) 3-16 = *KlSchr* III (1966) 35-47. G. Marschall, *Die Gottlosen des ersten Psalmenbuches* (1929). F. Horst, "Die Doxologien im Amosbuch," *ZAW* 47 (1929) 45-54 = *Gottes Recht,* ThB 12 (1961) 155-166. H. Gressmann, *Der Messias* (1929). B. Bomberg, "Die Vergeltungslehre in den Psalmen," *NKZ* 41 (1930) 539-566. S. Daiches, *Studies in the Psalms* (1930) C. R. North, "The Religious Aspect of Hebrew Kingship," *ZAW* 50 (1932) 8-38. K. F. Fahlgren, Sᵉdaka *nahestehende und entgegengesetzte Begriffe im Alten Testament* (1932). H. Birkeland, *'Ani und* anaw *in den Psalmen,* SNVAO II Hist.-Filos. Kl. (1933). Idem, *Die Feinde des Individuums in der israelitischen Psalmenliteratur* (1933). Idem, *The Evildoers in the Book of Psalms* (1955). Idem, *Myt och historia i Psaltaren* (1955). L. Gulkowitsch, *Die Entwicklung des Begriffs* hāsîd *im Alten Testament,* Acta et Commentationes Univ. Tartuensis (1934). A. Parenti, *Notae exegeticae in Psalmos selectos* (1934). Idem, *Notae introductoriae in librum Psalmorum* (1935). R. Galdos, "De Psalmis paenitentalibus," *VD* 16 (1936) 113-118. Idem, "De Psalmis sacerdotalibus," *VD* 16 (1936) 233-241. J. Cales, *La doctrine des Psaumes,* 2 vols. (1936). P. A. Munch, "Einige Bemerkungen zu den *'anijjīm* und den *reša'īm* in den Psalmen," *Le Monde Oriental* 30 (1936) 13-26. Idem, "Das Problem des Reichtums in den Psalmen 37, 49, 73," *ZAW* 55 (1937) 36-46. Idem, "Die jüdischen 'Weisheitspsalmen' und ihr Sitz im Leben," *AcOr* 15 (1937) 112-140. A. Causse, *Du groupe ethnique à la communauté religieuse* (1937) 243-258. S. Hylander, *Gamla Testamentets Psalmbok* (1937). A. Rinkel, *Psalter: Beschouwingen over de Psalmen,* 2 vols. (1937). A. Miller, "Das Ideal der Gottverbundenheit nach der Lehre der Psalmen," *Benediktinische Monatsschrift* 19 (1937) 153-173. Idem, "Fluchpsalmen und israelitisches Recht," *Angelicum* 20 (1943) 92-173. G. Dahl, "The Messianic Expectation in the Psalter," *JBL* 57 (1938) 1-12. A. Guillaume, *Prophecy and Divination among the Hebrews and Other Semites* (1938). P. Vulliaud, *Les Psaumes Messianiques: Traduction annotée d'après L'Hébreu* (1938). J. de Groot, *In de Binnenkamer van het Oude Testament, uitleg van tien Psalmen* (1939). H. Edelkort, *Stil tot God: De psalmen voor heden* (1941). N. H. Ridderbos, "De 'werkers der ongerechtigheid' in de individueele psalmen," diss., Amsterdam (1939). Idem, "De betuigingen van 'onschuld, rechtvaardigheid' in de psalmen," *Gereform. Theol. Tijdschr.* 50 (1950) 86-104. A. Kuschke, "Arm und reich im Alten Testament mit besonderer Berücksichtigung der nachexilischen Zeit," *ZAW* 57 (1939) 31-57. R. Gyllenberg, "Die Bedeutung der Wortes *Sela,*" *ZAW* 58 (1940/41) 153-156. G. von Rad, "Erwägungen zu den Königspsalmen," *ZAW* 58 (1940/41) 216-222. Idem,

" 'Gerechtigkeit' und 'Leben' in der Kultsprache der Psalmen," *Bertholet Festschrift* (1950) 418-437 = *GesStud*, ThB 8 (1971⁴) 225-247. M. Gierlich, "Der Lichtgedanke in den Psalmen," *Freiburger Theol. Studien* 56 (1940). V. Schönbächler, *Die Stellung der Psalmen zum alttestamentlichen Opferkult* (1941). A. Alt, "Gedanken über das Königtum Jahwes," *KlSchr* I (1953) 345-357. A. Guillaume, "Magical Terms in the Old Testament," *JRAS* (1942) 111f.; (1943) 251ff.; (1946) 79ff. P. A. H. de Boer, "Jahu's Ordination of Heaven and Earth," *OTS* II (1943). C. A. Keller, "Das wort *OTH* als 'Offenbarungszeichen Gottes,' " diss., Basel (1946). A. Bentzen, "Der Tod des Beters in den Psalmen," *Eissfeldt Festschrift* (1947) 57-60. B. N. Wambacq, *L'épithète divine Jahwé Sebaoth* (1947). A Bentzen, *Messias—Moses redivivus—Menschensohn*, ATANT 17 (1948). Idem, *King and Messiah* (1955). J. H. Scammon, "God in History according to the Psalms," diss., Harvard (1948). A. R. Johnson, *The Vitality of the Individual in the Thought of Ancient Israel* (1949). Chr. Barth, *Die Errettung vom Tode in den individuellen Klage- und Dankliedern des Alten Testaments* (1947). J. Paterson, *The Praises of Israel: Studies Literary and Religious in the Psalms* (1950). J. Ziegler, "Die Hilfe Gottes 'am Morgen,' " *Atl. Stud. f. F. Nötscher* (1950) 281-288. F. Puukko, "Der Feind in den alttestamentlichen Psalmen," *OTS* 8 (1950) 47-65. R. Weber, "La traduction primitive de *baptizein* dans les psautiers latins," *Vigiliae Christianae* (1950) 20ff. J. van der Ploeg, "Les pauvres d' Israel et leur piété," *OTS* 7 (1950) 236-270. J. Steinmann, *Les Psaumes* (1951). S. Aalen, *Die Begriffe 'Licht' und 'Finsternis' im Alten Testament, im Spätjudentum und im Rabbinismus,* SNVAO II Hist.-Filo. Kl (1951). M. Buber, "Recht und Unrecht. Deutung einiger Psalmen," *Sammlung Klosterberg* (1952). A. H. van der Weijden, *Die 'Gerechtigkeit' in den Psalmen* (1952). K. Koch, "*Sdq* im Alten Testament," diss., Heidelberg (1953). Idem, "Gibt es eine Vergeltungsdogma im Alten Testament?" *ZThK* (1955) 1-42. H. J. Stoebe, "Die Bedeutung des Wortes *häsäd* im Alten Testament," *VT* 2 (1952) 244-254. A. Gelin, *Les pauvres de Yahwé* (1953). H. Ringgren, "König und Messias," *ZAW* 65 (1953) 120-147. Idem, "Quelques traits essentiels de la piété des Psaumes," *Mél. A. Robert* (1957) 205-213. Idem, *Psalterens fromhet* (1957). H. A. Brongers, "De chasidim in het boek der psalmen," *NTT* 8 (1954) 279-297. J. de Fraine, *L'aspect religieux de la royauté israélite* (1954). H. J. Franken, *The mystical Communion with Jhwh in the Book of Psalms* (1954). J. Bauer, "Theologie der Psalmen," *BiLi* 23 (1955/56) 175-178. A. R. Johnson, *Sacral Kingship in Ancient Israel* (1955). H. E. Hill, "Messianic Expectation in the Targum to the Psalms," diss., Yale (1955). G. Widengren, *Sakrales Königtum im Alten Testament und im Judentum* (1955). G. S. Gunn, *God in the Psalms* (1956). P. J. N. Smal, "Die Universalisme in die Psalms," diss., Amsterdam (1956). J. L. McKenzie, "Royal Messianisme," *CBQ* 19 (1957) 27-52. J. Gray, "The Hebrew Conception of the Kingship of God," *VT* 6 (1956) 268-285. R. Martin-Achard, *De la mort à la résurrection d'après l'Ancien Testament* (1956). Idem, "Israel et les nations," *Cahiers Théologiques* 42 (1959). G. Sauer, "Die strafende Vergeltung in den Psalmen: Eine frömmigkeitsgeschichtliche Untersuchung," diss., Basel (1957). F. Hasselhoff, "Urmensch und König," diss., Hamburg (1957). J. Coppens, *De Messiaanse Verwachting in het Psalmboek,* Mededelingen v. d. Kon. Vlaamsche Acad. v. W. (1955). Idem, "Les psaumes des *Hasîdîm,*" *Mel. A. Robert* (1957) 214-224. P. Drijvers, *Les Psaumes; Genres littéraires et thèmes doctrinaux* (1958). M. Pierik, *The Psalter in the Temple and the Church* (1957). S. Grill, "Um die Theologie der Psalmen, ihre

Messianität und ihre 'Christianisierung,' " *Der Seelsorger* 27 (1956/57) 367-373. R. B. Y. Scott, *The Psalms as Christian Praise* (1958). P. A. H. de Boer, *De zoon van God in het Oude Testament* (1958). S. B. Frost, "Asseveration by Thanksgiving," *VT* 8 (1958) 380-390. M. Berchat, "La vie de foi du Psalmiste," *Cah. Univ. Cath.* (1958) 212-224. S. B. Frost, "The Christian Interpretation of the Psalms," *CJT* 5 (1959) 25-34. A. Luger, "Der Messianismus der Psalmen," diss., Wien (1959). M. Didier, "Une lecture des Psaumes du règne de Yahwé," *Rev. Dic. de Namur* 12 (1959) 457-470. N. E. Wagner, "רנה in the Psalter," *VT* 10 (1960) 435-441. J. Gray, "The Kingship of God in the Prophets and Psalms," *VT* 9, 1 (1961) 1-29. R. de Vaux, *Ancient Israel: Its Life and Institutions* (1961). W. I. Wolverton, "The Psalmist's Belief in God's Presence," *CJT* 9 (1963) 82-94. B. Gemser, "Gesinnungsethik im Psalter," *OTS* 13 (1963) 1-20. H. Ringgren, *Faith of the Psalmist* (1963). R. E. Murphy, *A Consideration of the Classification "Wisdom Psalms,"* VTSuppl 9 (1963) 156-167. S. du Toit, *Studies on the Psalms* (1963). H. A. Brongers, "Die Rache- und Fluchpsalmen im Alten Testament," *OTS* 13 (1963) 21-42. J. D. W. Watts, "Yahweh Málak Psalms," *ThZ* 21 (1965) 341-348. S. L. Terrien, "Creation, Cultus, and Faith in the Psalter," *Horizons of Theological Education* (1966) 116-128. H. Reinelt, "Die altorientalische und biblische Weisheit und ihr Einfluss auf den Psalter," diss., Freiburg (1966). G. Wanke, *Die Zionstheologie der Korachiten,* BZAW 97 (1966). J. Kühlewein, "Das Reden von Geschichte in den Psalmen," diss., Heidelberg (1966). R. A. F. MacKenzie, "The Psalms: A Selection," *OT Reading Guide* 23 (1967). W. Wilkinson, "Israel's Praise: A Study of the Psalms," *Approaching the Bible* (1967). L. Delekat, *Asylie und Schutzorakel am Zionheiligtum* (1967). N. J. McEleney, *The Melody of Israel: Introduction to the Psalms,* Pamphlet Bible Series 42 (1968). S. Amirtham, "To Be Near to and Far away from Yahweh," *Bangalore Theological Forum* 2 (1968) 31-55. W. J. Martin, "The Shepherd Psalm: Patterns for Freedom," *Christianity Today* 12 (1968) 14f. E. Beaucamp, "La théologie des Psaumes: Un dialogue avec le Dieu vivant," *Études Franciscaines* 18 (1968) 103-136. L. Monloubou, *L'âme des psalmistes ou la spiritualité du psautier,* Coll. "Paroles de vie" (1968). A. Rose, "Publications sur Psautier," *La Maison-Dieu* 93 (1968) 152-156. H. H. Schmid, *Gerechtigkeit als Weltordnung,* BHT 40 (1968). H. W. Huppenbauer, "God and Nature in the Psalm," *Ghana Bulletin of Theology* 3 (1969) 19-32. R. Martin-Achard, "Approche des Psalmes," *Cahiers Théologiques* 60 (1969). P. Vonck, "L'expression de confiance dans le Psautier," *Publications de L'université Lovanium de Kishasa* (1969) 1-51. W. Shottroff, *Der altisraelitische Fluchspruch,* WMANT 30 (1969). A. A. Anderson, "Psalm Study between 1955–1969," *Baptist Quarterly* 23 (1969) 155-163. H. Ringgren, *Psalmen* (1970). G. Wehmeier, *Der Segen im Alten Testament* (1970). H.-J. Kraus, *Die Biblische Theologie: Ihre Geschichte und Problematik* (1970). D. Vetter, *Jahwes Mit-Sein: Ein Ausdruck des Segens* (1971). C. Barth, "Die Antwort Israels," *Probleme biblischer Theologie: G. von Rad zum 70. Geburtstag* (1971) 44-56. K. Heinen, *Das Gebet im Alten Testament* (1971). H.-J. Kraus, *Biblisch-theologische Aufsätze* (1972). O. H. Steck, *Friedensvorstellungen im alten Jerusalem* (1972). L. Perlitt, "Anklage und Freispruch Gottes," *ZThK* 69 (1972) 290-303. N. Airoldi, "L' antico mondo poetico dei Salmisti," *BiOr* 14 (1972) 97-105. I. R. M. Parson, "Suffering in the Psalms," *ABR* 20 (1972) 49-53. D. Eichhorn, *Gott als Fels, Burg und Zuflucht* (1972). J. Kühlewein, *Geschichte in Psalmen* (1973). H. H. Schmid, "Schöpfung, Gerechtigkeit und Heil," *ZThK* 70 (1973) 1-19. L. Ruppert, *Der leidende*

Gerechte und seine Feinde: Eine Wortuntersuchung (1973). H. Goeke, "Die Anthropologie der individuellen Klagelieder," *BiLe* 14 (1973) 13-29, 112-137. R. Albertz, *Weltschöpfung und Menschenschöpfung* (1974). W. H. Schmidt, *Alttestamentlicher Glaube und seine Umwelt* (1975). F. Crüsemann, "Jahwes Gerechtigkeit im Alten Testament," *EvTh* 36 (1976) 427-449. W. Dietrich, "Rache: Erwägungen zu einem alttestamentlichen Thema," *EvTh* 36 (1976) 450-472.

Additional bibliographical data are to be found in §1-8 of the Introduction and in the Literature sections of the treatment of the individual psalms. We call attention also to the following surveys: M. Haller, "Ein Jahrzehnt Psalmenforschung," *ThR* NF 1 (1929) 377-402; J. A. Montgomery, "Recent Developments in the Study of the Psalms," *ATR* 16 (1934) 185-198; J. J. Stamm, "Ein Vierteljahrhundert Psalmenforschung," *ThR* NF 23 (1955) 1-68; J. Hempel, "Neue Literatur zum Studium des Psalters," *ZAW* 56 (1938) 171ff.; S. Mowinckel, "Psalm Criticism between 1900 and 1935," *VT* 5 (1955) 13-33.

Psalm 1

The Truly Happy Person

Literature

H. Schmidt, "Grüsse und Glückwunsche im Psalter," *ThStKr* 103 (1931) 141-150. N. H. Snaith, *Five Psalms (1; 27; 51; 107; 34): A New Translation with Commentary and Questionary* (1938). E. R. Arbez, "A Study of Psalm 1," *CBQ* 7 (1945) 398-404. P. Auvray, "Le psaume I: Notes de grammaire et d'exégèse," *RB* 53 (1946) 365-371. H. W. Wolff, "Psalm 1," *EvTh* 1949/50, 9, 385-394. H.-J. Kraus, "Freude an Gottes Gesetz: Ein Beitrag zur Auslegung der Psalmen 1, 19B und 119," *EvTh* 1950/51, 8, 337-351. M. Buber, "Recht und Unrecht: Deutung einiger Psalmen," *Sammlung Klosterberg*, Europ. Reihe, 1952. I. Engnell, "Planted by the Streams of Water: Some Remarks on the Problem of the Interpretation of the Psalms as Illustrated by a Detail in Psalm 1," *Studia Orientalia Ioanni Pedersen . . . dicata* (1953) 85-96. G. Botterweck, "Ein Lied vom glücklichen Menschen (Psalm 1)," *ThQ* 138 (1958). M. Weis, "Via Thorae" (Hebr.), מעיבות 6 (1958). L. Roussel, *Le psaume 1: Texte, Traduction, Commentaire* (1959). F. C. Fensham, "Malediction and Benediction in Ancient Near Eastern Vassal Treaties and the Old Testament," *ZAW* 74 (1962) 1-9. W. Janzen, "'Ašrē in the Old Testament," *HTR* 58 (1965) 215-226. J. Dupont, " 'Beatitudes' égyptiennes," *Bibl* 47 (1966) 185-222. S. Bullough, "The Question of Metre in Psalm 1," *VT* 17 (1967) 42-49. R. Bergmeier, "Zum Ausdruck אצת רשעים in Ps. 1:1 . . ." *ZAW* 79 (1967) 229-232. E. Lipiński, "Macarismes et Psaumes de Congratulation," *RB* 75 (1960) 321-367. J. A. Soggin, "Zum ersten Psalm," *ThZ* 23 (1967) 81-96. C. Schedl, "Psalm 1 und die altjüdische Weisheitsmystik," *Deutscher Orientalistentag* 1 (1968) 318-333. H.-J. Kraus, "Zum Gesetzesverständnis der nachprophetischen Zeit," KAIROS 11 (1969) 122-133. W. Käser, "Beobachtungen zum alttestamentlichen Makarismus," *ZAW* 82 (1970) 225-250. G. W. Anderson, "A Note on Psalm 1:1," *VT* 24 (1974) 231-234. R. Lack, "Le Psaume 1: Une analyse structurale," *Bibl* 57 (1976) 154-167.

Text

1:1 Happy [is] the one who walks not in the counsel of the wicked,[a]
nor stands in the way of sinners,
nor sits in the circle of scoffers;

2 but who has delight in Yahweh's instruction,[b]
and, reading his Torah, he meditates day and night.

3 He is like a tree
  planted by streams of water,[c]
  that always yields its fruit,
  whose leaves do not wither.
  [No matter what he does, he brings it to a successful
    conclusion].[d]
4 That is not the way of the wicked, 'No';[e]
  They are rather like chaff that the wind blows away.[f]
5 Therefore the wicked cannot stand in the judgment,
  nor sinners in the congregation[g] of the righteous.
6 For Yahweh knows about the way[h] of the righteous,
  but the way of the wicked leads to destruction.

1a Syr transposes בעצת and בדרך. This reading shows that the expression הלך בדרך was more at home in Hebrew usage than הלך בעצת. Just the same, we should read with MT and interpret the phrase transmitted there in the sense: "to follow the advice" (2 Chron. 22:5; Micah 6:16; Ps. 81:13; Jer. 7:24). For the tenses used in Psalm 1, cf. D. Michel, *Tempora und Satzstellung in den Psalmen* (1960) 108ff. Already G. Bergsträsser had recognized: "In poetry, especially in later poetry, a further expansion of the use of the perfect with a present or future meaning led to a complete blurring of the differences between the meanings of the tenses and to an anomalous promiscuity in the use of all tense indications . . . respecting the present and the future. Examples of changing tense for the expression of the present and the future without evident reason: . . . Ps. 1:1ff . . ." (*Hebräische Grammatik*, 2/1 [1926], 29). D. Michel concludes: "These difficulties now resolve themselves as soon as we no longer interpret the tenses as expressions of points of time" (108). A conjecture concerning the character of tenses: " . . . the actions expressed by the perfect show accidental character in relation to the acting person"; " . . . the actions expressed by the imperfect show substantive character in relation to the acting person" (110).

2b Against the advice of stylists and aesthetes, who consider it unusual that in two parallel members of a verse the same word תורה is used and who want to introduce a חקות or a יראת (De Lagarde), we ought to follow MT. "Thus in spite of everything, there seems to be an emphasis here on the word תורה that is stronger than the rules of poetry. We must respect the fact that it was more important for the poet than his rule of style" (H. W. Wolff, 389).

3c The construct פלגי is missing in Jer. 17:8. It is apparent, however, that in postexilic times, especially in wisdom poetry, מים מלגי was a current phrase: Ps. 119:136; Prov. 5:16; 21:1 (Lam. 3:48; Isa. 32:2).

d The words of this line give an explanation of the metaphor applied before. The subject is not the tree but the צדיק. What we have here is a supplement from Josh. 1:8 in a verse that also metrically cannot be incorporated.

4e At this point Gk introduces, with emphatic assertion, an οὐχ οὕτως which can provide occasion for inserting לא כן in the MT, especially since it is this addition that provides this part of the verse with its shape.

f The addition in Gk, ἀπὸ προσώπου τῆς γῆς ("from the face of the earth"), is to be thought of as a decorative appendage.

5g Gk obviously read בעצת instead of בעדת and translated ἐν βουλῇ, but MT is unquestionably to be preferred.

6h The deletion of the double דרך, often done by textual critics, fails to recognize the peculiarity of expression and style of wisdom teaching, which here contemplates the "two ways."

Form

The first psalm was at one time placed at the head of the collection of the Psalter as an introduction, a preamble. This fact is confirmed by a noteworthy variant reading for Acts 13:33. At the citation of the second psalm the reading has εν τῷ πρώτῳ ψαλμῷ ("in the first psalm"). It is thus presupposed that our modernP-salm 1 in its role as preamble was not counted at all. For the understanding of Psalm 1 in the framework of the Psalter, this observation will be of no little importance. Without foundation is the conception of W. H. Brownlee that Psalms 1 and 2 are to be taken and interpreted as belonging together to form a "coronation liturgy." Brownlee has reference to Deut. 17:14-20, the Deutero-nomic law of the king, in which the king is ordered to read and keep the Torah (Deut. 17:19f.). But there is no indication in Psalm 1 that the statements there could refer to a king. For the hypothesis, see W. H. Brownlee, "Psalms 1-2 as a Coronation Liturgy," *Biblica* 52 (1971) 321-336. Also cf. J. A. Soggin (90ff.) in conversation with I. Engnell.

In its composition Psalm 1 is easily analyzed. Verses 1-3 deal with the righteous man, vv. 4-5 with the ungodly, and v. 6 summarizes and speaks of the fate of the two ways. But in the shape of its text Psalm 1 presents a picture that is difficult to clarify. This is shown by a metrical analysis. Already v. 1 contains formidable difficulties. The arrangement $3+3+3$ would be completely sense-less. At best, we arrive at the accentuation $2+2+2$ (Sievers, Gunkel). Of course, then a clear $3+3$ meter would attach itself to v. 1. In the remaining verses the following meters then remain disproportionate: v. 2: $4+4$; v. 3: $3+2$ (?) and $3+2$ (?); the last line of v. 3 would be a secondary addition and goes beyond the possibility of metrical assimilation; v. 4: $3+4$; v. 5: $4+3$; v. 6: $4+3$. No doubt this diagnosis of the meter yields an unsatisfactory result; yet every correction of the text on the basis of metrical considerations would be senseless and indefensible. One could easily surmise that the psalm moves along in a kind of prose with a hymnic elation (S. Bullough, "The Question of Metre in Psalm 1," *VT* 17 [1967], 42-49).

The psalm is to be assigned to the thematic form group of didactic poetry (see above, Introduction §6, 5). It is, in addition, marked by the following elements: (1) the introductory formula אשרי האיש, which is characteristic of a "congratulatory text." This formula for wishing happiness has taken the place of the old blessing formula ברוך (Jer. 17:7); (2) terms and conceptions of the teaching of wisdom, which are easily recognizable in the individual verses (Gunkel and Begrich, *EinlPs* 381-397); (3) the typical terminology and view-point of the Torah psalms, which celebrate the revelation of Yahweh's will as the source of all knowledge and as the indispensable guide (cf., above all, Psalms 19B and 119, but also Psalms 34; 37; 49; 73; 111; 112; 127; 128; 139). On the Torah psalms as a group, see G. von Rad, *Wisdom in Israel* (1970) 49. But we will have to consider that the Torah in later times was more and more attached to חכמה: Yahweh's instruction is understood to be the source of wisdom (e.g., Ps. 119:98).

Setting

If the didactic poetry of Psalm 1 is thematically influenced basically by the conceptual elements of חכמה and especially of תורה, we should expect to find the writer of the psalm in the circle of teachers of wisdom and Torah. The time of composition can hardly be determined. Even the statement that Psalm 1 is more recent than Jeremiah 17 (R. Kittel) could be challenged (M. Buber). In any case, in view of the total effect of the psalm, we could certainly think of postexilic times. H. W. Wolff considers references to conditions in the kingdom of the Ptolemies in the 3rd c. B.C. H. Gunkel reminds us of the repudiation of the

Samaritans and the dissolution of mixed marriages (for the understanding of the first verse). B. Duhm finally dates the psalm in the last century B.C.and leaves room for the possibility that the preamble of the Psalter could have been taken from an older Torah scroll. In any case, the autonomy of the individual that is becoming apparent in Psalm 1 is most noteworthy. Among the people of God a cleavage and division of unimaginable proportions and effects has taken place. Groups and movements have opposed one another. The individual, lone צדיק ("righteous") stands opposed to the ungodly. The "congregation of the righteous" (Ps. 1:5) is no longer all of Israel but a circle of those who have come out through decisions and separations, a group that thinks of itself as opposed to the mass of the ungodly. This is the situation to which Psalm 1 belongs. In the form of a didactic poem the psalm extols the צדיק who is rooted in Yahweh's Torah as the truly fortunate person. A cultic "Sitz im Leben" is not discernible—even though a number of conceptions and terms of Psalm 1 are derived from the area of worship, as can be demonstrated in individual cases.

Commentary

[1:1] The congratulatory formula אשרי occurs frequently in the Psalms: Pss. 2:12; 32:1f.; 33:12; 34:9; 40:5; 41:2; 65:5; and frequently; it occurs particularly in the wisdom poetry: Prov. 3:13; 8:34; 20:7; 28:14; Job 5:17; Sir. 14:1f.; and frequently. As the opposite formula we should probably name הוי ("Woe!"): W. H. Wolff, *Amos' geistige Heimat*, WMANT 18 (1964) 16ff. On the formula of well-wishing, see F. C. Fensham, "Malediction and Benediction in Ancient Near Eastern Vassal Treaties and the Old Testament," *ZAW* 74 (1962) 1-9; W. Janzen, "'Ašrê in the Old Testament," *HTR* 58 (1963) 215-226; E. Lipińske, "Macarismes et Psaumes de congratulation," *RB* 75 (1968) 321-367; K. Koch, *The Growth of the Biblical Tradition* [1969] 20-22, and *THAT* vol. 1, 257ff. (additional bibliography there).

אשרי is a plural construct form that lends a noun character to the "formula of well-wishing" (BrSynt §7a). The well-wishing is, however, not so much a wish or a promise directed at an individual. It is rather "a joyous exclamation and an enthusiastic observation": "Oh, how fortunate is the man!" (M. Buber, *Recht und Unrecht* 65/66). The "secular" אשרי is to be distinguished from the solemn liturgical ברוך (Jer. 17:7). The English commentaries therefore correctly prefer "happy" (A. Cohen, E. G. Briggs) to "blessed" (G. Scroggie). Exclamation and comment at the beginning of v. 1 have in wisdom poetry noticeably taken the place of the former word of admonition (W. Zimmerli, *ZAW* 51 [1933], 185f.). Formerly the wisdom teachers' exhortation first called for obedience; now the course of the truly fortunate life in the power of the Torah becomes the object of the glorifying, congratulatory statement. But what are the "characteristics" (*notae*) of the truly fortunate person? That is the question answered in vv. 1-3, first in negative descriptions (v. 1), then in positive. The truly fortunate person separates himself from conduct that is at enmity with God. He does not accept advice from the רשעים ("wicked"), does not walk the way of sinners, and does not sit in the circle of scoffers. The climax is worth noting: ישב—עמד—הלך ("walks," "stands," "sits"). The strict separation from the nations is a commandment from Israel's oldest period (Num. 23:9). But as an intra-Israelite exhorteation, this command to be separate is emphasized particularly in the circle of wisdom teachers: Prov. 1:10-19; 4:14-19. A wise person will avoid all concourse with scoffers, the wicked, and fools. In the Torah-relation of our psalm it is the צדיק whose distinctive characteristic is separation from those whose intention is hostile to God (Ps. 26:4).

Psalm 1

We must now define more precisely from whom the man who is to be judged truly fortunate, the צדיק, is to separate himself. The רשע is originally one who has been proved guilty in respect to an accusation in court (L. Köhler, *Old Testament Theology*, 171f.). In addition, however—and this is of basic importance for an understanding of Psalm 1—the רשע is one who has been found guilty before the Torah of God, one who is excluded from the sanctuary by order of a priest (Psalm 15; Ps. 5:15 compared with Ps. 5:8). The רשעים despise the Torah of Yahweh; they have their own principles of life and their own maxims (עצה). The חטאים ("sinners") are known for a specific offense against a given commandment or prohibition (L. Köhler, *OT Theol*, 168). Therefore the reference is to their "way." Their error is recognized in what they have done. Finally, the לץ ("scoffer") has a preference for the "circle," the association, in which he is incited to emit strong, mocking words directed at God. His manner of speech and thought may in the OT be deduced from Isa. 28:15; Ps. 73:8-11; and Mal. 3:14. In wisdom poetry the "scoffer" is a figure that occurs again and again. From all these people hostile to God the צדיק separates himself. This separation is the prerequisite for true good fortune. It is not "Pharisaism" in the narrow sense but faith's prerequisite for life, which is emphatically demanded also in the NT (2 Cor. 5:11; 6:14-18; 2 Thess. 3:6).

[1:2] In v. 2 the description of the characteristics of the צדיק, that is, the truly fortunate person, emphasizes the positive side. "His positive characteristics are (1) an affect: his reaction to the revelation of God's will is one of joy, and (2) he maintains an unbroken life-relationship with this revelation" (G. von Rad, " 'Gerechtigkeit' und 'Leben' in der Kultsprache der Psalmen," *Bertholet-Festschrift* [1950], 421). Our comprehension of this verse and of the whole psalm now depends on the interpretation of the term תורה (Torah). We must reject the traditional translation, "law," which immediately imports all kinds of nomistic prejudices and reflections. תורה is "instruction" in the sense of the "merciful revelation of the will of God" (cf. G. von Rad *OT Theol*, 1:190ff.). In Psalm 1 this merciful revelation of the will of God is presupposed as something fixed and written. For an understanding of this view of תורה we must in the first place adduce the late Deuteronomic, or Deuteronomistic, conception. The תורה is the complete, written revelation of the will of God, which may be read in public (Deut. 31:9-11) or in private (Josh. 1:7). This expression of God's will, which primarily contains God's law, also includes historical pronouncements (Deut. 1:5; Ps. 78:1; Neh. 8:13ff.). Of course, the center of the תורה is and remains the law of God transmitted by Moses (Mal. 4:4). In any case, however, the תורה in this sense is the authoritatively valid "Sacred Scripture." The scope of "Sacred Scripture" presupposed in Ps. 1:2 cannot be determined. Is the reference to Deuteronomy, to the Pentateuch, or even to the (partly) completed canon? This question is related to the uncertainty of the dating of Psalm 1. Indeed, in its nature as a preamble to the Psalter, the concept תורה in any case—and even primarily—includes the scriptural scroll of the Psalms.

The concept תורה that is to be presupposed in Psalm 1 has its origin in Deuteronomic theology. In it there is not only mention of commandments, ordinances, and statutes, but also the multiplicity of the disparate commandments of God is referred to as the "Torah of Yahweh," and therefore as a unit complete in itself. That made possible a breakthrough to a new understanding. "All the individual directions are now looked on as parts of a basically indivisible revelation of the will of Jahweh. At the same time, however, as the result of this, the concept of Jahweh's revelation finally outgrew the sphere of the cult. It was in the cult that older Israel encountered commandments and series of commandments, as well as the priestly *Toroth*. But 'the' Torah was a matter for theological instruction, and its *Sitz im Leben* now became more and more the heart of man'' (G. von Rad, *Theol OT*, 1:200). The Torah of Yahweh is to be present in a person's life at all times (Deut. 6:6f.; Josh. 1:18). One is to think about it continuously; it is the embodiment of joy and good fortune. Without doubt, a decided change, stimulated by the Deuteronomic-Deuteronomistic theology, has taken place. It corresponds to what was outlined above (''Setting'') concerning the cleavages and divisions among the people of God. The Torah ceased to be understood as the dispensation of salvation of a specified group ''(the cultic community of Israel) linked to it by the facts of history'' (G. von Rad, 201). Was this associated with a tendency toward a ''legalistic'' view? Did ''the law'' become an ''absolute and unconditioned object'' (M. Noth)? For the first we shall have to emphasize that the translation of the word תורה with ''law'' is unsuitable and deceptive. The תורה is and remains Yahweh's merciful ''direction'' (M. Buber), no matter under what presuppositions and in what connections it may be used. No matter how its scope may have been constituted, as Yahweh's merciful direction the Torah is the fountain of revelation for the צדיק. As he meditates on it and reads it, he prays that he may with open eyes see ''wondrous things out of thy law'' (Ps. 119:118). An intense, fervid expectation meets the promise that Yahweh speaks in the Torah.

But if the term תורה points to the Holy Scriptures in this manner as the medium and witness of divine revelation, then every attempt to narrow it down to the concept ''law'' and every judgment of ''Jewish nomism'' must be rejected. In the תורה the צדיק perceives the living speech of God (Psalm 119). It is a reviving (Ps. 19:7) and cheering (Ps. 19:8) power; it radiates forth light and brightness (Ps. 119:105, 130). These experiences with the תורה therefore also are the ones that give rise to joy and ''delight'' (חֵפֶץ) for the revelation of the will of God. In Psalm 119 the relation of the צדיק to the תורה is described with the concepts שַׁעֲשׁוּעִים (''delight,'' ''enjoyment'': Ps. 119:24, 77, 92, 143, 174) and אהב (''love'': Ps. 119:97, 165). This taking delight (*delectari*) in the revelation of the divine will is the determining and effective disposition of the truly happy life (Ps. 112:1).[1] The continuity of the relation of the inner life to the תורה is then expressed in the second half of the verse. הגה denotes the soft, murmuring reading of Scripture to oneself. הגה can also denote the growling of the lion over its prey (Isa. 31:4) or the moaning of a pigeon (Isa. 38:14). Vg translates *meditari*. The צדיק reads the תורה pensively ''day and night.'' The phrase יומם ולילה means as much as ''all the time,'' ''constantly'' (cf. Ps. 119:97, 98: לעולם).[2]

---

1. ''From these words we may learn that forced or servile obedience is not at all acceptable to God, and that those only are worthy students of the law who come to it with a cheerful mind, and are so delighted with its instructions, as to account nothing more desirable or delicious than to make progress therein. From this love of the law proceeds constant *meditation* upon it'' (John Calvin, *Commentary on the Book of Psalms*, on Ps. 1:2, trans. James Anderson [Grand Rapids: Eerdmans, 1949]).

2. '' 'And on His Law he meditates day and night.' This meditation is not beyond criticism unless the will comes first, for love itself will teach meditation. Truly, as we despair of our own strength, we must through humble faith in Christ pray (as I have said) that the desire be sent down from heaven. Note this well: It is the mode and nature of all who love, to chatter, sing, think, compose, and frolic freely about what they love and to enjoy hearing about it. Therefore this lover, this blessed man, has his love, the Law of God, always in his mouth, always in his heart and, if possible, always in his ear. 'He who is of God hears the words of God' (John 8:47); and 'Thy statutes have been my songs in the house of my pilgrimage' (Ps. 119:54); and again, 'I will delight in Thy statutes' (119:6)'' (Martin Luther, *Luther's Works*, vol. 14 [St. Louis: Concordia, 1958], on Ps. 1:2, pp. 297f., trans. composite).

[1:3] After the characteristics of a truly happy person—the "marks" (*notae*) of the צדיק—have been described, both negatively and positively, the good fortune of such a person is now graphically portrayed in a simile. He is like a tree planted near a stream of water. The comparison of a person to a tree is not infrequent in the OT (cf., e.g., Jer. 11:19; Ezek. 17:5ff.). Above all, Ps. 92:13-15 should be adduced as a parallel passage. But we must carefully consider the history of the tradition of the picture now emerging in Ps. 1:3.

In the חכמה tradition we find the oldest witness to the picture outside the OT in "The Instruction of Amen-em-ope." There we read:

> (But) the truly silent man holds himself apart.
> He is like a tree growing in a *garden*.
> It flourishes and doubles its yield;
> It (stands) before its lord.
> Its fruit is sweet; its shade is pleasant;
> And its end is reached in the garden. . . .
> (*ANET* 421f.)

In the Egyptian text the happy, ideal existence is that of the "truly silent person." He is then also the blessed, successful person who is compared to a tree.

In the OT we find the simile (probably antedating Ps. 1:3) in Jer. 17:7-8—in a text most commentaries have rightly credited to the wisdom tradition. The differences between Jer. 17:7-8 and Ps. 1:3 are worth noting. Jer. 17:7-8 begins with the liturgically important ברוך ("blessed"), while Psalm 1 is characterized by the more secular אשרי ("happy"). The blessed man in Jeremiah 17 is he who puts his trust in Yahweh (בטח ביהוה), while he who is pronounced fortunate in Psalm 1 is the צדיק who is rooted in the תורה. On the basis of this difference H. Gunkel in his commentary has made inferences for the history of piety that are altogether inadequate. He contrasts the lively prophetic religion of trust to the coldly legalistic religion of the letter of Psalm 1. (1) In this judgment the author overlooked the fact that the picture of a tree in full sap may be applied to various modes of existence in the wisdom tradition, and that in every case the description must be carefully understood from the context. But the צדיק of Psalm 1 does not fit into a scheme of the history of piety that contrasts a prophetic height of religion with a nomistic religious abyss (see above). (2) We need to take note that the opening formula of Psalm 1 does not at all indicate a tendency toward a sacral ossification of the ברוך, but, quite to the contrary, it reveals a surprising relaxation. "We should from the start be aware of the fact that those who definitely belong on the side of Yahweh should know that they are 'blessed' not only in a spiritual . . . way, but that also from the viewpoint of all that is desirable in a worldly way they may simply be called 'happy' " (H. W. Wolff, 386).

His fortunes of life are rich who has his "delight" in the תורה and lives in it. Such a person is like the tree that is planted "by streams of water." פלג (Akkadian, *palgu*) denotes the artificial water course. The water therefore at all times nourishes the roots of the tree, so that בעתו (literally, "in its time," i.e., regularly, constantly) it bears its fruit and does not wither in its foliage. In a transferred sense, then, the reference is to the certainty of the "harvest of life" (cf. Ps. 92:12ff.). The combination with the element of life guarantees a "fruitful existence" in every respect.

To this illustration is added an insertion that soberly states a fact and makes a transition from illustration to fact: he who is rooted in God's תורה will prosperously bring to conclusion all that he undertakes.[1] This added part of the

---

1. "However, beware that prosperity is not understood as prosperity of the flesh. This prospering is hidden; it is so deep within the spirit that if you do not hold fast to it in faith, you might rather call

verse is modeled after Josh. 1:8—a text that is parallel to Ps. 1:2. In Josh. 1:8 Joshua receives the promise כִּי־אָז תַּצְלִיחַ אֶת־דְּרָכֶךָ ("for then you shall make your way prosperous").

[1:4] While vv. 1-3 treated the marks and the essence and value of the צַדִּיק as the truly fortunate person, vv. 4-5 now paint the somber opposite picture of the fateful life of the רָשָׁע. The life of the wicked person is emphatically contrasted to that of the righteous one. The difference cannot be presented too crassly (Mal. 3:18), especially since there is always the tendency to make allowances and to undermine the צְדָקָה (Mal. 3:14). The רָשָׁע is like chaff which is carried away by the wind when grain is winnowed, while the heavy kernels fall to the ground (cf. Ps. 35:5; Job 21:18; Isa. 17:13; Hos. 13:3; G. Dalman, *AuS* 3, 126-139). Over against the image of that which is firmly grounded and enduring (v. 3) we have the image of that which is blown away and disappears (v. 4). In the teaching of wisdom this black-white technique doubtlessly has a pedagogical purpose: it is to be pointed out unmistakably how the life of the צַדִּיק differs from that of the רָשָׁע. Here we must not overlook the fact that the צַדִּיק bears the features of archetypal solitude, while the רְשָׁעִים in their profusion have the character of a *massa perditionis* ("mass of the lost").

[1:5] In v. 5 we face a difficult exegetical problem that begins immediately with the translation of the קוּם בְּ. Most often it is translated without another thought: "Therefore the godless do not stand [or 'will not stand'] in the judgment." In that connection then the question is asked: Does the מִשְׁפָּט refer to the final judgment (Duhm, Kittel) or to the "continuous righteous government of God" (Gunkel in reference to Eccles. 12:14)? But when this question is asked, an important, precise translation of קוּם בְּ has already been passed over. A statement of L. Köhler deserves to be noted here. He translates: "The wicked may not stand in the legal assembly" and then surmises "that the accused waited during the discussion of his guilt kneeling or lying on the ground" (L. Köhler, *Hebrew Man* [1956], 155). But we shall probably have to look for the interpretation in still another direction. In the commentary on v. 1, in an explanation of the concept רָשָׁע (see above), we pointed out that we could derive the designation רָשָׁע not only from the area of the legal community but also from the area of the cultic community that is influenced by Yahweh's תּוֹרָה. The רָשָׁע is a person who by Yahweh's תּוֹרָה has been proved to be guilty and therefore is excluded from the worship of God in the holy place (Pss. 15; 5:4-5). In a sacral juridical act it is established in Israel "who shall dwell on God's holy hill" (Ps. 15:1). In Ps. 24:3 the question is asked: "Who shall ascend the hill of the Lord? And who shall stand in his holy place?" In the second half-verse of this passage, Ps. 24:3, we encounter the expression קוּם בְּ. Here a significant connection may be revealed. Ps. 1:5, in view of Ps. 24:3, provisionally must be translated,

---

it the greatest adversity. For just as the devil violently hates the 'leaves' and the Word of God, so he also hates those who teach it and listen to it; and he persecutes them with the help of the powers of the whole world. So you are witness to the greatest of all miracles when you hear that everything prospers which the blessed man does. For what is more wonderful than that the believers increase when they are destroyed, that they multiply when they are diminished, that they overcome when they are subdued, that they enter when they are cast out, that they are victorious when they are defeated? . . . Thus God exalts his saints, that the height of misfortune becomes the height of prosperity" (*Luther's Works*, 14, p. 304, trans. composite).

"therefore the wicked will not enter the judgment court, nor sinners the congregation of the righteous." And the meaning would be as follows: The רְשָׁעִים do not have access to the act of sacral judgment (מִשְׁפָּט), which is the presupposition for access to the sanctuary, and therefore also do not arrive at the עֵדָה of the צַדִּיקִים, that is, the congregation that praises God in the holy place (Pss. 118:19, 20; 111:1). But why do the wicked not enter this area? Because their lives—like the chaff in the wind—already earlier drift away. The conjunction with עַל־כֵּן reinforces this translation and interpretation. Of course—and we must now emphasize this strongly—it is probably not at all conceivable that the sacral-legal and the cultic institutions still have a real significance for our psalm. The concepts and formulations are indeed molded from that model, but they have largely been spiritualized. The sacral-juristic institution of מִשְׁפָּט mentioned in Psalm 1 and the עֲדַת צַדִּיקִים transcend the empirical reality of the cultic-sacral and are made transparent entities that affect all of existence and point to the end-time. Thus those conceptions would finally be proved to be correct which speak—perhaps too quickly and too rashly—of מִשְׁפָּט as of the "final judgment" and of עֵדָה as the "messianic congregation of the new world." Gunkel's explanation, that מִשְׁפָּט is the "continuous righteous rule of God," generalizes and breaks up the concrete ideas we have to investigate (especially in the peculiar juxtaposition of the terms מִשְׁפָּט and עֵדָה). But F. Nötscher completely obliterates all the contours of the OT message when he writes, "The course of the world itself takes on the effect of judgment. The wicked do not live very long; they soon disappear from the community."

[1:6] In the conclusion, the content both of vv. 1-3 and of vv. 4-5 is summarized in a formula of the doctrine of the two ways: Yahweh "knows about" the way of the צַדִּיקִים, but the way of the רְשָׁעִים "leads to destruction." Here it is appropriate to offer a brief interpretation of the concept צַדִּיק that has been introduced from the very beginning. As a parallel to the interpretation of the term רָשָׁע, we may first note that the צַדִּיק is the kind of person who, in concrete social relationships regarding the legal order, has proved to be a "righteous" person, one who could not be called guilty. In the sacral-legal relationship respecting the תּוֹרָה of Yahweh this interpretation can be repeated—except that the social order is now defined as pertaining to the covenant of God and the justice of God. The question of sacral justice concerning the צַדִּיק is found, e.g., in Ezekiel 18 and in Psalms 15 and 24. The concept צַדִּיק is to be understood on the basis of this double background of the social order stemming from the juridical community and the cult community. Still, the expression in Psalm 1 receives its distinctive nuance through this specific context: the צַדִּיק is recognized in that he avoids all relationships that tear him away from Yahweh and that he turns his attention to the תּוֹרָה as the sole effective and determinative element of life. The life of the צַדִּיק is characterized by a desire and love for Holy Scripture. The צְדָקָה of the צַדִּיק therefore encompasses and determines his entire life. This צַדִּיק, a truly fortunate person rooted in the תּוֹרָה of God, is "known" by Yahweh. יָדַע here has the meaning "to take care of a person," "to attend a person with affectionate concern," "to be close to a person," "to provide for a person": Ps. 34:15ff. That the verb "belongs not so much to the area of contemplation as rather to that of contact" is emphasized especially by M. Buber. Cf. Ps. 37:18ff. While the way of those who live their life in the light of the תּוֹרָה is also directed in the light of Yahweh (Prov. 4:18), the way of the רְשָׁעִים dashes down to destruction (Prov. 13:13).

Purpose and Thrust

On the basis of the summarizing final verse, Psalm 1 has often been given the theme "the two ways." Again and again reference is then made to the thorough-going theology of recompense of the nomistic wisdom teaching that infiltrates into Psalm 1. Moreover, in the צדיק the "ideal of the Pharisee who is loyal to the Law and isolates himself" is generally seen. Psalm 1 is then appraised as a document of Judaism based on nomism. Is this conception correct? Does it correspond to the intention of the entire psalm?

To begin with this point, it can surely be no secret to anyone that the wisdom of our psalm cannot be that of "Hercules at the crossroads." The psalm certainly does not point to the "two ways" in this sense, as if the way of the רשע were also a practical possibility that is up for discussion. This is definitely rejected and vanishing, and is basically not an alternative way at all. The dreadful lot of the רשעים, that is, of those that have separated themselves from the "direction" of God, is only the somber contrast to a life that alone is worth recommending and truly happy. For that reason the psalm as a whole can be understood correctly only from this viewpoint. In that case, all attention is immediately focused on the צדיק, whose way of life is characterized and presented under the joyful exclamation and the enthusiastic declaration expressed in the formula אשרי האיש, "How fortunate is this man!" He knows that the רשעים tear him down to ruin; therefore he separates himself from them. He is rooted in the life-giving soil of the תורה in joy and constant deepening. This תורה, however, is not the killing νόμος ("law") but the life-giving, salutary revelation of Holy Scripture as then constituted (cf. Psalm 119). The צדיק is not an imitator who, for want of living prophetic speech, has succumbed to a "religion of observance" and now, in keeping with his own (as is said, "typically Jewish") piety, with the enthusiasm of a scribe, tries to keep alive a message that has become a mere letter. The life-style of the צדיק, especially his all-encompassing love and delight in the תורה, is sustained rather by the Torah's own lively power to communicate and influence (Psalms 19B and 119).[1] But everything that is stated in Psalm 1 about the צדיק basically entails a character that transcends any one individual. "In spite of the personal style, they are out and out type expressions, and as such they definitely transcend human, psychological, and moral possibilities" (G. von Rad, *OT Theol,* 1:382). The picture of the fortunate צדיק definitely bears the features of the super individual, the paradigmatic person. The "Pharisee," with his utmost rigoristic obedience to the Law, cannot fill out this picture. The NT declares that Jesus Christ, "whom God made our . . . righteousness" (1 Cor. 1:30), is the fulfillment of this original picture that the OT psalm had in mind and already joyously embraced. His food was to do the will of him who sent him (John 4:34). Through him and in him the congregation of the new covenant recognizes and experiences that joyful lifelong relation to the Bible that is founded alone on the imparting and bestowing power of God—as it is described in Psalm 1. In him and through him the Christian participates in the fortunate manner of existence of the new creature of the צדיק.

---

1. "But it is one thing to be in the law, another under the law. Whoso is in the law, acteth according to the law; whoso is under the law, is acted upon according to the law; the one therefore is free, the other a slave" (Augustine, "Commentary on the Psalms," Oxford trans., ed. A. Coxe, *Nicene and Post-Nicene Fathers,* vol. 8 [1888], Psalm 1).

Psalm 1

But, finally, we must not forget that Psalm 1 is the preamble of the Psalter. That person is pronounced happy who, in his reading and reflection about the Psalms, lets himself be guided by the message that shows the path.[2]

---

2. "I know that whoever becomes practiced in this will find more by himself in the Psalter than all the interpretations of other men can give him" (*Luther's Works* 14, p. 311, trans. composite).

Psalm 2

Yahweh's King and the Nations

Literature

A. Schulz, "Bemerkungen zum 2. Psalm," *ThGl* 23 (1931) 87-97. G. E. Closen, "Gedanken zur Textkritik von Ps. 2:11b-12a," *Bibl* 21 (1940) 288-309. R. Köbert, "Zur ursprünglichen Textform von Ps. 2:11-12a," *Bibl* 21 (1940) 426-428. G. von Rad, "Erwägungen zu den Königspsalmen," *ZAW* 58 (1940/41) 216-222. H. H. Rowley, "The Text and Structure of Psalm II," *JTS* 42 (1941) 143-154. I. Sonne, "The Second Psalm" *HUCA* 19 (1945/46) 43-55. G. von Rad, "Das jüdische Königsritual," *ThLZ* 72 (1947) 211-216. J. de Fraine, "Quel est le sens exact de la filiation dans Ps 2, 7," *Bijdr* 16, 4 (1955) 349-356. P. A. H. de Boer, "De zoon van God in het Oude Testament," *Leidse Voordrachten* 29 (1958). G. Cooke, "The Israelite King as Son of God," *ZAW* 73 (1961) 202-225. H. Cazelles, "*Nšqw br* (Ps 2,12)," *Oriens Antiquus* 3 (1964) 43-45. R. Tournay, "Le Psaume (de la Fête du Christ-Roi) Ps 2: Le Roi-Messie," *Assemblées du Seigneur* 88 (1966) 46-63. W. Vischer, *Der im Himmel Thronende lacht*, EvThBeih (1966) 129-135. B. Lindars, "Is Psalm 2 an Acrostic Poem?" *VT* 17 (1967) 60-67. G. Sauer, "Die ἀκροστιχίδες Psalm 2 und 110," *ZDMG* 118 (1968) 259-264. J. A. Soggin, "Zum zweiten Psalm," *Wort, Gebot, Glaube: W. Eichrodt zum 80. Geburtstag* (1970) 191-207. W. Thiel, "Die Weltherrschaft der judäischen Könige nach Psalm 2," *Theologische Versuche III* ed. J. Rogge and G. Schille (1971) 53-63. H. Gese, "Natus ex Virgine," *Probleme biblischer Theologie: G. von Rad zum 70 Geburtstag* (1971) 73-89. O. H. Steck, *Friedensvorstellungen im alten Jerusalem*, TheolStud 111 (1972).

Text

2:1 Why do the peoples murmur
and the nations plot in vain?

2 There is a marshaling[a] of kings of the earth,
and rulers are conspiring,[b]
[—against Yahweh and against his anointed one].[c]

3 "Let us tear their bonds to shreds
and cast their cords[d] from us!"

4 He who is enthroned in heaven laughs;
the Lord[e] mocks them.

5 In good time he addresses them in his anger
and frightens them in his wrath:

6 "I myself have solemnly installed my king[f]
on Zion, my holy hill!"

7 I will announce Yahweh's[g] enactment:
He said to me: "You are my son,
I myself have begotten you today!

8 Ask of me,[h]
And I will give you[i] nations as an inheritance
and the ends of the earth as your possession.

9 You may smash[j] them with an iron rod,
like pottery dash them to pieces."

10 Now then, you kings, act wisely!
Be warned, you judges of the earth!

11 Serve Yahweh with fear
'and with trembling kiss his feet!'[k]

12 Lest he be angry, you perish in your intention,
for his wrath kindles very quickly.
Happy [are] all those who trust him!

2a יתיצבו in the sense of marshaling forces for battle (1 Sam. 17:6; Jer. 46:4) provides good sense and avoids a correction to יְתִיצָּו (so corresponding to Ps. 83:3, Graetz, Lagarde, and Gunkel).

b נוֹסְדוּ, from סוּד (KBL 386). Also cf. Ps. 31:13 = "conspire" (to form a סוֹד). Targ and Gk συνήχθησαν). The emendation to נוֹעֲדוּ, from יעד, is not necessary.

c This line is very likely a secondary addition that announces the purpose of the hostile coalition and seeks to explain the plural suffix ("their cords"). Gk has a סֶלָה at the end of v. 2.

3d Although Syr with עָלֵתִימוֹ and Gk with τὸν ζυγόν suggest an emendation of the text, we should probably prefer the plural עבתימו, parallel to מוסרותימו in MT.

4e Whether the proper name יהוה transmitted in many Mss is "more effective" (Gunkel) cannot be determinative in textual criticism. On the background of the יהוה versions, אדני is the more foreign reading.

6f The emendation frequently undertaken (since Wellhausen) that changes the words of God to words of the king ("I have been established as his king on Zion, his holy hill") is hardly justified. The decision must be made on the basis of an explanation of the form of the whole psalm. The reasons for the emendation are some Mss in Gk: ἐγὼ δὲ κατεστάθην βασιλεὺς ὑπ' αὐτοῦ. This would correspond to a Hebrew text: נסַּכְתִּי.מַלְכּוֹ. But we will stay with MT for reasons discussed below, on "Form."

7g The emendation undertaken in v. 6 (see under f) usually involves additional changes in v. 7 that are entirely unsupported, especially since they insist on "improving" the strange-sounding but now easily explained חק. Example: אֹסִפְךָ אֶל־חֵקִי ("I will take you on my lap"). We leave MT unchanged.

8h On metrical grounds people try to delete שְׁאַל מִמֶּנִּי. The justification for this procedure will have to be investigated (see below, on "Form").

i That the suffix of the second person (following Gk δώσω σοι) must be supplied (וְאֶתְּנָךְ) cannot be maintained with certainty, since the object of giving is implicit in the suffix of the noun and a double application of the suffix would be contrary to good style).

9j תרעם, from רעע II, "smash." What we have here is an Aramaic form for the Hebrew רצץ (Mic. 5:5; Jer. 15:12; Job 34:24). That the first verb in v. 9 is incorrectly pronounced תִּרְעֵם by Gk but correctly by MT תְּרֹעֵם (poel of the Aramaic רעע = Hebrew רצץ) is proved by the parallel נְפֵּץ (cf. B. Duhm).

11k MT literally: "and exult with trembling," and at the beginning of v. 12: "kiss the son." The text is problematic both in view of the "trembling exultation" and also the inexplicable idea of kissing the בר (an unintelligible Aramaism! In v. 7 we have בֵן). The text is corrupt. An evident textual conjecture, after much groping (G. E. Closen), was proposed by A. Bertholet in *ZAW* 28 (1908) 58f.: the two last words of v. 11 and the first two words of v. 12 are to be exchanged. In this way (disregarding the *mater lectionis*, the vocalization, and the separation of words) the following original and factually well-founded text results: בְּרַגְלָיו נַשְּׁקוּ בִּרְעָדָה, "Kiss his feet with trembling!" This conjecture also shows consideration for the parallelism of members.

On the tenses in Psalm 2 and their meaning in their syntactical framework, cf. D. Michel, *Tempora und Satzstellung in den Psalmen* (1960) 94f.

Form

In the collection of the Psalter, Psalm 2 originally was counted as Psalm 1, for Psalm 1 was considered a preamble. In an important variant reading for Acts 13:33 Psalm 2 is cited with the words ἐν τῷ πρώτῳ ψαλμῷ.

The organization of the psalm hardly provides any problems if we follow MT. It is not easy to see how the organization and sequence of thought of the text would become more meaningful with an emendation of v. 6 (in agreement with a number of Mss in Gk). If we follow MT, the picture we get is as follows: in vv. 1-3 we hear of the world revolution of the foreign nations (against Yahweh and his anointed one). In striking contrast, the reaction of Yahweh to this revolt is described (vv. 4-6). The passage in v. 6 contains a declaration of God—that statement announced in v. 5 as the future answer to the plans of the hostile nations and their kings. This future statement of God (v. 6) is then in vv. 7-9 in the fabric of the text effectively supported by the calling of the king to his investiture. And following this reference to the present, effective full power of the king—and at the same time to the coming wrathful intervention of Yahweh— an ultimatum is presented to the rebellious kings (vv. 10-12). The entire psalm is so clear and transparent in its organization that every emendation has to create confusion. But who is the speaker? The answer can only be: the king enthroned on Zion. Amazed, he points out the hostile revolt of the nations and their kings (vv. 1-3), gives Yahweh's reaction (vv. 4-6), proclaims his own investiture (vv. 7-9), and presents the ultimatum to the hostile rulers (vv. 10-12). In the psalm, formal statements are combined that the king still had to proclaim, that is, promulgate at an occasion still to be determined.

Psalm 2 belongs to the thematic form group royal psalms (see above, Introduction, §6, 3). The royal psalms, clearly designated a special group in Ps. 45:1, have as their common theme the term "king." The "Sitz im Leben" of these psalms is to be determined case by case (see below, Setting).

First, the metrical situation is to be examined. Precise double triple verses may be identified in vv. 1, 2 (with the exception of the words probably added, "against Yahweh and against his anointed one"), 3, 4, 6, 7 (with the exception of the introduction "I will announce Yahweh's decree"), 8 (with the exception of the first two words, "ask of me"), 9, 10, 11, and 12 (with the exception of the closing formula "happy [are] all those who trust him"). Only v. 5, the future statement of God, which is very prominent also in its thought content, is to be read 4 + 3. The parts of verses listed as exceptions above need to be discussed briefly. If that part of the sentence "against Yahweh and against his anointed one" is an expansion, as indeed it seems likely to be, then these words drop out of the metrical analysis. But the introduction in v. 7 is a good triple verse that justifies its isolated position as a solemn announcement of the חֹק יהוה. In v. 8 the words שְׁאַל מִמֶּנִּי could be separated from the double triple verse following. A duple metrical construction would do violence to the unusually agitated psalm by means of an undue schematization. The closing formula, "happy [are] all those who trust him," formally and suddenly (in terms of content) opens up the possibility of a positive mode of existence and concludes the psalm on a short optimistic note. There is hardly room here for thinking of an interpolation.

Setting

We have stated that Psalm 2 belongs to the group "royal psalms." Now, how is the "Sitz im Leben" of this characteristic psalm to be determined? In most of the newer commentaries the explanation is given that Psalm 2 was sung in Jerusalem at the occasion of a king's enthronement festival. But it is in no way possible to reconstruct from this text, let us say, the course of an enthronement festival or the ritual of the crowning. We cannot divide the psalm among various speakers; the text layout does not permit it. The singer and speaker is the king only. But does the view prove right that the ruler in Jerusalem presented the psalm at the festival of his accession? The uprising of previously subject nations described in vv. 1-3 would speak for this interpretation. We know from the history of the ancient Near East that vassal states had a way of taking advantage of a change in rule to throw off the yoke of powers that enslaved and oppressed them. If an enthronement festival in this sense were to be thought of as the "Sitz im Leben," the interpretation given by O. H. Steck (23) would be suitable: "The psalm assembles standard phrases which the king is obliged to speak after he has taken his place on the throne in the palace. The psalm is the ritual expression of the statement that the Jerusalem king, because of Yahweh, is unassailable and invincible; therefore we have in vv. 1-3 the contrast of a renewed chaotic revolt of the nations, but one which because of Yahweh's subduing of the chaos of nations . . . is indeed doomed to fail from the start." But the reference to the investiture formula for the enthronement allows us to think also of another connection as the "Sitz im Leben." We could think of an "annual enthronement festival," after the manner of the *Sed* festival which was for a time celebrated every 30th year in Egypt, or of a "royal Zion festival" (H.-J. Kraus, *Die Königsherrschaft Gottes im Alten Testament* [1951], §4; also cf. the excursus on Psalm 132).

As for the time of origin of the psalm, we should certainly think of the era of the Jerusalem monarchy in Judah, with the reservation, however, that in the course of the history of tradition there were intrusions into the statements. The exact determination of the age of the psalm is made difficult by the use of conventionalized language. Still, the Aramaisms (רגשׁ and רעע in v. 9) seem to point to the later intrusions alluded to.

M. Treves represented the theory that Psalm 2 is to be thought of and interpreted as originating in the year 103 B.C.—that the psalm contains an acrostic allusion to Jannaeus (*VT* 15 [1965], 81-90). This view has been challenged, with good reason, by B. Lindars, "Is Psalm II an Acrostic Poem?" *VT* 17 (1967) 60-67.

What can we contribute on the question of authorship? If the king is the speaker, he could also have been the poet. But we could also look for the poet in the circles of court prophets who wrote for the king, for Psalm 2 is undoubtedly permeated by a strong prophetic power (so also Gunkel).

Commentary

[2:1] A pronounced prophetic character is displayed immediately in v. 1 in the question introduced by למה. The singer is astonished and surprised that the foreign nations, which (so we presuppose, according to v. 3) up to now had been subject to the king of Jerusalem, are risking a revolt. This astonishment arises from the knowledge about the sovereign power of Yahweh (v. 3), who indeed has given the foreign nations into the power of his chosen king (v. 8). Therefore, how can these powers dare to rebel against Yahweh and his "anointed one" (v. 2)? The question introduced by למה is thus not accompanied by worried anxiety but by a surprised certainty concerning the presumptuousness of the foreign nations. In v. 1 the dull murmuring (רגש) and whispering (הגה) of the revolting powers is described impressively; but it is from the very beginning "vain" and "useless" (ריק). (In the depictions of the situation the perfect tense can stand next to the imperfect [BrSynt §4li].) "World revolution against world rule" (H. Schmidt)—that is the situation bursting all seams into which vv. 1-3 place the hearer. And since v. 8 later once more speaks of the world domination of the king of Jerusalem, an interpretation of this conception will now first provide an opening to the understanding of the psalm.

The commentaries almost unanimously declare that the conception of world domination of the Judahite king, as it is expressed also in Pss. 18:43-47; 72:8-11; 89:25, stands in strongest contradiction to historical reality, and that David himself did not rule over a world empire (Gunkel). So we revert to the explanation that these passages of the Psalter represent an imitation of foreign poems of pomp and circumstance or the excessive claims of glory in ancient Near Eastern "court style" (H. Gressmann, *Der Messias* [1929], 1-64). In the more recent interpretations the statements about world dominion of the ruler are viewed within the parameters of the so-called ancient Near Eastern "royal ideology" and its mythical-sacral basis (I. Engnell, G. Widengren).

But this approach affords no access to the essential message of Psalm 2. Rather, we must consider three points: (1) In Israel there are without doubt concrete historical points of departure for a greatly expanded conception of rule. Here we must disagree with Gunkel. A. Alt has demonstrated that David was king over an empire which played an important role in the history of empire-building in the ancient Near East (A. Alt, "Das Grossreich Davids," *KlSchr* 2, 66-75). Alt writes: "You may call it 'court style' when, let us say, in the psalms for the beginning of the reign of a new king of the house of David, he is wished a rule 'from sea to sea and from the river (Euphrates) to the ends of earth,' or with similar words a universal reign is held in prospect for him (Ps. 72:8). But, exaggerated as such formulations sound in comparison with the actual power or weakness of the Davidites after Solomon, they are not chosen thoughtlessly or simply taken over from the stock of formulas of other great kingdoms, but from the very beginning are applied to the historical reality of the kingdom of David that was expanded to universal proportions, a reality which is now to be held up to the successors as an ideal and a postulate" (*KlSchr* 2, 75). We have an important point of departure when we take this historical reality into consideration. For Judean kings the model of world empire is the empire of David.

(2) We shall have to consider that in the royal psalms the conception of a large kingdom has been expanded to a conception of world empire. For the moment let it be unresolved whether the tendency of this exaggeration is pomp or "court style," ideal or postulate; in any case, we should note that a conventionalized, stock language of figures of speech accomplishes the gigantic expansion. There is no denying that the Jerusalem king's court participates in the ideas and representations of ancient Near Eastern "royal ideology" (of course, in detail much changed). The great king stands in the center of a universal world area. But in the ancient Near Eastern royal ideology this universal aspect arises at the point where mythical cosmology and sacral enthronement intersect. The ruler is "divine king" and for that reason also ruler of the world. This is the decisive point.

(3) The ancient Near Eastern ruler is "divine king" in the sense of the mythical-sacral pretenses of the time—but the ruler on Zion is Yahweh's chosen king. His

world dominion can be understood only from the viewpoint of the Creator and Lord of the world, Yahweh (cf. above, Introduction §10, 1). The conception of universal rule is founded on the OT at the point when the teachings of creation and of the election of David or his dynasty intersect; in its factual origin it is neither pomp nor court style, neither ideal nor postulate, but the occasion of a comprehensive mandate which Yahweh as Creator and Lord of the world conveys to his chosen king. To the God of Israel, to the אדני (vv. 4; 8:1), belong the peoples and the "ends of the earth" (Pss. 24:1-2; 47:2, 8; 89:8; Isa. 6:3), therefore he can give them over to his chosen king (Ps. 2:8). Even if the conventionalized figurative language concerning the world dominion of the king in Israel and those in the ancient Near East are very similar, the decisive question is, What right does any given king have to declare that he has taken over world dominion, inherited it, or received it as a commission? To whom does the ruler appeal? Who is God? Yahweh or the religious powers?

In the course of the history of Israel it could well happen that a king of Jerusalem, in the midst of his meager and endangered official possessions, lay himself bare to the point of becoming ludicrous when he spoke of his "world dominion." And yet Yahweh, the Creator and Lord of the earth, stood behind him. This discrepancy increases in the New Testament to the point of the "scandal" of the complete hiddenness of the lordship of God over the world in the Messiah, Jesus of Nazareth.

When we see the royal psalms in this connection, then the question is quite different: Who finally has rightly understood the royal psalms, the New Testament and the messianic-Christological exegesis that is found in NT texts, or those modern interpretations which, with premature history-of-religions deductions derived from the similarity of the conventionalized figurative speech, have robbed the OT psalms of their real witness and, in a sense, completely emptied them? We must agree with G. von Rad, who writes: "The royal psalms depict the kingdom and office of the anointed one according to his— still hidden—divine *doxa* ('glory'), which for them he now already has, and which may any moment become manifest" (*ZAW* 58 [1940/41], 219/20).

[2:2-3] The poet of Psalm 2 visualizes the hostile kings and "dignitaries" (thus technically רוזנים; cf. Judg. 5:3; Isa. 40:23; Hab. 1:10) as plotting together in the great world revolution against the world dominion of Yahweh and his anointed one. Even if the phrase "against Yahweh and his anointed one" is an explanatory addition, still this complement matches the sense of the whole psalm perfectly. משיח ("anointed")) is the king of God who has been earmarked by anointing and who is untouchable (1 Sam. 2:10, 35; 12:3, 5 and often; Pss. 18:50; 20:6; 28:8; 89:38, 51; 132:10, 17). The hostile powers want to be autonomous, independent of Yahweh and the one who represents his lordship. The "bonds" and "cords" represent their subordination and subjection. The foreign powers want to be free and independent.

[2:4] In v. 4 it becomes apparent why the singer, in the question in v. 1, observed the rebellion of the peoples with such amazement and why all the enterprises of the foreign powers were from the beginning described as ריק ("vain," "empty"): the king of Jerusalem knows Yahweh as the God who is over the whole world and who is enthroned in heaven (cf. Isa. 18:4), who laughs about the schemes of the rebels (Pss. 37:13; 59:8). Some of this laughter of God is suggested already in v. 1, in the amazed question of the singer. The shrill anthropomorphism characterizes Yahweh as the God who experiences a lively reaction to the goings-on on earth and enthusiastically takes part in them (L. Köhler, *OT Theology* 24). But to counter this anthropomorphism, there is the conception of a heavenly throne, high above all worlds. Behind the king of Jerusalem stands not any mythical power, but the אדני, the Lord who is in command, who has all things in his hands (Ps. 8:1), and who "mocks" the mad display of power on the part of the rebels. This vision of a laughing, mocking heavenly Lord is a message of unheard-of prophetic force.[1] For Yahweh's laughter is an expression of his sovereignty, majesty, and loftiness (cf. H. D. Preuss, *Verspottung fremder Religionen im Alten Testament*, BWANT 92 [1971], 150).

[2:5] But Yahweh does not let things go their own way. He bides his time (Isa. 18:4) but will "in good time" (v. 5) in his anger come face to face with the rebellious forces and terrify them with a sudden eruption of his message. The question whether אז ("then," "in good time") is to be understood as looking backwards or to the future is clearly to be decided in favor of the future sense: cf. Mic. 3:4; Zeph. 3:9. A. Bentzen's interpretation of אז as a reference that looks back to an ancient human foundation of royal ideology comes to grief in a twofold way in face of the parallel of Ps. 89:20 that he himself adduces, for (1) in Ps. 89:20, in distinction from Ps. 2:5, the perfect tense is used and (2) in the parallel passage the אז in no way refers to the ancient human foundation of the monarchy but to the historical election of David (A. Bentzen, *Messias—Moses redivivus—Menschensohn* [1948], 11-15).

[2:6] The speech with which Yahweh will "in good time" frighten and angrily turn back the rebels is now reported literally in v. 6. It contains the statement that Yahweh himself has "established" the king enthroned on Zion (נסך means "pour out a libation," "dedicate"). What is in the offing is the revelation of a fact that is still hidden from the foreign powers or in any case not known to them in all of its consequences. God professes his loyalty to his chosen king before all the nations. That this revelation takes place in "anger" and "wrath" (v. 5) is noted by a number of exegetes with embarrassment. But we will have to ask whether this fact does not correspond to the prophetic message that sees the coming of the Messiah as a judgment over contemporary political principles (Isaiah 7). The revelatory speech of God is a radical, clarifying end-event that of course should not be understood in terms of a fixed eschatology, remote in time, for God's angry eruption is very near (v. 12); it is imminent. Worth noting, incidentally, is the reference to the fact that God's king is "established" on God's hill. Both suffixes of the first person singular refer to the double theme of the election of the dynasty of David and the election of Jerusalem (cf. the excursus to Psalm 132; H.-J. Kraus, *Die Königsherrschaft Gottes im Alten Testament*, 65-70).

[2:7] While v. 6 presents the revelatory speech of Yahweh with which "in good time" the universal investiture of the king of Jerusalem is manifested before all nations, in v. 7 the ruler enthroned on Zion proclaims the investiture under which even now his kingly authority may be seen and understood: "I will announce Yahweh's enactment." חק is a term from sacral royal law. It denotes the

---

1. "So now, by the lofty title of *He that dwelleth in heaven*, he extols the power of God, as if he had said, that power remains intact and unimpaired, whatever men may attempt against it. Let them exalt themselves as they may, they shall never be able to reach to heaven; yea, while they think to confound heaven and earth together, they resemble so many grasshoppers, and the Lord, meanwhile, undisturbed beholds from on high their infatuated evolutions" (J. Calvin, on Ps. 2:4, trans. J. Anderson [Grand Rapids: Eerdmans, 1949]).

document of legitimacy, the royal protocol that was written down at the enthronement and thereafter identified the legitimate ruler.

The explanation of the term חק in connection with royal law has been given by G. vonRad in his essay "Das jüdische Königsritual," *GesStudAT* 1, 205-213. Parallels in the Egyptian ritual of the king confirm this interpretation of חק. Amon-Re of Karnak says to Hatshepsut: "My dear daughter . . . I am your dear father. I confirm your position as ruler of both countries. I am writing your protocol for you" (Roeder, *Urkunden* 4, 285, cited by von Rad, 209). More significant, and important especially for the viewpoint of a later repetition of the protocol of the enthronement, is the following passage: "At that time then the Lord of all wrote the protocol S.M. as the beneficent king in the area of Egypt, he who seizes lands and determines their needs. S.M. spoke as he wrote the protocol for the repetitions of the jubilees. . . ." The function and significance of the "protocols" in the Egyptian cult of the king has been precisely grasped and described by W. Helck, "Ramessidische Inschriften aus Karnak," *Zeitschr. f. ägypt. Sprache und Altertumskunde* 82, 2 (1958) 98-140. Worth noting is the fact that kings' names were written down on a tree. In connection with this practice, undertaken by Atum, the divine declaration is issued: "I have proclaimed you king on my throne since you lay at the breast. You will remain as long as the heavens remain, as long as my name is secure to all eternity" (120). Also Thoth, who also writes kings' names "in the tree," declares: "Thoth, Lord of the words of God, says: 'I have made your great name and the protocol endure in power and strength while all foreigners are subject to your terrors and the circle of the heavens is under your supervision . . .' " (126). Helck considers the "list of names" the primary expression of the protocol. In the OT that would correspond to Isa. 9:6. But the ritual act of writing down lists of names, which can be documented in Egypt, is accompanied by proclamations in which it is solemnly declared that (1) the king is chosen and designated as the ruler of the divinity on its own throne; (2) the "great name" which the divinity conferred will endure in power and strength; (3) the ruler is given power to subjugate all foreigners.

    In the OT the "protocol" in the form of a proclamation is called חק in Ps. 2:7, עדות in 2 Kings 11:12. The translation of חק as "enactment" emphasizes the apodictic, legitimizing nature of the proclamation of the protocol.

    The content of the "enactment of Yahweh," which the king now announces as the proof of his investiture (ספר with the here unusual preposition אל), is: "You are my son, I myself have begotten you today." This statement, fixed by protocol, has solemnly been communicated to the king at the enthronement (carried out some time ago or just now); to it the ruler appeals in view of the world revolution. The problems of the words of investiture—a first-person statement of Yahweh obviously spoken by a prophet—should be discussed in detail. The idea was common in the ancient Near East that the king is "God's son." The presuppositions, however, under which the sonship of God is to be viewed and understood must be precisely determined in each case. In the history-of-religions school, but also in the more recent postulate of the phenomenology of religion of a schematic "royal ideology" (Engnell, Bentzen), the differences and nuances have largely been blurred. A conspicuous difference exists already between the Egyptian and the Mesopotamian perspectives (a difference that already illustrates how unallowable are generalization of ideas that should be historically differentiated). For the following discussion, cf. H. Frankfort, *Kingship and the Gods* (1948), and C. J. Gadd, *Ideas of Divine Rule in the Ancient East* (1948). In Egypt sonship with God is most consistently understood as mythological. The Pharaoh is *Deus incarnatus*. Cf. H. Jacobson, "Die dogmatische Stellung des Königs in der Theologie der alten Ägypter,"

Ägypt Stud., Booklet 8 (1955) 19. The god Amon has begotten him with the queen mother. Contrary to that, in Babylonia and Assyria the king is most often understood to be a servant called, installed, and empowered through a "statement" by the gods.

A few examples for the Mesopotamian conception: "An, in his overflowing heart, has called him (King Lipitishtar) to be king, has in faithfulness spoken to him, the royal offspring: 'Lipitishtar, I have granted you power—may you proudly lift your head to heaven like a violent storm; may you be clothed in fearful brightness against all your enemies; may the rebellious foreign country be overclouded by your storms!' " This is a Sumerian piece (Falkenstein and von Soden, *Sumerische und akkadische Hymnen und Gebete* [1953], 103/104). To quote from another Sumerian song: "The god who causes seed to sprout, the father of all, spoke to the king the definitive decree, decided his fate for him: 'Chosen cedar, pride of the court of Ekur, Urninurta, may the land Sumer fear your shadow, may you be the good shepherd of all lands . . .' " (Falkenstein and von Soden, 106). Concerning the kingship of Israel in the light of the ancient Near Eastern conception of kings: K. H. Bernhardt, *Das Problem der altorientalischen Königsideologie im Alten Testament*, VTSuppl 8 (1961); A. R. Johnson, *Sacral Kingship in Ancient Israel* (1967); J. Schubert, *Heilsmittler im Alten Testament und im Alten Orient* (1964); J. S. Soggin, *Das Königtum in Israel*, ZAWBeih 104 (1967); J. Gray, "Sacral Kingship in Ugarit," *Ugaritica* 6 (1969) 289-302.

The words of investiture addressed to the king of Jerusalem—phenomenologically considered—lie between the Egyptian and the Mesopotamian conceptions. The emphasis on the king's sonship with God (cf. in the OT also Ps. 89:26, 27; 2 Sam. 7:13, 14; 1 Chron. 28:6) is akin to the Egyptian custom of applying the name—without, however any semblance of a mythically oriented conception of a physical begetting. The OT king becomes "son of God" rather through the call and the announced installation. In this respect the process of enthronement in Jerusalem is like the Mesopotamian ritual (especially the Sumerian). But in this respect there is another important perspective: the sonship of the Jerusalem king is based on a process of adoption. *Per adoptionem* the ruler is declared to be "Son of God" in a sacral legal act (cf. with this legal act, outside the context of royalty: Gen. 30:3; 50:23). Here then lie the final profound depths of that investiture which was expressed in the חק. The prophetic address, "You are my son, I myself have begotten you!" reveals itself as a creative word, one that originates a new existence. The chosen king is drawn to the side of God, he becomes the heir and representative of his rule. Thus, in the OT "the king was not by nature 'son of God,' nor did he enter the sphere of divinity by the nature of things through his enthronement; but at the accession to his kingship he was declared to be the son by the definitive will of the God of Israel" (M. Noth, "Gott, König, Volk im Alten Testament," *GesStudzAT* 222). Finally, we should refer to the fact that the prophetic oracle of investiture has its foundation—even if not verbally (2 Sam. 7:13, 14 does not belong to the original shape of Nathan's speech)—in that statement which the prophet Nathan made to David and his dynasty for all times in 2 Samuel 7.

The father-son relation between Yahweh and the ruler chosen and solemnly installed by him merits examination in detail. In Israel's surrounding world the king was thought of as "son of God." This is well known and has been emphasized again and again. Above all, in ancient Egypt this sonship was mythologically/physically determined. The king can declare: "He is truly my physical father" (G. Roeder, *Kulte, Orakel und Naturverehrung im alten Ägypten* [1960], 200ff.). Amon-Re says to Amenhotep III: "My living image,the creation of my members!'' ''You are my beloved son, issued from my members, my image, which I have installed on earth!'' (W. H. Schmidt, *Alttestamentlicher Glaube und seine Umwelt* [1975], 195).

In contrast to that, Ps. 2:7 means to announce the occurrence of an adoption. In the Codex Hammurabi (170f.) the father recognizes the children of the female slave with the words: ''You are my children!'' The word ''today'' therefore in Ps. 2:7 refers to the enthronement and its act of declaration. To be sure, we should not permit ourselves to be bound too much by the (significant) concept of adoption. For the proclamation of Ps. 2:7 quite literally contains and reveals an act of choosing. The context of the father-son relation between Yahweh and Israel with its clear component of choosing cannot be overlooked: ''Israel is my first-born son!'' (Exod. 4:22); ''You are the sons of Yahweh, your God'' (Deut. 14:1). Also Isa. 42:1 and other statements of Deutero-Isaiah respecting election, in which the phrase ''my servant'' occurs, would have to be taken into consideration.

. A different aspect is suggested by Isa. 9:6: ''To us a child is born, to us a son is given; and the government will be upon his shoulder. . . .'' H. Wildberger (BK X 380) understands Isa. 9:6f. ''as a prophetic imitation of a customary proclamation of the court at Jerusalem which soon after the birth of a royal child announced his accession to the title of crown prince.'' A more probable solution is to let Isa. 9:6 refer to the act of adoption and election that is also recognizable in Ps. 2:7 (cf. A. Alt, ''Jesaiah 8:23—9:6: Befreiungstag und Krönungstag,'' *KlSchr* 2, 206-225, especially 216ff.). The proclamation of the series of names (Isa. 9:6) corresponds to the Egyptian rite of enthronement, and is evidence for a connection (see above). But if we view Ps. 2:7 in this wider context, then the following is true for the act of enthronement: ''In the assumption of the role of king on Zion, Israel saw a realistic birth of the world king enthroned on Zion, who had entered this world and taken residence here'' (H. Gese, *Natus ex virgine*, 81). And in another respect also Gese is to be followed: ''It is by all means correct that people in Jerusalem would most likely have called this sonship of God of the Davidites an adoption if they had been willing to give it legal and natural precision. But that would be too much to ask of the citation of the divine oracle at the climax of the ceremonies surrounding the enthronement formulations, which has a purely negative and inhibiting nature. In this most solemn moment of the highest promise of well-being, the object is not to let a statement that has been perceived as too strong evaporate again in the concluding sentence . . . Rather, the word 'today' has by all means a positive meaning: now, in this solemn moment of the enthronement, the birth is taking place . . .'' (80).

[2:8-9] One of the privileges of the chosen and empowered king must have been that of free request (שְׁאַל מִמֶּנִּי; 1 Kings 3:5ff.; Pss. 20:4; 21:2, 4; 2 Sam. 24:12; cf. G. von Rad, *OT Theol*, 1:324f.). But the concrete request mentioned in v. 8 is prompted by a promise given before. Yahweh intends to transfer to the chosen king ''the nations'' as an inheritance and ''the ends of the earth'' as his possession. The ''Father'' is the Lord over the peoples and over the whole earth; the whole universe belongs to him; he is the Creator. The ''son'' is the heir (Gal. 4:7; Matt. 21:38; Mark 12:6ff.). To him world dominion is conveyed (cf. the excursus to Ps. 2:1). Together with the inheritance conveyed, also the power to preside over the judgment of the peoples is awarded to the ''son'' in v. 9. The picture of dashing pottery to pieces has a far-reaching significance. In the Egyptian coronation and jubilee rituals the king demonstrated his worldwide power by symbolically smashing earthen vessels that bore the names of foreign nations (cf. Egyptian execration texts) or by symbolically shooting four arrows into the four directions of the heavens (H. Kees, *Der Gottesglaube im alten Ägypten* [1941], 103). In a similar sense the Mesopotamian texts frequently mention the fact that a ruler smashes nations ''like pottery.'' Thus it is said of Sargon that ''he shattered the lands like pottery and bridled the four corners of the earth.'' Thus the conception in any case tended toward "universal, judiciary absolute power."

[2:10-12] After the king of Jerusalem has given notice of his installation and investiture (vv. 7-9), he presents an ultimatum to the revolting foreign powers: "Now then, you kings, act wisely! Be warned, you judges of earth!'' This admonition is not spoken by some overenthusiastic ruler who has become too big for his boots, but by Yahweh's king, to whom all power is given. The hostile kings, who put on airs as "judges of the earth,'' see themselves pitted against the ruler whom Yahweh has equipped with complete, ultimate judgmental power (v. 9). But how should the kings act? What might it mean to "act wisely''? The answer is given in v. 11: to serve Yahweh in fear. The son directs the foreign powers toward the "Father''; he does not claim honor for himself. Kissing the feet is a sign of servile subjection (Isa. 49:23). In view of the formulation נַשְּׁקוּ־בַר, the suggestion should at least be considered whether perhaps, with consideration for the Ugaritic root *brr*, we should translate: "Kiss the pure one,'' or "kiss the shining one.'' Cf. H. Cazelles, "*nšqw br* (Ps. 2:12),"*Oriens Antiquus* 3 (1964) 43-45.

The challenge to the kings of the peoples is really an ultimatum; for if the rebels continue on their way and carry out their designs (vv. 1-3), they will perish in the midst of their activity. The outbreak of divine anger announced in v. 5 can happen very quickly, "unexpectedly'' (כִּמְעַט). Psalm 2, however, does not close with this somber warning, but with the possibility of a good and blissful existence: All who trust Yahweh (literally, all who seek shelter in him, who seek protection and refuge with him) will be blessed.

Purpose and Thrust

First, we will again refer to the statement of G. von Rad: "The royal psalms depict the kingdom and office of the anointed one according to his—still hidden—divine *doxa* ('glory'), which for them he now already has, and which may at any moment become manifest'' (*ZAW* 58, 219/20). In the OT this *doxa* concealed itself more and more—until in Christ *sub contrario crucis* ("under the opposite of the cross'') it appeared most darkly veiled. The NT witnesses, however, believed in this glory and recognized that above the hiddenness of the Messiah, Jesus of Nazareth, the message of the OT now for the first time really shines forth, because the crucified one is the resurrected one. To him has been given all authority in heaven and on earth (Matt. 28:18); he is the Son and heir (Matt. 21:38). He is the true Son of the Father (Heb. 1:5; 5:5). In Jesus Christ the NT sees the king of God who in the comprehensive sense has approached and fulfilled the kingdom and office of the OT anointed one. It is significant that Acts and Revelation cite Psalm 2 (Acts 4:25f.; 13:33; Rev. 2:26-27; 19:15) in the contests between Christ the exalted king with the hostile Gentile nations.

But to what extent does the NT interpretation do justice to the essential message of Psalm 2? The aim of the message of Psalm 2 could be summarized thus: The revolt of the nations and kings against the universal lordship of God and his anointed one is a senseless undertaking—this rebellion is viewed here only with amazement. And immediately, in view of the universal power of God and the effective investiture of his king, an ultimatum calls people to rethink the situation. The NT citations also aim in the direction of this appeal, since indeed Jesus Christ is seen as God's eschatological king.

Finally, we shall broach four questions that may contribute to elucidating the correspondences between the Old and the New Testaments:

(1) In his book *Messias—Moses redivivus—Menschensohn* (1948) A. Bentzen writes: ''The psalm—phenomenologically viewed—is a parallel and a type of the Christmas gospel: The Savior is born'' (p. 16). This explanation is not appropriate. It applies ('in phenomenological ways') to the birth of Jesus the myth of a physical begetting that is sloughed off already in Ps. 2:7. The NT correspondence to the installment and investiture in Ps. 2:7 could possibly be found in the story of the baptism of Jesus (Matt. 3:17). There, too, the absolute power of the ''sonship'' is proclaimed by a statement of God. But we must immediately ask the basic question whether this corresponds to the essential message of Psalm 2 in only a single point. At the center of Psalm 2 there are statements concerning the relation of the foreign powers to the lordship of Yahweh and his anointed one. This main theme we will have to keep in view consistently. It must not be dissolved through associations with prominent history-of-salvation points of reference of the NT.

(2) That brings us to a delicate point. In his commentary Gunkel writes on Psalm 2: ''The Christian congregation will be able to edify itself only with considerable parings with such a psalm, which, to their sensibilities, has more than one 'earthly remnant' clinging to it.'' The norm for this critical conception (and that could be characteristic for an entire epoch of theology) is a Christianity that is spiritualized to the utmost and viewed idealistically. Forgotten was the fact that the Christ of the NT is Lord and king of the nations, indeed of all of creation. In this way every inner relation to the real facts of the OT and the NT was lost. On the foil of the spiritualized gospel people saw everywhere in the OT painful ''earthly remnants'' which could be interpreted and possibly even praised only in terms of an aesthetic and lyrical understanding. Under these presuppositions no point of contact could be found between Psalm 2 and the NT citations in Acts and the Revelation of John. Theology's task is to inquire about the OT message on the basis of an understanding of the actual content of the NT.

(3) But where are we concretely to see the correspondences between the NT and Psalm 2? In his commentary H. Schmidt writes: ''How foreign to the picture of the crucified is that of the king who smashes peoples with an iron rod!'' In this contrast pictures are suggested, but no effort is made to find practical correspondences. In the context of Psalm 2 the picture of the smashing of the earthen vessels has the signification of pointing out the absolute judicial power of the ''son'' as the heir of the world and its nations by means of a metaphor that was well known in the ancient Near East. Does the NT really have nothing to say about the power of Jesus for judgment over the nations (Matt. 28:18)? Then also this contrast is in error. But the correspondence of the message lies in the ultimatum, the call expressed also in the NT, that the nations already are under the power of God and his Christ (Rev. 12:10ff.) and that they have no longer room for a life that is independent, turned away from God, or hostile to God. In the eschaton of the new covenant everything is intensified to the utmost: ''Happy are they who seek refuge with God.''

(4) Great difficulties in biblical-theological perspective result when the statement σήμερον γεγέννηκά σε in Luke 3:22 (variant; see also Heb. 1:5; 5:5) is understood in terms of adoption in connection with and in reference to Ps. 2:7. Yet the interpretation of Ps. 2:7 in the strict sense of an adoption represents a stricture (see above). For one thing the aspect of election is to be introduced; for another, the important interpretations of H. Gese are to be adopted (see above). Moreover, if we consider that Jesus of Nazareth is not a Judean king who is to be enthroned, then for the NT (particularly for Luke 3:22) nothing would stand in the way of the interpretation: ''. . . the 'this day' is . . . the day of God

which cannot be fixed chronologically, the νῦν *aeternitatis* of his election which is now proclaimed'' (K. Barth, *Church Dogmatics* 4/4, 64).[1]

---

1. "Although that day may also seem to be prophetically spoken of, on which Jesus Christ was born according to the flesh; and in eternity there is nothing past as if it had ceased to be, nor future as if it were not yet, but present only, since whatever is eternal, always is; yet as 'today' intimates presentiality, a divine interpretation is given to that expression, 'Today have I begotten Thee,' whereby the uncorrupt and Catholic faith proclaims the eternal generation of the Power and Wisdom of God, who is the Only-begotten Son'' (Augustine on Ps. 2:7, Oxford trans., *NPNF*, VIII, 3.

Psalm 3

Surrounded by Enemies

Literature

J. Botterweck, "Klage und Zuversicht der Bedrängten: Auslegung der Psalmen 3 und 6," *BiLe* 3 (1962) 184-189. W. Beyerlin, *Die Rettung der Bedrängten in den Feindpsalmen der Einzelnen auf institutionelle Zusammenhänge untersucht*, FRLANT 99 (1970) 75-84.

Text

A psalm of David, when he fled from Absalom his son.

3:1 Yahweh, how numerous are my foes!
Many rise up against me!

2 Many are they who say to me,
"For him there is no help[a] before God!"[b] *Selah.*

3 Yet you, Yahweh,[c] are my shield about me;[d]
you are my glory; you lift up my head.

4 When I cry aloud to Yahweh,
he answers[e] me from his holy hill. *Selah.*

5 I lay down and went to sleep,
—I awoke, for Yahweh sustains me.

6 I am not afraid of a crowd of ten thousand[f]
that besiege me round about.

7 Arise, Yahweh! Help me, O my God![g]
Indeed, you have smitten all my enemies[h] on their cheeks,[i]
you broke the teeth of the wicked.

8 Help is with Yahweh!
May your blessing be upon your people. *Selah.*

2a For the ending תָה, often used in poetry, cf. Ges-K §90g.
b The variant reading transmitted in the Gk, ἐν τῷ θεῷ αὐτοῦ = באלהיו, would lend an even stronger flavor to the mocking, but the translation in Gk takes up only the dative לו. MT is accordingly to be preferred.
3c יהוה is not to be deleted on metrical considerations (against Buhl and Duhm). "The new break begins with the livelier seven-unit meter instead of the usual double triple

meter. The same is to be found in Pss. 44:18, 24; 100:5; 102:13f.; 103:19; and often''
(Gunkel).

d Gk here offers the text ἀντιλήμπτωρ μου εἶ . Did it read סַעְדִּי?

4e In the apodosis it would be better to read וְיַעֲנֵנִי rather than וַיַּעֲנֵנִי, in accordance with
α΄, ε΄, Jerome (Lagarde).

6f Targ here reads the construct מְרִיבֵי.

7g The isolated half-verse has often been thought of as troublesome, because it seems to
interrupt the even flow of the song. Still, against all metrical schematization, we have to
adhere to the existence of individual exclamations unaccompanied by any parallelism,
interrupting items, etc.

h Following a number of Mss, we should probably delete אַת, especially since that would
clear up the meter.

i Gk here reads ματαίως, which would correspond to the Hebrew חִנָּם. But the reading in
MT is secured by the parallelism of members.

Form

With Psalm 3 the Psalter begins the group Psalms of David (Psalms 3–41). For
the Psalter as a collection, see above, Introduction §3.

As far as the text is concerned, Psalm 3 offers no difficulties. Also the
meter presents no problems for us. Basically we have double triple meters,
relieved only by a 4 + 3 meter in v. 3. And in v. 7 we come up against an isolated
half-verse with four accented syllables. Moreover, the organization of the psalm
is easily analyzed, but of course it needs detailed exegetical explanation.
Immediately after the added explanatory note of the title, the psalm begins with
the statements of complaint in vv. 1-2. Then expressions of trust follow in vv.
3-6. With the words ''Arise, Yahweh! Help me, O my God!'' the psalmist then
prays for the intervention of God in the worst distress. Yahweh's actual
intervention, averting all dangers, is then expressed in the same verse: ''Indeed,
you have smitten all my enemies on their cheeks, you broke the teeth of the
wicked.'' In v. 8 the psalm then closes with a confession and a blessing.

There can be no doubt that Psalm 3 belongs to the theme-oriented form
group of prayer songs, traditionally the laments of the individual (Gunkel and
Begrich, *EinlPs* §6). On the prayer songs as a group, cf. above, Introduction
§6, 2. The petitioner presents to Yahweh the great distress in which he finds
himself (vv. 1-2). Expressions of assurance and trust arise in vv. 3-4, but also—
in a manner still to be explained in detail—in vv. 5-6. In v. 7aα the plea for help,
which asks for Yahweh's intervention, emerges clearly. V. 7aβ.b looks back
upon Yahweh's intervention and is definitely to be separated from the preceding
(see below). V. 8 is to be considered a closing statement added for the liturgical
use of the psalm, an epiphonema (J. Botterweck, 188).

Setting

Who is the petitioner? This question entails difficulties that can hardly be cleared
up completely. H. Gunkel considers the petitioner of the psalm a ''private
citizen'' who in grandiose metaphors that extend even to military affairs
endeavors to picture the seriousness and the extent of the danger in which he is
caught. R. Kittel, however, thinks of a general of the armies of Israel who
presumably has come into a dangerous situation in his conduct of the war. B.
Duhm (with the late dating typical of his commentary on the Psalms) places the
psalm in the partisan battles and struggles of the time of the Maccabees; he insists
on thinking of the singer as a person in high station and of great reputation (''No
private citizen can speak of ten thousand opponents, even if he expresses himself

in hyperbole''). Finally, A. Bentzen defines our text as a ''royal psalm'' and advocates the position that all ''psalms of lament that expressly mention the king,'' or may be transposed to a situation typical for kingship, must be classified as belonging to this type (A. Bentzen, *Messias—Moses redivivus—Menschensohn* [1948], 20). A. Weiser goes even farther in this explanation of the Psalms in terms of royal ideology that is becoming more and more prevalent today; he writes: ''The psalm presumably belongs to the kingly ritual, in which the conception of Yahweh's battle against the enemies forms the history-of-salvation framework that is of importance for understanding the specific situation of the petitioner.'' The multiplicity of interpretations corresponds to the themes and pictures that turn up in the short psalm.

In any case, we will have to leave out of consideration an interpretation of the psalm in the light of the late editorial introduction in the title. We cannot consider it justifiable that the interpretation that emphasizes the ''royal ideology'' appropriates the assertions of the title as arguments for its case. On the other hand, the conception that a ''private citizen'' is speaking in the prayer songs of the Psalms is becoming more and more questionable. Rather, we will have to think of preformed liturgies (to avoid the term ''ritual,'' which is hardly suitable). Cf. E. Gerstenberger, ''Der bittende Mensch: Bittritual und Klagelied des Einzelnen im Alten Testament,'' diss., Heidelberg. The prayer formulas then incorporated metaphors and conventionalized idea forms, institutional procedures (W. Beyerlin), and ordinary life experiences. The enemies of the petitioner (cf. above, Introduction §10, 4) can then, for example, be compared to the siege of an entire army. In this respect the petitioner who takes up the formulary of prayer may be transposed to a ''kingly situation'' which transcends his own individual fate and so encircles it that he can find a place for himself there.

The Uppsala school and many followers of the myth-and-ritual school are of the opinion that older psalms that were designed for the ''royal ideology'' and composed for the king were in the course of time ''democratized.'' But the process of transmitting and developing prayer formularies and liturgies is by means of such an interpretation insufficiently grasped, and distilled to an unsuitable formula.

We are still far from being able practically to grasp and describe the process of development of the prayer formulas. Because of their magical and conjurative nature, ancient Near Eastern ritual parallels can be adduced only conditionally and with great caution. These are the limitations of the study of E. Gerstenberger, already referred to.

Sometimes Psalm 3 is given the title ''a morning song.'' This title refers to v. 5 and infers from the content of this verse that the whole psalm was sung early in the morning. Not infrequently a pious lyricism is combined with this explanation. More likely is the possibility recognized already by S. Mowinckel, that the psalm refers to a temple incubation (vigil) (*PsStud* 1, 156) and leads to this situation after a night watch in the sanctuary. W. Beyerlin has seen the ''institutional connection'' more clearly (see below).

It is impossible to assign a date to the psalm; if Psalm 3 is understood to be a ''prayer formulary,'' the date can be given only approximately. Therefore it is appropriate to speak of the psalm's derivation from the epoch of the first Jerusalem temple rather than from preexilic times (W. Beyerlin).

Commentary

[Title] The explanatory note in the title attempts to fit Psalm 3 as a ''Psalm of David'' (on מזמור לדוד, cf. above, Introduction §4, 2) into a specific situation in the life of David: 2 Samuel 15–18. This application is proved to be erroneous by the psalm itself and does not help to elucidate the text. For the singer of our psalm does not flee like David and evinces not a trace of mourning (for Absalom). The divergence in detail is obvious.

The explanatory note is a later editorial addition. "The editor is obviously not so much concerned about giving the impression of an exact historical fact by means of a historicizing title; rather, he wants to find a situation taken from the history of his people, a place in the history of election, from which the psalm may always be understood. Accordingly, we should think of the psalm titles as evidence of the first exegetical activity" (K. H. Bernhardt, *Das Problem der altorientalischen Königsideologie im Alten Testament* [1961], 11).

[3:1-2] As is customary in many prayer songs, the singer begins with the address to Yahweh (in the vocative case). The solemn affirmation מה ("how") points to the seriousness of the danger and the inescapable distress of the petitioner. Similar complaints about the profusion of enemies are found often in the Psalms: Pss. 22:16; 25:19; 31:13; 38:19; 56:2; 69:4; 119:157. Also the comparison to a large army is not infrequent. The petitioner is surrounded by opponents who rise up against him in hostility (that is the meaning of קום על in Pss. 54:3; 86:14; and often). The passionate repetitions in vv. 1-2 (רבו—רבים—רבים) want persistently to set forth the seriousness of the danger and to persuade Yahweh to intervene. Then the petitioner expresses the derisive charge of his adversaries before Yahweh: "For him there is no help before God!"[1] אמר ל means "to say about someone" (Gen. 20:13; Lam. 4:20), and נפש is simply to be translated "I," without any specific meaning; this word in the widest sense signifies "that which is vital in man" (G. von Rad, *OT Theol*, 1:153). The reference to the scornful speech of the enemies is to induce Yahweh to prove his divine power against all the secure prognoses of the adversaries. ישע in its etymology probably has the meaning "to be wide, roomy" (cf. Arabic *wasi ʿa*) and would in the causative *hiphil* have to be translated with "to make wide, roomy," "to make room for someone" (Chr. Barth, *Die Errettung vom Tode* [1947], 27; S. Mowinckel, *Religion und Kultus* [1953], 63). The opposite would be צרר, "to be crowded together, compressed." Luther: "As distress is our narrowness that presses in on us and makes us sad, so the help of God is our expanded room that makes us free and happy." On סלה, cf. above, Introduction §4, 13.

[3:3] With ואתה, "yet you," a contrast is introduced. In the prayer songs the transition from the complaint to the expressions of trust is introduced in this way. It is worth noting that the statements of trust begin, not with "I," but with "you." Trust has its foundation in Yahweh, not in the believing human being. The petitioner knows that he is surrounded as with a shield by the presence of God and sheltered in God's protection (cf. Ps. 27:5, 6). "An ordinary shield covers only one side, but Yahweh protects from all sides" (Gunkel). On בעד, cf. Ps. 139:11. That Yahweh protects his own like a shield is recorded often in the

---

1. "Christ certainly heard this on the cross [Matt. 27:43]: 'He trusts in God; let God deliver him now, if he desires him,' as it is also predicted in Ps. 22:7-8: 'All who see me mock at me, they make mouths at me, they wag their heads; "he committed his cause to the Lord; let him deliver him, let him rescue him, for he delights in him."' For this confidence, mocking, jeering, insulting, this victory song, this eulogy on the part of the adversaries, as if over a defeated and completely hopeless enemy, is the final and most bitter part of the tribulation" (Luther, WA 5, 78, 19ff.).

Psalms, e.g., Pss. 18:2; 28:7; 119:114. The petitioner is now completely sure that Yahweh restores his כבוד and lifts his head. כבוד in this context does not necessarily have to refer to a person of "eminent rank" (Duhm), whose "dignity" is restored. The Hebrew concept in its widest sense signifies "what is influential about a person," "what makes him respectable" (G. von Rad, *ThW* 2, 240ff.). In suppression and derision a person's dignity is taken away (Job19:9). But the petitioner trusts that Yahweh will restore it. In connection with מרים ראשי H. Schmidt thinks of a court action in which the judge raises up from the floor and thereby pronounces free a defendant who has prostrated himself (cf. Lev. 19:15; Ps. 82:2). This interpretation then leads Schmidt to important results: Psalm 3 is understood to be a "prayer of one accused" (H. Schmidt, *Das Gebet des Angeklagten im AT*, ZAWBeih 49 [1928], 26). This view suggests itself, because one can understand the lifting up of the head in a legal action.

W. Beyerlin has even more lucidly illumined the situation that is basic to the psalm. He places Psalm 3 into the context of an action in the court of God. The petitioner has arrived in the area of asylum and protection at the temple. He knows that he is protected by Yahweh as by a shield against those who persecute him and contest his rights. Now he looks forward to the verdict of God by which his human dignity is restored and (by the lifting up of his head) the contested rights that he has looked for from Yahweh are given back to him. The precise accusation issuing from the enemies is not known.

[3:4] The second sentence of trust reveals the certainty of being heard. The petitioner cries aloud to Yahweh. קול appears syntactically "as the effected object with instrumental meaning" (BrSyn §93n). The "holy hill" (Zion) is the place of the presence of God. From here the hearing emanates (Pss. 14:7; 20:2; and often). Here the turn of fortune is to be awaited. The certainty of being heard is solid and unassailable. The oppressed does not doubt that Yahweh will intervene and help.

[3:5-6] In v. 5 the petitioner looks back. He lay down and went to sleep. Where? In the workaday life? Somewhere in the land "in the face of the enemies"? There are many indications that the protective area of the temple is meant, where the petitioner has entered and where he has retired. The prayer formulary refers to this frequently recurring connection. "The taking of refuge, which makes it possible to spend the night in safety and to be without fear in spite of the enemies round about, is understood as the protection of the temple, which removes the afflicted from the clutches of his enemies until the court of God should reach its verdict. Taking refuge is not itself a permanent solution but is accompanied by the desire to find relief by a drastic act of rescue on the part of God. This is also the only way in which the efficacy of that refuge-taking becomes practically intelligible" (W. Beyerlin, 77). Of course, we must carefully evaluate exegetically the way the institutional connection is understood. For although the temple is indeed a refuge, none of the expressions of trust spoken by the petitioner attributes the protection to the holy precincts as such. Indeed, this petitioner does not call out: "The temple of the Lord, the temple of the Lord, the temple of the Lord is here" (Jer. 7:4). He puts his trust entirely and exclusively in Yahweh. Yahweh is his protection. Him he trusts. "Yahweh sustains me!" On this basis we may affirm that the prayer formula—no matter what its connection with the institution of temple refuge and the expected verdict of God may be—was separable from cult and rite and perhaps in the history of tradition was in fact thus separated. For the references to what is institutional are only dimly recognizable; they have to be detected by a combination of techniques.

On the expression of trust in v. 5, cf. Ps. 23:5. Fearlessly the petitioner beholds an entire army drawn up for battle.[2] For עַם as "troops," cf. Num. 20:20; Ps. 18:44. The petitioner sees himself besieged round about and encircled. But he is not afraid, for Yahweh will hear him; Yahweh is present (Psalm 46). שִׁית seems to be a technical military concept (cf. Isa. 22:7). Fearless security is based—we must emphasize it once more—on the trust expressed in v. 3.

[3:7] After the words of trust, the plea of extreme distress of the petitioner surrounded by enemies now breaks out in v. 7a: "Arise, Yahweh! Help me, O my God!" On the significance of this plea as an extreme call of distress, cf. Jer. 2:27 and Pss. 7:6; 9:19; 10:12; 17:13; 44:26; 74:22. On יָשַׁע, cf. v. 2. It is possible that the conception of קוּם and of God's entrance was connected with the ark, the empty throne of God. As a ruler gets up from his throne and intervenes, so may Yahweh arise and come to aid (Num. 10:35).

In v. 7aβ.b the decision about the sense and meaning of the verse depends on the interpretation of the tenses. How is the perfect tense to be understood? As an expression of "unshakable certainty of being heard" (J. Botterweck, 188)? As a statement of an experience that the petitioner has had? "Since Yahweh has in the past always given evidence of his help, therefore the petitioner, sure in his faith, knows that he will help in actual distress now too" (J. Botterweck, 188). The situation of the tense is cleared up by D. Michel, *Tempora und Satzstellung in den Psalmen* (1960) 61ff.: "The Perfect Tense in Reports of Deliverance." In any case, the two half-verses are to be translated: "You have smitten all my enemies on their cheeks, you broke the teeth of the wicked." This statement contains "the triumphant certainty based on help experienced" (H. Schmidt). Also cf. W. Beyerlin, 78ff. Accordingly, 7aβb clearly must be separated from 7aα. Between these two parts of the verse lies the occurrence of actual intervention and aid on the part of Yahweh. The turn of events has come. Was a word of God issued in the form of an "oracle of salvation"? Cf. J. Begrich, "Das priesterliche Heilsorakel," *ZAW* 52 (1934) 84.

The statement is enough: In keeping with the confession of trust in v. 4, Yahweh has really intervened. He has defeated the enemies. In the OT the slap on the cheek stands for a disgraceful, degrading punishment: 1 Kings 22:24; Job 16:10; Mic. 4:14; Lam. 3:30. When mention is made of breaking teeth, we will have to consider the fact that in the Psalms, especially in the prayer songs, we have rather frequent mention of the mouth, throat, tongue, lip, or teeth of the adversaries: Pss. 5:9; 10:7; 31:18; 52:2; 57:4; 58:6; 59:7; 140:4. The mouth, from which issued the mocking statements of the enemies, has been smashed (v. 3). The enemies are considered רְשָׁעִים, they are in essence characterized by wickedness and godlessness (cf. above, Introduction §10, 4).

[3:8] The psalm ends with a closing statement (epiphonema) added for liturgical use. Trust and confidence on the part of the petitioner of the psalm sound forth

2. "Thus he is weak and overpowered according to appearance and in the eyes of men, but before God and in spirit he is very strong, and also in the strength of God he exults with confidence" (Luther, WA 5, 81, 36ff.).

in a timeless, creedal theological statement (J. Botterweck). With Yahweh, everyone who trusts in him and calls on him in need and distress will find help. Such well-being is prayed for in the form of a comprehensive bestowal of blessings for the entire people of God. This makes it evident at the same time that the rescue and help that came to the individual took place in Israel. From this history-of-salvation series of events the life of an individual petitioner cannot be isolated.

Purpose and Thrust

The petitioner of the psalm was threatened by a host of enemies and persecutors. His position must have seemed hopeless. The mocking voices of his adversaries, conscious of victory, threatened to cut off the last avenue of escape for this man as he sought refuge with his God and prayed to him for rescue. These enemies and persecutors were so sure of their position that they arrogated to themselves a judgment concerning God's word and deed: "For him there is no help before God!" (v. 2). But it was God's rescuing word and his liberating deed that the petitioner longed for. These hostile actions and the statements concerning Yahweh's deeds, so definitively presented, all calculated to thrust the one they persecuted into final God-forsakenness—these the petitioner of the psalm meets with an unshakable confidence in the present and effective power of God to protect him. He is certain that God—in spite of all assertions and prophecies to the contrary—will find help. With his כבוד ("glory") Yahweh will intervene for the honor of him who is ostracized and rejected by men; he will (by the symbolical act of lifting up his head, v. 3) restore justice to him who had already been condemned by humans. This person will be justified—even in the sight of his enemies (cf. Isa. 49:4; 50:8). Clearly and unconditionally the certainty of being heard comes into evidence (v. 4). To be united with Yahweh in such certainty of being heard, even in the face of a host of adversaries and contradictions—in the Psalter this is called faith. This faith is free of fear, even if they number ten thousand who threaten to lay siege to life and destroy it (v. 6). The prayer petition is expressed in an appeal that advances into the Holy of Holies of the self-revelation of the God of Israel (v. 7aα). The "God of the ark" is addressed, and his theophany is awaited.

But then the turning-point is reached.[3] We are not told when, where, and how it took place. If v. 5 should refer to the institutional act of taking advantage of the protection of the temple, we could easily suppose the original situation to have been the occurrence of a self-manifestation on the part of Yahweh (perhaps mediated through a priest or temple prophet) in the sanctuary. Still, the concrete contours of such an occurrence are indeed remote in the present psalm text. Above all, we would have to consider that v. 7aβ.b bears witness to an occurrence that transcends all dimensions of anything institutional. Restraint would therefore be indicated. Only the echo, only the testimony of a turn of events that has taken place is discernible in v. 7β.b. The enemies have been

---

3. It is amazing how clearly Calvin saw the problem of the tenses in v. 7. He writes on this verse: "What follows concerning the smiting of his enemies may be explained in two ways: either that in praying he calls to remembrance his former victories, or that, having experienced the assistance of God and obtained the answer of his prayers, he now follows it up by thanksgiving; and this last meaning I am much inclined to adopt. In the first place, then, he declares that he fled to God for help in dangers and humbly prayed for deliverance; and after salvation had been granted him, he gives thanks, by which he testifies that he acknowledged God to be the author of the deliverance which he had obtained" (Calvin, on Ps. 3:7, trans. James Anderson [Grand Rapids: Eerdmans, 1949]).

defeated, the adversaries overcome. Persecutors, confident of victory, who presumed to know God's judgment and to anticipate it (v. 2), are unmasked and branded as רשעים. What is proved and demonstrated in this event is: "Help is with Yahweh!" (v. 8). This is the enduring reality among the people of God, who live under the promise of blessing and therefore under the promise that this reality will become real.

The prayer formulary of Psalm 3 transcends and encompasses every affliction and persecution of individual persons. And yet, in this formulary the invitation is extended to sufferers and persecuted people to take refuge in this broad expression and to articulate each specific affliction in its own language. In the fulfillment of the NT Jesus Christ is the sole and first one who prays the Psalms. He is the "royal human being" (K. Barth). He is the persecuted one, the one who (before human beings) is thrust and cast off into hopeless forsakenness of God. But he is also the one who trusts, who prays, who is united with the Father, who is justified by God, who is arisen. Christians pray Psalm 3 ἐν Χριστῷ. The wide scope of expression of the language of the psalm is fulfilled in the reality of Jesus Christ.

In Spite of All Accusations,
Safe and Secure with God

Literature

L. Dürr, "Zur Datierung von Psalm 4," *Bibl.* 16 (1935) 330-338. M. Mannati, "Sur le sens de *min* en Ps. 4:8," *VT* 20 (1970) 361-366. W. Beyerlin, *Die Rettung der Bedrängten in den Feindpsalmen der Einzelnen auf institutionelle Zusammenhänge untersucht,* FRLANT 99 (1970) 84-90.

Text

For the choirmaster. With string accompaniment. A psalm of David.
4:1 When I call, answer me,[a] God of my righteousness!
—In (my) distress you created[b] room for me.—
Be gracious to me and hear my prayer!
2 You distinguished people, how long will my honor suffer shame,[c]
how long will you love what is vain and seek after lies? *Selah.*
3 Know indeed that Yahweh has shown great 'grace to me.'[d]
Yahweh hears when I call to him.
4 'Just think things over in your hearts'[e]—but do not miss the mark!
Just 'be angry'[e] on your beds—but be silent! *Selah.*
5 Present right sacrifices and put your trust in Yahweh!
6 There are many who say: "Who lets us see what is good?
'Gone'[f] from us is the light of your[g] countenance!"
7 You, 'Yahweh,'[h] put more joy in my heart
than they have who are rich in grain and wine.[i]
8 In peace I go to sleep as soon as I lie down,
for you[j]—lonely though I am—let me dwell in safety.

1a Gk reads εἰσήκουσιν. According to that, we would have to read עָנֵנִי, and the tenses in v. 1 would all have to be adjusted accordingly and be made to refer to past time. But we should perhaps conjecture that Gk has already toned down the imperative to a perfect tense in בצר הרחבת לי, the part of the verse that has the effect of a parenthesis, while in

MT the parallel half-verse for בקראי ענני אלהי צדקי is probably to be found in חנני ושמע תפלתי.

b The suggestion now to change the perfect הרחבת to the imperative הַרְחֶי בֶה and thus to accommodate it to the imperatives ענני and חנני ושמה convinces one as little as the correction proposed under letter **a**. This part of the verse has a peculiar position (like that of an interpolation).

2c In Gk we find the text ἕως πότε βαρυκάρδιοι; ἵνα τί. This would correspond to Hebrew כִּבְדֵי לֵב לָמָּה. But this would destroy the organization of the verse. MT literally: "How long (is) my honor for shame?"

3d MT translated literally: "that Yahweh has chosen a pious person for himself" (הפלה, Mss הפלא). This interpretation of the text is hardly possible syntactically, and it is also questionable in context. In Ps. 31:21 we find the idiom that clears up the text: הִפְלִיא חַסְדּוֹ לִי (also cf. Ps. 17:7). Correction: הִפְלִיא חֶסֶד לִי, "He has showed wondrous grace to me."

4e In its construction, i.e., in the arrangement of the parallelism of members, the text before us in MT presents difficulties. These can best—without violence to the wording— be cleared up by a transposition of the word order: by an exchange of רגזו and אמרו בלבבכם. The impulse for a likely change of position of בלבבכם before על־משכבכם would be explained by a reference to the fact that the conception of "thinking things over on the bed" lay very close (cf. Ps. 36:4; Mic. 2:1). The commentaries mostly employ a very circumstantial and hardly well-substantiated process according to which the word בלבבכם is inserted after רגזו (although אמר בלבב is a common phrase), and אמרו is corrected to הָמְרוּ, הָמְרוּ, מרו.

6f We can hardly think of נסה as being an unusual way of writing נְשָׂא, or שָׂא (in the sense of Num. 6:26). Very likely the Hebrew text once read נָסְעָה. In the parallelism of members this would make good sense. The preposition עַל would then have to be understood in the sense of Ps. 81:8 ("from over," G. R. Driver, *VT* 1 [1951], 247).

g Syr recommends the suffix of the third person פָּנָיו and thus probably smoothes the way toward the verb נשׂא for a text under consideration.

7h It would agree with the context (and the meter) if יהוה as a vocative were to be read at the beginning of v. 7 rather than at the end of v. 6.

i מֵעֵת as a comparative is probably to be translated literally: "as at the time when . . . ." More freely (and giving precedence to the suffixes that prevail logically): "than they when they . . . ."

8j יהוה in this verse is very likely a secondary addition that could be expunged on metrical grounds. לבדד = "lonely though I am" (H. Schmidt) is more secure textually; Gk κατὰ μόνας.

Form

Psalm 4 belongs to the group of Psalms of David (Psalms 3–41). Budde is of the opinion that Psalms 3 and 4 belong together and at one time formed a unit. This conception—which has been discussed often—is without foundation.

In its textual and metrical form the psalm presents a number of difficulties. The transposition in v. 4 is mandatory (see textual notes). Corrections must be undertaken in vv. 3, 6, 7, and 8. Accordingly, the following metrical picture results: v. 1a is an isolated quadruple meter followed by a double triple meter. The 4 + 4 meter is accordingly present in vv. 2, 3, 4, 6, 7, 8. The corrections on metrical grounds in vv. 7 and 8 are insignificant. V. 5 may be thought of as an isolated quadruple meter.

The arrangement of the psalm under the presuppositions so far developed (see textual notes) presents no difficulties. Transpositions of verses (E. Baumann, "Struktur-Untersuchungen im Psalter I," *ZAW* 61 [1945/48], 114ff.) are unnecessary and hardly meaningful. V. 1 contains a prayerful address to Yahweh which already reverts to the experience of the help of God (cf. v. 3). But the petitioner is still threatened and therefore in vv. 2-5 addresses the enemies that persecute him (with reference in v. 3 to the grace given him). In closing, in vv. 6-8 the attitude of people who impatiently complain (v. 6) is contrasted to the trusting security of the petitioner (vv. 7-8).

From this overview of the structure and content of the psalm we arrive at the assertion (which in the commentary is still to be defined and explained more in detail): Psalm 4 belongs to the theme-oriented form group of prayer songs, traditionally called "individual laments" (Gunkel and Begrich, *EinlPs* §6). For the group of prayer songs cf. above, Introduction §6, 2. Precisely in view of Psalm 4, the question arises whether the traditional type classification that results in the designations "lament" or "song of trust" may still be maintained (thus correctly: W. Beyerlin, 89). Therefore we ought simply to speak of a "prayer song" (תפלה) and develop the more detailed explanations in the process of exegesis.

Setting

The situation in which the petitioner of the psalm finds himself becomes recognizable first in vv. 1 and 3: Yahweh has shown grace to the petitioner and in a dangerous experience of persecution and temptation has created room for him. Still the enemies continue to revile him, to defame him (v. 2), and to plan mischief against him (v. 4). As the "Sitz im Leben" we easily assume an experience in the temple; for this, especially the reference to the sacrifice in v. 5 gives occasion. Thus it would be in place to suggest the interpretation that an innocent person who has been persecuted and accused has had his rights restored through a divine verdict in the temple. The psalm transfers us to the cultic-institutional scene of a divine court procedure (H. Schmidt, E. A. Leslie, W. Beyerlin). The cultic character is underlined by the reference to the act of sacrifice. Of course, the singularity of the presumed procedure is that the persecutors and oppressors are not willing to accept the divine verdict and therefore to respect the outcome of the procedure. We must be dealing with highly placed, influential persons (v. 2) who, even after the intervention of Yahweh has already taken place, do not cease to present their accusations (v. 2) and probably also invent new arguments (v. 4). From this perspective the outlines of the psalm become very sharp and clear. V. 8 would then have to be interpreted in connection with the situation already set: the petitioner lies and sleeps in the protective area of the temple (cf. the commentary on Ps. 3:5).

The interpretation of the psalm as an "evening song" fails to recognize the concrete reference of the statement in v. 8 and borders on pious lyricism.

In comparison with the situation to be observed, or to be deduced by inference, in Psalm 3, the following picture emerges: the petitioner in Psalm 3 is in vv. 1-7a confronted with the experience of the divine court procedure. The turning point brought about by Yahweh's intervention is treated in v. 7aβ.b only very briefly by looking back and witnessing to the fact that the enemies have been overcome. In Psalm 4, on the other hand, the deciding verdict of the divine court action has been rendered (vv. 1 and 3). But this verdict is not acknowledged by the enemies and persecutors of the petitioner. In other words, the justification by Yahweh of the accused is contested. God's acquittal, God's verdict, is not accepted by the "distinguished" people (v. 2). The oppressors set themselves up as superior to the verdict of God, and they continue their accusations and defamations (cf. W. Beyerlin, 85).

About the writer and petitioner of the psalm a great variety of opinions has been expressed. In most cases people began with an exaggerated view of the concept כבוד and thought of the "dignity" of a leader of the people (Wellhausen and others), a king (Baethgen), or a high priest (Duhm). But it is hardly correct to take כבוד in this exclusive sense (see below, "Commentary"). In trying to answer the question about the person of the petitioner, we might find a clue in the address in v. 2 and then in v. 7: he belongs to the poor, uninfluential people; he is not rich in grain and wine; he has to look up to the "distinguished" people who possess power and claim rights as their own. But the question about the "person" is immaterial. Psalm 4 is a prayer formula written for an extraordinary occasion: for the attack on a divine verdict in a court procedure in the temple.

On the question about the time of composition there are few clues. In every respect the psalm can equally well be preexilic and postexilic (W. Beyerlin, 84). But without doubt the psalm refers to the cultus (sacrifice; institution of divine court procedure) and was there transmitted.

Commentary

[Title] On the designations in the title cf. the following references: למנצח, above, Introduction, §4, No. 17; בנגינות, Introduction, §4, No. 9; מזמור לדוד, Introduction §4, No. 2.

[4:1] The psalm begins in v. 1 with petitions which are significant for a prayer song: it asks that its petitions be heard. Although Yahweh has "created room" and "shown great grace" (v. 3)—as the psalm as a whole lets us know and as we have stated in our analysis of the situation—the oppression of the enemies has not abated as yet. The corrections not infrequently undertaken in the commentaries, changing the imperatives to perfect tenses, do not do justice to the situation and the content of the psalm. In extraordinary distress, the petitioner calls to Yahweh for help and rescue.[1] The name of God, אלהי צדקי, points to the fact that the right of the petitioner, the declaration of his innocence over against all accusations and defamations, proceeds from Yahweh, from God's verdict: Pss. 17:2; 35:23; 37:6; 69:28 (cf. G. von Rad, " 'Gerechtigkeit' und 'Leben' in der Kultsprache der Psalmen," *GesStudAT* I 225-247). Yahweh is called "God of my righteousness" because he has espoused the cause of the oppressed person with a liberating verdict and, against all claims to justice by influential men of power, has incorruptibly confirmed the fidelity of his covenant and of his association with the poor man. Yahweh's righteousness takes sides; it devotes itself to the helpless person who trusts in him and calls to him. The special situation of the petitioner in Psalm 4 is that he has already received a restoration of his right and his dignity from the אלהי צדקי (v. 3) but that this his right is nevertheless still contested, namely, with new arguments (v. 4). Therefore the address "God of my righteousness" is a designation based on trust which entails the hope of further confirmation of the righteousness of Yahweh.

---

1. "Moreover, he calls him *the God of his righteousness,* which is the same thing as if he had called him vindicator of his right; and he appeals to God, because all men everywhere condemned him, and his innocence was borne down by slanderous reports of his enemies and the perverse judgments of the common people. And this cruel and unjust treatment, which David met with, ought to be carefully marked. For while nothing is more painful for us than to be falsely condemned, and to endure, at one and the same time, wrongful violence and slander; yet to be ill spoken of for doing well is an affliction which daily befalls all saints" (Calvin, on Ps. 4:1, trans. James Anderson [Grand Rapids: Eerdmans, 1949]).

The words "In distress you created room for me" indicate that the decisive intervention on the part of God has already taken place. צר denotes the straits, the oppression that chokes off life. הרחבת, however, is a concept of "nomadic feeling for life" (Gen. 26:22) that sees the expanse and the liberty of unrestricted possibilities before it. In the Psalms this concept repeatedly illustrates the liberating rescue from oppression (Pss. 18:19; 31:8; 66:12; 118:5).

[4:2] After the petition has been addressed to Yahweh, the singer of our psalm turns directly to his adversaries. For this kind of address to others that leaves the song for a moment, cf. Pss. 6:8; 52:1f.; 58:2; 62:3; 119:115. בני איש is very likely a term for respected and prominent people. In Egypt and Babylonia influential proprietors were called "sons of a man," to distinguish them from the poor (E. Meyer, *Geschichte des Altertums* I, 250, 514; B. Meissner, *Babylonien und Assyrien* I, 371ff.). Thus in Psalm 4 we would have before our eyes the practice frequently castigated in OT prophecy, that influential people accuse and condemn the poor under false charges. They deprecate his כבוד (cf. the commentary on Ps. 3:3) and thus destroy the dignity of his life before God and man. The oppressed now accuses his opponents that they loved ריק (here probably: the baseless, groundless accusation) and invented lies, that is, that they took refuge in slander. Cf. M. A. Klopfenstein, "Die Lüge nach dem Alten Testament," diss., Berne (1964) 224.

On סלה, cf. above, Introduction, §4, No. 13.

[4:3] In v. 3 the adversaries addressed are now challenged to acknowledge the fact of the bestowal of grace on the part of Yahweh. On חֶסֶד, cf. the commentary on Ps. 5:7. We are here dealing with an "expression of realization that is connected with a portentous demonstration of proof" (W. Zimmerli, *Erkenntnis Gottes nach dem Buch Ezechiel*, ATANT 27 [1954], 56). The fact that Yahweh "has shown great grace" to the petitioner must have been expressed in a concrete word of God or in a portentous occurrence. The adversaries therefore are challenged to acknowledge and to honor this happening; that is the meaning of ידע. In the parallel part of the sentence the imperfect denotes the certainty of being heard in the present time—in the face of the constant lack of discernment on the part of the enemies. This certainty is to be thought of as an expression of trust corresponding to v. 1. The accused confesses in the face of his enemies that God hears his complaints and attends to his cause.

[4:5] In v. 4 it is now plainly presupposed that the opponents are devising schemes and looking for arguments to see how they may take advantage of him whose rights God has restored. אמר בלבב describes the scheming and planning, רגז the sullen excitement. With boldly challenging imperatives the petitioner of our psalm invites the slanderers to continue their hostile contemplations but warns them against transgression (before Yahweh). חטא expresses the thought of making a dreadful mistake. He advises them to be silent under all circumstances, probably intending to say that they invent no new accusation. Also the challenge of v. 5 should probably be understood in this connection. For the first, the verse probably presupposes that the entire altercation between the accused and his adversaries takes place in the area of the sanctuary. If now זבחי־צדק may be connected with אלהי צדק (v. 1)—and that is obvious—then we are dealing with sacrifices by means of which the justice proceeding from Yahweh is acknowledged (cf. Ps. 5:3). Very likely also Ps. 51:19, the passage often cited as a parallel passage in the interpretation, may be interpreted and understood in this sense (cf. the commentary on Ps. 51:19). But such an offering acknowledging the justice of God must be accompanied by trust and confidence among those who present it (cf. Ps. 5:3). That is why we have the challenge בטחו אל־יהוה.

Against this interpretation of צבחי־צדק objection has been raised, above all by R. Schmid, *Das Bundesopfer in Israel,* StANT 9 (1964) 40. Schmid is of the opinion that the interpretation offered is hardly in keeping with the purport of Ps. 51:19; "the question is rather about right sacrifices, the rightness of which is based on this, that they satisfy the cultic prescriptions or, much more preferable, that they proceed from the right spirit, a sincere attitude toward Yahweh" (40). Yet this interpretation, which reflects the conception of many interpreters, "definitely does not prove right" (W. Beyerlin, 87). We should first take up the interpretation given by W. Beyerlin, which could define more closely the interpretation expressed above: "צדק in this context refers much more to the salutary gift that enables the human being to abstain from all unrighteous acts, to put aside the breach of the peace, and to restore the כבוד of him who is falsely accused. The sacrifices demanded are to be understood as a means of conveyance of the צדק. When they are performed, those who offer them become partakers of the salutary gift of the צדק and are by them enabled to contribute their part to overcoming injustice and social adversity (W. Beyerlin, 87, with reference to K. Koch, "*Sdq* im Alten Testament: Eine traditionsgeschichtliche Untersuchung," diss., Heidelberg [1953], 32, 42, 76, et passim). This interpretation is to be stated yet more sharply. In this effort we begin with the fact that after the event of Yahweh's intervention those who were rescued celebrated the great deeds of Yahweh in the common meal (זבח) and (as former outcasts, persecuted and ostracized people) were visibly and effectively received into the community of God's people (Pss. 22:26; 34:8; and often). In this connection it can only have been the meaning of זבחי־צדק to bring the persecutors and the persecuted into a new social relation at a sacrifice after Yahweh's declaration of justice and into a social relation that corresponds to the bestowal of צדק by Yahweh. Here lies the inner connection between אלהי צדק and זבחי־צדק in Psalm 4.

If this interpretation of the challenge in v. 5 is adequate, the sense of vv. 4-5 should be given as follows: The enemies and persecutors of the petitioner should not commit sin in their protesting and slanderous efforts against Yahweh's declaration of righteousness (which brought liberation for the oppressed). Rather, they should now present the required זבחי־צדק, enter the community with the one who was declared free, and trust Yahweh. In this connection the phrase ובטחו אל־יהוה has the meaning: to agree with Yahweh's declaration of righteousness, to accept this declaration, to yield to it. "To trust," accordingly, is to be in agreement with the word and deed of the אלהי צדק. If the distinguished people were to resist the presentation of the זבחי־צדק and their participation in it, it would be distrust of the righteousness of Yahweh and impugnment of his declaration.

[4:6] In vv. 6-8 the restless inquiring and demanding of those who do not trust (cf. בטח in v. 5) is now contrasted to the petitioner's certainty and security founded on Yahweh. For the first, v. 6 speaks of people who bicker about their fate. The words of the grumblers are cited in direct discourse—as is sometimes customary in the Psalms (Pss. 3:2; 11:1; and often). It is significant now that these people do not address Yahweh, but without direction, that is, without trust (בטח in v. 5), wail about their dismal existence. They do not see what is good; they perceive no sign of a turn toward God that would brighten life with good fortune. They lament about the fact that the light of the countenance of God (i.e., his illuminating presence) has departed. Even though the reproduction of these words of lamentation probably does not represent a direct quotation of the opponents on the part of the psalmsinger, still the oppressed person certainly sees their view of life as under the influence of such a disoriented complaint against fate.

[4:7] Over against the unrest of that tormenting inquiry of v. 6, v. 7 now presents the certainty of him who already has received טוב. Yahweh has given joy in heart to the petitioner. When God shows wondrous grace (v. 3) and together with a grant of his help "creates room" (v. 1), that means: שׂמחה, joy, that fills the innermost recesses of a human being. This joy is more glorious than the time (עת) in which the בני איש (v. 2), as the prominent and the rich, have grain and wine in abundance. Significantly, in this passage all the blessed gifts of natural life are disregarded, and only the joy of being turned to Yahweh's salvation is lauded (cf. Ps. 63:3, כי־טוב חסדך מחיים). All earthly blessings vanish in the face of the gracious love (חסד in v. 3) of God.

[4:8] The good fortune of this joy is accompanied by the certainty of permanent security: יחדו in the complex sentence of v. 8 has the meaning: "the moment I lie down, I am asleep." He who is blessed with Yahweh's joy rests in peace. He does not toss about in worried, sleepless unrest (cf. Ps. 3:5). He rests securely. No matter how lonely he may be, God lets him dwell in safety. The word לבדד refers to the critical situation of the petitioner, who without influence and all alone stands face to face with the בני איש. Still he is not afraid (Ps. 3:6); the help he has experienced from God is the reason for an unassailable security. As in Ps. 3:5, we should emphasize that this consciousness of being protected is provided not by the temple's area of asylum and protection as such; the determining factor is trust in Yahweh, the אלהי צדקי, who gives to the lonely and repeatedly oppressed person security and victory over his dangerous isolation. שׁלום is the gift of God that proves itself also in, and precisely in the face of, acute attacks and threats. Dwelling securely is not a sacral, self-evident thing but a gift of the God of Israel.

Purpose and Thrust

Psalm 4 is a testimony to the invincible security and certainty which, amid the marvelous experience of the grace of God's comfort, defies all enmity and defamation. In Isa. 50:8-9 the עבד־יהוה speaks the words: "He who vindicates me is near. Who will contend with me? Who is my adversary? Let him come near me. Behold, the Lord God helps me; who will declare me guilty?" These sentences correspond to the message of Psalm 4. In the NT they are taken up in the powerful closing words of Rom. 8:34. He for whom God provides righteousness cannot be touched by any hostile power. The OT testimony has been taken up in the NT proclamation of justification. Here the eschatological framework becomes visible, in which all those concrete events are to be viewed in which the servants of God on earth have their rights and their honor (כבוד) spurned and denied, but in which God intervenes for those that are his (cf. Psalm 5, "Purpose and Thrust"). In the NT, this miracle of God's bestowal of salvation takes place in Jesus Christ, whose life-giving help, however, always becomes effective only in the event of the actual consolation that is trustingly grasped.

Psalm 5

Prayer for the Demonstration of the Righteousness of God

Literature

L. Krinetzki, "Psalm 5: Eine Untersuchung seiner dichterischen Struktur und seines theologischen Gehaltes," *Tübinger Quartalschrift* 142 (1962) 23-46. G. W. Anderson, "Enemies and Evildoers in the Book of Psalms," *BJRL* 48 (1965) 18-29. O. Keel, "Die Schilderung der Feinde in den individuellen Klage- und Lobpsalmen," diss., Freiburg (1967). N. A. van Uchelen, " אנשי דמים in the Psalms," *OTS* 15 (1969) 205-212. W. Beyerlin, *Die Rettung der Bedrängten in den Feindpsalmen der Einzelnen auf institutionelle Zusammenhänge untersucht*, FRLANT 99 (1970) 90-95.

Text

To the choirmaster. For flute accompaniment(?). A psalm of David.

5:1   Hear my words, O Yahweh; give heed to my groaning!

2   Give attention to my loud crying, O Yahweh, my King and my God!
    For to you do I pray

3   ' '[a] in the morning; you will hear my crying.
    In the morning I get ready for you and look out "after you."[b]

4   For you ' '[c] do not take pleasure in wickedness, no evildoer
      abides with you.

5   The boastful may not appear before your eyes.
    You hate all evildoers,[d]

6   You destroy[e] the liars.
    A murderer and a deceiver Yahweh abhors.[f]

7   But I, thanks to your great favor, enter your house,
    pray toward your holy temple, in fear before you.[g]

8   O Yahweh, lead me in your righteousness because of my
      enemies,
    make your path even[h] before me![i]

9   For there is nothing truthful in "their"[j] mouth, their heart
      is destruction.
    An open grave is their throat, their tongue smooth talk.

151

10 Let them pay for it, O God, and fall[k] by their own schemes!
   Because of their many wicked deeds, cast them away, for they
      have rebelled against you.
11 But let those who trust in you rejoice, let them continually
      shout for joy, '. . . . . .'[l]
   and may they exult . . . who love your name.
12 For you bless the righteous one, O Yahweh . . .,[m]
   "you cover"[n] "him"[o] as with a shield, crown[p] him with favor.

3a For the sake of the meter v. 2c and v. 3a will have to be combined. In that case we would have to read אֶתְפַּלָּל at the end of v. 2, יהוה would have to be bracketed, and בֹּקֶר would have to be combined in a five-pulse meter with the first half-verse (for the justification of this textual criticism on metrical grounds, see below on ''Form''). **b** There is a metrical foot missing, one that would have to be inserted or added as the object of וַאֲצַפֶּה—perhaps according to Mic. 7:7, בָּךְ. **4c** For the meter of Psalm 5, it is generally demonstrable, v. 4a is too long. Omission of אַל (demonstrable in the Mss) would clear up the text also in meaning. **5d** As in v. 2c/3a, so now in v. 5c/6a a supplemental addition in the meter is necessary. **6e** Gk reads πάντας additionally. A corresponding complement in the MT would of course disturb the meter. **f** Occasionally יתעב is changed to תְּתָעֵב, because Yahweh is addressed in the whole psalm. But it is easily conceivable that this is a paraphrase and that we ought to read the third person. **7g** It is possible that בִירָאַתְךָ once stood in the first half-verse (cf. Syr and v. 9). **8h** Kethib הוֹשַׁר, Qere הַיְשַׁר. Hiph also in Isa. 45:2. **i** The correction of the suffixes of לְפָנֶיךָ and דְּרָכֶי suggested in 2 Mss and the Mss of Gk, and rather frequently adopted, simplifies the Hebrew text, which is to be retained. דרכך is parallel to בצדקתך and is to be understood accordingly. **9j** The suffix in the plural בפימו is to be demanded on the basis of the parallelism קרבם. **10k** Also the variant יַפְּלוּם מעצותיהם (''ruin their schemes'') would be possible. **11l** In vv. 11 and 12 the meter that is generally demonstrable is significantly disturbed. 11c is too long, 12c disproportionately short. In the context, ותסך עלימו in v. 11c is disturbing, whereas these two words (as has been recognized a long time) form a splendid complement before כצנה in v. 12c. This transposition would solve the textual problems. **12m** According to the metrical laws predominant in Psalm 5, the first half-verse in v. 12 would have to read כי אתה תברך צדיק. But then there is obviously a word missing after יהוה. Sometimes, although without adequate reason, בשלום is added. **n** Cf. note 1. **o** Upon the insertion of ותסך עלימו the suffix would have to be accommodated to the new context: עָלָיו. **p** Very likely the piel תְּעַטְּרֶהוּ is to be read in this passage (Pss. 8:5; 103:4).

Form

An investigation of the meter of Psalm 5 leads us, together with E. G. Briggs and H. Gunkel, to the conviction that the double five-pulse meter dominates the entire poem. Parallelisms of similar thought-content regularly correspond to each other in two verses that are to be read in the $3+2$ meter. This meter is so clearly demonstrable that only slight corrections ''for the sake of the meter'' are required to restore the original arrangement also in those verses that in the present MT depart from the poetical consistency (cf. textual criticism). Among the critical emendations worth noting in this connection are above all the completion of v. 2c by means of v. 3a and of v. 5c by means of v. 6a, and then also the transpositions in vv. 11 and 12. The bracketing of the word יהוה in v. 3 and of the word אַל in v. 4 is insignificant. Perhaps also האבד in v. 6 would have to be removed "for the sake of the meter." Supplementation is necessary in vv. 3, 8, 11c, and 12b. Whereas v. 3 provides a clue for the addition of the בְּךְ on the basis of Mic. 7:7, the completions of the meter in vv. 8, 11c, and 12b remain hypothetical. On the whole, however, Psalm 5 provides a text whose metrical order is easily analyzed and undoubtedly provides occasion for reconstruction.

From the series of double five-pulse meters the organization of the psalm can also be developed in vv. 4-7 by the petitioner from the reference to the fact that wicked people are not allowed to appear before Yahweh but that he himself, the plaintive, has access to the sanctuary of God. Then follows in v. 8 the prayer for Yahweh's guiding path of righteousness. This is accompanied by the indictment against the enemies (v. 9) and a demand for decision (v. 10). Vv. 11 and 12 then close by treating of the joy and blessing of the righteous.

The psalm belongs to the theme-oriented form group of prayer songs. Concerning this group of prayer songs, cf. above, Introduction §6, 2. The type description "lament of an individual" has proved to be inadequate; the psalm does not have the character of a lament (Beyerlin, 95). As a תפלה it is sufficiently clear in perception and has a clear form of address. The petitioner prays for Yahweh's intervention in the face of a threatening hostile persecution and an obvious, existing (false) accusation that is to be equated with malevolent slander. The psalm probably served as a formulary in a definite situation still to be defined in detail (vv. 2 and 3). It is difficult to determine to what extent this formulary has in the course of tradition departed from the concrete "Sitz im Leben" that is discernible (see below). In any case, it is probably a part of the historical influence of the psalm that it was prayed, also outside its institutional relations in real-life situations that correspond to its contents.

Setting

The situation, the "Sitz im Leben," that is discernible in the psalm is easily grasped and reconstructed. The petitioner gained entrance to the temple area (v. 7); thereby he has experienced a first bestowal of grace on the part of Yahweh. In the face of threatening danger from accusing and persecuting enemies, who possibly are also present in the area of the sanctuary, the oppressed petitioner prepares a sacrifice early in the morning (v. 3). He prays for a revelation of Yahweh's help, consisting of a word of God. The cultic institution of the court of God is the context of Psalm 5. If it is a prayer formulary, every possibility of a detailed description of the petitioner is to be rejected. There is no evidence, for instance, that a king or a priest was the petitioner. Still, it may probably be assumed that such prayer formularies were composed by the temple priesthood and in the case of a specific application were dictated word for word.

For obvious reasons, it is hardly possible to suggest a timeframe for this prayer. Is the temple mentioned in v. 7 the temple of Solomon or the temple of postexilic times? That question has no answer. Even individual observations, such as the fact that Yahweh is called "King," do not help. Still, we can assert "that nothing in the text of this psalm precludes a provenance from the era of the preexilic Zion temple" (W. Beyerlin, 90).

Commentary

[Title] The (editorial) heading contains a number of technical terms. On למנצח, cf. above, Introduction §4, No. 17. On אל־הנחילות, see §4, No. 10; and on מזמור לדוד, see §4, No. 2. We must point out that the statement (still current in

153

fundamentalist circles) that the psalm was composed by David has to come to grief at the very fact that the temple is mentioned in v. 7.

[5:1-3] The psalm begins in the characteristic style of a prayer song. Yahweh is addressed and implored to give attention to the sighing of the petitioner. הגיג, as in Ps. 39:3, is imploring, pitiable pleading. The petitioner cries aloud to Yahweh[1] and calls him "my King and my God" (Pss. 44:4; 68:24; 74:12; 84:3). The meaning of this address is closely allied to the interpretation of the so-called "psalms of Yahweh's enthronement" (cf. Pss. 47; 68:24; 93; 96; 97; [98]; 99). But it is obvious in any event that we think of the conception of "King Yahweh" enthroned above the ark of the covenant and present in the Holy of Holies (cf. Isa. 6). To the enthroned judge Ps. 9:7 is addressed. Unheard-of boldness is displayed in the address "My King and my God"; it shows that—no matter in what timeframe we place it—the individual is sure of this, "Yahweh in the power of his dominion can be addressed by me; he is there for me." On אלהי, cf. O. Eissfeld, " 'Mein Gott' im Alten Testament," *ZAW* 61 (1945/48) 3-16. The lamenting prayer is brought before Yahweh early in the day (cf. Ps. 88:13) and is accompanied by a sacrifice. ערך here probably has the meaning: to prepare a sacrifice, to lay the pieces of the offering in order (Lev. 1:8f., 12). The priest would then present the offering laid out. But ערך, probably connected with מלין, may also have the meaning: "prepare words," "present words" (Job 32:14), or in the phrase ערך משפט it can have the meaning: "to present a case at law" (Job 13:18; 23:4; Ps. 50:21). But the context, especially the verb צפה, suggests the idea of presenting an offering. Thus—in connection with the cultic judgment of God—we should have to imagine that early in the morning the petitioner brought an offering that accompanied his prayers and pleas for a divine verdict. H. Gunkel thinks of an omen-offering, in the course of which the petitioner awaits God's decision, a sign of God's favor. Still, the idea of an "omen" inherent in the offering or accompanying the act of sacrificing is inept. This expectation, characteristic of the cultic practice of Mesopotamia, is not found in the OT. The petitioner anticipates the help of God in the morning (cf. J. Ziegler, "Die Hilfe Gottes 'am Morgen,' " *Festschrift f. F. Nötscher,* BBB 1 [1950], 281ff.). But how is this help manifested? From Num. 23:1ff. we can learn that a vision was expected at the offering. But Numbers 23 involves a unique (cult-) prophetic practice. By contrast, however, it is significant that the petitioner of Psalm 5 "is on the lookout" and "waits" (יחל; cf. the parallel concepts in Mic. 7:7), expecting that a דבר of Yahweh (Ps. 130:5), a divine word, sent through the mouth of the priest, will be transmitted to him (J. Begrich, "Das priesterliche Heilsorakel," *ZAW* 52 [1934], 81-92). Thus it is not without significance in vv. 1-3 to recognize the attitude of anticipation that accompanied the sacrifice. The sacrifice (and, certainly, we are to think of a burnt offering) is the visible side of the loud crying, the pleading, and the petitioning. It indicates the time at which the entire life, threatened by persecution and distress, turns to Yahweh—and that

---

1. While many commentaries take the view that the loud crying of the petitioner of the Psalms originated in the naive conception that the loud calling had to bridge the distance between man and God, Calvin writes in his Commentary on the Psalms: "Again, the word *cry,* which signifies a loud and sonorous utterance of the voice, serves to mark the earnestness of his desire. David did not cry out as it were into the ears of one who was deaf; but the vehemence of his grief, and his inward anguish, burst forth into his cry" (Calvin, on Ps. 5:2, trans. Anderson [Grand Rapids: Eerdmans, 1949]).

in anticipation of a final decision, an effective acquittal. Since ancient Israel court decisions were made early in the morning (2 Sam. 15:2; Jer. 21:12; Ps.101:8), so the divine decision was awaited early in the morning (cf. L. Delekat, ''Zum hebräischen Wörterbuch,'' *VT* 14 [1964], 8f.). As we can conclude from Ps. 3:5 and Ps. 4:8, the night before the crucial morning was spent at the temple, after which the important preliminary decision of admittance to the area of the sanctuary was made (cf. v. 7).

[5:4-7] The assurance of being heard is now won by the petitioner from the fact that the wicked are not allowed to appear before Yahweh, whereas he himself, the petitioner, has access to the sanctuary (vv. 4-7). Disregarding the sacral-judicial backgrounds that are to be considered in vv. 4-7, Gunkel here remarks: ''That certainly is a rather easy way of becoming sure of one's own righteousness.'' But the sacral-judicial presuppositions let the text appear in a different light. According to Psalm 15, only he is allowed to enter the area of the sanctuary as ''guest and refuge-taker'' (גור is the corresponding verb in Ps. 15:1) who has satisfied certain definite statutes of the Torah that can be fulfilled and has accordingly been declared צדיק (G. von Rad, '' 'Gerechtigkeit' und 'Leben' in der Kultsprache der Psalmen,'' *Bertholet Festschrift* [1950], 418-437). This ''barrier'' of a strict, sacral-juridical discipline the petitioner of our psalm has evidently crossed (v. 7) with a so-called ''oath of cleansing'' (cf. Job 31). He is now standing in the holy area and knows that in this place an evildoer is not allowed to ''abide'' (גור). In a רשע Yahweh has no pleasure. The הוללים, those whose conduct is ''boastful,'' ''foolish,'' or ''insane'' (cf. Pss. 73:3; 75:4), are not allowed to appear before God. התיצב (with לפני or לנגד) is a standing phrase for the cultic gathering that takes place in the sanctuary (Josh. 24:1; 1 Sam. 10:19); with על it is a technical term for cultic service (Zech 6:5; Job 1:6; 2:1). Yahweh hates evildoers and liars. The question ought to be asked whether the terms חפץ and שנא are perhaps taken from the language of cultic-sacral condemnations (cf. Amos 5:21-22, and regarding it, E. Würthwein, ''Amos 5:21-27,'' *ThLZ* 72 [1947], 143-152). Murderers and deceivers Yahweh abhors. The רשע is excluded from worship in the holy place (cf. the comment on Ps. 1:5). The צדיק (v. 12), on the other hand, is allowed to enter the sanctuary of God (Ps. 118:19-20). This admittance the petitioner ascribes to the favor of Yahweh. חסד in its essential meaning is ''the relationship of goodwill and conformity to the covenant obtaining between a ruler and his people'' (M. Buber, *Der Glaube der Propheten* [1950], 164). חסד, therefore, describes a concept of relations that gives expression to ''affection and solidarity'' (N. Glueck, *Das Wort* חסד *im alttestamentlichen Sprachgebrauch,* 1927). But now the benevolent favor of Yahweh reveals itself in a real act of grace and reception (in Ps. 4:3 the real act is the turn to salvation taking place in the verdict of God). The distressed person may now present his petition in the holy area facing the temple as the place of the royal presence of Yahweh (also cf. Pss. 28:2; 138:2). He does so ביראתך, i.e., in the attitude that is appropriate for the living presence of God.[2]

The various names for enemies and evildoers that appear in Psalm 5 provide occasion to take note of the full orientation on this subject presented in

---

2. ''For in the full sense of the concept, fear means necessarily to expect the cessation of one's existence at the hands of someone or something. Where the expectation is anything less, or less than necessary, we have not really learned to fear. What we do not fear above all things we do not properly fear at all'' (K. Barth, *CD*, 2/1, 35).

the Introduction §10, 4. In any case, in Psalm 5 we are dealing with the enemies of the צדיק, with the persecutors and accusers who have driven the petitioner into the situation in which he seeks the verdict of God. They are "liars" (v. 6) because they defame the oppressed person with a false accusation. They are "murderers" (v. 6) because they aim to bring about the death sentence for the צדיק with their accusation.

[5:8] After the petitioner of Psalm 5 has expressed the certainty of being heard with a reference to the exclusion of the evildoer from the holy area (vv. 4-6) and his own entrance to the holy place (v. 7), the real petition for Yahweh's directive legal help is presented. Here from the very beginning צדקה and דרך should be understood as two terms that complement and interpret each other. On צדקה, cf. G. von Rad, *OT Theol*, 1:370ff. In our context צדקה is the "bestowal of salvation" (*Heilserweisung*, v. Rad, 372ff.), which becomes visible in the act of revelation of the guiding legal help for him who laments. The manifestation of the צדקה presupposes the coming of God (for the deep roots of the צדקה in the event of revelation and theophany, cf. K. Koch, "*Sdq* im Alten Testament," diss., Heidelberg (1953): "צדקה is a domain . . . . to be placed into it means to experience its power to provide salvation," 38). The petition for this bestowal of salvation that encompasses the existence of the petitioner is directed against the enemies. They are to learn that Yahweh provides "justice" for him who laments. The verse that runs parallel to v. 8ab, that does not have the full form of a five-pulse unit, should be translated (without correction of the suffixes): "Make your way even before me!" The "way of Yahweh" is a standing concept in the Psalter: Pss. 25:4, 5, 12; 27:11; 32:8; 86:11. Involved is the concrete instruction which Yahweh gives to the individual (Ps. 25:12). The "way of Yahweh" is synonymous with the "answer of God," which is revealed to the petitioner (Pss. 32:8-9; 27:11) and through which the future revealed by God opens up before his eyes (לפני). Basically, therefore, the petition expressed in v. 8 is the crucial prayer that Yahweh may declare his faith in his servant and by his bestowal of help grant him a new possibility of existence that is anchored in God's legal counsel that points the way.

[5:9-10] Upon the petition in v. 8 follows an accusation against the enemies (v. 9) and a demand for a verdict (v. 10). The lie and calumny of the enemies is pointed out before the eyes of God. "Nothing truthful is in their mouth." נכונה would be that which proves to be "steadfast" and "reliable."

Their "inner being" is filled with forces that bring about "destruction" (on הוות, cf. Pss. 38:13; 52:2; 55:11). The mouth of the slanderers is called an "open grave" (Jer. 5:16)—in other words, the place of death and ruin, a place that continues to receive the dead. And their tongue the slanderers have "made smooth," i.e., they ruin a person through dangerous words (concerning dangerous flattery that brings people down to ruin, cf. Prov. 2:16; 7:5; 28:23). From these accusations it becomes abundantly clear that the enemies of the petitioner are insidious slanderers against whose attack the one afflicted is seeking protection and help from Yahweh.

The demand for a verdict, attached in v. 10, asks that Yahweh "let them pay for it."[3] האשימם is an unusual *hiph.* of אשם (*qal*, cf. Ps. 34:21, 22). The

---

3. "A Hebrew word which has been translated 'judge them' Jerome translated 'condemn them.' Properly he indicates this judgment by which they are revealed for what kind of people they are, once

adversaries should fall from their insidious schemes. Here we may certainly not as yet presuppose the very abstract conceptions in the sense of *excidere consilio* = "to have no luck with one's schemes" (Sir. 14:2). The thought is rather of actually "overthrowing" the slanderers (on נפל, cf. Pss. 20:8; 27:2; 36:12). The same is indicated also in the word הדיחמו = "cast them away," which occurs in the parallel five-pulse meter. It is a matter of the expulsion of those who have sinned by slandering man before Yahweh. פשע, a word that entails "the true profundity of the OT concept of sin" (L. Köhler, *OT Theology* 170), carries the meaning "rebellion," "insurrection." The guilt of the enemies assumes immeasurable proportions by the very fact that they dare to present their case resting on lies and deception in the area of the sanctuary and before Yahweh. מרה denotes callous defiance (Lam. 1:20; 3:42; Ps. 78:8). The question has been raised whether this demand for a verdict by the lamenting petitioner does not contradict some "moral value of the gospel." This, however, fails to recognize that in the OT it is always a matter of the actual demonstration of the power and aid of Yahweh. The verdicts do not apply to a future age but to this world. For the presence of God on Zion is not an imaginary presence of some numen, but it is the royal reign of God that intervenes in human life and history. For the one who prays in the OT, the complaint and call for a verdict raised on Zion is an extremity, something critical. Yahweh's help is not a mere "comfort" in spite of which the afflicted person finally perishes anyhow, but it is a radical turning point. That is the faith of the psalmsingers. Therefore the realism of OT legal aid ought not to be degraded by means of a spiritualized "gospel"; rather, the NT faith ought to regain its this-worldly power from the OT. Only when we have considered that, may we ask the question whether, in view of the cross, where Jesus prays for his enemies, a demand for judgment is still possible in the new covenant.

[5:11-12] The bright contrast to the accusation and judgment of the evildoers (vv. 9-10) is given in vv. 11-12. Whoever seeks shelter with Yahweh and takes refuge there (חסה); let him be glad! The last verses have the form of a wish, an invitation to all who with an upright heart put their trust in Yahweh. Their life is under the banner of joy (Ps. 4:7) and of jubilant exultation (עלץ, cf. Akkadian *elêsu*). עלץ בְ has the meaning "exult in . . ." (Ps. 9:2; 1 Sam. 2:1), whereas "exult over . . ." would be עלץ לְ (Ps. 25:2). He who finds shelter with Yahweh exults in the realm of his presence. The צדיקים are called אהבי שמך. Here שם is an alternate term for יהוה in the language of worship (O. Grether, *Name und Wort Gottes im Alten Testament*, BZAW 64 [1934], 35-37). "The שם denotes the side of Yahweh that is turned toward mankind, the revelatory side. It means Yahweh as *deus revelatus*, who is revered by human beings as such" (Grether, 40). The צדיק is the one who is blessed by Yahweh; and here ברך indicates "the enhancement of the power of life" (F. Horst, "Segen und Segenshandlungen in der Bibel," *EvTh* [1947], 23-27). For צדיק, cf. the commentary on Ps. 1:6.

their wickedness is revealed, in which sense Paul also writes, 2 Tim. 3:9: 'But they will not get very far, for their folly will be plain to all, as was that of those two men,' as if the prophet were saying: 'See to it that, just as now they are approved, loved, and praised by all, once their folly has been revealed, they will be hated, rejected, and detested, so that men may see that they were wrong in approving what you condemned.'

    "Therefore this not only refers to the final judgment, but this is a prayer that truth may triumph with God as the judge, truth that those people suppressed while man's day was the judge. You judge us, O God, because human beings judge badly" (Luther, WA 5, 153, 6ff., 19ff.).

Against all the oppression of the enemies the צדיק is hedged round as with a shield. צנה is the shield that covers the entire body (Ps. 35:2). At the same time the צדיק is crowned with רצון, the bestowal of God's grace and gift of salvation. The closing verses therefore in wish and invitation at the same time contain the confidence of the petitioner that he is among those who exult and therefore among the blessed of Yahweh.

Purpose and Thrust

The prayer for the demonstration of the righteousness of God (v. 8), which is the focal point of Psalm 5, is addressed to the King and God from whom the petitioner expects to receive help and good fortune for his life. We could state the assurance that is expressed in vv. 4-7 thus: "To be sure, I have the documented (sacral-judicial) right to pray in your presence for your guiding legal help." The sacral-judicial institution of the OT, together with the sacrifices, is abrogated in the NT through Jesus Christ. In him the Christian has "confidence to enter the sanctuary" (Heb. 10:19), in him he also has "confidence" (παρρησία) for prayer. (Just the same, we should observe how strongly the legal element of "church discipline" is allied to the Christ event in the NT.)

But is the prayer for guiding legal help in the new covenant still possible? Does not the word of Paul apply here: "To have lawsuits at all with one another is defeat for you. Why not rather suffer wrong?" (1 Cor. 6:7). No doubt all juridical problems and all litigations of a Christian acquire an entirely new point of disposition through the judgment pronounced on Jesus Christ on the cross. But there remains that sinister slander that separates from God and precipitates in the midst of the congregation divisions that must be endured until the End. In this sense the Reformers understood the OT laments that are voiced because of legal problems. For them there is here a battle between the true community of God and the elements of destruction in the church which want to separate the Christian from his Lord by means of false accusations. This contest can not and may not be postponed; it is settled before the eyes of the living God in the midst of this world (cf. Luther on Ps. 7:8; see also below, on Ps. 7:8). In this battle things may go so far as to give expression to a demand for judgment on the enemies: "We must pray that truth may triumph" (Luther). In any case, this may be found in the commentaries of Luther and Calvin. Included in the justification before God is the right to life of the true community of God on earth and their victory over the lies and deceptions of the adversaries that arise in the church (cf. the commentary and Psalm 7, "Purpose and Thrust").

Psalm 6

Prayer for Averting
the Anger of God

Literature

J. Coppens, "Les Psaumes 6 et 41 dépendant-ils du livre de Jerémie?" *HUCA* 32 (1961) 217-226. J. Botterweck, "Klage und Zuversicht der Bedrängten: Auslegung der Psalmen 3 und 6," *BiLe* 3 (1962) 184-193. J. A. Soggin, "Osservazioni filologiche ed exegetiche al Salmo VI," *Studi sull' Oriente e la Bibbia* (1967) 293-302. N. Airoldi, "Note critiche al Salmo 6," *RBiblIt* 16 (1968) 285-289. R. Martin-Achard, "Approche des Psaumes," *Cahiers Théologiques* 60 (1969) 49-65. H. C. Knuth, "Zur Auslegungsgeschichte von Psalm 6," *Beitr. z. Geschichte d. biblischen Exegese* (1971). K. Seybold, *Das Gebet des Kranken im Alten Testament: Untersuchungen zur Bestimmung und Zuordnung der Krankheits- und Heilungspsalmen*, BWANT 99 (1973).

Text

To the choirmaster. With strings on the eighth. A psalm of David.

6:1 O Yahweh, rebuke me not in your anger,
and chasten me not in your wrath!

2 Be gracious to me, O Yahweh, for I am languishing;
heal me ' ',[a] for my bones have 'fallen to pieces.'[b]

3 My soul is thoroughly frightened
—but you, O Yahweh, oh, how long!

4 Turn again, O Yahweh, save my soul;
help me for the sake of your grace!

5 In death there is no remembering[c] you;
in Sheol, who praises you there?

6 From moaning I am totally exhausted, . . . ,[d]
every night I flood my bed [with weeping],
I sprinkle my couch with tears.

7 My eye is dimmed with grief,
entirely worn out[e] because of all my "woe."[f]

8 Depart from me, all you evildoers,
for Yahweh has heard my weeping!

159

9 Yahweh has listened to my pleading;
Yahweh accepts my prayer.
10 Shame and shock sorely assail
all my enemies, and they must ' 'ᵍ desist in an instant.

2a יהוה in the first half-verse may not be expunged. But the divine name in the second half-verse should probably be dropped, as also in Gk.
b The MT would have to be translated: "they have been frightened." In the parallelism of members and in the thematic structure of the language of the Psalms נבהלו עצמי is unusual. According to Ps. 32:3, the emendation בָּלוּ עצמי is obvious. This would yield good sense in the parallelism of the members. The slip of the pen in the MT could be influenced by נבהלה in v. 3 (another suggestion for emendation: נָבְלוּ, cf. Isa. 24:4; Ezek. 47:11).
5c Gk reads ὁ μνημονεύων σου and has therefore read the participle זֹכְרֶךָ . Considering the אין, this is surely the original reading.
6d The two words at the beginning of v. 6 are to be separated from the following complete verse. This is either a fragment of a complete line or an addition.
7e Gk, α´, σ´, and Jerome read עָתְקָתִי and thereby syntactically separate the second half-verse from its relation to עיני.
f צוררי = "those who press in upon me" is probably to smooth the way to vv. 8-10. It would be best to read בכל־צָרָתִי (Bertholet) in the parallelism of members, with Ps. 31:9.
10g The יבשו occurring twice in v. 10 is unlikely. Perhaps the second יבשו is a variant of ישבי (Gunkel) and should therefore be eliminated.

Form

Psalm 6 is not completely uniform in its metrical form. The 3 + 3 meter is ascertainable in vv. 1, 3, 5, 6, 7, 9, 10. Only in v. 10 does a textual emendation contribute to establishing this meter. If we should expunge יהוה in vv. 2 and 4 and if ממני in v. 8 is eliminated, then (with the exception of the first two words in v. 6, which refuse to yield to any metrical system) we would encounter only double triple meters in the entire psalm (Kittel). It would be more prudent to leave vv. 2, 4, and 8 in the 4 + 3 meter, since the reasons for emendation are not conclusive.

A closer analysis of the structure could lead us to the following result: v.1, call to Yahweh; vv. 2-5, petitions of the prayer; vv. 6f., description of the situation of distress; vv. 8-10, witness to being heard (for the basic outline: N. Airoldi). H. Gunkel would point out v. 5 especially as the "motive for Yahweh's intervention." In vv. 6f. the petitioner describes the excessive load of his suffering. An unexpected, abrupt reversal ("change of mood") is then revealed in vv. 8-10. In this connection the petitioner in triumphant assurance slams the door in the face of the enemies that harass him.

The psalm belongs to the theme-oriented form group of songs of prayer (תפלה). Vv. 8-10 correspond as proof of being heard. These verses may not be removed from Psalm 6 and addressed as a "new prayer," as H. Schmidt tries to do. As the interpretation will still show more succinctly, the event of God's hearing and being inclined takes place between vv. 7 and 8 (cf. the comment on Ps. 3:7f.). This event is impressively emphasized by the twofold שמע יהוה (for the tense, cf. D. Michel, *Tempora und Satzstellung in den Psalmen* [1960], 62f.). The prayer song Psalm 6 is in its detail to be classified among the psalms characterized by the theme "sickness and healing." R. Martin-Achard (49) counts Psalms 6; 38; 41; 88; and 102 among this cycle; K. Seybold distinguishes three categories: with certainty, Psalms 38; 41; and 88 belong to the psalms of "sickness and healing"; with relative certainty, Psalms 30; 39; 69; 102; 103; with likelihood, Psalms 6; 13; (31); 32; (35); 51; (71); (73); 91. In all casesPsalm 6 is to be classified among the prayer songs of "sickness and healing." Cf. above, Introduction, §6, 2.

Setting

We might name the temple in Jerusalem as the locale for the prayer song (R. Kittel). The psalmist prays in bitter suffering. His sickness has brought him to the brink of the grave. This situation is completely lost sight of if the sufferings expressed in the psalm are understood to be an expression of "pain of the soul" and if the added comment is made that Near Easterners have a way of depicting distress of soul with a lively fantasy. To what degree also a consciousness of guilt is expressed in Psalm 6 and whether therefore the psalm can be classified among the traditional seven "penitential psalms" of the church we must leave for a later consideration (the seven penitential psalms are Psalms 6; 32; 38; 51; 102; 130; 143).

It is hardly possible to date the psalm. But its presence as a prayer formulary in the temple cult in Jerusalem permits preexilic composition to be viewed as not impossible. A dependence on the book of Jeremiah (thus J. Coppens) can hardly be maintained; we should rather point to common conventionalized formulations and conceptions in Psalm 6 and the book of Jeremiah.

Commentary

[Title] For the technical terms of the (redactional) title of Psalm 6 the following references should be given: for למנצח, cf. above, Introduction, §4, No. 17; for בנגינות, cf. §4, No. 9; for על־השמינית, cf. §4, No. 25; and for מזמור לדוד, cf. §4, No. 2.

[6:1-2] For the understanding of the entire psalm the following fact is determinative: the petitioner knows that he stands under the wrath of God. This fact gives the real shape to the suffering and sighing, to the praying and pleading. "Wrath of God" means that Yahweh turns away from the human being, forsakes him, and casts him away (Ps. 27:9). This wrath is frightful. On its account the earth may shake, and mountains may collapse (Jer. 10:10); no one can "still" it (Job 9:5). Human beings fade away and languish when the wrath of God takes hold of them (Ps. 90:7; Job 17:1). In his anger Yahweh reveals himself as judge; יכח basically means: "to act as judge." In the physical suffering of which the petitioner speaks somewhat later, he therefore recognizes a consequence of the judicial wrath of God that avenges the violation of the covenant. And thus the prayer for averting the anger is joined to pleading for healing from sickness (v. 2). In the OT the association of guilt and sickness is indissoluble (Pss. 32:1ff.; 38:2ff.; 39:8,11; and often. Cf. G. von Rad, *OT Theol,* 1: 274ff. In sickness, guilt becomes manifest both as human perdition and as divine wrath. With physical distress Yahweh "chastizes" the human being (יסר, Pss. 38:11; 118:8). The coincidence of divine anger and human mortality provides the unfathomable depth of temptation.[1]

---

1. "Therefore it is true that when this conflict is present, nothing but hell is visible, and no redemption appears. All things that are felt are thought of as eternal. For the anger is here felt to be not that of a human being, which may some time subside, but that of the eternal God, which may

With this background the petitions become rather accessible. The lamenting singer pleads that the judgment of wrath be taken away from him. But that means that he is praying that Yahweh have mercy on his languishing, crumbling life and heal him. Only God can heal (Exod. 15:26; 2 Kings 5:7), therefore the prayer is addressed to God (Ps. 41:4; Jer. 17:4; for corresponding statements in other psalms, cf. Pss. 30:2; 103:3; 107:20; 147:3). The distress of the petitioner is great. מלל = "wither away" (Ps. 37:2; Job 14:2; 18:16) and— very likely—בְּלוּ = "go to pieces" are the verbs that speak of the suffering as being near to death.

The prayer in sickness was probably spoken according to fixed formularies. The question about the cultic situation here causes some difficulties. Where, when, and how did the prayer come into being? In Sir. 38:9f. we read: "My son, when you are sick, do not be negligent, but pray to the Lord, and he will heal you. Give up your faults and direct your hands aright, and cleanse your heart from all sin. Offer a sweet-smelling sacrifice, and a memorial portion of fine flour, and pour oil on your offering. . . ." This is a reference to the practice of restitution which doubtless took place at the cultic center and was introduced with an act of atonement of ritual character (K. Seybold). Sir. 38:12 enjoins us also to let the physician have access to us and not to resist his treatment (cf. Isa. 38:21). Still, the sick person relies first and foremost on the healing provided by Yahweh, the healer (Exod. 15:26). The sentence about Yahweh the healer "sounds both programmatic and polemical. It proclaims that human life with all its derangements finds its unity before God, and it rejects the notion that the future is to be won other than in dialog with him" (H. W. Wolff, *Anthropology of the OT* [1974], 148).

[6:3-4] The inner excitement and emotional impatience of the petitioner is expressed in v. 3. For נפש we can often simply insert "I" in the translation; in our case we could of course agree with L. Köhler: " 'My soul' is the I as it were in a special context and degree and in a particular respect—the I in a private and unitary capacity" (*OT Theology* 144). נפש may also be described as "the self of the needy life, thirsting with desire" (H. W. Wolff, *Anthropology of the OT* [1974] 25). The entire shocked and frightened existence here rises up to an insistent cry: את יהוה עד־מתי. This is the cry of one who is passing away under the wrath of God (for the עד־מתי standing alone, cf. Isa. 6:11; Hab. 2:6; Ps. 90:13). V. 4 contains also another pleading petition that God may intervene. שׁובה we may probably not take in the sense of Exod. 32:12; 2 Kings 23:26; and Jonah 3:9 as "desist from wrath." Rather, the imperative שׁוב as a petition that Yahweh may "again turn toward" him who is forsaken belongs to the topicality of the language of the Psalms (Pss. 90:13; 80:14). The context, too, shows this. God is entreated to intervene and to help. For חסד, cf. Ps. 5:7, "Commentary," but especially H. J. Stoebe in *THAT* 1, 600-621 (additional bibliography there).

[6:5] That the lamenting singer of our psalm is near death was apparent already in vv. 2-3. Now death and Sheol are mentioned. In death we do not think of (the great deeds of) Yahweh. זכר refers to thinking of the great deeds of God in praise (Pss. 111:4; 145:7). In Sheol there is no thankful glorifying of Yahweh; it is an area remote from worship. שׁאול is the "not-land," the "land which is not a land," the area that is not (L. Köhler, *Hebrew Man* [1956], 113). Beyond life is this soulless, shadowy existence which is far, far removed from God (G.

---

never find an end. 'Rebuke me not in your anger,' he says; to be rebuked in the temporal anger of a temporary human being is not enough. Then all the things of hell are put into action" (Luther, WA 5: 210, 13ff.).

von Rad, *OT Theol* 1, 369). Thus the petitioner expostulates with Yahweh: Let me not sink away to Sheol, for I have found the meaning and substance of my life in glorifying and praising you! This reason for entering presented to God lets us recognize that in the OT all decisions are made on this side of the boundary of death. We could say: all the soteriological and eschatological facts of the NT are in the OT attached to life in this world. Death and Sheol are areas far removed from life. For this, cf. Pss. 30:9; 88:10ff.; 115:17; Isa. 38:18f.

[6:6-7] These verses describe the situation of the suffering person. He is completely exhausted with sighing. ב יגע = "to be tired out by . . ." (Ps. 69:3; Isa. 57:10; Jer. 45:3). The sickbed is sprinkled over and over with tears. This hyperbolic manner of speaking wants to give expression to the unfathomable depth of the hurt. For מטה and ערש, cf. G. Dalman, *AuS* 7:185ff. Weeping and wailing have dimmed and tired the eyes; cf. Ps. 31:9. None of the statements of the psalm reveals with which sickness the petitioner was afflicted. But it probably also belongs to the formulary character of these psalms that they present descriptions in which suffering from every type of sickness could be expressed and subsumed.

[6:8-10] But at v. 8 the great change now closes in.[2] Suddenly the petitioner lifts his head with a triumphant shout. This sudden change is so incisive that some have even thought of a completely new song beginning in vv. 8-10.

But how will we have to think of the sudden change that lies between vv. 7 and 8? In vv. 8 and 9 we learn through the shout שמע יהוה that the lamenting singer has been heard. This means: Yahweh has turned his wrath away from him and has healed the sick. Obviously that word of God for which the petitioners of the Psalms wait (Ps. 130:5) has here been spoken in the holy place. In Ps. 107:20 we read ישלח דברו וירפאם. This occurrence must be presupposed also before vv. 8-10, for the sending of the דבר conveys the assurance שמע יהוה. Accordingly, we are not to think of an oracle or an omen at the offering after the manner of the cultic practices of Mesopotamia. The change of fortune that the דבר (transmitted through priests) occasions is easily seen in the formula שמע (יהוה) in many psalms: Pss. 22:24; 28:6; 34:6; 66:19 (also cf. Pss. 10:17; 31:22; 40:1). The petitioner has heard the "Fear not." He has received the assurance that Yahweh will not desert him. Such a promise conveys the certainty of being heard. It provides occasion for trust and hope. The prayer has been accepted by Yahweh (v. 9). The repeated emphasis on this event makes its weight felt and shows the joy of him who has been heard and rescued.[3] The whole outlook on life is changed. For immediately the petitioner—in the assurance of his being heard—turns to face his enemies. These enemies are presumably not the cause of the sickness, as perhaps through witchcraft (Mowinckel); neither are they a group

---

2. "After David has disburdened his griefs and troubles into the bosom of God, he now, as it were, assumes a new character" (Calvin, on Ps. 6:8, trans. Anderson [Grand Rapids, Eerdmans, 1949]). It is worth noting how firmly Luther is determined to deduce the perfect tense, "Yahweh has heard," from the faith and hope of the petitioner alone: "Since it is certain that he is speaking in hope and in spirit, and is not yet placed before God face to face, it is at the same time certain that he has been saved by hope and that, being comforted in hope, he sounds forth this whole collection of things, by which he chases away a most troublesome swarm of those evils." A few lines further on we read: "As is the hope, so are the tangible results" (Luther, WA 5; 215, 19ff.).

3. "A frequent repetition of the same thought reveals not, as it were, the need of a narrator, but the impression of one who is in exultation; for so those who are happy are accustomed to speak: it is not sufficient to state but once what it is that makes them happy" (Augustine, on Ps. 6:8-9).

which in the party strife of later times caused mental anguish for the pious (Kittel); they are instead people who wanted to separate the mortally ill from God through their accusations and opinions. Cf. above, Introduction, §9, 6. It is possible that the פעלי און filled up the measure of suffering in that they increased the visible wrath of God for the sufferer by means of an effective imprecation of their own. But once Yahweh has heard the petitioner, the adversaries have been put in the wrong; then they can be routed with the triumphant challenge סורו ממני. For such an address to the enemies, cf. Pss. 4:2f.; 52:1ff.; 58:1f.; 62:3; 119:115. The certainty of being heard is in v. 9 expressed in the words, "Yahweh accepts my prayer" (לקח). It is worth noting how the tense changes here. This change indicates that the singer recalls a single outstanding occurrence of the past with particular liveliness (BrSynt §42e). But if Yahweh has taken up the prayers of the petitioner, then that spells "shame" and "shock" for the enemies. All those who have harassed the sufferer so far must very suddenly (רגע) desist. In the fate of the enemies the petitioner comes to recognize the reality of his pardon. Cf. the comment on Ps. 5:9-10.

In the act of restitution the humiliation of the enemies becomes evident in the fact that the healed person is permitted to take part in the worship of the community and in the smaller circle to experience communion with members of God's people and with Yahweh himself (K. Seybold). For the enemies this is a visible demonstration that the person they accused and ostracized has been accepted.

Purpose and Thrust

Duhm writes regarding Psalm 6: "As a reading at a Christian sickbed this psalm is not suitable." And almost unanimously the recent commentaries declare that Psalm 6 has to be deleted from the church's traditional list of penitential psalms. These opinions regarding the contents are then occasionally also joined by criticisms of form that deny any poetic power to this "mediocre poem."

But one thing all these critical opinions of Psalm 6 overlook is that here a human being bears the whole burden of the anger of God and the frailty of earthly existence, so near to death. The Reformers recognized that. Luther freely declares: "Nor is there anyone who would understand this great affliction (to say nothing of worse ones) unless he has experienced it, and that is why we cannot adequately describe it." The weight of incalculable affliction is increased by the import of a this-worldly decision. To be separated from God or blessed by God for good—that is the either-or in Psalm 6. Here the decision cannot be postponed to "the other world"; it must be made on earth (Ps. 27:13). But to be separated from God would mean to be condemned under God's wrath to death as the "non-world," far from God. But to be blessed by God means to hear his well-directed, life-giving, and healing word that is directed to the praying and pleading human being. Psalm 6 teaches the "idealized Christian" (Duhm) to perceive the seriousness of the decisions of his life.[4] It teaches the church, which

---

4. "But this we should know, that for people who suffer such things the teaching of this psalm ought most diligently to be preserved, so that they do not go astray, complain, or look for the comfort of human beings, but take a firm stand by themselves, take the hand of God, and with the prophet turn nowhere but to God, saying: 'O Lord, rebuke me not in your anger.' Unless they excel in this good sense (as the priests of this matter wish it), they will to their great harm slip from the hand of the healing and atoning God, while they take refuge in their petty creaturely comfort, just as when clay, while it is being formed, slips from the hand of the potter and is the worse for the beating, until it becomes completely useless or so bad that it deserves only to be discarded" (Luther WA 5; 204, 34ff.).

often prays in colorless penitential formulas, to recognize in the strident images of the individual laments the either-or of its existence in this world.

These petitions want to penetrate all the way to the triumph that is expressed in vv. 8-10, the triumph over all powers that would separate the believer from God through accusation and judgment.

If we in this way try to explain the purpose and thrust of the psalm, we do so in conscious distinction to all declarations of the *totaliter aliter* which might be claimed to proceed from the NT. Thus H. C. Knuth (19) writes: "The New Testament does not witness to a new possibility of interpretation but preserves the possibilities hitherto existing through a final interpretation of our psalm. Even if we may over against this antithetical view of relationships between the Old Testament and the New Testament interpose that the New Testament possibilities were also always given already in the Old Testament—which we do not intend at all to deny—the specifically new element in the New Testament message is that it pits a single criterion, namely, Jesus himself, precisely against the plethora of possibilities." But we should ask, to what extent is "Jesus himself" a "criterion"? How else does the message of the NT come down to us than in the multiform kerygma of the witnesses of Jesus Christ? The antithetical determination of relations suggests a fulfillment factor that can be proved in a single line. But this overlooks the fact *that* and *how* in the NT the witnesses of Christ Jesus use the language of the OT in order to be able to interpret what is "basically new" in the context of its prophecy. Everything depends on the self-witness of the Old Testament actually being heard and on the interpreter then being exposed to the biblical-theological question about the Old Testament textual statement in the light of the fulfillment in Christ. Like antitheses, so also syntheses are to be avoided strictly. References and allusions must be subjected to questioning and determination anew.

In this process the literal citation cannot always be the determining factor. Matt. 7:23 and Luke 13:27 cite Ps. 6:8 in this way, that Jesus confronts those who say "Lord, Lord," but do not do the will of God the Father with the rebuff and denunciation: "Depart from me, workers of lawlessness!" (ἐργαζόμενοι τὴν ἀνομίαν). In the light of Psalm 6, those who say "Lord, Lord" appear as enemies of the sufferer. Jesus confronts them as the judge who brings to light what is hidden. These features are important for Matt. 7:23 and Luke 13:27. For the interpretation of Psalm 6 they do not amount to much. This psalm will rather have to be developed in its own profile and grasped in keeping with its declaration of purpose. This is what we have tried to do.

Psalm 7

Appeal to the
Righteous Judgment of God

Literature

N. Lohr, "Psalm 7; 9; 10," *ZAW* 36 (1916) 225-237. G. J. Thierry, "Remarks on Various Passages of the Psalms," *OTS* 13 (1963) 77-82. J. Leveen, "The Textual Problems of Psalm 7," *VT* 16 (1966) 439-445. W. Beyerlin, *Die Rettung der Bedrängten in den Feindpsalmen der Einzelnen auf institutionelle Zusammenhänge untersucht*, FRLANT 99 (1970) 95-101.

Text

A *shiggaion* of David, sung by him before Yahweh in behalf of the Benjaminite Cush.

7:1 Yahweh, my God, with you I seek refuge;
      save me from 'my pursuer'![a]

2 lest he rend my life like a lion
   and 'no one'[b] save and rescue.

3 Yahweh, my God, if I have done this,[c]
   if wrongdoing sticks to my hands,

4 if I have done wrong to my friend[d]
   and have robbed[e] him who harassed me without a cause,

5 may the enemy persecute[f] my soul and overtake it!
   May he trample my life to the ground
   and lay my honor[g] in the dust. *Selah.*

6 Arise, Yahweh, in your anger!
   Be uplifted against[h] the wrathful flare-up of my enemies!
   And awake toward me![i] —You have announced judgment.[j]

7 May the multitude of the peoples[k] be stationed around you,
   may you be 'enthroned'[l] above them!

8 —Yahweh judges the peoples.—[m]
   Judge me, O Yahweh, according to my righteousness
   and according to my innocence![n]

9 May there be an end° of the wickedness^p of the transgressors,
but lift up the righteous!
You who try the hearts and minds,
O righteous God!

10 A shield 'above me'^q is God
—a savior of those who are of upright heart.

11 'Yahweh'^r is the advocate of the righteous
and a God who chastizes every day.^s—

12 Indeed, again he sharpens his sword,^t
draws his bow, and sets his sights.

13 But he has aimed murderous weapons at himself
and has given fire to his arrows.

14 Behold, he conceives wickedness, becomes pregnant
with mischief, and gives birth to the lie.

15 He dug a pit, hollowing it out,
but he fell into the hole that he had made.

16 The mischief turns on his own head,
on his own pate does the wickedness descend.

17 I will praise Yahweh, for he is righteous,
I will sing to the name ' '^u of the Most High.

1a In the essential parts of Psalm 7 only one single enemy of the lamenting petitioner is mentioned. For that reason we should probably have to read מֵרֹדְפִי.

2b The question arises whether פָּרֵק belongs to the first half-verse (emendation: יִפְרֹק) or should be included in the second half-verse, as in Gk and Syr (Gk: μὴ ὄντος λυτρουμένου μηδὲ σῴζοντος = אֵין פרק). The decision depends on the meaning of the verb פרק. Does this verb have the meaning "to rob" (Gunkel), or must we translate "to extricate," "to rescue"? The passages documenting פרק unanimously speak for the second conception: Ps. 136:24 (Gk: ἐλυτρώσατο), Lam. 5:8 (Gk: λυτρούμενος). Therefore we will have to read אֵין פרק ואין מציל.

3c It is an impermssible simplification to read גֵּאוּת instead of זֹאת (Grimme, Schlögl, Gunkel).

4d Gk has read the plural τοῖς ἀνταποδιδοῦσίν μοι = שֹׁלְמַי (also cf. Jerome). But the context confirms the MT.

e Gk: ἀποπέσοιμι ἀπὸ = וָאֲחַלְּצָה (so also Syr and Targ). The context speaks for the MT.

5f For the pointing יְרַדֹּף the readings יִרְדֹּף and יְרַדֵּף are alternates; both are possible.

g The suggestion כְּבֵדִי = "my liver" can hardly be justified, since כבוד is a standing term in the language of the Psalms; cf. on Ps. 3:3.

6h The difficulties seen in the second half-verse and presumably obviated in various emendations vanish immediately when בְּ is understood in the meaning of the inimical "against" (BrSynt §106h).

i The change of the pointing to אֵלִי (Gk even has: κύριε ὁ θεός μου) simplifies the text without a reason for it. Rather, cf. Ps. 59:4: עוּרָה לִקְרָאתִי.

j This verse fragment is disturbing—especially with the perfect tense צִוִּית. Perhaps we ought to read צַוֵּה. Then the words יהוה ידין עמים from v. 8, where they, too, disturb the verse organization, could be added as the second half-verse (in the 4 + 3 meter).

7k לְאֻמִּים conjures up a conception that is substantiated throughout in the Psalms (immediately in the context we read: יהוה ידין עמים; cf. also Pss. 9:8; 96:10; 98:9; and often), but also in Deutero-Isaiah (e.g., Isa. 43:8ff.). The archaic, mythological picture of Yahweh as the heavenly judge surrounded by אלהים, based on Ps. 82:1 and Job 1f., a conception that led to the emendation of לְאֻמִּים to אלהים (Budde, Gunkel), must yield to the former.

l שׁוּבָה = "turn back" does not make good sense ("Should he complete the judgment on earth and then return to heaven? Or, should he have left the heavenly judgment seat before the judgment?" Gunkel). More to the purpose would be שְׁבָה. On ישׁב in the sense "be enthroned for judgment," cf. Ps. 9:4. Concerning the exchange of שׁובה and שבה in the MT: Num. 10:36; Ps. 116:7; Isa. 30:15.

8m Cf. the comment on v. 6, n. **i**.

n An emendation or complement for עלי is unnecessary (Wellhausen: עֲנֵנִי for עלי; Kittel: גָּמְלֵנִי; Graetz: וכתם פעלי) עלי (to intensify the suffix) denotes the power of innocence which (like a weight that cannot be removed) rests on the petitioner.

9o יִגְמָר is the pointing to be preferred. The verb has intransitive meaning here.

p The better pointing here is רֵעַ rather than רַע (Schlögl, Löhr, Gunkel, Schmidt).

10q MT ("my shield is on God") is unintelligible. Syr ("my shield is God") would be suspect metrically. The best reading would be עָלַי, cf., e.g., Ps. 3:3.

11r If in the parallel half-verse we have אֵל, we will have to reckon with an intrusion of an Elohistic redaction already in v. 6 (Gunkel); an original יהוה will have been changed. So perhaps also already in v. 10.

s The criticism of many commentaries concerning the words וְאֵל זֹעֵם stems from the contextual sense and therefore has to be taken up in the commentary (see below). None of the emendations proposed does justice to the textual data.

12t The emendations of the text in the commentaries, some of them radical (as in v. 11 on וְאֵל זֹעֵם) address themselves to the contextual sense. They are very bold and problematic. One should first attempt a literal translation.

17u יהוה will probably have to be eliminated "for the sake of the rhythm" (but also in consideration of the presence of יהוה in the first half-verse).

Form

Psalm 7 belongs to the group Psalms of David. We will have to reject the supposition that the psalm should be combined with Psalm 9 and 10 to form a larger unit (M. Löhr, *ZAW* 36 [1916], 225-237). Related themes and motifs do not provide a right to reconstruct literary complexes. But while M. Löhr goes beyond Psalm 7 to achieve a larger unit, a number of other interpreters undertake a division on grounds of literary criticism within the psalm. For instance, B. Duhm and E. G. Briggs think of vv. 6-11 as foreign elements. Duhm segregates these verses as an independent song. But an accurate examination of the shape of the form and of the "Sitz im Leben" will lead to the conclusion that Psalm 7 is a closely knit unit—a song whose structure is easily understood from the situation from which it arises.

The textual and metrical circumstances are marked by some unevennesses. Difficulties in respect to the text transmission occur especially in vv. 5, 6, 8, 11, 12. In vv. 5, 6, and 8 we encounter half-verses that cannot be coordinated (or can be coordinated with one another only by transpositions). As double triple meters we may read vv. 13-17, and additionally vv. 2, 4, 5 (with the exception of the four-meter verse: יִרְדֹּף אוֹיֵב נַפְשִׁי וְיַשֵּׂג), 6a, 7, 11. Vv. 1, 3, 12 are to be taken in the meter 4 + 3. And, finally, the meter 3 + 2 is to be established in v. 8 (with the exception of יהוה יָדִין עַמִּים).

These first observations on the form of the text lead to the question about the organization. For the first, an attempt to catch hold of the organization by concentrating on the contents yields the following picture: the title contains a classifying superscription. In vv. 1-2 the petitioner approaches Yahweh with pleading, solemnly affirms his innocence in vv. 3-5, and appeals to God's righteous justice in vv. 6-9. After the assertion of trust and certainty in vv. 10-11, the petitioner speaks about the attack (v. 12) and the fate (vv. 13-16) of his enemy and closes with thankful praise (v. 17).

The textual emendation suggested by J. Leveen (440) fails to convince; and M. Dahood's interpretive effort (420) to smooth things out is hardly justified. The following exegesis will show that the investigation of the form presented above will lead to an appropriate interpretation of the text.

Psalm 7 belongs to the form group of prayer songs (תְּפִלָּה). We have had constantly mounting evidence to show that the type classification that has so far been determinative in the sense of an "individual lament" (Gunkel and Begrich, *EinlPs* §6) does not really conform to the distinctive shape and form of expression of the psalm (thus also Beyerlin, 101). But the individual component parts of the prayer song must be grasped and defined more succinctly. In this effort it becomes evident that these components have emerged from the "Sitz im Leben" of the prayer song. The affirmation of innocence in vv. 3-5 has the characteristic form of an oath of cleansing presented among statements of self-imprecation, an oath that needs still to be interpreted (see below). Vv. 6-9 are to be understood as an appeal to Yahweh, the judge. Elements of a "judgment doxology" appear in vv. 10-11. The cohortative formulation of v. 17 contrasts the verse to the customary interpretation that in it a *toda* ("thanksgiving song of an individual") is expressed; rather, we ought to think of a "form of vow" pronouncing praise (thus F. Crüsemann, *Studien zur Formgeschichte von Hymnus und Danklied in Israel*, WMANT 32 [1969], 275). For an insight into the "prayer songs," cf. above, Introduction §6, 2.

Setting

The situation to which Psalm 7 points is easily recognized. The psalm presupposes the institution of the court of God, into which one who is accused and persecuted by enemies has come to receive the verdict of Yahweh. This "Sitz im Leben" leads us to the area of the temple of Jerusalem. On the research regarding this setting, cf. H. Schmidt, *Das Gebet des Angeklagten im Alten Testament*, BZAW 49 (1928) 17; and especially W. Beyerlin, 96f. The petitioner is persecuted by the adversaries. He flees to the sanctuary, affirms his innocence (with the formulary of an oath of cleansing), and appeals to Yahweh as the righteous judge. The cultic situation is described as follows in 1 Kings 8:31ff.: "If a man sins against his neighbor and is made to take an oath, and comes and swears his oath before thine altar in this house, then hear thou in heaven, and act, and judge thy servants, condemning the guilty by bringing his conduct upon his own head, and vindicating the righteous by rewarding him according to his righteousness." This describes the situation exactly. We would have to assume that the most diverse petitioners at various times entered into this act of God's judgment. And they will have used Psalm 7 as their formulary. When H. Gunkel in his commentary presumes to be able to determine "that in it echo the words of the king," we have to remember that the prayer formularies adopted conceptions and metaphors that transcend every individual destiny (cf. Psalm 3 and the explanations given there). The chronological connections can be arrived at only by deduction. The prayer song probably originated in preexilic times. In many ways it gives the impression of being archaic, and it can be dated very early.

Commentary

[Title] For שִׁגָּיוֹן cf. above, Introduction, §4, No. 6. The explanatory (redactional) reference to the situation providing a recollection of the slander (?) of the Benjaminite Cush is no longer intelligible. This can hardly be a reference to the narrative of 1 Sam. 18:21ff. Very likely the writer of the note that introduces a historical referent has in mind an occurrence not transmitted in the OT. H. Gunkel suggests an unknown legend.

[7:1-2] Against his persecutor the petitioner of our psalm seeks refuge with Yahweh (cf. Ps. 11:1). חסה ב denotes the act of looking for protection and sheltering oneself in the realm of the presence of God. More frequently in the

Psalms we hear of "wings" or the "shadow of the wings" of the cherubim under which the petitioner looking for help flees (e.g., Pss. 57:1; 61:4). On אלהי, cf. O. Eissfeldt, " 'Mein Gott' im Alten Testament," *ZAW* 61 (1945/48) 3-16. The persecuted one asks Yahweh for help—and (as v. 8 will show) for legal help. The enemy of the lamenting writer is compared to a ravenous lion. Such a metaphor illustrates the seriousness of the danger (cf. above, Introduction §10, 4). Like a beast of prey, the persecutor wants to tear the petitioner to pieces. נפש could in this passage have the original meaning "gullet" (H. Schmidt). By means of the depiction of the distress the petitioner wants to persuade Yahweh to intervene. Above all, the reference to complete helplessness is intended to move God to intervene.

[7:3-5] To the pleading complaint is now joined the important oath which the petitioner presents to affirm his innocence. The meaning of the statements of vv. 3-5 is to be grasped by means of a precise form-critical investigation.

In the oath of the innocent the stylization is worth noting in the first place. זאת refers to the accusations brought forward by the persecutor. Then follow two further subordinate clauses introduced by אם, clauses that refer to a possible case of trespass. To these statements of casuistry the self-imprecation is then joined. A passage parallel to this oath of the innocent in vv. 3-5 is found in Job 31. In that passage several items are assembled. The characteristic sentences, introduced by אם, are easily recognized: Job 31:5-8, 9-10, 16-22, 24-28. In Pss. 17:3-4; 26:4-6 the form type clearly recognizable in Psalm 7 and Job 31 is blurred, whereas in Ps. 137:5-6 it appears outside the court area. The procedure for oathtaking customary in the cultus could be imagined as follows: in a difficult court case that cannot be settled, the litigants visit the central sanctuary (Deut. 17:8-10). There an authorized דבר המשפט (Deut. 17:9) or a תורה (11) from the mouth of the priest is awaited. He who declares himself innocent is put under oath: נשא־בן אלה להאלתו (1 Kings 8:31). The cited formulation exactly covers the procedure of the affirmation of innocence and the self-imprecation. This oath of the innocent is taken לפני מזבח (1 Kings 8:31). Very likely this sacral act was accompanied by the symbolic washing of hands and a procession around the altar (Ps. 26:6). On *abiuratio,* cf. F. Horst, "Der Eid im Alten Testament," *EvTh* [1957], Nos. 8/9, 366-384. On the oath of cleansing in the area and organization of the institution of the judgment of God, cf. W. Beyerlin, 96ff.: "The wording of the oath in vv. 3-5 with its parallelisms possesses a solemn poignancy, to be sure; still, in its strict concentration on one thought, it gives the impression of being quite natural. One thing should especially be noted, namely, that in the first of the conditional dependent clauses the object of the accusation is represented by the reflexive demonstrative pronoun זאת: 'If I have done *this* . . .' (3a). Since the preceding verses of the psalm do not reveal what accusation was leveled at the psalmist, only one deduction is possible, namely, that the complaint had been stated expressly before he began to pray" (W. Beyerlin, 97).

In vv. 3-5 the oath of the innocent first refers to accusations made by his persecutor. The specific image in the formula אם־יש־עול בכפי could be understood as the washing of hands (probably) to be undertaken at the time of the oath of cleansing (Ps. 26:6; Isa. 1:15-16). עול in the OT is often the iniquity that stains the hands (1 Sam. 24:12; Isa 1:15; 59:3,6). An insight—at least a brief one—into the misdemeanors with which the petitioner is charged we get at v. 4: the one persecuted is supposed to be guilty of having betrayed a trust. The word שולמי could refer to the person "who keeps the peace of the same house with a person" (H. Schmidt). In this meaning (cf. also Ps. 41:9; Jer. 38:22) the term would be parallel to the word רע. But the betrayal of the trust is now thought to consist of the idea that the accused committed an offense against the property of his friend . חלץ denotes robbery or plunder in a very intensive sense, so that we should have to think of sustained embezzling. But the hands of the petitioner are empty, and he is persecuted without cause (ריקם): this solemn affirmation already sounds through the casuistic formulations of the dependent clauses. In the self-imprecation (v. 5) the accused then declares that he is ready to take on himself the persecution of his enemy and to lose life and honor if the alleged and sworn possible offenses should turn out to be true. On כבוד, cf. Ps. 3:3; on נפש, Ps. 6:3-4.

[7:6-8] The oath of the innocent is obviously the presupposition for the appeal to Yahweh, the judge, which now follows. God is invoked with the three imperatives עורה, הנשא, קומה. The concepts and images of the expressed appeal suggest the thought of the ark of the covenant as the judicial throne of God. The following details should be noted: (1) Yahweh is enthroned as king and judge on the ark (Ps. 99:1; Isa. 6:1ff.; Ps. 94:1ff.), but his majestic presence extends far beyond the cubic space of the holy of holies (Isa. 6:1ff.). As Yahweh is enthroned on earth, so is he also in heaven (Ps. 11:4). Therefore the sanctuary on Zion can be described as "built like the high heavens" (Ps. 78:69; Isa. 2:2-5). Ps. 7:6-7 refers to these conceptions. The God who is present on Zion is the king who is enthroned in heaven—on this, cf. above, Introduction, §10, 1). (2) To this majestic king and judge the peoples are subject. He judges and rules them (Pss. 9:8; 96:10; 98:9; and often). That the God-King who is enthroned above the ark and in heaven is ruler and judge of the world is proclaimed in Jerusalem time and again (cf. above, Introduction §10, 1). To these presuppositions especially Ps. 7:7-8 makes reference. It is unnecessary to detach these conceptions with the picture presented in Ps. 82:1. (3) The ark of the covenant (even after its reception in the Jerusalem temple at the time of Solomon) remained imbued with the traditions of the holy war, into which it was once carried as a palladium (Num. 10:35-36; 1 Sam. 4:3). The God-King enthroned above the ark is and remains the "hero in battle" (Ps. 24:8). Obviously, Ps. 7:6 must be interpreted in connection with these conceptions. The call יהוה קומה is anchored in the old marching orders of the ark in Num. 10:35-36. And the petition for God's wrathful intervention against the enemies (plural!) causes the prayer formula of a king to reecho, in which the king pleads with Yahweh, the hero in battle, to intervene. In sum: the petitioner of Psalm 7 addresses his appeal to Yahweh, the enthroned ruler of the peoples and the hero in war, whose presence above the ark in Jerusalem is a reality.

More strange, and to be distinguished from the traditional conceptions of the ark, is the view hidden behind the address עורה. Sleep is a mythical and ritual state of the deity of vegetation (1 Kings 18:27). עורה is in this religious sphere a cultic wake-up call which calls back to life the numen that has died with the vegetation. It could not be maintained, however, that even a trace of a relevant mythological conception is associated with the call עורה addressed to Yahweh (contrary to G. Widengren, "Sakrales Königtum im Alten Testament und im Judentum," *Franz Delitsch-Vorlesungen* [1952, 1955], 67). The lively mythological background of the nature cult behind the call עורה in Ps. 7:6 is completely dead and gone. The God of Israel "neither slumbers nor sleeps" (Ps. 121:4). The imperative עורה has entered the language of appeals without any mythical specific import of its own.

What does the petitioner with his appeal to Yahweh, the judge, now expect? He hopes for an answer (cf. the appeal in Job 31:35); he waits for Yahweh to "take care of his case" (Ps. 35:23). The answering voice of God could perhaps have the content of Ps. 12:5; indeed, basically it is even a theophany that the appellant with his weighty forms of appeal expects (Ps. 18:7ff.). On הנשׁה, cf. Ps. 94:2; Isa. 33:10. The prayer of the individual here too entirely becomes a part of the traditions of the ark and the theophany that are alive on Zion. These connections are denied by the criticism of those commentators who consider it "presumptuous" and very serious when an individual calls down God's judgment of the world on his enemies (A. Cohen, on the contrary, rightly calls attention to Gen. 18:25). The petitioner makes reference to living cultic traditions and conceptions; he steps into them with the decisive call שׁפטני יהוה כצדקי (v. 8; cf. also Pss. 26:1; 35:24; 43:1). The verb שׁפט unquestionably first points to a judgmental decision. But L. Köhler is right when he incorporates the idea of giving assistance to justice in the concept (*Hebrew Man* [1956] 156ff.). The appellant is sure that his מׁשפט emanates (יצא, Ps. 17:2) from Yahweh. Once more he refers emphatically to his righteousness and innocence in this connection. Under no circumstances does this express a presumptive moral self-qualification. Rather, what is involved is a very concrete declaration of loyalty that has its foundation in the oath of vv. 3-5. The petitioner clings to the innocence (תמי עלי) and righteousness that gird him round and (like a weight) hang over him (cf. Job 27:6).

The psalm petitioner's appeal to his own righteousness has, since the Reformation, become a problem of an acute theological difference. Calvin asserts concerning this problem: "The solution is easy, because this does not treat the question how he should respond if God should demand an explanation of his whole life; but, comparing himself with his enemies, he asserts, not without reason, that he is righteous compared with them" (Ps. 7:8). Luther (on Ps. 7:8), in his *Operationes in Psalmos, 1519-1521*, goes into the theological problem more precisely. He writes: "In the Holy Scriptures my righteousness and God's righteousness are two different things, because the former is each one's own righteousness, by which he is without blame before other people and in his own conscience, although this does not suffice before the judgment of God; the latter, however, is the grace and mercy of God that justifies us before God." In our own time, K. Barth has very thoroughly dealt with the "voice of extraordinary confidence" with which OT petitioners "boast of their own righteousness before God and man" (*CD* 4/1, 570).

There are numerous history-of-religions parallels of an appeal to the gods in the ancient Near East. Thus a person seeking justice prays to Shamash and Adad in the following words: "I offer incense to the image of your great godhead; satiate yourselves with the [aroma of] cedar; may the great gods satiate themselves with [aroma of] cedar as a gift. Be seated to administer justice to me, and let me have justice! At my word, at my lifting up of hands, may there be justice in all I do and in the words I pray!" (Falkenstein and von Soden, *Sumerische und akkadische Hymnen und Gebete* [1953], 278). A prayer for a model offering to Ninurta contains petitions of a priest: "Do not look down [on me], approach and decide the case of justice; accept my pleading and hear my prayer! For all the things I had resolved, provide a decision (for me), so that on the basis of your reliable 'Yes' I may give direction!" (Falkenstein and von Soden, 277). From a prayer to Girka: "You provide the administration of justice for him and her who are deprived of their rights. In my legal case come to me like the warrior Shamash and render jurisdiction in my case and make the decision for me!" (Falkenstein and von Soden, 348). Also in Mesopotamia the person in legal distress waits for a word of the god and for a militant intervention on the part of the divinity, but the dominating factor is the expectation and the granting of an omen at the sacrifice. As for the rest, we will probably have to consider the statements of K. Barth: "The fact that the 'innocence motif' is also found in

Babylonian Psalms finally does not alter in the slightest the fact that in the Psalms of Israel it has its meaning and right and necessity only from Israel's gracious election, on the basis of which God willed to set up and maintain His covenant with Israel'' (*CD* 4/1, 571).

In the affirmation of innocence and righteousness by the petitioners of the psalms of Israel we are not at all dealing with a moral self-qualification, or with what we usually call self-righteousness. Rather, we are dealing with the category "guilty" or "not guilty" that must be rendered as a decision in the institution of divine judgment in view of the concrete accusations brought forward by the accusers and persecutors. In 1 Kings 8:31ff. the situation is clearly distinguished. Everything is decided by the judgment of God, in which Yahweh himself declares "guilty" or "not guilty" (= צדיק). This declaration has an alternative. Therefore if a petitioner declares his innocence, if he considers himself "righteous," then these declarations are formulations that go before the declarative judgment of Yahweh and hasten to meet it. We are here dealing not with the *iustificatio impii* but with the *iustificatio iusti*, in other words, with the fact that God brings to light the righteousness of the righteous against all questioning and temptation. The appropriate NT analogy is given in Rom. 8:31ff.

[7:9] The petition שפטני יהוה is made explicit in v. 9 to the effect that God would make an end of the רשעים but lift up the צדיק. In the OT the decisions of God always end in a concrete act. The evidence of Yahweh's help is produced visibly and palpably. For such a deed the petitioner of the old covenant can credit God. He does it in trust and confidence. The hymnlike formula בחן לבות וכליות (cf. Ps. 17:3; Jer. 17:10) is an element of the "doxology of judgment," in which Yahweh is praised as the righteous judge (F. Horst, "Gottes Recht," *GesStud* [1961], 155-166). God looks into that which is concealed and knows the spirit of man. אלהים צדיק is here an emphatic designation (BrSynt §19c) in which Yahweh's community-directed healing activity is addressed doxologically. On צדיק, cf. G. von Rad, *OT Theol,* 1:379f.

[7:10] This verse also has a doxological and trusting base note. The "shield" is the symbol for the protective legal aid that surrounds the ישרי-לב. If the emendation עלי is correct, we could give the explanation that the petitioner knows that the protective legal aid of the "shield" is already above him and that he awaits its descent.

[7:11] Likewise v. 11 (like the participial formula in v. 9b) would best be understood as an element of the "doxology of judgment." The God who judges is glorified as the legal helper of the צדיק and as the perpetual punitive agent for the רשעים. Such doxologies of judgment distinguish themselves from the pragmatic connection of the events that especially apply to the petitioner; they praise God's authority as judge, which is always valid and unchangeable. These points of view have not been taken into consideration in regard to the numerous conjectures suggested for v. 11. The doxology of judgment basically differs from the experiential sequence, which scholars have tried to reconstruct step by step in Psalm 7 according to psychological viewpoints; it encompasses circumstances which lie beyond the distress of the petitioner but which signify comfort and uplifting certainty to him.[1]

---

1. "But although he does not immediately execute his judgments, yet, as no time passes, yea, not even a day, in which he does not furnish the clearest evidence that he discerns between the righteous and the wicked, notwithstanding the confusion of things in the world, it is certain that he never ceases to execute the office of judge" (Calvin, on Ps. 7:11, trans. Anderson [Grand Rapids: Eerdmans, 1949]).

[7:12-16] After the doxological statement, in which the petitioner looks for comfort and confidence, v. 12 now follows—unusually abruptly—with a reference to the dangerous arming of the enemy. There has been much puzzlement about the meaning of the introductory אִם־לֹא. The wording of an oath cannot be involved—that has rightly been emphasized again and again. But it would be possible for אִם־לֹא to have a secure position in the sacral appeal to justice. Also in Job 31:31 a sentence is introduced with אִם־לֹא in the course of declarations under oath. Obviously, reassuring references to a fact that is important before the court begin with אִם־לֹא. Therefore also v. 12 could be understood as such a "reassuring reference." But the verb יָשׁוּב, which (of course, with certain reservations) has been translated literally, remains a strange item. Did a call for repentance at one time have a place here? (cf. Job 6:29). Or was שׁוּב in this passage once appraised in the sense of v. 17? Every textual criticism that permits itself to be influenced by such considerations must undertake radical and basically indefensible emendations. Now, in any case, v. 12 speaks about the enemy who is lifting his head in a threatening manner. "Sword" (Pss. 37:13f.; 55:21; 57:4; 63:10; 64:3) and "bow" (Pss. 11:2; 37:14; 57:4; 64:3; 120:4) are in his hand. These are כְּלִי־מָוֶת (v. 13) with which the petitioner is threatened. Military pictures and metaphors from the hunting scene illustrate the death-dealing snares of the persecutor in vv. 12-16. Even the fiery arrows (used in sieges) are mentioned (v. 13). Essential for the understanding of the passage vv. 13-16 are above all two questions: (1) How are we to understand it that the hostile undertakings of the persecutor fall back on him himself? (2) How does the petitioner gain the assurance that the enemies bring judgment on themselves with their baseless snares?

1. Vv. 13-16 had earlier been viewed as the expression of a coarse dogma of retribution that had been intensified by OT "legalism." In his essay "Gibt es ein Vergeltungsdogma im AT?" (*ZThK* 52 [1955], 1ff.), K. Koch took issue with this thesis. He begins with the observation that in the OT the idea is prevalent that every evil deed falls back on the doer with dire consequences and that every good deed brings him blessings. The Hebrew language has no term for "punishment." Rather, in the "synthetic view of life" of antiquity, the factors that appear separated in the idea of retribution—"deed/punishment" or "deed/reward"—form a closed unit. Koch speaks of "a sphere of action which creates fate" (cf. also G. von Rad, *OT Theol*, 1:384). This "immanent nemesis" (von Rad) is now integrated with "Yahweh's causality of all things" in the OT. By that process the problem so far addressed by the theme "retribution" turns up in a new appearance. Of course, the question remains whether the wholesale integration of the "area in which deeds influence destiny" into "Yahweh's causality of all things" is not in need of a careful theological description. Just what is the personal reaction of God to the ontological sphere of the "immanent nemesis"? It is instructive and important to hear a number of voices from the history of interpretation regarding this question. Luther declares: "This is the incomprehensible manner of divine judgment, that God does not catch the wicked except properly in their own scheme and leads them to the ruin they have themselves devised" (WA 5; 246, 26f.). In Calvin we find the statements: ". . . By the wondrous providence of God things have been turned to the opposite goal"; "by the hidden governance of his hand, God turns it back on their own heads." And, finally, Franz Delitsch reminds us of God's "giving them up" (Rom. 1:24) with his definition "sin's self-punishment." All these

theological qualifications will have to be taken into consideration in studying the statements of the text in vv. 13-16.

2. But how did the petitioner of Psalm 7 arrive at the conviction that the evil persecution of his enemy falls back upon him with dire consequences? H. Schmidt conjectures that vv. 12-16 are an integral part of a song of thanksgiving appearing in v. 17. In that case, the event of God's gracious turning to the praying petitioner would have to be stated between vv. 11 and 12. That is hardly possible. We would also have to ask whether Schmidt's inclusion of v. 12 (with heavy conjectures) is justified. According to the interpretation given above, v. 12 would be understood as an affirming reference to the dangerous attack of the enemies. The break would therefore have to be made between vv. 12 and 13.

Of course, against this whole interpretation it must be said that v. 17 is to be thought of not as a definitive song of thanksgiving but as a "vow of thanksgiving" ("I will praise Yahweh . . ."). In that case, vv. 13-16 would have to be understood as statements of a dauntless certainty, and this certainty again would have its foundation in the words of the doxology of v. 11, uplifted above all legal problems. Such an interpretation would, moreover, also be defensible if v. 17 were to be understood as a "verse of thanksgiving" (as it were, as an appendix to the words of dauntless certainty in vv. 13-16).

The conceptions of vv. 14-15 are found in the OT also outside Psalm 7. For v. 14, cf. Job 15:35; Isa. 59:4. The picture of the pit into which the digger himself falls is taken from the hunter's life. The hunter tries to catch game in a pit. Finally, in v. 16, we will have to imagine a stone hurled aloft as falling back on the head of the hurler (Prov. 26:27; Sir. 27:25). Behind all the statements and pictures lies the conviction that the built-in nemesis will let dire consequences result in return as the deed of the persecutor had planned them.

[7:17] In its cohortative formulation, v. 17 is to be thought of as a "vow of praise" (see above, "Form"). The thanksgiving as it is expressed in the *todah* formulations is not executed as yet but is announced for the future (F. Crüsemann, see above).

wdu here has the meaning "legal aid," "bestowal of salvation" (Calvin on Ps. 7:17). And כ expresses the agreement (BrSynt §109c). But תודה, which we translated "praise," really means "confess," "aver"; the verb most often refers to a specific demonstration of salvation (G. von Rad, *OT Theol* 1:357). עליון is a designation of God that in Jerusalem had a traditional meaning and very likely goes back to pre-Israelite, ancient Canaanite times (cf. also Gen. 14:18; Pss. 47:2; 78:35; and often). H. Schmidt thinks of the "high-towering God" (1 Chron. 21:16), of the אל of the holy rock of Jerusalem (*Der heilige Fels in Jerusalem,* 1933, 86). Still, extrabiblical sources point to a divinity that was common as the "Baal of heaven" everywhere in the Syrian-Canaanite area, especially in Phoenicia. Under the name אל־עליון a locally confined numen could rise to the realm of the great universal divinities and in its worship be identified with the God of heaven (O. Eissfeldt, *ZAW* 57 [1939], 3ff.). In the OT עליון is an honorific appellation of Yahweh that has an archaic-hymnic quality. Very likely this designation comes from pre-Davidic Jerusalem (H. Schmid, "Jahwe und die Kulttradition von Jerusalem," *ZAW* 68 [1955], 168ff.).

Purpose and Thrust

1. The petitioner of Psalm 7, in need of justice, looks for refuge with Yahweh (vv. 1ff.). The God of Israel is a God of justice, to the area of whose presence persecuted and defamed people may flee and seek shelter.

2. To look for refuge with Yahweh in times of need for justice means to throw oneself upon his dominion "for good or evil." The oath of the innocent, with its self-imprecations, is a sign of such complete surrender.

3. The persecuted person calls to the judge of the world in his need for justice. But the judge of the world looks after every single person. The doxology of justice honors him as the righteous God, who always intervenes effectively. The petitioner is certain that Yahweh helps.

4. The statements that lead to the verse of thanksgiving (vv. 13-16) give expression to the bold certainty that the enemy is already judged.

The question is repeatedly asked of the significance the OT affirmations of innocence still have in the NT community. Has not the sacral institution of an appeal to the judgment of God that was customary in the cultus been completely superseded? Is not the Christian's entire need for justice given a completely new orientation by means of the judgment spoken at the cross of Jesus Christ? (cf. 1 Cor. 6:7). It is instructive at this point to consult the interpretation of the Reformers. But the basic point to be interpreted will be this: In the prayer songs such as Psalm 7 we are not concerned with the "justification of the sinner" but with the "justification of the righteous"; in other words, that God brings to light the righteousness of the righteous against all questioning and temptation (cf. Rom. 8:31ff.). In this area Psalm 7 is of lasting importance and can become a prayer formulary for Christians.

Luther recognizes the importance of Psalm 7 in that (1) every Christian must under all circumstances fight for truth and justice and may therefore not withdraw as a sufferer. (2) It will be an urgent task in theology and church to settle—polemically, if necessary—the question about guilt and innocence. On the first point, Luther writes: "Thus we see that it is not enough that if someone suffers for a just cause or for the truth, he commits the matter to God and is ready to yield and to be turned to dust together with his glory, but he should diligently pray that God judge and justify the cause of the truth, not for the petitioner's own advantage, but for the service of God and the salvation of the people; for their salvation is not without danger nor without your culpability if on account of stupid humility you do not most solicitously pray for the preservation and restoration of truth and justice. For you should not only take care how humble and dejected you can be and to what extent the people are alienated from the truth and from justice and may be ensnared by lies and wickedness" (WA 5; 233, 26ff.). On the second point Luther, in his interpretation of Psalm 7, very emphatically refers to 1 Cor. 4:2ff. The apostle Paul affirms his innocence. Then we read on Psalm 7: "Such fear and humility are necessary today too because we are fighting for the soundness of theology and the power of the church." "We must pray that the truth may triumph" (WA 5; 227, 28ff.).

Psalm 8

The Glory of the Creator
and the Dignity of Human Beings

Literature

P. S. Fair, "De genuina lectione Ps. 8:2," *Bibl* 23 (1942) 318-322. J. Lindblom, "Bemerkungen zu den Psalmen I," *ZAW* 60 (1943) 1-13. P. A. H. de Boer, "Jahu's Ordination of Heaven and Earth. An Essay on Psalm VIII," *OTS* 2 (1943) 171-198. L. Köhler, "Psalm 8:5," *ThZ* Basel 1 (1945) 77f. J. Morgenstern, "Psalm 8 and 19A," *HUCA* 19 (1945/46) 491-523. C. Louis, *The Theology of Psalm VIII* (1946). J. J. Koopmans, "Psalm 8," *ThT* 3 (1948) 1-10. Th. C. Vriezen, "Psalm 8,2 en 3," *ThT* 3 (1948) 11-15. S. Mowinckel, "Metrischer Aufbau und Textkritik an Ps 8 illustriert," *Studia Orientalia Joanni Pedersen . . . dicata* (1953) 250-262. A. Deissler, "Zur Datierung und Situierung der 'kosmischen Hymnen' Ps. 8; 19; 29," *Lex tua Veritas: Festschr. f. H. Junker* (1961) 47-58. J. Hempel, "Mensch und König: Studie zu Psalm 8 und Hiob," *FuF* 35 (1961) 119-123. C. Schedl, "Psalm 8 in ugaritischer Sicht," *FuF* 38 (1964) 183-185. M. Tanner, "Ps 8,1-2: Studies in Texts," *Theology* 69 (London, 1966) 492-496. J. L. Koole, "Bijbelstudie over Psalm 8," *GThT* 66 (1966) 1-8. J. A. Soggin, "Salmo 8,3: Osservazioni filologico-esegetiche," *Bibl* 47 (1966) 420-424. H. Graf Reventlow, "Der Psalm 8," *Poetica* I (1967) 304-332. O. Loretz, *Die Gottebenbildlichkeit des Menschen* (1967). B. S. Childs, "Psalm 8 in the Context of the Christian Canon," *Interp.* 22 (1968) 20-31. A. Gelston, "A Sidelight on the 'Son of Man,' " *SJTh* 21 (1968) 189-196. W. H. Schmidt, "Gott und Mensch in Ps. 8: Form- und überlieferungsgeschichtliche Erwägungen," *ThZ* 25 (1969) 1-15. R. Martin-Achard, "Remarques sur le psaume 8. A propos de l'hymnologie israélite: Approche des Psaumes," *CTh* 60 (1969) 71-85. J. A. Soggin, "Zum achten Psalm," *ASTI* 8 (1970/71) 106-122. E. Otto, "Der Mensch als Geschöpf und Bild Gottes in Ägypten," *Probleme bibl. Theologie: G. von Rad zum 70. Geburtstag* (1971) 335-348. R. Tournay, "Le Psaume VIII et la doctrine biblique du nom," *RB* 78 (1971) 18-30. V. Hamp, "Psalm 8, 2b.3," *BZ* NF 16 (1972) 115-120. H. Ringgren, "Psalm 8 och kristologien," *SEÅ* 37/38 (1972/73) 16-20. J. du Preez, "Bible Study on Psalm 8: A Prayer of Praise on the Glory and Greatness of God," *NGTT* 14 (1973) 206-213. K. Gouders, "Gottes Schöpfung und der Auftrag des Menschen," *BiLe* 14 (1973) 164-180. W. Beyerlin, "Psalm 8: Chancen der Überlieferungskritik," *ZThK* 73 (1976) 1-22. W. Rudolph, "Aus dem Munde der jungen Kinder und Säuglinge . . ." (Ps. 8:3), *Beiträge zur alttestamentlichen Theologie: Festschrift W. Zimmerli* (1977) 388-396.

Text

To the choirmaster. According to The Gittith. A psalm of David.

8:1 O Yahweh, our Lord, how glorious is your name in all the
world!
You who have 'laid'[a] your splendor on the heavens.

2 From the mouths of children and infants
you have built up a bulwark
because of[b] your foes, to put an end
to the enemy and the avenger.

3 When I behold your heavens,[c] the work of your fingers,
the moon and the stars that you have placed there,

4 —what is man that you think of him,
and the son of man, that you take care of him!

5 You made him a little lower than heavenly beings
and did crown him with honor and glory.

6 You appointed him ruler over the work of your hands,
everything you laid at his feet:

7 sheep and oxen altogether
and also the beasts of the field,

8 the birds of the heavens and the fish of the sea
—whatever traverses the ways of the waters.[d]

9 O Yahweh, our Lord, how glorious is your name in all the
world!

1a MT אשר תנה = "which give" is possible neither syntactically nor according to sense. Gk proposes the text ὅτι ἐπήρθη. Starting with this Greek verb, people have made efforts at conjecturing the Hebrew text and, among other things, settled on a verb תנה = "praise in song." But these attempts remain problematical. Here ("you who have laid") Syr and Targ have read נָתַתָּה—perhaps even the short form תַּתָּ(2 Sam. 22:41), which could have been the reason for a copyist's error to תנה. The version in Jerome, Syr, and Targ without doubt has the best foundation, especially since the much criticized אשר at the beginning of the sentence can serve as the continuation of the hymnic description (Pss. 84:3; 95:9; 115:8; 129:6; 135:10; 146:5). Other emendations: נְתַן (Lindblom), נָתְנָ (Weiser). Doubtful in view of the refrain confirmed by v. 9 is every emendation that cuts off הארץ־ בכל and then forms a new parallel member with a corrected v. 1b: among others, אַדַּרְתֶּךָ בכל־הארץ. Worth mentioning would be the possibility that תנה has been exchanged for the יסדת of v. 2, for עז הנה is documented, for instance, in Ps. 86:16, while יסדת could easily be inserted in v. 1b. The problems of textual criticism were taken up anew by H. Donner (*ZAW* 79 [1967], 324ff.). Donner rejects the possibility of explaining תנה with a reference to the Ugaritic verb *tny* ("whose glory is praised in the sky"). He concurs in B. Duhm's brilliant conjecture, אשרה נה ("I will sing the praises of . . ."), but goes even further in his conjecture (326f.). A summary of the wealth of suggestions for emendation of Ps. 8:1 is given in F. Crüsemann, *Studien zur Formgeschichte von Hymnus und Danklied in Israel*, WMANT 32 (1969) 289 A.2 (cf. also V. Hamp and W. Schmid).
2b למען צורריך is most often deleted as a secondary addition. But by that operation a half-verse is torn from the organization of the sentence. This disturbance should hardly be compensated for by further reduction of the text (elimination of ויונקים and עז). For the connection עוללים ויונקים, cf. 1 Sam. 15:3; 22:19; Jer. 44:7; Lam. 2:11. It will hardly be possible to clear up the flow of the text without encroachments. A possibility would be the transposition למען השבית צוררי; then two 5-pulse meters would result.
3c Gk has τοὺς οὐρανούς. The suffix is missing in Gk; thus the text is smoothed out.
8d Considering the parallelism of members and the usual variation, we should have to read מָיִם instead of ימים.

Form

There is no one obvious solution to the textual difficulties in vv. 1 and 2. Text-critical and metrical problems are mutually intertwined and make the decision difficult. In any case, we can hardly bypass the fact that the refrain of v. 9 stands in need of its own metrical version in v. 2. A suitable explanation could be given with the metrical unit 2 + 2 + 2 (cf. Ps. 1:1). V. 1b would then have to be thought of as a free-standing 4-unit meter. For v. 2, cf. textual note **b**; but one would still have to exercise restraint. V. 3 could be read as a double 4-unit meter, while double triple meters determine the metrical scheme of vv. 4-7. In v. 8 we have the metrical scheme 4 + 3, and in v. 9 (as in v. 1a), 2 + 2 + 2. In view of the whole, this is a very uneven and agitated picture of the form of Psalm 8. Perhaps the metrical variations may be attributed to the antiphonal singing that prevails in the song (see below). For the problems of parallelism and meter, with an attempt at a new solution, cf. H. Reventlow, 311ff.

Psalm 8 belongs to the group songs of praise (תהלה), on which cf. above, Introduction §6, 1. Still the distinctiveness of the psalm is to be grasped more precisely. The song of praise is entirely formed and molded by addressing Yahweh in the second person. This hymnic style of direct address is relatively rare (cf. Exod. 15:1-18) and, according to H. Gunkel, first penetrated the Israelite hymn only at a late time (Gunkel and Begrich, *EinlPs 47*). At any rate, the real principal subject of the psalm can be called "hymn of an individual" (F. Crüsemann, *Studien zur Formgeschichte von Hymnus und Danklied,* 294f.). This song of praise of an individual is framed by a choral refrain (vv. 1a and 9), so that a cultic antiphonal song may have been at the base of it. But in the "hymn of the individual" the rhetorical question (v. 4) forms the center.

In more recent times exegetes have become more and more aware of the various elements of form of Psalm 8, thus, among others, of the elements of lament and thanksgiving (H. Reventlow, 310f. and 330), but also features of wisdom (W. H. Schmid, 9f.). The "purity of form" so highly rated by H. Gunkel as a criterion of authenticity certainly is not present. Still, the basic hymnic aspect is hardly in doubt. At the same time, we should take note of the wisdom characteristics recognized by W. H. Schmidt. Thematically, Psalm 90 is parallel to Psalm 8. The rhetorical question "What is man?!" (Ps. 8:4) should certainly be understood to be an exclamation of amazement, but it could also be understood in the light of the prayer expressed in Ps. 90:12: "Teach us that we may get a heart of wisdom!" Wisdom reflects the mystery of the greatness and frailty of man. That is its theme. As a parallel thematic exposition to Psalm 8, Sir. 17:2ff. could be quoted. In both texts we have reflections of Gen. 1:26ff. Still, we ought to hold on to the form classification: Psalm 8 is a song of praise of an individual framed by choral verses (refrain).

Setting

This determination of form makes it obvious that we assume a cultic "Sitz im Leben." We might think of a festival at night, in the course of which the song of praise was intoned antiphonally. For such worship at night, cf. Ps. 134:1; Isa. 30:29; 1 Chron. 9:33. But also a number of other considerations are necessary; they have to do with the dating of the psalm. J. Hempel is of the opinion that Psalm 8 is based on a Canaanite song that was sung by the royal representative of the cultic congregation (perhaps in honor of Hadad) but was then in Israel applied to man. This explanation is an attempt to air the mystery of the (archaic) "royal ideology" that darts forth from Psalm 8. But, in the first place, there should be no doubt that Psalm 8 has reference to Gen. 1:26ff. In its text the psalm is later than Gen. 1:26ff.; thus, e.g., the address אדנינו (vv. 1, 9) occurs only in postexilic times (Neh. 10:30; Pss. 135:5; 147:5). Also all observations regarding form and theme point to a relatively late time. But this dating does not preclude the fact that older elements in the history of tradition come into play in Psalm 8 (W. H. Schmidt, 12A.25). This is a phenomenon worth noting, one, e.g., that is also observed in the interpretation of the book of Daniel: old, Canaanite (Ugaritic) traditions turn up in later times (cf. also the conception of God in Daniel 7). On the questions concerning the history of tradition, particularly those concerning the criticism of transmission, cf. W. Beyerlin, *ZThK* 73 (1976) 1ff. This investigation opens up the entire set of problems.

But how is the (cultic) situation of the psalm to be understood in relation to these statements? "No trace of a specific, unchangeable situation, the experience of which could be the basis of Psalm 8, is now discernible. The 'I' . . . is not to be thought of as biographical" (W. H. Schmidt, 9). Therefore an "exemplary I" would have to be assumed as the one who raises his voice in a song of praise, framed by the choral song of the congregation. The statement of this "exemplary I" is characterized by wisdom reflections which, while making cautious use of old traditions," principally refer to Gen. 1:26ff. And here it would easily be conceivable that we have in Psalm 8 a song that had its "Sitz im Leben" in the worship of the postexilic sanctuary. To be sure, even now the "I" which raises its voices in Psalm 8 should be defined precisely in such a way that it has reference to an "archetypal I" as the (cultic) representative of the first-created, the primeval man (*Urmensch*).

Commentary

[Title] The title provides (redactional) directions and explanations which, among other things, have to do with cultic technicalities. On למנצח, cf. above, Introduction §4, No. 17. On על־הגתית, cf. above §4, No. 23. On מזמור לדוד, cf. §4, No. 2.

[8:1] Yahweh is called אדנינו by the singing congregation. "Our lord" is in the OT a characteristic address for the king (1 Kings 1:11, 43, 47). In Ps. 97:5 the God-king Yahweh is called אדון כל־הארץ. Pss. 135:5 and 147:5 speak of his greatness and might. The Lord of Israel is Lord of creation (cf. above, Introduction §10, 1). He is the universal ruler (Ps. 2:4). Accordingly, Psalm 8 does not treat of the glory of creation but of the glory of the Lord of Israel, the Lord of all things created. שם preserves the exclusiveness of his might and thereby also the uniqueness of the revelation of glory which in the self-presentation to Israel had become the basis of the knowledge of God. In its majestic greatness the name of the Lord of Israel comes into prominence in all the world. In astonishment and amazement, the hymn establishes the immeasurable power of the God who has decided to make the chosen people the realm of his rule. The self-presentation of Yahweh in Israel (Ps. 76:1) makes possible the recognition of his self-representation in the whole creation. That is because the name as the embodiment of the revelation and presence of Yahweh in his people decodes the mystery of the creation (cf. also R. Tournay).[1]

---

1. "For the name of God is the name of the Lord of all life. To hear his voice is to be confronted

Corresponding to "the world" (אֶרֶץ), in which the glory of the name radiates, there are (in the parallelism) שָׁמַיִם, the heavens, on which the brightness of God is reflected. For the interpretation of these statements of choral verse, cf. Pss. 104:1f. and 19:1 (cf. the commentary).

This glorification of the God of Israel as the Lord and Creator of all the world will have to be understood as resulting, not from a certain spontaneous "festival enthusiasm" (thus H. Schmidt), but from certain given cultic data. The "Yahweh Sebaoth" who is present and appears in a theophany is in the liturgical tradition of the Jerusalem temple celebrated as the king of all worlds: Isa. 6:3; Psalm 99 (cf. above Introduction §10, 1). This expansion of the divine area of rule has a history-of-religions parallel in the elevation of certain local numina to the highest gods in heaven and kings of creation. Even if a divinity has but little importance, this elevation and expansion can take place. So, for instance, the weather god Ishkur could be addressed in song in an ancient Sumerian hymn as follows: "Father Ishkur, Lord, you who ride on a storm wind, your name extends to the end of heaven. Father Ishkur, you who ride on a great storm wind, your name extends to the end of heaven" (Falkenstein and von Soden, *Sumerische und akkadische Hymnen und Gebete* [1953], 81).

[8:2] But now, what is the meaning of v. 2? The content of this verse is in the OT without even the remotest parallel passage. Therefore it does not surprise us when this statement is regarded as strange, sometimes even as a foreign element. But all emendations are of no avail. We must hazard an interpretation. מִפִּי will in the context of the hymn have to be considered a brachylogy—and that in the sense of "from the praise of the mouth . . .." But here questions begin to rise: Did children sing along in this song of praise? Or does the singer have something like a parable, or even an episodic conception, in mind? These possibilities can only be suggested, for every attempt to delineate them ends in a tortuous interpretation. But certainly we may subscribe to the trend of the statement with Gunkel: God "performs his great deeds through apparently insufficient means, so that his power may be revealed all the more plainly" (cf. 1 Cor. 1:27).[2] But what do the great things consist of that God accomplishes through the mouths of children? Out of the stammering praise of the children Yahweh builds a bulwark, erects a lasting power, that is directed against the enemies of God and puts an end to them. Here we can adduce as explanation two conceptions from the Psalter: (1) The presence of despisers and enemies of God is in the creation hymns perceived as a piercing cacophany. And how can there be room in the radiant realm of God's lordship for the sinister nonbeing of self-willed, anarchic godless

by the decision which has been taken on life as a whole, and by which it is determined and ruled in both its aspects. And to hear God and to assent to this fulfilled decision is to be forced to recognize the goodness of existence as determined and ruled by him" (K. Barth, *Church Dogmatics*, 3/1, 379).

2. "The meaning, therefore, is, that God, in order to commend his providence, has no need of the powerful eloquence of rhetoricians nor even of distinct and formed language, because the tongues of infants, although they do not as yet speak, are ready and eloquent enough to celebrate it." "And when he not only introduces babes as witnesses and preachers of God's glory, but also attributes *mature strength* to their mouth, the expression is very emphatic. It means the same thing as if he had said, These are invincible champions of God who, when it comes to the conflict, can easily scatter and discomfit the whole host of the wicked despisers of God, . . . We should observe against whom he imposes on infants the office of defending the glory of God, namely, against the hardened despisers of God, who dare to rise up against heaven to make war upon God, as the poets have said, in olden times, of the giants" (Calvin, on Ps. 8:2, trans. Anderson [Grand Rapids: Eerdmans, 1949])."

creatures? Cf. Ps. 104:35. The enemies are burned up by God's majestic beam of fire (Ps. 97:3, 4). This theme, "the end of all anarchy in God's realm of creation," is worthy of our attention. (2) But it is characteristic that in Psalm 8 the termination of all enmity in God's creation is by way of the mouth of children. By this path Yahweh erects עֹז. In Ps. 86: 16-17 an individual petitioner prays that God may give him עֹז in the contest against his enemies that the foe may be put to shame and be defeated. The final overcoming of all enemies through the intervention of God therefore has its hidden antecedents in the deliverance that Yahweh bestows on individual petitioners.

Thus also that bulwark which Yahweh erects by means of the praise of children would be such a hidden prelude to the final defeat of the enemies—of course, a prelude that has long sounded forth and produced its effects.

It still remains true that the statement of v. 2 is unique in the OT. Perhaps we may assume that wisdom reflection was involved here and wanted to show that and how the power of the enemies is broken by the voice of weak children. In Matt. 21:16 the verse is quoted and applied to the praise of the children.

[8:3-4] Beginning at v. 3, the voice of a single singer, who looks up into the sparkling Near Eastern starry heaven, is raised. It is God's heaven of which he sings (for the suffix, cf. Pss. 20:6; 115:16; 144:5; Lam. 3:66). In this area no other power has room or right of possession. Yahweh has created heaven (Pss. 33:6; 95:5; 102:25; 136:5). It is "the work of his fingers," i.e., all of it bears the "personal mark" of God's creating and working. The constellations have been "placed there" (כוננתה) and fixed in the vault of heaven. Gen. 1:17: הרמים ברקיע . . . ויתן. Isa. 40:26: ברא אלה. But now the singer does not linger even for a moment to behold the beaming sky. The כי at the beginning of the verse already announces that the hymn is hastening on to a perception that is gained through contemplation of the huge noctural vault. But in place of the consecutive clause "I must exclaim," usually expected after the introductory כי, we have the exclamation itself, introduced by the astonished מה. In the vast expanse of the creation that witnesses to God's glory and greatness, the singer becomes conscious of the utter depths of his being as a human. Yet, as the creative power of God is in all the world revealed only through the medium of the greatness of the revelation of the שם (v. 1), so the psalmist recognizes the mystery and wonder of human existence in the certainty taken to heart from God's self-revelation: "He thinks of me (זכר); he takes care of me" (פקד). Accordingly, it is not a relation immanent in the world through which the essence of the human being is prevailed on in spontaneously seized, intuitive recognition.[3] That God bends down to man and provides him with the certainty of God's goodwill to him—this fact under the starry sky as the witness to the immeasurable greatness of God opens up the profound mystery of human life. אנוש often carries the connotation of a frail, impotent being (Pss. 9:20; 90:3; 103:14), and בן־אדם designates the earthborn (אדמה), earthbound human nature in the sense of its characteristic property (for this meaning of בן, cf. BrSynt §74c). The weak human being, lost under the lofty heaven of God is incomprehensibly the

---

3. "It is therefore a sublime wonder that man—who, by himself and in the eyes of all forsaken, hopeless, godforsaken, thinks of nothing less than that God should remember him—is actually remembered by God. And the heart of man ought to and can receive and believe this, that God is agreeable, propitious, pleasant, although he thinks of him only as angry, terrible, and unbearable. Who would not be amazed? Who would not say: 'What is man that you think of him?' The works of God are incomprehensible except through faith" (Luther, WA 5; 270, 17ff.).

pardoned, accepted human being (Ps. 144:3; also cf. Job 7:17; 14:3). But the fact that God "thinks of" (זכר) human existence and "takes care of" it (פקד) is grounded in a long-standing and ever-valid act of the Creator.

[8:5] About this deed vv. 5-6 sing. The psalmist reminds himself of a basic arrangement of God, according to which human beings have their place in creation מעט מאלהים. Curiously enough, the point of comparison for frail human existence in the lost depths below heaven is the lofty heavenly beings. Because the psalmist addresses Yahweh (v. 1) (but also in view of the plural summons "let us . . .," with which God in Gen. 1:26, at the creation of human beings, links himself together with the אלהים-beings), we will presumably have to translate אלהים with "divine beings," "heavenly beings." Gk translates אלהים logically with ἄγγελοι (also cf. Heb. 2:5, 7). The meaning therefore is: human beings have their station, given to them by God in creation, immediately below the heavenly beings that surround Yahweh's royal throne (1 Kings 22:19; Job 1:6; Isa. 6:1-3). They are created—to use OT terminology—like Elohim (G. von Rad, *OT Theol*, 1: 146). Radiant splendor (כבוד) and majestic honor (הדר) rest on them like a crown (עטר). כבוד והדר are the marks of the king (Ps. 21:5). From this (but also from the epithet "Lord" in v. 6) A. Bentzen urges the conclusion that our psalm has to do with the "primal king" and "primal man" in the sense of a sacral king ideology (*Messias—Moses redivivus—Menschensohn*, ATANT 17 [1948], 12. 39). But it is also said of God himself that he appears in כבוד והדר (Pss. 29:1; 104:1). Accordingly, the song is to be about the royal and divine grandeur that rests on human beings. The little, frail human being (v. 4) belongs to God's world according to Yahweh's determination and arrangement. As the glorious name of God becomes manifest on earth and God's grandeur illuminates heaven, so also from the human being as the one allied to the אלהים-world the radiant majesty of God emerges. In the creation, the *theatrum gloriae Dei* (Calvin), in which everything shines and sparkles, the lowly human being is no exception.

[8:6] On the contrary: even the dominion over all the works of the Creator is assigned to the human being. With emphasis the second half-verse says: everything (הכל, cf. Isa. 44:24; Eccles. 3:1) has been laid at the feet of the human being (like booty). The Creator and world ruler Yahweh assigns the world to the human being as to a king installed by God (cf. Ps. 2:8). And yet the scope of the rule of the human being is markedly distinguished from that of a royal regent. The king has peoples and enemies of the historical area subjected to him (Ps. 110:1); man has animals subordinated to him (Gen. 1:28ff.). Here no "sacral king ideology" is unfolded, but the hidden backgrounds of everyday human life are revealed. The shepherding and the slaughtering of animals, the hunting and catching of wild game and fish is a sovereign right emanating from God by which the superiority of the human being over all created things—even more, their אלהים-stature—is revealed.[4]

If the text before us in vv. 5-6 is interpreted in the manner in which we have just done it, then every reference to the so-called "royal ideology" has rightly been

---

4. "It is certainly a singular honor, and one which cannot be sufficiently estimated, that mortal man, as the representative of God, has dominion over the world, as if it pertained to him by right, and that to whatever quarter he turns his eyes, he sees nothing wanting which may contribute to the convenience and happiness of his life" (Calvin on Ps. 8:6, trans. Anderson).

eliminated. It is the human being that is being dealt with (v. 4). And yet this human being who raises his voice in Psalm 8 is the representative of the first created human being (Gen. 1:16ff.). He is the archetypal man, the primal man. We cannot deny that the background perspective of the history of the tradition of Psalm 8 makes room for the appearance of conceptions of an ancient Near Eastern "royal ideology." Even though the verb "tocrown" (v. 5) does not have to be taken in the strict sense, still the concepts כבוד and הדר refer to the context of the language of the ancient Near Eastern king's court (Pss. 21:5; 110:1). Even more important and pregnant with connections is the fact that in ancient Egyptian texts the king was thought of and celebrated as the image of God. Thus the *imago Dei* theology that gains expression in Psalm 8 (in analogy to Gen 1:26ff.) is referred to the history-of-religions context of ancient Egyptian conceptions of royalty. H. Wildberger above all called attention to this ("Das Abbild Gottes," *ThZ* 21 [1965], 245-259, 481-501). On a stela of King Amenhotep II of Amada, the Pharaoh is praised as "the beloved physical son of Re, lord of foreign lands . . . beneficient god, the creation of Re, the lord, who came from the body already strong; the image of Horus on the throne of his father; great in power . . . " (quoted by H. Wildberger, 485). Formerly there was no documentation for the fact that the king bore the name "image of God." Now we know that since the 17th century B.C.the Pharaoh was considered the image of the creator and sun god—all the way to Hellenistic times. The following idioms are common: "Image of Re, Amon, Atum"; "holy image"; "living image on earth" (cf. W. H. Schmidt, *Alttestamentlicher Glaube in seiner Geschichte* [1975], 195f.). The Egyptian parallels are deserving of an entirely new consideration (cf. E. Otto, "Der Mensch als Geschöpf und Bild Gottes in Ägypten," *Probleme biblischer Theologie: G. von Rad zum 70. Geburtstag* [1971], 335-348). For an explanation, the ancient Near Eastern "royal ideology" moves closer to the OT texts, especially to Psalm 8. Thus one could certainly come to the following reflection: "The exalted position of the human being reveals itself in his lordship over the entire animal kingdom (vv. 6ff.). Even this statement does not completely lie outside ancient Near Eastern 'royal ideology'; for even power over nature can be ascribed to the king (cf. Jer. 27:6; 28:14). Accordingly, it is not necessary to consider that Psalm 8, in the 'democratization' of the royal dignity, transferred the sphere of influence from the world of human beings to the animal kingdom; perhaps it merely narrowed down existing conceptions" (W. H. Schmidt, "Gott und Mensch in Ps. 8:12"). But probably we ought to eliminate entirely the concept "democratization," for what is obviously at stake is the reception and integration of royal conceptions into the picture of the first-created human being, the primal human being. Here the relationships were close in any case ("primal man and king"). It is significant how carefully and circumspectly the royal depictions and concepts are included in Psalm 8—and yet are expressed in such a way that they serve to express the glory of the primal human being. Therefore it is highly appropriate to distinguish between the interpretation of the psalm in the text as we have it and the method of analysis and tradition-historical findings that rest on inference.

[8:7-8] In vv. 7-8 "the psalmist examines with elation the area of human jurisdiction, similar to the king's singer" (Gunkel). צנה designates a herd of small livestock; אלפים originally means oxen that are serviceable to human beings, and here it surely refers to large cattle (G. Dalman, *AuS* 6, 172). כלם, as an all-embracing generalization, wants to have us understand both groups of domesticated animals previously named. But not only in the area of house and home are animals subservient to human beings. Also the "beasts of the field" belong to this area of rule. גם clearly points beyond the group named in the first half-verse and probably refers to all animal life beyond the areas of human dwelling and pasturage (with the exception of birds and fish, which are mentioned in v. 8). Instead of בהמה after גם one would really expect חית השדה (Gen. 1:24; 2:20; 3:14; and often), but for בהמות השדה in a comprehensive plural, cf. Joel 1:20; 2:22. And more and more is the area of human power

expanded: also the birds and the fish belong to it. In connection with מים עבר
ארחות we should probably think of the large sea animals which in the ancient
world had about them the nimbus of invincibility.

[8:9] In reference to v. 9 the only question now is why v. 1 is not cited in its
entirety. Refrains that consist of more than one member are otherwise repeated
in their entirety (cf. Pss. 24:7-10; 46:3,7,11; 67:3,5; 80:3,7,(14),19; 99:5,9). E.
Baumann is probably right when he points to the fact that the abbreviated
repetition is inherent in the train of thought of the psalm: ''The thoughts of the
psalmist in vv. 2-8 essentially deal only with the earth'' (cf. on the contrary,
e.g., Psalm 148; E. Baumann, ''Struktur-Untersuchungen im Psalter I,'' *ZAW*
61 [1945/48], 116-125).

Purpose and Thrust

Psalm 8 deals with the glory of the Creator and the dignity of the human being.
The hymn sings first about the manifest self-presentation of the name of God in
all the world, so that the mystery and wonder of human existence may come into
prominence in marvelous contemplation. In general, we ought to notice that the
entire song of praise exhibits the marks of wondering awareness (cf. מה in vv.
1 and 5). In the adoration, life-determining perceptions are revealed. The world
and the human being are permeated by the radiating power of divine creation and
ordaining. Yet the insight into this permeation awakens in the event of the
revelation of salvation, in which Yahweh as אדנינו has come to meet Israel in a
self-presentation by name and in which at the same time he turns (זכר and פקד)
to each individual human being.

But how are these great expressions of the dignity of the human being in vv. 5-8
to be understood? Here we have the pivotal question of the interpretation of our
hymn. In this commentary, Franz Delitsch very pointedly asked whether those
are really valid assessments that are expressed in vv. 5-8; whether, rather, some
brokenness (Genesis 3), in which the dignity of the human being has been
perverted, would not in all seriousness have to be considered. It is strange: the
guilt of the human being comes into the picture of the hymn of Psalm 8 as little
as it does in the story of creation in chapter 1 of Genesis. And it would only be
a monumental mistake to speak, in the language of traditional dogmatics, of an
''original state'' to which the hymn and the doctrine look back. Rather,
everything that is said in Genesis 1 and Psalm 8 about the dignity of the human
being is a reference to the absolutely valid and irrevocable ordaining of God (for
the continued effectiveness of the אלהים-figure, cf. Gen. 5:3; 9:6b). Where
Yahweh in his שם steps forth from obscurity, where he is praised as אדנינו, and
where finally he ''thinks of'' the human being and ''takes care of him,'' there the
miracle of human existence—which, regarding guilt made no sense but now
comes to be quite determinative—is recognized with amazement. Human beings
belong to God's world. God has blessed them with incomprehensible rights to
rule, and they are crowned with honor and glory. In Heb. 2:5 these things are
applied to the world to come (τὴν οἰκουμένην τὴν μέλλουσαν), and Jesus
Christ is named as the Son of man (υἱός ἀνθρώπου, Heb. 2:6), who was for a
little while made lower than the angels but was then crowned with glory and
honor and installed as the ruler of the universe. The NT thereby concentrates the
entire mystery of human existence that is brought to light in Psalm 8 on the Son
of man come from heaven (Daniel 7), Jesus Christ, and on the coming age that

has dawned through his humiliation and exaltation. In this kerygma of fulfillment, the hidden "eschatological" sense of the OT hymn becomes manifest.
Heb. 2:6-9 proclaims that Psalm 8 basically deals with the new world, in which
no disturbances hostile to God or estranged from God find room any longer (Ps.
8:2); it speaks of the new Adam, Jesus Christ, who was lowered to the frail being
of אֱנוֹשׁ and to whom alone as the exalted king the rule over the entire universe
is due (also cf. Eph. 1:22 and 1 Cor. 15:27). However, in Psalm 8 there is not
even a trace of this eschatological-messianic message of the NT. For the amazed
psalmsinger, the "new world" is without reflection or search present; it is
neither otherworldly nor future. For worshiping faith it is already visible in total
this-worldliness. This is where the whole weight of OT proclamation lies, which
of course comes to astonishing and overwhelming reality only when it is
considered from the eschatological-messianic unveiling—just as the mystery of
the creation and of the human being was disclosed to Israel in no other way than
by the electing condescension of Yahweh. (For the biblical-theological perspective, cf. B. S. Childs, 20-31.)

The position of human beings vis-à-vis the gods was in antiquity the object of very diverse
assessments. Mythological systems and emphatic self-evaluations determine the picture of
the assertions. Worth noting are two basic principal features of ancient Near Eastern
anthropology: (1) The king alone is in the fullest sense human. In ancient Sumer he is
called *lugal* = "great man." The king stands in closest relationship to the gods. He is
begotten by heavenly powers, nursed and raised by goddesses. The divine king alone
wears the halo of the heavenly world. He can be called "image of the gods" (B.
Meissner, *Babylonien und Assyrien* 1 [1920], 46ff.; F. M. Th. De Liagre Bohl, *Das
Menschenbild in babylonischer Schau*, Supplements to *Numen*, 2 [1955], 28-48). The
gods formed the Egyptian king "according to their own beauty" (Hierat. Pap. Berlin
3048, col. IV 2.3—VII 2.1; cf. *Religionsgeschichtliches Lesebuch*, 10, 11ff.). The divine
king is therefore the perfect man. He is "the image of god living on earth" (A. Erman,
Die Religion der Ägypter, ihr Werden und Vergehen in vier Jahrhunderten [1934], 52).
G. Widengren (*Religion och Bibel* [1943], 59 A.1) and A. Bentzen (*Messias—Moses
redivivus—Menschensohn*, 12, 32) have tried to introduce into the interpretation also of
Psalm 8 the observations schematically scraped together in the religio-phenomenological
thesis about the "sacral king ideology." For a criticism of this interpretation, see above.
(2) The individual human being recedes completely behind the king. Also in the myths
about the origin of the world the figure of the primordial king and the primordial man is
dominant. Only in a very relative sense is there mention of a direct physical connection
to the world of the gods, in which every human participates. The blood of gods—by the
mediation of the royal archetypal man—courses through the veins of all mortals (Th. C.
Vriezen, *TheolAT;* B. Meissner, *Babylonien und Assyrien* 2 [1925], 106). As a "heavenly
dowry" a "divine soul" is operative in man (Meissner, 2, 135). All statements are
encased in the theogonies and cosmogonies that basically lie on the same level. That the
human being is in essence of divine lineage and divine descent sounds through the myths
like a muffled notion and would be graphically portrayed. Yet, by contrast, these
expressions stand in stark contrast to the self-judgments that turn up in cultic hymns.

From the intellectual area of the Greek world the saying of Sophocles from *Antigone* is
repeatedly cited on Psalm 8: "Much that is mighty is alive, but nothing is mightier than
man." Still, in Heraclitus, for instance, in a passionate rejection of all anthropomor-
phisms that might affect the image of God, we read: "Compared with God, the most
beautiful human being is an ape" (W. Jaeger, *Die Theologie der frühen griechischen
Denker* [1953], 145).

These are a few examples from the immense field of ancient anthropology, so
variegated in detail, that indicate the horizon of mythical interpretation and strong
self-criticism from which the OT record stands apart (cf. W. Zimmerli, *Das Menschenbild*

des ATs, Theol. Ex. heute N.F. 14 [1949]; W. Eichrodt, *Das Menschenverständnis des ATs,* ATANT 40). Here, finally, two aspects of OT anthropology should especially be mentioned: (1) Humans are destined to praise God. This becomes evident in consideration of the archetypal human being in Psalm 8. "The man in Psalm 8, who discovers his superiority in the world, is unable to express this fact through praise of himself; he can only find words of praise addressed to God" (H. W. Wolff, *Anthropology of the OT* [1974] 228). (2) Human beings are destined for ruling. Here Psalm 8 "leads to the final, decisive and all-embracing recognition by emphasizing that the crowning of man to be steward over the world is (in view of his minuteness in relation to the universe and his pitiable need of providing care) anything but a matter of course, and certainly does not have its ground in man himself " (H. W. Wolff, 327).

Yahweh as the Savior
of the Poor and Afflicted

Literature

K. Marti, "Zu Psalm 9:14," *ZAW* 36 (1916) 245-246. J. Leveen, "A Note on Psalm 10:17-18," *JBL* 67 (1948) 249. H. Junker, "Unité, composition et genre littéraire des psaumes IX et X,"*RB* 60 (1953) 161-169. R. Martin-Achard, "Yahwé et les *'anāwīm*," *ThZ* 21 (1965) 349-357. G. Schuttermayr, "Studien zum Text der Ps 9-10 und 18," diss., Munich (1966). J. Becker, "Israel deutet seine Psalmen," *SBS* 18 (1966) 61ff. W. Beyerlin, "Die *tôdā* der Heilsvergegenwärtigung," *ZAW* 79 (1967) 221ff. W. G. Simpson, "Some Egyptian Light on a Translation Problem in Ps 10," *VT* 19 (1969) 128-131. P. R. Berger, "Zu den Strophen des 10. Psalms," *Ugarit-Forschungen*, 2 (1970) 7-18.

Text

To the choirmaster. According to *'alūmot.'* A psalm of David.

9:1 I thank 'you,'[a] Yahweh, with all my heart,
I want to tell of all your wonders.

2 I want to rejoice and shout for joy concerning you,
I want to sing to your name, O Most HIgh.

3 For my enemies turned,
stumbled, and perished before you.

4 You have been in charge of my rights and my case,
you have taken your seat on the throne, a righteous judge.

5 You have rebuked nations and destroyed the wicked,[b]
their names you have blotted out forever and ever.

6 The enemy is gone,[c] ruined[d] forever.
Cities you have depopulated,[e] their glory is at an end.

7 'Impassioned,'[f] 'Yahweh'[g] has 'established himself'[h] forever,
has set up his throne for judgment.

8 He judges the earth in righteousness,
pronounces judgment on the nations with equity.

9 Then Yahweh became[i] a fortress for the oppressed,
   a fortress in times 'of need,'[j]
10 And those who know your name 'put their trust'[k] in you,
   for you will not forsake those who seek you, O Yahweh.
11 Sing to Yahweh, who is enthroned on Zion,
   proclaim his deeds among the nations!
12 For he is an avenger of blood and thinks of them;
   he does not forget the cry of the poor.
13 Yahweh 'was'[l] gracious to me, he 'saw'[m] my distress
   —he 'who lifted me up,'[n] raised from the gates of death,
14 that I may tell of all your glory,
   may exult about your help in the portals of the daughter of Zion.
15 Sunk are the nations in the pits that they have dug;
   in the net that they have spread their own feet got caught.
16 Yahweh made himself known, executed judgment;
   in the work of their own hands the wicked 'got caught.'[o]
   —*higgaion. Selah.*
17 May the wicked go down to Sheol
   —all the nations that forget God!
18 For the poor man will not be forgotten forever,
   Nor will the hope of those in distress vanish forever.
19 Arise, O Yahweh, so that human beings may not be defiant,
   so that the nations may be judged before you.
20 O Yahweh, inspire "fright"[p] in them
   that the nations may know that they are but human beings. *Selah.*

10:1 Why, O Yahweh, do you stand afar off,
   why do you hide in times of 'distress'?[a]
2 In 'arrogance'[b] the wicked persecute the poor;
   they are caught in schemes which they have devised.[c]
3 For he exalts 'wickedness,'[d] ' '[e] the greed of his gullet,
   he praises 'profit,'[f] despises Yahweh.
4 The wicked man [thinks] arrogantly:
   "He does not avenge; there is no God."
   'Before him'[g] [lie] all his plans,
5 'of long duration'[h] at all times are his ways.
   On high up there are your judgments, far removed from him;
   against all his adversaries he puffs away.
6 He says in his heart: "I shall not waver
   —from generation to generation immune[i] to misfortune."
7 Full of cursing is his mouth, full of deceit and oppression
   —under his tongue mischief and iniquity.
8 He sits in the ambush of enclosures,
   stealthily he murders the innocent.
   His eyes are on the lookout for 'the weak person,'[j]
9 he lurks in hiding like the lion in the thicket.[k]
   He lies in wait to catch the poor man;
   he seizes the poor, draws him into his net.
10 'He was on the lookout and waited,'[l] crouched down,
   and 'through his schemes'[m] the weak[n] fall.
11 He says in his heart: "God has forgotten it,
   has hidden his face, does not see it for all eternity."
12 Arise, O Yahweh, ' ',[o] lift up your hand,
   do not forget the lowly!

13 Why may the wicked despise God,
say in his heart, "You do not avenge"?
14 You have ' ' [p] seen harm and affliction;
you do look and take it in hand.
On you the weak person,[q] the forsaken, relies;
you are still the one to help.
15 Break the arm of the wicked and the evil man;
avenge his wickedness, that he may 'vanish'![r]
16 Yahweh is king forever and ever;
gone from his land are the nations.
17 The desire of the poor you have heard, O Yahweh;
you firm up their heart, you incline your ear
18 to provide justice for the forsaken and the oppressed,
so that man on earth will no longer engage in violence.

9:1a In the style of the Psalter's laments and songs of thanksgiving, יהוה is vocative. Accordingly, we have to read אוֹדְךָ (Pss. 86:12; 138:1) with Gk (ἐξομολογήσομαί σοι).
5b Gk and Jerome have אָבַד. But there is no compelling reason to correct the MT.
6c תמו refers to the collective term האויב.
d חרבות לנצח is coordinated with האויב תמו—as אבד זכרם is to the verse fragment וערים נתשת. That חרבות can refer to האויב is to be gleaned from 2 Kings 19:17; Isa. 37:18; 60:12 (against Gunkel). Otherwise, all radical attempts at emendation in v. 6 are without foundation. The reconstruction of a ד-strophe in an acrostic (e.g., דָּמוּ אוֹיֵב לְחָרְבוֹת) can only be thought of as an experiment. But the ד-strophe has probably dropped out.
e נתשׁ denotes plucking out or eradicating plants, but then—applied to peoples and lands—it has become a technical term for deportation or depopulation (Jer. 1:10; 12:14ff.; 18:7 and often).
7f המה at the end of v. 6 is not a strengthening of the suffix of זכרם but (corresponding to the meter and the ה-strophe due in the acrostic pattern) the first word in v. 7. But at the beginning of v. 7 הֵמָּה does not make sense and is best pointed הֹמָה (= "impassioned," Prov. 7:11) in agreement with Gk (μετ' ἤχους), (For the thought, cf. Ps. 7:6).
g In connection with הֹמָה we must read יהוה instead of ויהוה.
h The pointing יָשַׁב (Ps. 29:10) is suitable for this passage.
i In the context the pointing וַיְהִי is to be preferred.
9j As a construct connection together with לעתות, it is better to read הצרה instead of בצרה.
10k In the context: וַיִּבְטְחוּ.
13l An imperative would disturb the flow of thought, therefore we should point חֲנָנֵנִי.
m Cf. **l** and point רָאָה.
n MT = "of those who hate me" is impossible. We must read מְנַשְּׂאִי. K. Marti corrects: חנני יהוה ראה עניי שׂאני מרום משערי־מות ("Be gracious to me, Yahweh, look upon my distress, lift me up from the portals of death") *ZAW* 36 (1916) 245-246.
16o Following Gk, α', Syr, Targ, Jerome, read נוֹקֵשׁ.
20p Following α', θ', Jerome, Targ, and Mss MT read מוֹרָא.
10:1a Cf. the comment on Ps. 9:9, note **j.**
2b In the context of the verse, we should point בְּגֵאוּת.
c The emendation in יִתָּפְשׂוּ and חָשַׁב is not absolutely necessary. The plural forms can refer to the collective nouns רשׁע and עני.
3d MT: "for the wicked exalts according to (?) the desire of his soul, and the greedy curses for gain." Gk reads in the passive: ἐπαινεῖται and ἐνευλογεῖται (also cf. Syr, Targ). In any case, the text in vv. 3-5 has fallen into disarray. The acrostic alphabetical sequence can hardly be reconstructed. Gk begins v. 25 with παρώξυνεν τὸν κύριον and makes possible the reconstruction of the נ-strophe. But with this transposition v. 3 is shortened excessively and v. 4 is lengthened intolerably. We should probably follow MT. But then there are difficulties. How is על to be translated? How are the individual parts of the verse to be understood syntactically? The suggestion of Ehrlich, to read רֶשַׁע and

וּבֶצַע, is good. The עַל would in any case have to be deleted.

e Cf. note **d.**

f Cf. note **d.**

4g Gk completes: לְפָנָיו

5h On the translation of יחילו, cf. Job 20:21.

6i The reconstruction of the פ-strophe by means of including אלה in v. 6 can hardly mitigate the difficulties of the very corrupt text in vv. 4-11. The result is conjectures in v. 6b. Gunkel: אַשְׁרֵי לֹא־תַכְרִיעַ אָלָה ("No curse assails my footsteps"). MT is probably to be retained. אֲשֶׁר לֹא־בָרַע can be translated and understood in accordance with Gk ἄνευ κακοῦ.

8j חלכה in the OT is found only in Ps. 10:8, 10 (חלכאים), 14. Gk: τὸν πένητα (from πένομαι: "to be poor, needy," "to lack"). Gk for v. 14 (9:35): ὁ πτωχός.

9k MT has "in his thicket." Jerome has בְּסֻכָּה "in the thicket."

10l וְדָכָה (from דכה?; perhaps יִדְכָּא = "he is knocked out") is hard to understand in view of ישׁח (cf. Job 38:40). If we can proceed from the fact that a צ-strophe is due in the acrostic pattern, the conjecture suggested by Duhm would be possible: צָפָה יַחְמֶה. Gunkel's suggestion is different: צדיק ידכא ישׁח = "the righteous man is knocked down and falls."

m MT = "and through his strong men the poor falls (fall)." This is scarcely intelligible. Duhm suggests בְּצַמִּיו = "by means of his cords." Better is Gunkel's suggestion בְּמוֹעֲצֹתָיו = "by means of his plans."

n Cf. v. 8, note **j.** Is the word developed from חֵל כָּאִים? We will probably have to read חלכים.

12o In the unusual doubling יהוה אל, אל should probably be eliminated (very likely אל got into the text in view of v. 11).

14p The ר-strophe is interrupted by a disturbing כי אתה, which at one time may have preceded ראיתה. Beyond that, there is the question whether v. 14 has not been materially disturbed in its original order. לתת בידך can only with strong reservations be translated, " . . . to take it into your hand." By means of transposition of the individual parts of the verse and lesser supplementation, Gunkel arrives at the translation of the text, "You of course behold affliction and misery, for you look at the weak 'and' forsaken; to you he entrusts it, to place it into your hands, for you are of course 'his' helper."

q Cf. v. 8, note **j.**

15r Syr תִּמָּצֵא = "that it [the wickedness] may not [any longer] be found." For other emendations of the text in v. 15, cf. Gunkel and H. Schmidt.

Form

Psalms 9 and 10 are to be thought of as a unit (so also J. Becker, 61ff.). In favor of this conception (recognized a long time already) are especially the following observations and conclusions: (1) Psalms 9 and 10 are throughout governed by the alphabetical sequence of the acrostic pattern (for the form of the acrostic in general and as applied to Psalms 9 and 10 in particular, see below). (2) The Septuagint combines Psalms 9 and 10 into a single psalm and therefore subsequently departs from the numbering of the Hebrew Bible. (3) Psalm 9 closes with the liturgical-technical mark of separation, סלה (on which, cf. above, Introduction, §4, No. 13). This indication is otherwise used only within a psalm. (4) Psalm 10 in the MT does not present the (redactional) title expected in the group, psalms of David. (5) The diction and style common to Psalms 9 and 10 is an important argument for the unity (cf. לעתות בצרה in 9:9 and 10:1, for example).

Songs like Psalm 9/10 that are alphabetically organized are found in the OT in Psalms 25; 34; 37; 111; 112; 119; 145; Prov. 31:10-31; Lamentations 1–4 (Nah. 1:2-8). In these songs the order of the alphabet entirely or in part determines the form by means of the first letter of the first word of each verse or strophe. The meaning of this curious element of form has heretofore not been very clear. Among other things, there was the thought of a magic relevance of the alphabet (Lohr). But now the discoveries in Ras Shamra shed light on the problem. It has been established as fact that in ancient Ugarit the alphabet was very early drawn upon for educational purposes; cf. W. F. Albright, "Alphabetic Origins and the Idrimi Statue," *BASOR* 118 (1950) 11-20; W. F. Albright, "The Origin of the Alphabet and the Ugaritic ABC Again," *BASOR* 119 (1950) 23-24; E. A. Speiser, "A Note on Alphabetic Origins," *BASOR* 121 (1951) 17-20. That alphabetical order in a poem can serve as a mnemonic device is obvious. In any case, alphabetism carries with it a formative force that with a schematizing organizational force exerts an influence on the poetry to which it is applied (cf. H.-J. Kraus, BK 20 6f.).

In Psalm 9/10 the reconstruction of the alphabetical sequence precipitates a number of difficulties. The ד-strope is missing. The מ-strophe could at one time have begun with in 10:5. However, vv. 4-11 present so corrupt a text that every restoration between ג and ק is virtually impossible. The emendations and conjectures—some of them very radical—are hypothetical and not infrequently very daring. In vv. 4-11 one may, for better or for worse, follow MT and then—with restraint—consider the possibilities of reconstructing the alphabetical organization. In vv. 12-17 the sequence ק to ת is then assured. For every "strophe" beginning with the applicable letter of the alphabet there are two complete verse lines, the meter of which fluctuates very much in the general picture. This is in part related to the corruptness of the text, but it also has some basis in the change of *Gattung* and in the contents of the statements. In the meter 4+4 are included Ps. 9:5, 6,10, 13-16, 18, 20; Ps. 10:2, 3, 7, 15, 17. In the meter 4+3 are Ps. 9:1 7-9, 11, 12, 19; Ps. 10:1, 13, 14 (second line), 16, 18. Also meters 3+4 are to be reckoned with: Ps. 9:4; Ps. 10:5 (from מרום on), 6, 8-11. Double triple meters are to be found in Ps. 9:2, 3, 17; Ps. 10:4, 5 (up to עת), 12, 14.

A survey of the structure and contents leads to the identification of the following sections and thematic groups: Ps. 9:1-4 (the petitioner thanks Yahweh for help bestowed), 5-8 (Yahweh as judge of the peoples), 9-10 (Yahweh is the fortress of the oppressed), 11-14 (grateful proclamation of the help experienced), 15-16 (nations have fallen through Yahweh's judgments), 17-20 (petition for God's judgment on the godless nations); Ps. 10:1-11 (the proud and secure evildoer, who succeeds in everything, becomes an assailant of the psalmist), 12-15 (prayer for Yahweh's legal help for the poor man), 16-18 (Yahweh as king is judge of the nations and savior of the poor). This overview immediately demonstrates that principally three themes are dealt with in Psalm 9/10: (1) the rescue of the helpless and poor man from the hand of the enemies; (2) Yahweh's worldwide judgment and kingship over the nations; (3) the self-assured evildoer as an assailant of the faith of the weak. The constant exchange of these three themes, above all the remarkable rebound in the progress of the psalm at the beginning of chap. 10, has let the interpreters again and again come to the conclusion that the contents of the text are "artificial" (Gunkel), that the sum total of it produces a "double impression" (H. Schmidt), and that the "heterogeneous tone" (Kittel) can hardly be explained adequately. The continuously changing pictures and conceptions are in most instances attributable to the constraints of the acrostic form.

The observations concerning the structure and contents are matched by results that may be achieved in a form-critical analysis when the thematic structuring is similarly studied and contemplated. In the first place we should call attention to the formal elements of a song of praise that proves to be a thanksgiving song of an individual (cf. above, Introduction §6, 1). These elements of form are revealed especially in Ps. 9:1-4, 13, 14, but also in vv. 5-12, 15-16, while vv. 17-20 should be designated a prayer song (תפלה; see above, Introduction §6, 2). Vv. 17-20 has its continuation (also determined by the form) in Ps. 10:1-11, then again in vv. 12-18; but vv. 16-18 run out to a song of praise. Almost abruptly at times the form types are broken off and replaced by new elements. Thus H. Gunkel criticizes not without reason this "vacillation between the types" that seems characteristic of the work and of the author who is bound to the alphabet and who works according to a scheme.

It seems doubtful that in Psalm 9/10 the *todah* is to be understood and thought of as a visualization of salvation (so W. Beyerlin, 221ff.). There are two reasons for this view: (1) The psalms listed by Beyerlin are not so congruous and analogous in form and content that we could speak of a definite type (he lists Psalms 9/10; 26; 40; 71), and altogether too quickly he determines that there are "differing acts in the same liturgical connection" (223); (2) Psalm 9/10 is an artificial construction, a relatively late formation consisting of a combination of elements from which a general theory concerning form and cultic act can hardly be extracted.

Setting

If in our inquiry about the situation in Psalm 9/10 we begin with the song of thanksgiving (song of praise) of an individual, that is, with those expressions that belong to the theme "rescue from the hand of the enemies," then the situation in which such a song of praise and thanksgiving was intoned is definitely recognizable in Ps. 9:14. The one who has been rescued from dire affliction "tells" (Ps. 9:14) of God's "acts of glory" and praises Yahweh. He stands in the temple area and "bears witness to" Yahweh's acts of rescue. This grateful witness and praise to God, typical of the thanksgiving songs of the individual in the Psalter, has in the history-of-tradition development now in part assumed the form of an extensive instruction for the audience (cf. Ps. 34:11). And this is now the opportunity that provides an entrance for the most dissimilar messages, which, going beyond the experience of personal rescue, are presented in other types. In Psalm 9/10 the themes "Yahweh's worldwide judgment and kingship over the nations" and "the self-assured evildoer as assailant of the faith of the weak" have found their way into the song of thanksgiving of an individual. It is by no means necessary to explain this process as "painting over private experience with a hand that touches up," as H. Schmidt does. Schmidt is of the opinion "that a song of thanksgiving by one who has been acquitted became available to a secondary author and was revised, recast, and extensively amplified." But it would be just as plausible to think of the expansive "telling" as a genuine exposition, which would of course have to be assigned to a late (postexilic) time. The psalmist would in that case—proceeding from the song of thanksgiving—make use of the most varied traditional illustrations, conception, and formulations. His presentation, tending toward the didactic, would, e.g., take up problems which, through the poetry of Job and Psalm 73, were made contemporary in postexilic times (Ps. 10:1-11). But we would also have to reckon with older elements. Worth noting is the relationship to Lamentations 3 (cf. H.-J. Kraus, BK 20, 46ff.). Of course, it is impossible to decide whether one should suggest a date in "a very late age" (Gunkel), perhaps even as late as Hellenistic times (Duhm, Bertholet, Schmidt). We should observe that the acrostic form enjoyed a particular popularity in the sixth century B.C.

In its present form the song of praise and thanksgiving as we have it in Psalm 9/10 is a very artistic structure. The formulary character of the songs of praise and thanksgiving has been introduced into a structured whole. Both this shaping as well as the didactic trend of the whole point to a possible wisdomlike adoption of older elements.

Commentary

[Title] The redactional technical heading begins with למנצח (cf. above, Introduction §4, No. 17). On עלמות לבן, see above, §4, No. 24. Gk has read עֲלָמוֹת ("that which is secret" or "the strength of youth"?). On מזמור לדוד, see §4, No. 2.

[9:1-2] In vv. 1-2 we have the characteristic forms of expression that introduce the song of thanksgiving of an individual. Characteristic are the five verbs. The petitioner wants to thank Yahweh "with all his heart" for the wonders (נפלאות) he has experienced. The song at one and the same time contains praise, confession, and narrative. For the beginning of the song, cf. Pss. 111:1; 138:1. The glory is entirely Yahweh's. שמך עליון—this name of God very likely goes back to pre-Israelite, ancient Canaanite times (Pss. 7:17; 47:2; 78:35; and often; Gen. 14:18). עליון is the name for the universal divinity that holds the rank of "Most High God," "God of Heaven," and "God-King" (cf. above, Intro. §10, 1). In the OT this epithet always carries with it the corresponding conceptions of grandeur belonging to the judge of the world and the Lord of all nations. Therefore also in Psalm 9/10 we may not a priori declare the theme "Yahweh as the judge of the nations" a late, eschatological proclamation; instead, we have here an archaic conception that is most intimately connected with Yahweh the אל־עליון and מלך (Ps. 19:6) of Jerusalem. These elements of tradition very likely derive from the pre-Davidic Jerusalem cult (H. Schmid, "Jahwe und die Kulttradition von Jerusalem," *ZAW* 68 [1955], 168ff., and W. H. Schmidt, *Königtum Gottes in Ugarit und Israel*, 1966²).

[9:3-4] After the introit (vv. 1-2) to the song of thanksgiving, the principal subject follows immediately in vv. 3-4. Here the wonderful works of God announced in the word נפלאותיך are now named. The singer was persecuted by enemies, took refuge in the sanctuary, sought his rights with Yahweh, and experienced God's intervention. The enemies had to yield (on שוב אחור, see Pss. 44:10; 56:9). They stumbled and perished, for Yahweh had shown himself to be the "righteous judge." ישבת לכסא is probably an old theophanic formula that refers to the appearance and effective intervention of God. The preposition לְ (otherwise עַל) means "direction toward a target" (BrSynt §107a). The song of thanksgiving praises the divine deliverer who defeated the enemies (see above, Intro. §10, 4). About the method and manner of Yahweh's intervention we hear nothing.

[9:5-8] In vv. 5-8 the horizon gradually expands. יהוה is עליון (v. 2). The realm of his power is now described by the terms גוים (v. 5), ערים (v. 6), תבל and לאמים (v. 8). Political and universal conceptions come to the fore. The God of Israel, with whom the individual who is persecuted by enemies takes refuge, is the king and judge of the nations. We cannot say: "The poet loves to generalize the individual case to produce a judgment of the nations'' (F. Nötscher); rather, what we have is a cultic tradition of Jerusalem without exceptions to which the singer goes back (cf. the comment on Psalm 7). Thus the psalmist, while disregarding the rescue he himself experienced, now celebrates in song the נפלאותש of the אל־עליון, who is enthroned on Zion. He recapitulates the cultic exaltations that in Jerusalem are presented to Yahweh as the ''hero in battle'' (Ps. 24:8) and the universally mighty king of the earth (on תבל in v. 8, cf. Ps. 24:1). Thus גער (v. 5) is an expression of mythology:[1] Pss. 68:30; 76:6; 80:16; 104:7; Isa. 17:13; 66:15. It is worth noting that the terms גוים and רשע regularly are identical in meaning. The גוים are the embodiment of a foreign power that lives outside of the covenant and the divine order. In connection with the statements of v. 6 we should not think of concrete historical events. Here the cultic exaltations of Yahweh, the ''Lord, mighty in battle'' (Ps. 24:8), have found their literary expression. The central point of all the exaltations is Yahweh, the judge of the nations enthroned on Zion (vv. 7-8), who appears ''impassioned'' (on הֵמָה, cf. Ps. 7:6) and has established his throne of judgment for all times (לעולם). תבל is a cosmological concept that designates the lighted, life-sustaining ''mainland'' (Akkadian *tābālu*) (Ps. 24:1). On the theme ''Yahweh as judge of the nations,'' cf. Pss. 7:8; 96:13; 98:9; 1 Sam. 2:10; Acts 17:31.

[9:9] The power of Yahweh celebrated in vv. 5-8 is a ''fortress'' (מִשְׂגָּב) and a place of refuge. The emendation often suggested, לעתות הצרה, could be thought of as unnecessary if W. F. Albright's conjecture is correct, that עתות has the meaning ''omens.'' Albright explains that עתות ''is either originally identical with *'anatu-ettu* or is a parallel word from the same stem'' (on עתות, reference is also made to Ps. 31:15: W. F. Albright, *Archaeology and the Religion of Israel* [1942] 195, n. 14).

[9:10] בטח and דרש are characteristic verbs to express the trusting desire and expectation of people who have taken refuge in Yahweh's protectorate. יודעי שמך designates those people who walk in trusting association, in confidential communion with Yahweh's presence.

[9:11-14] The section vv. 11-14 begins doxologically. Yahweh, enthroned on Zion, is to be praised by all. The personal experience of rescue (vv. 3-4) and the worship experiences of the congregation (vv. 5ff.) flow together in the adoration of יהוה ישב ציון, whose glorious deeds are to penetrate to the world of the nations and become known there. Yahweh is the דרש דמים (''avenger of blood''). As שופט צדק (v. 4) he avenges the bloody schemes, persecutions, and deeds of violence. He hears the cries of the ''poor.'' Such a saving bestowal of help the psalmist himself had witnessed, therefore he comes back to his personal experience in vv. 13-14. The bestowal of grace occurred as the sufferer was extricated ''from the gates of death.'' שערי מות (cf. Ps. 107:18; Job 38:10; Isa. 38:15; Matt. 16:18)—this picture designates the ''sphere of death'' and the total

---

1. ''I was thinking that we would hear the clash of arms and some four-footed tumult of horses and riders. And behold, the sound and chiding of a word produces the means for such a great effect. He merely chides, and all things are done. Who would not marvel? This is what that means: Out of the mouth of babes and infants he perfects strength. This is what that means, that the Spirit of truth convinces the world of sin, of righteousness, and of judgment; by the word alone he does all things'' (Luther, WA 5; 294, 22ff.).

separation from God (Chr. Barth, *Die Errettung vom Tode* [1947], 78). Over against that the שַׁעֲרֵי בַת־צִיּוֹן (v. 14) represent the sphere of life and nearness to God. In the temple area the thankful psalmist celebrates and relates the help received. He has experienced the fact that Yahweh rescues "the poor." Regarding the self-designation of "the poor" and "the distressed," we need only state at this point: The certainty that Yahweh is inclined in a special way to, and looks after, the "underprivileged," those with inadequate legal protection, and the handicapped in the struggle of life goes back to a most ancient time in the history of Israel. One can observe that the term "poor" embraced a veritable legitimate claim to Yahweh's attention and help. From this the qualifying self-designation of the petitioners before Yahweh emerged (cf. Pss. 12:5; 14:6; 18:27; 35:19; 116:8; 140:12; 146:7; 149:4). The "poor" understand that they are the first and the real claimants of the bestowal of salvation by the God of Israel. In their helplessness and defenselessness they have only one refuge and confidence: Yahweh. Their poverty consists of the fact that they are unable to help themselves and therefore raise their petitions in absolute dependence on being rescued. These poor people carry with them the dark shadow, the very opposite picture: they are persecuted by enemies and violent men who want to trample on the right to life and the right to receive help that is promised to the poor by Yahweh, and who want to destroy the afflicted totally (Pss. 10; 35:10; 37:14). On the designation and self-designation of the "poor," see above, Intro. §10, 3. On the expression "enemies," see Intro. §10, 4.

[9:15-16] Yahweh's legal aid shows itself in the life of the individual and in the fortune of the peoples in the form of a hidden "immanent nemesis." The nations fall into the pit they have dug, they themselves get entangled in the net they have laid out for others. "Pits" and "nets" are the traps the hunter sets for wild game (G. Dalman, *AuS* 6, 334f., 338). Regarding the "immanent nemesis" and the theological problems tied to this ancient conception, cf. Ps. 7:13-16. Vv. 15-16 deal with God's intervention in the characteristic hymnic form that describes a definitive (eschatological) event. Gunkel is right in calling vv. 15-16 elements of the "eschatological hymns." But a comprehensive investigation will be necessary to show whether or not "eschatological" is the appropriate term here.

At the end of v. 16 the cultic-technical terms *higgaion* (see above, Intro. §4, No. 12) and *selah* (see above, §4, No. 13) point to the conclusion of a thematic section.

[9:17-20] In vv. 17-20 two elements converge: the plea for final destruction of the enemies (nations) and the declaration of trust on the part of the poor. רְשָׁעִים and גּוֹיִם are thought of as on the same level (as in vv. 5f.). They are characterized as the שְׁכֵחֵי אֱלֹהִים (cf. Ps. 50:22). For these hostile forces that have turned away from God, the singer wishes a "return" to Sheol—the realm of separation from God beyond Yahweh's area of lordship (Ps. 10:16). שׁוּב here has the meaning "depart for," "turn to." On v. 17, cf. Pss. 31:17; 55:15, 23; 63:9. The "poor man," on the other hand, may depend on God's inclining to him to rescue him even in the worst desolation. The section vv. 17-20 closes with a cry of appeal (cf. the comment on Ps. 7:6). In a typifying concept all enemies of God are called אֱנוֹשׁ, where the conception of a frail, impotent essence of "humankind" echoes along (Pss. 8:4; 90:3; 103:15). Under the demonstration of

God's power of judgment, the nations are to recognize their nothingness.

[10:1-11] The ל-strophe of the acrostic pattern furnished the poet occasiontoinclude a question and lament introduced by למה. In the "literary form"(Gunkel) of an individual lament, vv. 1-11, in part a very corrupt text, deal with the arrogance and security of the רשע. But the "poor man" experiences the hiddenness of God (v. 1) in the midst of the terrors of persecution (v. 2). On v. 1, cf. Ps. 22:1; on לעתות בצרה, cf. Ps. 9:9. The enemies of the individual appear as arrogant men of wickedness, who hatch dangerous schemes for the annihilation of the עני. Their praise extends to misdeeds, limitless greed, and (unlawful) gain (v. 3); the רשע despises Yahweh. His attitude is expressed in the words בל־ידרש אין אלהים. This does not express theoretical atheism, but the secure view that Yahweh does not intervene (Ps. 14:1; Jer. 5:12; Zeph. 1:12; Th. Boman, *Hebrew Thought Compared with Greek* [1960] 48). As in Ps. 9:12 and Ps. 10:13, דרש has the meaning "avenge." The thinking and the attitude of the רשע is for the עני the object of oppressive temptation: the godless man succeeds in all his plans and enterprises, the judgment of God is "far removed from him," and he can say in his secure way: בל־אמוט. The expression יפיח בהם (v. 5) is unique. Is this a matter of "magic effect by breath" (Mowinckel, Gunkel)? Or are we simply to translate: "he puffs away at them"? In view of אלה in v. 7 we may perhaps think of an effective curse which the רשעים unscrupulously emit against the עני in order to ruin him. In v. 7 we hear of the dangerous words of the wicked man. His mouth is an arsenal full of deadly weapons (Rom. 3:14). Vv. 8-9 describe the ambushes of the רשע. Like a lion in the thicket, so the enemy lies in wait for his weak prey (cf. Pss. 17:12; 37:32; 56:6; 59:3). He who is pursued is called נקי, עני, and חלכה. The treacherous attack is especially vividly visualized in v. 10. And in v. 11 the lament about the arrogant, self-assured wicked person concludes with a renewed reference to the challenging statement of the רשעים: "God has forgotten it, has hidden his face, does not see it for all eternity" (cf. v. 4). In the inquiring and lamenting prayer of the afflicted, this challenging attitude of the enemies is to move Yahweh to intervene. The distress revealed in v. 1 is to be relieved. And so v. 12 immediately begins with the call to address and waken Yahweh. But it will be important to look back at vv. 1-11 to take note of a number of biblical-theological contexts. Didactically applied, Psalm 9/10 obviously deals with the situation in which a petitioner who seeks refuge with Yahweh does not receive a sign of a bestowal of rescue from God. The enemy triumphs, his plans and ambushes succeed. But Yahweh is silent. He has forsaken the עני and has hidden himself (v. 1). In view of this distress there arises an urgent lament and inquiry. But at the same time the problem arises that is dealt with in Psalm 73 and in the book of Job: Why does he who despises Yahweh succeed in all his enterprises, while the helpless עני (in spite of the privileges he has of calling to God) looks in vain for a sign of Yahweh's intervention? Viewed according to the history of tradition, the "problem poetry" of Job and Psalm 73 originated in this situation of delay in the demonstration of God's salvation.

[10:12-15] Based on the insights expressed by the psalmist in vv. 1-11, the appeal to God's righteous judgment is now made with particular emotion (for the cries of appeal introduced by קומה, cf. Ps. 7:6) that Yahweh intervene as righteous judge. The lifting up of the hand of God could be interpreted as a gesture accompanying an oath, but very likely it is considered only a sign of intervention. In Egypt the lifting of the hand is a symbolic gesture of the god of war and of the king-god (H. Jacobsohn, *Die dogmatische Stellung des Königs in der Theologie der alten Ägypter,* Ägypt. Stud. 8, 1955). The suffering of the "poor" and the challenging defiance of the wicked are expressly presented to Yahweh. With agitated words the petitioner prays for proof of the power of God for judgment by which all the false hopes of the רשעים are to be refuted (v. 15). The demeanor of the עני, who has committed his lot to Yahweh without reservation, is described in the significant words עליך יעזב חלכה (v. 14). The helpless person trusts that Yahweh is עוזר. But the help of Yahweh would reveal itself in an actual, visible intervention. In this regard, OT thought is always solidly this-worldly. And precisely this waiting for a sign of God's effective intervention is then also the element that made the temptation among those who waited·and the weight of the problem unbearably heavy.

[10:16-18] The conclusion (vv. 16-18) praises Yahweh's royal power in hymn form; it expresses a glowing assurance of being heard. On יהוה מלך, see above, Intro. §10, 1. The appellations of God מלך—שופט—עליון in Psalm 9/10 lie on the same level. They proclaim the loftiness of the God who is enthroned on Zion. Yahweh overcomes all enemies; with this assurance, voiced in hymnic style, the psalm closes. In his area of lordship the גוים, hostile to God, cannot establish themselves. As in Psalm 9/10 as a whole, so the two themes "Yahweh as judge of the nations" and "Yahweh as juridical helper of the individual" also flow together in this concluding piece. The "poor" person knows that God is a God of the poor and the orphaned. The helpless enjoy the privilege of his salvation. And again—as in Ps. 9:15-16—v. 18 has the ring of the definitive, the eschatological. אנוש—since Ps. 9:19 a general term for the frail world of man—shall no longer (עוד) exercise power, for Yahweh is King (cf. Pss. 29:10; 145:13; 146:10).

Purpose and Thrust

The commentary has shown that the sometimes very depreciatory evaluations of the commentators on Psalm 9/10 are not justified. If from the very beginning we start from the fact of a "didactic extension" of an individual song of thanksgiving, then the conceptions and thematic sections that differ a good deal from one another do not become the prey of criticism that sunders, but rather we come to realize that the sum and total of it forms a unit. The analytical separation of forms and conceptions has in most cases lost sight of the center of the multiplicity of various statements. The center of Psalm 9/10 is Yahweh as עליון (Ps. 9:2), שופט (Ps. 9:4, 8, 16, 19; Ps. 10:5, 18), and מלך (Ps. 10:16). He is the judge of the peoples. This doxological statement of high dignity concerning the ישב ציון (Ps. 9:11) is a cultic element of the worship in Jerusalem; like a red thread it pervades Psalm 9/10. Yahweh, who has humbled himself to dwell on Zion, is אל־עליון, God Most High and the judge of the world (cf. Acts 17:31). But on Zion the עני, the helpless and persecuted one, comes into the presence of the judge of the world. On the one hand, Psalm 9/10 lets it be known what miracles (Ps. 9:1) of rescue and bestowal of salvation are performed for the שמך ידעי (Ps. 9:10). But on the other hand, the psalm also indicates what anguish then is precipitated when the signs of God's help fail to appear (Ps. 10:1-11). And so the "didactic extension" of the individual song of thanksgiving is characterized, on the one hand, by hymnic expressions, and by lamenting and pleading, on the other. Godforsakenness and triumph are juxtaposed in one and the same psalm, and that quite abruptly. Jubilation and lament permeate the song. Two experiences lie adjacent to each other, just as they are met with under the world reign of God on Zion: wondrous rescue and incomprehensible delay. But it is important to hear the voice of anguish exactly. Beneath the burden of a delayed bestowal of salvation there is no proliferation of despair. An emotional cry and at the same time a solid trust characterize the statements of Ps. 10:12-15. But in the hymnically oriented closing words (Ps. 10:16-18) the anguish of the waiting sufferer is incorporated in the eschatological hymn. It is not blended in hymnically, but it is taken up in a definitive solution of all mysteries that lie with the מלך Yahweh. Thus the cultic transmission that Yahweh is judge and king over all nations is something final for the person of faith. It cannot be surpassed by any other power. This "solution" of the "problem of Job" that bursts forth in Psalm 10 should especially be noted. This proves that already in the OT there are relations between individual lives and definitive eschatological factors that determine and influence faith.

Psalm 11

Yahweh Is My Refuge

Literature

I. Sonne, "Psalm Eleven," *JBL* 68 (1949) 241-245. J. Morgenstern, "Psalm 11," *JBL* 69 (1950) 221-231. W. Beyerlin, *Die Rettung der Bedrängten in den Feindpsalmen der Einzelnen auf institutionelle Zusammenhänge untersucht*, FRLANT 99 (1970) 101-105.

Text

To the Choirmaster. Of David.
11:1 With Yahweh I have taken refuge. How can you say to me,
    " 'Flee to the mountains like a bird'![a]
   2 For behold, the wicked—they bend the bow,
     have already placed their arrow on the string
     to shoot in the dark[b]at those who are upright in heart.
   3 If the foundations have been broken down,
     what can the righteous person do?"—
   4 Yahweh resides in his holy temple.
     Yahweh—in heaven is his throne.
     His eyes are looking,[c] his eyelids test the human beings.
   5 Yahweh tests the righteous[d] and the wicked.
     His soul hates him who loves violence.
   6 On the wicked he lets fiery 'coals'[e] and brimstone
     rain down—a scorching wind is the lot of their cup.
   7 For Yahweh is righteous, and he loves righteous deeds;
     righteous people behold his countenance.[f]

1a MT (*kethib*): "Flee into your hills, you birds." Gk, α´, Syr, Targ, Jerome, Q and several MSS read נוּדִי. Besides, in GK, α´, Syr, Targ, Jerome we have the version הר כְּמוֹ צִפּוֹר " . . . to the mountain like a bird." In this way the difficult summons of the MT is woven into the sense of the text. Graetz, Budde, Gunkel, and Schmidt go even further and reconstruct as the "original text": נוּד מַהֵר כְּמוֹ צִפּוֹר "flee quickly like a bird." In this way the accommodation of the Hebrew is carried too far. Perhaps an old proverb is present in the MT (*kethib*) (Ewald, Wellhausen, Weiser). But an emendation after the manner of GK, α´, Syr, Targ, Jerome can hardly be avoided here.

2b For במו אפל Gunkel suggests the ingenious emendation כְּמוֹ עוֹף (interchange of א and ע because of auditory misapprehension, ל as dittography). But thereby an important nuance in the description of the malicious stratagems of the persecutors in the MT is lost.

4c Supplying an object (εὸς τὸν πένητα ἀποβλέπουσιν or εἰς τὴν οἰκουμένην) simplifies the Hebrew text; it is to be rejected.

5d A transposition צדיק ורשע יבחן is indispensable.

6e MT = "He lets it rain as fire and brimstone are falling." This text is hardly possible. We should probably have to read פֶּחָם אֵשׁ (perhaps פַּחֲמֵי־אֵשׁ, according to Bickel).

7f MT = "Righteous people [collective] behold their countenance." Here we probably have to read פָּנָיו.

Form

In textual form and in the meter Psalm 11 shows a number of slight unevennesses. V. 2b is to be understood as an isolated half-verse. The meter of this half-verse is that of a four-meter verse. As 4 + 3 meters we are to read: vv. 1 (with the exception of the heading), 2a, 7. In vv. 5 and 6 we have the meter 4 + 4. Sporadic in appearance are: 3 + 3 in v. 4; 3 + 2 in v. 3; and 2 + 2 + 2 in the second part of v. 4 (אדם . . . עיניו). The organization of the psalm, on the other hand, is simple and clear. Immediately after the cultic-technical title the psalmist speaks of his trust in Yahweh and rejects the advice of well-meaning friends, as cited in detail in vv. 1b-3. Vv. 4-7 then speak about Yahweh as the righteous judge and juridical helper of those who are persecuted.

This psalm must be assigned to the form group of prayer songs (תפלה; cf. above, Intro. §6, 2). Conspicuous are the expressions of trust, which earlier gave rise to the idea of classifying Psalm 11 in the *Gattung* "songs of trust." Such expressions of trust dominate also in Psalms 16; 23; and 27. The song of prayer, strictly speaking, is present only in vv. 4ff. and contains significant formulations of confession—Yahweh is referred to in the third person! In it an address to a group of people who had evidently advised the petitioner to flee to the wilderness hill country to find protection there (v. 1b) is joined to an initial expression of confidence and confession in v. 1b. From this unique arrangement of the psalm we may already infer that the classification "prayer song" can only be a very general, comprehensive, temporary, and preliminary description, one that is in need of clarification and concretization by means of inquiry into the situation of the psalmist.

Setting

The situation of Psalm 11 is clearly shown in vv. 1 and 4. The petitioner has found refuge from persecuting enemies in the temple area. At the sanctuary he obviously meets those people who recommended a different way to him, namely, not the way of refuge with Yahweh but that of flight to the hills. There can be no doubt that the psalm is to be attributed to the cultic institution of God's juridical authority (cf. Psalms 3; 4; 5; 7; 17, and often; on this, see W. Beyerlin, 103). The verb חסה in v. 1 is characteristic of the way of looking for protection in the asylum area of the temple (L. Delekat, *Asylie and Schutzorakel*, 1967; E. Gerstenberger, *THAT* 1, 621f.). But the speaker in the psalm is devoted not to the area of protection as such but to Yahweh alone; with him he has sheltered himself. We cannot recognize in detail which stages of the legal proceedings the seeker of protection has already passed through (W. Beyerlin, 103). The only thing that seems to be established is that he has not as yet heard the actual verdict of Yahweh. Confession and confidence are devoted to the righteous judgment and activity of the God of Israel and hopefully already look forward to the hour of decision.

We can hardly speak of a "king's ritual" when we look at Psalm 11. A. Bentzen (*Messias—Moses Redivivus—Menschensohn* [1948], 20) has taken the view that the psalm is to be assigned to a king in a dramatic cultic act. For the meaning of conceptions and statements that transcend the lot of individual petitioners, cf. the commentary on Psalm 3. We shall have to assume that Psalm 11 was available as a formulary in the temple archives and there also experienced changes (spiritualizations?) that were determined by the history of tradition. On observing the spiritualizing of statements, see W. Beyerlin, 102.

A dating of the psalm is, in accordance with what has been said about its form, hardly possible. There can hardly be any doubt that the formulary belongs to the realm of the temple and of the cultic act of the jurisdiction of God. A preexilic origin is possible. But in such a dating the perspective of the history of tradition is not to be curtailed.

Commentary

[11:1] On למנצח, see above, Intro. §4, No. 17. On לדוד, see §4, No. 2.

The psalm begins immediately. The singer has sheltered himself with Yahweh. חסה in the Psalter is the characteristic concept to denote the search for shelter by those who are persecuted (Pss. 7:1; 31:1; 64:10; 71:1). The way to the realm of the presence of God on Zion has become—and that is characteristic of Psalm 11—an act of trust and confession. Opposed to the singer are people who recommended an altogether different procedure to him who is threatened and persecuted. They considered fleeing to the hills expedient. With an indignant question introduced by איך, the psalmist takes his advisers to task. In their advice they doubtlessly pursued a good purpose, for people in Israel have often been able to find safety in the pathless, rugged hill country. Above all, the singer of our psalm is indebted to his advisers for informing him of the dangerous purposes of his enemies.

[11:2] In v. 2 the well-meaning advisers give reasons for their suggestion that the singer flee. The exclamatory הנה calls attention to a deadly scheme on the part of malicious persecutors. The enemies are depicted by means of images of the hunter, or the armed warrior (cf. Pss. 7:12ff.; 10:8; 37:14; 64:2ff.; above, Intro. §10, 4). "One bends the bow by 'stepping on' (דרך) the string, one 'places' (כונן) the 'arrow' (חץ) on the 'string' (יתר) in order to 'shoot' (ירה)" (G. Dalman, *AuS* 6, 330). But these dangerous practices—so the advisers report it— take place "in the dark." The activities of the enemies are sinister and destructive. Here we can think of slander or deceitful snares. But the target of this deadly activity knows that he belongs among the ישרי־לב , among those who are of a clean heart and innocent (cf. the comment on Ps. 7:3ff.).

[11:3] That the persecuted one is צדיק , also the advisers bear witness (v. 3). But these persons, so ready to help, consider the situation of the persecuted person hopeless. The sentence כי השתות יהרסון, with the term שת ("foundation"?) that is hard to interpret, we may be allowed to understand in the sense of Ps. 82:5 (F. Nötscher). When all law and order is overturned and chaos in the form of raw violence breaks out—what can the "righteous" do then? "The perfect tense (פעל) after an imperfect establishes coming events and situations that are to be expected as sure'' (BrSynt §41f). Accordingly, the advisers consider it completely without hope that in view of the abysmal schemes of violence of the enemies there would still be a chance to rescue the צדיק. But in a clear statement this prudent and reasonable advice is unmasked and indignantly rejected by the singer of the psalm as an attack on his faith, as faint-hearted self-help (v. 1). In full trust, the persecuted person shelters himself with Yahweh. "He who believes will not flee" (Isa. 28:16). This trust is a confession to God's ability to protect and a rejection of all self-help.

[11:4] In v. 4 the hymnic elements enter the song of trust. In words of praise the singer proclaims the God with whom he finds shelter. Abruptly juxtaposed are two statements: "Yahweh resides in his holy temple" and "Yahweh—in heaven is his throne." How are these two conceptions to be interpreted? It is the basic worship tradition of the Zion sanctuary (cf. Psalm 132) that Yahweh has chosen Zion (2 Sam. 6) and has taken up residence in the temple (1 Kings 8). On this basis such cultic invocations as Hab. 2:20 and many psalm statements are to be understood. Yahweh is the ישב ציון (Ps. 9:11). But he is at the same time "Most High God" (אל־עליון, see the comment on Ps. 7:17), world judge (see the comment on Ps. 7:6ff.), and King (cf. above, Intro. §10, 1). The history-of-religions phenomenon of the elevation of local numina to "Most High deities," which is frequently encountered in the Syrian-Canaanite world, is in the Jerusalem worship a definite doxological, confessional, and kerygmatic tradition which in its conceptual forms very likely was transmitted through the pre-Davidic cultus. Thus in the testimony of the Psalms the statement of condescension about Yahweh's election of, and residence on, Zion and the statement of exaltation about God's reign in heaven and about his universal office of judgment lie immediately next to each other and among each other. The innocent persecuted person who entrusts his case to Yahweh on Zion is confident because he stands before the heavenly judge (cf. Ps. 7:6ff.). The heavenly judge has insight even into the tangled and impenetrable legal situation, from the chaotic depths of which well-meaning tongues suggest fleeing (v. 1) (cf. Pss. 33:13f.; 102:19; 139:1ff.).[1] On the juxtaposition of two statements, "Yahweh resides in his holy temple" and "Yahweh—in heaven is his home," cf. M. Metzger, "Himmlische und irdische Wohnstatt Yahwehs," *Ugarit-Forschungen* 2 (1970) 139-158.

[11:5-7] The singer of the song of trust is sure that Yahweh in his probing and penetrating way sees through the צדיק and the רשע. On צדיק and רשע, cf. Psalm 1. In emotional sympathy God's נפש (that is, his vitally sympathetic "I") "hates" everyone who loves violence. V. 5 contains the creed of him who as an innocently persecuted person has given his lot into the hand of Yahweh. His conception of God's intervening legal aid is revealed in v. 6: "On the wicked he lets fiery coals and brimstone rain down." The prototype of this conception of

---

1. "If God reigns in heaven, and if his throne is erected there, it follows that he must necessarily attend to the affairs of men, in order one day to sit in judgment upon them. Epicurus and such like him as would persuade themselves that God is idle and indulges in repose in heaven, may be said rather to spread for him a couch on which to sleep, than to erect for him a throne of judgment. But it is the glory of our faith that God, the Creator of the world, does not disregard or abandon the order which he himself at first established. And when he suspends his judgment for a time, it becomes us to lean on this one truth—that he beholds from heaven" (Calvin, on Ps. 11:4; trans. Anderson [Grand Rapids: Eerdmans, 1949]).

the destructive intervention of Yahweh is, on the one hand, the narrative of the destruction of Sodom and Gomorrah (Gen. 19:24) and, on the other, the theophanic tradition as it is expressed, for instance, in Ps. 18:12ff. The latter passage, especially, must be considered. Into the traditional picture of Yahweh's appearance, volcanic conceptions find their way. In other words, the singer of our psalm is thinking of an epiphany through which the wicked are annihilated "from heaven above." The psalmist, with his trusting expectation and certainty (cf. Ps. 140:10), enters into a sphere that far transcends the life of the individual, one that a person might prefer to associate with the king and with his wars (A. Bentzen). The "scorching wind" (רוח זלעפות) accompanies the destructive intervention from heaven—that is the "lot of the cup" or "cup allotment" of the enemies. The curious conception of the מנת־כוסם has most often been interpreted with a reference to the picture of the father of the house as he distributes and pours out. But there are surely more profound, cultic-sacral events in the background. There is the "cup of salvation" (כוס־ישועת, Ps. 116:13) which Yahweh pours; cf. Ps. 23:5. But there is also the "cup of wrath" (כוס חמתו, Isa. 51:17, 22; Lam. 4:21, 32, 33; and often). This either-or lets us think of a divine decision that perhaps was once reached in an ordeal (Num. 5:26ff.). But here it is a matter of standing metaphors, the specific original sacral connection of which has faded away. The psalmist sharply contrasts God's reaction to the misdeed of the wicked (v. 6) with God's love for the צדיק and his upright way of life (v. 7). The background for the statements about Yahweh's "hating" and "loving" could have been cultic declarations (cf. the comment on Ps. 5:5). Traces of so-called judgment-doxology form are unmistakable (cf. the comment on Ps. 7:9f.). While the רשע now is ruined, the צדיק, or ישר, may "behold the countenance of God." The background of this formulation is the viewing of the image of the god in pagan cults (cf. F. Nötscher, *Das Angesicht Gottes schauen* [1924]). In the OT this expression extends to the theophany, or to the event of God's presence in the temple (Pss. 17:15; 27:4). That Yahweh is "righteous" (v. 7) is a most concrete reality for the petitioner, the demonstration of which he enthusiastically anticipates. On the righteousness of God, cf. above, Intro. §10, 1. Otherwise, the statement of v. 7 perfectly agrees with what is stated in Ps. 5:4 ff. Reference should be made to the interpretations there advanced.

Purpose and Thrust

Psalm 11 deals with the mystery and wonder of trust in the God of Israel. Where well-meaning advisers can think only of flight and personal rescue as a way out of the abysmal distress, there the singer of the song of trust shelters himself with the God who has condescended in space and time and yet at the same time is the heavenly judge and savior. The definitive solution of the confused and tangled situation the psalmist thinks of as lying in God's hands. In keeping with OT faith, it is certain that a decisive and completely this-worldly intervention is imminent.

The NT proclaims Jesus Christ as the "place" of God's presence. To him is given all authority in heaven and on earth (Matt. 28:18). In him the eschatological judgment is at one and the same time both apparent and hidden. In the NT community the individual will seek the confident shelter of which Psalm 11 speaks in Jesus Christ alone. The ὀλιγόπιστοι (Matt. 8:26), who despair in the face of chaos, are called to complete trust in his power to overcome all hostile forces. But when considering a psalm such as this, we ought to realize that it opens up a possibility of an ecclesiological reception. Viewed thus, the psalm could become a song of confession and trust for the *ecclesia pressa* (church militant), which knows that every self-willed path of escape and shelter (v. 1b) is cut off for it and which places its confidence in the righteousness and help of God alone. If Psalm 11 was a formulary available to many generations, in which countless persecuted people and members of God's people whose rights were threatened could find a place for their distress, then the ecclesiological relation is unmistakable. The Psalms are the prayer songs of the people of God.

Psalm 12

Yahweh's Saving Word
in a World of Wickedness

Literature

M. Buber, *Recht und Unrecht: Deuting einiger Psalmen*, Sammlung Klosterberg. Europ. Reihe (1952). Jörg Jeremias, *Kultprophetie und Gerichtsverkündigung in der späten Königszeit Israels*, WMANT 35 (1970) 112-114.

Text

To the choirmaster. On the eighth. A psalm of David.

12:1 Help, O Yahweh, for the godly[a] are done for,
the faithful among human beings are 'cut off.'[b]

2 They speak deceitfully, one to another;
with smooth tongue and double heart they express themselves.

3 May Yahweh cut off all smooth lips,
the tongue that utters boasts;

4 Who declare: "With our tongue we are powerful,
our lips help us; who can be lord over us?"—

5 "Because of the oppression of the poor and the groans of
the weak
I will now arise," says Yahweh.
"I will place him in safety who is hard pressed."[c]

6 Yahweh's statements are pure words,
refined silver,' '[d] purified seven times.

7 You, O Yahweh, will keep them,
will protect him[e] against this[f] generation forever—

8 even though the wicked may walk round about
'and'[g] vileness may lift its head among the people.

1a With a reference to Hos. 4:1 (Jer. 7:28) and to the context of the psalm an emendation of חֶסֶד instead of חסיד is frequently suggested, an emendation not sufficiently substantiated. But on אבד חסיד, cf. Mic. 7:2; Isa. 57:1.

b פסו is not documented otherwise in the OT. The verb, in *parallelismus membrorum*, must have the meaning "cease." But that is a postulate. Perhaps סָפוּ (Ps. 73:19) can be adduced as an emendation.

5c The translation of יפיח לו had for a long time been disputed. It was usually translated: "for which he longs." Better is: "against whom people fret and fume"(= "who is hard pressed"); cf. Ps. 10:5 and Hab. 2:3 for the meaning of the verb and its construction with לְ. But we will also have to take into consideration the suffix of the third person singular in תצרנו (v. 7). There are textual emendations, for instance, following Gk (παρρησ-ιάσομαι ἐν αὐτῷ): אוֹפִיעַ (Ps. 94:1). But we expect to see the object of אשׁית. Gunkel: מְיַחֵל לִי.

6d Great difficulties are precipitated by the phrase בעליל לארץ (perhaps added as an explanatory note). GK has: δοκίμιον τῇ γῇ. According to Targ, we would have to translate "in the crucible" or "in the workshop." Were some completely unintelligible marginal readings incorporated in the text at this point? (Gunkel). It could be that בעליל לארץ denotes a procedure in the process of smelting: perhaps the "planting" of the molten mass into the earthen form.

7e The MT reading "you will protect him" is not to be corrected to תצרנו, following Gk. The suffix refers to יפיח לו in v. 5. In תשמרם the suffix refers to אמרות in v. 6.

f On זו without an article, cf. GesK §126y.

8g The addition of the second half-verse with כְ is hardly correct. With a few Mss we should read בְּרוּם (in a free translation, with "and").

Form

In its meter Psalm 12 exhibits an even form. The double four-pulse meter predominates: vv. 2, 3, 5, 7. If we should venture with Gunkel to supply וכל before לשׁון in v. 3b, then 4 + 4 would be read there too. The speech of God in v. 5 stands out in relief as a three-member four-pulse meter on its own weight. The psalm closes with two double three-pulse meters in vv. 7 and 8. The quotations in vv. 4 and 5 give the song a feeling of liveliness. The organization is easily visualized: vv. 1-2, the lamenting call for help by the petitioner; vv. 3-4, the wish that the wicked might be annihilated; v. 5, the saving word of God; vv. 6-8, the trusting answer to Yahweh's statement in v. 5.

For a long time great difficulties complicated the question of the *Gattung* (form group) of the psalm. The prevailing views tended toward thinking of Psalm 12 as a "lament of an individual" and toward understanding the statement of God in v. 5 as a "priestly oracle of salvation" (J. Begrich). But the strongly generalizing manner of speech in which the misdeeds "of the wicked" and the sufferings "of the poor" are expressed has also led to the supposition that there is a collective aspect to the psalm. Accordingly, people spoke of a "lamenting folk song" or of a "cultic liturgy" (H. Gunkel, A. Weiser). However we may decide on the details, in any case it is a good idea to settle on a prior determination of form with the general, inclusive declaration: Psalm 12 is a prayer song (cf. above, Intro. §6, 2) in which an utterance of God (v. 5) has been incorporated. More detailed statements can be introduced only in combinations. Especially Jörg Jeremias has materially advanced the understanding of the psalm by means of his investigations. He interprets Psalm 12 (as also Psalms 14 and 75) as a "cultic-prophetic liturgy of lament" and in our psalm sees the form represented in its most unequivocal shape. According to Jeremias, the cultic prophet is the speaker of the whole psalm, but especially of the word of God in v. 5, which he transmits as the message of salvation. "The word of God in v. 5 is by its linguistic independence from the preceding lament, by the lack of an address, and by the emphasis on the 'now' in the action of Yahweh clearly distinguished from the 'priestly oracle of salvation,' as J. Begrich has developed it'' (113). These characteristics closely connect Ps. 12:5 with Hab. 1:6ff.—as in general we must establish a close agreement of the psalm with the cultic-prophetic liturgy in Habakkuk 1.

Setting

Classifying the prayer song as a ''cultic-prophetic liturgy'' establishes a connection between Psalm 12 and the worship of Israel and begins with the assumption that a cultic prophet was the speaker of the liturgical pieces, in other words, not only of the words of God in v. 5 but also of the laments and petitions spoken in the name of the community. There are no ''we-laments.'' The prophet speaks as the representative of his afflicted people (J. Jeremias, 113). Parallel forms of expression and intentions should be noted in OT prophecy: Hos. 4:1; 7:4; Isa. 9:16; Mic. 7:2; Jer. 5:1ff.; and often. This conception rules out all psychologizing or individualizing attempts at interpretation. Also, there is no discernible trace of a cultic drama with a king at its center (A. Bentzen). The cultic-prophetic liturgy of lament opens up new possibilities of interpretation for the whole. However, it may not be embraced so narrowly and exclusively as to preclude the possibility of thinking of Psalm 12 as a prayer formulary, which this psalm doubtlessly was in its subsequent history. The cultic liturgical definition can and must be undertaken within the framework of the more general, more comprehensive understanding and must there have its place.

The question when the psalm originated has been investigated by Jeremias on the basis of word statistics. He came to the conclusion that both the early years of the monarchy and also the late postexilic dating are excluded. Thus, a late preexilic estimate is a possibility (the time of Habakkuk).

Commentary

On לַמְנַצֵּחַ, cf. above, Intro. § 4, No. 17. On the formulation עַל־הַשְּׁמִינִית, see §4, No. 25. And on מִזְמוֹר לְדָוִד, see §4, No. 2.

[12:1] Psalm 12 begins with a supplication uttered in face of the worst distress (''the godly are done for'') and that begs for Yahweh's saving intervention (cf. Ps. 3:7; 6:4; 7:1; and often). The חָסִיד threatens to be devoured by enemies hostile to God. In its background חָסִיד had become a decidedly collective term that denoted membership in the covenant with Yahweh (L. Gulkowitsch, *Die Entwicklung des Begriffes ḥāsîd im Alten Testament* [1934], 22). חָסִיד is now the person who lives a life that is true to the community and in keeping with the covenant, one who may also be called צַדִּיק (see above, Intro. §10, 3). The speaker in Psalm 12 intercedes for those members of the people of God who are persecuted innocently (cf. Psalm 7), for the poor and those without rights. He lifts his voice for the אֱמוּנִים, who remain true to Yahweh and his convenant (on the root אָמַן, cf. H. Wildberger in *THAT* 1, 177ff.; additional bibliography there).

[12:2] The activity of the violent and the persecutors is for the first indicated in a general way in v. 2. They speak ''deceitfully,'' they express themselves with ''smooth tongue and double heart.'' We are presumably to think of slanderous accusations and rumors allowed to circulate cleverly. שָׁוְא denotes that which is empty of meaning, shallow (M.A. Klopfenstein, ''Die Lüge nach dem Alten Testament,'' diss., Bern, 1964, 310ff.). The reference is only to the enemies' power of words; so also in v. 4. Obviously there is to be a contrast, which comes to light with the characterization of the words of Yahweh in v. 6a. On the activity of the enemies, see above, Intro. §10, 4. חלקות are the smooth, insidious speeches that lead to downfall (Isa. 30:10; Dan. 11:32). With psychological awareness, the speaker recognizes that the lying and slanderous words of the persecutors arise from a divided, split heart. לב אחד (Jer. 32:39; Ezek. 11:19; 1 Chron. 12:39; Acts 4:32) is the "conscious, perfect unification of will, thought, and feeling" (Franz Delitzsch, *System der biblischen Psychologie* [1855], 206). By contrast, the expression בלב ולב denotes the ἀνήρ δίψυχος (James 1:8). For the sake of illustration, F. Nötscher calls attention to Deut. 25:13, where אבן ואבן denotes false weight. In the intentional lie the center, the personal nucleus, of human existence is split. Persons of this stamp predominate; their machinations leave their stamp on the course of life, and it is a badly split and torn existence. The power of prophetic speech that permeates the whole is unmistakable.

[12:3-4] In view of the torn and dangerous situation, the speaker prays for Yahweh's intervention and appeals to his effective judgment. The slanderers, who pride themselves on their unrestrained, insidious ("smooth") power of speech, are to be destroyed and extirpated. As in Ps. 10:4, 6, the speaker cites the high-sounding talk of the enemies for the purpose of persuading Yahweh to intervene. One might be inclined to take the statements of v. 4 as magic curses emanating from the רשעים (S. Mowinckel). But these could also intend in a general way to represent the presumptuous and self-assured talk which is to intimidate and beat down the poor (cf. Ps. 73:8-9). The ground is being prepared for a contrast: opposite the words מי אדון לנו in the proud talk of the wicked stands the powerful action of Yahweh, outlined in vv. 5 and 7f.

[12:5] The focal point of the prophetic liturgy is the message of Yahweh transmitted by the cultic prophet (v. 5). Franz Delitzsch was still able to assert that Psalm 12 shows "how the writer of the psalm, while in spiritual excitement, graduates to the tone of a prophet who perceives the word of God directly and is accordingly inspired." And yet we are actually dealing with a prophetically transmitted statement (that is to be separated and distinguished from the priestly oracle of salvation (J. Begrich). Characteristic of the prophetic type of the דבר is the acutely historical announcement: "I will now arise!" We must also take note of this "arising." Yahweh intervenes not only for an individual persecuted person but "because of the oppression of the poor." His judgment affects the whole people of God. Nevertheless, in v. 5 we are dealing with evidence of prophecy of salvation. The statement of Yahweh transmitted by the cultic prophet brings salvation to the oppressed and the weak.

The parallelism with the cultic-prophetic liturgy of Habakkuk 1 is worth noting. Also in that text the prophetic speaker cries and prays for help in view of violence and suppression (v. 2). He has to witness evil; oppression and violence are perpetrated before his eyes (v. 3), and justice is perverted (v. 4). But then a change takes place, for which v. 5 provides the preparation. The prophetically transmitted word of God in vv. 6ff. announces God's intervention in a first-person address by God. The subject is an incursion by the Chaldeans. To be sure, in contrast to Ps. 12:5, Habakkuk 1 basically deals with a word of judgment (cf. v. 12), but in any case it also deals with the announcement of God's intervention in face of the collapse of justice and the corrupt living conditions of the people of God.

It was with the plea קומו (cf. Ps. 7:6) that Israel prayed for Yahweh's intervention in its cry for help. Consequently, אקום would have to be interpreted as the announcement of the arising of God that is now taking place and is to be expected immediately (Ps. 18:7ff.). עתה entails the zenith of prophetically announced actuality. "With this 'now' the manifestation of salvation breaks out into the open in the worst time of adversity, a manifestation that is not still to come but is always present and needs only to become active" (M. Buber, 14).[1]

Of course the question is whether the formulation "always present" is appropriate. The accent is on the immediate presence of the salvation. אשית בישע is a pointed promise of God's words. Literally, we would have to translate: "I will transport to the sphere of salvation." The object of this intervention of God's that changes the whole situation is יפיח לו. Here (as, for example, also in Ps. 10:5) S. Mowinckel thinks of the magic breath and translates: "who has been breathed upon" (*PsStud* 1, 23, 54f.). But even if this should refer to a magic gesture of imprecation, we would still have to assume that it is fading away or would have to be understood as speaking about the raging and dangerous fumings of the persecutors that furiously assail the oppressed.

[12:6-8] Vv. 6-8 deal with the meaning of God's words in v. 5, and this meaning decides and determines everything. The reference to the אמרות indicates and, in the style of a confession, asserts that all the utterances of Yahweh are proved and reliable. In contrast to the deceptive, empty talk of the proud and boastful wicked, the word of God has not the slightest deceitful admixture. Yahweh's statements are pure and genuine, and one can depend on them. For the syntactical arrangement of the sentence in the MT, cf. BrSynt, §126a. Like frequently refined precious metal are the promises of Yahweh, without a trace of anything false or spurious. This sincerity and integrity of the words of God is demonstrated by the fact that Yahweh "keeps" (for שמר, cf. Jer. 1:12) his word. V. 7 is a prayer address to Yahweh which not only is applied to the cry for help in v. 1 as the conviction that it will be heard but also extends immediately to the assent given in v. 5. הדור qualifies the entire generation now alive in the sense of vv. 1ff. This manner of speaking is taken up in the NT: cf. Matt. 11:16; 12:41f.; 23:36; and often. But Yahweh's promise of salvation signifies protection for the poor, even when he is surrounded by the wicked (cf. Ps. 3:1ff.) and when malice reigns everywhere.

Purpose and Thrust

The center of the psalm is without question the prophetically transmitted saying of God in v. 5. It occurs in the context of a cultic-prophetic liturgy in which the speaker expresses himself first in the function of intercession. This speaker appears before Yahweh as the representative of the community. He intercedes for the poor and the oppressed of his people. Intercession was a chief function of the cultic prophet (G. von Rad, *OT Theol*, 2:46f.). The prayer song is influenced by the prophetic office. The prayer goes far beyond the fate of an individual; it extends to the distress of the people of God. In this context the wicked are

---

1. "There is also great emphasis in the adverb *now*, by which God intimates that, although our safety is in his hand, and, therefore, in secure keeping, yet he does not immediately grant deliverance from affliction; for his words imply that he had hitherto been, as it were, lying still and asleep, until he was awakened by the calamities and the cries of his people. When, therefore, the injuries, the extortions, and the devastations of our enemies leave us nothing but tears and groans, let us remember that now the time is at hand when God intends to rise up to execute judgment. This doctrine should also serve to produce in us patience, and prevent us from taking it ill, that we are reckoned among the number of the poor and afflicted, whose cause God promises to take into his own hand" (Calvin, on Ps. 12:5, trans. Anderson [Grand Rapids: Eerdmans, 1949]).

exposed in their ruinous dealings (as in a prophetic speech of indictment). And yet the words of Yahweh stand in the center of the cultic-prophetic event. The specific and realistic (עתה, v. 5) promise of rescue and of intervention protrudes as a power that snatches a persecuted and despairing life from the realm of destruction. Yahweh arises in majesty and turns to the helpless. The psalm shows how all things depend on God's word and how reliable and helpful this word actually is. All of this, in the final analysis, centers on the path of the people of God. The context in which Psalm 12 wants to be received and make its point is an ecclesiological one.

Psalm 13

Questions and Laments at the Abyss of Death

Literature

E. Baumann, "Struktur-Untersuchungen im Psalter I," *ZAW* 61 (1945/48 114-176). C. Barth, *Die Errettung vom Tode in den individuellen Klage- und Dankliedern des Alten Testaments* (1947). L. Wachter, *Der Tod im Alten Testament* (1967).

Text

To the choirmaster. A psalm of David.

13:1 Yet how long, O Yahweh? Will you forget me forever[a]?
How long will you hide your face before me?

2 How long am I to carry sorrows[b] about in my soul,
grief in my heart day after day[c]?
How long will my enemy rise up against me?

3 Behold me, hear me,[d] O Yahweh, my God!
Enlighten my eyes that I may not fall asleep in death[e]!

4 That my enemy may not say, I have subdued[f] him!
That my adversary may not exult because I am shaken.

5 Yet I—I trust in your goodwill,
May my heart exult in your help!
I want to sing to Yahweh, for he has done[g] good
things for me.

1a The word נצח (Gk εἰς τέλος) after עד־אנה or עד־מָתַי designates the impatience of waiting and of lamenting: Pss. 74:10; 79:5; 89:46.

2b עצות (Gk βουλάς) in the sense of "sorrows" is documented in Prov. 27:9 and Sir. 30:21. Still, the reading עַצֶּבֶת or עַצְּבוֹת is frequently conjectured.

c Gk and Syh supply וָלַיְלָה but this is probably more a matter of instinctive supplementation.

3d Another reading thought of as possible, עָנְיִי (Pss. 9:13; 25:18; 119:153), is hardly to be preferred to the MT.

e The suggestion to read אִשָּׁנָה מָוֶת (Baethgen and others) is to mitigate the offense of the article. But cf. Ges-K §117r, n. 2.

4f יכל usually with ל: Gen. 32:26; Num. 13:30; and often; therefore Gk translates ἴσχυσα πρὸς αὐτόν. Accordingly, we should perhaps read יָכֹלְתִּי לוֹ. But cf. BrSynt §90a.

5g Gk adds: καὶ ψαλῶ τῷ ὀνόματι κυρίου τοῦ ὑψίστου (cf. Ps. 7:17).

Form

Psalm 13 belongs to the group, Psalms of David. In its arrangement it presents a clear picture. After the technical preliminary remarks in the title, the song begins with a series of desperate questions, vv. 1 and 2. These questions change into lamenting petitions in vv. 3 and 4, and confidence and thanksgiving are heard at the close in v. 5. There is no way of proving a strophic organization. The meter is unsettled. If we follow the MT, we must read 4 + 4 in vv. 1 and 3, 4 + 3 in vv. 2 and 4; 3 + 3 in v. 5. Half-verses without a corresponding parallelism of members are present as simple fours in vv. 2 and 5. The question remains whether the additions to the text in Gk are original. If so, a second parallelism of members would have to be set up in v. 5. All emendations "for the sake of the meter" remain unsatisfactory patchwork.

Psalm 13 is to be classified as belonging to the form group, prayer songs (תפלה; cf. above, Intro. §6, 2). H. Gunkel classified the psalm as an individual lament (Gunkel and Begrich, *EinlPs* 6) and was of the opinion that Psalm 13 is a particularly clear model of this *Gattung*. Nonetheless, the concept of lament must be abandoned. The petitioners of the psalms do not lament, neither do they complain. They openly declare their distress before Yahweh and pray for his intervention. This is justly called a prayer. Accordingly, Hebrew tradition calls such a prayer song תפלה. In the עד־אנה-questions in vv. 1-2, the distress of long standing disclosed by the petitioner before Yahweh is revealed. In vv. 3 and 4 there follow the strained imperatives of the plea which exhibit great urgency in view of the pursuing enemy (v. 4). In v. 5 we are to distinguish two intentions. V. 5a contains an expression of trust, summarized in the statement "I trust in your goodwill"; combined with this expression of trust is the confidence and wish that the heart of the petition may exult in Yahweh's help (his concrete intervention). In contrast to this, v. 5b looks back to the salvation already bestowed and in the style of a song of praise of an individual expresses thanksgiving (*todah*) for the rescue already experienced. Features of a "report of praise" are suggested (cf. D. Michel, *Tempora und Satzstellung in den Psalmen* [1960], 63, 65).

Setting

What is the situation of the psalmist? Does the prayer song reveal any clues at all that may answer this question? V. 3 has again and again become the center of attention in this matter. Obviously, the petitioner is near death. His vitality, broken down by suffering of long standing (vv. 1f.), is blighted. Thus we could think of a person mortally ill. Still, there is really not a trace of concrete evidence that points to a sickness, or of the nature of the suffering. H. Schmidt's suggestion that we might think of a person afflicted with a disease of the eyes depends on inappropriate interpretation of the plea "enlighten my eyes!" (see below). The real distress in which the petitioner of the psalm utters his groans is the separation from God, that is, his experiencing of the wrath of God. And yet, we must surely also give attention to the appearance of the enemy (v. 4), whose purpose is to ruin this weak person (by means of slanderous accusation? by means of disclosures of the guilt that is presumed to be at the bottom of the sickness?). Basically, however, H. Gunkel is right in emphasizing that it is not the physical pain of the petitioner that is the heart of the matter, but rather the fact that "his hope in God seems to come to grief and that his faith does not seem to come into its own."

It is completely beside the point to think of hidden "messianic" motives, in connection with title לדוד, and to interpret Psalm 13 as a "royal psalm" in the context of a dramatic rite of lament (so A. Bentzen).

The powerful prayer song could be very old, but dating is hardly possible. The psalm would have been intoned in the sanctuary and probably had some importance as a prayer formulary.

Commentary

[Title] On למנצח, cf. above, Intro. §4, No. 17. On מזמור לדוד, see §4, No. 2.

[13:1-2] To begin with, the questions and laments in vv. 1-2 reveal a remarkable peculiarity so far as their formal organization is concerned. Four times the questions begin with עד־אנה. Metrically considered, there are always sets of four involved. Therefore one may be tempted to ask whether the second half-verse in v. 2a should perhaps have to be expunged altogether "for the sake of the meter" because of its troublesome triple meter. In that case, we would have to read four four-pulse units beginning with עד־אנה. Such a reconstruction would claim as a precedent a Babylonian parallel.

> In a lament of Nebuchadnezzar I we read:
> Yet how long with me,
> Yet how long in my land,
> Yet how long in my people?
> Until when, Lord of Babylon,
> This groaning and depression?
> This weeping and grieving?
> This lamenting and weeping?
> Do you tarry in the camp of the enemy?

This text expresses the fourfold question ("yet how long?") in 2+2, or 4, stresses. The song was adapted by H. Zimmern (*AO* 7, 7/8) and in the interpretation of Psalm 13 is adduced for the reconstruction of an original text by E. Baumann (*Struktur-Untersuchungen im Psalter 1*, 126f.). Even though the formal parallel structure is remarkable, we should presumably preserve some restraint in the reconstruction of the "original state" of Psalm 13. The Babylonian royal lament and communal lament, after all, have their own identity, in terms of form and of content. Baumann recognizes these distinctions, but nevertheless goes rather far afield in his structural analyses based on the parallels.

The desperate questions עד־אנה are witnesses to the unbearable afflictions that the petitioner had to suffer a long time. Cf. Pss. 6:3; 35:17; 74:10; 79:5; 94:3; 80:4; and often. Yahweh is addressed. Accordingly, all affliction is traced back to him. The person whom Yahweh "forgets," whom he forsakes, must bear the unbearable affliction of which Psalm 13 speaks.[1]

---

1. "Doesn't he who perceives God everywhere to be turned away, contrary, implacable, inexorable, and eternally angry describe this most desperate and bitter state of mind with fitting words? For here hope despairs and at the same time despair has hope, and there is alive only that indescribable groaning by which the Spirit intercedes, moving over the face of the waters of darkness, as Genesis 1 tells us. No one understands these things who has not experienced them; these things do not take place in what meets the eye or in open appearances, such as spectators can play with at their leisure,

The primary and worst agony dealt with in our lament is the state of being forsaken by God (Ps. 22:1). This is the thrust of the word נצח. In the contradictory "how long—forever" F. Nötscher wants to see a crystallized form of expression which he contends is a contradiction logically but not psychologically. Even though a person may question whether the imputation of a "crystallization" is appropriate, still he will probably be able to consider Nötscher's interpretation as correct—insofar as its intention coincides with the meaning of the following explanation of Franz Delitzsch: "It is part of the essence of the wrath of God that the perception of it is always accompanied by the impression of eternity and therefore as a foretaste of hell" ("hell" = absolute abandonment by God). On נצח, cf. Jer. 15:18; Amos 1:11 (Ps. 16:11). But of course in the צד־אנה-questions we may see not only signs of a stormy impatience but also signs of a great patience, which never ceased to call on Yahweh in suffering of long duration. But now, because of excessive affliction this patience has turned to desperate hopelessness that can no longer endure unending abandonment by God: "Yet how long will you hide your face before me?"

פנים in the OT is a manner of visualizing in which Yahweh reveals himself (L. Köhler, *OT Theology* 123f.). If Yahweh now hides his countenance, then the human being is forsaken by God. He is alone with his עצות (v. 2). He torments himself with worrisome thoughts and "conjures up disquieting conceptions": F. Delitzsch, *System der biblischen Psychologie* (1855) 161. These עצות presumably constantly center on the problem of the connection between grief and guilt, on the basic question of all distress: Why must I suffer all this? Parallel to עצות is the expression יגון בלבבי; it cautions against every emendation for the word עצות (cf. also Prov. 27:9; Sir. 30:21). V. 2a deals with the self-examining, self-condemning, and scrupulous considerations that arise in the experience of abandonment by God and worsen the suffering immeasurably. And here also the "enemy" of the petitioner immediately enters the picture. On the problem of "the enemies of the individual," cf. above, Intro. §10, 4. The enemy of the individual is a force that separates from God, for which the interpretations have a definite character (Ps. 3:2). The enemy reasons: You are cut off from God—your life, given over to death and ruin, is proof of it! The petitioner asks at the brink of the grave: עד־אנה.

[13:3-4] The questions and complaints now develop into pleas (vv. 3-4). The imperatives are ultimate, extreme cries for help. הביטה in the OT is a characteristic cry of prayer (cf. Isa. 63:15). The petitioner who knows he is "forgotten" by God (v. 1) now prays for God's sympathy and attention.[2] He prays for an answer—very likely for a specific word from God, an "oracle of salvation" (J. Begrich, "Das priesterliche Heilsorakel," *ZAW* 52,1934, 81-92). On אלהי, see O. Eissfeldt, " 'Mein Gott' im AT," *ZAW* 61 (1945/48) 3-16. But may the attention and the answer of Yahweh turn into a rescuing act—that is the

---

but in the innermost recesses of immortal life, that is, in the perception of the soul" (Luther, WA 5; 385, 17ff.)..

2. " 'Have regard' according to the style of Scripture denotes the accomplishment of God when he has pity, just as he said about the verb 'arise' in the foregoing psalm, and it signifies a more immediate and more welcome accomplishment than just to have remembered, as for instance: do not remember or have regard for the more bitter (aspect)" (Luther, WA 5: 388, 11f.).

prayer of the petitioner. האירה עיני means "revive my power to live!" Cf. Chr. Barth, *Die Errettung vom Tode in den individuellen Klage- und Dankliedern des Alten Testaments* (1947) 35.[3] In grief and illness the glow of life is extinguished in the eyes, and they become dull and tired (Pss. 6:7; 38:10; Lam. 5:17). Invigorating nourishment can restore the glow (1 Sam. 14:27, 29). But above all, it is Yahweh's power of life that lets the eyes sparkle again" (Ps. 19:8; Prov. 29:13). As in Psalm 13, now the prayer for God's attention and answer stands opposite the experience of being forgotten (v. 1), so the prayer for restoration of the power of life will correspond to that frightful experience in v. 1b that Yahweh hides his countenance: If Yahweh lets his countenance "shine" again (Num. 6:25), then the eyes that are becoming lifeless will also receive the light of life. "Enlighten my eyes!" This prayer call means to say: "Let me see the light of life!" Cf. H.-J. Kraus, "Hören und Sehen in der althebräischen Tradition," *Biblisch-theologische Aufsätze* (1972) 84ff. The situation is clearly discernible in v. 3: the petitioner is near death. Death is portrayed as sleep (cf. Jer. 51:39; Job 3:13; 14:12), as a condition in which a person is far removed from the life before God. Cf. Ps. 6:5 and the commentary on this verse. For the afflicted, death would be the sealing of an irrevocable separation from Yahweh. It would be the triumph of the enemy, whose entire effort is directed toward overwhelming the sufferer with clearly defined judgments. If the petitioner were to stagger and collapse, that would call forth a shout of jubilation from the adversaries. The forces that have parted company with God would win the day. Is that the way it should be? Should God not be able to intervene? The prayers of the lamenting petitioner contain an appeal to the honor and power of God.

[13:5] The expression of trust beginning with ואני has the force of an emphatic affirmation: Even though everything points to death and the end, I trust in your goodness. On חסד, cf. the interpretation of Ps. 5:7. The petitioner trusts in God's readiness to help, promised in the covenant. He permits no power to force him away from Yahweh's benevolent declaration of salvation. His trust in v. 1a is not spun out of thin air. His request and his confidence already look forward to the coming turn of events—the request that his heart may rejoice in the experience of deliverance. V. 5b—sounding forth in a single sentence—contains the *todah*-hymn of the individual: the song of praise that looks back on Yahweh's completed intervention and reports concerning it that "good things were done" for the sufferer. How the turn of events happened we are not told. It is enough that it did happen and that it is attested in a song of praise.

Purpose and Thrust

At the center of the first part of the psalm (vv. 1-2) stands the unfathomable affliction of abandonment by God. The reference is not to the illness possibly present in its life-threatening outward form but only to the break in the communion with God. The petitioner is crushed by the wrath of God (cf. the

---

3. "To enlighten the eyes signifies the same thing in the Hebrew language as to give the breath of life, for the vigor of life appears chiefly in the eyes. . . . In short, David confesses that unless God causes the light of life to shine upon him, he will be immediately overwhelmed with the darkness of death, and that he is already as a man without life, unless God breathe into him new vigor. And certainly our confidence of life depends on this, that although the world may threaten us with a thousand deaths, yet God is possessed of numberless means of restoring us to life" (Calvin on Ps. 13:4, trans. Anderson [Grand Rapids: Eerdmans, 1949]).

comment on Psalm 6). Luther declares: "Christ bore the same tribulation on the cross" (WA 5: 386, 26). In this statement Luther points to the full realization of abandonment by God (Matt. 27:46), on the basis of which alone our psalm can be understood correctly. But the prayer for rescue from death (v. 3) in the OT has the meaning that the force that separates from God (Ps. 6:5) be deprived of its power in the midst of this life. If the enemies of the individual do not find opportunity for exultation over one who has been ruined, this too is a triumph over the forces that want to separate the petitioner from Yahweh (v. 4). In trust and hope the prayer song looks forward to the moment when the exultation over God's intervention will break out. Yet it is amazing that the accomplished turn of events is clearly announced in v. 5b. The song of praise is not only a thing hoped for; it already is intoned in the midst of the abyss of forsakenness by God described in vv. 1ff. Thereby the center of attention is not the change of fortune but the saving God alone, who rescues from the realm of death, enlightens the eyes (v. 3), and does good things (v. 5b).

Psalm 14

The Help of God in a World Dominated by Corruption

Literature

C. H. C. Torrey, "The Archetype of Psalms 14 and 53," *JBL* 46 (1927) 186-192. K. Budde, "Psalm 14 and 53," *JBL* 47 (1928) 160-183. M. Buber, *Recht und Unrecht: Deutung einiger Psalmen* (Sammlung Klosterberg, Europ. Reihe) 1952. E. San Pedro, "Problemata philologica psalmi XIV," *VD* 45 (1967) 65-78. J. Jeremias, *Kultprophetie und Gerichtsverkündigung in der späten Königszeit Israels*, WMANT 35 (1970) 114-117.

Text

To the choirmaster. Of David.

14:1 The fool says in his heart:
"There is no God!"
They do what is wicked[a] and corrupt.[b]
No one does what is good.

2 Yahweh[c] looks down from heaven
on the children of men,
to see whether there be one who is wise,
one who (still) inquires about God.

3 They are all unfaithful,
altogether depraved;
there is no one who does good,
no, not a single one.[d]

4 Have they really no insight,[e] all[f] those evildoers
who devour my people (as) one eats bread,[g]
who do not call on Yahweh?[h]

5 (And yet) then they are terrified enormously,[i]
for God is with the righteous.[j]

6 In the plan against the poor man[k] you will go to pieces,
for Yahweh is his refuge.

218

7 Oh, that Israel's salvation[l] would appear from Zion!
   When Yahweh turns the fate of his people,
   Jacob will exult, and Israel will be glad.

1a In Ps. 53:1 and Targ: וְהִתְעִיבוּ. And yet the asyndetical connection without וֹ is far more effective; the copula simplifies the text.

b In Ps. 53:1 and Targ: עֲלִילָה עָוֶל ("the activity") is colorless in comparison with עוֹל and could involve a tendency to simplify.

2c In Ps. 53:2, in the Elohistic Psalter, we have אלהים.

3d Gk here interpolates the verses attested in Rom. 3:13-18 in the NT (but not in Psalm 53). This raises the suspicion that these verses were added later from Romans 3 by Christian hands.

4e Gk, σ´, Jerome, and Targ have יָדְעוּ. Still, the perfect tense in MT, occurring in the context with the other perfect tenses in Psalm 14, ought to be retained.

f כל־ is missing in Ps. 53:4.

g The אָכַל (Gk βρώσει ἄρτου) of Gk, Syr, and Jerome tries to decode the (difficult) abbreviating idiom in the MT ("as one eats bread"). The textual difficulties begin at v. 4 and extend to v. 6. Problematic is the attempt to combine לחם יהוה as a construct form, to supply שְׁמוֹ and to apply v. 4 to the priests (H. Gunkel, H. Schmidt). With this correction, fraught with many consequences, the purpose of the entire psalm is shifted. The godless priests suddenly appear at center stage. For this text-critical encroachment Gunkel imputes to the phrase "a genuinely prophetic leap."

h Ps. 53:4 (in the Elohistic Psalter): אלהים.

5i In Ps. 14:5 and Ps. 53:5 we now have texts that markedly deviate from each other and are especially difficult to understand:

Ps. 14:5: שם פחדו פחד כי אלהים בדור צדיק
עצת־עני תבישו כי יהוה מחסהו

Ps. 53:5: שם פחדו פחד לא־היה פחד כי־אלהים פזר עצמות חנך
הבשתה   כי־אלהים מאסם

Our attention should first of all be directed to the dependent clauses introduced by כי. Here it becomes apparent that Ps. 14:5 with its parallelisms provides a clearer picture than does Ps. 53:5. The latter: "There they are terrified enormously—there was [up to the present?] no terror—for God scatters the bones of him who besieges you; you put to shame [whom?], for God repudiates them." The meaning of this statement, hardly discernible without bold constructions, is to be found by way of the simple, transparent sentences of Ps. 14:5. Here above all the question comes up, how is שָׁם to be understood? Certainly not in a temporal sense ("at that time" or "then"). Rather, in the context, it is obvious to refer שָׁם to the local datum of the misdeeds brought to light in Ps. 14:4. "There, under those circumstances" (namely, the goings-on described in v. 4) "they [the evildoers] are terrified enormously." This emergence of judgment, which (as the parenthesis in Ps. 53:5 lets us notice) was heretofore hidden, has changed Ps. 53:5 into an address (cf. Ps. 14:6; תבישו). But here MT in Ps. 53:5 is probably thinking of a (promissory) address to afflicted persons: "Yahweh scatters the bones [perhaps better: עֲצוֹת 'the plans,' corresponding to Ps. 14:6] of the besieger." We would have to think of "the besieger," the violent man, whom God "repudiates" (plural) as the direct object of הבשתה.

j דור in the sense of "class of men," "group of human beings," recedes into the background in the translation.

6k עצת־עני in the context is very likely parallel to שָׁם and essentially refers to v. 4. Accordingly, this would be a matter of an abbreviated way of speaking. But all of this is only an attempt to understand the corrupt text in close connection with the MT.

7l *Athnaḥ* is uncorrectly written under the construct form יְשׁועַת. Unfortunately—and that goes for textual criticism on Psalm 14 as a whole—the reconstructions of an original text by C. C. Torrey and K. Budde are too radical and in part also too arbitrary.

Form

The text of our psalm is transmitted once more, with slight variations, in Psalm 53. Obviously, the song was present in two collections that were included in the Psalter (cf. Intro. §2). The form of the text in Psalm 53 (especially in Ps. 53:5) is more complicated and less transparent than in Psalm 14. It is therefore advisable to base the interpretation and exegesis on Psalm 14. The textual notes have already surveyed the divergencies in Psalm 53. Difficulties, which can be unraveled only slightly and with great caution, remain in Ps. 14:4-6 and Ps. 53:4-5, in any case. On the whole, B. Duhm has clearly pointed out that the divergent readings of Psalm 53 are in all points secondary over against Psalm 14 (with the exception of Ps. 14:4, which is influenced by the Elohistic redaction).

In its meter, Psalm 14 presents a number of difficulties, which can, however, be explained better than is commonly assumed. Disregarding the heading למנצח לדוד, we have in vv. 1 and 2 four 3 + 2 verses. In v. 3, two 2 + 2 verses follow. Corresponding to the translation presented above, v. 4 divides into three parts that would have to be read as 3 + 3 + 2. If we then proceed from the observation that in vv. 5 and 6 we again have the meter 3 + 2, we could be inclined to think of the words אכלו עמי אכלו לחם text-critically disputed as they are, as a later addition. But that is hardly possible. The text in vv. 4-6 presents difficulties that cannot be eliminated. In v. 7 a solitary four-pulse meter is followed by a close that must be read as 4 + 4.

In its arrangement Psalm 14 is easily analyzed. Following the editorial heading, vv. 1b-4 contain an independent section that laments the depraved conditions among the people of God; as a result, v. 4 ends with a question of despair. V. 5 certainly reveals a sudden change, which will have immediate consequences (v. 6). V. 7 could perhaps be a later addition (J. Jeremias, 115); the form-critical analysis will generally have to leave this verse out of account.

The form-critical investigation of our psalm has in its research so far led to considerable differences. Worth noting is the manner in which H. Gunkel and H. Schmidt have carried out the analysis of form. Three component parts have been isolated: a prophetic invective in vv. 1-3, a prophetic threat in v. 6, and the added "sigh" in v. 7. In this way a preponderantly prophetic character is assigned to the psalm. The first form observations of H. Gunkel and H. Schmidt have been confirmed in remarkable manner by J. Jeremias. Jeremias has recognized cultic-prophetic liturgies in Psalms 12; 14; and 75. Habakkuk 1 is to be added. In all these liturgies two basic ingredients are ascertainable: the lament of the prophetic speaker and the citation of, or the reference to, the word of Yahweh (cf. the comment on Psalm 12). In Psalm 14 the situation is such that in the first place the ruinous circumstances among the people of God are expressed in "starkly objective sobriety" (vv. 1-3). The lament, which certainly is comparable to prophetic indictment, reaches its climax in the question of despair in v. 4. Afflictions among the people of God are not the subject of any "individual lament"; they gain expression in prophetic revelation. "My people" (v. 4) is not the expression of an individual, but that of a prophet. The lament in Ps. 12:5 and Hab. 1:6ff. is followed by the word of God transmitted by the prophet. In Ps. 14:5 the procedure is different. The prophetic speaker "in v. 5 reports in formal ['prophetic'] perfect tenses the destruction of the wicked as seen in a vision, a destruction initiated by Yahweh's intervention . . ." (J. Jeremias, 115). As in Ps. 12:5 (עתה), the suddenness of the event is emphasized. V. 6 addresses the wicked and announces their destruction.

Setting

As with Psalm 12, also Psalm 14 should be set in a cultic situation of the late preexilic time (cf. the striking parallel to Habakkuk 1). But details cannot be provided. That a Zion tradition is involved is apparent from the fact that v. 7 is added. But the psalm with its radical disclosures must have developed into a prayer song of knowledge and confidence in all places where, dislodged from its cultic-liturgical situation, it was adapted for use in a new way. Especially v. 7 clearly reveals that a special prayer petition and basic insight were required when the psalm was recited in the worship of the community.

Commentary

[14:1] On למנצח, cf. above, Intro. §4, No. 17. On לדוד, §4, No. 2.

The psalm begins immediately with a striking reference to the thinking and reasoning of the נבל. Concerning the style element אמר נבל, cf. נאם־פשע in Ps. 36:1. The opening of the psalm therefore immediately draws attention to a type of human being that lives under the secret assumption, אין אלהים. The person who thinks thus is in the OT otherwise usually called רשע. The term נבל is borrowed from the חכמה tradition and tends toward an intellectual way of thinking which, however, immediately expresses itself in ruinous and abominable actions. This type, the נבל, dominates all of communal life. The prophetic speaker unexpectedly lashes out in a general judgment (cf. Ps. 12:1f.): אין עשׂה־טוב. Where God is not present, there is no good deed either.[1] אין עשׂה־טוב corresponds to אין אלהים.

It has properly been pointed out again and again that the judgment אין אלהים entails, not a theoretical, but a practical atheism. "There is no God," according to Ps. 10:4, 11, means: "He does not avenge," "he has hidden his face," "he does not see." He who denies God contests not the existence of God but the concrete activity of God. With the judgment לוא הוא he combines the contention: "No evil will come upon us" (Jer. 5:12). The godless person "knows no fear of God" (Ps. 36:1). The antithesis to אין אלהים would be דרשׁ את־אלהים (Ps. 14:2). The נבל does not call on God (Ps. 14:4). Here a serious decision may be involved, which becomes a reality if Yahweh does not intervene (Job 2:9). "The assumption that God exists is the Old Testament's greatest gift to mankind. In the Old Testament God's existence is entirely a foregone conclusion, always presupposed; reference is continually being made to it; it is never denied or questioned. The fool says in his heart 'there is no God', Ps. 14:1, Ps. 53:1, and the foolish women may speak like that (Job. 2:10); or man may deny Him and say 'this is not He', לא הוא, Jer. 5:12. But these are the words of people who are lacking in understanding, so lacking that they can be described in the same breath as corrupt and having done abominable works. They speak like that not in order to deny God but in order to evade His judgment and His claims upon them. They call in question His action as it affects their lives, but they do not call in question His existence. It is practical atheism, as the sinner practices it; not theoretical atheism. The latter is unknown to the Old Testament" (L. Köhler, *OT Theology* [1957] I §1, opening paragraph).

[14:2-3] The lament and statement uttered in v. 1 is given its underpinning in vv. 2-3 by means of a verdict of the heavenly judge. Whenever the Psalms speak of the heavenly throne of Yahweh and of the scrutinizing look of God, they always

---

1. "It is therefore important for us, in the first place, to know, that however much the world applaud these crafty and scoffing characters, who allow themselves to indulge to any extent in wickedness, yet the Holy Spirit condemns them as being fools; for there is no stupidity more brutish than forgetfulness of God" (Calvin, on Ps. 14:1, trans. Anderson [Grand Rapids: Eerdmans, 1949]).

have in mind Yahweh's office of judgment that is above all worlds: Pss. 9:7f.;
11:4f.; 33:13; 102:19. Under this horizon, the circle of those who are judged
widens immediately. Yahweh is the judge of the whole world (Ps. 7:6ff.); he
looks down עַל־בְּנֵי־אָדָם (cf. also Ps. 11:4). This broadening, according to the
history of tradition, emanates from the conception that the God who is enthroned
on Zion is the אֵל עֶלְיוֹן, the אָדוֹן, the מֶלֶךְ, and the שׁוֹפֵט of the entire world.
Accordingly, we may not speak of "exaggerations of emotion" (Gunkel)
orhyperbolic generalizations in vv. 1-3. On the tradition, see above, Intro. §10,
1. Before the scrutinizing look of Yahweh no one can stand. There is nowhere
a מַשְׂכִּיל who could prove his wisdom by asking about God (cf. Ps. 12:1f.). All
are unfaithful (סָר) and depraved (נֶאֱלָחוּ). The judgment of Yahweh confirms the
statement that is put proleptically in v. 1: אֵין עֹשֵׂה־טוֹב. And there follows a
declaration that precludes exceptions: אֵין גַּם־אֶחָד. That means of course: the
depravity of the נָבָל holds sway in the world. The prophetic speaker (if his
statements are compared with Psalm 12 or Habakkuk) goes his own way, in the
sense that his lament "lets the scathing judgment of the people of Israel of his
time uttered by the prophet in v. 1 be confirmed in still harsher words in v. 3 by
Yahweh as the judge after a celestial act of examination" (J. Jeremias, 115).
"There is no one that does good, no, not a single one!"

[14:4] Upon this radical statement, as it is confirmed through the verdict of the
heavenly judge, the desperate question of the psalmsinger now arises in v. 4:
"Have they really no insight, all those evildoers who devour my people (as) one
eats bread, who do not call on Yahweh?" In place of נָבָל we now have the more
concrete term פֹּעֲלֵי אָוֶן, which in the Psalms most often designates the enemies
of the individual (see above, Intro. §10, 4). The psalmsinger complains about the
blindness of the "evildoers" who put their beliefs into practice in Israel. The
perfect tense יָדְעוּ indicates repeated acts, in other words, a continuous lack of
insight (BrSynt §41a). Continuously the פֹּעֲלֵי אָוֶן "annihilate," "devour"
(אָכְלוּ, again in the perfect) "my people." In עַמִּי, an expression that can only be
thought of as suitable in the mouth of a prophet, we have clear proof that a
representative of the people of God is speaking (cf. Psalm 12). The wicked in the
picture appear like huge monsters that devour Israel; they devour the members of
the people of God "as callously and indifferently as one eats bread" (H.
Gunkel). Cf. Mic. 3:3; Prov. 30:14. In any case, v. 4 represents the climax of
lament in the form of a desperate question uttered before Yahweh.

[14:5] Corresponding to the parallel structure in Psalm 12 and Habakkuk 1, the
turn of events initiated by Yahweh and reported in v. 5 is to be expected. It is
indicated not by a prophetically transmitted word of Yahweh (as in Ps. 12:5) but
by the description of a vision (J. Jeremias, 115). In this connection we might ask
where and how the prophet became aware of the event described in v. 5.
However, this question, which basically has to do with the problem of cultic
prophecy, cannot be answered from the text. Concerning this problem, see S.
Mowinckel, *PsStud* III; A. R. Johnson, *The Cultic Prophet in Ancient Israel*
(1944); A. Haldar, *Associations of Cult Prophets among the Ancient Semites*
(1945); on Haldar's book, cf. H. H. Rowley, "Ritual and the Hebrew
Prophets," *JSS* (1955) 338ff.
    It is in prophetic perfect tenses that the speaker expresses the inviolable
validity and actuality of what has been seen. The wicked, who "know no fright

before God'' (Ps. 36:1), are overtaken by terror irspired by God that breaks out suddenly as in a holy war. And Yahweh shows his presence among the righteous; he steps over to their side and becomes manifest among them.

[14:6] From the (visionary) perception of the intervention of Yahweh and the assurance of a turn of events thus given, the address to the פעלי און emerges, which begins spontaneously with תבישׁו, ''you will go to pieces.'' This going to pieces begins already in their plans. The purposes do not come to fruition. The breviloquence עצת־עני refers to an undertaking nipped in the bud. It is the poor for whom Yahweh intercedes (see above, Intro. §10, 3).

[14:7] As Psalm 12, which is similar to our psalm in its organization, closes with an ardent prayer, so also Psalm 14 ends in an insistent request: May the ישׁועת ישׂראל appear! The petition מי יתן, presented in the form of a question, extends to all of Israel, or the people addressed by the speaker as ''righteous'' and ''poor'' (cf. עמי in v. 4). The closing petition prays for a new order of all things, a turn of events that provides a blessing. On שׁוב שׁבות, cf. E. L. Dietrich, שׁוב שׁבות (1925). If Yahweh brings a blessing to his people and makes all things new, then exultation and joy will reign in a community which now still lies in the dark shadows of the statements and laments of v. 1.

Purpose and Thrust

To gain a proper understanding of the distinctive assertions of Psalm 14, two facts must be noted carefully:

    1. In vv. 1-3 the ''foolish'' thinking and striving of all human beings (בני־אדם) is brought to light. There is noticeable, as it were, a primal movement and everywhere a decisive whisper: אין אלהים. Under this determining signature of all human existence no one does what is good, no, not a single one. The inclusiveness of this judgment is based on the tradition and the proclamation of Yahweh's worldwide office as judge (also cf. Gen. 6:5). This is not changed by the fact that Ps. 14:4-6 has in mind the sacrifices of the wicked, at which God is present and involved. Also, we may not think of the inclusiveness of the judgment as emotional exaggeration (Gunkel). Rather, it corresponds to the radical and total disclosure of guilt of the OT, which may not be relativized by conceptions of a different kind (Ps. 143:2)! In this sense and with this purpose the apostle Paul cites the first part of Psalm 14 in Rom. 3:10ff. ''Jews and Greeks'' are under the power of destruction: οὐ γάρ ἐστιν διαστολή· πάντες γὰρ ἥμαρτον καὶ ὑστεροῦνται (Rom. 3:22, 23).

    2. To the questions: Where does this godless and ruinous activity that governs the whole world have an end? Where is God? Psalm 14 answers: God is, amazingly, among the righteous and the poor. Here the wicked suddenly comes up against limits. Here he meets God as the judge who intervenes on earth—in the weakness of the helpless. Here the schemes that were put into action under the signature of ''אין אלהים'' come to grief. But the NT then proclaims that the righteous and the poor of the old covenant were only anticipations of the Christ, in whose weakness God brings proud security down to ruin (1 Cor. 1:27). The crucified, the sacrifice of the wicked, is the judge (Rev. 1:7). Henceforth he embraces all the ''poor.'' And every hostile act against them assails him himself (Matt. 25:40)—the one who will act as judge (Matt. 25:41ff.).

    Finally, one must come to realize how shocking the assertions of Psalm

14 actually are. Its ecclesiological high point we will not be able to deny: God's people—a people consisting of godless folk and evildoers, in which no one does what is good, no, not even a single one. Among the people of God, the mighty ones, the wicked are at work. They devour the weak and the poor like bread. Only the intervention of God will save the true Israel and make it known. The true people of God are the poor, whose refuge is their God. Yet the scenery is dominated by those who do not ask about God, who, though they are members of God's people, live and act according to the conviction "There is no God!" And so judgment must begin "with the household of God" (1 Peter 4:17). Without doubt, Psalm 14 proves to be a prophetic psalm, whose assertions are to be seen and understood in the context of OT prophecy (Mic. 7:2; Jer. 5:1ff.; 8:6; Isa. 59:4). The fact that this prophetic psalm is found among the songs and prayers of the OT provides occasion for reflecting anew on the importance of prophecy in worship, and for not simply liturgically absorbing or singing over the terror (v. 5) that emanates from this text for the congregation of God.

Psalm 15

The Conditions
for Entering the Sanctuary

Literature

G. von Rad, " 'Gerechtigkeit' und 'Leben' in der Kultsprache der Psalmen,'' *GesStud* I, 225-247. K. Koch, *Tempeleinlassliturgien und Dekaloge: Studien zur Theologie der alttestamentlichen Überlieferungen* (1961) 45-60. J. L. Koole, "Psalm 15—Eine königliche Einzugsliturgie?'' *OTS* 13 (1963) 98-111. V. W. Rabe, "Israelite Opposition to the Temple,'' *CBQ* 29 (1967) 228-233. O. Garcia de la Fuente, "Liturgias de entrada, normas de asilo o exhortaciones proféticas: A propósito de los Salmos 15 y 24,'' *Aug.* 9 (1969) 266-298. J. A. Soggin, "Il Salmo 15. Osservazioni filologiche ed esegetiche,'' *BibOr* 12 (1970) 83-90.

Text

A psalm of David.
15:1 O Yahweh, who may sojourn in your tent,[a]
who[b] may dwell on your holy hill?
2 He who walks blamelessly and does what is righteous
and sincerely means it in his heart.
3 He who does not spread[c] slander with his tongue,
does not do to his fellow human being what is evil
and does not bring shame on his neighbor,
4 to whom the rejected[d] is contemptible,
but who honors those who fear Yahweh.
Who does 'not'[e] swear to an evil deed
and does not change ' . . . ' .[f]
5 He does not put his money out at excessive interest,
does not take a bribe against the innocent.—
He who acts thus will never waver.

1a Several Mss: בְּאׇהֳלֶיךָ; these versions are thinking of the tents that are pitched in the area of the sanctuary by the pilgrims.
b Gk, Syr, and Jerome use the conjunction to simplify the asyndetic connection in MT.
3c On the meaning of רגל = "make the rounds as a slanderer,'' cf. 2 Sam. 19:27; Sir. 5:14.

4d נמאס = "the despised," "the rejected." According to the parallelism of members, we should really expect מוֹאֵס, or perhaps מְנָאֵץ ("the slanderer"). Gk: πονηρευόμενος. Yet נמאס in the sense "rejected (by God)" is documented in Isa. 54:6.

e The text is corrupt. In MT the second half-verse is missing. But Ps. 24:1-6, to be consulted as a parallel text to Psalm 15, suggests that we think of Ps. 15:4b as the mutilated remainder of a parallelism of members in which the first half-verse was introduced by לֹא and the second by וְלֹא (cf. Ps. 24:4). Accordingly, we could insert לֹא before נשבע and assume an omitted word after ימר. By means of לְהָרֵעַ (τῷ πλησίον αὐτοῦ) Gk and Syr attempt to remedy the difficulty precipitated by the omission of לֹא. The translation of the MT "he keeps his oath even when it harms him" is hardly possible.

f Obviously, a word has dropped out in this passage. Rearrangements (thus H. Schmidt) do not solve the problem.

˙Form

Psalm 15, listed among the psalms of David in the collection of the Psalter, is very clearly laid out in its arrangement. The question asked in v. 1 is answered in vv. 2-5. In the meter the triple 3-pulse dominates (vv. 1, 3, 4, 5). V. 2 is to be read in the 4 + 3 meter. The first half-verse of v. 3 is an incomplete 3-pulse meter. In v. 4b we will very likely have to think of the mutilation of a complete verse (see above).

The first consideration concerning the form of Psalm 15 will probably have to concentrate on v. 1. Yahweh is addressed, and to him the question is put. The style of a prayer song could seem obvious; but it turns out that the psalm is preponderantly molded by the answer given in vv. 2-5. We will have to give full attention to the correspondence of question and answer. H. Gunkel was the first to point out that Psalm 15 is based on the conception of the תורה -consultation customary in Israel. A person goes to the priest and asks him for an "instruction" transmitted in the name of Yahweh. As examples of such Torah-consultations we might name the following passages: Zech. 7:1ff.; Hag. 2:1ff.; 2 Sam. 21:1ff. As the question, in the last analysis, is addressed to Yahweh, so also the answer is given on behalf of Yahweh. But now it becomes evident that Psalm 15 can in no way be understood to be the inquiry of an individual. The question in v. 1 concerns itself in a comprehensive way with the conditions for entry to the sanctuary. And the answer in vv. 2-5 enumerates a number of stipulations of OT divine law, obedience to which the presupposition for participation in worship directs (for these stipulations, cf. K. Koch, 46ff.). The process of the Torah-consultation has accordingly been transferred to a ritual of the worshiping community. And this process will have to be viewed in a larger context, the "Sitz im Leben" of which is to be investigated. Even here we could introduce as an appropriate explanation the form designation "torah liturgy" or—as we will still have to show in detail—"entrance liturgy." Such liturgies belong to the worship on Zion and are obvious for this circle of themes. Cf. above, Intro. §6, 4. Still, Psalm 15 will have to be coordinated with the events reported in Psalm 24 (which see), and therefore will belong to the context of the entry procedures.

Psalm 15 is not isolated in the OT. It is to be associated closely with Psalm 24 (as we have already noted). Additional parallels to be adduced are: Isa. 33:14-16; Mic. 6:6-8; and Ezek. 18:5ff. (On this passage, see K. Koch, 51ff.). Koch sees the oldest form represented in Psalm 15 and Mic. 6:8. He arrives at the tradition-history statement: "The development of the originally simple, positively oriented entrance requirements by means of the adoption of Decaloglike statements . . . was completed in the time of the monarchy'' (58). The interpretation of Psalm 15 will have to refer to the parallel passages mentioned.

Setting

The setting of Psalm 15 can be reconstructed on the basis of its combination with Psalm 24. At the time of entrance into the sanctuary in Jerusalem, a liturgical act took place (cf. above, Intro. §6, 6). The participants in the worship stand at the portals of the worship area and ask the question: "O Yahweh, who may sojourn in your tent, who may dwell on your holy hill?" From the inside a priestly speaker answers them with the declaration of the conditions of entrance (cf. Ps. 24:3ff.; cf. K. Koch, 46). Only then does the entry begin (Ps. 24:7ff.). The designation of Psalm 15 as the "torah liturgy" or "liturgy of entrance" is accordingly suitable from the viewpoint of the "Sitz im Leben" of this psalm. Psalm 15 belongs to the traditions of the Jerusalem temple ("your holy hill," "your tent," Ps. 15:1). Its composition and use in the preexilic cultus can hardly be doubted. Later as a prayer song, the psalm probably brought home to the petitioner the characteristics of the צדיק and became an ingredient of the תורה piety of Judaism. But Psalm 15 also had an effect on the early Christian tradition.

In the ancient Near Eastern cultus, the laying down of certain conditions can everywhere be noted, conditions the cultic participant had to know at the entrance to the sanctuary. In a holy area in Egypt the inscription is found: "Who enters here should be clean, and he should cleanse himself the way he cleanses himself for the temple of the great god." Above all, "clean hands" of the cultic participant are required (A. Erman, *Die Religion der Ägypter* [1934] 190). In an Akkadian prayer of repentance the especially serious guilt is confessed thus: "In my unclean state I again and again entered the temple. That which is the greatest abomination to you I did again and again" (Falkenstein and von Soden, *Sumerische und akkadische Hymnen und Gebete* [1953], 273). And then from Egypt, from the Book of the Dead, entire series of reassurances are known which the person presents in the form of an oath of cleansing in order to declare his acceptability: "I have not sinned against human beings, I have not made human beings miserable, I have not slaughtered God's cattle, I have not sinned at the place of truth, I did not know of base things, I have not done evil things . . . " (on this chain of assurances, see E. Lehmann and H. Haas, *Textbuch zur Religionsgeschichte* [1922], 273f.). The formularies with the series of assurances were available as a "confessional mirror" (K. Galling, *ZAW* 47 [1929], 125). In the OT we find significant examples of a "confessional mirror" or an "oath of cleansing" in Deut. 26:13ff. and Job 31. The "entrance liturgies" present in Psalms 15 and 24 belong directly to this entire complex. These psalms contain the liturgical elements of an established rite of purification that took effect at the entrance or the entry into the sanctuary. In Psalms 15 and 24 the Torah-answer outlines the "*notae* of the צדיק" (G. von Rad, *"Gerechtigkeit" und "Leben" in der Kultsprache der Psalmen,* 228). The picture of an "exemplary צדיק" (von Rad) is sketched (for this, cf. Ezek. 18:5-7). The צדיק is the proper participant in worship in Israel. The עדת צדיקים (Ps. 1:5) may enter the sanctuary of Yahweh: Pss. 5:7; 24:3ff.; 118:19-20; Isa. 26:2. In recent times the religion-history investigations on Psalm 15 have been expanded and new parallels have been adduced. Cf. especially O. Garcia de la Fuente, 270ff.

Commentary

[**Title**] On מזמור לדוד, cf. above, Intro. §4, No. 2

[**15:1**] At the beginning of Psalm 15 the question of who may enter the sanctuary and sojourn there is addressed to Yahweh. The pilgrims who stand at the gates of the sanctuary turn to Yahweh himself. The God present in the temple alone decides who may appear before him. The verbs גור and שכן refer to theconception that the participant in worship who has been admitted to the sanctuary is under the protection of God (Ps. 61:4) and receives "citizen's rights" in the sacred precincts (Eph. 2:19; Phil. 3:20). Where Yahweh is present, there "devouring fire" (Isa. 33:14) reigns. Who may sojourn here? The place of the presence of Yahweh is indicated by two terms which clearly point to the sanctuary in Jerusalem: אהלך and הר קדשך. אהל as a name for the temple (also cf. Ps. 61:4; Isa. 33:20) is not in the first place an archaizing or poetic parlance. Rather, in this name the tradition of the tent sanctuary of Yahweh (2 Sam. 7:6) lives on. On הר קדשך, cf. Pss. 2:6; 3:4; 43:3; 48:1; and others.

[15:2-5] To the liturgical question of the congregation praying for entrance vv. 2-5 now give the answer. The cultic attendants announce the conditions of entry in the name of Yahweh, as statements of OT divine law are proclaimed. Considering in the first place the formal nature of these statements of divine law, we cannot agree to the view of H. Schmidt and F. Nötscher that—as in the Decalog—ten statements are involved. For we must distinguish between the basic, general assertion in v. 2, on the one hand, and the explications in vv. 3-5 that penetrate to individual specific details, on the other. Also, apart from this fact, it is problematic to view the parallel statements of a complete verse as having the form of two different sentences (thus H. Schmidt and F. Nötscher). This conjecture therefore drops out. Worth noting, however, is the sentence structure with לא presented in vv. 3-5 (with the exception of v. 4a). For 4b, cf. the textual notes.

From the series of statements of rules the closing statement, עשה־אלה לא ימוט לעולם, clearly distinguishes itself as a promise. If we now consider the incongruity of the question in v. 1 and the answer in v. 5 (closing promise), we would have to acknowledge that the logical structure of the entire psalm between vv. 2 and 3 is sundered. The answer to v. 1 is given in v. 2. But the explication of v. 2 in vv. 3-5 already tends toward the closing promise in v. 5.

[15:2] Thus the liturgical question in v. 1 is in essence answered in v. 2. Here the condition for the sojourn in the holy place is identified in very basic words. Three assertions in participial form stand next to one another. הולך תמים refers to one's being tied into the life of a community in whose ordinances a blameless walk is required; cf. L. Köhler, *OT Theology*, 167f. פעל צדק is the central formulation of the Psalms that speaks of the actual basic condition of admittance. Only the צדיק[1] may enter Yahweh's sanctuary. Only the person who lives according to the covenant and keeps (פעל) the ordinances of the mutual relationship between Yahweh and his people—only this person may enter the

---

1. "But as hypocrites, in order to promote their own interests, are not sparing in their attention to a multiplicity of external religious observances, while their ungodliness, notwithstanding, is manifested outwardly in the life, seeing they are full of pride, cruelty, violence, and are given to deceitfulness and extortion; the Psalmist, for the purpose of discovering and drawing forth into the light all who are of such a character, takes the marks and evidence of true and sincere faith from the second table of the law. According to the care which every man takes to practice righteousness and equity toward his neighbors, so does he actually show that he fears God" (Calvin on Ps. 15:2, trans. Anderson [Grand Rapids: Eerdmans, 1949]).

sacred precincts. For a more detailed description of the צדיק, or the פעל צדק, cf., among others passages, Ezek. 18:5-7. This proper, irreproachable conduct vis-à-vis the ordinance of the covenant ordained by Yahweh is aimed at a person's innermost being: דבר אמת בלבבו. דבר בלבבו refers to the thoughts and the meditations of the heart. Are the innermost movements of thought and directions of the will "faithful" and "reliable"? Are they אמת? The penetration of the word to the innermost recesses of human existence is attested in Deut. 6:4. Therefore, without reservations, the whole person is involved. צדקה is a thing complete, a totality. "If a person was a צדיק, he was not so in an inchoate or approximate way, but he was so completely" (G. von Rad, "*Gerechtigkeit*" *und* "*Leben*" *in der Kultsprache der Psalmen*, 232). Therefore the מי -question of v. 1 is answered with a reference to a holistic, irreproachable type that corresponds to the covenant order of Yahweh. In a paradigmatic sense the archetypal picture of the צדיק is drawn—an exemplar.

The theological question that arises in view of v. 2 cannot be overlooked: In Psalm 15 is the perfection of the צדיק the presupposition for entrance to nearness to God and for the reception of salvation?

In the commentaries deliberations are presented in various ways about the way in which morality and cultus are related to each other in Psalm 15. Most often the thought is about the incursion (occurring at a late date) of prophetic morality into the area of the cultus. H. Gunkel remarks concerning v. 2: "Here we clearly recognize the influence of the prophetic movement, which has completely brushed aside the sacrifices and sacred practices and in their stead instituted morality." The assumption of such a "prophetic influence," of course, affects the dating of our psalm: in postexilic times—so it is said—the prophetic morality was able to gain influence in the cultus. But in this connection the nomistic-conditional expression of the prophetic morality is deplored, which is said to lean toward the typically Jewish attitude and toward the "oath of the Essenes" (B. Duhm). If these declarations are right, then Psalm 15 would be a perfect model of a legalistic piety that makes perfect obedience the presupposition for the reception of salvation. Concerning this problem G. von Rad writes: "We do not have to conclude from this that in ancient Israel the fulfilling of the commandments was in principle antecedent to the reception of salvation in the cult, since those seeking admission were certainly not coming before Jahweh for the first time—they had been members of the community of Jahweh from the beginning. But this much becomes clear: those who came to worship were asked for something like a declaration of loyalty to Jahweh's will for justice. These commandments were regarded as perfectly capable of being fulfilled, and indeed as easy to fulfil. The question whether those who sought entrance avowed themselves to be loyal to them now, and had been so in the past, was therefore nothing but the question of their צדקה. Hence 'the gates of righteousness' are spoken of, through which only 'righteous people' enter" (G. von Rad, *OT Theol*, 1:378). We need to refer to Ps. 118:19f.; Isa. 26:2. Thus the entrance liturgy confronts every individual cultic participant always anew with the question whether in the interim between festivals he has lived and acted in conformity to the ordinances of God. In Israel worship and life are most intimately associated. Already in most ancient times the customary covenant responsibility culminates in a confession that applies to the whole life (Josh. 24:15, 21, 24). The law of God was in Israel originally the essential content of worship. Therefore it will not be allowable to consider the entrance liturgy a late result of a confluence of prophecy and cultus. The prophets do not bring morality into the cultus as something new and revolutionary; they are rather renewers, reformers of a festival cultus that in the course of time has severed itself from the law of God. In Psalm 15 the law of God still belongs essentially to the cultus. But when the prophet Jeremiah is to enter the gate of the temple to proclaim the law of God to "those who enter" (Jer. 7:1ff.), this mission presupposes that the institution of the torah liturgy has fallen into ruin.

[15:3] Beginning with v. 3 the assertions in v. 2 are now explained. Individual concrete ways of behavior in everyday life are mentioned and called to remembrance for the participants in worship as the acknowledged law of God. There is in vv. 3-5 no mention of the gross transgressions with which Jeremiah, for instance, is to confront the entrants in the form of a reprimanding address that is to lay bare their guilt (Jer. 7:5ff.). It is assumed to be self-evident that the simple, great basic commandments are in force. Only individual infractions are addressed in the entrance liturgy—and such, too, as, removed from normal jurisdiction, are done in secret. In this respect the series of legal sentences in Psalm 15 is related to the apodictic law of God, for the apodictic commandments apply to deeds and areas of life that do not become judicial cases, or which, under certain circumstances, do not come under the purview of jurisdiction. But the direction of the assertion in Psalm 15 is different. In the apodictic law Israel meets the proclamation of the will of the one who is Lord in Israel as it is addressed directly to the community. In Psalm 15—on the basis of the law of God that is familiar to the congregation—the *notae* of the צדיק, the marks of him who is admitted to Yahweh's sanctuary, are outlined. The צדיק does not make the rounds (רגל) in order to slander, he does not do to his neighbor what is evil, and he does not bring shame on his neighbor by false rumors or wicked machinations. In v. 3, therefore, the subject is the relation to the neighbor. Here, in daily life, irreproachable conduct—the practice of righteousness and the purity of inner impulses—proves itself (v. 2).

[15:4] There is a rift in Israel. There are people whom Yahweh has rejected (who despise Yahweh?), and there are people who fear him. In v. 4 the attitude of the צדיק to these two groups is now addressed. It is a matter of considering him "contemptible" who has been rejected (by God), of avoiding the area of his influence (cf. Ps. 1:1). On the other hand, the יראי יהוה are to be honored (כבד). Here a confession in matters of daily associations is required of the צדיק. This theme is dealt with above all in Psalm 1.

If the corrupt text in v. 4b has been emended correctly (see above, textual notes), then false swearing is now the subject discussed. In Ps. 24:4 the corresponding passage reads: אשר לא־נשא לשוא נפשו ולא נשבע למרמה. The subject is the thoughtless, vain swearing by which one intends to accomplish (להרע) some injustice; cf. Lev. 5:4. The verse can no longer be completely reconstructed.

[15:5] The subject is traffic in money. The צדיק does not enrich himself in a dishonest way. On money loaned he does not impose usurious interest, and he does not take bribes. The lending of money according to OT law is understood exclusively as a service of assistance: Exod. 22:24; Lev. 25:36f.; Deut. 23:20. From ancient Near Eastern traffic in money we know of monstrously high interest rates. In Babylonia 33.3% was demanded, in Assyria even up to 50% (B. Meissner, *Babylonien und Assyrien*, 1: 156, 364). Such unjust enrichment is not to be possible in the community constitution of Israel. פעל צדק (v. 2) means: to be helpful with the proceeds of a loan and not to practice usury.

Bribery is referred to in the OT divine law in Exod. 23:8; Deut. 16:19; 27:25. The צדיק intercedes for the rights of the נקי. Thus the condition for entry into the sanctuary mentioned in v. 5 also shows that the interest is always in the correct way of behaving in everyday communal life. The participant in worship on Zion before Yahweh, who is a God of justice and aid, shows his צדקה in the hidden deals and business transactions which are not accessible to the intervention of any judicial agent. The gift of salvation in the OT cultus is not a magic center of power, and it is not dispensed in impersonal fullness at every festival. Every visitor of Zion is asked to give a declaration of loyalty: Do you also conduct your life in accordance with the covenant of Yahweh? Is Yahweh the Lord of your everyday life? At this point the OT shows that the עבד of the community of Yahweh does not refer to cultic skills and special arrangements, to ritual conduct and esoteric rules, but to one's entire life (Josh. 24:15, 21, 23). The doer of the word (James 1:21ff.) receives the promise לא ימוט לעולם. But what is the meaning of לא מוט? We may not prematurely speak in a general way of "blessing" or "aid in the face of calamity" (Herkenne). Specific conceptions are basic to the language of the Psalms. The entering congregation of צדיקים marches into the area in which Yahweh is present as the "eternal rock" (Isa. 26:2-4). In the cultic tradition of Zion, cosmic conceptions from time immemorial of a world foundation, firmly founded and reaching to the skies, are combined with the holy rock of the Jerusalem temple mount (H. Schmidt, *Der heilige Fels in Jerusalem* [1933] 94ff.). These conceptions (very likely originating in pre-Israelite times) have been transferred to Yahweh. Yahweh himself is the "eternal rock," Pss. 31:3; 42:9. The one, therefore, who enters the sanctuary is stepping on ground which the great cosmic catastrophes cannot touch; it "does not waver," Pss. 26:12; 61:2-4; and others. This event of having a part in Yahweh the "eternal rock" is understood to be something continuous, something that influences and determines the life of human beings, Ps. 112:6. The לעולם in v. 5 is to be understood in this sense (cf. also Ps. 16:8).

Purpose and Thrust

Yahweh, who is enthroned on Zion, is a God of all that is right. Yahweh's cult is no naturalistic, magical grant of power to the assembled community. Whoever enters the realm of God's presence is interrogated regarding his everyday manner of behavior and is called to account. The worship in the sanctuary begins with a decisive question about obedience. The "conditions" for admittance to the temple area destroy all cultic frenzy; they turn the attention back to the cult participant—back to daily life. "Not those who say, 'Lord, Lord,' but the ones who do the will of God have familial privileges and rights with him" (Franz Delitzsch).

The NT community, however, will have to consider two viewpoints especially: (1) Zion in the OT has the character of an ultimate reality (Isa. 2:2ff.) that far transcends all earthly living conditions. Every approach to this sanctuary occurs under the sign of an ultimate joy and an ultimate seriousness. The NT has consequently spoken of Zion "eschatologically" (Heb. 12:22). The "heavenly Jerusalem" of the Revelation of John is the final destination of all the paths of the congregation. Thus the church of the new covenant can speak of Zion only "eschatologically." The OT declarations already have an unmistakable transparency in the direction of this finality. Still, the NT community will have to ask itself how this final reality casts its image on every specific service of worship, its orders, liturgies, and proclamations. (2) When Psalm 15 states that only the פעל צדק has access to the sanctuary of God, and when the "marks" of this צדק, as of a prototype, are portrayed as so supraindividual and exemplary, then we are to take note immediately that Christ is the fulfillment: he is "made our righteousness" by God (1 Cor. 1:30). In him the supraindividual and exemplary prototype of the OT צדּיק emerges. Still, membership in the "new creation" means fellowship with Christ: life with him. Only the doer of the word participates with him (Rom. 2:13; James 1:22f.).[2] The apostolic word proclaims that the προσαγωγή to God is a happening only in faith in Jesus Christ (Rom. 5:2).

In the history of tradition it is significant and could give rise to further biblical-theological considerations that the NT passages concerning "entry into the kingdom ofGod" still speak of the demonstration of the δικαιοσύνη. The tradition and the pattern of the old gate liturgy, transmitted through Jewish channels, have had a lingering effect (cf. H. Windisch, *ZNW*, 1928, 177ff.).

2. "But note the expression 'worker of righteousness'; he does not say, 'He who speaks, thinks, and hears of righteousness,' because not hearers, but doers of the law will be justified" (Luther, WA 5; 432, 5f.).

Psalm 16

The Fortunate Fate
in the Face of Death

Literature

E. Zolli, "Die Heiligen in Psalm 16," *ThZ* Basel 6 (1950)149-150. H. W. Boers, "Psalm 16 and the Historical Origin of the Christian Faith," *ZNW* 60 (1969) 105-110. A. Schmitt, "Psalm 16, 8-11 als Zeugnis der Auferstehung in der Apostelgeschichte," *BZ* NF 17 (1973) 229-248.

Text

A *miktam* of David.

16:1 Protect me, O God, for I seek refuge with you!

2 I 'said'[a] to Yahweh, "You are my Lord,
my good fortune 'rests with you alone'."[b]

3 For the saints on earth 'is his desire,'[c]
in them 'he glorifies'[d] 'his'[e] entire will to save.

4 . . .[f]
great are their pains, the other (gods) court them.[g]
I do not like to administer their blood offering
or take their names on my lips.

5 O Yahweh, my portion and my cup,
you are he 'who establishes'[h] my lot.

6 For me the measuring cord has fallen on a pleasant place,
yes, 'my'[i] inheritance pleases me well.

7 I praise Yahweh, who has advised me,
even at night my innermost being exhorts me.

8 Constantly do I keep Yahweh before my eyes,
if he remains at my right hand, I do not waver.

9 Therefore my heart is glad, and my soul exults,
and also my body will dwell secure.

10 For you do not surrender my life to Sheol,
you do not permit your godly one to see the pit.

233

11 You show me the way of life.
Joy in fullness before you!
Delight at your right hand forever!

2a Some Mss have אָמַרְתִּי. Cf. Gk, Syr, Jerome.

b The text in MT presents difficulties. If אדני אתה is the first clause of the address to Yahweh, then טובתי בל־עליך is to be understood as the second clause. But בל as a poetic negative is probably in this context plausible only if the text, following σ´, Targ, Jerome (*non sine te*) is emended to בַּל בִּלְעָדֶיךָ (F. Baethgen). No correction of עליך would be required if על could be understood in the sense of BrSynt §110f. Driver emends to כָּלָּה עָלֶיךָ, "my good fortune rests entirely with you." An entirely different possibility of understanding the text would be the result if אדני were emended; in that case, the first clause of the address to Yahweh would be אתה טו. The negative בל־עליך would then have to be taken together with v. 3. But here new difficulties would then arise (see below).

3c The text in v. 3 is corrupt. Only one conjecture can be helpful. הֵמָּה at the end of the first half-verse is obtrusive. One expects a verb. Are we to read הָמָה at this point? Compare with המה (מעי) לְ in Jer. 31:20. But perhaps (cf. parallelism of members חפץ): חָמַד with לְ BrSynt §107c.

d ואדירי in MT is hardly possible. The construct construction presents an uncommon form. Gk reads a verb: ἐθαυμάστωσεν. That would provide a lead for an emendation to יַאְדִּיר (cf. Isa. 42:21).

e Gk has read כי־חפצו־בם and thereby gives a clue for a good possible understanding of the text.

4f V. 4, in contrast to v. 3, probably referred to idol worshipers. That may still be recognized from the context. The conjecture is possible that the first half-verse preceding the clause ירבו עצבותם אחד מהרו dropped out. The suffix in עצבותם surely refers to human beings mentioned earlier (רשעים in contrast to קדושים?).

g מהרו is disputed because the "courting" refers to the feminine sex (Exod. 22:15). Gk read מְהָרוּ (ἐτάχυναν). A number of commentaries also conjecture הֵמִירוּ as possible (cf. Jer. 2:11). In any case, אחר probably means אל אחר (Exod. 34:14).

5h A verb יָמַךְ, from which the *hiphil* form תּוֹמִיךְ could be developed, is unknown in the OT. Gk σὺ εἶ ὁ ἀποκαθιστῶν points to a participial construction (usual in the hymn): תּוֹמֵךְ, from תָּמַךְ.

6i Following Gk (τὴν κληρονομίαν μου) and Syr, we are certainly to read נחלתי here.

Form

Already in considering the formal aspects of Psalm 16 the corruptness of the text in vv. 3 and 4 presents difficulties. Only with the proviso that the understanding of the text presented in the translation is probably correct can the psalm be explained. The interpreter may not exclude the responsibility of considering also other possibilities of interpretation at given points.

If we follow the translation presented, the following picture of the organization of Psalm 16 comes into view; vv. 1-2, an expression of trust; vv. 3-4, a reflection on the position of Yahweh regarding the saints on the relation of the petitioner to the idol worshipers; vv. 5-8, trust and confidence in Yahweh; vv. 9-11, the certainty of rescue from death. If we are permitted to begin with this understanding of the organization and the analogous division of the whole, the first question is that of the metrical form. That we have very dissimilar verses before us in Psalm 16 is certainly the result of the general condition of the text. Still, the uncorrupted section of the text, vv. 5-9, shows the 4 + 3 (in v. 10: 4 + 4) meter throughout. In the rest of the verses the following accentuation is observable: vv. 1-2a, 4 + 4; v. 2b, triple meter without parallelism; v. 3, 3 + 3; v. 4, x + 4 and 3 + 4; v. 11, 3 and 3 + 3.

Psalm 16 is usually classified in the *Gattung* of laments of an individual (cf. Gunkel and Begrich, *EinlPs*, No. 1, 24). And yet, elements of the lament cannot be established. Therefore it is advisable to classify Psalm 16 as a prayer song (Hebrew תפלה). Cf. above, Intro. §6, 2. As we read through the individual verses, the form classification can be justified on the basis of the content. Vv. 2f. contain an expression of confession which is trustingly formulated in the address to Yahweh—as in general Psalm 16 contains a series of statements of trust and confession. In v. 7 the note of praise is heard (cf. above, Intro. §6, 1). The prayer song addresses Yahweh (vv. 2, 5, 10f.), but occasionally there is also mention of Yahweh in the third person (vv. 3, 7f.).

Setting

We can assume that Psalm 16 was intoned in the area of the sanctuary (in Jerusalem?) (v. 1). The petitioner has taken refuge in the protective area of the temple. On חסה , cf. E. Gerstenberger, *THAT* I, 621ff.; L. Delekat, *Asylie und Schutzorakel* (1967). An accurate inquiry as to who, precisely, might have been the petitioner—or, to put it more carefully, which life situation may be inferred from the prayer formulary of the psalm—can initially be answered only with a rough sketch. From the statements in vv. 4-6 one gets the impression that a priest is here speaking, a Levite (see the explanation below, under "Commentary"). If this explanation should be correct, we would have to conclude that the psalm refers to specific living conditions and is to be considered a priestly prayer. But it would certainly be possible that in the prayer formulary certain conceptions and terms from the world of the priestly life were generalized, in other words, that the authors of the formulary, who are to be looked for in the circle of the priesthood, incorporated elements of their theology in the prayer song—as certain aspects of royalty were adopted in Psalm 3 (which see). Questions of detail will come in for discussion only in the commentary on the text, with careful attention to the nuances.

In view of the manifold difficulties that stand in the way of establishing the setting, an attempt at dating the psalm can hardly be undertaken. Occasionally one thinks of the circumstances observable in Isa. 57:3ff.; 62:11f.; and 65:1ff., and one is then inclined to assign Psalm 16 to the situation of the postexilic diaspora (H. Gunkel), or one may conjecture a still later date (B. Duhm). A. Weiser pushes the psalm back into the context of a "preexilic cult of a national festival" that he has posited. But all attempts rest on an insecure foundation. Even on the basis of a statistical word study, a preexilic time of writing cannot be ruled out.

Commentary

[Title] On מכתם, see above, Intro. §4, No. 4. On לדוד, see §4, No. 2.

[16:1] Psalm 16 begins with a petition that is otherwise characteristic of the prayer songs of people suffering persecution and of those who are looking for the institution of God's jurisdiction (cf. Psalm 11). In any case, this means that confidence in Yahweh developed in the concrete rescue from a specific crisis. In vv. 9-11 it will become apparent that the petitioner is in mortal danger. Generalizing interpretations impair the meaning of the song. A person in trouble flees to Yahweh (i.e., in the sanctuary) to find refuge with him. On שמרני, cf. Pss. 17:8; 140:4; 141:9. On חסיתי, cf. Pss. 7:1; 11:1; 25:20; 31:1; 71:1; 141:8;

144:2. The verbs refer to the sanctuary's functions as asylum (Ps. 61:4).

[16:2] To the prayer for protection in v. 1, a trusting address to Yahweh is added in v. 2: אדני אתה. The God enthroned on Zion is אדון—so reads one of his names in the cultic tradition (see above, Intro. §10, 1). The individual may approach him (cf. Psalm 1). Immediately the petitioner realizes that his good fortune is only in the hands of Yahweh. Only what is "good" does he expect from God. He alone is the "highest good" of him who seeks protection. These words of trust receive an enduring interpretation in vv. 5-6. But even now we are to notice and to consider how emphatically the formulation "with you alone" corresponds to the exclusive demand of the First Commandment. "In a statement such as this we have the beginning of a veritable distinction between the fulfillment of life and the relation to God; for the petitioner seems to treasure the relation to God (v. 8; cf. Pss. 23:6; 27:4) above the gifts of life" (W. H. Schmidt, *Das erste Gebot*, TheolEx 165 [1970], 42).

Before v. 3 can be interpreted in the sense of the translation presented above, we must first give some consideration to the possible connection of the statements in vv. 2 and 3. In the conjecture concerning the corrupt text in v. 3, various attempts were undertaken to add בל־עליך to v. 3. Until now, these attempts do not satisfy, because later in v. 4 serious difficulties in understanding the text arise.

But the following attempt would be worth considering: if we begin with טובתי בל־עליך and reconstrue v. 3 (in immediate connection with this beginning) with a reference to Ps. 73:25, we could, by including the word לקדושים, translate: "My good fortune (is) not above you with the saints." After M. Noth has shown that we are above all to think of the "saints of the Most High" in the OT as heavenly creatures (M. Noth, *GesStudzAT* 274-290), such an interpretation could seem obvious. In Ps. 73:25 the petitioner asks: מי־לי בשמים. In connection with such a reconstruction we could now ask additionally, Has בארץ in Ps. 16:3 wrongly been applied to לקדושים? Could בארץ perhaps in an original text (as in Ps. 73:25) have modified the complementary parallel statement— let us say, in the sense, "and in all that is on earth I have no pleasure"? In that case חפצי would stand opposite טובתי. But then how is v. 4 to be understood? Does the petitioner suddenly join the idol worshipers, who do not put their trust in Yahweh and for that reason endure "great pain"?

That the possibilities of a reconstruction of the text in v. 3 are strongly influenced by the understanding of the word לקדושים has also been recognized by E. Zolli. Of course (following G. van der Leeuw, *Phänomenologie der Religion* [1933], 111), he is thinking of the "mighty dead," in an explanation conceptually not adequate for the OT. The statements of vv. 4ff. are then by Zolli applied entirely to this understanding of the term לקדושים (*ThZtschr* Basel 6 [1950], 149-150).

[16:3] If v. 3 is conjectured following Gk, then the subject is the petitioner's meditation on the direction of Yahweh's saving acts and favor. He turns to the "saints in the land." But who could be meant here by קדושים? Two possibilities may be considered: (1) The term קדושים serves as a name for the חסידים (Ps. 34:9; also cf. Ps. 16:10). Then we would have to translate: "the saints in the land." (2) The Levitical priests are the "saints," because Yahweh is in their midst (Num. 16:3). In this case we would have to translate "the saints on earth," for we would have to think of the terrestrial counterpart of the heavenly beings who surround and serve Yahweh. On the interpretation of the conception "the saints of the Most High" as the heavenly beings, cf. S. Mowinckel, *Religion und Kultus* (1953) 35; M. Noth, "Die Heiligen des Höchsten," *GesStudzAT* 274-290. The second interpretation is the more likely, for in v. 4 we should probably have to recognize the petitioner of our psalm to be a priest (see below). Also the (corrected) verb יַאְדִּיר would speak for that. The meaning would then be as follows: the trust of the (priestly) petitioner expressed in v. 2 is based on the confidence that Yahweh in a special way turns toward his priestly circle and in them puts into practice his saving will (חפץ). This interpretation of the meaning can appeal to the prerogatives of the Levites that clearly come into view in vv. 5-6 (see below).

[16:4] One can only carefully feel one's way through the statements of v. 4. If we for the first pass over the words ירבו עצבותם אחר מהרו, it will become apparent in v. 4 that the psalmsinger is obliged to perform cultic-ritualistic duties. He presents drink offerings and mentions the names of foreign people. In all probability this has to do with priestly functions, namely, with the libation and the procurement of an answer from God for someone else (1 Sam. 1:17), or with the intercession for him. Now the question is whether the petitioner of our psalm perhaps in v. 4 wants to prove that he is a faithful servant in the cultus by declaring—and now we will probably also have to include the mutilated extension of v. 4—"The blood offering [the forbidden libation of blood?] of the idol worshipers I have not administered, also their names [as cultic expedients] I have not taken on my lips." Understood this way, v. 4 would come close to the "oath of cleansing," here spoken by a priest. On the "oath of cleansing," cf. the comment on Ps. 7:3-5. But it could also be—and here we would have to emphasize the words ירבו עצבותם אחר מהרו—that the petitioner contrasts the saints, who trust in Yahweh, with the idol worshipers, who with their courting of strange gods heap great pains on themselves (for this meaning of עצבות, cf. Prov. 15:13; Ps. 147:3). Then the statement that follows in v. 4 would have the meaning that the petitioner knows that in all of his activities he is separate from these people (who do not trust in Yahweh).

We need to append the reference to the difficulties that result in view of the statement about the נסכים. For "the singular statement that this is supposed to have to do with נסכים of blood (מדם) is most unusual" (R. Rendtorff, *Studien zur Geschichte des Opfers im alten Israel*, WMANT 24, [1967], 171). Rendtorff expresses the suspicion that the text could be mutilated. And yet we should certainly have to consider that in Isa. 66:3 there is mention of a מנחה of blood. In any case, this is a very difficult passage.

[16:5-6] In vv. 5-6 hymnically treated expressions of trust on the part of the psalmsinger emerge. They connect up with the declaration "my good fortune rests with you alone" (v. 2). We should immediately survey the new range of terminology. We meet the words נחלה.—חבל—גורל—כוס—מנת־חלקי. Almost all of these terms are unmistakably associated with the institution of the distribution of land (cf. Josh. 14:4; 15:13; Num. 16:55; Josh. 17:5; Num. 18-21; Deut. 4:21; Josh. 13:23). Only the word כוס seems to depart from this frame of ideas. Still, when the cultic-sacral backgrounds of כוס are considered, this conception means as much as "decision," "lot," except that with the image of the cup an entirely different context must now be considered. For the cultic-sacral background of כוס cf. the commentary on Ps. 11:6.

But what does it mean that the petitioner of our psalm suddenly expresses his trust in Yahweh in the terminology of the institution of the distribution of land by lot? Is this a matter of "crude, almost childlike images"

(H. Schmidt)? The actual state of affairs is more profound. In Israel the land was assigned to the tribes in a sacral act of distribution by lot. This process is reported in the second part of the book of Joshua. Only Levi was exempt from this process of land distribution. In place of it, this group, above all other tribes, received a unique prerogative: "Yahweh is his inheritance (נחלתו)," Deut. 10:9; Josh. 13:14; "I am your portion (חלק) and your inheritance (נחלה)," Num. 18:20. "This prescription simply contains a regulation for the maintenance of Levi, and is consequently to be understood in a perfectly material way (Deut. 18:8): Levi does not maintain itself by work on the land; it does not in fact hold any land, but lives from the shares in the sacrifices and other cultic payments (G. von Rad, *OT Theol*, 1:404). In other words, this refers to a unique Levitical prerogative, which, however, already very early may have gone beyond the purely material understanding, for in Israel the נחלה means more than merely "real property for a livelihood." The נחלה in the widest sense is the means of livelihood bestowed by Yahweh. Accordingly, the Levite has the important privilege that this means of livelihood bestowed by Yahweh comes to him not in the saving gift of the possession of property but in the proximity to God in the sanctuary, in Yahweh himself.

On the basis of this, we must inquire whether G. von Rad understands Psalm 16 correctly when he sees a "spiritual exegesis" of the old statement of Deut. 10:9 and Num. 18:20 in the expression "Yahweh is my portion" and so renames the specific Levitical prerogative a generalized, secondary "spiritualised idea of asylum" (*OT Theol*, 1:403). After all, Psalm 16 is not spoken by just any petitioner who presumably has in a spiritualized way appropriated the old prerogatives of the Levites to himself. Here, in the first place, the Levite himself is speaking. And there is the second question, to what extent his song of trust was sung and prayed in the spiritual sense also by other participants in worship. Incidentally, very likely the marked corruption of the text in vv. 3-4 points to encroachments on the older state of the text which were undertaken in the history of the transmission and use of this—perhaps very old—Levitical song.

The statements in vv. 5-6 express a final trust, based exclusively on Yahweh. In Yahweh, the petitioner has received his formative foundation of life. The hymnic participal תומך in trust screens out the praise. Lovely (נעם) is this highest good fortune: to be privileged to live in proximity to Yahweh, to live in Yahweh himself (Ps. 84:3-4). In this passage the OT provides gentle hints of a "mystic" union with God. It is implicit in the peculiarity of the Levitical prerogative.

[16:7] In v. 7 praise in the style of an individual thanksgiving song (Gunkel and Begrich, *EinlPs* §7) emerges. ברך originally probably had the meaning: "to magnify the power of the gods." But in the Bible these dynamic root relations no longer play a role. Here ברך means: "in due form to recognize someone in his position of power and his claim of high position" (F. Horst, "Segen und Segenshandlungen in der Bibel," *EvTh* 1/2 [1947], 31). The laudatory "recognition" of the power of Yahweh refers in v. 7 to a helpful revelation of God. Yahweh has given advice (יעץ) to the petitioner who sought refuge with him (v. 1). For the interpretation of this verb we could probably adduce v. 11: Yahweh has "shown the way of life" to the petitioner; that is the content of the "advice." Thus we may therefore think of a word of God which the singer of our psalm has received (J. Begrich, "Das priesterliche Heilsorakel," *ZAW* 52 [1934], 81-92). The "way of life" (v. 11) has been revealed to one caught in the peril of death (vv. 9-10). From the context we may understand v. 7b in this way, that the "innermost being" constantly reminds the sufferer of the helpful revelation of Yahweh. כליות in the OT is the name for the innermost impulses of the soul (G. von Rad, *OT Theol*, 1:153; Ps. 73:21; Jer. 17:10). This interpretation is confirmed by v. 8. It is the characteristic of the song of trust before us in Psalm 16 that here a permanent security is announced on the basis of a revelation of God that has taken place once (vv. 7a, 11).

[16:8] תמיד = "perpetually" the petitioner lives in the certainty of the presence of Yahweh bestowed on him. When he now "constantly keeps Yahweh before his eyes" (v. 8a), we are not to think of a visionary imagination.[1] Rather, the reference is to the remembrance of the actual יעץ (v. 7a) that is always alive and present. Was it perhaps a theophany in which Yahweh encountered the singer of our psalm? And is this occurrence in which the word of God was given always taken up anew as a stay in subsequent times? In any case, the petitioner knows that Yahweh is always present. "He remains at the right hand." "At the right hand" stands the powerful protector (Pss. 110:5; 121:5). On the verb מוט cf. the commentary on Ps. 15:5.

[16:9-10] Because Yahweh intervened with helpful advice (v. 7) and is continuously present (v. 8), exulting joy enters the life of the sufferer together with trust—even when the body (apparently, even now) is threatened by death. The deciding exegetical question in vv. 9-10 is: Is the singer speaking of a rescue from death, or do we hear words that refer to a hope of resurrection?

A survey of the history of interpretation may provide orientation. In the NT Ps. 16:9-10 is applied to the resurrection of Jesus Christ: David "foresaw and spoke of the resurrection of the Christ, that he was not abandoned to Hades, nor did his flesh see corruption" (Acts 2:31; 13:35f.). This interpretation of the NT fixed the exegesis of Psalm 16. Also Luther and Calvin expressed themselves as favoring the messianic-Christological interpretation. Still, Calvin sees that another interpretation would be possible: one could also think of a temporal rescue from death. But Calvin quickly denounces such a conception with the following statement: "But how small and how slender a consolation this would be, to breathe on briefly until death finally should swallow us up without hope of salvation!"

Among modern researchers, G. Beer ("Der biblische Hades," *Festschrift für H. J. Holtzmann* [1902], 27) believed to have found in Ps. 16:10f. the late Jewish doctrine concerning the reception of the pious "into the heavenly paradise." For understanding our passage in the sense of a statement about immortality, cf. the following OT scholars: E. Sellin, R. Smend, F. Baethgen, and (with certain reservations) R. Kittel. For a more recent interpretation along these lines, cf. J. J. Stamm, *ThR* NF 23/1, 65f. But, regarding these declarations, Chr. Barth rightly states: "All these assertions are open to criticism, even because they provide no answer to the question of what actually is to be understood by eternal life in the hereafter. In the interpretation of the Psalms, in which this concept is in any case not something self-evident, the attempt at a corresponding definition would probably have been in place. Because such is not to be found, the appearance is given that these exegetes, without regard for vv. 1-9, which clearly deal with this life, wanted to

---

1. "To set God before us is nothing else than to keep all our senses bound and captive, that they may not run out and go astray after any other object. We must look to him with other eyes than those of the flesh, for we shall seldom be able to perceive him unless we elevate our minds above the world; and faith prevents us from turning our back upon him" (Calvin, on Ps. 16:8, trans. Anderson [Grand Rapids: Eerdmans, 1949]).

postulate a continuation after death'' (*Die Errettung vom Tode in den individuellen Klage-
und Dankliedern* [1947], 154). Since W. Nowack and B. Duhm, the interpretation in the
sense of a belief in resurrection or immortality has been contested more and more
vehemently (according to these scholars, vv. 9-10 speak of a rescue from the danger of
death), but the remarkable interpretation of Franz Delitzsch is still worth noting. He writes
first of all: ''It is the hope of not dying that David expresses in v. 10''; but then we read
further: ''Physical freedom from death is only the external aspect of that which David
hopes for in his own case''; according to the inner man it is ''life from God, with God,
in God the living one,'' and that in contrast ''to death as proof of the wrath of God and
as separation from him.'' This wise aloofness from a complete resurrection interpretation
is characteristic for the exegete Franz Delitzsch, who thoroughly weighs the assertions of
the text.

Psalm 16 does not deal with resurrection, or even immortality, but with
the rescue from an acute mortal danger. This is clear from two observations: (1)
In the style of a prayer song, Psalm 16 begins with the prayer for protection and
sheltering against the danger of death. Accordingly, the subject is an acute threat
to life, such as is described also elsewhere in connection with persecution or
sickness. And vv. 7 and 11 also show that he who has sought refuge with
Yahweh has received an answer. The ''way of life'' has been shown to him. (2)
The assertions about the rescue from death in vv. 9-10 do not materially differ
from the corresponding descriptions in other psalms. Here Chr. Barth, in his
study *Die Errettung vom Tode*, has convincingly clarified the exegesis of the
Psalms. Concerning Ps. 16:9ff. his view is that ''the author hopes and trusts that
he, as a member of the community of Yahweh, will be able to proceed on his
life's way through all dangers'' (154). We should seek an appropriate understanding of the text along the lines of this interpretation.

The petitioner is sure that his ''body will dwell secure'' (9b). בשׂר is the
''human stuff'' of human existence (L. Köhler, *OT Theol*, 135). Physical
existence is accordingly threatened (v. 1). Yet the petitioner is completely sure
that his ''body will dwell secure,'' that he is protected and sheltered by the
presence of Yahweh. שׁכן לבטח in the OT always refers to the undisturbed life
in this world, but above all we may think of ''dwelling secure'' in the realm of
the sanctuary (Ps. 15:1, 5). Accordingly, we should have to begin in the first
place with this thought: the petitioner is sure that the great danger that a sudden
death might sever his connection with God is overcome. Yet the assurance
bestowed on him continues ''infinitely further'' (G. von Rad, *God at Work in
Israel* [1980], 205ff.). Yahweh's acts know no limits. Therefore also the trust in
him is not a trust with limitations. Cf. H.-J. Kraus, ''Vom Leben und Tod in den
Psalmen,'' *Biblisch-theologische Aufsätze* (1922) 258-277. The understanding of
נפשׁ in v. 10 tends to point to surrendered, indigent human life in all its infirmity.
On נפשׁ, see above, Intro. §10, 4. The petitioner is sure: Yahweh will not
surrender the נפשׁ to שׁאול (cf. the commentary on Ps. 6:5). שׁאול as the
''underworld'' is the non-world. The חסיד will not see the pit. In all these
assertions the most concrete facts of the life here on earth and of the deliverance
from threatening death are in the foreground. And yet the ''endless background''
is not excluded thereby. The assertions of trust are transparent as they view the
sovereign possibilities of the God of Israel. Basically, the problem of death is not
solved in the OT, and yet it is clear in which direction the assertions of trust
point: man is destined for life. He learns to know Yahweh's liberating power
which knows no limits. Cf. H. W. Wolff, *Anthropology of the OT* [1974], 223f.

If the psalm is interpreted in line with the more detailed priestly conceptions suggested by vv. 5f., then we will be able to take for granted that a priest threatened by death is, in his avowal of the Levitical prerogatives that apply to him, but above all in his trust in Yahweh's helpful revelation (v. 7), certain that Yahweh sustains his life and guards against death. Meanwhile, however, also the further possibility indicated under "Setting" should be brought into the discussion: It is thinkable that conceptions and elements of speech belonging to the priestly prerogatives fashioned and molded a prayer formulary that could be adopted by those persecuted (v. 1), those threatened with loss of life, the sick, and those marked for death, as a means of expressing their situation in prayer.

[16.11] Yahweh shows the way to life. He leads the petitioner through the—obviously still persisting—threats of death. Then there is fulsome joy in the proximity of Yahweh (cf. v. 8). The closing verse speaks of the bliss of the nearness to God, which in the midst of death opens up a way of life, on which one may walk with joy.[2]

Purpose and Thrust

Let us now begin at v. 7: Yahweh has revealed himself to the petitioner who is seeking protection, and he has done so by means of gracious advice, by a helpful word of God. The reaction to this revelation once taken to heart is trust, assurance, praise, and a constant reminder of the salvation bestowed. The avowals of the Levitical prerogatives (vv. 5-6) and the assertions in v. 8 try to describe the entire mystery and miracle of security with God and in God. The petitioner can never forget that Yahweh through his word revealed himself as the God who points to life (v. 11) and is gracious. He lives only on the basis of the foundation of life, Yahweh himself.

In place of the ביהוה of the OT, in the fulfillment of the new covenant the ἐν Χριστῷ has entered. In Christ all priestly prerogatives fall away, prerogatives in which in the OT only the mystery of the final communion with God showed itself in silhouette.

The singer of Psalm 16 outlines the importance of the nearness of God that embraces the existence of the human being by viewing the concrete dangers that threaten him. Physical life is girded round by the present God. And when v. 10 reads, "You do not surrender my life to Sheol, you do not permit your godly one to see the pit," here the thought is certainly in the first place only of preservation from an evil death (G. von Rad, cf. *OT Theol*, 1:405). Every premature spiritualization blunts the point of the essential assertion of our psalm. Rightly does H. Gunkel remark: "The historical understanding of such passages (also cf. Pss. 118:17; 49:15) is safeguarded beyond all doubt by the counterpart in the songs of thanksgiving (such as Pss. 9:13; 30:3). The forces of death assail the petitioner. But from the word of God he knows: My life is sheltered, it is not surrendered to the power of death, Sheol, that exerts its influence so powerfully

---

2. "In this verse the psalmist commends the inestimable fruit of faith, of which Scripture everywhere makes mention, in that, by placing us under the protection of God, it makes us ready not only to live in the enjoyment of mental tranquility, but, what is more, to live joyful and cheerful. The principal, the essential part of a happy life, as we know, is to possess tranquility of conscience and of mind; as, on the contrary, there is no greater infelicity than to be tossed amidst a multiplicity of cares and fears" (Calvin, on Ps. 16:9, trans. Anderson [Grand Rapids: Eerdmans, 1949]).

in this world—it is protectively surrounded on all sides (Ps. 139:5). The concrete dimension that must first be noticed and entered into has a lasting meaning: ''In a world in which survival is threatening to become increasingly improbable, the biblical insight into man's destiny is ground for a new expectation of life'' (H. W. Wolff, *Anthropology of the OT* [1974], 225). Man is destined for life. ''You do not surrender my life to Sheol!'' People may live in this conviction. Thus the life that has come to light in Christ Jesus is the power that now and today embraces human life. ''In the midst of death we are encompassed by life'' (Chr. Blumhardt). The body of man is sustained and kept by God in the midst of the realm of death. The fact that God's power brings even the dying person through death into the life of the new world of God—this assurance, founded on the resurrection of Christ Jesus, was still hidden from the people of the OT. Only the power of unlimited trust let them hope beyond the final border. Therefore the expressions of trust in the prayer songs are characterized by that unique transparency which then, in the pattern and witness of the certainty of the resurrection in the NT, played an important role (cf. H. W. Boers, A. Schmitt). In the language of the OT prayer song in Acts 2:24ff. the resurrection of Christ Jesus is announced. But thereby it is revealed that the assertions of trust by the psalmsingers provided the early Christian witness for Christ with the language and the categorical conceptions in which also the ultimate could be expressed: the resurrection from death.

Psalm 17

The Call for Help
by One Persecuted,
Though Innocent

Literature

H. Schmidt, *Das Gebet des Angeklagten in Alten Testament*, BZAW 49 (1928). J. Lindblom, "Bemerkungen zu den Psalmen I," *ZAW* 59 (1943) 1-13. D. Gualandi, "Salmo 17 (16), 13-14," *Bibl* 37 (1956) 199-208. J. Leveen, "The Textual Problems of Psalm 17," *VT* 11 (1961) 48-54. J. van der Ploeg, "Le psaume XVII et ses problèmes," *OTS* 14 (1965) 273-295. L. Hardouin-Duparc, "Je suis là, je t'appelle (Ps. 17,6 Is 42,6)," *Vie Spirit* 120 (1969) 129-137. W. Beyerlin, *Die Rettung der Bedrängten in den Feind-psalmen auf institutionelle Zusammenhänge untersucht*, FRLANT 99 (1970) 105-111.

Text

A prayer of David.
17:1 Hear, O Yahweh, 'my righteousness,'[a] attend to my cry,
  take note of my prayer from lips free of deceit!
2 From you my righteousness proceeds.
  Let your eyes[b] see what is right!
3 You try my heart, investigate it at night,
  test me—you find no 'shameful deed in me.'[c]
  My mouth[d] does not overflow [4] at[e] the deeds of men;
  to the words of your lips I have attended.
  'From'[f] the ways of the robber
5 my steps 'have desisted';[g]
  in your paths my steps did not waver.
6 I call to you, for you hear me, O God;
  incline your ear to me, listen to my word!
7 Show the wonders of your goodness, O Savior of those who seek
    refuge
  from those who rebel against your laws![h]

8 Protect me like an apple of the eye,[i]
 hide me in the shadow of your wings

9 from the wicked, who have done violence[j] to me,
 from my enemies, who greedily surround me!

10 'Their hearts they have unfeelingly'[k] closed up,
 with their mouth they speak arrogant things.

11 'They lie in wait for me'[l]—now 'they surround me,'[m]
 they seek to throw (me) to the ground.

12 He is like a lion, eager for prey,
 like the young lion that lies in hiding.

13 Arise, O Yahweh, confront him, throw him down,
 rescue me from the wicked person with your sword!

14 May 'a cruel death'[n] at your hand, O Yahweh,
 a cruel death 'put an end'[o] to their portion in life!
 'What you have put in store for them'[p]—(with that) fill their belly,
 so that their sons may (still) have their fill
 and bequeath a remainder to their children!

15 But I will behold your face in righteousness,
 when I awake, I will satisfy myself with your form.

1a Gk (δικαιοσύνης μου) read צדקי. Or ought we to read אל־צדקי (Ps. 4:1)? יהוה צדק in MT is unusual and hardly original.

2b MT is confirmed by the context of v. 3. Gk: οἱ ὀφθαλμοί μου.

3c According to the versification, which can also be determined from Gk, α´, σ´, and S. זמתי belongs to בל־תמצא. Accordingly, read זַמֹּתִי (Ps. 18:24).

d עבר here in the sense of "run over" (cf. Ps. 73:7). The statement, which is not easily interpreted, probably wants to say that the composer of the psalm has kept himself free of every sin of speech. Cf. the context in v. 4.

4e For the possible meaning of לֹ in this passage, cf. BrSynt §107c.

f If ארחות פריץ is taken with v. 5, then תמֹךְ is not possible in this passage. MT: "The paths of the robber held fast my steps." In the corrupt text a conjecture suited to the contextual sense would probably have to be: "From the ways of the robber my steps have desisted." That would yield the following Hebrew text: מֵאָרחות פריץ תָּעַמֹד אשורי.

5g On עמד מן, cf. Gen. 29:35; Jonah 1:15.

7h בימינך can hardly be dependent on חוסים; accordingly, this word is to be referred to ממתקוממים.

8i אישון בת־עין is here probably a compound concept (Deut. 32:10; Prov. 7:2; Lam. 2:18). We can hardly think of two separate concepts.

9j שדד as in Prov. 13:3; Job 12:6; 15:21.

10k MT: "Their fatness they have closed up." Very likely we are to read חֶלֶב לָבָמוֹ: "With fatness they have closed up their hearts" (cf. Ps. 119:70; Job 15:27).

11l The text is scarcely intelligible: "Our steps—now they have surrounded me (*Ketib; Qere:* 'us')." Gk: ἐκβάλλοντές με is oriented to the Aramaic אשדוני. S: אַשְׁרוּנִי. Perhaps the first word in the parallelism of members may be corrected to יְשֻׁרְנִי, "they keep an eye out for me," "they lie in wait for me." The correction remains an experiment. J. Lindblom suggests אשרימו: "Now their steps surround me" (*ZAW* 59 [1943], 9f.).

14m *Ketib:* סבבוני.

n this verse makes for difficulties—especially the double occurrence of the word ממתים, which would literally have to be translated "men," "human beings." But in this interpretation of the text the repetition of the word and the context remain obscure. When Gk translates ממתים מחלד with ἀπὸ ὀλίγων ἀπὸ γῆς, we have here only an emergency combination (ὀλίγων = מתי in Ps. 105:12; γῆς = חלד in Ps. 49:1). All conjectures advanced so far are problematic. It would easily be possible to recognize in ממתים a defective spelling of the intensive plural מְמוֹתִים (Jer. 16:4; Ezek. 28:8). In that case, for instance, we could read ממתים מידך (by haplology of מ): "a cruel death at your hand."

With this understanding of מְמִתִים the emphatic repetition would become intelligible.

o In keeping with the reconstruction of the verse, we would at this point expect a verb. Was there at one time an imperfect (jussive) *piel* or *hiphil* of חדל (with interchange of consonants)?

p *Ketib* וּצְפִינֶךָ. *Qere* וּצְפוּנְךָ.

Form

Psalm 17, which is to be counted among the psalms of David, presents no difficulties regarding its organization. In vv. 1-2 a petition is presented to Yahweh. In vv. 3-5 a profession of innocence follows. In vv. 6-9 the petition again emerges, which, in view of the enemies, is directed to God in vv. 10-12. In vv. 13-14 the petitioner appeals to Yahweh's judgment, and v. 15 finally expresses a wish and a certainty which the singer of the psalm cherishes for himself.

Let us consider the meter of Psalm 17. The verses are not consistent, and in part they contain problems that carry over into the criticism of the text. The meter 4 + 4 is to be found in vv. 1, 3bβ—4abα, 4bβ—5, 6, 7, 9, 13. The meter 4 + 3 can be established in vv. 3abα, 8, 12, 15. Vv. 2 and 10 are in the 3 + 3 meter, while the meter 3 + 4 is determinative in vv. 11 and 14. The second part of v. 14, beginning with וּצְפִינֶךָ, presents difficulties. The condition of the text does not permit a metrical determination. On the other hand, it is hardly possible to initiate text-critical measures on the basis of the meter.

Even the first analysis that has to do with form and structure very definitely shows that in Psalm 17 we are dealing with a prayer song that is preponderantly marked by petitions. For the form group תפלה, cf. above, Intro. §6, 2. The supplication addresses Yahweh in the second person (vv. 2ff., 6ff., 13ff.). The usual designation of type, that we have here a "lament of an individual" (Gunkel and Begrich, *EinlPs* § 6, 26), does not prove to be right. There are no traces at all of a lament. Rather, we ought to note that in vv. 3-5 the declaration of innocence is stressed in a special way, and that the petitioner refers to accusers and persecutors. Thus a particular situation is indicated, one that demands a detailed explanation. Already H. Schmidt (*Das Gebet des Angeklagten im Alten Testament*, 19f.) called attention to this.

Setting

The situation in which the petitioner of Psalm 17 finds himself is to be recognized, or inferred, from individual statements. As we see from v. 8, the psalmist looks for refuge "in the shadow" of the wings of the cherubim (see below). He is persecuted and surrounded by enemies (vv. 7, 9, 11). But the decisive demand is expressed in v. 1. And v. 2 may be rendered in a literal translation:

> From your countenance the verdict of my righteousness proceeds.
> Your eyes behold what is righteous.

He who is petitioning and seeking protection accordingly awaits the verdict of Yahweh in the cultic institution of the divine dispensation of judgment (W. Beyerlin, 105ff.). Thus a situation is indicated such as is reflected also in Psalms 3; 4; 5; 7; 11; and often. Obviously, the speaker of the psalm expects an ongoing grant of temple protection (v. 8), but he prays above all for the saving verdict of righteousness (vv. 13-14). From v. 15 it follows that he who is looking for protection is spending the night in the temple (cf. Ps. 3:5), in fact, that he has lain down for an *incubatio* ("lying in") and has committed his innermost being—in his sleep—to probation by Yahweh (S. Mowinckel; H. Schmidt). Especially in

vv. 2f. is the request for a verdict expressed (cf. Psalm 139). We will still need to investigate whether we can on that account speak of a "prayer of incubation."

Concerning the time of composition we can hardly provide information that is even approximately adequate. A late date is not to be suggested without qualification—certainly not the claim that we have to deduce from v. 5 that the petitioner belongs to the strict, legalistic Jews of late OT times (H. Duhm). Rather, we may probably assume that the psalm belongs to the cultic traditions of Jerusalem (cf. v. 8) and that it was associated as a prayer formula with the institution of divine dispensation of judgment. But with that consideration we have also immediately opened up the perspective of transmission, and we have before us the question to what extent Psalm 17 may still be applied to that institution and whether we have to think of a spiritualizing prayer song that developed from the cultic connections.

G. von Rad was of the opinion that the statement in v. 8 had disengaged itself from a specific cultic connection; that it had in a "spiritualized sense" entered the general language of prayer *(OT Theol*, 1:402). Parallel passages cited are Pss. 57:1; 59:16; 61:4; 64:10. By contrast, W. Beyerlin asserts: "The text of Psalm 17 so perfectly corresponds to an institutional procedure of divine judgment consisting of various acts, that a classification among such a procedure seems very likely. A psalm disengaged from it would hardly still imitate the contours of the individual acts of the procedure which are so indelibly and so definitely distinguished from one another. To be sure, we can say of individual motifs in the psalm text before us that they are disengaged from the institutional roots and that, understood in a spiritualized sense, they are used as elements of the general language of prayer. But about a well-organized succession of several motifs still sharply delineated we can speak much less emphatically. In this case the assumption of an undiminished connection to the institution actually lies closer" (107). This problem deserves a detailed and comprehensive elucidation. Yet the alternatives could not be presented so sharply as is done here. Finally, we have to proceed from the fact that also the psalms rooted in the soil of the cultus, in the process of their adoption as prayer songs, have been disengaged from their original ground. Even when we are of the opinion that we can by synthetic procedures discern a "well-organized succession" of scenes and motifs relating to the institution, finally the hard fact remains that in the collection of the Psalms no actual rituals are transmitted. Research oriented toward the cultus has a limitation here which precisely then should not be exceeded or forgotten when in a synthetic process conclusions are drawn and issues are reconstructed. In this point the Psalms of the OT differ essentially from the cultic texts known to us from the surrounding world.

Commentary

[Title] On תפלה, cf. above, Intro. §4, No. 8. On לדוד, cf. §4, No. 2.

[17:1-2] With a plea the persecuted petitioner comes before Yahweh, who in his godhead is the essence of צדק. He is אלהי צדקי (Ps. 4:1). The concept צדק in v. 1 implies what is stated in v. 2a: מלפניך משפטי יצא. Yahweh is the God who through saving intervention restores confused situations to order again. The appeal to his "righteousness" is a summons to his saving verdict of justice. In this urgent plea the psalmsinger already serves notice that he is innocent. His תפלה comes from "lips free of deceit"—so he confesses. From v. 2 we clearly discern that he who is innocently persecuted awaits the verdict of God. In legal situations that are not transparent the Israelite visits the sanctuary (Deut. 17:8-11; 1 Kings 8:31ff.). In the face of hostile persecutions and accusations the petitioner hopes for Yahweh's acquittal, for his verdict of righteousness. And yet the presupposition is that he who is looking for help completely surrenders to God. He points to his righteousness, that is, to his innocence. This statement has nothing to do with "self-righteousness"; it refers, rather, to the specific accusation that threatens his life. But what righteousness consists of, whether he who cries from depths of woe is declared צדיק—that is determined by Yahweh alone. From the ritual of Gen. 15:6 and Deut. 6:25, which forms the background of Ezek. 18:5ff., this is clearly discernible. Therefore the petitioner also waits and hopes that his righteousness may "proceed" from Yahweh, that is, may appear in a manifest declaration (cf. Ps. 37:6). In this situation of a disputed and contested righteousness—and that is what Psalm 17 is about—everything depends on the specific revelation of God, on God's word, God's declaration. The reference to one's own righteousness and innocence can accordingly gain expression in the prayer only from the side of the petition. Declaration and imputation of the צדקה are the free gift of grace on the part of the God of Israel. And yet, in reference to the specific accusation that has assailed the one who is seeking protection, an investigation through the eyes of Yahweh is prayed for in the complete surrender of self.

[17:3-5] It is possible, even probable, that the investigation of the accused took place during the lying-in at the temple (cf. v. 15). But what takes place is decisive. A trusting address to Yahweh indicates that he who is persecuted knows that he is an open book to Yahweh. God "investigates" the center of human existence, the core of all thinking, reasoning, planning, and doing: the heart (לב). This "investigating" is a matter of taking a look at the depths of reasoning and of "evaluating" (צרף) the thoughts. This בחן and צרף takes place at night. In this connection we may probably think of an "incubation" in the holy place. The God who is present visits the petitioner who has surrendered to him and "investigates" him; both elements (visiting, investigating) lie in the root פקד. Probably the conception is that the human being in his sleep no longer has the potential of hiding his thoughts.[1] The innermost recesses are laid bare. This self-presentation of man in a temple incubation, in addition to the oath of cleansing (cf. the commentary on Ps. 7:3-5), must have played an important role in procuring the verdict of God. He who is innocently persecuted is certain: "You find no shameful deed in me." This declaration we cannot, with H. Herkenne, describe as "juridical and relative" under the aegis of a theologically comprehensive concept of innocence. That would be to deny the final seriousness of that solemn affirmation which is stated before Yahweh. In the "juridical" process there are always acts of life-determining consequences. The enemies (vv. 10-12) want to separate the one who prays the psalm from Yahweh, want to declare him a רשע and cast him out. Always at stake in the "juridical and relative" processes is something final: the communion with God.

When the petitioner now expresses himself as being closer to his innocence, this takes place at first in a negative formulation, later in a positive

---

1. "The time when he declares God to have visited him is during *the night,* because, when a man is withdrawn from the presence of his fellow creatures, he sees more clearly his sins, which otherwise would be hidden from his view; just as, on the contrary, the sight of men affects us with shame, and this is, as it were, a veil before our eyes, which prevents us from deliberately examining our faults. It is, therefore, as if David had said, 'O Lord, since the darkness of the night discovers the conscience more fully, all coverings then being taken away, and since, at that season, the affections, either good or bad, according to men's inclinations, manifest themselves more freely, when there is no person present to witness and to pronounce judgment upon them; if thou then examinest me, there will be found neither disguise nor deceit in my heart' " (Calvin, on Ps. 17:3, trans. Anderson [Grand Rapids: Eerdmans, 1949]).

one. "It does not enter my mouth at the deeds of men." This solemn affirmation obviously wants to say that the petitioner has not sinned in his speech. " 'I do not break out in heated words.' The poet is thinking of the temptation to utter irresponsible, bitter words that can elicit the misdeeds of the enemies" (J. Lindblom, *ZAW* 59 [1943], 8). Does this interpretation want to point out that the petitioner did not save himself? That he did not anticipate the judgment of God with profanity? On the contrary, the positive statement of v. 4 points out that he who was persecuted always heeded the words of Yahweh. Here we are very likely to think of the expression of God's will in the Torah. At v. 4bβ another negative statement begins, which is again followed by a positive declaration. We must be sure to take note of this parallelism of two declarations, each negatively and positively oriented.

When we take note of this parallelism, it seems doubtful that J. Lindblom is right when in the text-critical reconstruction of vv. 4bβ and 5a he begins with the presupposition that here only positive declarations are present. Lindblom considers ארחות פריץ a "marginal note intruding on the text" and so constructs a double triple meter in v. 5 that is positive in content.

In vv. 4bβ and 5 the petitioner confesses that he has not walked "on the ways of the robber." Very likely this is to reject a specific accusation that has been launched against him who has been persecuted. Has there been an accusation that he has been guilty of robbery? The accused confesses, "In your paths my steps did not waver"—i.e., "I did not depart from the way which your will prescribed." In their content these protestations remind us of the "oath of cleansing" (cf. the comment on Ps. 7:3-5), but in the form of their diction they are structured differently. The decided rejection is always followed by a declaration of loyalty to Yahweh's juridical will.

[17:6-9] Now in vv. 6-9 the psalmsinger prays that Yahweh may take note and intervene. He is confident: כי־תעננני אל. The salutary intervention of God, which in v. 2 was expressed in the formula מלפניך משפטי יצא, he now prays for with the words: תפלה חסדיך. חסד denotes a kind disposition that in spontaneous love brings affection into action: N. Glueck, *Das Wort* חֶסֶד *im alttestamentlichen Sprachgebrauch,* BZAW 47 (1927); H. J. Stoebe, "Die Bedeutung des Wortes חֶסֶד im Alten Testament," *VT* 2 (1952) 244-254. This intervention of Yahweh's, by which he proves his benevolent affection, is a wonderful event. The root פלא denotes that which is unusual, extraordinary (KBL 759). In the prayer for wonderful intervention Yahweh is called מושיע חוסים. This expression points out a standing activity of God. He "makes room" (for this meaning of ישׁע, cf. the commentary on Ps. 3:2) for those who in adversity and fear seek shelter with him. The poor and the helpless find protection with Yahweh (see above, Intro. §10, 3). The adversaries of him who is innocently persecuted, in v. 9b called איבי, are in v. 7b described as מתקוממים—as "rebels" against Yahweh's power (בימינך). V. 8 then shows the function of the sanctuary as asylum. He who is persecuted prays for careful and mindful attention ("like an apple of the eye") and wants to hide under the shadow of the wings of God. צל in ancient Near Eastern metaphorical language is an expression for the immediate area of protection. He who lives "in the shadow of the king" enjoys his power to protect him (cf., beside many Egyptian texts, Lam. 4:20). The term כנפיך very likely refers to the extended wings of the cherubim above the ark of the covenant, which are thought of as a symbol of God's protection (Pss. 36:7; 63:7). The reference of this statement to the holy of holies in the temple, in which the cherubim were located, may be recognized without difficulty (cf. especially Ps. 80:1). Cf. J. Meier, *Das altisraelitische Ladeheiligtum,* BZAW (1965) 53f.; M. Haran, "The Ark and the Cherubim," *IEJ* 9 (1959) 30-38; R. E. Clements, *God and Temple* (1965) 31. Still, this figurative manner of speech was able to prevail in a spiritualized form in the later adoption of the prayer song (see above).

In v. 9 the situation of threatening enemies clearly comes into view. For the statements about the "enemies," see above, Intro, §10, 4. The persecutors surround the accused and press in on him. Their fanaticism, their "greed" is expressed in the word בנפש. In this connection the original nuance of meaning of נפש is easily recognized: "gullet," "greed" (Isa. 56:11; Ezek. 7:19). Cf. H W. Wolff, *Anthropology of the OT* (1974) 10ff.

[17:10-12] In his supplication the psalmsinger in vv. 10-12 presents a description of the activities of his enemies. Characteristic of his persecutors is the unfeeling secretiveness (חלב לבמו) and the proud self-assurance of speech (פימו דברו בגאות, cf. Ps. 73:9). The persecution already hinted at in v. 9 is then still more urgently presented in vv. 11-12. The persecutor is like the lion hungry for prey (cf. Ps. 10:8-10). By means of this description of the activity of the enemies Yahweh is to be moved to quick intervention. For that reason the petitioner now also (as in Ps. 10:12) immediately moves to an appeal to Yahweh.

[17:13-14] קומה יהוה is the address to the judge (cf. the comment on Ps. 7:6). Yahweh is asked to intervene and drive back the רשע. No matter how we reconstruct v. 14 with its textual difficulties, undoubtedly what is involved here is the plea that Yahweh as judge might carry out a verdict against the enemies of the petitioner. If we read ממתים as a defective form in the sense of the textual note above, then the psalmist prays for the death of his persecutors—and here the second part of v. 14 is perhaps borrowed from the conception of the deadly poison of an ordeal (Num. 5:19ff.). The divine sentence of death, however, is to befall not only the persecutors but also their progeny (v. 14b). For this judgment, in effect for generations, cf. Exod. 20:5. We must here realize that the usual conception of the plea in v. 14 in terms of revenge is not applicable. The point in Psalm 17 is not that a human being gives vent to his desire for revenge before God. A persecuted person pleads for his rights (v. 2) and for bestowal of the grace of God (v. 7). In the OT these decisions are carried out in this world. The demonstration of the intervention of God occurs in complete this-worldliness and is always hoped for anew as a miracle (v. 7). The appeal to the juridical intervention of Yahweh has therefore in the OT the character of final judgment on which everything depends. For that reason we may not, from the perspective of the NT, set "reconciling love" in contrast to "vengeful hatred." Such confrontations usually arise from an interest in setting up the dualism "Old Testament—New Testament" that is nontheological in its foundation. Rather, the appeals and pleas for judgment (as seen from the NT) are preludes to the final judgment. The OT petitioners are sure that the judgmental power of Yahweh becomes effective in the midst of life. Those who are persecuted and helpless pray that God may provide evidence of his saving activity and at the same time of a curb against wickedness. They believe that God is Lord in this world and that the רשע has forfeited his right to life in Yahweh's sphere of power, for the רשעים are, after all, members of Israel.

[17:15] When it now happens, that the deciding verdict is issued by Yahweh (מֹשׁפֹט יצא, v. 2) and that God provides wondrous divine favor (הפלה חסד, v. 7), then the petitioner stands בצדק—he is in the kingdom of salvation (K. Koch, "*Sdq im Alten Testament*," diss. Heidelberg [1953], 38). The psalmsinger expresses the wish and the hope that he may, as one blessed with the grace of Yahweh, see the countenance of God בצדק. The parallel concept to פניך is תמונתך. "Seeing God" therefore has to do with a concrete figure (Num. 12:8). Thus the suggestion here is obviously of a theophany, possibly in the sense of Isa. 6:1ff. But בהקיץ should probably be taken in connection with לילה (v. 3). In the morning after the night of testing by God, he who was accused and persecuted would like to have the satisfaction of the ultimate meeting with Yahweh in a theophany.

The interpretation of v. 15 has always been heavily disputed. Formerly in the history of interpretation, the interpretation usually favored the resurrection on judgment day. Luther declares: "And beautifully has he brought in a word of resurrection, 'when I awake,' that is, from the sleep of death, so that he might point out that our fulfillment is not in this life but in the life to come" (WA 5; 489, 39f.). Calvin, on the other hand, already recognized that this widely held interpretation is not possible. He understands the sleep from which the petitioner would like to awaken and see God to be the relaxing of acute affliction: "But to me it seems more suitable to refer the word *awake* to David, and to view it as meaning the same thing as to obtain respite from his sorrow. David had never indeed been overwhelmed with stupor; but after a lengthened period of fatigue, through the persecution of his enemies, he must needs have been brought into such a state as to appear sunk into a profound sleep. The saints do not sustain and repel all the assaults which are made upon them so courageously as not, by reason of the weakness of their flesh, to feel languid and feeble for a time, or to be terrified as if they were enveloped in darkness. David compares this perturbation of mind to a sleep" (Calvin, on Ps. 17:15, trans. Anderson [Grand Rapids: Eerdmans, 1949]).

That there is great difficulty in applying Ps. 17:15 to the resurrection was recognized also by Franz Delitzsch. And yet he expresses himself in favor of such an interpretation: "That all who lie in their graves will eventually hear the voice of him who wakes the dead, as we are taught in the postexilic time, Dan. 12:2, David of course did not know as yet. But why should this truth of revelation, toward which prophecy in Isa. 26:19 and Ezek. 37:1-14 proceeds with gigantic steps, not become articulate also already in the Psalms of David, as later in the book of Job, as a bold postulate of faith, as the hope wrenched from the disconsolate conception of Sheol?" While in more recent times text-critical measures were frequently undertaken to interpret the difficult בהקיץ appropriately, S. Mowinckel and H. Schmidt paved the way for the exegesis based on the idea that what is involved is the morning after the incubation. J. Lindblom opposes this interpretation, as he understands אחזה פניך to mean, "I will enjoy life in its fullness" (cf. Job 33:25f.). But in view of the parallel תמונתך, this interpretation is untenable. Also, the general conception of a merciful intervention of God in the morning (Lam. 3:23; Pss. 30:5; 46:5) cannot be of any help in the interpretation of v. 15, since this general conception probably grew out of this very specific procedure of the word of God that went out early in the morning (against Lindblom, *ZAW* 59 [1943], 12).

Purpose and Thrust

For the most important theological questions concerning the prayer of one who is falsely accused and persecuted, let us first of all refer to the "Purpose and Thrust" discussions on Psalm 7. Characteristic of Psalm 17 are the individual formulations in which the petitioner affirms his innocence and asks for God's intervention. The psalm statements culminate in the prayer for the judgment of the enemies (v. 14) and the wish to behold Yahweh's countenance of righteousness. The emphatic אני in v. 15 places the personal fate in sharp contrast to the fate of the enemies. Over against the "cruel death" (ממתים), the most abject verdict of rejection of those judged, stands "beholding God," the highest good fortune of those pardoned. Seen thus, we can understand it when the exegesis that interprets in NT categories viewed this "greatest good fortune" as something ultimate, something announcing the resurrection. Such interpreters can appeal to Rev. 22:4. For an understanding of the OT data, however, it would be important to recognize the real presence of the last judgment and the final pardoning in the present life.

Psalm 18

A Song of Thanksgiving
of the King
after a Victorious Battle

Literature

E. Baumann, "Struktur-Untersuchungen im Psalter I," *ZAW* 61 (1945/48) 131-136. F. M. Cross and D. N. Freedman, "A Royal Song of Thanksgiving," *JBL* 72 (1953) 16ff. F. Schnutenhaus, "Das Kommen und Erscheinen Gottes im Alten Testament," *ZAW* 76 (1964) 1-21. Jörg Jeremias, *Theophanie: Die Geschichte einer alttestamentlichen Gattung,* WMANT 10 (1965). G. Schuttermayr, "Studien zum Text der Psalmen 9/10 und 18: Probleme der Textkritik und Übersetzung und das Psalterium Pianum," diss. München (1966). D. Eichhorn, "Gott als Fels, Burg und Zuflucht," *EHS. T* 4 (1972) 30ff.

Text

To the choirmaster. Concerning the servant of Yahweh. Of David, who spoke to Yahweh the words of this song on the day when Yahweh rescued him from the hands of all his enemies and from the hands[a] of Saul.

18:1 And he said,
"I will 'extol you,'[b] O Yahweh, my strength,

2 ' '[c] my rock, my fortress, my savior,
my God, my shelter to which I flee,
my shield and horn of my salvation." ' '[d]

3 'Pierced through,'[e] I cried to Yahweh—
and I was rescued in the sight of my enemies.

4 'Billows'[f] of death had encompassed me,
and torrents of ruin had frightened me.

5 The cords of Sheol enveloped me,
the snares of death fell over me.

6 In my distress I cried to Yahweh
and called to my God.
He heard my crying from his temple,
and my call ' '[g] made its way to his ears.

7 Then the earth tottered and trembled,
the foundations of the earth shook—
and they trembled, for he was angry—.[h]

8 Smoke rose up from his nose,
and a consuming fire issued from his mouth—
glowing coals flamed up before him.—[i]

9 He let heaven descend and swooped down,
with darkness of clouds at his feet.

10 He rode along, flying on the cherub,
and soared on the wings of the storm.

11 He made darkness his cloak,' '[j]
and dark waters ' '[k] his abode.

12 Out of the radiance before him ' '[l] came
hail and fiery coals.

13 Thunder did Yahweh cause to boom in the heavens,
the Most High let his voice resound.' '[m]

14 He shot his arrows and scattered them,
'hurled'[n] bolts of lightning and let them race about.

15 Then the depths of 'the sea'[o] became visible,
the foundations of the earth lay uncovered—
before your rebuke, O Yahweh,
before the fuming of the storm of your wrath.

16 He reached down from on high, took hold of me,
and plucked me out of the vast waters.

17 He rescued me in the sight of 'my enemies, who were strong,'[p]
in the sight of those who hated me, who were stronger than I.

18 They descended on me in the day of my misfortune,
but Yahweh became my support.

19 He brought me out into the wide expanse,
rescued me, for he took delight in me.[q]

20 Yahweh dealt with me according to my righteousness,
according to the cleanness of my hands he rewarded me.

21 Indeed, Yahweh's ways I observed,
I did not fall away from my God.

22 Indeed, all his statutes stood before me,
and his commandments I did not reject.

23 Also, I was blameless before him
and guarded against wickedness.

24 Therefore Yahweh rewarded me according to my righteousness,
according to the cleanness of my hands before his eyes.

25 Over against the pious[r] you show yourself gracious,
over against the upright 'man,'[s] genuine.

26 To the pure you show yourself as pure,
but to the deceitful as perverse.

27 For you will save a lowly people,
but haughty eyes you will bring down low.

28 Indeed, you are ' '[t] my lamp, O Yahweh.
My God turns my darkness into light.

29 For with you I take fortifications by storm,
and with my God I leap over walls.

30 God—his way is perfect,
The word of Yahweh is genuine.
He is a shield to all who take refuge with him.

31 For who is God beside Yahweh?

And who is a rock?—Surely only our God!

32 God—he girded[u] me with strength,
   he made my way blameless.

33 He made my feet like those of the hinds,
   and he let me walk on (my) heights.

34 He taught my hands to wage war,
   so that my arms drew the metal[v] bow.

35 You gave to me the shield of your aid,
   —your right hand supported me,[w]
   'your encouragement'[x] made me strong.

36 You made room for the steps I took,
   and my ankles did not weaken.

37 I pursued my enemies and overtook them
   and did not turn back until I had annihilated them.

38 I smashed them, they could not get up,
   they fell beneath my feet.

39 You girded me with might for the battle,
   forced my adversaries under me.

40 My enemies had to turn their back to me,
   those who hated me I was able to annihilate.

41 They cried out—but there was no savior—
   'to'[y] Yahweh, but he did not hear them.

42 I beat them down like dust before the wind,
   I 'trampled on them'[z] as on dirt on the street.

43 You have rescued me from a 'numberless'[aa] army,
   and you are appointing me head of the nations.
   Nations whom I did not know became subject to me—

44 as soon as they heard of me, they became obedient to me. '   '[bb]

45 The sons of foreign lands languish
   and come trembling from their dungeons.

46 Yahweh lives! Praise be to my rock!
   Exalted be the God of my salvation!

47 God—he let me have revenge,
   forced peoples under me.

48 He rescued me from my angry enemies,
   exalted me above my adversaries,
   snatched me from the grips of the man of violence.

49 Therefore I will praise you
   among the peoples, O Yahweh,
   and sing to your name.

50 He granted strong aid to his king
   and bestowed grace on his anointed one:
   David and his seed forever.

---

a 2 Sam 22:1, וּמִיד מִכַּף. could have the meaning ''and especially'' (Ges-K §154a).
1b רחם as an expression of the love for God is documented only here in the OT and therefore is questionable. Consistent with the hymnic beginning of the song of thanksgiving (see below on ''form'') would be the verb אֲרֹמִמְךָ, which can be documented in Pss. 30:1; 145:1; Isa. 25:1. The beginning of Psalm 18 differs from that of 2 Samuel 22 respecting the condition of the text and the arrangement of the parallel verses. While 2 Samuel 22 lacks the half-verse ארחמך יהוה חזקי (Ps. 18:1), we notice in Psalm 18 the lack of the verse part ומנוסי משעי מחמס תשעני (2 Sam. 22:3bβ).
2c 2 Sam. 22:2 begins with the address יהוה, which in the text of Ps. 18:2 has an intrusive effect, because here all the nouns in v. 2, including חזקי in v. 1, are appositives to יהוה in v. 1.

d Because Psalm 18 is almost throughout dominated by the double triple meter (see below), מִשְׂגַּבִּי should probably be eliminated on metrical grounds as a variant reading within the text.

3e MT מְהֻלָּל, "praised," is hardly possible, syntactically as well as in terms of content. In v. 3 we would have to reconstruct something that corresponds to v. 6. Perhaps we may be permitted to read מְחֹלָל (Isa. 53:5). Such a statement would correspond to the descriptions in vv. 4ff. The emendation מְמַהֲלַלִי is a pale, pedantic complement to the parallel word מִן־אֹיְבִי.

4f חֶבְלֵי־מָוֶת, "cords of death," is a frequent construct combination in the OT, which in this passage has probably been brought about by חֶבְלֵי־שְׁאוֹל (v. 5). The parallelism of members and 2 Sam. 22:5 suggest an emendation. Instead of חבלי we ought to read מִשְׁבְּרֵי.

6g לפני is not present in 2 Sam. 22:7 and is to be eliminated as an intrusive interpolation.

7h That we have a gloss in 7b we can deduce not only from the explanatory and pedagogical character of the statement but also from the conspicuous disruption of the double triple meter.

8i Here too we probably have a complementary addition.

11j The text of v. 11 is peculiarly crowded and in the wording doubtful. In 2 Sam. 22:12 סתרו is not present; in Gk, however, this word is transmitted. As parallel complementary terms, we have סתרו and סכתו, as well as the objects חשׁךְ and the double description חֶשְׁכַת־מַיִם עָבֵי שְׁחָקִים. The question arises where supplementation of a possible original text (in a double triple meter) has been undertaken. In the first half-verse (the *atnaḥ* is in the wrong place) סביבותיו could have been added.

k In the second half-verse there is a variant—perhaps עָבֵי שְׁחָקִים—probable as a duple representation within the text.

12l MT: "Before the radiance before him, his clouds raced along." עביו is not present in 2 Sam. 22:13 and should probably be eliminated. עביו is perhaps a variant of נגדו.

13m V. 12b once more turns up as dittography in v. 13b (unintelligible in the train of thought).

14n According to 2 Sam. 22:15 we ought to read בָּרָק here (cf. also Ps. 144:6).

15o 2 Sam. 22:16 reads יָם.

17p In MT the construction מֵאֹיְבַי עָז is striking; conspicuous, too, is the suffix in the singular; S reads the verbal form עָזוּ instead of עָז. That would correspond to parallelism of members; the ו is then mistakenly placed before מִשֹּׂנְאַי. In addition, we should probably—in keeping with the parallelism of members—have to supply כִּי before עָזוּ (haplography?). In מֵאֹיְבַי, corresponding to v. 3, the suffix is to be read in the plural.

19q Gk here adds ῥύσεταί με ἐξ ἐχθρῶν μου δυνατῶν καὶ ἐκ τῶν μισούντων με. Cf. v. 17.

25r Here, in keeping with the parallelism of members, we should very likely supply אִישׁ (Gunkel); such a complement is suggested also for metrical reasons.

s On גבר as the Aramaic form for גֶּבֶר, cf. Ges-K §93s.

28t תָּאִיר is not present in 2 Sam. 22:29 and should also on metrical grounds be eliminated. Most likely, the interpolation was introduced as a verbal equivalent for יגיה in the parallelism.

32u The MT reading in Psalm 18 is in any case to be preferred to מְעוּזִּי in 2 Sam. 22:33.

34v In line with the double triple meter, נְחוּשָׁה would have to be eliminated here.

35w 2 Sam. 22:36 does not have וִימִינְךָ תִסְעָדֵנִי. This part of the verse would have to be thought of as an addition.

x MT עֲנֹתְךָ, "your humility," makes no sense. Gk, S, and θ´ translated ἡ παιδεία σου. That would correspond to the *piel* infinitive עַנֹּתְךָ; but also this version is not possible. 2 Sam. 22:36, עֲנֹתְךָ = "your answer," "your hearing," "your oracle," your encouragement."

41y In agreement with 2 Sam. 22:42, we should here read אֶל instead of עַל.

42z אֲרִיקֵם in MT = "I emptied them." This form is impossible in the context. Following 2 Sam 22:43, we should read אֲדִקֵּם אֶרְקָעֵם.

43aa מֵרִיבֵי עָם in MT, "from battles of the people," is a very rare construct combination,

Psalm 18

one that must be elucidated by Pss. 3:6; 68:9. In this passage we must read מֶרְכְּבוֹת עָם according to the topicality of the language of the Psalms.

44bb In the half-verses בְּנֵי־נֵכָר יְכַחֲשׁוּ לִי and בְּנֵי־נֵכָר יִבֹּלוּ we obviously have variants within the text. V. 44b should very likely be set aside.

Form

In its meter, Psalm 18 almost throughout reveals the form of the double triple scheme. Slight variations should be noted in the following verses: In vv. 7 and 8, as well as in vv. 30, 35, 48, and 50, and 3 + 3 meter is exceeded by a further half-verse. In vv. 7, 8, 30, and 35 we would have to think of elucidating additions (glosses). In vv. 48 and 50 the conclusions could have brought on the expansion. V. 49 is best read, with Sievers and Gunkel, in the 2 + 2 + 2 meter. For the remaining verses we should note that v. 25 in MT would have to be read in the 2 + 3 meter. Still, in the first half-verse אִישׁ should probably be supplied. An exception in v. 34 (3 + 4) can hardly be eliminated.

Before the text is understood according to content and arrangement, certain basic questions must first be considered. The parallel transmission of Psalm 18 in 2 Samuel 22 has to be given careful consideration. A comparison of the two versions shows that Psalm 18 is closer than 2 Samuel 22 to the prototype that is to be arrived at by textual criticism. However, 2 Samuel 22 provides valuable details.

In more recent times, there have been doubts whether Psalm 18 can even be considered a unit. H. Schmidt divides the psalm into two parts: Psalm 18A, vv. 1-30; Psalm 18B, vv. 31-50. In form criticism, literary critical probes are accompanied by type classifications. Thus H. Schmidt is of the opinion that Psalm 18A is a "lament of the falsely accused," while Psalm 18B may be termed a "royal psalm." In agreement with this view is, among others, E. Baumann ("Strukturuntersuchungen im Psalter I," *ZAW* 61 [1945/48], 131-136). The division of Psalm 18 into two psalms is always based on the following arguments: (1) The two different reports of the psalmist in vv. 3ff. and 31ff. are so definitely at variance that they cannot be molded together to a single unit; (2) in vv. 20ff. there are Deuteronomic reflections that seem to make an early derivation of the first part impossible, or at least show that an early text was later amplified; in view of this, the second part would have to be thought of as an independent song (from earlier times). However, there are difficulties in Psalm 18 not only in the basic question of its partition, but also in details. The flow of speech changes often and abruptly. The literary form is not clear. Sections like vv. 7-15, which describe a theophany, must additionally be considered a type all their own and have a history peculiar to them. The interpretation can therefore proceed only very cautiously; it must leave many questions unanswered.

Against a partition of the psalm into two songs, especially the following should be considered: (1) It is altogether possible that in a song of thanksgiving of an individual (on this form group, see below) the rescue to which the thankful person looks back is described in two phases of narrating and reporting; (2) the Deuteronomistic pieces could be understood as later interpolations; they provide no data for the question of whether an independent prior song may be assumed or even must be assumed; (3) the factual connections to which the statements of vv. 20ff. belong will have to be developed in detail (see below); (4) the fact of the unified parallel transmission of the entire psalm in 2 Samuel 22 urges caution.

The following is a preliminary overview and outline: title; laudatory introduction, vv. 1-3; narration of God's great acts of rescue, vv. 3-19; thoughts on the question, why does Yahweh rescue? vv. 20-26; concerning the wondrous bestowal of power, vv. 27ff.; developed from that: a new narration of the wonders of the rescue, vv. 35-48; conclusion, vv. 49-50.

From this preliminary overview and outline we may conclude, by form-critical analysis, that we have in vv. 1-30 the song of thanksgiving of an individual; cf. above, Intro. §6, 2aβ. Still the *todah* in the first part of the psalm is "in every respect an exception among the OT songs of thanksgiving" (F. Crüsemann, *Studien zur Formgeschichte von Hymnus und Danklied in Israel*, WMANT 32 [1969], 254; which see, on individual questions). Also in vv. 31-49 the basic features of the song of thanksgiving of an individual, especially in the form and type of the account, are unmistakable. Of course, the hymnic features are much more in evidence there. Also v. 50—if this is not an interpolation—refers to the king. Thus we could here have a royal psalm (see above, Intro. §6, 3) or, more precisely, "a royal song of thanksgiving" (F. Crüsemann, 256). We can build on these findings only hypothetically, for we cannot silently pass over the difficulties which everywhere stand in the way and permit our every step to be valid only as a probe. Especially, after all that has been said so far, the question arises anew how the psalm may be interpreted and understood as a unit. But to provide an answer, new attempts at interpretation are necessary.

Setting

At which occasion was the song of thanksgiving intoned? Where was it sung? Who is the author and singer? Such questions, in the case of Psalm 18, have provoked an especially lively discussion. If the psalm is divided into two parts, the answer is: Part A is the "song of thanksgiving of an ordinary person" (Baumann) or of any accused person whatsoever (Schmidt) who presents his thanks in the sanctuary—very likely in connection with a festival; Part B, on the other hand, has to be understood as the "song of thanksgiving of a king." In the holy place the king thanks Yahweh for a victory. This view of the psalm could appeal to the fact that in vv. 31ff. the contours of royal ruling and dealing come into prominence more sharply than in vv. 4ff. But is such a judgment to the point? In vv. 3ff. we meet with pictures and conceptions that belong to the sphere of experience that transcends all limits of this-worldly relations. Here we have primeval, powerful images that move about in the polarity "Sheol/God's heavenly world." He who suffers distress descends to the lowest point of separation from God—but Yahweh intervenes from the height of heaven.

If now Part B clearly shows the features of a royal song of thanksgiving, could not the images of Part A also be applied to the king? It is natural to proceed from the viewpoint of unity of the whole song (see above). But then the questions mentioned at the beginning of this section ("setting") are to be repeated with emphasis. That Psalm 18 has been sung in the sanctuary is evident from v. 6 and from the "Sitz im Leben," which may be documented also in other songs of thanksgiving. The king sings the psalm in the holy place. But at which occasion is the song of thanksgiving intoned? The answers of the commentators vary between the historical and the mythical. While earlier interpretations searched for a historical event, H. Gunkel was ready to speak in a very general way of a royal "festival of thanksgiving for a victory," H. Schmidt saw connections to a festival of enthronement of Yahweh, and the Scandinavians uncovered mythological backgrounds (descent into hell and revival in the context of a nature cult). Gunkel is probably on the right track: the song of thanksgiving refers to a victory that Yahweh has granted his chosen king. Here we are to assume from the very beginning that this song of thanksgiving for a victory was used not once but— as a formulary—repeatedly, and later made the transition from the area of royalty to the use of the entire congregation (cf. the comment on Psalm 3). This history of a psalm in worship makes it impossible to propose precise answers to the question about authorship and time of composition. The gamut of frequently repeated conceptions basically reflects a changing history of tradition: W. F. Albright is of the opinion that Psalm 18 "we may provisionally attribute" to the 10th century (*Archaeology and the Religion of Israel* [1942] 129). O. Eissfeldt considers the possibility "not quite excluded" that David could have been the author (*The OT*, 452). But H. Gunkel, in view of the latitude of expression and the frequent repetitions, points to the last years of Judah (Josiah). All these interpretations grasp at phases of the tradition of Psalm 18. Certainly, we could assign the original form of the psalm, which probably could not be ascertained, to early times, perhaps even to the 10th century. The research of F. M. Cross and D. W. Freedmann ("A Royal Song of Thanksgiving," *JBL* 72 [1953], 16ff.) has exhibited ancient Canaanite elements, including even orthographic peculiarities. And yet, Gunkel's observations on style are not to be put aside: Psalm 18 bears the marks of later reformulation. Of course, we must reject as inappropriate Gunkel's criterion that long psalms are always to be assigned to a later time, while the short psalm exhibits the marks of extreme old age. Such a conception is disproved by the Song of Deborah (Judges 5), for instance.

Commentary

[Title] The heading of Psalm 18 is more detailed than that of any other psalm of David. On למנצח, cf. above, Intro. §4, No. 2. On לדוד, Intro. §4, No. 2. In the additional remarks David is called עבד־יהוה (cf. Pss. 36, title; 144:10). The entire song of thanksgiving is assigned to him. This is in any case the earliest commentary, one that asserts that Psalm 18 is to be viewed as in a frame that leads from the explicit naming of the king in the title ("David spoke the words of this song") to v. 50—in other words, to that verse in which the king, David, and all of his seed are mentioned. Could it be that an original form of the psalm goes back to David himself and that the "accretions of transmission," i.e., the possible expansion that the song experienced, are to be credited to the interest those who transmitted it had in this particular material of tradition? We can only ask the question. The statement of the situation in the title remains a general one: "When Yahweh rescued him from the hands of all his enemies." " . . . And from the hand of Saul"—these words give the impression of a later qualification which, however, is in no position to shed light on the "historical problems" or to indicate a setting that can be helpful in interpreting the text (cf. the comment on Psalm 3, title).

[18:1-2] The introit of the song of thanksgiving shows all the marks of hymnic elation. The emendation ארממך instead of ארחמך is based on formal and practical considerations. In the hymnic introduction Yahweh is "extolled" (Pss. 30:1; 145:1; Isa. 25:1). רחם as an expression of human love of God is impossible in this passage, for רחם in the OT denotes the compassion that originates in God's innermost being. The abundance of predicates of God in the introit has a hymnic character. All the designations of Yahweh refer to the savior and helper. מפלטי

258

is accordingly the central term about which the expressions of the sacral right of asylum and of Jerusalem cultic language are grouped. Thus the term צוּר, for instance, alludes to an important sacral tradition of Jerusalem. With the sacred rock of the Jerusalem temple mount there are associated in the cultic tradition of Zion cosmic conceptions of the foundation of the world that is solidly grounded and lifted up on high: H. Schmidt, *Der heilige Fels in Jerusalem* (1933) 94ff. These traditions (very likely originating in pre-Israelite times) have been applied to Yahweh. Yahweh himself is the "eternal rock" (Pss. 31:3; 42:9). To him as the "fortress," "shield," and "horn" all those who are in distress and danger flee for refuge; cf. D. Eichhorn, 30ff. On קֶרֶן־יֵשַׁע, cf. 1 Sam. 2:10; Ps. 132:17; Luke 1:69.

Thus the hymnic introit glorifies Yahweh as the constant God of protection for all the oppressed.

[18:3-6] At v. 3 begins the first narration that reports the wonderful rescue. Up to v. 6 we have for the most part a description of the distress and oppression. From the very beginning we must realize that the stories about Sheol and about the intervention of Yahweh transcend every possible historical situation. In mythlike ciphers and images the specific distress of the petitioner is described.[1] An event that is supraindividual, penetrating into the most remote dimensions, is called upon to illustrate the secret and the wonder of the work of God. One could therefore in the interpretation of Psalm 18 occasionally get the impression that the subject was not at all a human king who suffers and is rescued but rather a god (H. Schmidt). The entire event is sketched to form an archetypal happening in whose vast realm the petitioner "finds a place" for himself and his specific distress. If we view the entire narrative phase of vv. 3-19 with this understanding, then all historicizing inquiries, on the one hand, and the mythologizing hypothesis, on the other, are thwarted. The (royal) petitioner enters a conventionalized, archetypal area of conception. In vv. 3-6 the unfathomable mystery of distress that is understood to be separation from God is described in a picturesque way. In the hour of distress the singer fell into the sphere of שְׁאוֹל (Chr. Barth, *Die Errettung vom Tode in den individuellen Klage- und Dankliedern* [1947], 76ff.). All of the images illustrate this situation. מְחֻלָּל also in Isa. 53:5 denotes extreme suffering, the state of being mortally shattered.

But the singer of the psalm of thanksgiving does not for a moment let doubt take over: in this distressful situation he called to Yahweh (v. 3) and was rescued. This proleptic expression is characteristic of the song of thanksgiving, which is a result of the help experienced.

The enemies here in Psalm 18 are without question foreign powers (see above, Intro. §10, 4). Yet their activity is seen in their revolt against the צַדִּיק (vv. 20ff.), against the one who belongs to Yahweh. The sea of chaos is the

---

1. About the picturesque language of Psalm 18, Calvin declares: "The Holy Spirit, to contend against and make an impression upon the wicked and perverse dispositions of men, has here furnished David with eloquence full of majesty, energy, and wonderful power, to awaken mankind to consider the benefits of God. There is scarcely any assistance God bestows, however evident and palpable it may be to our senses, which our indifference or proud disdain does not obscure. David, therefore, the more effectually to move and penetrate our minds, says that the deliverance and succor which God had granted him had been conspicuous in the whole framework of the world. This his intention it is needful for us to take into view, lest we should think that he exceeds due bounds in expressing himself in a style so remarkable for sublimity" (Calvin, on Ps. 18:5, trans. Anderson [Grand Rapids: Eerdmans, 1949]).

essence of dangerous, godless power. Therefore the threatening ruin is described in v. 4 with the metaphors of the mythology of Tiamat (cf. Psalm 93): Ps. 69:1f., 14; Lam. 3:54; Jonah 2:4, 6; Pss. 42:7; 88:7; 93:4. מות and בליעל are the powers that rage in the sphere of שאול. The insidiousness of the ruinous powers is illustrated by means of images of the hunt (v. 5): G. Dalman, AuS 6:337, 339. In this distress (בצר) the petitioner of the psalm cried to Yahweh. He cried and experienced the miracle of being heard. For the cry of distress made its way to the ear of Yahweh, who is enthroned in the temple (of Jerusalem) (Jonah 2:8). מהיכלו probably does not refer to the heavenly palace, but to the temple, in which the song of thanksgiving is presented.

[18:7-15] Here we now have a powerful depiction of a theophany. From the highest heavens Yahweh inclines to the petitioner, who is oppressed in the lowest area of. שאול. Here we clearly recognize supraindividual polarity. The appearance of God is ushered in by an earthquake (v. 7). This announcement of God's coming is characteristic of depictions of theophanies in the OT: Judg. 5:4ff.; Deut. 33:2f.; Isa. 30:27ff.; Hab. 3:4ff.; Ps. 97:2ff. The quake affects also the מוסדי הרים, the archetypal foundations of all that is durable and solid. The whole heavenly world of power descends (v. 9). We should here take note of ירד as the technical term for divine "condescension": Gen. 11:5, 7; 18:21; Exod. 3:8; 19:11, 18, 20; 34:5. The allusions of this description to the Sinai theophany should not be overlooked. "Darkness of clouds" envelops God in his appearance. As the coming one, God is veiled. As the *revelatus* God remains *absconditus;* cf. also v. 11 (Exod. 19:16, 18; Ps. 97:2; Ezek. 1:4). The codelike description of God in his appearance mentions the כרוב as the "vehicle" of the approaching theophany. In the OT Yahweh is enthroned above the cherubim of the ark (Ps. 80:1; Ezekiel 1; Ps. 99:1; 1 Sam. 4:4). Are these cherubim guards at the throne of the Holy One, or are they a "personification" of the thundercloud? This question cannot be answered unequivocally on the basis of our passage. Very likely, sacral elements of depiction of the chariot throne of the ark (Ezekiel 10) have been joined to the phenomenon of cloud formations. We can no longer penetrate the great variety of the symbols of antiquity. In any case, we should note that כרוב and כנפי־רוח in the parallel member are synonymous concepts.

Although the appearing God veils himself (v. 11), a dazzling brilliance precedes him as he goes (cf. Deut. 33:2; Hab. 3:4). This flashing brilliance of light represents the real wonder of the theophany (Ps. 50:2). Hail and fiery coals rain down (v. 12). The activities of a mighty thunderstorm and a volcanic eruption are telescoped into each other: Isa. 30:30; Pss. 97:5; 104:32; and Pss. 11:6; 140:10. Verse 13 (cf. Psalm 19) describes the booming thunder as the sound announcing the appearance of God. Yahweh is called עליון, the God of heaven (see above, Intro. §10, 1). God sends down bolts of lightning like arrows (v. 14; Hab. 3:9, 11; Ps. 77:17f.), and in his appearance he reveals the אפיקי מים. Here the description of the theophany reaches over into the conceptual world of primeval chaos and the origin of the earth (H. Gunkel, *Schöpfung und Chaos in Urzeit und Endzeit²*, 102f.). Yahweh's intervention disperses the powers of chaos (cf. v. 4) and institutes the מוסדות תבל. Here we are dealing with cosmological terms that refer to the foundations of the land area freed from the sea of chaos. The booming thunder of the theophany (Psalm 29) is combined with the word of power uttered in primeval times by means of which God has repelled the forces of שאול (Ps. 104:7).

In many respects the theophany descriptions of the OT still represent an impenetrable problem. What especially concerns the conceptual elements of these descriptions are two blocks of images that are here telescoped: the notions of the epiphany of the god of the thunderstorm, familiar from the Hadad-Rimmon myth, and the metaphors that point to volcanic areas. In a hymn addressed to the god of the thunderstorm we could read: "Father Ishkur, lord, he who rides along on the storm, that is your name, supreme god; Father Ishkur, lord, he who rides along on the mighty lion, that is your name, supreme god; Ishkur, lion of heaven, lofty steer, radiant one, that is your name, supreme god. Your name covers the world like a cloak, at your thunder the high hill totters, Father Enlil, at your roaring the great Mother Ninlil trembles" (H. Gressmann, *AOT* 249). On the other side, the volcanic conceptions point to traditional relations from the northeast and all the way to the farthest southeast (beyond the Gulf of Aqaba). The events of the thunderstorm or volcanic eruption as a sign were contained already in the picture of the Sinai theophany (Exodus 19), and from there onward they had an effect on the descriptions of the divine appearances in the OT. But at times even pre-Israelite and extra-Israelite rudiments of conception play into the OT theophanies. They serve as poetic and prophetic illustrations of the coming of God. But here the question immediately arises how a theophany is to be imagined concretely. That the appearance of God is a narrative and prophetic ingredient of the Sinai tradition probably has no need of more detailed documentation (G. von Rad, *The Problem of the Hexateuch and Other Studies* [1966]). But did this theophany also have a meaning in the cultus of that time? S. Mowinckel and A. Weiser have stated it as their opinion that in the dramatic course of worship we have to take for granted also a representation of a theophany. Is this conception appropriate?

We are not in a position precisely to reconstruct the actual procedures in the worship of Israel. For this our sources do not provide a foundation. Thus the assumption of a dramatically presented theophany must be thought of as an experiment. But we must ask the question, How do we imagine such a representation of a theophany to have been presented? Is it conceivable that Israel let itself be carried away to such physical manifestations in worship? Should we not rather with proper restraint consider whether perhaps with a procession of the ark (2 Samuel 6; 1 Kings 8; Psalm 132) a reference was made to the coming and appearing of God in the style of a kerygmatic proclamation? Psalms 50 and 97 we could understand to be such cultic proclamations of the appearance of God. But Psalm 18 would then have borrowed its conceptions from the kerygma in worship.

The type and subject of the descriptions of the theophany have been prepared and presented in a comprehensive way by Jörg Jeremias in *Theophanie* (1965). The book contains a significant presentation and interpretation of the history-of-religions materials (pp. 73ff.). The influences from Israel's surroundings and the origin of the individual conceptions are indicated. The description of the theophany in Psalm 18 is interpreted in detail (pp. 34ff.). Here Jeremias arrives at the following summary: "In this powerful theophany text certain entirely different conceptions have been fused together to form a description of the coming of Yahweh. Yahweh's coming with fire (v. 8) has no direct relation to his approach on descending thunderclouds (v. 9). Again, we have to distinguish from that his hurried advent in a gale (v. 10b). Volcanic elements (v. 12b) and thunderstorm appearances (vv. 13f.) have no immediate connection with his appearance in glory (v. 13a). Yahweh was not the God of a single appearance in nature." On theophany, also cf. F. Schnutenhaus, 1ff.

[18:16-19] These verses deal with Yahweh's intervention and the actual rescue. God, descending from heaven in a theophany, now intervenes in the depths of ruin (cf. also Ps. 144:7). From the realm of chaos (מִמַּיִם רַבִּים) Yahweh plucked him who was lost.[2] From the hand of the mighty foe and despiser, against whom

---

2. "Here there is briefly shown the drift of the sublime and magnificent narrative which has now

the person in distress no longer knew of any powers of his own that he might use, God has rescued him. Verse 18 indicates that the king who now expresses thanks was attacked and overpowered on a dark day. That also in vv. 1-30 we hear of a situation of a royal army leader cannot be doubted. But Yahweh came to the support (לְמִשְׁעָן) of him who was lost. In v. 19 the rescue is described in graphic terms. The distress (צר) is a "narrow place," the help of God a "liberating expanse" (cf. the comment on Ps. 4:1). The gift of Yahweh is liberation.

[18:20-26] Here the singer inquires about the reason for God's intervention. Why, exactly, did Yahweh help me? This question, though not stated in so many words, stands at the head of our section. Now, the opinion has always prevailed that vv. 20-26 in the texture of the song of thanksgiving represent a "Deuteronomistic," if not even a Jewish-nomistic, relapse into all kinds of self-righteous reflections. This view arose when people let themselves be misled by individual concepts. The section vv. 20-26, however, should not be understood as "Deuteronomistic" or "nomistic"; rather, the foundations for an appropriate understanding are to be found in Psalm 15 and the institution of the Torah liturgy to be presupposed there (cf. the comment on Psalm 15). "Citizenship" on Zion is only for the צדיק, the Israelite who lives according to the precepts of the covenant of Yahweh. He alone has a claim to the protective power of God (cf. the comment on Ps. 15:1). The רשע has no right to appear before Yahweh; God is opposed to him (Ps. 5:5ff.). Thus vv. 20ff. draw a picture of the צדיק who is adjusted to the covenant and admitted to the sanctuary. And again this description launches forth into that which is archetypal and supraindividual (G. von Rad, *OT Theol,* 1:377f.). The emphasis on obedience over against the תורה and the profession of a righteous life are basically a reference to the declaration of loyalty on the part of the worshiper usually given upon entering the sanctuary (vv. 20-23). It is also worth noting that the king here enters the archetype of the צדיק—a conception attested also elsewhere in the OT (Jer. 23:5; Zech. 9:9). The expressions as such are related to Psalms 1 and 119. The sentences beginning with כי in vv. 21 and 22 correspond to the affirmations of an oath of cleansing. All the terms that denote Yahweh's expressions of will and direction are to be noted: דרך, מִשְׁפָּט, חק. The archetype of the צדיק is paraphrased with the words תמים, חסיד, נבר. In vv. 20 and 24 the petitioner confesses that Yahweh acted in conformity to the צֶדֶק of the petitioner. The causative (*hiphil*) ישיב gives occasion to the concept that the צדקה is a sphere of salvific power in which Yahweh lets "an immanent retroaction" take place: the צדיק is met with צדק = "salvation" (cf. H. Koch, "Gibt es ein Vergeltungs-dogma im Alten Testament?" *ZThK* 1955, 1ff.). Yahweh's "causality in all things" sees to it that in the salvation area of the צדקה the effects of God's protection and rescue reach the צדיק. On the basis of these precedents we are to understand also the statements of vv. 25 and 26. There is a single great correspondence: the דסיד experiences God's חסד.[3] And yet, the עקש experiences

---

passed under our review, namely, to teach us that David at length emerged from the profound abyss of his troubles, neither by his own skill, nor by the aid of men, but that he was drawn out of them by the hand of God. When God defends and preserves us wonderfully and by extraordinary means, he is said in Scripture language to send down succor from above; and this sending is set in opposition to human and earthly aids, on which we usually place a mistaken and undue confidence" (Calvin, on Ps. 18:16, trans. Anderson [Grand Rapids: Eerdmans, 1949])

3. Calvin does not want the assertion "To the pure you prove yourself pure" to be understood as a

Yahweh's destructive activity. Here we are dealing neither with the principles of strict retribution (F. Nötscher) nor with the tenets of the *ius talionis* [the right to provide punishment equal to the injury, trans.] (H. Gunkel). Rather, he who belongs to Yahweh's congregation and lives within the regulations of God's covenant, he by that very fact lives in an area of salvific power. But he who despises Yahweh excludes himself from the area of salvation. All these are regulations of the community of Yahweh that takes salvation for granted.

[18:27] In v. 27 it is once more emphasized that Yahweh helps the עַם־עָנִי. All the helpless and distressed have the great privilege in Jerusalem of a special bestowal of salvation that applies to all צדיקים here (see above, Intro. §10, 3). Therefore, as the petitioner goes back to the archetypal צדקה of the Torah liturgy, he at the same time mentions the privileges of the "poor," who enjoy God's special legal aid.[4] But when the king subjects himself to the privileges of the עַם־עָנִי, we are here reminded of Zech. 9:9. And this is worth noting in Psalm 18: the king numbers himself among the congregation of the צדיקים and the עֲנוים. The fact that he has been blessed with a rescue he credits not to his privileged royal station but to his solidarity with the "righteous" and the "poor" of his people. Actually, a note is here introduced that is foreign to the other royal psalms. Is this that king speaking who has humbled himself under the ancient Israelite institutions? Who brought the ark to Jerusalem and probably also strictly observed the ancient rules for access to the "tent"-sanctuary (Ps. 15:1)? Is this David speaking? The sometimes strongly archaic language with its captivating, archetypal conceptions permits us at least to ask the question. A sure answer cannot be given and perhaps also not be expected.

[18:28-34] Yahweh's help is in v. 28 compared to a light that is carried into the darkness. Yahweh himself was the light. Before him the darkness disappeared. The verse introduced by כי has the sound of an affirming, doxological confession. Only the presence of Yahweh brought about the change. A distinctive modification is experienced in vv. 29ff. by the concept of the holy war (cf. G. von Rad, *Der Heilige Krieg im Alten Testament,* ATANT, 1951). In the Israel of the time before the kings, Yahweh stood by his people as the "God of battles," but now his helpful activity concentrates on one single man, the king. God is at his side—as he once stood near the charismatic leader. Walls and protective ramparts do not ward off when Yahweh is present (v. 29). The guidance (דרך) of God, his oracular directive (אמרת־יהוה) is perfect proof of his

---

general statement, but he wants to apply it strictly to the context: "For, in the first place, we must adapt the words to the scope of the whole discourse, and view them as implying that God, in so often delivering an innocent man from death, when it was near him, showed, indeed, that he is merciful towards the merciful, and pure towards the pure . . . provided they wait for his aid with meekness and patience." "The scope of the discourse is that the people of God should entertain good hope, and encourage themselves to practice uprightness and integrity, since every man shall reap the fruit of his own uprightness" (Calvin, on Ps. 18:25-26, trans. Anderson [Grand Rapids: Eerdmans, 1949]).

4. "Thus he in an excellent way repeats the essence of all that has been said before and preaches the just judgment of God. For he sanctifies the saints because he makes the lowly well, and therefore the saints are the lowly, that is, the poor and the worthless; and he confutes the perverse because he brings down low the eyes of the haughty, and therefore the perverse are the haughty, those who have been honored and made much of. It is as if he were saying: This is the fairness of your judgment, in fact, this is your nature, to exalt the lowly and to be with them, but to humble the haughty and to be against them. About this subject we have said many things, and Scripture is full of them" (Luther, WA 5; 524, 5ff.).

Psalm 18

helpful presence (v. 30). As behind a shield, the king can conceal himself with the *deus praesens* (v. 30b). A hero's strength, good fortune in war, swiftness, and versatility—these are the gifts of Yahweh (vv. 32-34). The song of thanksgiving again and again in its praise and confession extols the unique power that is presented to the king in charisma (v. 31; 1 Sam. 2:2; Ps. 144:1). From this description of this wonderful grant of power, a second report is now developed in the royal song of thanksgiving.

[18:35-48] Yahweh protected and supported the king who had got into trouble. He heard his cries (v. 6) and answered him. In v. 35b we are to read עֲנֹתְךָ = "your answering." By means of his answer, his salutary encouragement, Yahweh has brought about the change (Ps. 35:3). As already in v. 30, so here we will have to think of an oracle which the king has procured in the midst of the battle: 1 Sam. 32:2; 28:6, 15; 30:8; Isa. 45:1ff. Yahweh made room for the steps of the distressed (v. 36), and the pursued he turned into a pursuer (vv. 37-39). The second phase of narration concentrates entirely on the battle and reports especially concerning the wonderful victory over the enemies (vv. 39ff.; cf. 1 Sam. 2:4). The adversaries were annihilated (v. 40); (cf. Exod. 23:27). Their crying to Yahweh had no success (v. 41).

In vv. 40-41 we could think that the terms קָמַי, אֹיְבִי, and מְשַׂנְאַי extended to an event within Israel. Above all, the crying of the enemies "to Yahweh" (v. 41) could be understood in that way. Probably, in the course of time, the psalm was refined at this very point. If the song of thanksgiving was later sung also by the community, then certainly conceptions of "the enemy of the individual" were inserted at this point (see above, Intro. §10, 4). But it is altogether possible that already the royal song of thanksgiving dealt with contests within Israel.

The king ground the enemies down like dust and trampled on them as on dirt: v. 42 (for the picture, cf. Isa. 10:6; Mic. 7:10). From the lowest distress Yahweh has lifted his king to the highest heights (v. 43). He who lay defeated became the רֹאשׁ גּוֹיִם. Nations became subject to him (vv. 43-45). Here is struck the usual theme of royal psalms, "world dominion of the anointed of Yahweh" (cf. the comment on Ps. 2:8). Those who have been subjected bow down in obedience, and those who have been defeated tremble in the dungeons. A complete change has taken place. And at this point in the song of thanksgiving the hymnic accents become stronger and stronger. חַי־יְהוָה must here certainly mean: "Yahweh lives!" (v. 46). On the problems touched on with the theme חַי־יְהוָה, in its details and in its broad context, cf. H.-J. Kraus, *Der lebendige Gott: Biblisch-theologische Aufsätze* (1972) 12f.; W. H. Schmidt, *Alttestamentlicher Glaube in seiner Geschichte* (1975²) 156f.

G. Widengren thought of formulations of sacral language that are present in v. 46. In his estimation the locutions are embedded in the cultic drama—and that originally in the fertility cult. "In the Ugaritic cultic texts *El* testifies to his knowledge that *'Al'iyān Ba'al* after his death and his sojourn in Hades again returned to life, and he does so in the following words:

Yes, I know that *'Al'iyān Ba'al* lives,
that the prince, the lord of the earth, exists.

This cultic formula is as follows: חֵי אַלְאִין בַּעַל, *'Al'iyān Ba'al* lives! It seems to be of greatest importance that in Psalm 18, in a royal psalm, the same cultic formula recurs when the praying king says, "Yahweh lives!" (Ps. 18:46). Here חַי יְהוָה corresponds to

264

the Ugaritic formula חי אלאין בעל. As we have become convinced that the conceptions of sleep and awakening of the deity represent an ancient Canaanite heritage, so we must assume the same for the formula in which the certitude is expressed that the deity has come back to life. Also in this case it is of importance that the formula turns up in a context characterized by Canaanite influences; for Psalm 18 belongs to those psalms most filled with Canaanite expressions'' (G. Widengren, ''Sakrales Königtum im Alten Testament und im Judentum,'' *Franz Delitzsch Vorlesungen* [1952, 1955], 69). We will have to keep these associations in mind at every turn. Still, Widengren concedes too strong a relevance to the Canaanite component so far as content is concerned. Is it not the case that in Ps. 18:46 there is a mere adoption of an archaic formula? Could we really assume that nature-mythological backgrounds and the cultic-dramatic backgrounds are still alive in the OT? Th. C. Vriezen calls such formulations as חי־יהוה even an ''antithetical correspondence to the Canaanite faith in the dying and rising gods of fertility religion'' (*TheolAT* 143).

The living activity of Yahweh that is attested in the exclamation חי־יהוה does not refer to nature-mythological and cultic-dramatic data, but to God's saving activity in history, to the wonderful intervention of Yahweh in the distress of his chosen ones. Yahweh is called the אלוהי ישעי. These divine predicates, especially the word צור, point to Zion as the place of the presence of God.

Regarding the form, by the way, we should note that the song of thanksgiving at this point speaks of Yahweh in the third person. Here we recognize the transition from a report with thanksgiving to a doxology. Verse 47 then begins (as vv. 30 and 32 did) with the exclamatory האל. God is glorified as the giver of victory. This hymnic conclusion of the second narrative phase of the song of thanksgiving culminates in v. 48 in a summarizing sentence of confession and praise. Yahweh ''rescued'' and ''exalted.'' The verse fragment מאיש חמס תצילני could be a secondary addition which originated in the communal use of the prior song of thanksgiving and was formulated in the sense of the conception of ''enemies of the individual'' (cf. above, Intro. §10, 4).

[18:49-50] V. 49 exhibits the typical marks of a hymnic conclusion, which with על־כן points back to the narratives of Yahweh's saving intervention. The praise of the king lets itself be heard by an audience of nations. The singer calls the divine act of deliverance of the ''anointed one'' חסד and ישועות. משיח is the one marked by anointing, God's untouchable king (1 Sam. 2:10; 12:3, 5; Pss. 2:2; 20:6; 28:8; and often). Finally, the demonstration of Yahweh's help is anchored in David and his dynasty. Verse 50 thus underlines the fact that Psalm 18 treats the king's salvation.

Purpose and Thrust

The main lines of the kerygma in this song of thanksgiving should, in view of the events reported, first be stated in a threefold way: (1) From the abode of his presence, Yahweh hears the cry of distress and the prayer of him who is hard pressed (vv. 6, 25). His answer becomes real in an immediate, powerful intervention. (2) Yahweh's highest heavenly power bows down to the outermost depths of the realm of death, to the area of Sheol, and snatches the afflicted one out of all danger (vv. 4, 5, 9ff.). (3) Yahweh rescues from defeat by providing not only victory but also wonderful exaltation (vv. 18, 43f.).

In this event the attention is drawn to the figure of the king: he is the one who suffers (vv. 3ff., 18). His distress is illustrated in images and conceptions that transcend all situations in the world. The king undergoes archetypal suffering. But in it he turns out to be the one who prays—a human being who

265

Psalm 18

trusts in Yahweh alone (v. 6). The sufferer does not appeal to royal privileges or
divine attributes. He takes shelter under the loyalty declaration of the צדיקים (vv.
20ff.) and appeals to the rescue prerogatives of the עם־עני (v. 27). When
Yahweh now grants his aid, the suffering king becomes a charismatic hero,
carried along by God's military power (vv. 29ff.), who defeats all enemies. The
sufferer turns into one exalted above all nations (vv. 43f.).

Accordingly, Psalm 18, in its type, song of thanksgiving, describes
God's wonderful act of rescue of his royal servant (עבד, heading). Mythical
metaphors and formulations are mixed into the narration. But neither the myth
nor the cultic drama predominates. The secret of the OT royal psalms lies in the
historical dimension. Mythical rudiments from the realm of the cults of dying
and rising gods illustrate the presence of God's salvation in historical life. The
path of interpretation therefore leads us through between myth and history on a
wire edge. There is danger both of mythologizing and historicizing. While in
former times the interest lay in pointing out relations to the "story of David,"
today, under the guidance of the history-of-religions parallels, the tendency often
is toward a mythicization of the psalm. The kerygma of Psalm 18, however,
opposes both. It is a free expression that, via Isaiah 53, points to the NT. Against
any phenomenology that strives to bring the mythical and cultic-dramatic
element of dying and rising again in the divine cult of kings directly into relations
with the Christ event of the NT, the historical intention of the song of thanksgiving, which refers to actual events, of course offers resistance.

Finally, we should point out that Psalm 18 reveals traces of its being
used by the OT community. The ordinary petitioner subsequently enters the area
of royal statements and thereby places himself on the foundation of immovable
saving acts that in his distress are received as effective (cf. the comment on
Psalm 3).

Psalm 19

Yahweh's Revelation
in the Heavens and on Earth

Literature

O. Schroeder, "Zu Psalm 19," *ZAW* 34 (1919) 69-70. L. Dürr, "Psalm 19," *Festschrift E. Sellin* (1927) 37ff. J. Morgenstern, "Psalm 8 und 19A," *HUCA* 19 (1945/46) 491-523. H.-J. Kraus, "Freude an Gottes Gesetz," *EvTh* 11 (1951) 337-351. A. Jirku, "Die Sprache der Gottheit in der Natur," *ThLZ* 76 (1951) 631. D. Focos-Fuchs, "Psalm 19:5," *I Goldziher Mem. Vol. II* (1958). K. H. Bernhardt, "Zur Bedeutung der Schöpfungsvorstellung für die Religion Israels in vorexilischer Zeit," *ThLZ* 85 (1960) 821-824. M Weippert, "Mitteilungen zum Text von Ps 19,5 und Jes. 22,5," *ZAW* 73 (1961) 97-99. J. v. d. Ploeg, "Psalm XIX and Some of Its Problems," *Jaarsbericht v. h. Vooraziatisch-Egyptisch Genootschap 'Ex Oriente Lux'* 17 (1963) 193-201. A. H. van Zyl, "Psalm 19," *Biblical Essays 1966* (1967) 142-158. J. A. Soggin, "La radive HWH II in ebraico, con speciale referimento a Ps 19, 3b," *Annali dell' Istituto Universario Orientale die Napoli* NS 17 (1967) 1-8. N. Sarna, "Psalm XIX and the Near Eastern Sun-God Literature," *Fourth World Congress of Jewish Studies I* (1967) 171-175. H.-J. Kraus, "Zum Gesetzesverständnis der nachprophetischen Zeit," *Biblisch-theologische Aufsätze* (1972) 179-194. D. J. A. Clines, "The Tree of Knowledge and the Law of Yahweh (Psalm XIX)," *VT* 24 (1974) 8-14.

Text

To the choirmaster. A psalm of David.

19A:1 The heavens declare the glory of God,
and the firmament proclaims the work of his hands.

2 One day transmits words to another,
and one night reveals knowledge to another.

3 Without words and without speech—
with a voice that cannot be perceived.

4 To all lands their sound[a] goes forth,
and to[b] the end of the world their speech.
He has prepared a tent in them[c] for the sun.

267

5 It is like a bridegroom coming forth from his chamber,
   exulting like a hero to run the race.
6 From the end of the heavens it goes forth
   and runs again 'to'ᵈ its end—
   and nothing remains hidden to its heat.

19B:7 The instruction of Yahweh is perfect,
   it revives the soul.
   The testimony of Yahweh is dependable,
   it makes fools wise.
8 The statutes of Yahweh are right,
   they delight the heart.
   The commandment of Yahweh is pure,
   it brightens the eyes.
9 The 'word'ᵉ of Yahweh is genuine,
   it remains forever.
   The laws of Yahweh are truth,
   they are altogether righteous—
10 they, who are more precious than gold,
   than much fine gold;
   and sweeter than honey
   and honey in the comb.
11 Your servant also lets himself be warned by them;
   he who keeps them has a rich reward.
12 Errors—who takes note of them?
   Absolve me of that of which I am unaware!
13 Also against the wickedᶠ protect your servant,
   that they may not rule over me!
   Then I am blamelessᵍ and free
   of serious offenses.
14 Let the words of my mouth please you,
   and may the thoughts of my heart come to you,
   Yahweh, my rock and savior!

4a Here קַו does not belong to the concept קָו, or קָו = "line," "plumbline." In Isa. 28:10, 13, קַו is an onomatopoetic word (KBL 830). Gk: φθόγγος; Jerome: *sonus*. However, no emendation of לְקוֹלָם should be undertaken.
b α´ recommends the preposition לְ, but בְּ is entirely possible (BrSynt §106a).
c The rather frequent correction of בהם to בָּיָם is unnecessary. בהם refers to הַשׁמים (v. 1) and is also factually proved correct by v. 6: The sun goes forth from the end of the heavens.
6d In agreement with Mss and Gk (ἕως ἄκρου), עַד is to be read instead of עַל.
9e יראת = "fear" could be retained; yet Ps. 119:38 supports the reading אִמְרַת. In the variations of the תורה concept, יראת is intrusive.
13f We might consider whether we ought not read זָדוֹן = "presumption," "defiance," "wickedness" instead of זדים = "presumptive people," "wicked people." In that case we would have a contrast to the inadvertent errors and unintentional sins mentioned in v. 12. But the correction involved interferes too much with the condition of the text of the MT in v. 13.
g *Atnaḥ* is in the wrong place and should be placed under בִי (cf. the meter).

Form

It has been recognized for a long time already that Psalm 19 is composed of two psalms. Section A deals with hymnic praise of Yahweh in nature, Section B with the glory of the תורה. The differences between the two parts of the psalm are so conspicuous that for the present no explanation is necessary. Still, it would be impractical to treat Psalms 19A and 19B as two completely disparate texts. Tradition has welded the two together. For that reason we have the obligation in connection with an interpretation of the two parts to inquire into the reason for the combination and for its meaning.

Not only in content but also even in the metrical form it becomes apparent that Psalms 19A and 19B are different entities. The meter in Psalm 19A is to be analyzed as follows: vv. 1, 2, and 5: 4 + 4; vv. 3 and 5a: 4 + 3; v. 6a: 3 + 3. Isolated short verses (without parallelism) are found in v. 4b as a 4-pulse meter and in v. 6b as 3-pulse meter. By contrast, Psalm 19B is to be read predominantly in the 3 + 2 meter: vv. 7-9 and 11-13 (v. 13a, it is true, has the 4 + 2 meter; here disturbances are present in the text). In v. 10 a verse in the 4 + 4 meter appears, and in v. 14, after the double triple meter, a single triple meter will be found.

With respect to the form-critical classification of Psalm 19A difficult questions arise. Of course, it has long been recognized that this part of the psalm is to be classified in the *Gattung* of hymns (Gunkel and Begrich, *EinlPs* 2, 13), and yet, the argumentation is by no means conclusive. Rather, an exact investigation shows that Psalm 19A exhibits altogether singular forms and in this respect is to be compared with Psalms 114 and 68. All these psalms are found to be "completely outside the usual form language of the hymn" (F. Crüsemann, *Studien zur Formgeschichte von Hymnus und Danklied in Israel*, WMANT 32 [1969], 306A.1). Nevertheless, we will have to classify Psalm 19A in a wider sense among the form group: songs of praise. See above, Intro. §6, 1. We will probably have to consider the special (archaic) traditional type of the three remarkable and isolated psalms and ask questions about their origins.

Psalm 19B is to be set in a different context. We could speak of praise of the Torah and thus point out the hymnic characteristics. Yet, vv. 12ff. definitely suggest a prayer song; Yahweh is addressed in the second person. In addition, form characteristics of didactic poetry (see above, Intro. §6, 5) make their appearance. The form group to which Psalm 19B would have to be assigned can accordingly by no means be determined clearly. But in respect to thematic considerations we would have to classify this part of the psalm in the group of Torah psalms. Cf. G. von Rad, *Wisdom in Israel* (1972) (also see the comment on Psalm 1).

Setting

While Psalm 19A exhibits all the signs of great age, Psalm 19B should probably not be dated before the time of Ezra. Praise of the תורה presupposes that the תורה as a complex entity, codified in written form and of high authority in the life of the OT community, played a special role (see below). But both parts of the psalm were probably intoned as cultic songs in the worship of Israel: Psalm 19A at the exaltation of Yahweh as the Creator (cf. Psalms 8; 104; 148); Psalm 19B probably in connection with the reading of the תורה, which could be presumed to have been a cultic custom in accordance with Nehemiah 8. Both cultic hymns in all likelihood belong to the cycle of autumn festivals.

Commentary

[Title] On למנצח, see above, Intro. §4, No. 17. On מזמור לדוד, see Intro. §4, No. 2.

[19:1] In v. 1 the hymn begins with a description of the song of praise of the heavens. The heavenly realm and the "firmament" appear as live powers that "declare" (ספר) and "proclaim" (הגיד). הרקיע as a cosmological concept denotes the plate (Latin: *firmamentum*) by which the blue sea of the ocean of the heavens is held up and confined (Gen. 1:6ff.; Ezek. 1:22ff.; Ps. 150:1). The praise of this heavenly area is intended for the כבוד־אל and the מעשה ידיו. The chiasm in the word order of this powerful introit is very effective. כבוד semantically contains the notion of weightiness, of weighty prestige (*gravitas*). The OT uses this concept most frequently to indicate "something that may be experienced in a striking way" (cf. G. von Rad, *OT Theol*, 1:239). When the subject of Yahweh's כבוד comes up, the impressive concepts of the theophany are awakened. The song of praise of the heavens turns to God, who is enthroned above the heavens (cf. Ps. 29:9, 10), who is present on Zion, and whose brilliant light fills all the lands (Isa. 6:3). מעשה ידיו are the constellations (Ps. 8:3). Thereby v. 1 already announces the hymn of the sun emerging in v. 4b. The content of the heavenly hymn of praise accordingly is Yahweh's glory in his appearance and at the same time God's work of creation. "The glory which God has granted to creation as an image of his own glory is reflected back and, as it were, given back to God as a confession" (Franz Delitzsch).

Already in view of v. 1 the question arises whether anything can be ascertained in the religious environment of Israel regarding the origin of Psalm 19A. Since v. 1 mentions אל, the possibility suggests itself that this might be evidence that the land was originally intended for the Canaanite god El (thus W. H. Schmidt, *Alttestamentlicher Glaube in Seiner Geschichte* [1975], 153). A. Jirku points out relations of the psalm to the Baal-Anat cycle; but H. Donner challenges the claim that such a relation is present ("Ugaritismen in der Psalmenforschung," *ZAW* 79 [1967], 330). Uncertain, too, is the association of our psalm with specific texts in the literature about sun deities, even though these parallels do have to be investigated. That is, we would merely have to inquire whether the pre-Israelite local tradition of Jerusalem together with the associations with the divinity El also carried along traditions that have to do with the sun, traditions that are hinted at in Solomon's speech at the dedication of the temple (1 Kings 8:12).

[19:2] New verbs in v. 2 describe the "declaring" and "proclaiming" on the part of the heavenly realm. הביע ("to bubble forth") denotes ecstatic, bubbling, excited speech. חוה, an Aramaic verb, again has the meaning "proclaim" (Job 15:17; 32:6, 10, 17; 36:2). In other words, four verbs denoting excited, proclaiming speaking describe the hymn of the heavens in vv. 1 and 2. It is worth noting that the specific verbs of singing and praising are absent. As we can gather from v. 3, it is a singular message that is transmitted in the heavenly world. In v. 2 this message is presented with the terms אמר and דעת. The narration of the heavens is "word" (אמר) and entails "theological knowledge." דעת in Hos. 4:1; 6:6 contains the conception of a special familiarity (of a priest) with the law of God; we could speak of an "original form of theology" (H. W. Wolff, "'Wissen um Gott' bei Hosea als Urform von Theologie," *GesStudAT* 182-205). Immediately the question arises whether in such a priestly דעת also the theology of creation can be included (Genesis 1). In that case, a priestly conception would have been projected into the heavenly proclamation. Just as on earth there is a "theological creation tradition," so also a knowledge concerning the Creator and his work is transmitted by the heavenly powers. the text states that one day transmits this דעת to another day and one night to another night, "like two choruses that take turns" (F. Nötscher). The hymn sees an equally mysterious and wondrous chain of transmission at work. Incidentally, Hos. 2:23f. reports in a different way about a continuing chain of effects in the realm of nature. Verses 1 and 2 give the impression that the singer transferred the hymnic and didactic tradition of creation of the priestly circles of Israel to the heavenly realm. The intuitive interpretation of B. Duhm, that this is a "glosso-lalia of living works of God," and the explanation of H. Gunkel, that in this text we have to presuppose the "music of the spheres," do not agree with the facts.

The problems present in v. 2 have been taken up anew by G. von Rad, who has tried to elucidate them in a larger context. G. von Rad is of the opinion that, while speech on the part of an area of creation does appear as a concomitant phenomenon to divine self-revelation, yet it is unlikely that the heavens were empowered to provide a witness only in connection with this event and were mute before. Then he says: "We encounter the idea that the world is not dumb, that it has a message, in the hymn. The world proclaims itself before God as a created thing; the heavens 'tell', the firmament 'proclaims' (Ps. 19:2). 'All his works praise God' (Ps. 145:10). Within the context of the description of a theophany, it could be said, 'The heavens proclaim his (God's) righteousness' (Ps. 97:6)" (G. von Rad, *Wisdom in Israel* [1972], 162. Accordingly, certain elements of creation would be media of revelation which communicate the mystery of creation. And in the transmission of wisdom, according to G. von Rad, corresponding conceptions can then be identified: the scheme of the universe calls to man, it communicates itself to him. H. Donners sees it differently: "The psalmist does not seriously think that the heavens 'declare' and the firmament 'proclaims'; rather, he clothes the religious experience in which he participates in the cloak of metonymy" (*ZAW* 79 [1967], 328). The problem is very difficult. If we were to agree with von Rad, "natural theology" would have to be broached anew (cf. G. von Rad's reference to K. Barth, *CD* 413). But as we consider the statement in v. 2, we dare not overlook the context in v. 3.

[19:3] The statement in v. 3 is unique. After the descriptions of vv. 1 and 2, it has the character of a paradox. The transmission of the praising and knowing "word" (אמר in v. 2) takes place אין־אמר ואין דברים. Efforts have been made to offset this paradox through textual criticism. H. Gunkel rightly deplores such rationalistic manipulations, but he falls into the opposite extreme: mystification. The meaning of the offensive half-verse 3a clearly emerges from the explanatory parallelism of members. The "word" (אמר) and "speech" (דברים) of the heavenly powers are not audible to human ears. The negations, therefore, in v. 3a point to a unique process, without analogy, of proclamation by the remote areas of creation, a proclamation which is high above human beings and cannot be picked up. The entire weight of this conception is implicitly comprehended in the concept דעת—to the degree that already in the priestly realm there is "secret knowledge" that is not accessible to everybody (J. Begrich, *Die priesterliche Tora,* BZAW 66 [1936], 72, 86f.). How completely different the heavenly דעת must be!

[19:4a] The unique, unanalogous process of proclaiming by the heavenly דעת is in v. 4 called קו. According to Isa. 28:10, 13, this concept is an expression for the stammering utterance of ecstatic prophets, akin to glossolalia. Such sounds are unintelligible (Isa. 28:11); they are a "strange sound." The singer of Psalm 19A hears how this hymnic—and at the same time overwhelmingly instructive—

"sound" of the heavens goes out to all lands (cf. Isa. 6:3). Also to the end of the earth does this (unintelligible) speech penetrate. The Aramaic word מליהם should be understood on the basis of the parallel קום. תבל is a cosmological concept which denotes the bright, life-sustaining "dry land" (Akkadian: *tābālu*) (Pss. 9:8; 24:1). The entire creation is filled with a mighty and yet inaudible intelligence that extols the כבוד־אל and the מעשה ידיו.

[19:4b] At v. 4b a section now suddenly begins that refers to the sun and its radiating course. Perhaps we should assume that a sentence has dropped out between v. 4a and v. 4b. Verse 4b begins very abruptly. The suffix in בהם could refer to a word in the sentence that—according to our supposition—has dropped out. There should be no doubt that in the present text the suffix refers to השמים (cf. the suffixes in v. 4a and the statement in v. 6a). The sun is one of the מעשה ידיו (v. 1b). It now comes to center stage. Ancient indeed are the conceptions of the שמש (masculine), which (like the heavens in v. 1a) appears as a living power and reminds us of the Babylonian sun god Shamash in appearance. But the point of all mythological references is immediately lost when v. 4b asserts that God has prepared a tent for the שמש. The שמש accordingly is no independent great power, but one of the works of the hands of God (v. 1b). As in Gen. 1:17, control is exercised over the sun. A place is assigned to the sun. אהל reminds us of an ancient way of life. The sun does not have a palace (היכל), but a tent. Perhaps these archaisms were deliberately retained by Israel in order to form an appropriate contrast to the כבוד־אל. אהל in the conception of our text is the night quarters of the שמש. In the morning the sun then leaves its chamber (for the use, cf. G. Dalman, *AuS* 6, 35) in the radiant brightness of the bridegroom, the "newly married" (L. Köhler, *Hebrew Man* [1956], 38). Exulting and like a hero, the שמש makes its appearance. Light and joy belong together (cf. Psalm 104). The title גבור for the שמש is taken from ancient Near Eastern mythology. In a Sumerian hymn the sun god is called the "hero who goes out" (O. Schroeder, *ZAW* 34, 70). ארח (Akkadian: *arḫu*) is a common Semitic verb that has the meaning "circle, orbit" (W. F. Albright, *Archaeology and the Religion of Israel* [1942] 150). The sun begins its "circuit" (Sir. 43:1ff.). This circuit extends עד־קצותם . . . מקצה השמים. Also v. 6c is derived from the Shamash-tradition of the Babylonian hymns, for the sun god is considered the highest judge, the one who has insight into all the deeds of men.

The relationship of the sun hymn in Ps. 19:4b-6 with ancient Near Eastern myths and hymns about the sun deity needs to be reviewed for orientation. Both in Mesopotamia and also in Egypt, the sun deity assumes a high rank, and most often the highest rank, in the pantheon of the gods. In Sumer Utu and Babbar are the ones to whom the hymn of the worshiping community is addressed. In Babylonian-Assyrian mythology Shamash is the sun god who is honored with ardent hymns (A. Ungnad, *Die Religion der Babylonier und Assyrer* [1921] 185ff.; H. Gressmann, *AOT* 242ff.; A. Falkenstein and W. von Soden, *Sumerische und akkadische Hymnen und Gebete* [1953] 240ff.). According to the conceptions of the Babylonian mythology, Shamash every morning "emerges from the great hill," "opens the huge door of the radiant heavens," and "in countless hours rushes along through unknown distant regions"; at night he descends to the underworld. Shamash is at the same time the highest judge and the god of the oracle and of letters (B. Meissner, *Babylonien und Assyrien* 2, 20, 166).

About the Egyptian worship of the sun in Heliopolis, H. Kees writes: "Every morning the god repeated his appearance when his rays hit the well-gilded peak of the obelisk. The chthonian archetypal hill thereby became a 'place of appearance' of the sun god'' (*Der Götterglaube im alten Ägypten* [1941], 232).

In Israel traditions concerning creation that refer to the sun are without doubt very old. Already Solomon's statement at the dedication of the temple (1 Kings 8:12) speaks of the creation of the sun (cf. the text-critical apparatus in BHS). Traditions from outside of Israel have been transferred to Yahweh the Creator. In the process the relevant myths are eliminated. "Among other peoples a 'myth' arises when, for instance, what the sun does or experiences in the present is traced back to a first, archetypal act and experience, and so a story about a single occurrence is created; but here (in Psalm 19A) we are not dealing with an event, but with an activity, with a deed and a will of a sovereign Creator; therefore there emerges a report concerning an act—not a myth, a history—not a poem regarding destiny'' (B. Duhm). Finally, an entirely different striking parallel to Psalm 19A from ancient Ugarit has been discovered (A. Jirku, "Die Sprache der Gottheit in der Natur," *ThLZ* 76 [1951] 631); this parallel refers to vv. 1ff.

[19:7-14] Psalm 19B contains a song of praise for the תורה, which in its perfections and effects is the subject of blissful meditation. In the explanation of the foundational understanding of the תורה, the later Deuteronomic (or Deutero-nomistic) conception must be adduced: תורה is the exclusive, written revelation of the will of God that is read publicly (Deut. 31:9-11) and privately (Josh. 1:7; Ps. 1:2). In this expression of the will of God, which above all contains the law of God, also the historical proclamations are included (Deut. 1:5; Ps. 78:1; Neh. 8:13ff.). But the Law of God transmitted through Moses (Mal. 4:4) is and remains the real center of the תורה. In any case, however, especially since Ezra, the תורה is the authoritative official "Holy Scripture."

An exhaustive study of the תורה concept has been presented by G. Ostborn, *Tora in the Old Testament, A Semantic Study* (1945). The question about the theological conception of the תורה in Psalms 1, 19B, and 119 is under debate. B. Duhm unhesitatingly credits the hymns on "the Law" to the Pharisees and scribes of the latest times. About the "Judaism" of this "law-piety" there have then been critical remarks time and again. In his treatise *The Laws in the Pentateuch,* M. Noth has investigated the relationships between "covenant" and "law" in the OT. In Psalms 1; 19B; and 119 he misses the Torah's being founded on the greatness of the "covenant." According to his opinion, "the Law" has become an absolute power, valid without presuppositions. Concerning the statements of Psalm 19B, we read in Noth: "In these and similar cases the phrases show how 'the law' had become something *which man evaluates for himself;* and a personal attitude towards the law is expected of every man. On the other hand a man must then bear the consequences of his attitude'' (p. 97).

In view of all this, we will have to adhere to three observations: (1) The term תורה in the OT is not in the first place associated with the strictly nomistic conception, which we easily bring into the interpretation together with the translation "the law." תורה is Yahweh's merciful expression of his will, which as an "instruction" (Östborn, 9) comes to human beings and marks off the way for them, from which one may not depart either to the right or to the left. (2) Psalms 1; 19B; and 119 are in agreement in showing that the תורה is no stark, lifeless quantity which only through human "evaluation" is elevated to an absolute validity. Rather, human beings confront the תורה as a working power. In it they have perceived the living address of God (Psalm 119), by it they have been revived (Ps. 19:7) and delighted (Ps. 19:8). The תורה radiates light and brightness (Ps. 119:105, 130). The hymn in Psalm 19B is an echo, an answer to the event that has been introduced by the תורה (cf. the comment on Ps. 1:2). (3) The attitude of human beings to the תורה, which is distinguished by "joy," "love," and "cheerfulness," is not characterized by a nomistic obedience, or by being bound without presuppositions. We will have to ask what meaning texts like Deut. 30:11-14 and Jer. 31:31-34 had for the postexilic understanding of the תורה. In Ps. 40:7, 8 and Ps. 37:30, 31, the petitioner of the psalm pointedly makes reference to the reality of the new covenant proclaimed in Jer. 31:31-34. H. Gunkel remarks on Ps. 40:8: "Even under the dominion of the law . . . the spirit of the prophets lived on in certain pious circles of the laity, and these people were unbiased enough to combine the respect for the law and the prophets' thoughts with each other: they read the *torah* in the prophetic sense. . . ." And K. Barth adds the question to Ps. 40:7—"Who is the man who can take to himself the words of Ps. 40:8f.: 'Then said I, Lo, I am come; in the roll of the book it is written what I must do. I delight to do thy will, O my God: yea, thy law is within my heart'? To be sure, this was said by a member of the later Jewish Church, but in what dimension was he thinking, in what hidden sense—pointing up and away from himself—was he speaking, unless we are to take it that he was most strangely puffed up and self-deceived? . . . The Psalmist was no doubt speaking of himself, but in so doing he obviously did not focus his gaze upon the place to which he finally addressed that prayer. In these verses we have an almost verbal reminiscence of the well-known promise of Jer. 31:31ff. concerning the new covenant of the last day. When and as God establishes this new covenant, it will come to pass that 'I will put my law in their inward parts and in their heart will I write it.' The subject is obviously what Jer. 32:39 speaks of as 'another heart,' and Ezek. 11:19; 36:26 as the promised 'new spirit'—the future I that lives and works only by the grace of God and that is promised to the Israelite by the grace and Word of God" (Karl Barth, CD 2/2: 604). According to that, in man's attitude toward the תורה (the translation "law" should be avoided as much as possible) we ought to consider presuppositions that exclude every thought of nomism, Judaism, and narrow observance. Cf. H.-J. Kraus, "Freude an Gottes Gesetz," *EvTh* 8 (1951) 337-351; idem, *Zum Gesetzesverständnis der nachprophetischen Zeit*, 179ff.

[19:7] The תורה is praised as being תמימה in v. 7. תמים is properly a term belonging to the language of sacrifices. The flawless, spotless animal is called תמים. Here the word denotes the sufficiency of "Holy Scripture" (cf. Deut. 32:4). The effect of this perfect תורה is seen in this, that it "brings back" the נפש. This means to say that it restores the power of life (cf. Lam. 1:11, 16). A restorative strength emanates from the תורה. It is נאמנה ("dependable") and transmits wisdom to the פתי—the simple, those who are easily led astray (Prov. 1:22; 7:7; 9:6; 19:25; 21:11; Ps. 119:130). Conceptions of the חכמה-theology combine with the postexilic תורה-understanding also in Psalms 1 and 119. Life and wisdom stream forth from the instruction of God. The Torah is instruction for life.

The explanation of D. J. A. Clines, that vv. 7-9a contain a meditation about the Torah in the light of Genesis 3 and that this meditation points to relationships with the theme "Creation" (Genesis 1) and can explain the juxtaposition of Psalm 19A and Psalm 19B, is hardly convincing (*VT* 24 [1974], 8-14).

[19:8-10] In variations, as found especially in Psalm 119, different turns of expression for תורה occur: פקודים (21 times in Psalm 119), אמרה, מצוה (correction in v. 9a), and משפטים. All these correlative terms especially emphasize the lament of the Torah's instruction in the law. In constantly new words the perfection of the divine instruction is praised. It "delights the heart" (v. 8a), it "brightens the eyes" (v. 8b), that is, it provides new strength of life. The word which Yahweh speaks by means of the תורה remains לעד ("forever," v. 9a). All the משפטים ("instructions in the law") are proved true (אמת) and in a comprehensive sense "right" (צדק). Verse 10 deals with the great value and the life-giving benefit of תורה, while v. 11 strikes the note of a lament.

[19:11-13] In v. 11 the singer expresses a kind of declaration of loyalty. He lets himself be "warned" by the תורה and "keeps" it at all times—so he says. Such a life, led by the direction of God, knows that it is richly rewarded. However, there are infractions and unintentional failures that give rise to accusation (v. 12). Praise (vv. 7-10) suddenly turns into a petition: that Yahweh may absolve "his servant" of all the failures of which he is unaware. Here overtones of formulas of the oath of cleansing ring through—as in general the content of the psalms exhibits a connection with the Torah-liturgy (cf. Psalm 15) and with the declaration of loyalty of the צדיק (cf. the comments on Psalm 1).

An essential motive of the individual lament is the petition for deliverance from the wicked. This is expressed in v. 13 and contextually joined to v. 12. For the enemies are thought of as the cause of unintentional lapses. Like Psalm 1, Psalm 19B also refers to the archetype of the צדיק, who lives according to the direction of God. An unclouded vitality flashes up that makes its appearance like a new age. The wicked who do not know the תורה are thought of as disturbing and tormenting. They are a threat to the close relationship of man, who derives all of his life strength from the instruction of God and who lets the תורה alone guide him. In Psalm 19B this close relationship is expressed by the term עבדך (vv. 11, 13).

[19:14] Psalm 19B closes with a formula of dedication (cf. Ps. 104:34; 119:108). Such formulas were spoken during the presentation of the sacrifice, and now they form a conclusion to the hymnic song. "Prayer is the sacrifice of the inner man" (Franz Delitzsch).

Purpose and Thrust

Psalms 19A and 19B have been combined in the transmission of the text. This fact needs to be explained. H. Schmidt suggested that "the former is a poem in which the mysterious life force in nature and the stars and the sun appears before us as witness to the glory of God; the latter speaks of another mysteriously living entity—'the law,' the unbreakable demand of the moral commandment. And here, too, the glory of God reveals itself." This intuitive synopsis, which, following I. Kant, speaks of the "starry heavens above" and of the "moral law within" as of a "divine unity," is found in many commentaries as the explanation of Psalm 19. Does it comprehend the statements correctly?

We should not overlook the fact that the prodigious "transmission" (v. 2) of the hymn of creation of which Psalm 19A speaks is a message that cannot be perceived by humans. Verse 3 expressly reports: אין־אמר ואין דברים. The teaching and praising of nature, which powerfully penetrates heaven and earth, remains an unfathomable secret: בלי נשמע קולם (v. 3b). Correctly, therefore, Wis. 13:1ff. and Rom. 1:19-20 declare that we do not recognize God from the works of creation. Indeed, a powerful message comes our way, but we do not understand it. The glossolalian ciphers of transmission in the heart of nature, which praise and teach the Creator, no one can perceive. The cosmos celebrates God's כבוד, but it does not teach his will. For that reason Psalm 19B has been added as a decisive direction, as it were, to reveal the deciphered code word. In the תורה—there God is perceivable, that is where we recognize who God is. That is where the manifestation of God's will reaches us.[1] It effects what nature

---

1. "But as, although surrounded with so clear a light, we are nevertheless blind, this splendid representation of the glory of God, without the aid of the word, would profit us nothing, although it

is not able to effect: it leads us as the עבד־יהוה, it raises up the one who despairs, and it breaks a path through the realm of guilt. The תורה-understanding of Psalm 19B has nothing to do with nomism; rather, this psalm should always provide a new impetus to think about the mystery and the wonder of the revelation of God in his word, that is, about the word that contains both encouragement (*Zuspruch*) and demand (*Anspruch*). This word is the place where God himself as the Creator meets human beings in life-giving and life-sustaining fidelity. In this word, that becomes perceivable which the utterances of the created world are unable to communicate but yet never cease to proclaim.

---

should be to us as a loud and distinct proclamation sounding in our ears. Accordingly, God vouchsafes to those whom he has determined to call to salvation special grace, just as in ancient times, while he gave to all men without exception evidences of his existence in his works, he communicated to the children of Abraham alone his Law, thereby to furnish them with a more certain and intimate knowledge of his majesty" (Calvin, on Ps. 19:9, trans. Anderson [Grand Rapids: Eerdmans, 1949]).

Psalm 20

Prayer for the King

Literature

W. H. Schmidt, *Alttestamentlicher Glaube in seiner Geschichte* (1975) 180ff. (additional bibliography there on the theme of "kingship").

Text

To the choirmaster. A psalm of David.

20:1 May the Lord hear you in the day of trouble,
    may the name of the God of Jacob protect you!

2 May he send you aid from the sanctuary,[a]
    and from Zion may he stand by you!

3 May he remember all your gift offerings,
    and 'ask'[b] about your burnt offerings![c] *Selah.*

4 May he give you[d] what your heart desires
    and fulfill all your planning!

5 Then we shall exult concerning your prosperity
    and 'rejoice'[e] over the name of our God.
    —May Yahweh answer all your petitions!

6 Now I have learned 'for sure'[f]
    that Yahweh comes to the aid of his anointed one.
    He hears him from his holy heaven
    with helpful deeds of his right hand.

7 Some (trust) in chariots, some in horses,
    but we call on the name ' '[g] of our God.

8 They stumbled and fell,
    but we got up and stood upright.

9 O Yahweh, come to the aid of the king![h]
    May he hear us on the day when we call!

2a S has read מקדשׁוֹ and also has taken the copula in ומציון with מקדשׁ.

3b MT would have to be translated: "May he declare it fat." A. Weiser considers this verb a technical term of the language of ritual. For this view there is of course no supporting parallel passage in the OT. Ehrlich reads יִדְרְשֶׁנָּה = "May he ask about it."

Accordingly, we would have to assume that a ר has dropped out. This reading has the advantage that it is endorsed by the parallelism.

c The plural וְעוֹלֹתֶיךָ is given in 4 Mss, S, T.

4d Five Mss, Gk^Aal, S, supply יהוה.

5e MT from דָּגַל = "we will lift up the banner" (?). Gk μεγαλυνθησόμεθα. In agreement with Gk a correction נַגְדִּיל or נְגַדֵּל would be meaningful, also in the parallelism (Bicknell, Wellhausen). Still, we probably ought to read נָגִיל and to translate accordingly (cf. H. Bardtke, BHS 11). Less probable is the suggestion of P. Haupt (*JBL* 37 [1918], 229ff.) and G. R. Driver (*HThR* 29 [1936], 174f.), to proceed from the Akkadian *dagālu* ("to wait for"); cf. the parallelism.

6f If the parallel half-verse begins with כִּי, then certainly a word has dropped out in the first part of the verse. For the sake of the meter, the intensifying absolute infinitive יָדֹעַ will probably have to be supplied.

7g By יהוה, which is not present in Gk^A, the second half-verse is expanded beyond the meter; יהוה is to be eliminated.

9h *Atnah* is in the wrong place and has to be entered under הַמֶּלֶךְ.

Form

Psalm 20 embraces two parts. After v. 5 a new thought begins. The layout presents the following picture: title; vv. 1-5, intercession for the king; vv. 6-8, certainty that the prayer will be heard; v. 9, repetition of the intercession. The double triple meter dominates, but in vv. 3 and 7 we are to read the 4 + 4 meter. A single 4-pulse meter occurs in v. 5b.

The question about the form-critical classification of Psalm 20 faces some difficulties. First, we will have to reckon with the fact that in vv. 1-5 a number of speakers make an appearance (v. 5a), whereas a single speaker takes the floor in vv. 6ff. In this exchange the liturgical character of the psalm is revealed. This situation needs to be explored further (see below). The section vv. 1-5 is a prayer song (see above, Intro., §6, 2). More precisely, a group which, we may assume, represents the community of Israel at worship intercedes for the king in its prayer. On the other hand, in v. 6 we may recognize the song of thanksgiving of an individual (see above, Intro., §6, 2a); the speaker and singer of this song of thanksgiving is the king. Accordingly, we have before us a form schema similar to the one in Psalm 18.

The circumstances established by the form analysis will have to be augmented by the observation that Psalm 20 deals with the king throughout (מְשִׁיחוֹ, v. 6; מֶלֶךְ, v. 9). The liturgy is accordingly to be classified among the "royal psalms" (see above, Intro. §6, 3).

Setting

From the observations of the analysis of the type we deduce in the first place that Psalm 20 is to be classified as a cultic act at the center of which are the king and the Lord of the temple at the sanctuary of Zion (v. 2). Difficulties arise immediately when the question is asked, At which occasion was the bidding liturgy intoned? Almost all the newer commentaries emphasize the thought that it is impossible to mention a specific historical date. Calvin already stated this understanding.[1] In an attempt to establish the situation, we should consider

---

1. "Many interpreters view this prayer as offered up only on one particular occasion; but in this I cannot agree. The occasion of this composition at first may have arisen from some particular battle which was about to be fought, either against the Ammonites, or against some other enemies of Israel. But the design of the Holy Spirit, in my judgment, was to deliver to the Church a common form of prayer, which, as one may gather from the words, was to be used whenever she was threatened with any danger" (Calvin, on Ps. 20:1, trans. Anderson [Grand Rapids: Eerdmans, 1949]).

especially two conceptions: (1) Psalm 20 could have been the liturgy of a "dayof prayer before war" (H. Gunkel). This involves the assumption that the liturgy "may have been performed repeatedly at occasions occurring similarly" (S. Mowinckel, *PsStud* 3, 73). (2) Some say that Psalm 20 might have been a part of a ritual of the festival of the enthronement of the king (B. Duhm) or of the celebration of the enthronement of Yahweh (H. Schmidt, A. Weiser). The view of H. Schmidt and A. Weiser refers to a problematical set of circumstances, but the suggestions of H. Gunkel and B. Duhm are both worth considering. Because of the uncertain diction in Psalm 20, a definite choice between them will be impossible. However, the late date assigned by Duhm (see below) is to be rejected in any case. In favor of Gunkel's interpretation is the relation of the contents to Psalm 18; in favor of Duhm's the relation to Psalm 2.

In the determination of the cultic situation, a number of details are important. The intercession (vv. 1-5) has been accompanied by sacrifices (v. 3). It is possible that the number of singers in vv. 1-5 is to be explained by reference to priestly temple singers (H. Gunkel). In that case, the singing of the priests would have accompanied the sacrifice. Between vv. 5 and 6 we would have to presuppose the occurrence of a Torah sacrifice or an "oracle." On the Torah sacrifice, cf. E. Würthwein *ThLZ* 72 (1947) 147f., and R. Rendtorff, *Die Gesetze in der Priesterschaft* (1954) 74f. On the oracle, cf. J. Begrich, "Das priesterliche Heilsorakel," *ZAW* 52 (1934) 81-92. It is less likely that a "cultic theophany" was responsible for the certainty of being heard that emerges in vv. 6ff. (A. Weiser's theory).

In the dating of Psalm 20 opinions vary between the time of David (Weiser) and the era of the Hasmonean kingdom (Duhm). But probably Gunkel has found the right explanation in suggesting a late preexilic time. Conspicuous is the heavily profiled שם-theology, which leaves the impression of a Deuteronomic slant. And yet it would be conceivable that this שם-theology in Jerusalem had become a permanent element of tradition of the central sanctuary even before the seventh century.

Commentary

[Title] On למנצח, cf. above, Intro. §4, No. 17; on מזמור לדוד, Intro. §4, No. 2.

[20:1] In vv. 1-4 the praying group speaks the liturgical prayer for the king in the form of verbal optative sentences (BrSynt §8a). In the first place there is the prayer that Yahweh hear the king "in the day of trouble." יום צרה is the name here given to the day of affliction on which the king, surrounded by enemies, cries to Yahweh (cf. Ps. 18:6). From the contents of Psalm 20 we cannot tell whether this ill-fated day might be immediately imminent or the reference might be to a catastrophe that could happen at any given time. In the former case our psalm would have been sung before the king's departure for battle; in the latter, a festival in connection with the cult of royalty (an enthronement? cf. the comment on Psalm 2) would have to be assumed. Verse 1a prays that the ruler may be heard. How the psalm conceives of the fulfillment of this being-heard we derive from v. 1b: May the name of the God of Jacob protect the king. The שם of God is mentioned three times in Psalm 20: vv. 1b, 5a, 7b. The underlying thought here is the conception related to Deuteronomy and the Deuteronomistic writings that Yahweh himself is enthroned in heaven, while on earth only his שם is present (R. Kittel; O. Grether, *Name und Wort Gottes im Alten Testament*,

BZAW 64 [1934], 46). But the שֵׁם does not (as in the heathen world round about) operate as a magic power (F. Nötscher). It is the protective power working on earth with which Yahweh, upon the king's request, can answer and prove his presence.[2] This "name theology," which is closely connected with the central sanctuary and with the *praesentia Dei* there active, plays an important role in the Psalms: Pss. 44:5; 54:6; 118:10-12; 124:8. The שֵׁם is a protective rampart (Prov. 18:10). The root שָׂגַב arouses the conception of something lofty, impregnable. In the *piel* the verb has the meaning "protect," "save" (Pss. 69:29; 91:14). The intercession prays for the protection of the שֵׁם אֱלֹהֵי יַעֲקֹב. It sounds as if the old divine name of the time of the patriarchs, אֲבִיר יַעֲקֹב, had given rise to the tradition of the strong protective power of the "God of Jacob" (Ps. 46:7, 11).

[20:2] The שֵׁם of Yahweh is present in the sanctuary of Zion. The intercession expresses the wish that Yahweh's עֹז, his protective power present in the שֵׁם, be sent out from the holy place like a saving figure and be of assistance to the king (cf. Ps. 18:6). Formerly, Yahweh himself went forth into battle with the sacred ark (1 Sam. 4:3ff.; Ps. 44:9); now he should take part in the battle from the station of the ark—from the place where his שֵׁם dwells. The cultic fixing of the ark permits the old conceptions of the "holy war" to emerge only indirectly (cf. also Ps. 24:8).

[20:3] The prayers of the singing group accompany the sacrifice of the king (v. 3). These sacrifices could be such as were presented before going to war (1 Sam. 7:9; 13:9ff.; 1 Kings 8:44f.); but there is also the possibility that the reference is to sacrificial activities of the regularly recurring worship of the king (2 Sam. 6:18; 1 Kings 8:5; 2 Kings 16:15). On the connection of sacrifice and being-heard, cf. Ps. 66:13-15.

מִנְחָה is the "gift offering," in which payments from the herd, later from the crops of the field, are presented (L. Köhler, *OT Theology* 184); accordingly, מִנְחָה can have the meaning "flour offering" (Gunkel). עֹלָה is the "gift of homage" that rises up (in fire), the burnt offering (L. Köhler, 184). Therefore v. 3 clearly speaks of the "power of the sacrifice," with which the OT prophets energetically refused to be occupied exclusively. But we should not overlook the fact that sacrifice and prayer commonly being together in the OT (cf. Pss. 4:5; 5:3). The abuse of the sacrifice consists of a use of magic powers that is isolated from the word and life of man. On the question of the "sacrifice" in v. 3, cf. R. Rendtorff, *Studien zur Geschichte des Opfers im Alten Testament*, WMANT 24 (1967) 193.

[20:4] In v. 4 reference is made to the fact that the king has the right of free prayer before Yahweh. This important ingredient can easily be documented: Pss. 2:8; 21:2, 4; 1 Kings 3:5ff. (on this matter, cf. G. von Rad, *OT Theol*, 1:320). Among the privileges of the chosen king, of the father-son relationship created at his induction (Psalm 2), was the special right to candid prayer. Verse 4 prays for constant validity and efficacy of this special right. The fulfillment of the

---

2. "*The name of God* is here put for *God himself,* and not without good reason; for the essence of God being incomprehensible to us, it behooves us to trust in him, in so far as his grace and power are made known to us. From his name, therefore, proceeds confidence in calling upon him" (Calvin, on Ps. 20:1, trans. Anderson [Grand Rapids: Eerdmans, 1949).

king's plans lies in Yahweh's hands. Accordingly, we will not be allowed to add v. 4 to v. 3 with the idea that the ruler receives the hearing and fulfillment of his prayers as a reward for his sacrifices. In v. 4 there is reference to a standingprivilege.

[**20:5**] To the prayers of the group of singers already presented in vv. 1-4, v. 5 now adds a vow that points in the direction of the song of thanksgiving: if help is afforded for the king by means of Yahweh's intervention, then jubilation is to resound about this יׁשועה. In thankfulness the protective power of the שֵם is to be praised in song. The first person plural in the verb form refers to the (priestly) singers who, we may assume, are speaking vicariously for the assembled congregation. It is worth noting that the יׁשועה—corresponding to v. 1b—is credited entirely to the שֵם. Verse 5b should not be moved to a position directly behind v. 4 (with proper regard for an intact sequence of thought). This verse fragment, at the close of the first part of the psalm, once more takes up the most important thought: May Yahweh indeed fulfill all the petitions of the king!

[**20:6**] With the sudden appearance of עתה we are transported to a new situation. The prayer in vv. 1-5 has been followed by a sign of fulfillment. Yahweh has notified the praying community that he will bestow יׁשועה on the king. The event of this presentation is hidden from the reader. As already indicated, a Torah of sacrifice or an "oracle of salvation" may be involved. ידעתי denotes taking due notice of the comfort (W. Zimmerli, *Erkenntnis Gottes nach dem Buche Ezechiel,* ATANT [1954], 44). The perfect tense הוׁשיע establishes an event that is to be awaited as sure (BrSynt §41f.).

The king is called מׁשיחו. He is the chosen one of God, distinguished by anointing and untouchable (Pss. 2:2; 18:50; 28:8; 89:38, 51; 132:10, 17). The statement יענהו מׁשמי קדׁשו serves notice that Yahweh himself is enthroned in the heavenly sanctuary, hears the bidding prayer there, and finally carries out his saving interventions from on high. In v. 6 an individual singer steps forth from the choir (v. 5) and jubilates concerning the hearing of the prayer.

[**20:7-8**] That the psalm as a whole refers to a military event (and not to a dramatic-mythic cultic act) is definitely indicated in vv. 7-8. Contrasted are those who rely on war chariots and horses and "we who call on the name of our God." אנחנו without doubt refers to the community that prays and trusts in Yahweh. Their strength is the שֵם of their God. But those who trust in "chariots" and "horses" are obviously the alien forces whom the king meets on the יום צרה (v. 1). Weapons are of no avail; but those who trust in the שֵם hold the line in the battle. Here echo the avowals of the "holy war" (G. von Rad, *Der Heilige Krieg im alten Israel,* ATANT 20 [1951], 82). To the chosen kingship are joined the central faith of the (long extinct) institution of the "holy war": Pss. 18:40; 144; Isa. 7:1ff. The confidence that all weapons are shattered before the present might of Yahweh has always been preserved in the OT: Isa. 30:15, 17; 31:1; Zech. 4:6.

[**20:9**] In the conclusion, the real petition of the psalm is once more taken up in v. 9. This is appropriate to the form (Gunkel). Individual psalms return to their beginning in their final sentence (Ps. 8:9; 2 Sam. 1:27; Ps. 21:13). May Yahweh help the king—that is the main theme of the liturgy, which is understood in its essence as "our cry" (קראנו), that is, as the bidding prayer of the community.

Purpose and Thrust

The liturgy of Psalm 20 is characterized by the faith that Yahweh's chosen king can endure only through the ישועה and through the protective power of thedivine שם in the decisions of war. Because all human potential in weapons accomplishes nothing, the congregation—through its priestly singers—prays for the ruler. It receives the promise, and with it the certainty, that Yahweh is intervening (v. 6) "from heaven above" and is helping the king.

The question arises what meaning Psalm 20 has in the community of the new covenant. Luther transfers the statements of the psalm directly—without any Christological application—to the "princes of the peoples," who in Psalm 20 are presumably advised to think about the true battle power, to renounce confidence in weapons and to trust in God.[3] But Calvin, on the other hand, wants Psalm 20 understood exclusively in view of the "kingdom of Christ." For only to the "kingdom of Christ," in his view, do the promises apply from which v. 6 draws such unrestrained confidence and assurance. Both interpretations will have to be noted, but in such a way that absolute priority is given to the understanding set forth by Calvin. The "princes of the peoples" receive the full power of prayer and the actuality of the promise exclusively from the revealed reality of the bestowal of salvation in the OT and in the "kingdom of Christ."

Of course, in stating the situation precisely, the difference should also be clearly indicated. The NT community does not intercede in prayer for its king, Christ; on the contrary, he is the high priest who intercedes for his own. This striking difference is to be adhered to. Just the same, the intercession in vv. 1-5 can be understood in such a way that it refers to the real matter at hand, and therefore to the kingdom of the Christ. Accordingly, the ecclesiological application of the psalm should receive special attention.

---

3. "But the entire psalm, almost throughout the individual verses, wants to make this point, that a prince of the peoples should not be confident in any strength, should not trust in any resources, should not depend on any plans of his own, as that passage in Psalm 33[:16-17] says: 'A king is not saved by his great army, a warrior is not delivered by his great strength. The war horse is a vain hope for victory, and by its great might it cannot save.' But let him await help from heaven, let him know that victory comes from above, let him hope alone in the name of the Lord, and let him fight in prayer like Moses. Thus the prophet at the same time prays and shows that instruction is truly necessary, which only few princes take note of" (Luther, WA 5; 569, 8).

The Welfare
of the Chosen King

Literature

E. Beaucamp, "Le psaume 21 (20), psaume messianique," Coll. Bibl. Lat. 13 (1959).
F. J. Morris, "Psalm XXI, 10—An Example of Haplography," *VT* 18 (1968) 558-559.

Text

To the choirmaster. A psalm of David.

21:1 O Yahweh, about your strength[a] the king is glad,
and about your salvation—how[b] greatly he exults![c]

2 The desire of his heart you have granted him,
and the request of his lips you have not denied. *Selah.*

3 Indeed, you met him with a wealth of blessing,
you put on his head the golden crown.

4 Life he requested of you—you granted it to him,
length of days—forever[d] and eternally.

5 Great is his glory through your help;
with majesty and might you equip him.

6 For you make him a blessing forever,
you let him[e] rejoice with gladness before[f] your countenance.

7 For the king trusts in Yahweh,
and because of the favor of the Most High he will not waver.

8 Your hand will find all your enemies,
your right hand will find[g] those who hate you.

9 You will make them an oven of fire when you appear: '   '[h]
'your'[i] wrath will consume them, and fire will devour them.

10 Their offspring you will exterminate from the earth,
their seed from among the children of men.

11 Even if they have directed mischief against you,
have devised intrigues—they shall accomplish nothing!

12 For you will put them to flight,
with your bow you will aim at their face.

283

13 Arise, O Yahweh,ʲ in your might.
and we will sing and make music over your great deed!

1a The word עֹז= ''might'' will have to be assumed in this place; the concept is assured by v. 13.

b מה is not present in Gk, S, Jerome; in these versions we doubtlessly have a simplification of the text.

c *Ketīb* יָגִיל; *Qere* יָגֵל.

4d A number of Mss read לְעוֹלָם.

6e The Aramaizing verb חדה ought not to be corrected (H. Gunkel: תְּרַוֵּהוּ = ''you refreshed him'').

f T simplifies the text with the reading מֵאֵת.

8g We are advised again and again to vary the repeated תמצא by means of text-critical interference. This move is unfounded. If we are dealing with an oracle (see below) in vv.8ff., then the expressive emphasis of תמצא as the answer or explanation of God may have a very specific meaning. The laws of style in Hebrew poetry are certainly overestimated by far (cf. the comment on Ps. 1:2).

9h MT literally in v. 9: ''You will make them an oven of fire; may your countenance (at the time of your appearance), Yahweh, consume them in your wrath, and may the fire devour them.'' The comprehension of the unduly expanded verse can follow only tentatively. The *atnah* would then have to be placed under פָּנֶיךָ, and יהוה would have to be eliminated. An aid to understanding the text might be the suggestion to read לְעֻמַּת (''You will make them like a fiery oven before your countenance'') instead of לעת. Cf. F. J. Morris, *VT* 18 (1968) 558-559.

i Gkᴬ ὀργῇ σου, though ב would probably have to be crossed out: אפך. Thus v. 9b in its chiastic position would then be the interpretation of v. 9a.

13j The transposition בעז יהוה is unfounded.

Form

In considering the arrangement in Psalm 21, our attention will have to be focused on two formally completely different main sections and a short bidding verse. After the cultic-technical heading the psalm itself begins with a song that exalts the well-being of the king (vv. 1-7). Over against that, the promises in vv. 8-12 address the king. Verse 13 contains a bidding prayer of the congregation. In its meter Psalm 21 presents uneven forms. As double triple meters we are to classify vv. 6, 7, 10, 11, 12, 13. In the 4 + 4 meter we are to read vv. 1, 4, 9; in the 4 + 3 meter vv. 2, 8; in the 3 + 4 meter vv. 3, 5. The text has been transmitted in relatively good condition; difficulties are encountered only in v. 9.

Like Psalm 20, Psalm 21 also presents a number of difficulties in its multilayered structure and variety of form. But this is clear: In vv. 1-6 we have a song of praise (see above, Intro. §6, 2a), comparable to that part of Psalm 20, but also of Psalm 18, which is dedicated to thanksgiving. Prayers of the king have been answered (v. 2). Under the privilege accorded him of free access through prayer, the king has experienced answer and help. We may assume that an individual speaker performed this song of thanksgiving. In v. 7 a basic declaration is made about the king: he trusts in Yahweh and will therefore not waver. This verse should be understood as the conclusion of the song of thanksgiving. Verses 8-12 contain the message of a promise of help and prosperity addressed to the ruler. This promise will likely have been transmitted through a cultic prophet (cf. Jörg Jeremias, *Kultprophetie und Gerichtsverkündigung in der späten Königszeit Israels,* WMANT 35 [1970], 188f.). We can adduce 1 Kings 22:5ff. in order to bring to mind the possible situation, but a regular cultic celebration is also conceivable (see below). In v. 13 a bidding prayer is given in a terse style of presentation; it runs out to a concluding vow of praise. Accordingly, the entire psalm could be called a "liturgy," although we could here think of only an excerpt from the actual ritual (which is not fully revealed).

Setting

If we proceed from the assumption that liturgical pieces are here assembled (song of thanksgiving, prophetic proclamation of salvation, bidding prayer, and vow of praise), the vexed question about the "Sitz im Leben" still remains for discussion. Does Psalm 21 reflect the program of a festival, a ritual, from which individual parts have been excerpted? Which cultic act, which ritual could be involved? In an earlier stage of research interest lay in a possible historical reference, and we thought of a "song of victory," but since B. Duhm the prevailing view has been that Psalm 21 belongs to the ritual of the royal court in Jerusalem. Of course, we will not be able to share Duhm's view that the psalm has to be assigned to the time of the Hasmoneans. Worthy of note, however, is Duhm's opinion that we should think of an "anniversary celebration of the enthronement." H. Gunkel, too, directs our attention to a "royal festival" (Hos. 7:5; Gen. 40:20), without presuming to be able to provide more detailed connections. A. Weiser surmises that Psalm 21 contains the ingredients of a coronation ritual; he bases his interpretation especially on v. 3. Since this conception is more frequently held in more recent times, the relation to Psalm 2 and its statements must be considered (cf. the comment on Psalm 2). A precise statement of the situation will hardly be possible. Still, since a cultic act is to be presupposed, a celebration of an enthronement festival or a "royal Zion festival" could be involved (see above, Intro. §10, 1; and the comment on Psalm 132). Nor can we reject the conception of S. Mowinckel, that Psalm 21 (like Psalm 20) is a "liturgy for the day of prayer before the king's departure to war" (*PsStud* 3, 76). In view of Ps. 2:8f., whether connections with such a ritual would allow the promises of prosperity and help in vv. 8-12 to assume sharper contours still remains a question. Psalm 21 may be assigned to the time of the Judaic kingdom; at any rate, nothing excludes such a statement.

Commentary

[Title] On למנצח, cf. above, Intro. §4, No. 17. On the מזמור לדוד that follows, Intro. §4, No. 2.

[21:1] In vv. 1-7 the congregation gratefully contemplates the welfare of the king chosen by Yahweh. It sees the king enveloped in Yahweh's gifts of prosperity and the effects of his blessings. The protective power of God is round about him. עז in v. 1 has the same meaning as שם has in Ps. 20:1. About this protective power the king is happy; he rejoices over the prosperity (ישועה) that surrounds him. With the terms עז and ישועה the psalm announces its main theme.

[21:2] The situation of the song of thanksgiving is clearly pointed out in v. 2: the king has directed a prayer to Yahweh, and that prayer has been heard. Here we should first consider that in the OT God's chosen king had the privilege of free prayer (1 Kings 3:5ff.; Pss. 2:8; 20:4; G. von Rad, *OT Theol*, 1:320). He held an exceptional priestly position (Jer. 30:21). Concerning the contents of the king's prayer we hear details in v. 4.

[21:3] In this verse we are reminded of royal gifts that have been given to the ruler (on קדם = "to come to meet someone with something," cf. GesK §117ff.) and that now are decisive for his life. The chosen king has the privilege of having his prayers heard (v. 2); Yahweh has met him with a "wealth of blessing" and has put a golden crown on his head (v. 3). The last two statements we should interpret more precisely. ברכות טוב denotes the "enhancement of life" in a comprehensive sense (F. Horst, *EvTh* [1947], 29); it is promised to the house of David (2 Sam. 7:29).[1] The symbol of the powerful blessings coming from God and showered on the royal life is the golden crown. Unfortunately, we cannot imagine the appearance of this royal crown in detail. Very likely we should think of a diadem encased in a golden circlet (נזר: Ps. 132:18; 2 Sam. 1:10; 2 Chron. 12:30; 2 Kings 11:12) that was fastened to a headband. A. Weiser wants to infer from v. 3 that the reference is to a coronation ritual. This appears possible, but it is not an absolutely cogent conclusion. The act of crowning could conveniently be mentioned in connection with an "anniversary celebration of the coronation" (B. Duhm) or a "royal Zion festival" (cf. the comment on Psalm 132). The reference could also be possible in connection with a day of prayer before marching out to war (S. Mowinckel).

[21:4] The hearing of the prayer already mentioned in v. 2 now in v. 4 again becomes the center of grateful consideration. Now we hear of the content of the king's prayer. It was "life" (חיים) the king had prayed for, and this request had been granted. For the correspondence of the terms שאל and נתן, cf. Ps. 2:8. In the East the prayer for a long life was among the "basic prayers" of every ruler, and it turns up again and again in the OT too (1 Kings 3:11, 14; Pss. 61:6; 72:17). Still the prophecies of prosperity addressed to David (2 Sam. 7:13ff.) and the natural life expectancies of every king are closely interwoven. The perfect form of the verb in vv. 2 and 4 denotes something that has taken place definitively (BrSynt §41g), while the imperfect form in vv. 1ff. describes repeated events (BrSynt §42α).

[21:5] In v. 5 the majesty and sovereignty of the king blessed by Yahweh is emphasized. His כבוד acquires power and greatness in the area of divine ישועה.

[21:6] This verse clearly seems to refer to 2 Sam. 7:13ff. An establishing by Yahweh takes effect in the case of each ruler in David's line. Again (as in v. 3) the psalm speaks of ברכות (cf. Gen. 12:2; Isa. 19:24; Zech. 8:13; Ps. 37:26; Prov. 10:7). Above all, Ps. 72:17 must be adduced as a parallel passage. The king lives before Yahweh's countenance under God's special attention to his prosperity and blessing.

In this connection we need to think about the meaning of the concept of eternity vis-à-vis the king's existence. Both in v. 4 and v. 6 mention is made of the ruler's

---

1. In his commentary on the Psalms, Calvin interprets Psalm 21 with a reference to 2 Sam. 7:14. What ברכות means, we should be able to infer from that passage alone, he contends. Then he continues: "By *blessings* we are to understand abundance or plenteousness. Some translate the Hebrew word טוב *goodness;* but with this I cannot agree. It is to be taken rather for *the beneficence* or *the free gifts of God*. Thus the meaning will be, the king shall want nothing which is requisite to make his life in every respect happy, since God of his own good pleasure will anticipate his wishes, and enrich him with an abundance of all good things" (Calvin, on Ps. 21:3, trans. Anderson [Grand Rapids: Eerdmans, 1949]).

"eternal" life. In his study *Die Errettung vom Tode in den individuellen Klage- und Dankliedern des Alten Testaments,* Chr. Barth called attention to the fact that the concept "to have time for" always refers only to an existence that is substantially definite and full. "It is essential for life to have time for the realization and fulfillment of the purposes, expectations, and promises which on their part must be presupposed as given where life is actually to be realized. Life for its possessor means—so far as the required time is concerned—the possibility to be and to become what he is" (Chr. Barth, 23). Under these presuppositions also the "eternal" life of the king will have to be understood. Here the realization of a life according to the promises of God (1 Samuel 7) is prayed for and fulfilled. The perfection of life is realized in this, that the ruler stands and is active in communion with Yahweh before his countenance (את פניך, v. 6).

[21:7] For the predominant view of the kingship in Psalm 21, v. 7 is authoritative. The king is seen as the one who trusts, the one who is dependent on Yahweh exclusively. He lives in the "favor of Yahweh." Here the term חסד might refer to the חסדי דוד (Ps. 89:25, 29, 34; Isa. 55:3). Cf. G. von Rad, *OT Theol,* 1:310.

[21:8] In v. 8 the second section of the liturgy now begins. The form determination already given, that vv. 8-12 have to do with an "oracle of prosperity" (J. Begrich, "Das priesterliche Heilsorakel," *ZAW* 52 [1934], 81-92, is disputed. H. Gunkel sees optative clauses in vv. 8-12 ("May your hand find all your enemies . . ."). Against the view that the second section is an "oracle of prosperity" Gunkel advances the argument that the introductory formulas are absent. But this argument is inappropriate, for Gunkel himself considers a number of passages in the Psalms "oracles" which only in the rarest cases exhibit characteristic introductory formulas. "Promises of prosperity" in the majority of cases can, after all, be recognized only from the intention of the text and, especially in the liturgy, lack any kind of special introductory marks. We may now imagine that vv. 8-12 were addressed to the king by a cultic prophet. At which occasion? This question arises at every turn. The content of the promise of prosperity is the assurance that Yahweh's chosen king will overcome and annihilate all of his enemies. This theme is possible in the context of a regularly recurring festival of the king (cf. Ps. 2:8), but with S. Mowinckel one could consider that in Ps. 21:8-12 the "promise of a definite, specific situation" could be meant (*PsStud* 3, 76). It is difficult to give an answer to the question. Still, the "enemies" of the king would probably be foreign powers (see above, Intro. §10, 4). The ruler will "find" (מצא) them, so the promise says twice. Does the king have to fight against adversaries that again and again invade the country and cannot be made to stand for a decisive battle? Are these warlike desert tribes that quickly retreat into inaccessible regions?

[21:9] An annihilating judgment is to come over the enemies of the king. Especially in v. 9 do the picturesque illustrations speak of a cruel defeat of the hostile forces. Like a "fiery oven" (תנור אש) the adversaries are to burn. For the conception of תנור, cf. M. Noth, *The OT World,* 160. A consuming force is to issue from the chosen king—a force such as Yahweh himself causes to enter as judgment in the history of the nations (Mal. 4:1; Isa. 30:27; 33:11f.; Ps. 18:8). But the annihilation is to take place לעת פניך, at the time when the king appears. On פנים as an expression for the power of the king's appearance, cf. 2 Sam. 17:11. In the king's battle Yahweh sends annihilating judgment against the enemies and grants deliverance to his chosen one. Here traditions of the "holy war" enter the promise of the prophetic message; cf. G. von Rad, *Der Heilige Krieg im alten Israel*, ATANT [1951], 82. These conceptions are so powerful that already very early intrusions were made into the text of this passage and the promises of judgment assigned to the king were referred back to Yahweh. Perhaps that explains the confusion in the organization of the text and the appearance of the name יהוה.

[21:10-12] The annihilating judgment promised to the king is to extend to the complete destruction of all the descendants of the enemies (v. 10). None of the malicious plans and schemes are to come to fruition (v. 11). The prophecy בל־יוכלו reminds us of the promise which Isaiah gives to King Ahaz in the Syro-Ephraimite War: לא תקום ולא תהיה ("It shall not stand, and it shall not come to pass," Isa. 7:7). But, in Psalm 21, must we not think of a repulsion of specific hostile undertakings (S. Mowinckel)? Yet we must not overlook Ps. 2:2-4.

The promise to the chosen king is that he will put the enemies to flight and shoot them to pieces with the bow. "The strings of a number of bows are used as an illustration" (G. Dalman, *AuS* 6, 331). Gunkel considers that על־פניהם is in need of correction, for in a rout—so he reasons—you shoot the adversary not in the face but in the back. But these suggestions are wrong. The promise simply reaches its climax when the king is told: you will force the enemies to engage in battle, you will find them out (v. 8) and annihilate them "root and branch" (v. 10). Thus we must think of v. 12b as combat in which the routed party comes to grief.

[21:13] The "liturgy" comes to a close in v. 13 with a petitionary verse. Following the promise of the prophetic message (vv. 8-12), the congregation prays that Yahweh rise in his warlike power and—true to his prophecy—intervene. This brief petition is supplemented with a vow: "And we will sing and make music over your great deed!" This vow points to a new song of thanksgiving which the community will intone when Yahweh has let his promise come true. גבורה above all denotes the warring power of Yahweh, which becomes visible when God aids his chosen king.

Purpose and Thrust

The peculiarly indeterminate manner of expression of Psalm 21 makes for difficulty not only in recognizing the situation but also in discerning the kerygma. The statements have a kind of vaporous and exuberant quality about them. And so, to begin with, we can understand H. Gunkel's judgment: "A grandiose, truly Eastern description of the Israelite ideal of a king." Nevertheless, a few important details stand out in bold relief, and it is important to point these out. The chosen king lives a happy life in God's protective power (v. 1). His prayers are heard (vv. 2, 4). Yahweh grants the chosen ruler enhancements of life all the way to a presentation of his full majesty (vv. 3, 4, 5, 6). In this world of protection and blessing the king plays the part of one who displays trust (v. 7). He aligns his entire existence to agree with Yahweh's fundamental arrangements and repeated bestowals of blessing.—But to this king is promised victory over all his enemies. His kingdom is to triumph (vv. 8-12). Thus the "prosperity of a king" of which Psalm 21 speaks lets events become apparent that transcend OT occurrence. And yet, the biblical witness as a whole restrains us, so that we try to find the key to the interpretation of the statements not in a characteristically oriental ideal of a king but in the path that leads from 2 Samuel 7 to the NT.

For the biblical-theological connections and problems, cf. the comment on Psalm 2 (''Purpose and Thrust'').

Psalm 22

Rescued from Godforsakenness

Literature

W. E. Barnes, "Two Psalm Notes, Ps. 22,17; 95,6," *JTS* 37 (1936) 385-387. M. S. Seale, "Arabic and OT-Interpretation," *Expository Times* 66 (1954/55) 92f. C. Westermann, "Gewendete Klage, Eine Auslegung des 22. Psalms," *BiblStud* 8 (1955). H. de Saint-Marie, "Le psaume 22 (21) dans le juxta Hebraeos," *Collecteana Biblica Latina* 13 (1959) 151-187. J. Magne, "Le texte du psaume XXII et sa restitution sur deux colonnes," *Sem* 11 (1961) 29-41. R. Martin-Achard, "Remarques sur le Psaume 22," *VC* 65 (1963) 78-87. G. J. Thierry, "Remarks on Various Passages of the Psalms," *OTS* 13 (1963) 85ff. J. A. Soggin, "Appunti per esegesi cristiana della prima parte des Salmo 22," *BibOr* 7 (1965) 105-116. A. Jepsen, "Warum? Eine lexikalische und theologische Studie," *Festschrift L. Rost* (1967) 106-113. R. Kilian, "Psalm 22 und das priesterliche Heilsorakel," *BZ* 12 (1968) 172-185. H. Gese, "Psalm 22 und das Neue Testament," *ZThK* 65 (1968) 1-22. N. Airoldi, " 'Deus meus, Deus meus, quare me derelinquis?' Psalmus 22 (21)," *VD* 47 (1969) 96-103. E. Lipiński, "L'hymne à Yahwé Roi au Psaume 22,28-32," *Bibl* 50 (1969) 153-168). H. H. Schmid, " 'Mein Gott, mein Gott, warum hast du mich verlassen?' Psalm 22 als Beispiel alttestamentlicher Rede von Krankheit und Tod," *WuD* NF 11 (1971) 119-140. H. D. Lange, "The Relation between Psalm and the Passion Narrative," *Concordia Theological Monthly* 43 (1972) 610-621. R. Tournay, "Note sur le Pseaume XXII, 17," *VT* 23 (1973) 111-112.

Text

> To the choirmaster. According to "The Hind of the Dawn" (?).
> A psalm of David.

22:1 My God, my God, why have you forsaken me,
    are far from my 'crying,'[a] the words of my entreaty?

  2 [b]I call at daytime, and you do not answer,
    at night, and I find no rest.

  3 Yet you are enthroned as the Holy One,[c]
    you Praise[d] of Israel!

  4 In you our fathers trusted,
    they trusted, and you delivered them.

  5 To you they cried and were saved,
    in you they trusted and were not disappointed!

290

6 But I am a worm and not a man,
   the ridicule of men, despised by the people.
7 All who see me scoff at me,
   screw up their mouth, shake their head.
8 'He put it in the hands'ᵉ of Yahweh, let him free him,
   let him rescue him, for he is obviously well disposed to him!
9 You pulledᶠ me from the womb,
   sheltered me at my mother's breast.
10 On you was I cast from my mother's womb,
   from my mother's bosom you have been my God.
11 Be not far from me,
   for affliction is near,
   for no one helps.—
12 Many steers surround me,
   the strong ones of Bashan encircle me.
13 Their jaws they open wide for meᵍ—
   lions, ravening and roaring.
14 Like water am I poured out,
   out of joint are all my members.
   My heart has become like wax,
   dissolved in my inner parts.
15 'My throat'ʰ is dry like a potsherd,
   and my tongue sticks to my gums.
   Into the dust of death you lay me.
16 For 'many'ⁱ dogs surround me,
   a gang of evildoers encircle me.
   They 'bind'ʲ me hand and foot.—
17 I can countᵏ all my bones.
   They stare and gape at me.
18 They divide my clothes among themselves
   and cast lots for my cloak.
19 But you, O Yahweh, do not stay far from me;
   my Strength, hasten to help me!
20 Save my life from the sword,
   from the dogs my only possession!
21 Snatch me from the jaws of the lion
   and from the horns of the buffalo.
   —You have heard me!'—
22 (Now) will I announce your name to my brothers,
   will praise you in the midst of the congregation.
23 You who fear Yahweh, praise him,
   honor him, all descendants of Jacob
   —and prayᵐ before him, all you children of Israel!
24 For he has not disdained
   nor despised
   the affliction of him who is poor.
   He has not hidden his countenance from him,
   when he cried, he listened to him.
25 To you Iⁿ am indebted for my praise in the great congregation,
   my vows I fulfill before them who fear him.
26 The poor shall eat and be filled.
   They who look for Yahweh shall praise him.
   Your heartᵒ shall revive forever!
27 Of this all the ends of the earth shall think and turn, ' 'ᵖ
   'before him'ᑫ all generations of the peoples shall bow down!

28 For the kingdom belongs to Yahweh, 'he rules'ʳ
   over nations.
29 'Only to him'ˢ shall all pay homage who 'sleep'ᵗ in the earth,
   before him shall all bow down who went down to the dust,
   (and whose soul did not 'stay alive'ᵘ).
30 'My'ᵛ seed will serve him
   'and will tell'ʷ about the Lord
   'to the coming'ˣ generation.
31 'They will tell'ʸ of his saving deed
   to the peoples later born,
   for he has finished it!

1a MT = "far from my help are the words of my crying." Very likely the emendation מִשַּׁוְעָתִי—parallel to שַׁאֲגָתִי—will have to be undertaken.

2b אֱלֹהַי cannot be fitted into the meter; there is probably an interpolation.

3c *Atnah* is to be placed under יוֹשֵׁב; on קְדוֹשׁ יוֹשֵׁב cf. Isa. 57:15.

d Many Mss read תְּהִלֹּת. Gk, S, Jerome have the singular. Also cf. Deut. 10:21; Pss. 71:6; 109:1; Jer. 17:14.

8e Gk, S, Jerome have גֹּל. Also cf. Matt. 27:43. Targ translates יְשַׁבַּח and probably has read יָגִיל.

9f A correction of the word גֹחִי is not advisable. Occasionally, following Jerome, עֻזִּי (*propugnator meus* ["my champion"]) is emended.

13g It is really questionable whether פָּצוּ עָלַי פִּיהֶם has to be assimilated to the parallelism (פצה פיהו). The pictures in vv. 12ff. are arranged in a strangely asyndetic way.

15h כֹּחִי = "my strength" does not fit well with the predicate. There is probably a mistake in copying. It is probably better to read חִכִּי "the roof of my mouth" (also cf. the parallelism).

16i Following Gk, רַבִּים is to be supplied. With it the meter is filled out.

j MT = "like a lion my hands and feet." Gk, S, Σ offer a verbal form. Gk ὤρυξαν, S *laceraverunt*, σ´ ὡς ζητοῦντες δῆσαι. Very likely a verb כרה is to be supplied (Driver, KBL 454). כָּרוּ = "they tie together."

k Gk, S, Jerome read יְסַפֵּרוּ.

21l The makeshift emendations of the striking verb form עֲנִיתָנִי = "you have heard me" cannot avoid the odd fact that even before the beginning of the song of thanksgiving (vv. 22ff.) the certainty of being heard is definitely expressed. The verbal form עֲנִיתָנִי closes the lament and forms a transition to the song of thanksgiving.

23m *Ketib* Or, Gk read יָגוּרוּ.

25n MT = "from you my praise emanates." An emendation אֲמִתְּךָ = "your faithfulness" is without foundation.

26o Gk αἱ καρδίαι αὐτῶν (cf. also S).

27p אֶל־יהוה, surely an explanatory interpolation added to the verb שׁוּב, should be eliminated.

q Following Gk, S, Jerome, we should probably read לְפָנָיו here.

28r We may perhaps be able to read וּמְשְׁלוֹ. Cf. Gk, S.

29s The text in vv. 29-31 is badly corrupt. MT = "all the fat ones of the earth have eaten and have bowed down." This text—corresponding to the parallelism—is to be reconstructed. Instead of אכלו we should read אַךְ לוֹ.

t The emendation יְשֵׁנֵי would best suit the parallelism (Dan. 12:2).

u The genuineness of v. 29b is disputed. Perhaps there is an explanatory interpolation. In that case we should probably read חָיָה. In view of MT ("and he who does not revive his soul"), A. Weiser thinks of a later dogmatic addition. But which dogmatic sentence could be involved?

30v Gk, θ´. have זַרְעִי.

w Perhaps the emendation וְסִפֵּר can provide the connection to 30a.

x Gk applies יָבֹאוּ from v. 31 to לְדוֹר: γενεᾷ ἡ ἐρχομένη.

31y The copula in וְיַגִּידוּ could involve dittography. We ought to read יַגִּידוּ here.

Form

Already in the middle of the previous century it was established that Psalm 22 is composed of two different parts. Verses 1-21 deal with the distress of abandonment by God, while vv. 22-31 present praise and thanksgiving for Yahweh's help. We could come to the conclusion that Psalm 22 consists of two entirely different psalms (Duhm, Cheyne, Kautsch-Bertholet, H. Schmidt). But this conception is without foundation. It will become apparent later how the sudden change of vv. 22ff. is to be explained (see below).

Metrically, Psalm 22 presents many problems, most of which cannot be solved by text-critical means. If we observe the text carefully, we shall be able to identify the following meters: The double triple meter is present in vv. 4, 5, 6, 8, 9, 12-15a, 16a, 17-20, 22, 23a, 24aγ/b, 26a. The 4 + 4 meter is to be found in vv. 1, 25, 27, 29a; the 4 + 3 meter in v. 2; the 3 + 4 meter in vv. 7, 10; the 3 + 2 meter in vv. 3, 21. The three-member meter 2 + 2 + 2 is to be observed in vv. 11, 24aαβ, 30, 31. Verse fragments without parallel complements are present in vv. 15b, 16b, 23b, 26b, 28, 29b. In addition, the word עניתני in v. 21b will have to be eliminated from the metrical scheme. What is involved is an interjection that is very important for understanding the connection between vv. 1-21 and vv. 22-31. For a hardly likely process of reconstruction in two parallel columns, cf. J. Magne, pp. 29ff.

Form-critically, Psalm 22 belongs to the group called prayer songs (see above, Intro. §6, 2). The address to Yahweh, which immediately at v. 1 characterized the psalm, contains mainly descriptions of distress. The petitions become articulate in vv. 11 and 19-21. Regularly inserted again and again are expressions of trust: vv. 3-5 and 9-11. Worth noting is the sudden change appearing in vv. 22-31. In place of a description of distress, a cry, and a plea, we have thanksgiving. Great importance must be attached to the word עניתני ("you have heard me!") in v. 21. This word is proof of a change that has taken place and that has given rise to the song of thanksgiving (cf. the "commentary" on v. 21 below). In any case, the passage vv. 22-31 will have to be understood as the song of thanksgiving of an individual. For the *todah* in the Psalms, cf. above, Intro. §6, 2a.

Finally, we should also call attention to the formula ישב תהלות ישראל (v. 3), which (like the formulas in Pss. 80:1; 135:21; 2:4) turns up not only in hymnic contexts and which must definitely be distinguished from the hymnic participals (F. Crüsemann, *Studien zur Formgeschichte von Hymnus und Danklied in Israel,* WMANT 32 [1969], 125).

Setting

After the interpretation of Psalm 22 as referring to David (title) had been shown to be inappropriate, the opinion at first prevailed that the lamenting and thanking singer was "an ordinary member of the OT community." This conception was then contested by the representatives of the royal ideology (G. Widengren, A. Bentzen). In the cultic ritual the king represents the dying and reviving deity. This idea is thought to be inherent also in the laments of the individual. Cf. A. Bentzen, *Messias—Moses redivivus—Menschensohn,* ATANT [1948], 20. Accordingly, the person abandoned by God in Psalm 22 would be the "dying king" in the cultic ritual, and the thanking person (vv. 22-31) would be the "reviving ruler" in the worship drama. The exegetes who defend this interpretation reckon with a later "democratization" of the royal cultic words. The explanation that in Psalm 22 "an ordinary member of the OT community" is involved is insufficient to interpret the peculiarly fulsome expressions. The petitioner of Psalm 22 is weighed down with a variety of afflictions (G. von Rad, *OT Theol,* 1:399f.). The "archetypal affliction" of abandonment by God is at the root of all individual statements (cf. the comment on Psalm 18). The tendency to deal in types is unmistakable. Like the "poor man" (see above, Intro. §10, 3), so also the "sufferer" in Israel has become an archetypal figure that in its complaints and petitions participates in a conventional complex of language and conceptualization. A critical analysis of the individual expressions in Psalm 22 could identify that body of material in which the traditional motives form a preexistent whole. And yet, in Psalm 22 a number of sharp profiles can be isolated. The body of the petitioner is disfigured by disease (vv. 6f.). He is surrounded by the "demons of sickness" and "enemies" (see below, "Commentary"). In a fever he suffers the beginning throes of the final agony (vv. 14-15) and already sees that his death is being taken for granted (v. 18). Accordingly, the "archetypal affliction" of Godforsakenness is being suffered in a mortal sickness. Viewed thus, Psalm 22 is the outstanding example of the OT way of speaking about sickness and death (H. H. Schmid, 119ff.). And immediately we will have to decide what standing the psalm had as a prayer formulary among the OT people of God. There can be no doubt that at various times different petitioners have left their mark on this lament and prayer. Especially in the final verses, the psalm shows traces of expansion and new formulations. It is therefore hardly possible to set a date of origin. Finally, in an explanation of the setting we should also call attention to vv. 22 and 25. The petitioner and singer presents his lament and thanksgiving בתוך קהל ("in the midst of the congregation") or בקהל רב ("in the great congregation"). Accordingly, he has obviously appeared during a great festival and has intoned his psalm in the court of the temple. Very likely the psalm was sung at a meal associated with an offering, to which the "poor" were invited and assembled (v. 26).

Commentary

[Title] On למנצח, cf. above, Intro. §4, No. 17. On the formula על־אילת השחר, cf. Intro. §4, No. 20. On מזמור לדוד, Intro. §4, No. 2. It is interesting to note that Calvin already remarked (in his comment on the title of the psalm) regarding the formula על־אילת השחר: "It certainly seems plausible to me that it was the beginning of a popular song."

[22:1] The prayer song (vv. 1-21) begins with a repeated, insistent cry אלי אלי. The repetition of the address is a sign of the depth of the affliction from which the petitioner issues his cry to God. And yet the lamenter sticks to it: Yahweh is "my God" (cf. O. Eissfeldt, " 'Mein Gott' im Alten Testament," *ZAW* 61 [1945/46], 3-16); I have the right to expect help and salvation from him. The cry אלי is evidence of the individual appropriation of the promise of covenant and salvation given to Israel.

The heavy, unfathomable distress of being far from God and being forsaken by him (עזב) is introduced in the lament by the question "Why?" The God from whom help and salvation may be expected is the Hidden and Distant One (Jer. 23:23). Right next to each other are the trusting אלי אלי and the despairing למה עזבתני.[1] In the archetypal distress of abandonment by God he who laments clutches at "his God."[2] In the word עזבתני all distress issummarized. Yahweh is far removed from the lamenting and crying of the petitioner. In שאג, a verb that otherwise denotes the roaring of the lion (Isa. 5:29), we have a dark picture of the worst pain of the affliction. Into this worst of afflictions the crucified Christ entered (Matt. 27:46; Mark 15:34). On v. 1, cf. A. Jepsen, 106ff., and N. Airoldi, 96ff. On the biblical-theological problems of adaptation, cf. H. Gese, 6ff.

[22:2] This verse deals with ceaseless crying and lamenting. The suffering extends over a long period of time. Yahweh does not answer. This is where the real bitterness of forsakenness lies. And yet he who laments does not renounce God (Job 2:9), but he clings to "his God" and does not come to rest. On דמה, cf. Lam. 3:49; Jer. 14:17.

[22:3-5] The support for the trust expressed in the cry is Yahweh's constant display of power and blessing in Israel (vv. 3-5). Yahweh is unchangeably the same God. He is enthroned as the Holy One. קדוש יושב reminds us of יושב כרובים (Pss. 99:1; 80:1), who is enthroned on Zion as the קדוש (Ps. 99:3; Isa. 6:3; 57:15). On this conception, see above, Intro. §10, 1. The enthroned God is תהלת ישראל (cf. Deut. 10:21; Pss. 71:6; 109:1; Jer. 17:14). Yahweh is .surrounded by the thanksgiving and praise of Israel. He is the cause, the object, and the essence of the תהלה; and, to be sure, because from time immemorial those who trust in him have experienced the power of the קדוש יושב in the concrete bestowal of help and rescue (v. 4).[3] The verb בטח sheds light on the intention of the lamentation introduced by אלי אלי.

The sense of the statements in vv. 3-5 is clear: the lamenting petitioner consoles himself with the fact that Yahweh has up to the present helped those who trusted in him. Israel's experience of deliverance (v. 3) is the consolation of the individual. Yahweh's power has proved itself among the fathers, and the sufferer can console himself with this fact. And yet everything depends on the attitude of בטח, by which the unchangeably present saving power is released. But בטח means: to cry day and night, never to come to rest (vv. 2, 5).

[22:6-8] In v. 6 the lamenter points to the fact that his life has been dislocated and that human honor has been trodden underfoot (C. Westermann). לא־איש means to say: I have lost every semblance of humanness (cf. Isa. 52:14; 53:3).

---

1. "There is not one of the godly who does not daily experience in himself the same thing. According to the judgment of the flesh, he thinks he is cast off and forsaken by God, while yet he apprehends by faith the grace of God, which is hidden from the eye of sense and reason; and thus it comes to pass, that contrary affections are mingled and interwoven in the prayers of the faithful" (Calvin, on Ps. 22:1, trans. Anderson [Grand Rapids: Eerdmans, 1949]).

2. "And so we are far from salvation when we suffer, but he is nearby to help, because what to us is impossible and subject to despair is to him possible and easy; so that the universal separation is on account of our suffering weakness, that is, our sin, and that is nothing else than that very feeling of torture" (Luther, WA 5; 607, 5ff.).

3. "Some think that the eternal and immutable state of God is here set in opposition to the afflictions which David experienced; but I cannot subscribe to this opinion. It is more simple and natural to view the language as meaning that God has always shown himself gracious to his chosen people. The subject here treated is not what God is in heaven, but what he has shown himself to be towards men" (Calvin, On Ps. 22:3, trans. Anderson [Grand Rapids: Eerdmans, 1949]).

I am like the worm that creeps along in the dust (for the picture, cf. Job 25:6; Isa. 41:14). But immediately the "enemies" (see above, Intro. §10, 4) attack this humiliated and disfigured man. Scorn and ridicule attempt to put their seal on the humiliation and to separate the sufferer from God.[4] יניעי ראש denotes a gesture of derision (Pss. 44:14; 64:8). The mocking advice of the "enemies" is then quoted in the lament: Let him put his distress into the hands of Yahweh (for this meaning of גלל, cf. Ps. 37:5; Prov. 16:3); may he save him from his hopeless situation, for he is obviously well disposed to him! This mocking suggestion carries with it the accessory notion: may Yahweh help him who boasts concerning himself that Yahweh takes delight in him. חפץ hints at a declaratory act. On this "suggestion of scorekeeping," cf. R. Rendtorff, *Studien zur Geschichte des Opfers im alten Israel,* WMANT 24 (1967) 259.

[22:9-10] As in vv. 3-5, so now in vv. 9 and 10 the lamenting petitioner looks for support. In v. 9 the assurance is expressed: You gave me life. And in v. 10 this assertion is supplemented with the certainty: From the moment of birth my life is in your hands. It could seem plausible that in these declarations of the petitioner we are reminded of royal prerogatives as they are given by the "adoption" of the ruler to be the "son of God" (cf. the comment on Ps. 2:7). But we could not at the same time use this observation as a reason for assigning Psalm 22 to the royal cult (thus A. Bentzen, *Messias—Moses redivivus— Menschensohn,* 20). Rather, the petitioner, in his words of trust, adopts conceptions from the king's language of well-being. A different conception of the statements in vv. 9 and 10 could be introduced on the basis of Ps. 139:13ff. (with reference to the creation of humans).

[22:11] In any case, the complaints of vv. 1-10, twice interrupted by expressions of trust (vv. 3-5 and 9-10), end in an urgent plea in v. 11: May the "distant God" (v. 1) bring the Godforsakenness of his servant to an end! The distress (צרה) close at hand is like an independent force, and (except for Yahweh) no helper is available.

[22:12] In this verse the description of the "near affliction" (v. 11) begins with illustrations and symbolic words. "Steers" and "strong ones of Bashan" surround the sufferer. אבירי בשן probably refers to a particularly powerful breed of steers of the area of Bashan (cf. Amos 4:1; Deut. 32:14; G. Dalman, *AuS* 6, 170f.).

Because the affliction of the petitioner in vv. 12ff. is illustrated by means of images of beasts that charge and hem in, we should first clarify the significance of these metaphors. H. Gunkel explains in his commentary: "The comparisons to beasts do not strike the sensibilities of antiquity as something abusive; but the poet wants to say that powerful, eminent people are here involved, people whose wrath is fearful." Thus

---

4. "Thus you see that one who confesses Christ and is a preacher of the gospel of God has to be one who is not surprised if all men and the whole population hates and loathes him; in fact if he is not hated, he is not yet a complete confessor of Christ. For to be the scorn of men and an outcast among the people is a proof of his salvation. For so also Jer. 20:8 complains: 'For the word of the Lord has become for me a reproach and derision all day long.' And Christ too says [Matt. 10:22]: 'You will be hated by all for my name's sake.' And in Matt. 5:11 he said: 'Blessed are you when men revile you and persecute you and utter all kinds of evil against you falsely on my account' " (Luther, WA 5; 615, 31ff.).

Gunkel begins with the idea that in the final analysis the beast metaphors describe people—namely, the powerful and eminent "enemies of the individual" (see above, Intro. §10, 4). There can be no doubt, in fact, that the raging of hostile people can be described by means of metaphors referring to animals (Pss. 7:2; 10:9f.; 27:2; 35:21f.). But we will have to keep in mind that these "enemies" in the laments always represent demonic powers that separate from God. Therefore it will be necessary to take into consideration another dimension in the interpretation of the animal metaphors. In Mesopotamia there were poems for purposes of conjuration in which demonic powers, which were considered responsible for sickness and suffering, were represented in the shapes of animals. Thus, for instance, in an "exorcism of the demon Samana" we may encounter: "Enuru-exorcism: Samana, he of the lion's muzzle, he of the dragon's tooth, he of the eagle's claws, he of the scorpion's stinger, Enlil's wild lion, Enlil's lion who cuts off the throat, the lion of Ninnisinna with the maw dripping blood, the lion of the gods with mouth wide open . . ." (A. Falkenstein and W. von Soden, *Sumerische und akkadische Hymnen und Gebete,* 214). Accordingly, the demonic forces hostile to human beings advance against them in the forms of animals. And here various types of pictures crowd in on one another to describe the distorted essential characteristics of the alien force (S. Moscati, *Geschichte und Kultur der semitischen Völker* [1953], 57f.). There is also a report concerning the common motifs in G. Widengren, "The Accadian and Hebrew Psalms of Lamentation as Religious Documents," diss. Uppsala, 1936 (1937).

[22:13-15] Verse 13 is to be understood in terms of a mingling of the most varied types of pictures. The dangerous forces open their mouths wide; like lions, roaring and ravenous, they approach the sufferer. That vv. 13 and 14 perhaps deal with the demons of sickness is suggested by the following v. 15. Vv. 14 and 15 both describe the agony: the passing and dissolution of the body in the heat of the fever. The present perfect (Gunkel and Begrich, *EinlPs* 215) describes the process in drastic similes: "like water" (cf. Josh. 7:5; Ezek. 7:17; 21:12), "like wax" (cf. Deut. 20:8; 2 Sam. 17:10). Both the exterior (עצמותי) and the interior (לב) "dissolve." The heat of the fever dries out the oral cavity (cf. Ps. 69:3). The sufferer stands at the immediate threshold of death (לעפר־מות).

[22:16] Like a pack of wild dogs, the עדת מרעים ("the gang of evildoers") surrounds the sufferer and binds (?) him hand and foot. Here the demonic forces again reveal the human face of the scoffers (vv. 7 and 8). They overwhelm him who is mortally sick. Unfortunately, the text is damaged in this passage. We are not sure whether כארי ידי ורגלי represent a metaphor or a real event. Has the sufferer been captured as a transgressor of the commandments of God (Ps. 107:10ff.)?

In כארי F. Nötscher wants to recognize a verb with the meaning "pierce" ("they pierce my hands and feet"), and he thinks of a crucifixion, but he is surprised that this passage is not included in the NT passion narrative. ("Were these words, in spite of the old translation, still not understood in this sense?" It is hardly possible to conjecture the text in this fashion. Only two possibilities remain: (1) The binding (?) of hands and feet develops the picture of the hunt further; in that case the dogs in v. 16a would be hunting dogs (cf. the illustration from Mesopotamia), and the sufferer would be the prey of a chase with hue and cry. (2) The wild dogs (v.16a) are a metaphorical illustration of the bustle of the "evildoers," who actually take captive the sufferer who is guilty (according to their view of cause and effect). This second explanation would seem more suggestive in the context (vv. 17f).

[22:17-21] Verses 17 and 18 indicate that the sufferer has been stripped of his clothes. There he lies—emaciated through sickness and worry (cf. Ps. 102:5; Job 19:20; 33:21). The evildoers "gape" at him. On רָאָה בְ, cf. BrSynt §106a. They have taken possession of the clothes of the dying, chained prisoner, and they are casting lots for their distribution. The last possessions are taken away from the one who is marked by God's judgment. The casting of lots tells the sufferer: You have died for us (Sir. 14:15). A song from Mesopotamia reads: "The coffin lay open, and people already helped themselves to my valuables; before I was even dead, the mourning was already done" (A. Ungnad, *Die Religion der Babylonier und Assyrer* [1921], 230.)

At this point of utmost need, we again hear (as in v. 11) the petition that Yahweh may not be far away but hasten to help. The petition extends to three verses (vv. 19-21). חרב ("sword") is probably a symbol for the power of death (Ps. 37:14), while כלב ("dog") refers to v. 16. Basically, the lamenting poet is pleading for rescue from the hand of the demonic powers that separate him from God. אריה ("lion") in v. 21 refers to v. 13. It is uncertain which wild animal is meant by רמים. Is this a reference to the unicorn, which can be documented frequently in ancient Near Eastern illustrations?

[22:21bβ] The remarkable interjection עניתני stands between the two principal parts of the psalm. It connects the lament with the song of thanksgiving and praise that follows in vv. 22ff. By means of a single word the singer declares: Yahweh has heard me. The sometimes abrupt transition from lament to thanksgiving in a number of psalms has in Psalm 22 been marked by the formula עניתני. Here the לא תענה of v. 2 is finally done away with. We may be permitted to assume that by means of an "oracle of rescue" Yahweh bestowed answer and rescue on the lamenting poet (Ps. 107:20; J. Begrich, "Das priesterliche Heilsorakel," *ZAW* 52 [1934], 81-92). When people have experienced such help, "they should thank Yahweh" (Ps. 107:21f.). Here the transition to vv. 22ff. is clearly marked.

A different conception is defended by R. Kilian (*BZ* 12 [1968], 172ff.). He is of the opinion that we should not presuppose an "oracle of rescue" and that we therefore also should not assume that an effective change has taken place. Rather, the section vv. 22ff. is understood as an expression of trust; a "perfection of trust" is assumed. But this conception is shattered by the form-critical findings that apply, which in the Psalms is very clear. On the tenses, cf. D. Michel, *Tempora und Satzstellung in den Psalmen* (1960), 63ff. Thus we will surely have to presuppose that the petitioner of the psalm "had heard the 'fear not' and then the assurance that Jahweh would not forsake him, but would be with him, and be his helper" (G. von Rad, *OT Theol*, 1:401).

In Mesopotamian prayers, too, the sick and suffering wait for an answer of the deity. They look forward to the "oracle of rescue," to the "reliable yes," in order to give thanks to the deity when the help has appeared. " . . . Upon your reliable yes, which cannot be overturned, may I, your servant, live and be healthy; then I will glorify your great deeds and bring you an ovation!" (A. Falkenstein and W. von Soden, *Sumerische und akkadische Hymnen und Gebete,* 347). The "yes" of the oracle of rescue may also consist of the priest's call "Enough!" (Falkenstein and von Soden, 338). But the helpful intervention of the gods is always followed by the thankful praise for the "great deeds" (Falkenstein and von Soden, 336, 338, 345, 348).

[22:22-23] אספרה שמך לאחי ("I will announce your name to my brothers") is not the formula of a vow that the lamenting poet utters in his affliction, but it is already the beginning of the song of thanksgiving and praise (Pss. 66:16; 109:30; 107:32).

The singer announces the שם of Yahweh as the only theme of his song before the worshiping congregation (קהל). שם is Yahweh's present power of rescue (cf. the comment on Ps. 20:1, 5, 7). The audience for the song are the אחי = fellow worshipers of the community of Israel (v. 3). On קהל as the term for the assembled cultic community, cf. Ps. 35:18; Exod. 16:3; Lev. 4:13ff., 21; Num. 10:7; 15:15; 17:12; 20:6; and often. Invited to join in the hymn of praise are all who have experienced Yahweh's reality (יראי יהוה). In this connection the constructs זרע יעקב and זרע ישראל have the force of calling on the "true Israel" for praise. Verse 23b emphasizes awe before the miracle by which Yahweh reveals his presence.

[22:24] In this verse the miracle of the rescue is expressed. Yahweh has not despised the affliction of the עני. The sufferer thinks of himself as among the "poor" (see above, Intro. §10, 3).[5] Regarding ולא־הסתיר פניו ממנו ("He has not hidden his countenance from him") one could ask whether at the oracle of rescue (v. 21, עניתני) a theophany played an auxiliary part (on the problem of the theophany, cf. Ps. 18:7-15). In v. 24b the interjection עניתני is expressed in the words ובשועו אליו שמע ("when he cried, he listened to him").

[22:25] The song of thanksgiving vv. 22-31 is in v. 25 called תהלה (in other words, not the expected תודה). The term תהלה in v. 25 is certainly to be applied to the name given to Yahweh in v. 3. The fact that Yahweh is תהלת ישראל is understood in v. 25 to mean that the praise of the petitioner emanates from Yahweh. In his acts Yahweh is a God who leads to praise. To his activity human beings can only answer with praise. קהל רב is the "full assembly" of the community at the time of the great annual festivals. At this occasion "vows are paid." On נדרי אשלם cf. Pss. 50:14; 61:8; 66:13; 116:14, 18. In distress the sufferer vows to bring offerings (Lev. 7:15-21) and thanks in the courts of the temple. "Such a vow in the midst of affliction is grossly misunderstood if we interpret it as a deal with God according to the motto: 'If you give me this, I will give you that.' Rather, it expresses the fact that the association between him who prays to God and God is not to come to an end when God has rescued him, but that after the rescue it is to continue in this, that he who has been rescued will tell his brothers about the rescue he experienced" (C. Westermann, "Die Geschichtsbezogenheit menschlicher Rede von Gott im Alten Testament," *Weltgespräch* 1 [1967], 21).

[22:26] We should probably assume that the song of praise and thanksgiving of vv. 22-31 was intoned at a meal for the poor in connection with an offering. At any rate, v. 26 could well be understood that way. The ענוים, among whom the petitioner of our psalm counts himself (v. 24), are to eat and be satisfied. But this wish, according to v. 26b, has an ultimate meaning: the poor may experience the

---

5. "Let him therefore be poor who will want to be the seed of Israel and rejoice because of the gospel. The statement stands firm: Our God is the kind who has regard for the poor. And note the variety of the prophet and the diligence. It is not enough to have said once: 'he has not disdained'; he adds 'he has not despised'; and again, 'he does not turn away'; and again, 'he listened' " (Luther, WA 5; 660, 26ff.).

full life of nearness to God for all times! On יחי לעד, cf. Chr. Barth, *Die Errettung vom Tode in den individuellen Klage- und Dankliedern*, 24.

[22:27-29] If now in vv. 27f. "all the ends of the earth" and "all generations of the nations" are called on for insight, repentance, and homage, this is not a matter of an enthusiastic intensification of the hymn, but of a tradition of the Jerusalem cultus associated with the קדוש יושב. The God enthroned on Zion is אל-עליון, Creator and Lord of the whole world (see above, Intro. §10, 1). About this fact, which is always valid, all the nations are to "think" (זכר) and "turn" (שוב). וישתחוו contains the conception of the homage of the nations. Especially in v. 28 the relation to the cultic tradition of Jerusalem becomes evident. Yahweh is honored on Zion as מלך and as משל (see above, Intro. §10, 1). He is the ruler of the world. Therefore the praise of the nations is due him. Even the dead are included in the great homage. This is the more curious as there is otherwise an insurmountable barrier in the OT: the dead have no connection to Yahweh, and they do not praise him (cf. Pss. 6:5; 88:10-12). שאול is a place far removed from the cultus. But now the barrier is broken down. Also those who sleep in the earth (Dan. 12:2) are drawn into the homage to Yahweh.

[22:30-31] The descendants of him who has been rescued are especially emphasized in v. 30. They are to serve Yahweh. As in v. 23, זרע denotes the immediate participation in God's effecting of the rescue. An unbreakable chain of tradition—so the singer assures us—shall be formed, one that transmits Yahweh's saving deed to the coming generations and the people yet to be born. On צדק, cf. G. von Rad, *OT Theol*, 1:370ff. Through the transmission of God's great deed (כי עשה) the coming generations would inherit the certainty which the petitioner of Psalm 22 expressed in vv. 3-5.

Purpose and Thrust

Psalm 22 traverses unimaginable dimensions. From the depths of abandonment by God, the song of the rescued person rises to a worldwide hymn that draws also the dead into a great homage of Yahweh.

We should probably at first note how closely the whole song is "tied to the community." The petitioner in the worst affliction draws confidence from the fact that the fathers of Israel gained an answer and a rescue from their lamentation (vv. 3-5). His life is encircled by the reality of the קהל. After he too has now been heard, he takes up the song of praise in the congregation (vv. 22, 25) and at the close gives the assurance that his descendants for generations to come will retain the event of the great deed of Yahweh in their tradition (vv. 30-31). This close relation to the קהל has its roots in the fact that the petitioner counts himself among the poor (v. 24). The "sufferer," the "poor man," is the most intensive visitor of Zion. He and his very existence are "cast" (v. 10) on Yahweh, and he waits for the healing help of God. In supreme joy he experiences the miracle of his rescue (v. 24) and in lament and praise refers to the reality of the royal sanctuary in Jerusalem that transcends his life.

In the New Testament, Psalm 22 is frequently quoted in the passion narrative: v. 1 in Matt. 27:46; Mark 15:34; v. 7 in Matt. 27:39; Mark 15:29; v. 8 in Matt. 27:43; v. 15 in John 19:28(?); v. 18 in Matt. 27:35; John 19:23-24. From these references of the passion narrative to Psalm 22, earlier churchly interpretations permitted themselves to conclude that Psalm 22 belongs to the "messianic prophecies." But this interpretation has been proved to be inappropriate. Psalm 22 does not deal with the "Messiah" (in the sense of an end-time king of salvation). Psalm 22 also is not a "prophecy." In this sense H. Gunkel, for instance, could state: "The 'messianic' interpretation, last represented by Delitzsch, has conclusively been dropped since it was recognized that the psalm actually contains no prophecy and, what is more, that the idea of a suffering Messiah is foreign to the Old Testament." This statement reflects an understanding that turns up almost everywhere in the more recent exegesis of the Psalms. Thus A. Cohen, in the "Soncino Books of the Bible," comes to this conclusion: "A christological intention has long been read into this Psalm, but modern Christian exegetes are agreed that it describes a situation then existing and does not anticipate an event of the future." The question must therefore be asked in a new way: What are the inner connections between Psalm 22 and the NT passion narrative?

We could begin with an explanation given by Franz Delitzsch in his commentary on the Psalms. He writes: "In Psalm 22 David with his lamentations descends to depths that lie beyond the depth of his own suffering, and with his hopes he ascends to heights that lie beyond the height of his own reward for suffering." This unique situation Delitzsch calls an "escalation of what is typical of the prophetic." Delitzsch has rightly recognized that "the statements of the mortally sick sufferer in Psalm 22 transcend every individual fate. What is typical and paradigmatic in the statements of suffering and praise, in their recourse to conventionalized means of speech and conception, catches hold of something that is archetypal and supraindividual. When Jesus now in the agony of the cross prays the first words of Psalm 22, two things happen: (1) Jesus enters the archetypal affliction of abandonment by God which was experienced in the OT by those who prayed and which is described in surpassing words and images. But this means that Jesus solidly identifies himself with the entire fullness of suffering. The path of the Son of man coming from heaven leads to the lowest depths of misery. (2) The first Christian community now saw associations between the fate of the OT petitioner in Psalm 22 and the death of Jesus on the cross. In the category "prophecy fulfillment" it took up correspondences of the outer and inner action because Jesus himself in praying Ps. 22:1 had showed the way.

H. Gese's detailed study (*ZThK* 65 [1968], 1ff.) has investigated the references of the NT to Psalm 22, especially the oldest report about the death of Jesus and about the institution of the Lord's Supper. Only two results of the study can be noted here: (1) "The oldest account of the central event of the death of Jesus is obscured under the veil of Psalm 22. Thus we would here not only have before us an old interpretation of the death of Jesus but, it seems to me, the *oldest* understanding of the event at Golgotha. Here we are not, as in Isaiah 53, dealing with expiatory sacrifice, in fact, not even with the Messiah, but rather with death, escalated to the highest degree of suffering, which, with an act of God that rescues from death, leads to the inbreaking of the eschatological βασιλεία τοῦ θεοῦ. He who proclaimed this βασιλεία in his life introduced it by his death" (p. 17). (2) "With the supper that instituted fellowship and a New Being, there must inseparably be associated the praise of Yahweh, the acknowledgment of Yahweh as the rescuer by means of the memorial of the saving event . . ." (p. 18). Gese clearly points out "that the Lord's Supper deals with the *todah* of the Risen One" (p. 22). To sum up, "We learn from Psalm 22 how the rescue from death is experienced in the light of revelation, how Israel escalated the experience of suffering to the experience of archetypal suffering, and how the divine blessing of rescue is apocalyptically awaited as the opening of the eschatological royal rule of God. We see that the realization of this takes place in the NT event. We understand the report of the death of Jesus, which was originally entirely dominated by Psalm 22, and the Lord's Supper as an acknowledgment of this event, the establishment of a New Being, in which the Risen One is present'' (p. 22).

Security in the
Goodness and Mercy
of Yahweh

Literature

Siegesmund, "Psalm 23 in palästinischer Beleuchtung," *PJB* 5 (1909) 97-100. P. Volz, "Psalm 23," *NKZ* 35 (1925) 576ff. J. Boehmer, "Der Reichtum von Psalm 23," *BZ* 23 (1935/36) 166-170. J. Morgenstern, "Ps 23," *JBL* 65 (1946) 13-24. T. J. Meek, "Old Testament Notes I: The Metrical Structure of Psalm 23," *JBL* 67 (1948) 233-235. E. Vogt, "The 'Place in Life' of Ps 23," *Bibl* 34 (1953) 195-211. L. Köhler, "Psalm 23," *ZAW* 68 (1956) 227-234. E. Pfeiffer, "Eine Inversion in Ps 23, 1bα?" *VT* 8 (1958) 219f. V. Maag, "Der Hirte Israels," *SThU* 28 (1958) 2-28. H. van Zyl, "Psalm 23," *Die ou Testamentiese Werkgemeenskap in Suid-Afrika* (1963) 64-83. G. Eaton, "Problems of Translation in Psalm 23, 3f.," *BiTrans* 16 (1965) 171-176. A. C. Merril, "Psalm 23 and the Jerusalem Tradition," *VT* 15 (1965) 354-360. J. J. Stamm, *Erwägungen zu Psalm 23*, *EvTh*Beih 44 (1966) 120-128. E. Beaukamp and A. Rose, Le Psaume 23 (22): Commentaire et lecture pour les chrétiens," *Feu Nouveau* 9, 11 (1966) 11-20. A. R. Johnson, "Psalm 23 and the Household of Faith," *Proclamation and Presence: Old Testament Essays of G. H. Davies* (1970) 255-271. O. Eissfeldt, "Bleiben im Hause Jahwes," *Beiträge zur Alten Geschichte und deren Nachleben: Festschrift F. Altheim I* (1969) 76-81. G. Schwarz, "Einen Tisch angesichts meiner Feinde? Eine Emendation," *VT* 20 (1970) 118-120. W. Beyerlin, *Die Rettung der Bedrängten in den Feindpsalmen der Einzelnen auf institutionelle Zusammenhänge untersucht*, FRLANT 99 (1970) 111-116.

Text

A psalm of David.

23:1 Yahweh is my shepherd, I shall lack nothing.

2 In green pastures[a] he lets me lie down.[b]
To[c] quiet waters he leads me.

3 He restores my soul.
He leads me on proper paths
for his name's sake.

4 Even when I wander in a dark^d valley,
I fear no harm,
for you are with me;
your rod and your staff—
they give me courage.^e
5 You spread a table^f before my eyes
—in view of my enemies.
You anoint my head with oil.
Full up is my cup.
6 Only goodness and mercy will follow me
all the days of my life,
and I 'will remain'^g in Yahweh's house
as long as I live.

2a In order to adjust the meter in v. 2a to 3 + 2 and thus gain a consistent picture in the meter, נאות is sometimes expunged "for the sake of the meter." But we should certainly have to be conservative in this case.

b Gk transmits the text: εἰς τόπον χλόης, ἐκεῖ κατεσκήνωσεν.

c על is by no means to be replaced by אל. The image of animals standing above the water could be present in על.

4d Gk has ἐν μέσῳ ˙ σκιᾶς θανάτου.

e The correction יַנְחֵנִי is surely introduced too quickly. Granted that נחם cannot have the meaning "to comfort" in this passage ("Comfort is the answer to harm," L. Köhler), yet Morgenstern (*JBL* 65 [1946], 17) correctly translates: "they reassure me."

5f E. Power (*Bibl* 9 [1928] 434-442) has assumed false dittography for שֻׁלְחָן נגד (שֶׁלַח instead of שֻׁלְחָן) and translates: "You hold the javelin at the ready in front of me" (also cf. J. Morgenstern and L. Köhler). L. Köhler is of the opinion: "Thus all difficulties of thought continuity vanish, and the picture of the shepherd is consistently the basis of the whole psalm" (*ZAW* 68 [1956], 233). But with this emendation and the consistency that is established, new problems are stirred up that still need to be discussed in detail (see below on "Form").

6g MT: "and I come back." This would refer to a vow of a pilgrimage. Better is Gk σ´ שֻׁבְתִּי ("and my dwelling"). Best of all: Jerome, S,T, וְיָשַׁבְתִּי ("and I dwell"); cf. Ps. 17:41.

Form

The condition of the text is excellent. The meter presents a clear picture. The meter 3 + 2 is determinative in vv. 2b/3a; 3bα/β; 4aα/β; 5aα/β; 5bα/β; 6aα/β; 6bα/β. Exceptions are the beginning, vv. 1b/2a in a 3 + 3 meter, and the conclusion of the first part of the psalm in v. 4 with its concluding 2 + 2 + 2 meter. However, the latter statement is disputed. Does the first part of the psalm really conclude with v. 4? This question, which—beyond its formal aspects—already precipitates extensive problems of content, is in need of a preliminary examination. L. Köhler maintains that Psalm 23 is a continuously uniform hymn in which only one single picture appears: that of the shepherd.

L. Köhler (in contrast to Siegesmund, PHB 5 [1909], 97ff.) begins with the conception that the change of pasturage is the determining metaphor of the whole psalm (on the so-called transhumance [seasonal movement of livestock between mountain and lowland pasturage], cf. M. Weber, *Das antike Judentum* [1921], 11; A. Alt, "Erwägungen über die Landnahme der Israeliten in Palästina," *PJB* 35 [1939], 28ff.; L. Rost, "Weidewechsel und alt-israelitischer Festkalender," ZDPV 66 [1943], 205ff.; and C. Westermann, *Genesis 12-36* [Minneapolis: Augsburg, 1985], 64, 77-79). In connection with changes of pasturage, long marches by day are made with the herd. In the light of this state of affairs, vv. 3 and 4 would easily be understood. In v. 5 the emendation suggested by E. Power is then introduced ("Over against my assailants you hold the javelin at the ready in front of me"; see above). Thus also v. 5a could be understood in connection with transhumance. Verse 5b is interpreted by Köhler as a device for dressing wounds (sheep easily wound their heads, and these wounds have to be treated with oil). After Köhler has progressed that far in bringing things together under the general theme of transhumance, has "removed" the "table" in v. 5, and has assigned the oil to the medical treatment of the animals, he still gets into difficulties, in the last analysis. Since when do sheep drink from a "cup"? And in v. 6: Does the transhumance of the herd end in the temple? But Köhler manages also these handicaps. In the cup there was oil—so he opines. And בית in v. 6 is corrected to בְּיָךְ. This understanding of Psalm 23, which is similarly presented also by J. Morgenstern, is original, to be sure, but can be carried through to the end of the text only by means of questionable encroachments on the text. This "unification" of the illustrative elements of the psalm eliminates itself.

The interpretation of Briggs and Weiser stands in contrast to that of Morgenstern and Köhler. Here Psalm 23 is divided into three parts and so also into three basic images: the shepherd (vv. 1-2), the wanderer (vv. 3-4), the host (vv. 5f.). Concerning v. 3 Weiser remarks: "In v. 3 the vivid phantasy of the Middle Easterner changes the image: God appears as the guide of the wanderer on his life's pathway." Is this explanation correct? Is it really a wanderer whom Yahweh guides in vv. 3 and 4? Actually, this is hardly possible, for שׁבטך ומשענתך ("your rod and your staff") unquestionably refers to the shepherd's protecting, guiding, and leading to pasture. Therefore the result is that Psalm 23 consists of two parts: vv. 1-4 (ending with the meter $2+2+2$) speak of the shepherd, Yahweh, and vv. 5f. deal with God, the host in the holy place.

Psalm 23 belongs to the form group of prayer songs. See above, Intro. §6, 2. Worth noting are the expressions of trust that caused the psalm to be classified in the type called songs of trust (Gunkel and Begrich, *EinlPs* §6, 27). Thereby a classification among the "laments of an individual" would become recognizable. But we must take note of the confessional formulations of vv. 2 and 3. They favor moving the prayer song near the song of thanksgiving uttered by an individual. For the *todah,* see above, Intro. §6, 2a. Details will have to be given when we take up the situation ("Sitz im Leben") of the psalm. The appropriateness of the statement that Psalm 23 is a prayer song is especially obvious in vv. 4f., in the address to Yahweh (in the second person). Verse 6 repeats the confessional statement.

Setting

Where was Psalm 23 intoned? At which occasion? Who is the composer? Let us take the last question first. If we follow MT in v. 6b, the singer of the psalm ought to be someone involved in the cultus, someone who in "the house of Yahweh" has experienced extraordinary blessings, who leaves the sanctuary trusting God and speaks the vow: "I will return to the house of Yahweh. . . . " But this reading does not agree with the topicality of the language of the Psalms (cf. Pss. 27:4f.; 52:8; 61:4; 63:2). We would no doubt have to read וישבתי (see above). But who is the singer in that case? Is this a matter of a "royal prayer" (G. Eaton, pp. 171ff.)? Was the petitioner of the psalm a king appearing at worship? A priest (H. Schmidt)? Or the representative of a "sublime cultic mysticism" (G. von Rad, " 'Gerechtigkeit' und 'Leben' in der Kultsprache der Psalmen," *Bertholet-Festschrift* [1950], 432)? The question can hardly be answered on the basis of v. 6. The outlines become somewhat clearer in v. 5. There we are told that the petitioner has "enemies"; but Yahweh provides him with a meal—obviously a meal in connection with a sacrifice (cf. בבית־יהוה in v. 6)—"in view of my enemies." S. Mowinckel thinks of a "banquet at a sacrifice of thanksgiving" (*PsStud* 1:126, 131), and E. Vogt goes a step further and (with reference to the "enemies") speaks of an accused person's banquet, arranged after his acquittal (*Bibl* 34 [1953], 195ff.). These interpretations are on the right track, and they have been elevated to a well-supported basis by W. Beyerlin (111-116). After the judgment of God has been rendered and the acquittal, declaring the falsely accused to be צדיק, has been published, a banquet in connection with an offering takes place, at which obviously also the enemies, i.e., the persecutors and accusers, take part. (On "enemies," see above, Intro. §10, 4.) This situation is clear from Ps. 4:5 (which see). Accordingly, Psalm 23 would have originated in such a "Sitz im Leben," in which the *todah,* the song of thanksgiving of an individual, was intoned. Characteristic of this celebration is a formulation of a confession that emanates from trust. If the petitioner trusts in Yahweh in a time of need and affliction, then he can praise the deeds of God in confessional expressions as soon as his fate has changed for the better.

Psalm 23 certainly belongs to the tradition of Jerusalem (A. C. Merril, 354ff.). It could be dated in preexilic times. But we would have to assume that this prayer song intoned at the meal in connection with an offering (v. 50) was used again and again. But the concrete situation that can be discerned in view of v. 5, compared with Ps. 4:5, removes the textual difficulties that have quite frequently been lamented (cf. the corrections in G. Schwarz, 118ff., who tries to provide relief by means of transposition).

Commentary

[Title] On מזמור לדוד, cf. above, Intro. §4, No. 2.

[23:1] יהוה רעי. How is this sentence, consisting of two nouns, to be understood? L. Köhler is of the opinion that v. 1 acquires a polemic connotation if רעי is considered the subject and יהוה the predicate. According to Köhler, the meaning would then be "to deny the falsehood that not Yahweh but another god is my shepherd" (*ZAW* 68 [1956], 228). Köhler considers this—up to now traditional—conception impossible. On the contrary, he sees יהוה as the subject and רעי as the predicate. The sentence would then be "inverted" and could be rendered either in a temporal or a causal version as follows: either, "as long as Yahweh is my shepherd . . .," or, "because Yahweh is my shepherd. . . ." But these syntactical declarations of Köhler's are not appropriate (E. Pfeiffer, "Eine Inversion in Ps 23, 1bα?" *VT* 8, 219f.). רעי is the subject, יהוה is the predicate. The statement about Yahweh in the third person has a confessional character. But confessions always have, among other things, also an antithetical character. They emphasize the שם (v. 3).

Now the picture of the shepherd originally applies to the people, who as the flock are being led and protected. In the cultic tradition of Jerusalem Yahweh is glorified as the רעה ישראל (Ps. 80:1). This conception goes back to a standing metaphor of the ancient Near East: the king is the shepherd of his people. Transferred to Yahweh, this conception is found in a number of OT passages: Pss. 79:13; 95:7; 100:3; Isa. 40:11; and often. In this metaphor the thought of a powerful and at the same time benevolent lordship is always determinative. Only rarely does the expression of trust of an individual in the OT depart from the picture of the shepherd and his flock (cf. Gen. 48:15). An individual member of the "flock" knows that he is sheltered under the benevolent and powerful lordship of his "shepherd"; he suffers no need (לא אחסר). The substance of the meaning of the Near Eastern metaphor forbids it that Psalm 23 be understood in an idyllically charming way (so, among others, H. Herkenne).

A text from Mesopotamia also can report about a deity's benevolent and powerful office of shepherd. In a hymn to Shamash we read, "You take care of the people of the lands altogether; whatever Ea, the king and ruler, caused to be brought forth is everywhere given over to you. All who have living breath you pasture" (A. Falkenstein and W. von Soden, *Sumerische und akkadische Hymnen und Gebete* [1953], 240f.).

[23:2] The shepherd leads his flock to the green pasturages (G. Dalman, *AuS* 6:211) and to the watering places. דשא simply means "the green place." The singer wants to emphasize that the shepherd leads his flock, not over sterile fields on which the sheep find only brush parched by the heat, but to succulent, ideal pasturages. And he also leads his flock to the best water holes. מי מנחות are the quiet, dammed-up watering places, where the animals may satisfy their thirst without haste. There is water in abundance. "He says 'quiet waters' for such as flow quietly because swift torrents are inconvenient for watering the sheep, and they are also very harmful" (Calvin). The singer therefore acknowledges the fullness of blessings which he as an individual has experienced among the people of God.

[23:3] In the pasturages and at the water holes the shepherd provides refreshment for his flock. נפשי ישובב literally means "to bring back the vigor of life, the vitality" (cf. Ps. 19:7; Lam. 1:11, 16, 19). Under the benevolent lordship of Yahweh the individual experiences the refreshment of God's care. When the flock is on the move, the good shepherd looks for מעגלי־צדק = "proper paths" that are beneficial for the flock. In the transferred sense this means: the petitioner is sure that Yahweh will protect him from every fall and lead him properly under his צדק. This expression of trust could be applied to the petition as it is expressed, for instance, in Ps. 5:8, יהוה נחני בצדקתך למען שוררי. The petitioner of Psalm 23 also finds himself in a contest with hostile powers (v. 5) that want to separate him from Yahweh and bring him down to ruin. But the singer trusts in the protective power of the divine שם (cf. Ps. 20:1), which considers it a matter of honor to find the right way. On למען שמו, cf. O. Grether, *Name und Wort Gottes im Alten Testament,* BZAW 64 (1934) 53f.

[23:4] Also v. 4 deals with the dangers of travel in which the protective power of the shepherd proves itself. Occasionally the flock, in its quest for good pasturage and water holes, must wander through dark valleys.[1] גיא צלמות literally means "the valley of death's shadows," the dangerous dark bottom of the valley. In the interpretation of these wanderings of the flock we must without

---

1. "Thus he does not promise himself continual pleasures; but he fortifies himself by the help of God courageously to endure the various calamities with which he might be visited. Pursuing this metaphor, he compares the care which God takes in governing true believers to a shepherd's staff and crook, declaring that he is satisfied with this as all-sufficient for the protection of his life. As a sheep, when it wanders up and down through a dark valley, is preserved safe from the attacks of wild beasts and from harm in other ways by the presence of the shepherd alone, so David now declares that as often as he shall be exposed to any danger, he will have sufficient defense and protection in being under the pastoral care of God" (Calvin, on Ps. 23:4, trans. Anderson [Grand Rapids: Eerdmans, 1949]).

question think of the long distances of the transhumance, as L. Köhler wants to interpret Psalm 23 (see above). But, to get back to the real point, even in the dark valley, on dangerous paths, the singer of our psalm fears no harm.

And now, for the first time, the song goes over to an address to Yahweh: כִּי־אַתָּה עִמָּדִי. This is the real central statement of trust (cf. Gen. 26:3, 24; 28:15; 31:3; Deut. 31:6f; and often). God is present with his mighty protective power. For the protection of his flock, the shepherd carries the שֵׁבֶט, an iron-shod cudgel (G. Dalman, AuS 6:238f.). With this weapon he beats back hostile animals and men (cf. 1 Sam. 17:43). At the same time, the shepherd carries a staff (מִשְׁעַנְתֶּךָ) in his hand, with which to urge the tardy sheep on and to bring the stray ones back to the flock. Accordingly, the protective weapon and the guiding staff inspire courage and fearless trust in those who are led—so the singer of the psalm declares. He knows he is under God's protection and guidance. In this, the expression "for you are with me" is a reflection of the promise of Yahweh: "I will be with you" (cf. H. D. Preuss, " ' . . . Ich will mit dir sein!' " ZAW 80 [1968], 139-173; on Pss. 23:4; 151).

[23:5] An entirely new picture comes into view in v. 5. Yahweh makes his appearance as the beneficent host who visibly sets the table for one who is persecuted and in this way takes him into the sphere of his protection. The guest has his head anointed with oil. His cup is filled to the rim. This picture of the host, who is ready to provide protection and who looks after one who is persecuted, should at the same time—from v. 6 on—be viewed in a special framework. The place where Yahweh dispenses the rights of protection and guest status is the בֵּית־יהוה, the temple (cf. Pss. 15:1; 6:14). There the "poor" and those who are persecuted, those who have experienced God's help and salvation are, at the sacrifice, associates of Yahweh's at the meal (Ps. 22:26). It is therefore easily possible to think of the picture presented in v. 5 in connection with the meal at a sacrifice of thanksgiving (S. Mowinckel, E. Vogt). Thus it is worth noting how visibly the preparation of the meal in v. 5a is described (on עָרַךְ שֻׁלְחָן, cf. Ps. 78:19; Prov. 9:2; Isa. 21:5). For the understanding of נֶגֶד צֹרְרָי, H. Gunkel quotes a noteworthy passage from the Amarna letters. A city prince subject to the supreme authority of Egypt addresses the request to Pharaoh, "May it please him to give gifts to his servant while our enemies look on" (Knudtzon, El-Amarna-Tafeln, No. 100, 33-35). Here, too, a visible gesture on the part of Pharaoh is to be involved by means of which this will become obvious to the enemies: this city magistrate is under the mighty protective power of the king. In v. 5, accordingly, the table fellowship with the host, Yahweh (at the sacrifice), means to say: I stand under the protective power of God, which is now demonstrated also to the enemies. Verse 5b speaks of the care of the host for the one who is persecuted. כּוֹסִי could allude to the כּוֹס־יְשׁוּעוֹת ("cup of salvation") mentioned in Ps. 116:13 (on this conception, cf. the comment on Ps. 11:6).

[23:6] The statement that follows in v. 6a is amazing. If we begin with the fact that one who was threatened and persecuted has found the protection of temple asylum while his enemies (see above, Intro. §10, 4) watch, the declaration of trust and confession in v. 6a now indicates a complete change: Not the enemies but טוֹב וָחֶסֶד "will follow" (רדף) the petitioner henceforth (כָּל־יְמֵי חַיַּי). The goodness and mercy (on חֶסֶד cf. the comment on Ps. 5:7) experienced in the sanctuary (בבית־יהוה) now run after him. The expression of trust and confession then goes over to the concluding statement, "I will remain in Yahweh's house— as long as I live." This is not "pious illusion, born of exuberance" (thus L. Köhler). Verse 6b could originally have been a Levitical confession (cf. the comment on Ps. 16:6f.). This Levitical confession would then have been spiritualized and recoined as a "sublime cultic mysticism" (G. von Rad," 'Ge- rechtigkeit' und 'Leben' in der Kultsprache der Psalmen," *Bertholet-Festschrift* [1950], 432). He who has experienced Yahweh's ישועה would forever like to stay in the area of salvation, in the sanctuary (cf. Pss. 27:4f.; 52:8; 61:4; 63:2). On the confession in v. 6, cf. especially O. Eissfeldt, 76ff. Naturally, it is hardly possible actually to discern the situation of the petitioner. Also, we will have to consider the "mode of adaptation" accorded v. 6 as the formulary was subsequently taken up.

Purpose and Thrust

Psalm 23 is not tangled up in the bliss of trust which is here displayed in idyllic and lovely pictures of pious submission. This lyric-romantic understanding of the song is determinative in most of the interpretations. The background of the psalm of trust represents a definite danger. The petitioner has enemies (v. 5), his life is threatened and persecuted. But in the temple, in the community of Yahweh, טוב וחסד has met the one persecuted. Now he knows that he is sheltered in the protective power of the שם. In his song of trust the singer at first takes hold of the image of Yahweh as the shepherd of his people (Ps. 80:1), as it is known in the communal tradition of Jerusalem, and he applies it to his own life. "Perfect refreshment" and "perpetual security"—these are the determining themes of the first cycle of images. In v. 5 the picture changes. As host, Yahweh demonstrates his protective power (v. 5a) in the fellowship of the meal (at a sacrifice?) over against the enemies, and Yahweh overwhelms the persecuted person with the fullness of his help. From this experience the petitioner knows that his life is always sheltered and surrounded by well-being.

H. Schmidt is right when he sees Psalm 23 as an illustration of the OT concept האמין (Isa. 7:9; 28:16; 30:15). It is true that the traditions to which Psalm 23 harks back clearly indicate that this faith is not something individual- istic. This trusting faith lives on the saving power of the place where Yahweh has revealed himself to his people. In the New Testament's message of fulfillment, Jesus Christ is ὁ ποιμὴν ὁ καλός (John 10:11ff.).

Psalm 24

The Entry of Yahweh,
the King of the World

Literature

I. W. Slotki, "The Text of the Ancient Form of Recital of Psalm 24 and 124," *JBL* 51 (1932) 214-226. J. D. Smart, "The Eschatological Interpretation of Psalm 24," *JBL* 52 (1933) 175-180. G. R. Deaver, "An Exegetic Study on Psalm 24," Th. M. Thesis, Dallas (1953). H. Schmidt, "Jahwe und die Kulttraditionen von Jerusalem," *ZAW* 67 (1955) 168-197. K. Koch, "Tempeleinlassliturgien und Dekaloge," *Studien zur Theologie der alttestamentlichen Überlieferungen* (1961) 46-60. M. Treves, "The Date of Psalm 24," *VT* 10 (1960) 428-437. A. Rose, " 'Attollite portas, principes, vestras . . .' Aperçus sur la lecture chrétienne du Psaume 24(23)B," *Studi G. Lercaro* (Rome, 1966) 453-478. W. Zimmerli, "Planungen für den Wiederaufbau nach der Katastrophe von 587," *VT* 18 (1968) 229-255. O. Garcia de la Fuente, "Liturgias de entrada, normas de asilo o exhortaciones proféticas. A propósito de los Salmos 15 y 24," *Aug* (1969) 266-298. P. R. Berger, "Zu Psalm 24,7 und 9," *Ugarit-Forschungen* 2 (1970) 335f.

Text

Of David. A Psalm.
24:1 To Yahweh does the world belong and its fullness,
    the land, and they who dwell[a] on it.
  2 For it is he who founded it on the sea
    and erected it solidly over streams.—
  3 Who is allowed to ascend to Yahweh's hill,
    and who is allowed to step into his holy domain?
  4 He who has clean hands and a clean heart,
    'whose'[b] soul does not judge according to vanity
    and does not swear deceitfully.
  5 He will receive a blessing from Yahweh,
    and righteousness from the God of his salvation.
  6 This is the generation of those who inquire after 'Yahweh,'[c]
    who seek the 'face of the God'[d] of Jacob. *Selah.*
  7 Lift up, O gates, your heads,
    be lifted up, O ancient portals,
    that the king of glory may enter in!

8 Who is this king of glory?
  Yahweh, the strong one, the hero!
  Yahweh, the hero in the war!
9 Lift up, O gates, your heads,
  'be lifted up,'ᵉ O ancient portals,
  that the king of glory may enter in!
10 Who, then, is the king of glory?
   Yahweh Sebaoth—
   he is the king of glory. *Selah.*

1a Gk: καὶ πάντες οἱ κατοικοῦντες ἐν αὐτῇ. But the addition of כָּל־, implied in this translation, is unnecessary.
4b Here we certainly must follow a number of manuscripts to read נַפְשׁוֹ. This correction is demanded by the context.
6c We must probably follow individual manuscripts of Gk and (also for the sake of the meter) read דֹּרְשֵׁי יהוה
d MT would have to be translated: "Who seek your countenance, O Jacob." This reading is hardly possible according to the parallelism and the context. The text in Gk reads: ζητούντων τὸ πρόσωπον τοῦ θεοῦ Ιακῶβ. Accordingly, we would have to correct the MT: פְּנֵי אֱלֹהֵי יעקב. Two manuscripts of S: פניך אלהי יעקב. Targ has פָּנָיו.
9e Following many manuscripts, we should read והנשאו in agreement with v. 7.

Form

Already in a consideration of the metrical proportions it becomes evident that we should divide Psalm 24 into two, if not even three, sections. The meter of v. 1 and v. 2 is marked by two double triple meters. In vv. 3-6 the meter is irregular: vv. 3 and 6 present the 3 + 4 meter. In v. 4 we first read the 4 + 4 meter; in v. 4b a half-verse without complement follows with three accents. The 4 + 3 meter is to be kept in v. 5. The metrical form of vv. 7-10 is entirely different. Verses 7-9 contain the 3 + 3 + 3 meters, while v. 10 closes with a 3 + 2 + 2 meter. Thus the entire psalm could be divided into two parts: vv. 1-6 and vv. 7-10, or even into three individual sections: vv. 1-2; 3-6; 7-10. Since the cleavage between vv. 6 and 7 is particularly striking, a number of commentaries start with the idea that two different psalms (Psalms 24A and 24B) are involved. But this assumption is not appropriate (as we shall show).

   An analysis of the elements of form and type discernible in Psalm 24 leads to the following findings: The psalm begins with an acknowledgment of the universal right of ownership extending to the entire created world (vv. 1f.). Against this statement about the world dominion and the creating power of Yahweh, the section vv. 3-6 stands in clear contrast. Verse 3 has the character and function of a Torah question that obviously occurs in a cultic and ritual connection (cf. vv. 7ff. and the comment on Psalm 15). Thus we could speak of a Torah liturgy, for the answer to the question in v. 3 is given in v. 4. In vv. 5f. are added promises of blessing that apply to those who correspond to the characteristics of the צדיק advanced in v. 4; v. 5 has the form of a prediction, a promise; while v. 6 demonstratively points to those who actually correspond to the characteristics of v. 4. In vv. 7-10, addresses, questions, and answers follow one upon another. The Torah liturgy is followed by a gate liturgy, which may have had its "Sitz im Leben" at the portals of the sanctuary (see below). All observations and investigations regarding the form of Psalm 24 lead directly to the question about the cultic "Sitz im Leben." On the relation of the liturgies for temple entrance of the Decalog, cf. K. Koch, 46ff.

Setting

In investigating the "Sitz im Leben" of Psalm 24, it is best to begin with the section vv. 7-10. A group of cultic participants is standing at the gates of the sanctuary. It wants to usher in the "king of glory," Yahweh Sebaoth. This group—obviously gathered for a procession—is twice addressed with the question: "Who is the king of glory?" This involves a cultic antiphonal song, a liturgical ceremonial, which doubtlessly is connected with an entrance of the holy ark to the temple in Jerusalem (see below). The situation of the liturgical addresses, questions, and responses is easily understood: the vanguard of the ark procession utters the address of vv. 7 and 9 before the gates of the sanctuary. Then each time the question "Who is the king of glory?" is heard from the inner area (of the temple or the sacred area) in vv. 8 and 10. The answers are given by the processional group desiring entrance. With this liturgical ceremonial before the gates of the sanctuary the Torah liturgy of vv. 3-6 can easily be coordinated. Prior to the entrance to the sacred area, the conditions for admittance are asked for and announced by the priests (cf. Psalm 15). Accordingly, v. 3 would then have been spoken by the members of the procession. In vv. 4-6 the priests give the answer. Finally, within the framework of this cultic course of events, also vv. 1-2 could be understood as a confession of the celebrating congregation. Thus Psalm 24 would contain individual pieces of a liturgy that accompanies the cultic act of bringing in the ark at the sanctuary. The psalm is to be thought of as a unity. On the fact that the hymn of vv. 1-2 and the bringing in of the ark in vv. 7-10 belong to this psalm, cf. Ps. 95:2-6. In reference to vv. 3-6, another explanation by Mowinckel should be cited: "As we can see from Psalm 24, it was a regular ingredient of the festival ritual for the festival procession to ask about the conditions of admittance and for the priest on duty at the temple gates to answer: Only he who has a clean heart and clean hands may 'visit Yahweh's holy hill' " (S. Mowinckel, *Religion und Kultus* [1953], 115). Also cf. above, Intro. §6, 6.

The question to which festival of Israel the bringing of the ark into the sanctuary belongs is in dispute. The late dating by B. Duhm (to a temple festival of the year 165 B.C.) is out of the question. It is based on an unrealistic prejudice regarding the history of the origin of the Psalms. On the other hand, the interpretation of Psalm 24 is still laboring under the impression of the "discovery" of the "festival of the enthronement of Yahweh" by P. Volz (*Das Neujahrsfest Jahwes*, Sammlung gemeinverständlicher Vorträge und Schriften aus dem Gebiet der Theologie und Religionsgeschichte 67, 1912) and S. Mowinckel (*PsStud* 2). In Intro. §10, 1, above, there is a detailed study setting forth whether the hypothesis of an annual "enthronement festival of Yahweh" is tenable in view of the text and the history of the cult. Also see H.-J. Kraus, *Worship in Israel* (1966) 205ff. But no matter how the question concerning the existence or nonexistence of a "festival of the enthronement of Yahweh" may be answered, in any case Psalm 24 will have to be assigned to preexilic times and to the tradition of the Jerusalem sanctuary. To be sure, we could with H. Gunkel conclude from the expression פתחי עולם ("O ancient portals," vv. 7, 9) that the earliest time of the kings (perhaps the time of Solomon) is not in question. The gates already are considered ancient and venerable. Or may the concept עולם not be interpreted as temporal? The heading of the psalm in Gk (τῆς μιᾶς σαββάτων) refers to a later use of the song in Jewish worship. This note is not an argument for the thesis of N. H. Snaith that the psalms proclaiming Yahweh

as king were "Sabbath psalms" (N. H. Snaith, *The Jewish New Year Festival*
[1947], 195ff.). About the later use of Psalm 24 we have no information. We
may, however, presume that the first part of the psalm in the style of a prayer
song led to the adoption of the Jewish Torah-piety. We cannot determine whether
the second part (vv. 7-10) played a role in connection with the festival of
tabernacles or that of the new year.

Commentary

[Title] On לדוד and מזמור, cf. above, Intro. §4, No. 2.

[24:1-2] In the hymnic section vv. 1-2, Yahweh is honored as Lord and creator
of the world. "To Yahweh does the world belong and its fullness." ל identifies
the possessor (BrSynt §107d). This comprehensive ownership is in a similar way
expressed in Pss. 50:12 and 89:11. In Ps. 97:5 Yahweh is called אדון כל־הארץ.
In all these expressions ארץ tends toward the idea of a universal area. This
statement is proved correct both by the summarizing term מלואה and by the
cosmological term תבל ("land"). On מלואה, cf. Deut. 33:16; Isa. 34:1; Mic.
1:2; Pss. 50:12; 89:11. The reference is to the total content of the created world.
תבל as a cosmological term (cf. Akkadian *tābālu*) refers to the bright,
life-sustaining "mainland" of "productive land," such as (according to the
ancient cosmogonies) was reclaimed from the sea of chaos (cf. especially Pss.
18:15; 77:16-18; 93:1). While מלואה refers rather to the material content of the
created world, the parallel term ישבי בה refers to the living beings, especially the
human beings. The universe is in Yahweh's hands. To him as the ruler does the
world belong. The כי (v. 2) that introduces the proof combines world dominion
(v. 1) and creation of the world. Yahweh, he (cf. the emphatic הוא) it was who
created the world, and he is therefore also its lord. Verse 2 takes up conceptions
of ancient Near Eastern cosmogony. Below the world lies the primal sea, which
is here indicated by the words ימים and נהרות (on the conception, cf. Gen. 1:6;
7:11; Exod. 20:4; Deut. 33:13). Like a house on stilts, the earth has been built
on piles in the water (cf. Ps. 104:5; Job 38:4ff.). The verbs יסד and כון (*polel*)
describe the founding and securing of the structure of the earth. The OT praises
Yahweh as the creator who through his work gave the world a firm solidity
(Psalm 93). How closely the glorification of the ruler and the creator of the world
belongs to the entry of the מלך הכבוד (vv. 7, 9) is discernible in Ps. 95:1-6. Very
likely the creation psalms belong to the hymns of great prostration before King
Yahweh (Pss. 95:6; 100:4). On the perfect tenses in the verbs of vv. 2ff., cf. D.
Michel, *Tempora und Satzstellung in den Psalmen* (1960) 118f. Michel is of the
opinion that the perfect tenses denoted "accessory acts."

[24:3-6] In v. 3 we now hear the question of the pilgrims as they enter the
sanctuary: מי־יעלה בהר־יהוה. הר־יהוה is the temple hill in Jerusalem (Ps. 2:6)—
the holy place, which in the parallelism is called מקום קדשו. עלה is the technical
term for the procession that leads up to the sanctuary on the hill (Ps. 47:5; 2 Sam.
6:12, 15; 1 Kings 8:4; 12:33; Isa. 2:3; and often). Aso קום ב should be
considered a customary term (cf. Ps. 1:5). With its question the procession about
to enter is asking for a תורה. The cultic conditions for admittance, which are
fixed as a sacral right in all the holy places of the ancient world (cf. the comment
on Psalm 15, "Setting"), are in the liturgical answer of the priesthood (v.
4)indicated and declared in a general statement rather than really expounded in

detail. The Torah of admittance in Psalm 15 is more expressive and more
specific. In Psalm 24 the statement of the priesthood in v. 4a is more generalized
and comprehensive. כפים and לבב (hand and heart)—here purity and cleanness
of external acts and the innermost movements of the heart are demanded. Psalm
15:2 corresponds to this principal demand. But the explication of the principal
demand in Psalm 24 (rather circumstantially introduced by אשר) is essentially
more terse than the corresponding elaboration in Ps. 15:3ff. Only two offenses
are mentioned that preclude participation in the worship: worship of idols and
perjury. On נשא נפש, cf. Deut. 24:15; Hos. 4:8; Prov. 19:18 (cf. above all נשא
את שמו לשוא in Exod. 20:7). The "vital force in a human being" (נפש) wants
to bow to the numina of the land, which in a judgmental term are indicated very
indefinitely and generally as שוא ("something vain," "something idle"). As in
Psalm 15, so also in the Torah of Psalm 24, the hidden and secret תורה
transgressions are mentioned exclusively. On the theme "cultus and ethos," as
well as on the theological problem of the ethical condition at admittance to the
sanctuary, cf. the comment on Ps. 15:2. The Torah answer of the priesthood
concludes with an observation. This observation contains a bestowal of blessing
(also cf. Ps. 15:5b). He who lives according to the covenant ordinances of
Yahweh has a part in the ברכה and the צדקה. From Yahweh (מאת יהוה) do
"blessing" and "righteousness" emanate. The "holy area" is no magic area of
good fortune. The worship of Israel is directed toward Yahweh's ruling will and
his gifts of good fortune as the center that is alone determinative. On ברכה, cf.
C. Westermann, *Der Segen in der Bibel und im Handeln der Kirche* (1968); C.
A. Keller and G. Wehmeier, *THAT*, 1:353-376. Since "blessing" and "righteousness" in v. 5 are used synonymously, we have to begin with צדקה as the
more concrete term. Corresponding to the Torah liturgy, it has a clearly shaped
meaning. From Yahweh the צדקה in the form of a declaration of imputation goes
out to the צדיק (cf. the comment on Ps. 17:2; G. von Rad, *OT Theol*, 1:37). The
declaratory act of imputation of righteousness must also have had an importance
in connection with the Torah liturgy, that is, in reference to the list of
characteristics in v. 4. But he who is declared "righteous" thereby receives the
blessing, and that means the full enrichment and fulfillment of the life in the
cultic area and in everyday life. The צדיקים are the blessed of God.

The "true Israel" consists of human beings who subordinate daily life to
the demands of the תורה. That is the way of the "generation" that is cultically
prepared and that appears before Yahweh (דור here has the meaning "type of
human being"). The "macarism" μακάριοι οἱ καθαροὶ τῇ καρδίᾳ, ὅτι αὐτοὶ
τὸν θεὸν ὄψονται refers to Psalm 24 not only in the first part of the sentence
but also in the dependent clause. The psalm tends toward the appearance (פנים)
of God (vv. 7-10). דרש and בקש are technical terms for the pilgrimage to the
sanctuary (Amos 5:5; 2 Sam. 21:1; Hos. 5:15; 2 Sam. 12:16). Still, the two
verbs, in connection with the demonstrative reference to the "true cultic
community," have a meaning that is more intensive than the usual one. Tying
the cult participant to the תורה has a cleansing effect in view of the understanding of worship as it is revealed in Psalm 24. It is worth remembering that the
אלהי יעקב, whose sanctuary was in Bethel, is now present in Jerusalem.

By means of the diaeretic סלה (cf. Intro. §4, No. 13) in MT the "Torah
liturgy" (vv. 3-6) is separated from the liturgical antiphony in vv. 7-10.

[24:7-10] The cultic ceremonial of the entrance of the ark into the sanctuary begins with an address in song to the gates (of the sacred area or of the temple?). On the address of a portal, cf. Isa. 14:31. With the ark the "righteous congregation" (cf. vv. 3-6) desires to pass through the gates into the sanctuary (Pss. 100:4; 118:19f.; Isa. 26:2). Yahweh as the entering king is introduced as the uplifted God (Isa. 6:1). Of course, the specific concept to be associated with the word ראשיכם ("your heads") cannot be ascertained. Is it that of the upper wings of the gates or the horizontal crossbeam of the gate area? The "venerable" (so Gunkel for עולם) gates are to grant entrance to the great king. We will, however, take into consideration that the cultic conceptions associated with "King" Yahweh cannot simply be identified with earthly dimensions. The "king of glory" (cf. Ps. 29:9f.) disperses all limited perceptions (Isa. 6:1); in its powerful dimensions it reaches all the way to heaven. In the cultic attitude of the ancient Near East the earthly and the heavenly sanctuary are always viewed together. Therefore we could be right in asking whether the words פתחי עולם are not intended to refer to the "gates of heaven" (in that case, עולם would have to be understood in the sense of "eternal," "heavenly"). Still, in the sanctuary the dimensions of the area are transcended and burst apart (cf. M. Metzger, "Himmlische und irdische Wohnstatt Jahwes," *Ugarit-Forschungen* 2 [1970], 145). To put it more precisely, "The God who in this place is (invisibly) enthroned bursts out of the confines of the area. This should hardly be understood as a spiritualized conception of God but is rather to be attributed to a religious understanding of space, for which in respect to the temple (the hill of God), the place of God's presence, the categories earthly and heavenly are set aside, because the sanctuary represents the entire cosmos" (J. Maier, *Das irdische Ladeheiligtum* [1965], 66f.). And this very representation of the entire cosmos is clearly expressed in Ps. 24:1f. Therefore we will also have to think of the cosmic breadth of the advent of God. It is not only Ugaritic parallels that allow us to gain a similar understanding. Also the Egyptian cultus reveals that kind of cultic-cosmic relations.

At the opening of the sanctuary in the Egyptian worship they sing, "The gates of heaven are being opened, the portals of the earth are laid open. The gates of heaven are being opened, and the nine gods are displayed in radiance . . ." (cf. K. Möhlenbrink, *Der Tempel Salomos*, BWANT 4, 7 [1932], 135; H. Schrade, *Der verborgene Gott— Gottesbild und Gottesvorstellung in Israel und im alten Orient* [1949], 50). Also cf. Gen. 28:17.

The מלך הכבוד wishes to enter (בוה). כבוד is "a characteristic of royal power and royal splendor and then denotes the king's majesty" (thus, with reference to Esther 1:4 and Ps. 21:5, B. Stein, *Der Begriff keᵇod Jahwe und seine Bedeutung für die alttestamentliche Gotteserkenntnis* [1939], 107). Cf. with the כבוד emanating from King Yahweh: Isa. 6:3.

From the inner recesses of the sanctuary the liturgical question is addressed to those seeking entrance: "Who is the king of glory?" The answer given in reply goes back to terms and conceptions that refer to the ark as the palladium of holy war. The name of the "war hero" Yahweh is used as the "password for admittance." The traditions of the ark sanctuary Shiloh are appealed to (1 Sam. 4:4; 17:45). Here we clearly see how significant those events which are described in the story of the journey of the ark from Shiloh to Jerusalem are for the cultic act of the entrance (cf. L. Rost, *Die Überlieferung von der Thronnachfolge Davids*, BWANT 3, 6 [1926], 4ff.). The "password for admittance'' emphasizes decisively that the entering God is the God of the old Israelite sanctuary at Shiloh, the ''war hero'' יהוה צבאות (v. 10). מלך הכבוד—that is a formal, hymnic title which does not open the portals of the sanctuary and therefore does not really lie at the center of the cultic event. Decisive are the names of the old Israelite God of the ark. Therefore Psalm 24 must deal with a worship act that reflects events of the time of David, i.e., of the period when for the first time amphictyonic traditions of the ark were transmitted to the area of Jebusite cultic traditions (cf. the comment on Psalm 132). The מלך הכבוד, the ''king of glory'' (Ps. 29:9f.), who is revered in Jerusalem since David's time—he is יהוה צבאות who comes from Shiloh (2 Samuel 6). On המלך יהוה צבאית, cf. Isa. 6:5. On particular details in vv. 7-10, the following references are recommended: on the epithet ''king'' as applied to Yahweh, see above, Intro. §10, 1; on worship on Zion, see above, Intro. §10,1 (H.-J. Kraus, *Worship in Israel*, 1964).

Purpose and Thrust

The liturgy of Psalm 24 celebrates Yahweh Sebaoth, the God of Israel, who is entering the sanctuary. He is Lord of the world (v. 1), creator of the world (v. 2), and ''king of glory'' (vv. 7, 10). He is accompanied and surrounded by the ''righteous'' (vv. 3-5), by the ''true Israel'' (v. 6). According to Psalm 24, the center of the entire creation is the place where Yahweh appears in his congregation and where he is present.

When Psalm 24 is read and adopted as an Advent psalm in the church of Jesus Christ, then the final valid element of the hymnic message of the OT liturgy has thereby correctly been recognized. The God who emerges from the hiddenness of ancient Israelite history comes forth into the brilliance of universal glorification. In the fulfillment of the NT, God himself in Jesus of Nazareth comes forth from the hiddenness of the history of Israel into the midst of his people and into the midst of the world. He is the king to whom all power in heaven and on earth is given. ''Already because at the coming of Christ that visible shadow vanished, it is not surprising that on Mount Zion no temple is seen whose extent takes in the whole earth'' (Calvin).

Psalm 25

Prayer for Forgiveness and Gracious Guidance

Literature

H. Möller, "Strophenbau der Psalmen," *ZAW* 50 (1932) 240-256. N. H. Ridderbos, "The Psalms: Style, Figures and Structure," *OTS* 13 (1963) 61ff. P. Vonck, "L'expression de confiance dans le Psautier," *Message and Mission: Publications de l'Université Lovanium de Kishasa* (1969). L. Ruppert, "Psalm 25 und die Grenze der kultorientierten Psalmenexegese," *ZAW* 84 (1972) 576-582.

Text

Of David.

25:1 In you 'is my hope,'[a] O Yahweh,
I lift up my soul 'to my God.'[b]

2 ' ' In you I trust, let me not be put to shame,
let not my enemies triumph over[c] me!

3 No one who waits for you will be put to shame;
but the faithless must 'go away'[d] empty-handed.

4 O Yahweh, let me know your ways,
teach me your pathways![e]

5 Let me walk in your faithfulness, ' '[f]
for you are the God of my salvation,
'and'[g] my hope is in you daily.

6 Be mindful of your mercy, O Yahweh,
and of your favor, for they are from eternity!

7 Remember not the sins of my youth, ' '[h]
but remember me according to your mercy—
for the sake of your goodness, O Yahweh![i]

8 Yahweh is kind-hearted and faithful,
' '[j] he shows the sinner the way.

9 He lets the oppressed come into judgment
and teaches his way to the oppressed.

317

10 All 'his'ᵏ pathways are kindness and faithfulness
    to them who keep his covenant and his testimonies.
11 For the sake of your name, O Yahweh,
    forgive my debt, for it is large!
12 Who is the man that fears Yahweh?
    To him he shows the way he should choose.
13 His soul will pass its time in prosperity,
    and his seed will inherit the land.
14 Yahweh's counsel (comes) to those who fear him,
    and his covenant (becomes known), to teach them.
15 My eyes always look to Yahweh,
    for he will pluck my feet out of the net.
16 Turn to me and be merciful to me,
    for I am lonely and miserable.
17 'Make wide'ˡ the straits of my heart,
    (and) lead me out of distress!
18 'Have regard'ᵐ for my misery and my trouble
    and forgive all my sins!
19 Just observe how numerous my enemies are,
    how they hate me with wicked hatred!
20 Protect my soul and rescue me,
    let me not be put to shame, for I trust in you!
21 May innocence and uprightness protect me,
    for I wait for you, 'O Yahweh'!ⁿ
22 Redeem Israel, O God,
    from all its afflictions!

1a V. 1 lacks the parallel half-verse. As a complement, אלהי is to be added from v. 2a. This procedure is suggested by Gk (there ὁ θεός μου is given at the end of v. 1). But also the alphabetical series of the acrostic pattern demands that v. 2 begin with ב. In the reconstruction of a parallel member we could be guided by F. Buhl, insert the verb קוה corresponding to v. 3a, and so read as follows: אליך קויתי יהוה נפשי אשא אל־אלהי.
b אלהי has been adopted in v. 1. Cf. note **a**.
2c. The combination of the verb עלץ with ל is unusual. But a correction to לעג (Gk, καταγελασάτωσάς μου) is not necessary on that account.
3d Difficulties arise from the peculiar phrase הבוגדים ריקם. יבשו in v. 2b, probably under the influence of יבשו in v. 2a, has become a mistaken dittography. Here the original may have been יָשֻׁבּוּ (Ehrlich, Buhl). Cf. 2 Sam. 1:22; Isa. 55:11; Jer. 50:9.
4e Gk [read] וְאָרְחוֹתֶיךָ.
5f ולמדני leaves the impression of extending the meter unduly and causing it to drag. Very likely the word was taken over from v. 4b by a slip of the eye.
g Following 4 Mss, Gk, and S, we must have regard for the alphabetical sequence at the beginning of each line of the song and read וְאוֹתְךָ.
7h The first half-verse is unduly extended by ופשעי. We will have to consider the word an addition (cf. S).
i The coordination of the half-verses in v. 7 is obviously disturbed. In keeping with the context and the sentence structure, v. 7b belongs to v. 7a as a parallel half-verse. It is conceivable that v. 7a once was the complement of the isolated half-verse in v. 5b and so in the course of the transmission of the text was transferred to a wrong place.
8j If we take into consideration the predominant 3 + 3 meter, על־כן could be a simplifying transitional particle which only later took its place in the sentence structure.
10k In the double triple meter that is determinative for Psalm 25, יהוה could be a complement explaining the suffix in the original אָרְחֹתָיו.
17l MT ("The straits of my heart make wide") makes no sense. The ending ו in הרחיבו should be read as the copula for ממצוקותי. In that case, we would have to read הַרְחֵב, "make wide" . . . "and" . . . .

18m Since the line beginning with ק must follow in v. 18, we had best read קְשֹׁר (or קְרֵה, קְחָה קֶדֶם) instead of ראה (cf. v. 19).
21n Following Gk, we should add יהוה for the sake of the meter.

Form

Psalm 25 is one of the acrostic psalms, i.e., that as to form are distinguished by the artificial device of lines beginning with successive letters of the alphabet. For these alphabetically arranged songs, cf. the discussion of Psalm 9/10, under "Form." Textual criticism (see above) is able to suggest corrections where the alphabetical sequence has been blurred by the transmission of the text and the attending harm. In v. 2 the line begins with בך (אלהי is to be taken with v. 1, as in Gk). Verse 5b would have to begin with the word ואותך and as a monostich very likely would have to be completed by means of v. 7aβ. In v. 18, the ק-line, קְשֹׁר would very likely have to be read instead of ראה. Verse 22 departs from the alphabetical arrangement. This may be an addition by a later hand. The double triple meter predominates. Changes for the sake of the meter stabilize the meter in vv. 8, 10, and 21. Only in vv. 15 (3 + 4) and 22 (3 + 2) will we have to abandon the idea of an assimilation of the meter.

The acrostic technique results in an undeniable rigidity of form. "The author lets the letter be his master," writes H. Gunkel. Repetitions are not infrequent, and a clear organization cannot be undertaken because of the lack of progress in thought. Nevertheless, a number of basic statements in a form-critical analysis can be made. We could classify the psalm in the form group "prayer songs" (תפלה). See above, Intro. §6, 2. The traditional conception that we have here an "individual's lament" (Gunkel and Begrich, *EinlPs* §6) must be abandoned. The psalm does not contain laments. On the contrary, the prayer song is preponderantly characterized by petitions and expressions of trust (P. Vonck). Verses 8ff. have the form of a confession, or a decidedly didactic message. Also vv. 12 and 13 show statements which are very close to the wisdom type of didactic poems (see above, Intro. §6, 5). Accordingly, the analysis of the forms confirms the conclusions of an unevenness of form reached at the beginning.

Setting

The situation in which Psalm 25 was sung can hardly be determined precisely. When A. Weiser thinks, for example, of a "cult of the covenant festival," his statement exaggerates the influence of vv. 10, 13, and 15. This psalm, to be dated relatively late (perhaps in postexilic times) because of linguistic and formal considerations, affords no indications of a precise determination of setting. A fusion of various traditions and conceptions of the situation has prevailed. The form analysis already makes this clear. Still, two observations should be considered especially. (1) The petitioner knows that he is surrounded by numerous enemies. He is persecuted with "wicked hatred" (v. 19); vv. 2, 15, and 17 must also presuppose this condition. Thus the singer of our psalm employs the conceptions, concepts, and statements of one who is persecuted, or "one falsely accused" (v. 21). On this, cf. H. Schmidt, *Das Gebet der Angeklagten im Alten Testament,* 49 (1928); W. Beyerlin, *Die Rettung der Bedrängten in den Feindpsalmen der Einzelnen auf institutionelle Zusammenhänge untersucht,* FRLANT 99 (1970). (2) The petitioner of the psalm knows he is guilty (v. 8). He prays for the forgiveness of his sins (vv. 7, 11); he reflects concerning the "God-fearing person" (v. 12) and the "righteous one," whom

Yahweh teaches and rescues. The words and conceptions of the Torah psalms suggest themselves (cf. the comments on Psalms 1; 19B; 119). But it would be absolutely out of place to assign to a cultic situation a psalm that points to a later (postexilic) time. In fact, here "the limits of psalm exegesis that are cultically oriented" are distinctly discernible (L. Ruppert). These limits begin "where the living prayer of Israel, at home in the cultic institutions or at least rooted in them, is detached by a literature of prayer" (Ruppert, 582). Thus, with Ruppert, we should establish the following facts: (1) Psalm 25 is a literary composition; (2) Psalm 25 points to a wealth of standard prayer formulas; (3) thematically Psalm 25 is determined largely by חכמה (578). Thus we have before us the artistically elaborated form of a prayer formulary.

Commentary

[**Title**] On לדוד, see above, Intro. §4, No. 2.

[**25:1-2**] In search of help in prayer, the petitioner of Psalm 25 turns to Yahweh. On נשא נפש, cf. Pss. 24:4; 86:4; 143:8. The purpose of the pleading and petitioning is the revelation of Yahweh's דרך (also cf. Ps. 143:8) and the bestowal of divine help in dire need (v. 19). On אלהי, cf. O. Eissfeld, " 'Mein Gott' im Alten Testament," *ZAW* 61 (1945/48) 3-16. The turn toward Yahweh takes place in trust (בטח). בטח denotes an attitude which is confident that all prayers will be answered (Ps. 22:5). To trust in Yahweh at the same time implies the earnest petition that the petitioner will not "be put to shame." The enemies of the petitioner lie in wait, hoping that he will not find help with Yahweh. The conceptions of the lament of one "innocently persecuted" can here be seen clearly. On עלץ ל, cf. שמח ל in Ps. 30:1.

[**25:3**] While בטח implies the motive of the certainty of fulfillment, קוה contains the conception of "restless attention to someone or something." On קוה, cf. C. Westermann, "Das Hoffen im Alten Testament," *Theologia viatorum* (1952). The trusting soul is confident that no one who waits intently for Yahweh's help will be put to shame. But the faithless must "go away empty-handed." בגד is a telling concept for faithless, traitorous defection. If the correction ישבו ריקם is right (see above), then this phrase descriptively clearly expresses the meaning of the verb בוש. As an expression of trust, v. 3 has confessional character.

[**25:4-5**] The psalmsinger pleads with Yahweh for a communication of his ways. The term דרך has a similar, almost parallel, history as the term תורה. דרך, too, is originally probably the "instruction" or the "direction" that is given upon request by the priest or the cultic prophet. דרך—that is the דבר that produces a fully authoritative clarification in ethical questions and opens up a new possibility of existence in dire distress (cf., for instance, Pss. 27:11; 16:11). But then דרך, singular or plural, has predominantly become a standing concept to designate the divine instruction of the תורה. The expressions of the will of the תורה are "Yahweh's ways" that he lets human beings know. In the Deuteronomistic use of language, this understanding of דרך is developed in a special way. Cf. Deut. 9:12, 16; 1 Kings 2:3; 3:14; Jer. 5:4. Finally, the concept דרך entered into the area of the teaching of wisdom (Prov. 3:17; 4:11; Ps. 1:6). Cf. A. Kuschke, "Die Menschenwege und der Weg Gottes im Alten Testament,"

Studia Theologica 5, 2 (1951) 106-118. In Psalm 25 דרך is the helpful, directive expression of the will of Yahweh, which is both a personal answer to him who petitions and also (in a supraindividual sense) a proclamation of the will to the congregation. With this explanation the real problem of Psalm 25 is indicated. The prayer song is no longer directed strictly to a single answer of God that is expected by the petitioner and applies only to him. The communication of the דרך is rather—in spite of all personal expectation—taken into the proclamation of the תורה. To be sure, the petitioner calls Yahweh אלהי ישעי (v. 5), but the act of the conveyance of salvation is nevertheless embedded in an event of the community (vv. 8ff.).

[25:6-7] In vv. 6 and 7 a prayer for forgiveness of sin comes into prominence. The petitioner appeals to Yahweh's mercy and goodness, which is proved to be מעולם. But forgiveness means no longer to remember the sins of youth. On the term חטאות נעורי, cf. Job 13:26. For the terminology and conceptions of the "forgiving" of Yahweh, see J. J. Stamm, *Erlösung und Vergebung im Alten Testament* (1940) 130. In v. 11 the petition for forgiveness of the debt is resumed, but for the first it is interrupted by statements about Yahweh that have a hymnic tone.

[25:8-10] That Yahweh is טוב־וישר is after v. 8 indicated in that he shows sinners the way. In other words, Yahweh comes to the "sinners' " help. Gk recommends a weakening reading חֹטְאִים which avoids the undoubtedly trouble-some fact that the חַטָּאִים (so MT; "the persistent sinners") perceive Yahweh's guidance. Verse 9 develops Yahweh's deed. God lets the ענוים enter במשפט. On ענוים, see above, Intro. §10, 3. משפט is either (as in Ps. 1:5) a spiritualizing remembrance of the sacral-legal institution of the Torah liturgy (cf. the comment on Psalm 15) or a reference to the divine judgment that is by Yahweh opened up as the new דרך (as the oracle of salvation) to the "poor" man, i.e., here the "falsely accused" person. Concrete conceptions of situations are toned down in v. 8. The "ways" that Yahweh shows are glorified in v. 10. They are in essence חסד ואמת, and they convey חסד ואמת to those who keep his covenant and his testimonies.[1] On חסד, cf. the comment on Ps. 5:7.

[25:11] Following the hymnic expositions in vv. 8-10, the phrase למען־שמך is to be applied to Yahweh's work of revelation. But this work aims at the glory of God. The psalmsinger takes up this situation with his petition (O. Grether, *Name und Wort Gottes im Alten Testament*, BZAW 64 [1934], 53). For the sake of his goodness revealed in his work of revelation, Yahweh is to intervene and forgive the huge debt.

[25:12-13] The question in v. 12 could be a late imitation of that question which in earlier times was expressed in the liturgy of the gate (Pss. 15:1; 24:3). Then Psalm 25 would take its place among the statements which describe the צדיק in the typical and exemplary sense (cf. the comment on Psalm 1). In Psalm 25, however, the term ירא יהוה takes the place of צדיק and the word דרך takes the

---

1. "The greatest of promises is most sweetly contained in this little verse: 'All the pathways of the Lord are mercy and truth to those who keep his covenant and his testimonies,' that is, God truly is merciful and kind toward his church, which embraces the Word transmitted by him and in the faith of that Word prays to him and worships him" (Melanchthon, on Ps. 25:10 [CR 13, 1055]).

place of the word תורה. The fact that "he who fears God" can *choose* the "way" is significant for the supraindividual form of the דרך. He who in obedience follows the indicated and chosen way will "spend the night" (תלין) in the realm of that which is good, i.e., he will at all times spend his time in good fortune (cf. Ps. 1:3). Also his descendants will be blessed and "possess the land" (cf. Matt. 5:5). The essence of the blessing is the perpetual enjoyment of the good yield of the land.

[25:14] Verse 14 contains a statement that is like a confession. Characteristic is the parallelism בריתו—סוד יהוה. Both concepts are a part of the effective realm of the revelation of the דרך. סוד therefore has the meaning "the decree to show the way" (cf. Amos 3:7). And ברית is the "revelation of the intention of the covenant of God" (cf. v. 10). In revelation, סוד and ברית come to human beings. לְ shows the direction: BrSynt §107a. In GesK 114i, v. 14b is therefore conceived of as follows: *et foedus suum manifestaturus est eis* ("and his covenant he is about to reveal to them").

[25:15] In v. 15 the psalmsinger confesses his trust in Yahweh. To him he looks up constantly (cf. also the comment on Ps. 16:8). And this looking up is connected with the hope that Yahweh will free the feet of him who is being persecuted. רשת here is a metaphor from the area of the chase (G. Dalman, *AuS* 6:335).

[25:16-21] At v. 16 the expressive petitions again resume. The petitioner takes shelter under the old legal privilege of "the poor" (see above, Intro. §10, 3). He thinks of himself as thrust into utter loneliness (H. Seidel, *Das Erlebnis der Einsamkeit im Alten Testament,* Theol. Arbeiten 29 [1969]). In this connection the petitions of v. 17 are revealing and graphic. In distress one's innermost being (לבב) is "in straits" (צר—צרר). By means of Yahweh's intervention, a widening, a liberation, is to take place. "As affliction is the narrow place that oppresses us and makes us sad, so God's help is the wide open space that makes us free and joyful" (Luther). "Make wide the straits of my heart!" "Here the pains of angina and its anxiety coincide. But in Ps. 119:32 talk about the 'enlarging' of the heart, that is to say, the relieving of its cramp, has already left the idea of physical recovery far behind . . ." (H. W. Wolff, *Anthropology of the OT* [1974], 44). Of course, there is the question whether this way of thinking established in Psalm 119:32 should be taken for granted already in Psalm 25. The petition in v. 17 surely has the meaning: "Set me free!" "Free me!" The afflictions that beset the petitioner are in v. 18 described with the terms עמל, עני, and חטאות. And in v. 19 the multiplicity of the enemies is emphasized. Verses 18 and 19 want to move Yahweh to intervene. With v. 20 the psalmsinger returns to the statements of v. 1, but he employs new concepts. This pleonasm is significant for the late date of origin of the psalm. Use is made of a wealth of previously existing traditional and formulary expressions. Finally, it is worth noting that in v. 21 the psalmist once more prays specifically for תם־וישר. The guilt should depart. In its stead the powers of a new life should enter.

[25:22] Whether v. 22 is a later addition we cannot say with certainty. In any case, at the close of the psalm that invariably had reference to the community of

"Israel" there is a prayer for the redemption and liberation of the entire people of God.

Purpose and Thrust

Insurmountable barriers stand in the way of a critical analysis of the terms, phrases, and conceptions of Psalm 25. This prayer song is overloaded with the most varied elements that are closely intertwined in severely limited space. In a concluding consideration of the whole that points up the essential message of the psalm, the interpreter will have to confine himself to the eminent, leading terms. In the first place the word דֶּרֶךְ will have to be emphasized here. A man threatened by enemies, whose way of life so far has been marked by "sins of youth," by failures (חטא), prays for forgiveness (vv. 7, 11, 18), for rescue (vv. 2, 15, 19f.), and, above all, for a new orientation of his life on Yahweh's "ways" (vv. 4, 5, 9, 12, 21). With these petitions the psalmsinger goes back to acts of rescue previously done by Yahweh (vv. 3, 6, 8, 9, 10, 14). The prayer has its proper place in the community—and that means in a community in which Yahweh's דֶּרֶךְ is proclaimed. The individual prayerfully and trustingly finds his place in this area. He waits "in hope" (קוה, vv. 1, 3, 5b, 21), in attentive expectation, for Yahweh to open up and show a "new way" in his existence. Psalm 25 is pervaded by a spirit of reversal. If we stay with the leading concepts, a clear picture will result, in spite of all the ramifications of the individual statements which are generally called for by the acrostic arrangement. H. Gunkel, however, judges that the psalm is "more a pious artistic exercise than a personal outpouring." But (1) with the help of the essential, leading terms, we must establish the fact that between "artistic exercise" and "personal outpouring" a clear kerygma is to be perceived from these statements. And (2) we must point out that the "personal outpouring" has been not so much overwhelmed by the "artistic exercise" as it has rather been expanded by the typical, exemplary, and tradition-filled statements.

Psalm 26

The Prayer and Confession
of One Oppressed, Though Innocent

Literature

H. Schmidt, *Das Gebet der Angeklagten im Alten Testament*, BZAW 49 (1928). E. Baumann, "Struktur-Untersuchungen im Psalter," *ZAW* 61 (1945/48) 114-176. L. A. Snijders, "Psaume 26 et l'innocence," *OTS* 13 (1963) 112-130. L. Wächter, "Drei umstrittene Psalmstellen (Ps 26,1; 30,8; 90,4-6)," *ZAW* 78 (1966) 61-68. M. Dahood, "Vocative *lamedh* in the Psalter," *VT* 16 (1966) 299-311. W. Beyerlin, *Die Rettung der Bedrängten in den Feindpsalmen der Einzelnen auf institutionelle Zusammenhänge untersucht*, FRLANT 99 (1970) 117-122.

Text

Of David.
26:1 Vindicate me, O Yahweh,[a]
    for I have walked blamelessly
    and have trusted in Yahweh—without wavering.
  2 Prove me, O Yahweh, and try me,
    test[b] my reins and my heart.
  3 For your goodness was before my eyes,
    and in your truth I walked.
  4 I did not sit with deceitful men,
    nor did I consort with the insidious.[c]
  5 I avoided the assembly of the wicked,
    and I did not sit with the wicked.
  6 I wash my hands in innocence
    and walk about your altar, ' '[d]
  7 to proclaim[e] the song of thanksgiving aloud,
    to tell of all your wonders.
  8 ' '[f] I love the abode of your house,
    the place where your glory dwells.
  9 Do not snatch my soul away with the sinners,
    and my life with murderers,

10 to whose hands iniquity sticks,
   whose right hand is filled with bribery.
11 But I walk in innocence.
   Redeem me[g] and be merciful to me!
12 My foot rests on even ground,
   in the assemblies I praise you,[h] O Yahweh.

1a This verse is undoubtedly more than full and, in the form before us in the MT, its exact meter is beyond our grasp. It has therefore been suggested either to eliminate שפטני יהוה כי or—perhaps even better—to remove וביהוה בטחתי. Both encroachments on the text remain problematical. For an attempt at elucidation and reconstruction, cf. L. Wächter. But it will remain difficult adequately to solve the problems present in v. 1.
2b *Ketīb:* צרוֹפָה; *Qere:* צָרְפָה.
4c A correction (מְעַוְּלִים, Ps. 71:4, instead of נעלמים) is not mandatory. נעלמים are the "hidden ones," i.e., those in concealment, the treacherous ones (KBL, 709).
6d The appended address יהוה should be viewed as an addition.
7e The Mss, Gk, and S read לִשְׁמֹעַ, but the MT is to be preferred.
8f The address יהוה is obviously an addition to the original shape of the text.
11g Gk adds יהוה and could thus contribute to filling out the double triple meter.
12h Gk: אֲבָרֶכְךָ.

Form

In the meter, only v. 1 presents difficulties. H. Gunkel reads (with omission of ביהוה בטחתי) $2 + 2 + 2$. But this metrical solution is unsatisfactory. Also E. Baumann's attempt to take שפטני as a marginal cue and to rearrange the text (sequence: vv. 2, 12, 1) does not help to clear things up. The trouble spots of the text will have to be taken over without interference. Otherwise the psalm displays a series of clear double triple meters. Only in v. 11 we would have to read $3 + 2$—unless also in this verse, by adding the address יהוה, a $3 + 3$ meter could be reconstructed, following Gk.

   Up to the present time Psalm 26 has generally been listed among the "laments of the individual" (especially by Gunkel and Begrich, *EinlPs* §6). But this explanation will finally have to be given up (cf. W. Beyerlin, 121). In the psalm there is no trace of lament. Rather, Psalm 26 will have to be classified in the broad framework of songs of prayer. For the תפלה, see above, Intro. §6, 2. The addresses and petitions in vv. 2 and 9 set the pattern for the whole picture. And yet, the analysis of the setting will more precisely show that Psalm 26 is the prayer song, or the appeal, of one who is accused (see above, Intro. §6, 2bβ). The protestations of innocence (vv. 4ff., 11) belong to this context. He who is oppressed by enemies looks to the future and awaits the moment when he will be able to intone the song of thanksgiving and to tell of Yahweh's wonders (v. 7). See above, Intro. §6, 2aγ. Very likely we will be able to remove v. 12 and declare it to be a part of the *todah* (see below). Or is this a matter of the certainty of being heard?

Setting

The situation in which Psalm 26 was sung is easily reconstructed. While H. Gunkel still was of the opinion that this lament was sung by one in serious sickness (cf. v. 9), H. Schmidt already was able to show a new way. Psalm 26 belongs among the prayers of one who is falsely accused (H. Schmidt, *Das Gebet der Angeklagten im Alten Testament,* BZAW 49 [1928] 12). Pursued by accusers, the petitioner flees to the sanctuary, finds asylum there, affirms his innocence, and appeals to Yahweh as the righteous judge. This is the situation that must be presupposed. Such a procedure takes place in the sanctuary in Jerusalem again and again. In 1 Kings 8:31ff. we read: ''If a man sins against his neighbor and is made to take an oath, and comes and swears his oath before thine altar in this house, then hear thou in heaven, and act, and judge thy servants, condemning the guilty by bringing his conduct upon his own head, and vindicating the righteous by rewarding him according to his righteousness.'' In connection with this exposition of ''Solomon's prayer,'' we should recognize in Psalm 26 the following procedures: (1) the appeal to Yahweh, the judge, by one who is accused, though innocent (vv. 1-2, 9-11); (2) the oath of cleansing (1 Kings 8:31) נשׂא־בו אלה, Ps. 26:4ff.; (3) the rite of a declaration of innocence before the altar (v. 6); (4) the expectation that Yahweh will declare as צדיק (1 Kings 8:32) such an accused person in accordance with his צדקה. For details, cf. the comments on Psalm 7.

The institutional connections are more precisely delineated in the monograph by W. Beyerlin (117). Accordingly, the subject of Psalm 26 is basically that an accused person is to be rescued from the oppression of enemies and persecutors by means of a verdict of divine judgment. The afflicted person is already present in the area of the sanctuary. He affirms his innocence, submits himself to the examination by Yahweh, and appeals to his righteous judgment. Here it would be conceivable ''that the petitioner of Psalm 26 offers resistance to the charge of apostasy (from Yahweh)'' (for the reasons, see W. Beyerlin, 118f.). Concerning the situation: ''Psalm 26 has been spoken in a relatively early stage of the procedure of divine judgment; the petitioner has already been received in the temple area, but without any sign that the protective effect of the sacred precinct is in play. The court inquiry is just getting started. Yahweh's epiphany for the act of judgment is still awaited'' (W. Beyerlin, 120). We may assume that the psalm was used as a prayer formula. Its oldest form points to the context of the (preexilic?) temple cultus. Closer than that we cannot get.

Commentary

[Title] On לדוד, see above, Intro. §4, No. 2.

[26:1] שפטני יהוה—with this plea, a persecuted and falsely accused person appeals to Yahweh's legal aid (cf. Pss. 7:8; 35:24; 43:1). The procedure of the appeal is very realistically described in Psalm 7 (cf. the comment on Psalm 7). The oppressed person affirms his innocence. תם designates the unsullied, pure attitude of the צדיק, who lives according to the covenant ordinances of Yahweh (cf. Pss. 7:8; 25:21; 41:12; 101:2). In Ps. 7:8 the term צדק is used parallel to תם. The petitioner measures his life (as he will show especially in vv. 3ff.) against the archetypal model of the צדיק. His appeal for legal aid originates in his trust (בטח) in Yahweh—a trust ''without wavering.'' לא אמעד is to be understood as a verbal sentence of circumstance, GesK §156g.

[26:2] Now the petitioner, praying for the legal aid of Yahweh, presents himself for examination by God. For this kind of ''proving,'' cf. Pss. 11:5; 17:3; 66:10; 139:23. From Ps. 17:3 we learn that the innocently accused laid his innermost heart bare to the scrutiny of God ''at night,'' (very likely at a temple incubation). The verbs צרף—נסה—בחן point to an activity that seeks to ascertain the ''true content.'' H. Gunkel reminds us of the tests of the "coin inspectors," which were originally designated by these verbs (cf., e.g., Jer. 6:27). Perhaps it would be even better to refer to the smelting of metals (Ps. 66:10). The innermost stirrings and movements of the human heart are "proved" by Yahweh for צרף and צדק. On כליות ולב, cf. Ps. 7:9; Jer. 11:20.

[26:3] We could either interpret v. 3 in connection with vv. 1-2 and, with regard to its meaning, set it alongside of ביהוה בטחתי, or—and this possibility would perhaps be preferable—v. 3 could also already be a component of the oath of cleansing that clearly emerges in vv. 4-5. In that case, v. 3 would, as it were, touch the positive side of the archetypal version of the צדיק, while vv. 4-5 present the negative side. In any case, the petitioner measures his life and his attitude (cf. the comment on Psalm 1) in comparison with the exemplary archetype of the צדיק. The "goodness" of Yahweh stood before him. He walked in Yahweh's "truth." On חסד as the merciful demeanor which characterizes Yawheh's loving attachment to his servant, cf. M. Buber, *Der Glaube der Propheten* (1950) 164; N. Glueck, *Das Wort* חסד *im alttestamentlichen Sprachgebrauch* (1927); and H. J. Stoebe, "Die Bedeutung des Wortes *häsäd* im Alten Testament," *VT* 2 (1952) 224-254. Also cf. *THAT* 1:600ff.; additional bibliography there. But how can Yahweh's חסד be "before the eyes" of anyone? What is the basic conception here? As a parallel we could adduce a passage such as Ps. 16:8. Does the gracious covenant-faithfulness of Yahweh reveal itself in a theophany? Does the petitioner refer to the occurrence of a manifestation of Yahweh's חסד that took place in worship? But "to walk" in Yahweh's אמת here surely means to live in the constant, trustworthy bestowal of the gracious covenant-faithfulness of God. חסד is experienced in the act of receiving attention; אמת provides the constancy and the permanence of the gracious demeanor of Yahweh.

[26:4-5] As v. 3 testifies positively to the manner of life of the accused, so vv. 4-5 delineate in negations the conscientious abstention from all associations of evil. The catalog reminds us vividly of the characteristics of the צדיק in Ps. 1:1. In connection with the terms מתי־שוא (cf. Job 11:11) and נעלמים, we could think of conjurors—of sinister manipulations, such as are condemned in Deut. 18:10ff. Has the petitioner of Psalm 26 been indicted with reference to misdeeds as a magician and a conjuror? Like a renunciation, v. 5 pronounces judgment on the "assembly of the wicked" and the רשעים. On רשע, cf. the comment on Ps. 1:4f. Worth noting are the tenses in vv. 4-5. In the first half-verse there is a perfect tense, in the second half-verse an imperfect tense. This change of tenses manifests the fact that the statements are true for all times. In general, the oath of purification in vv. 4-5 is formally not nearly so rigid and severely structured as in Ps. 7:3ff. It approaches the confessional statements concerning the features of the צדיק: cf. Ps. 18:25ff.

[26:6] In v. 6 the conventional rites at the oath of cleansing are discernible. Water as the symbol of that which is clean and cleansing washes the hands and serves as the proof of their cleanness (Ps. 24:4). On the usage, cf. Deut. 21:6; Ps. 73:13; Isa. 1:16; Matt. 27:24. The walk around the altar was very likely associated with petitions for being heard (1 Kings 18:26). According to 1 Kings

8:31, the oath of cleansing in the form of self-deprecation is presented at the altar.

[26:7] לֹ with an infinitive at the beginning of v. 7 points to the purpose of the petitions, affirmations, and rites: as one who has been heard and pardoned, the psalmsinger would like to present a תודה "with a loud voice" (בקול). The parallel half-verse makes the concept explicit. To intone a תודה means to recount the wondrous deeds of Yahweh (cf. Ps. 22:22ff.). Yahweh's helping intervention, with which he would declare the innocently accused צדיק (1 Kings 8:32), is considered a "wonder." נפלאות are the incomprehensible feats of God, before which human beings stand in awe (Pss. 9:1; 71:17; and often). The תודה contains thanksgiving for and acknowledgment of Yahweh's miracles of rescue.

[26:8] The love of the sacred place where the temple (בית) stands is expressed in v. 8. In the area of the sanctuary the one who was persecuted has found protection; here Yahweh's חסד has always come to him (v. 3); here he also now awaits the wonderful announcement of the helping presence of God. In a similar way Pss. 23:6; 27:4; and 84:1, 4 speak of the love for the sacred area of the *deus praesens*. The temple is the place where the כבוד of Yahweh "dwells" (שׁכן). The כבוד יהוה, a firmly entrenched element of tradition of the earliest times of Israel (G. von Rad, *OT Theol*, 1:239f.), at the moment of the ark's first entrance filled the temple (1 Kings 8:11).

[26:9] Verse 9 begins with a new petition. In the OT it is a certainty often stated that Yahweh destroys the "sinners" (Pss. 1:6; 5:6; 55:23; and often). Their death is a seal of a reprobate life. Now the psalmsinger prays that his נפשׁ (the vital powers in him) and his חיים may not be swept away with the חטאים and the אנשׁי דמים.

[26:10] His sole desire is by no means to perish in the same fateful death with those who have "unclean hands"! To the hands of sinners sticks זמה—defiling infamy. In the OT זמה is especially a significant term for sexual indecency: Lev. 18:17; 19:29; 20:14; Jer. 13:27; Ezek. 16:27; 22:9; 23:21; 24:13; and often. The payments of bribery fill the right hand of these (rich) people.

[26:11] The sharp contrast ואני introduces a sentence with which the petitioner once more emphasizes his own innocent walk. To this affirmation an immediate last cry for redemption and pardon is joined. פדה here has the meaning: to redeem from the fate of death of the חטאים (v. 9). On פדה, cf. J. J. Stamm, *Erlösen und Vergeben im Alten Testament* (1940) 14. The petition for legal assistance (v. 1) therefore ends in a plea for pardon.

[26:12] Verse 12 gives assurance of being heard. In v. 12a we have a metaphor that occurs rather frequently in the Psalms. The foot of him who has been freed and been pardoned by Yahweh "does not stumble," "is not caught in a net," "does not slip"—but stands firm (Pss. 31:8; 40:2; 56:13; 66:9; 121:3; and often). The psalmsinger is sure: he is standing on firm, even ground. Verse 12b announces the תודה (cf. v. 7). ברך has the meaning: "to acknowledge someone in his position of power and in his claim to greatness with all due formality" (F. Horst, "Segen und Segenshandlungen in der Bibel," *EvTh* 1/2 [1947], 31). The verb points to the hymnic intention of the תודה—but at the same time also to the public, formally executed glorification of Yahweh. The מקהלים are not the "choirs" (so H. Ewald), but the crowds that gather in the area of the sanctuary about the one who "tells of the wonders" of Yahweh "in the courts" (v. 7; Pss. 22:22; 35:18; 109:30; 116:14). Still, it would also be conceivable to separate v. 12 from the foregoing in such a way that this *todah* verse is an addition. In that case, the situation of a song of thanksgiving, hoped for in v. 7, has already begun. The petitioner would then already stand on a new foundation and would, as is customary in the *todah*, be praising (v. 12; cf. Ps. 22:5) the wonders of Yahweh (v 7.).

Purpose and Thrust

The petitioner of Psalm 26 and his very existence are under the threatening sign of accusation and indictment. If he has "unclean hands" and is guilty of association with the wicked—as it is obviously alleged—then his life is forfeit to the fate of the death of the חטאים (v. 9), then the bond between him and Yahweh is broken. In his struggle for proof of innocence, communion with God and the assurance of belonging to Yahweh are in the last analysis involved. Is this communion healthy and intact (תם), or is it actually broken and destroyed in a crucial area? Accused and charged, the psalmist rests his case with God. His prayers and cries are based on trust (בטח, v. 1), on the certainty of the "goodness" and "truth" of Yahweh (v. 3), and on his love for the place of God's presence (v. 8). The petitioner opens his innermost being before Yahweh, presents himself for a probing examination (v. 2), and affirms his life in the צדקה (vv. 4-5). He prays for God's wondrous intervention (v. 7) and for rescue from the fate of the death of the reprobate (v. 11). But in his praying, crying, and pleading, the psalmsinger hastens to get to the תודה—the glorification of Yahweh in a song of thanksgiving (vv. 7, 12). In this psalm the subject is not the self-qualification or haughty consciousness of innocence of one who wishes to justify himself (for the theological and history-of-religions problem of the so-called psalms of innocence, cf. the comment on Ps. 7:6-9). The psalm is prayed by one who is being tempted, accused. The covenant lies in the balance in the relation of the individual to Yahweh. Will the accused be separated from the חסד of Yahweh? The psalm is suffused with the confidence: Nothing can separate me from the goodness of God that shows itself active in the place of his presence (Rom. 8:33ff.). The church of the NT would take up and understand the psalm as looking to Jesus Christ—yet in such a way that in this struggle for righteousness none of the actuality of this life is removed. Cf. Psalm 5, "Purpose and Thrust."

Trust and Lament of One Persecuted, Though Innocent

Literature

I. W. Slotki, "The meter and Text of Psalm XXVII," *JTS* (1930) 387-395. H. Birkeland, "Zur Einheitlichkeit von Psalm 27," *ZAW* 51 (1933) 216-221. N. H. Snaith, *Five Psalms (1; 27; 51; 107; 34), A New Translation with Commentary and Questionary* (1938). M. Mannati, "*Tûb*-Yahwé en Psaume XXVII—La bonté de Yahwé, ou les biens de Yahwé?" *VT* 19 (1969) 488-493. J. Schreiner, "Vertrauen und Klage in höchster Bedrängnis. Meditation zu Psalm 27 (26), 1-14," *BiLe* 11 (1970) 41-45. W. Beyerlin, *Die Rettung der Bedrängten in den Feindpsalmen der Einzelnen auf institutionelle Zusammenhänge untersucht*, FRLANT 99 (1970) 122-129.

Text

Of David.

27:1 Yahweh is my light and my salvation,
whom could I fear?
Yahweh is my life's fortress of defense,
of whom could I be afraid?

2 If evildoers assault me,
to devour my flesh—
my opponents and my adversaries,
they must stumble and fall.

3 If an army camps against me,
my heart does not [a] fear.
Even if war is launched against me,
still I will be of good cheer.

4 One thing I have prayed for from Yahweh,[b]
that I desire:
to dwell in Yahweh's house
all the days of my life—[c]
to behold Yahweh's friendliness
and to look around in his temple.

5 For he hides me in 'his'ᵈ tabernacle
    in the day of adversity.
    He protects me in the shelter of his tent,
    to a high rock he lifts me up.
6 And now my head liftsᵉ itself up
    above my enemies round about.
    In his tent will I offer
    sacrifices, full of exultation.
    I will sing and make music to Yahweh.
        . . .
7 Hear, O Yahweh, I cry aloud,
    be merciful to me and hear me.
8 To you my heart holds up (your commandment):
    "Seek my countenance!"ᶠ
    Therefore I seek your countenance, O Yahweh.
9 Do not hide your countenance from me!
    Do not in anger turn away your servant!
    You are my help.
    Cast me not aside and do not forsake me,
    O God of my salvation!
10 Even if father and mother forsake me—
    Yahweh receives me.
11 Show me your way, O Yahweh!
    Lead me on an even way
    because of my enemies!
12 Do not give me upᵍ to the greed of my adversaries,
    for false witnesses rise up against me
    and 'rouse'ʰ injustice.
13 Alas, if I did not have the assurance to beholdⁱ
    the goodness of Yahweh in the land of the living—!
14 Hope in Yahweh!ⁱ
    Your heart be firm and strong!
    And hope in Yahweh!

3a 12 Mss: אִירָא.

4b A correction of מיהוה instead of מאת־יהוה is not mandatory.

c This five-pulse meter is by a number of commentators taken as a supplement from Ps. 26:6. That is quite probable. The line could as well be omitted (see below, "Commentary").

5d *Ketīb* in Gkᴮ, σ´: בְּסֻכָּה, "in a tabernacle" (cf. Ps. 31:20). But following *Qere* in α´, Jerome, T, S, we should read בְּסֻכּוֹ "in his tabernacle" (cf. Lam. 2:6; Ps. 76:2).

6e Gk, σ´, and Jerome have יָרִים, but we should read with the MT.

8f If we begin with the fact that in בקשׁו פני we have a command of God to which the petitioner appeals, then we have to assume that the introductory half-verse contains a shortened way of saying: "Toward you (לְ indicating direction: BrSynt §107a) my heart says"—i.e., "to you my heart holds up." We can hardly consider בקשׁו פני—as most often happens—a variant to v. 8b within the text and then take the first three words in v. 8a with v. 7. A correction often recommended is:

שׁמע־יהוה קולי   ביום אקרא
וחנני וענני אלי   כי מר לבי

(בקתו פני would then be eliminated as a variant reading). This conjecture has many problems, for it distorts the consonantal picture of the text and without good reason rids itself of a part of the sentence—בקשׁו פני.

12g Jerome here adds יהוה.

h Following S, we will do better to read וְיָפַח = וְיָפִיחוּ (cf. Prov. 6:19; 14:5, 25 ; 19:5, 9;

12:17). MT = "snorting" (?) from יִפַח?

13i לוּלֵא introduces a conditional clause and in most cases is used in the sentence structure "if not . . . then . . . ." But the apodasis can be omitted. In that case the sentence beginning with לוּלֵא takes on the character of a statement of certainty (Ges-K §159dd).

14j קַוֵּה אֶל־יְהוָה should not be eliminated. If there is an "oracle of salvation" (see below, "Form") in v. 14, then the striking statement should be retained under all circumstances (against all criticisms of form).

Form

The principal question in the form analysis of Psalm 27 comes up in view of the remarkable break that is to be noted between vv. 6 and 7. Whereas vv. 1-6 are replete with trust and confidence, vv. 7-14 have the sound of lament and prayer. The form-critical definition of "types" has so far come to the conclusion that vv. 1-6 contain an individual song of trust, while vv. 7-14 everywhere give evidence of elements of an individual lament. Finally, we should observe that v. 14 hardly represents self-encouragement on the part of the lamenting and praying singer, but must be understood as an "oracle of salvation" that comes to the psalmist (on "oracle of salvation," cf. J. Begrich, "Das priesterliche Heilsorakel," *ZAW* 52 [1934], 81-92). Of course, in many commentaries the two parts of Psalm 27 with their diversity of type lead to the conclusion that these are two completely different songs that have nothing to do with each other and therefore also have to be interpreted separately. Against this critical separation H. Schmidt has maintained, "The two psalms clarify each other. They are from the same hand and from the same situation." And F. Nötscher declares, "Both have in common the danger of malicious enmity, an unreserved trust in God, and a longing to be near God." These observations are appropriate but still lack precise definition.

We should begin by rejecting the usual type classification of Psalm 27 as an "individual lament." The psalm should preferably be assigned to the more general area of the form group of prayer songs (תְּפִלָּה; see above, Intro. §6, 2) and should more specifically be thought of as the prayer song of a person persecuted and accused (see above, Intro. §6 2bβ). Confession and confidence characterize the statements of vv. 1-6. Beginning with v. 7, the petitions emerge more and more clearly. An understanding of the psalm should be gained entirely from the situation in which it was spoken (see below). Individual parts should be interpreted from this vantage point; also the unity of the psalm will then reveal itself. But first the metrical problems must find an explanation compatible with the possibilities of comprehension. In respect to vv. 1-6, we have a fairly even picture here. The 3 + 2 meter dominates. Also in the second complete verse in v. 2 (after elimination of וְנָפְלוּ) a 3 + 2 meter may be assumed, while v. 6b shows a concluding 3-pulse meter without a parallel complement. In vv. 7-13 likewise the 3 + 2 meter sets the pace. Expections are represented by: v. 7 (4 + 3), v. 8b/9aα (3 + 3), v. 13 (3 + 3), and the isolated 3-pulse meter in v. 11aα and v. 12a. A text-critical correction for the sake of the meter would be possible in v. 9aα: by omitting the word מִמֶּנִּי the 3 + 2 meter could be reconstructed also here. For establishing the unity of Psalm 27, the predominant 3 + 2 meter is without doubt a not inconsiderable argument. Verse 14 should remain untouched by text-critical encroachments. The oracle of salvation addressed to the petitioner stands out in bold contrast both in content and form (2 + 3 + 2).

Setting

The really basic question, the answer to which can then also help to solve the problem of the unity of the psalm, is this: On the basis of which situation are the various parts and forms of Psalm 27 to be understood? How do these elements form a unit?

But first we must ask the question about the speaker or singer of the psalm. Who is involved here? H. Ewald thought of the leader of an army (v. 6). B. Duhm (quite fancifully) conjures up the picture of a high priest. And A. Bentzen (and with him the exegesis of the Psalms oriented toward the ideology of a king) points to a king (*Messias—Moses redivivus—Menschensohn*, ATANT [1948], 20). In all of these explanations, individual possible references of the psalm have been used with mistaken consequences for the whole. Clarity was first brought to the picture by H. Schmidt (*Das Gebet der Angeklagten im Alten Testament*, BZAW 49 [1928], 15f., 27f.). The psalm deals with a person who is persecuted and innocently accused (cf. vv. 2f., 12). He has taken refuge in the area of the temple (vv. 4f.) and is now sure that Yahweh protects him (v. 1). He is not afraid (vv. 2f.); on the contrary, he knows that he will present an offering of thanksgiving to Yahweh as the God of his rescue and his salvation (V. 6). The petition of vv. 7ff. has the character of an appeal. At the close another word of cheer is heard by which the petitioner is encouraged to cling to Yahweh (v. 14). Thus in the course of the psalm three phases are reflected: the trust of him who is threatened (vv. 1-6), the petition and appeal in the sanctuary (vv. 7-13), and the answer of God (v. 14), to which we can surely assign the significance of an oracle of salvation. The contours of the institutional connections have been sharpened by W. Beyerlin (122f.). In its entirety the psalm is a self-contained combination that was available as a formulary for people who were falsely accused and persecuted in Jerusalem. There are no specific clues for a dating. But it could easily be possible to assign Psalm 27 to preexilic times. In any case, nothing stands in the way of such an understanding. As a formulary the song of prayer later experienced phases of adaptations in which the development of the custom no longer played a role.

Commentary

[Title] On לדוד, see above, Intro. §4, No. 2.

[27:1] Verse 1 radiates confidence and confession. According to Isa. 10:17; 60:1, there was in Jerusalem a traditional designation of Yahweh as אור־ישראל. As in Ps. 23:1, this predicate for Yahweh (very likely current in the cultic tradition) is now taken up in the song of trust by an individual petitioner. אור (as the synonymous ישע shows) designates the God of salvation (Amos 5:18, 20; Mic. 7:8f.; Isa. 9:1; Pss. 97:11; 112:4). The confident appropriation of salvation authorizes the oppressed person to ask the bold question ממי אירא.[1] Yahweh is "my life's fortress of defense." On מעוז־חיי, cf. Sir. 51:2 (on מעוז: Pss. 28:8; 31:4; 37:39; 43:2; 52:7). The petitioner knows that he has been received into Yahweh's protective power of salvation; it embraces him even when he is far from the sanctuary—in the midst of oppression and danger.

---

1. "The term *light*, as is well known, is used in Scripture to denote joy, or the perfection of happiness. Further, to explain his meaning, he adds that God was *his salvation* and *the strength of his life*, as it was by his help that he felt himself safe, and free from the terrors of death. Certainly we find that all our fears arise from this source, that we are too anxious about our life, while we

[27:2-3] The enemies of the individual are called מרעים, צרי, and איבי (see above, Intro. §10, 4). Like wild animals, they want to devour the flesh of their prey (cf. Pss. 7:2; 17:12; Job 19:22). In the face of this threat before his very eyes, the singer is confident that the persecutors will stumble and fall. Another, still more powerful, picture of the threatening danger is drawn in v. 3. It is assumed that an army encampment is drawn up against the oppressed person and a war is started. But also here, in this case of the worst threat, the singer is confident (cf. Ps. 3:6). Verses 2 and 3 show us that the song of trust has recourse to descriptive pictures that portray the worst threats to life. From these metaphors no conclusion regarding the person of the psalmist can be drawn. He who is persecuted and falsely accused takes up extensive illustrations of ill will. From v. 2 to v. 3 we can observe a development that reaches even into the conceptual world of the king.

[27:4] In v. 4 the song of trust lets us hear the prayer of appeal which the petitioner in his distress uttered while still far away from the sanctuary. And now we should initially assume that the line שבתי בבית־יהוה כל־ימי חיי from Ps. 23:6 (''I will remain in Yahweh's house as long as I live'') has made its way in here; both syntactically and in terms of content it fits poorly into the context. The longing of the singer is to the effect that he wishes to see Yahweh's friendliness. On נעם, cf. Pss. 90:17; 135:3. What he means is God's loving way of turning to him for deliverance, to which he looks forward in vv. 1-6. Does this bestowal of deliverance take the form of a theophany, so that it could accordingly ''be viewed''? The OT petitioners in most cases expect an ''oracle of salvation'' (J. Begrich, ''Das priesterliche Heilsorakel,'' *ZAW* 52 [1934], 81-92). But what do the words in the parallel half-verse ולבקר בהיכלו mean? How are we to translate and understand the word בקר? No doubt, the meaning often adopted, ''to examine,'' ''to behold,'' or ''to enjoy'' (KBL on בקר) does not satisfy. We will have to think of a more specific, cultic activity (also cf. 2 Kings 16:15). Thus already S. Mowinckel represented the idea that בקר refers to witnessing the offering (*PsStud*, 1:146). In Nabatean, *mubaqqiru* is a term for a cultic officiant, probably one who witnesses the offering (C. F. Jean, *Dictionnaire des Inscriptions Sémitiques de l'Ouest* [1954]; *CIS* 2:2118, 2593, 2661, 2667ff.). It would therefore quite well be possible that בקר had the same meaning as צפה in Ps. 5:3 and Hab. 2:1. A concept might be involved which formerly described the detecting of an omen at an offering (cf. Gen. 15:11), a concept which, however, in the OT cultus for the most part described looking for and expecting a word of God, an ''oracle of salvation'' (cf. Hab. 2:1 and the comment on Ps. 5:3). At all events, the psalmsinger longs for a sign of salvation in the temple of Yahweh.

[27:5-6] The longing petition (v. 4) is accompanied by confident trust: Yahweh will hide me in his ''shelter'' and protect me in his ''tent'' (v. 5). סכה and אהל are archaizing metaphors that preserve an ancient Israelite tradition: once Yahweh dwelt in a ''tent'' (2 Sam. 7:2). This tradition was kept alive on Zion

---

acknowledge not that God is its preserver. We can have no tranquility, therefore, until we attain the persuasion that our life is sufficiently guarded, because it is protected by his omnipotent power. The interrogation, too, shows how highly David esteemed the Divine protection, as he thus boldly exults against all his enemies and dangers. Nor assuredly do we ascribe due homage to God, unless, trusting to his promised aid, we dare to boast of the certainty of our safety'' (Calvin, on Ps. 27:1, trans. Anderson [Grand Rapids: Eerdmans, 1949]).

by means of a cultic act (cf. Ps. 132:3f.). The temple (היכל, v. 4) plays the role of the אהל of the God of Israel (Ps. 15:1) and of the סכה (Ps. 76:2; Lam. 2:6). The psalmist knows that Yahweh will Zion''shelter'' and ''hide'' him at the place of Yahweh's presence. This is a clear reference to the function of the sacred area as asylum (cf. the comment on Ps. 15:1; 1 Kings 1:50; Exod. 21:12ff.). The persecuted and falsely accused finds refuge in the area of nearness to God. רעה יום is here evidently the name for the day on which the slanderous accusations against the one oppressed were made in the sacred area (v. 12). The psalmsinger has no doubt that in this critical hour he will not only be sheltered near Yahweh, but also ''be lifted up to a high rock.'' In the tradition of the sanctuary of Zion, צור is that mythically surrounded archetypal rock which the breaking waves of chaos could not reach (Is. 30:29; Pss. 28:1; 61:12).

Also in v. 6 the certainty is expressed that Yahweh will grant the persecuted person salvation and with it a triumph over all his enemies. The ''lifting up of the head above the enemies'' is a symbol for victorious exaltation (cf. Pss. 3:3; 83:3; 110:7). With the intention of a vow, the psalmsinger declares that he plans to present זבחי תרועה in Yahweh's ''tent,'' i.e., in Yahweh's temple. תרועה is the ''jubilation of the festival'' (cf. P. Humbert, *TEROU'A, Analyse d'un rite biblique* [1946]). As Franz Delitzsch rightly recognized, תרועה is here synonymous with תודה (Ps. 26:7). In Ps. 107:22 the offerings brought forward amid jubilation and thanksgiving and belonging to people who had experienced Yahweh's gift of salvation are called זבחי תודה. The תרועה expresses itself in שיר and זמר. Certainty, trust, and vow are blended together in the statements of v. 6.

[27:7-8] In v. 7 begins the bidding prayer which the persecuted person presents before Yahweh in the holy place. With a loud voice he prays for being heard and begs for mercy and a hearing. But the entire prayer that now follows is characterized by the trust expressed already while he was still far removed from the sanctuary (vv. 1-6). In v. 8 the lament and petitions present a quotation: the command of God בקשו פני, to which the petitioner obviously appeals as he approaches Yahweh. On בקש פנים, cf. the comment on Ps. 24:6; in addition, 2 Sam. 12:16; 21:1; Hos. 5:15; Amos 5:4; et al. The pressing call to seek the face of Yahweh in all troubles must have played an important role in the life of the people of God: Amos 5:4; Jer. 29:12ff.; and especially Ps. 50:15. On the basis of the last passage (Ps. 50:15), the citation in v. 8 could be understood without any difficulty. Now the petitioner, in keeping with the call and invitation of Yahweh, seeks ''his countenance,'' i.e., he calls to the *deus praesens*.

In the Amarna letters we can document a parallel passage that is noteworthy according to form and content:

> You give me life
> and you give me death—
> to your countenance I look!

(J. A. Knudtzon, *Die El-Amarna-Tafeln* [1915], No. 169, 7-9; cf. F. M. Th. De Liagre Böhl, *Opera minora* [1953] 378).

[27:9-10] Hiding and covering the countenance would be a sign of rejection and anger. The petitions of v. 9 plead with Yahweh as the judge and savior that he may not reject him who seeks help. אל־תט—from a form-critical perspective this petition belongs to the context of legal jurisdiction such as cannot deny a demand for rights (Isa. 19:21; Amos 5:12; Mal. 3:5; Prov. 18:5). Before the אלהי ישעי (cf. v. 1) the petitioner appears with the self-designation עבד, which indicates a belonging to Yahweh that is ready for service (Ps. 19:11). He who has been cast out by his closest relatives (v. 10) looks for refuge with Yahweh, for the accusation obviously branded him as a רשע unworthy of association. But the sheltering area of the sanctuary gives the one who appeals and pleads firm confidence: "Yahweh will receive me" (cf. v. 5). A Bentzen is of the opinion that v. 10 points to elements and conceptions of the "royal ideology." In the sacral act of adoption in the enthronement (cf. Ps. 2:7)—so Bentzen assumes— the statement of v. 10 has its place (cf. A. Bentzen, *Messias—Moses redivivus— Menschensohn* [1948] 20). This interpretation overestimates the relevance of the metaphorical element. If the adoption motif would really have a place in the verse, a participation in the lofty proceedings of the royal world (as in Ps. 22:10) would have to be presupposed (so also in v. 3).

[27:11-13] With the petition for showing the right way (v. 11) the psalmsinger pleads for the opening of a new possibility for life through Yahweh's intervention in a saving word. On דרך, cf. the comment on Pss. 5:8; 16:11; 25:4; 86:11; 143:10. The "greed" (on נפש in this meaning, cf. the comment on Ps. 17:9) wants to ruin the person persecuted (v. 2); it wants to separate him from Yahweh and have him be declared an outcast. At the holy place the accusers rise up against the oppressed one (ביום רעה, v. 5). עדי־שקר, lying witnesses, slanderers, are introduced for the purpose of loosing חמס ("injustice," "violence"). For these procedures, cf. the comment on Pss. 5:9; 7:3ff.; 10:2; 12:3; and often. The petitioner waits for "his rights to come forth" from Yahweh (Pss. 17:2; 7:6ff.). It would be inconceivable for the psalmsinger in such a dire threat to his very existence not to cling to Yahweh firmly and confidently (v. 13). האמין is the characteristic verb that emphasizes the confidence that appears already in vv. 1-6. The petitioner has "established," "solidified" his existence in Yahweh— that is the meaning of האמין here. If the verb has its original place in the "holy war" (thus G. von Rad, *Der Heilige Krieg im alten Israel*, ATANT [1951], 31), then the connection of the term with the conceptions in v. 3 is evident. At the same time it becomes apparent that the psalmist takes the perspective of the breadth of Yahweh's saving activity in behalf of his people, a perspective that breaks through all limits of personal existence. In his specific distress the petitioner is sure: I will not die, but live (cf. Ps. 118:17); I will not be expelled into the "sphere of death" (Chr. Barth, *Die Errettung vom Tode in den individuellen Klage- und Dankliedern des Alten Testaments* [1947], 76ff.), but behold the "goodness of Yahweh" in "the land of the living." טוב־יהוה is to be understood as synonymous with נעם־יהוה in v. 4b. Both words radiate the wonder of the bestowal of salvation and of life (cf. Ps. 16:10f.). The sentence introduced by לולא lets us sense from a distance the unimaginable catastrophe that would have set in if the firm trust in Yahweh had not carried life through the dangers. But the incomplete sentence bears witness all the more powerfully to the wonder of assurance.

M. Mannati wants טוב יהוה understood as a plural. The translation would then yield the following picture: "I have the assurance to behold the good things that Yahweh brings forth in the land of the living" (*VT* 19 [1969], 488ff.). But for the meaning of טוב in the construct formation, cf. H. J. Stoebe, *THAT*, 1:652ff.

[27:14] Two attempts at explanations for v. 14 should be eliminated immediately. The address קוה אל־יהוה is not "an admonition by itself" (thus H. Gunkel in reference to Ps. 42:5). It does not read נפשי (Ps. 42:5), but לבך. But from this observation concerning the suffix we also cannot on the other hand conclude that an encouraging address is directed toward others (as, e.g., in Ps. 2:12). It surely is still most immediate to think of a word of God by which the petitioner is encouraged to be firm and strong (cf. 1 Sam. 1:17). This passage could then of course be understood only as a reference to a final "oracle of salvation." But this is without question a yes, an encouraging answer that resounds from v. 14 (cf. the comment on Ps. 22:21). On קוה, cf. C. Westermann, "Das Hoffen im Alten Testament," *Theologia viatorum* 1952.

Purpose and Thrust

For the right understanding of Psalm 27 we must presuppose that a human being (an anonymous individual) is persecuted by hostile forces and threatened by slanderous accusations (v. 12). The adversaries want to separate the "servant of Yahweh" (v. 9a) from God. He is already expelled—also by his closest relatives—and sees before him death as the realm of abandonment by God (vv. 9, 13). With this in the background, trust (vv. 1-6) and pleading (vv. 7-13) are to be understood. Even though still far from the sanctuary, the psalmsinger puts his confidence in Yahweh. He longs for the redeeming bestowal of salvation in the temple area and for being sheltered in the holy place (v. 4). But the God of salvation (אלהי ישעי, v. 9b) is also present in the midst of the battle, in the midst of the external danger of his servant (vv. 1-3). Even the mightiest levy of the persecutors can therefore no longer inspire fear. This assurance is in control also in the bidding prayer and is announced by means of the striking verb האמין (v. 13). The oppressed person has anchored his life entirely in Yahweh. For that reason no hostile power can overwhelm him and separate him from the God of salvation (vv. 1, 9b). Behind the prayers of those accused who have trustingly held to Yahweh as legal aid and rescuer one could again and again see the NT word: τίς ἐγκαλέσει κατὰ ἐκλεκτῶν θεοῦ; θεὸς ὁ δικαιῶν (Rom. 8:33). those who have been threatened with death still are sure that nothing can separate them from God. Even though they are expelled by their closest relatives (v. 10), God receives them and opens for them a way of salvation (vv. 11, 13, 14). Under all circumstances we must observe the this-worldly nature (v. 13) of this certainty (as in Rom. 8:33).

Psalm 28

Call for Help and Thanksgiving of One Threatened by Death

Literature

A. Urban, " 'Herr, schweige nicht hinweg von mir!' Meditation über Ps 28 (27)," *BiLe* 8 (1967) 196-201. D. Eichhorn, "Jahwe als Fels, Burg und Zuflucht," *EHS*.T 4 (1972).

Text

Of David.

28:1 To you, O Yahweh, my rock, I call.
Do not turn silently away from me,
so that you become dumb before me and I become
like those who have sunk into the pit!

2 Hear[a] the voice of my supplication
when I cry to you,
when I lift up my hands
to your holy of holies!

3 Do not take me away with the wicked
and with the evildoers,
who speak friendly words with their neighbors
but carry mischief in their hearts!

4 Reward them[b] according to their works,
according to the wickedness of their acts!
According to the works of their hands give to them;
recompense their misdeeds!

5 For they have no regard for Yahweh's 'doing'[c]
and for the work of his hands.
'Therefore'[d] 'Yahweh' will tear them down
and not (any longer) build up.

6 Praised be Yahweh, for he has heard
the voice of my crying!

338

7 Yahweh is my might and my shield,
   in him my heart trusts.
   I was helped, then my heart[e] exulted,[f]
   and with my song I will thank him.
8 Yahweh's might is the might 'of his people'[g]—
   and the protection and salvation of his anointed.
9 Help your people and bless your heritage;
   shepherd and carry them forever!

2a Gk[Mss] and Jerome add יהוה. But we should read the MT.
4b Gk[α] adds יהוה, but we ought to read the MT.
5c Following 10 Mss of α´, we will do better to read פְּעֻלַּת.
d A rhythmically complete verse is here present in a mutilated form. If we should start with the idea that ולא יבנם is the second half-verse, we would have to complete יהרסם by conjecture. Perhaps—in accordance with the context—עַל־כֵּן יהוה may be added.
7e Gk: ἡ σάρξ μου καὶ ἐκ θελήματός μου. Thereby a change of grouping in the text would come about: בְּשָׂרִי וּמִלִּבִּי. All these variants obviously depend on a different text tradition, which can hardly correct the MT.
f Gk, θ´ has ἀνέθαλεν, S has *germinavit*, ε´ has ἐκρατύνθη = וַיַּחֲלֵף.
8g Eight Mss Gk and S have לְעַמּוֹ.

Form

The construction of Psalm 28 is easily analyzed: vv. 1-2, address to Yahweh and petition to be heard; vv. 3-5, prayer (in view of the fate of the wicked); vv. 6-7, thanksgiving; vv. 8-9, confession and intercession. Separating the song into two psalms (vv. 1-5; 6-9), as B. Duhm does, fails to take into consideration important form-critical data (see below).

In the meter, there are a number of difficulties. If we begin with the observation that the $3 + 2$ meter dominates, then a reconstruction of the verses not transmitted in a five-pulse meter could be undertaken. In v. la we could eliminate יהוה, and so two five-pulse meters would have to be read in v. 1. Verse 2b would have to be amplified by one word; H. Gunkel suggests that we supply הַבִּיטָה: "Look up when I lift up my hands . . . !" Thus also v. 2 would contain two five-pulse meters. Verse 3 contains two five-pulse meters. To achieve the same picture in v. 4, תֵּן לָהֶם in v. 4aγ could be understood as not original, being a repetition of the invitation from v. 4aα; הָשֵׁב would then have to be counted with the first half-verse of the second five-pulse meter of v. 4. In v. 5 כִּי would have to be eliminated. For the reconstruction of v. 5b, cf. the conjecture (see textual note 5d). Hardly any corrections at all seem possible "for the sake of the meter" in vv. 7-9.

Psalm 28 belongs to the form group of prayer songs. On תפלה, see above, Intro. §6, 2. In detail, the following construction is to be observed: After the address in vv. 1f., the petition is presented (vv. 3-5). But then a remarkable caesura is to be noted after v. 5. We must assume that previous to the song of thanksgiving of an individual, beginning in v. 6, an "oracle of salvation" has to be supposed as having occurred (on "oracle of salvation," cf. J. Begrich, "Das priesterliche Heilsorakel," *ZAW* 52 [1934], 81-92). Yahweh has heard the voice of the petitioner (v. 6b). Now his song of thanksgiving praises the rescuing God (cf. the comment on Pss. 6:8; 22:21; on *todah,* see above, Intro. §6, 2aγ). The song of thanksgiving closes with a confession (v. 8). Attached is an intercessory prayer in v. 9.

Setting

In dealing with the question about the person of the petitioner, we may not take our cue from vv. 8-9. A. Bentzen (*Messias—Moses redivivus—Menschensohn* [1948], 20) and S. Mowinckel (*Offersang og sangoffer* [1951], 84) declare that Psalm 28 is a royal psalm. Here observations from vv. 8-9 are wrongly transferred to the whole psalm. The question about the person and about the situation of the petitioner is to be answered and developed on the basis of vv. 1-7. The answer can, of course, not be unequivocal, because the actual fate of the lamenting and praying person appears only as under a veil. From the term יורדי בור (v. 1) and on the basis of a text emended in accordance with Gk, S, and ε′ in v. 7, H. Schmidt concludes that a gravely ill person approached Yahweh with his psalm. But it would also be possible to think of a person who is falsely persecuted and who is taking refuge in God's sanctuary (cf. vv. 3-5 and the parallels in Ps. 27:9, 10, as well as 7). In any case, lament and thanksgiving have been intoned in the sanctuary (v. 2). And from vv. 8-9 we could infer that Psalm 28 is to be dated in the time of the kings (so Baethgen, Briggs, Gunkel) and could possibly be very ancient (H. Schmidt). Psalm 28 was probably available and was used as a prayer formulary in a great variety of afflictions.

Commentary

[Title] On לדוד, see above, Intro. §4, No. 2.

[28:1] The psalmsinger cries to Yahweh and calls him "my rock" (צורי). On צורי, cf. Pss. 18:2, 46; 19:14; 62:2, 6; 92:15; 144:1. Does this appellation apply to the "holy rock" above which the temple was erected? (H. Schmidt, *Der Heilige Fels in Jerusalem* [1933], 87). Is there a reference here to the "holy of holies" (דביר), mentioned in v. 2, as the cell that encloses the "rock"? In the language of the psalms צור is the firm "archetypal place," the indestructible "refuge." The petition אל־תחרש ממני pleads for Yahweh's bestowal of salvation in a דבר, in a saying that brings salvation, one that comes from the mouth of a priest (cf. Pss. 35:22; 39:12; 83:2; 109:1; 143:7). The petitioner stands within the confines of the area of death; if Yahweh remains silent and forsakes him (Ps. 22:1), he will be like the יורדי בור. In Pss. 30:3 and 88:3f., בור is used as a synonym of שאול and therefore designates the "realm of death," the "depth of death." On יורדי בור, cf. Pss. 30:3; 88:4; 143:7; Prov. 1:12; etc. It is from the state of being forsaken by God that the petitioner calls. He pleads for being heard (v. 2). For קול תחנוני, a significant term of the lament, cf. Pss. 86:6; 116:1; 130:2; 140:6. The petitioner lifts his hand in prayer. Originally this was a gesture of one who sought protection (H. Gressmann, *AOB* 137), which later everywhere is familiar as the gesture of a person at prayer (*našû kâtâ*: B. Meissner, *Babylonien und Assyrien* 2 [1925], 80f.). "Prayers with uplifted hands" are familiar from Mesopotamia (Sumerian, *šu'illa:* A. Falkenstein and W. von Soden, *Sumerische und akkadische Hymnen und Gebete* [1953], 19). On the gesture in the Psalter, cf. Pss. 63:4; 134:2; 141:2 (Lam. 2:19; 3:41; Neh. 8:6; and, in the NT, 1 Tim. 2:8). The direction in which the petitioner addresses his laments and petitions is in v. 2bβ called: אל־דביר קדשך. Involved is the holy room, the "holy of holies" (1 Kings 6:5, 16, 19-23, 31; 7:49; 8:6, 8; 2 Chron. 3:16; 4:20; 5:7, 9; K. Möhlenbrink, *Der Tempel Salomos,* BWANT IV, 7 [1932], 131ff.). Here in the cell, Yahweh is present above the ark: 1 Kings

8:6f., 13. On the direction of prayer, cf. Pss. 5:7; 134:2; Lam. 2:19; 1 Kings 8:35.

The mention of Yahweh the "rock" (v. 1) and the "holy of holies" (v. 2) refers to the context of ancient Jerusalem traditions. Here the designation of Yahweh as "rock" points back to ancient, pre-David traditions, while the "holy of holies" belongs to the temple tradition. At present, our purpose is to deal with the theme "rock." Here we have to refer to the monograph of D. Eichhorn, *Jahwe als Fels, Burg und Zuflucht* (1972). Eichhorn correctly declares that the "holy rock" is the place where Yahweh actually reveals himself as the one who protects his people, who intervenes against the powers of chaos and against "the nations" (91). Over against the use of צור (which obviously goes back to the oldest stages of history-of-religions development), the utilization of the word סלע has receded (95). And now we read, literally, "צורי in the form of an address and a predicated reference to God which is particularized by the suffix of the first person singular is encountered in the mouth of an individual only in those psalms which, without prejudice to the variety of the traditional type classifications and without prejudice to the identification of the petitioner, . . . are in their structure applied to a revelation of Yahweh which is transmitted through the petitioner whose relation to Yahweh is determined for him by means of Yahweh's being the צור and which is qualified by the relation of Yahweh so characterized" (45f.). So far we can follow Eichhorn. But his insistence on an institutional office of mediator in this connection has not been proved sufficiently. For the office of mediator, cf. especially pp. 25ff.

[28:3-5] The petitioner fears that he will be taken away with the "wicked" (רשעים). Without a declaration of his צדקה, he is in danger of lapsing into the mortal fate of the רשעים (cf. the comment on Ps. 26:9-10). One easily thinks of a person who is falsely accused, one who fights for his צדקה (cf. the comment on Psalm 7, "Setting"). For an understanding of the terms רשעים and פעלי און, which point to the enemies of the individual, see above, Intro. §10,4. The meaning of the statements of vv. 3-5 is surely that the psalmsinger wants to see himself exempted from the רשעים. The judicial demands made on the "wicked" potentially contain the plea: But I am not a רשע! The petitioner has no part in the abysmal falseness of the "wicked" (v. 3)! The demand is rightly made that Yahweh react to the misdeeds of the רשעים. On the "thought of paying back," cf. the comment on Ps. 7:13-16, but we should note that in Psalm 28 the judgmental reaction of the majestic person of Yahweh pushes the conception of an "immanent nemesis" to the very brink. Verse 5 speaks of פעלת יהוה and means the judgmental activity which the רשעים overlook and forget (cf. Pss. 10:4f.; 54:3; 73:17ff.; Isa. 5:12; 28:21; Hab. 1:5). In v. 5b there is certainty that Yahweh will—justly—tear down and no longer build up the "wicked" (cf. Jer. 24:6; 42:10; 45:4). Worth noting in v. 5 are the reminiscences of the prophecy of Isaiah (5:12) and Jeremiah (24:6; 42:10; 45:4). We cannot tell whether we here have an actual dependence or the reference to a conventionalized way of language.

[28:6-7] For the song of thanksgiving sounding forth in hymnic style in vv. 6-7, we have to presuppose that the petition of him who prayed has been heard (שמע קול תחנוני). This answer to prayer becomes apparent in an "oracle of salvation." Now the psalmsinger praises Yahweh. On ברוך יהוה in the song of thanksgiving, cf. Pss. 124:6; 144:1; in the hymn, Pss. 68:19, 35; 135:21. ברך means: to recognize someone in his position of power and in his claim to greatness (F. Horst, "Segen und Segenshandlungen in der Bibel," *EvTh* 1/2 [1947], 31). When Yahweh is glorified as עזי ומגני, these very terms show that the petitioner of Psalm 28 was in distress and was persecuted. Yahweh as

צוּר (v. 1) has proved to be a powerful protection. בּוֹ בָטַח לִבִּי, like הֶאֱמַנְתִּי in Ps. 27:13, identifies the manner of conduct of one who rests on Yahweh's power for salvation. He who experiences Yahweh's help finds that his heart jubilates in thankful song. There is a definite reference to the תּוֹדָה (cf. the comment on Ps. 27:6).

[28:8] Verse 8 is to be thought of as a confession to the recipients of salvation beyond the individual. The event of Yahweh's hearing prayer and bestowing salvation on an individual petitioner takes place in the actuality of the people of God and in the area of the royal sanctuary in Jerusalem. Therefore the psalmsinger in his confession praises the power with which Yahweh blesses his people and the salutary protection that is given to the reigning king. On מָשִׁיחַ, cf. the comment on Ps. 2:2. In this passage one can easily recognize how an individual constantly participates in a larger reality of salvation, one that encompasses and supports his individual fate. When Gunkel speaks of a "patriotic conclusion," we will have to pardon him for this extreme and extravagant polemic against the mystifications of a "messianic exegesis." The "messianic exegesis" was on the right track, but it allowed itself to be caught by a dogmatic picture of the מָשִׁיחַ. The Scandinavian "royal ideology," on the other hand, is not able to see the distinctive relation of "the individual participation in the mystery of the royal realm of salvation"; it broadens the "royal elements" and covers the individual laments with a fictitious ideological interpretive category.

[28:9] In v. 9 the confession (v. 8) develops into an intercession for the people of God. For Israel help and blessing are prayed for (on the meaning of intercession in the Psalms: F. Hesse, "Die Fürbitte im Alten Testament," diss. Erlangen [1951], 65ff.). נַחֲלָה as a designation for Israel is probably a term that developed from the theologoumena about the אֵל־עֶלְיוֹן (cf. Deut. 32:8f.; and above, Intro. §10,1). The conceptions of "shepherding" and "carrying" refer to the picture of the good shepherd (Ps. 80:1; Isa. 40:11; Pss. 23:1; 74:1; 79:13; 95:7). Thus the psalmsinger, in concluding, prays that the saving presence of Yahweh may yet remain with Israel, to eternity (לְעוֹלָם). Thus also this intercessory prayer shows once more how firmly the psalmist sees the help that he has experienced anchored in Yahweh's gracious attention to Israel.

Purpose and Thrust

After the parameters of form and content have been drawn, an appropriate understanding of Psalm 28 develops most easily from v. 8. For here the subject is the protective and salutary reality to which a person threatened by death flees in his distress and which he acknowledges with thanksgiving: the people of God and the king. There a person finds מָעוֹז, עֹז, and יְשׁוּעָה, for in the midst of this people of God, in the royal temple of Jerusalem, Yahweh is present in the holy of holies (v. 2). The NT community sees in this OT work of salvation of the *deus praesens* the σκιὰ . . . τῶν μελλόντων ἀγαθῶν (Heb. 10:1) which appeared in reality in Jesus Christ. He who is accused, tempted, and mortally threatened here looks for the unshakable "rock" (v. 1) and presents his lamentations and petitions. The center of the lament is the distress: I am being swept away into destruction by the stream of ungodly powers (רְשָׁעִים, v. 3). The word of salvation prayed for from Yahweh has this meaning for sufferers: deliverance from the fate of the death of the reprobate. This is the εὐαγγέλιον that is the subject of Psalm 28 (cf. Rom. 8:33f.). The dark foil of this salvation event is the judgment of the רשעים. The trusting soul (בטח, v. 7) finds an answer (v. 6) and thankfully rejoices over Yahweh's help.

The Powerful Appearance of Yahweh
in a Thunderstorm

Literature

K. Fullerton, "The Strophe in Hebrew Poetry and Psalm 29," *JBL* 48 (1929) 274-290. T. H. Gaster, "Psalm 29," *JQR* 37 (1946/47) 55-65. I. W. Slotki, "The Metre and Text of Psalm 29:3 and 9," *JTS* 31, 186-198. F. M. Cross, "Notes on a Canaanite Psalm in the Old Testament," *BASOR* 117 (1950) 19-21. D. Gualandi, "Salmo 29 (28)," *Bibl* 39 (1958) 478-485. E. Vogt, "Der Aufbau von Psalm 29," *Bibl* 41 (1960) 17-24. A. Deissler, "Zur Datierung und Situierung der 'kosmischen Hymnen' Pss. 8; 19; 29," *Lex tua Veritas: Festschrift für H. Junker* (1961), 47-58. E. Pax, "Studien zur Theologie von Psalm 29," *BZ* NF 1 (1962) 93-100. F. C. Fensham, "Psalm 29 and Ugarit," *OTWP* (1963) 84-99. B. Maggioni, "Osservazioni sul Salmo 29 (28), 'Afferte Domino,' " *BibOr* 7 (1965) 245-251. F. C. Fensham, "Ugarit and the Translator of the Old Testament," *BiTrans* 18 (1967) 71-74. N. Avan Uchelen, "De LXX-interpretatie van Ps. 29," *NTT* 24 (1969/70) 171-181. H. Strauss, "Zur Auslegung von Psalm 29 auf dem Hintergrund seiner kanaanäischen Bezüge," *ZAW* 82 (1970) 91-102.

Text

A psalm of David.[a]

29:1 Give to Yahweh, O sons of God,
    give to Yahweh glory and strength!

2 Give to Yahweh the honor of his name;
    prostrate yourselves before Yahweh at "his" holy appearance![b]

3 Yahweh's voice over the waters!
    (The God of glory is thundering),[c]
    Yahweh over the mighty waters!

4 Yahweh's voice resounds with power,
    Yahweh's voice with majesty!

5 Yahweh's voice shatters cedars,
    Yahweh shatters[d] the cedars of Lebanon.

6 He makes Lebanon "skip"[e] like a calf,
    Sirion like a young wild ox.

7 Yahweh's voice flashes flames of fire.[f]

8 Yahweh's voice makes the desert quake,
 Yahweh makes the desert of Kadesh quake.
9 Yahweh's voice brings the hinds to birthpains,
 makes the kids squirm with pain.[9]

. . . .

 And in his palace all cry out: Glory!
10 Yahweh is enthroned over the flood;
 Yahweh is enthroned as king forever.
11 May Yahweh give strength to his people;
 may Yahweh bless his people with peace!

1a Gk adds to the superscription: ἐξοδίου σκηνῆς ("At leaving the tabernacle").

2b The word הדרה, the translation and explanation of which has heretofore been sought in the lexica and commentaries as derived from הדר ("ornament"), has had new light shed on it by the Ugaritic texts. In KRT 155; 145, 5 *hdrt* is parallel to *hlm* ("dream," "vision"), and it obviously has the meaning "revelation," "appearance" (C. H. Gordon, *Ugaritic Handbook,* Analecta Orientalia 25 [1947], 3:225). This meaning is to be assumed also for Ps. 96:9; 1 Chron. 16:29, whereas the archaic concept already in 2 Chron. 20:21 tends toward the better-known OT meaning of the root הדר ("ornament"). Following Gk and S, it would probably be best to read קָדְשׁוֹ. Of course, Gk and S provides the text בְּחַצְרַת קָדְשׁוֹ ἐν αὐλῇ ἁγίᾳ αὐτοῦ.

3c The words אֶל־הַכָּבוֹד הָרַעִים are likely to be thought of as a dislocated half-verse (see note **f** below).

5d Worthy of note is the consecutive ו (Ges-K §111r), which should not be amended to a copulative ו.

6e The metrical verse arrangement is disturbed if we follow MT ("he makes them skip like a calf, Lebanon and Sirion like a young wild ox"). It is probably best to read וַיַּרְקֵד or וְיַרְקִיד (Bickel, Wellhausen).

7f Verse 7, an isolated half-verse, deserts the metrical pattern. We could consider combining v. 7 with the dislocated half-verse of v. 3, אֶל־הַכָּבוֹד הָרַעִים, to form a complete verse thus: קוֹל־יְהוָה חֹצֵב לַהֲבוֹת אֵשׁ אֶל־הַכָּבוֹד הָרַעִים.

9g The second half-verse contains problems which, with Driver (*JTS* 32, 255), we can clear up only tentatively by construing the *hapax legomenon* יְעָרוֹת as the plural of יַעְרָה (KBL 391) and by assuming the meaning "to bring to early parturition" for חשׂף (KBL 339). A different attempt at emendation reads אַיָּלוֹת (= אֵילִים) for אַיָּלוֹת and יְעָרוֹת (= יְעָרִים): "Yahweh's voice makes the oaks skip and strips the forests bare." But this suggestion is very problematic.

Form

In vv. 1-9 Psalm 29 extols the powerful appearance of Yahweh in a thunderstorm and describes the effects of the sound of thunder. Then in v. 9b the description of the glorification of Yahweh in the heavenly palace (as a reprise of vv. 1-2) begins abruptly with ובהיכלו. This abrupt entry could give credence to the supposition that something dropped out before ובהיכלו. In v. 11 a concluding prayer expresses a wish.

The metrical relations of Psalm 29 cannot yet be analyzed successfully. The effort to get at the meter on the basis of the Ugaritic texts is still in its very beginnings and is made more difficult by the condition of the text in the Ugaritic transmission. All the same, F. M. Cross attempts to reconstruct the following picture: Strophe 1 (vv. 1-2): 2+2, 2+2; 2+2, 2+2; Strophe 2 (vv. 3-6): 2+2+3; 2+2+3; 2+2, 3+3. For vv. 7ff. it is assumed that the psalm presents only a torso of the original text (F. M. Cross, *BASOR* 117, 20). On an experimental basis (following the structural analysis of Cross) we could assume a meter of 2+2, 2+2; 2+2+3 for vv. 8-9. Without doubt we have in Psalm 29 archaic meters that clearly stand out from other OT psalmic poetry. It is correct procedure to recognize the undeniable relation of Psalm 29 to ancient Canaanite texts (see below) and also to attempt an explanation of the meter corresponding to the facts.

Regarding the major form-critical question of the "type" (*Gattung*) of the psalm, we must take the findings of the history of religions as our point of departure. It has been recognized and impressively set forth (T. H. Gaster, F. M. Cross, F. C. Fensham, H. Strauss) that Psalm 29 is based on an ancient Canaanite song (represented by Ugaritic texts); compare also W. H. Schmidt, *Königtum Gottes in Ugarit und Israel*, BZAW 80 (1966²) 55ff. The archaic hymn form with which Psalm 29 begins must have been taken over from the Canaanite sphere; and it must be assumed in general that Israel took over the original form of the hymn from the immediate surroundings. In any case, Psalm 29, in keeping with its prelude, must be thought of as a song of praise (תהלה) and must be classified as belonging to this group. See above, Intro. §6, 1. Still, the imperative summons of vv. 1ff. leads over to the presentation of a theophany, which must be thought of as a "type" by itself (cf. J. Jeremias, *Theophanie: Die Geschichte einer alttestamentlichen Gattung*, WMANT 10 [1965] 30f.). While the summons in vv. 1f. addresses itself to the בני אלים (see below), the specific application of the psalm to Israel—if for the moment we disregard the insertion of the name of Yahweh—is not expressed until we come to the prayer supplication in v. 11. Therefore, from the very beginning we will have to consider the probability that a Canaanite Baal hymn with its description of a theophany was handed down without radical revision on the part of the OT tradents in Israel. The archaic, pre-Israelite themes and conceptions are recognized without difficulty.

Setting

Where could Psalm 29 have had its "Sitz im Leben"? A person would immediately think of a cultic situation. A. Weiser designates Psalm 29 a "theophany psalm" and takes the view that the appearance of God was the "climax of the festival worship." H. Schmidt refers the hymn to the "festival of Yahweh's accession to the throne" (H. Schmidt, "Die Thronfahrt Jahwes," *Sammlung gemeinverständlicher Vorträge*, 122 [1927] 26f.). These conceptions fall within the boundaries of S. Mowinckel's thesis that a festival of Yahweh's enthronement was celebrated in Jerusalem (S. Mowinckel, *Psalmen-Studien II*) and accordingly strongly emphasize the designation "king" for Yahweh in v. 10. Regarding the problem of the designation "king" for Yahweh, however, see above, Intro. §10, 1; also see H. J. Kraus, *Worship in Israel* (1964), 205ff. Besides, it would be difficult to assume a (dramatically represented?) theophany for the worship of Israel. Therefore we may hazard the guess that the cultic song taken over from the Canaanites and applied to Yahweh was intoned at the prostration before Yahweh the king, who had entered the sanctuary (cf. on Pss. 95:6; 96:9; 99:5; and see above, Intro. §10, 1). A reliable tradition could be preserved [in the title of this psalm] in the LXX, which points to the Feast of Tabernacles (but for the Targum-like paraphrases and interpretations of the Septuagint, cf. N. Avan Uchelen, 171ff.).

After all that has been said concerning the Canaanite provenance of Psalm 29, we may agree that the OT psalm was adapted very early. Yet it seems questionable that we could establish the details. Thus H. Cazelles assumes that an older layout of Psalm 29 belongs to the time of David, but that later, under the influence of the prophets, a new interpretation followed (H. Cazelles, *Une relecture du Psaume XXIX? A la rencontre de Dieu. Mémorial A. Gelin* [1961] 119-128). A. Deissler even thinks that he can present clues for concluding that Psalm 29 originated in postexilic times. Reliable clues, however, cannot be arrived at. Rather, the general opinion of T. H. Gaster may be considered as guiding: "Certain hymnic patterns, derived from these (sc. Ugaritic) earlier usages, survived in literary convention" (64). Above all, the traditions of the theophany represented an old Canaanite type of tradition (cf. J. Jeremias, 73ff.).

The images and concepts in Psalm 29 present Yahweh as a God of thunderstorms. Unquestionably, elements of the ancient Near Eastern veneration of the god of thunderstorms are here taken up and transferred to Yahweh. In the religious literature of Babylon we find hymns that exalt Enlil's mighty voice of thunder. The same concepts and glorifications are later transferred also to other gods, especially to Marduk:

The word that causes the heavens above to quake;
the word that makes the earth below to shake;
the word that brings the Anunnaki down to ruin. . . .
His word makes the heavens quake, makes the earth shake. . . .
The Lord's word is a rising flash flood that beclouds the countenance;
the word of Marduk is a flood that catches hold of the dam.
His word, it sweeps away huge lotus trees [?];
his word is a storm, it saddles all things with burdens [?].
The word of Enlil storms about without an eye seeing it.

Cf. B. Meissner, *Babylonien und Assyrien* II (1925) 158f. Worthy of note would be especially the Adad-Ramman hymns, in which the powerful appearance of the thunderstorm deity is described (H. Gressmann, *AOT²* 248f.). That Psalm 29 very likely goes back directly to a Canaanite Baal hymn and extols his numinous thunderstorm manifestation was first recognized by H. L. Ginsberg and documented by reference to Canaanite and Ugaritic parallels (H. L. Ginsberg, *Kitwe Ugarit: The Ugaritic Texts* [1936] 129f.). Cf. also T. H. Gaster, "Psalm 29," *JQR* 37, 55ff. and F. M. Cross, *BASOR* 117, 19ff. For Baal-Hadad, however, Yahweh is substituted. The polemical meaning that overcomes the Canaanite myth in this conception will have to be worked out in the interpretation.

In dealing with the data of comparative religions, we must of course notice that Yahweh does not take the place of just any Baal-Hadad, but that Psalm 29 very clearly lets the monarchical hierarchy of the pantheon of the gods become recognizable. The concept of a בעל שמם to whom the בני אלים are subordinate (v. 1) and the picture of the "King of Heaven" (v. 10) who is majestically enthroned above the מבול lie at the base of the hymn. In any case, Psalm 29 is very old—perhaps one of the oldest of all OT psalms.

Commentary

[29:1] On מזמור לדוד, see above, Intro. §4, No. 2.

In the hymnic prelude of Psalm 29 the imperatives are significant. At the very beginning a group, a choir, is called on to give glory to Yahweh. Those involved are "divine beings," the בני אלים. With this concept a mythological conception comes alive which we must investigate in respect to its presuppositions and its contexts. Two levels of meaning are here contained. (1) בני אלים reminds us of the pantheon of those gods that are subordinate to a kingly supreme godhead. The king god (v. 10) receives the homage of the lesser gods subordinated to him. Thus the subordinate gods of Babylon give honor to the king god Marduk. In the OT this picture of the heavenly pantheon shines through most clearly in Ps. 82:1 (see above, Intro. §10, 1). The gods and the powers are subject to Yahweh (Ps. 97:7). Yahweh assumes the place of the highest deity, which in ancient Canaan is called בעל שמם, מלך, and, אל־עליון. (2) In the OT this pantheon of gods, the בני אלים, was "demythologized" in that the godly powers were thought of as ministering spirits in the heavenly world (1 Kings 22:19; Isa. 6:2f.; Job 1:6; 2:1; 38:7; Ps. 89:7; 103:20; 148:1ff.). In this sense we must think of בני אלים also in Ps. 29:1 (on the meaning of בני, cf. BrSynt §74c). Still, the meaning first considered glimmers through. On the theme בני אלים, cf. W. Herrmann, "Die Göttersöhne," *ZRGG* 12 (1960) 242-251; G. Cooke, "The Sons of (the) Gods," *ZAW* 76 (1964) 22-47 (on Psalm 29, pp. 24ff.).

The "heavenly beings" are to "give the glory" to Yahweh (cf. Ps. 148:1ff.). The manner in which the call הבו כבוד is to be implemented becomes clear in v. 9. כבוד as a call, as a hymnic acclamation, is presumably an honorific cry of archaic vintage, in which original magic applications may have played a role: one's own כבוד is in acclamation dedicated to the stronger and mightier, is transferred to him in the powerful word of the hymn. But we must inquire about the specific meaning of כבוד. In doing so we will have to deal with the coincidence of two components in the OT: (1) כבוד has an undeniable inclination toward things in nature (a bias that goes back to pre-Israelite tradition), and it applies itself above all to the brilliant and fearful theophanies of the (Canaanite) numina of heaven and earth. (2) In the specifically Israelite understanding of כבוד we are dealing with the importance of Yahweh in his acts, an importance that must be respected (cf. C. Westermann, *THAT* I, 805f.). In any case, כבוד in the OT has become "something obviously capable of being experienced"; it is Yahweh's "power and standing, his honour . . . perceptible in the world in the most varied of ways" (G. v. Rad, *OT Theol,* 1:239). It fills the entire creation (Isa. 6:3). Terrestrial and celestial beings have the duty "in praise to ascribe to God this honour of his power" (G. v. Rad, ibid.). If Psalm 29 were to be considered a song for the solemn prostration before Yahweh (see above), then we would have to assume that a heavenly act would correspond to the earthly hymn of praise and prayer (cf. especially Psalm 148). In this connection the adaptation of the Canaanite psalms would make sense, above all the glaring demotion of the בני אלים to מלאכים (Ps. 148:2), which, if not explicitly, then at least implicitly may be assumed for the OT adaptation of Psalm 29. For the heavenly beings represent the court retinue of the king, Yahweh (v. 10; cf. Gen. 1:26ff.; Ps. 8:6).

[29:2] On כבוד שמו in v. 2, cf. O. Grether, *Namen und Wort Gottes im Alten Testament,* BZAW 64 (1934) 38f. In Psalm 29 the שם, the name יהוה, is at stake. He is king of the heavenly world, and no one else. The conceptions of the original Canaanite hymn are illuminated by the very presence of the name יהוה and by the reality of this God revealed in Israel. The homage of the heavenly world of power is due him alone. By means of Ugaritic texts the meaning of בהדרת־קדש (see textual note **b** above) has become clear. At the appearance of the king of heaven (in the thunderstorm) the homage to Yahweh is to resound.

[29:3] After the introit (vv. 1-2), the theophany in the thunderstorm is now described. קול is the voice of thunder, the booming word of power.

The hymns to the god of thunder (Adad Ramman, Baal Hadad) clearly indicate that the deity's word of power was heard in the thunderclap. In Ugaritic texts *kl* is the word of thunder: C. H. Gordon, *Ugaritic Handbook,* II, 141 (51, V, 70; 51, VII, 29-31). In the

Amarna texts the voice of the Pharaoh, his word of power, is compared to the thunder of Adad: *să id-din ri-ig-ma-šu i-na šămē ki-ma addi ù ta(r)-ku-ub gab-bi mâti⁻ᵗⁱ iš-tu ri ig-mi-šu* (J. A. Knudtzon, *Die El-Amarna-Tafeln: Vorderasiatische Bibliothek* 2 [1915] 608). In the OT these conceptions have found a remarkable echo. The power of Yahweh expresses itself in thunder (Ps. 18:14; Isa. 30:30; Job 37:4f.). From the heavens the voice of thunder (Ps. 68:34) booms forth as the judge's word of power (Amos 1:2; Joel 4:16; Jer. 25:30). As in the ancient world the belief that the supreme god is the judge and the creator is joined to the conception of the highest god and the king of heaven, so also קול is the thundering word of power, the voice of the Judge (Ps. 46:7; Isa. 30:30) and of the Creator (Pss. 77:18; 104:7).

When v. 3 states that the thunderous voice of Yahweh resounds "over the waters," the reference is certainly to the מבול mentioned in v. 10. In the mythical-cosmological term מבול the "sea of heaven" is comprehended: Gen. 6:17; 7:6ff.; 9:11 (J. Begrich, *Zeitschrift für Semitistik,* 6 [1928] 135ff.). המים are, in keeping with the definition in Gen. 1:7, המים אשר מעל לרקיע. This therefore means: in the highest heavens the thunderous voice (קול—הרעים) of Yahweh, the אל־הכבוד, is booming. With this, cf. מלך הכבוד in Ps. 24: 7ff. and, in the NT, ὁ θεὸς τῆς δόξης (Acts 7:2).

[29:4-6] כח and הדר, "power" and "majesty," the voice of Yahweh is emitting (v. 4); it descends to the earth with destructive force (v. 5). The cedars of Lebanon, symbols of all that is lofty and proud (Isa. 2:13), tokens of all that is luxuriant and stable (Pss. 92:13; 104:16), are shattered. Lebanon and Sirion "skip," they tremble at the roar and rumble of the voice of thunder (v. 6). The parallelism Lebanon—Sirion can also be documented in the Ugaritic texts (C. H. Gordon, *Ugaritic Handbook* II, 142:51; VI, 18-19, 20-21). What is involved is evidently a standing phrase that originated in the Phoenician area. But where is the שרין (Ugaritic *šryn*) to be found? Gordon thinks of the Anti-Lebanon (*Ugaritic Handbook* III, 274). But the explanation given in Deut. 3:9 is probably correct: the Phoenicians (צידנים) called Mount Hermon *Sirion*. For the picture in v. 6, cf. Ps. 114:4.

[29:7-9]. With להבות אש (v. 7) the strokes of lightning emerge in the description of the thunderstorm theophany. Compare Pss. 18:9; 97:3f.; Isa. 30:27. The conception is as follows: the voice of thunder "flashes forth" (literally, "splits," חצב) flames of fire. Verse 7 gives the impression of having been inserted between vv. 6 and 8, and (with the addition of the words אל־הכבוד הרעים in v. 3) it could have been placed after v. 2 or before ובהיכלו in v. 9. In any case, the geographical combination of Lebanon (v. 6) and Kadesh (v. 8) belongs closely together and lets us recognize a geographical orientation that is not chosen *ad libitum* (F. Nötscher) but cast in a traditional mold. For the mention of the "desert of Kadesh" (*mdbr qdš*) in Ugaritic, cf. C. H. Gordon, *Ugaritic Handbook* II, 145:52, 65. The desert, too, trembles under the booming of the voice of thunder. Does the combination "Lebanon" and "Kadesh" (*ēn kdēs*) describe the jurisdiction of the מלך as the אדון כל־הארץ (cf. Ps. 97:5) in a possibly traditional ancient Canaanite understanding of space appropriate for the monarchical supreme godhead?

The last statement in v. 9 is applied to the animal world, which in trembling fear gives birth to its young prematurely. This association of earthquakes and birth pains is mysterious and below the surface. But now we should really expect a further discussion of the effects of the thunderous voice of

Yahweh on human beings. Yet at this very point the description suddenly comes to a close. Very likely some damage was sustained here in the course of the text tradition.

[29:9b-10] In its final section the hymn leads back to the situation observable in the introit (vv. 1-2). היכל is the heavenly palace (Ps. 11:4; Mic. 1:2; Hab. 2:20). This is the prototype and the otherworldly antitype of the temple. Here the great homage with the shout כבוד is paid to Yahweh (cf. Isa. 6:3; Pss. 19:2; 148:1; 150:1). "This verse, 9b, is the key-verse of the whole psalm—it leads us away from the commotions on the earth up to the heavenly sanctuary where the company of the heavenly beings recognises and glorifies these very occurrences on the earth as a revelation of the glory of Jahweh" (G. von Rad, *OT Theol*, 1:360). As מלך Yahweh here is enthroned (literally, "has taken his seat") above the מבול "forever" (Ps. 93:2). He is Lord of the world, who has threatening chaos lie at his feet (Ps. 93:3ff.). Elements of the theology of creation obviously are hinted at here (cf. H. Gressmann, *AOT²*, 111, 116f.).

It is immaterial at this point whether we consider v. 11 a later addition or an original part of the psalm; this verse is not a "patriotic appendage" (thus H. Gunkel, who never tires in his deliberate tendency to secularize). The wish in this prayer formally declares, in connection with the psalm, the conviction that the God who is mighty in his word is the Lord of his church. May he graciously turn all of the power described to the saving benefit of his chosen people.

Purpose and Thrust

In his book *Gott und Mensch im Alten Testament* (BWANT 3, 2 [1926] 38), J. Hempel, referring to Psalm 29, states: "There is no denying that in ancient times the faith in Yahweh's power in nature and history was rather one-sided because it focused essentially on the destructive and violent side of the divine activity." This classification is not in keeping with the facts. In this explanation there is an effort to reach behind the acutely polemical course of Yahweh's altercation with the monarchical claims of the supreme Canaanite deity, and the naturally destructive element of the deity that appears in the thunderstorm is subordinated to a criterion of its worth along the lines of the history of piety. But what is essential for the understanding of this hymn is:

1. All the statements of majesty and glory that in the Canaanite realm are due Baal-Hadad and the "King of Heaven" are exclusively transferred to Yahweh. He alone is the מלך הכבוד (vv. 9b, 10; Ps. 24:8ff.), to whom the heavenly powers render homage (vv. 1-2, 9b). To him alone all honor is due. It is significant that Israel invades the sphere of the claims of the "highest deity" and in the adaptation and surmounting of the archaic descriptions of power learns to experience Yahweh's reality anew. Thus it can in no way merely be a matter of Israel's simply usurping an originally Canaanite hymn (and with it a Canaanite theology) by simply substituting the tetragrammaton for the name Baal. Rather, Israel "formulated these and other similar texts literally 'in the name of Yahweh' and used and transmitted them as their statement of faith" (H. Strauss, 101).

2. The appearance of God in a thunderstorm has in the OT become an essential element in the description of a theophany. The revelation of Yahweh is always an event. In the eruption of the thunderstorm, the booming of the thunder and the flashing of the lightning, the appearance (הדרה, v. 2) of Yahweh occurs. That is the way the elements of threatening, dashing to pieces, and overwhelming in the coming of God, the "wholly Other," are signalized and coded. But

never is Yahweh represented in the OT as the God of thunderstorms. It is always a matter of a form of appearance from which Yahweh emerges in full personhood, speaking to human beings, promising and commanding. The name "Yahweh," the כבוד (v. 2) of his name, takes a position at center stage, decisive and dominating in such a way that the hymn and its descriptions of the theophany can be heard and understood properly only as coming from Yahweh and directed to Yahweh. At the same time we ought not to forget that Psalm 29 never stood alone in the worship of Israel but was always intoned in combination with other songs and prayers of Yahweh. Also, we surely cannot fail to recognize the polemically antithetic components that very pointedly militate against worshiping Canaanite deities. Psalm 29 gains circulation as a Yahweh hymn in a world characterized by Baal worship. Thereby the claim of the creator, Yahweh, on the world of heaven and earth becomes evident. *Yahweh* appears. *Yahweh's* כבוד radiates forth. *Yahweh's* voice resounds. *Yahweh* makes heaven and earth quake. To *him* all powers must bow in homage, and *him* must they serve.

3. But of course, the דבר with which Yahweh otherwise in the OT approaches human beings and reveals his majestic ego, in Psalm 29 resounds in the קול־יהוה that booms in the heavens, causes the earth to tremble, and frightens the animals. This "impersonal," "naturalistic" element in the קול־יהוה is conditioned by the pressing, close interchange with the alleged Canaanite hymn. But can any other voice be understood in Israel under the term קול־יהוה than this very voice of the God who has revealed himself to his people? Does not the OT person who prays, who joins in rendering homage to King Yahweh, always see in קול־יהוה only one single great illustration of the powerful and effective יהוהדבר־? To be sure, it is the shattering judge who manifests himself in his voice of thunder (cf. Amos 1:2; Joel 3:16); but can one set "judgment" and "salvation" against each other in a history of development the way Hempel attempts it?

4. It is to be noted that v. 11 prays that the entire might of Yahweh described in vv. 1-10 be granted to the assembly. It is to exercise itself in a *beneficial* way in the chosen people. No matter what point of time one may assign to the supplication of v. 11, whether it be original or—what may be more likely—secondary, the statement of v. 11 clearly sets forth what was inviolably valid and determinative for understanding each time Psalm 29 was intoned in OT worship: *Yahweh is the God of Israel*—known only in this relation. Yahweh is the God who with his might stands up for his people and therefore may be addressed and implored to bless his people with שלום from the fullness of his power as the God of Heaven and the ruling king.

Psalm 30

A Song of Thanksgiving
upon being Delivered from Death

Literature

J. Schildenberger, "Tod und Leben. Eine Auslegung von Ps. 30 (29)," *BiKi* 13 (1958), 110-115. L. Wächter, "Drei umstrittene Psalmstellen (Ps. 26:1; 30:8; 90:4-6)," *ZAW* 78 (1966), 61-68. E. J. Tromp, "Psalm 30 en de bijbelse bezinning op de dood," *Ons gestelijk leven* 44 (1967/68), 364-376. J. Schreiner, "Aus schwerer Krankheit errettet: Auslegung von Psalm 30," *BiLe* 10 (1965), 164-175. H.-J. Kraus, "Vom Leben und Tod in den Psalmen," *Biblisch-theologische Aufsätze* (1972), 258-277. W. Beyerlin, "Kontinuität beim 'berichtenden' Lobpreis des Einzelnen," *Wort und Geschichte: Festschrift K. Elliger*, AOAT 18 (1973), 17-24.

Text

A psalm. A song for the dedication of the temple. Of David.

30:1 I will extol you, O Yahweh, for you have lifted me up
and have not let my enemies rejoice over me.

2 O Yahweh, my God,
I cried to you;
you have healed me.

3 O Yahweh, you brought my soul out of Sheol,
called me back to life "from among those who had sunk
into the pit."[a]

4 Sing to Yahweh, you his saints,
and bring praises in remembrance of his holiness!

5 Indeed, his anger is but of short duration, but his grace is for a
lifetime;[b]
at evening " "[c] (there is) weeping, but in the morning—jubilation!

6 I said (at one time) in my prosperity,[d]
"Never will I waver!"

7 " "[e] By your grace "I was set"[f] on a "solid mountain."
You hid your countenance, and I was frightened.

352

8 To you, O Yahweh, I cried,
and made my prayer to my Lord:
9 How will you profit from my blood when I go down to the pit?
Will the dust praise you and declare your faithfulness?
10 Hear, O Yahweh, and have mercy!
O Yahweh, be my helper!
11 You have turned my mourning into dancing,
you have taken away my sackcloth and girded me with gladness
12 so that "my heart"ᵍ may sing and not be silent,
so that, O Yahweh, my God, I may praise you forever.

3a *Qere*: מִיָּרְדִי ("from my going down," "so that I may not go down"). Correct is *Ketīb* Mss Gθ´S מִיּוֹרְדִי־בוֹר (cf. Ps. 28:1).
5b Literally, one would have to translate: "Indeed, only briefly (does he act) in his wrath, but for a lifetime in his grace."
c The peculiarity of v. 5 is that there is a description of situations, or alterations of situations, under the rule of Yahweh, in four short sentences having two members each but without a single finite verb. יָלִין gives the impression that it was added to facilitate reading, and should therefore be eliminated because of the meter.
6d שַׁלְוִי is very likely a contraction or a mistake in spelling for שַׁלְוָתִי
8e On the textual criticism of v. 7, also cf. L. Wächter (*ZAW* 78 [1966]). יהוה should probably be eliminated because of the meter.
f MT is unintelligible ("you had stationed power for my mountain"?). *T* has לְהַרְרֵי עֹז = "on solid mountains." In that case, the emendation would presumably have to be הֶעֱמַדְתִּי or הֶעֱמַדְתָּנִי.
12g G has כְּבֹדִי.

Form

"From a poetic viewpoint, Psalm 30 is one of the best psalms, distinguished as it is for its light and flowing style in spite of a difficult meter, for its beautiful and appropriate images, for its clear outline, and for its uniform mood" (B. Duhm). The "clear outline" primarily yields the following picture: title; vv. 1-3, praise for Yahweh, who has rescued the petitioner from sickness and Sheol; vv. 4-5, call to all pious people to join in the praise, and a creedlike explanation (v. 5); vv. 6-12, description of the healing and help, together with concluding praise. The meter in Psalm 30, however, is exceptionally restless and excited. The dominating meter is 4 + 4: vv. 5, 7, 9, 11, 12. The meter 4 + 3 occurs in vv. 1 and 3; 3 + 3 in vv. 4, 8, 10; 3 + 2 in vv. 6 and 1; 2 + 2 + 2 in v. 2.

Psalm 30 belongs to the more general type, songs of prayer, and is clearly marked as an individual thanksgiving, as a *todah* (see above, Intro. §6, 2aγ; F. Crüsemann, *Studien zur Formgeschichte von Hymnus und Danklied in Israel*, WMANT 32 [1969], 235f.). V. 1 has the characteristic form of the *todah* formula. Characteristic is the style of address in vv. 4f. In the form of the imperative hymn, which contains an invitation to join in singing and giving thanks, people around the one who is singing and praying are encouraged to take part. Here it is worth noting that epigrammatic general statements concerning Yahweh's way of dealing are expressed. The actual occurrence is generalized and in its critical progress is encompassed in a sentence such as that in v. 5. Concerning the function of such verses, see L. Krinetzki (*ZThK* 83 [1961], 350ff.). In the prayer address to Yahweh the following is reported: the affliction (v. 7b), the pleading in prayer (vv. 8-10), and the turn toward the rescue (v. 11). The purpose of Yahweh's way of dealing in all that has taken place is noted in the concluding v. 12.

Setting

The singer of the psalm thankfully and worshipfully looks back to the occasion of healing and helping granted him by Yahweh. From v. 2 it clearly becomes evident that the psalmist was sick unto death and was healed (רפא). In vv. 6ff. he impressively describes how he at one time was torn from carefree days of good fortune (v. 6) and (in sickness) had the frightening experience of learning to know the hiddenness of God (v. 7). The pleading prayer that then rose to Yahweh from this position of distress and fear begins in vv. 9-10. But then thanksgiving and praise triumph in view of the wonderful change of fortune. One would have to suppose that the psalmsinger intones his song of thanksgiving as a תודה in a sacred place. Psalm 30 must be very old.

Commentary

[Title] On מזמור and לדוד, see above, Intro., §4, 2. The definition שיר־ חנכת הבית leaves the impression that it was secondarily inserted between מזמור and לדוד. As an individual song of thanksgiving, Psalm 30 evidently played an important role at the festival of the rededication of the temple since 165 B.C. (1 Macc. 4:52ff.; 2 Macc. 10:5ff.; John 10:22) and has therefore been transferred from individual experience to the community and its worship. The conjecture of Torczyner that שיר־חנכת הבית was at one time a subscript to Psalm 29 (*ZDMG* 64 [1912] 402) is hardly likely.

[30:1] With the hymnic exclamation אֲרוֹמִמְךָ יהוה the song of thanksgiving begins (cf. Ps. 18:1 corrected; Exod. 15:2; Isa. 25:1; Pss. 34:3; 99:5, 9; 145:1). Yahweh is "extolled" in praise because he has "lifted up" (דלה) a person who was suffering and sinking down into Sheol. As one draws the bucket out of the well (thus דלה *qal* in Exod. 2:16, 19; Prov. 20:5), so Yahweh has pulled (cf. also Ps. 18:16) a person sick unto death (see below) out of the depths (Ps. 130:1). The enemies (see above, Intro., § 10, 4) come forward at a significant point in the prayer songs of the sick. They pronounce judgment on the sufferer as one obviously "forsaken by God," they ferret out the cause of the sickness in a transgression, and they ridicule him as wasting away under "just punishment." The enemies also interpret the approaching death as the definitive separation from Yahweh and "rejoice" over the success of their analysis of life. But through the helpful intervention of Yahweh this "success" of the enemies is brought to naught. The powers that separate from God cannot triumph.

[30:2-3] In vv. 2 and 3 a first very brief and thankful report is made about the miracle of being heard and being rescued. For the address אלהי, cf. O. Eissfeldt, " 'Mein Gott' im Alten Testament," *ZAW* 61 (1945/48) 3-16. The "pleading" (שוע) of the lament and prayer (cf. vv. 9-10) was heard (on שוע אל, cf. Ps. 18:7; 22:24; 28:2; 31:22; 88:13). Yahweh "healed" the person sick unto death (cf. Ps. 6:2; 41:4; 103:3; 107:20; G. V. Rad, *OT Theol,* 1:274). To be sick unto death— that means in the OT and in the conception of the ancient Near East to hover in the "sphere of שאול" (Chr. Barth, *Die Errettung vom Tode in den individuellen Klage- und Dankliedern des Alten Testaments* [1947] 93ff.). By means of the saving healing, Yahweh has "brought out" (העלה) the נפש from the jurisdiction of שאול, that is, from harm's way in the nonworld, the underworld that devours life. נפש here is "life itself," the life of the petitioner (H. W. Wolff, *Anthropology of the OT* [1974] 18). On שאול cf. the comment on Ps. 6:5. The contrast between life and death is sharp-edged. Yahweh called the petitioner of the psalm away from the realm of death, from death itself. He drew him out of the group that is going down to the "pit." בור is a figurative expression that allows the concepts of grave and שאול to coincide. Thus the subject here is "the return to healthy life of the whole man who has, through his illness, already been exposed to the power of death" (H. W. Wolff, p. 20). Yet we must consider that the psalm not only describes an individual fate but has also served as a formulary for those who have experienced a rescue that corresponds to these extensive statements of prayer and thanksgiving and who now are giving thanks to Yahweh in the confines of the sanctuary. In this formulary, room could be found for many of the misfortunes of life: in the recognition and description of the depth of the distress and in the confession of the thanksgiving for the rescue experienced.

[30:4-5] To take part in his song of thanksgiving (vv. 1, 12) the singer of the psalm calls in the חסידים, who are by grace devoted to Yahweh. That was the custom in Israel. The תודה would turn to a group of fellow worshipers who were witnesses of the song of thanksgiving in the sanctuary (cf. Ps. 22:22ff.; 35:18; 40:9; 116:14). The individual's experience of rescue is introduced in the congregation. There praise and avowal is heard "in remembrance of his holiness." By means of the song of thanksgiving Yahweh's act of rescue is brought back to mind. זכר, often synonymous with שם, gives notice of the presence of God, which is honored in the cultic song. It is customary in the תודה that individual experiences are elevated to generally applicable, creedlike pronouncements. Verse 5 is to be understood in this way. Once Yahweh has granted help, the time in which God was angry, in which he "hid his face" (v. 7) and let the psalmist suffer in the "realm of death," shrinks down to a brief moment (רגע), whereas the extension of grace fills and determines the duration of a lifetime (cf. Isa. 54:7-8). The "normal work of God" (*opus proprium Dei*) determines the meaning of time (cf. K. Barth, *CD* 2/1, 416). Distress and weeping turn out to be events of yesterday, of the past. With the new morning, the point in time of Yahweh's intervention (cf. Ps. 46:5; 90:14; 143:8), jubilation breaks out as the spirit that determines the meaning of life henceforth. A person's relation to time is in the OT definitely determined by his nearness to God (Ps. 84:10). Here life receives its essential fullness which the meaning of existence entails. Also the "strange work of God" (*opus alienum Dei*), wrath and hiddenness, can only be explained in the light of the experience of salvation.[1]

[30:6-10] In vv. 6-12 the psalmsinger now describes the entire process once more and goes far back. He harks back to the days in which he enjoyed the

---

1. "Our condition in this world, I confess, involves us in such wretchedness, and we are harassed by such a variety of afflictions, that scarcely a day passes without some trouble or grief. Moreover, amid as many uncertain events, we cannot be otherwise than full of daily anxiety and fear. Whithersoever, therefore, men turn themselves, a labyrinth of evils surrounds them. But however much God may terrify and humble his faithful servants, with manifold signs of his displeasure, he always besprinkles them with the sweetness of his favor to moderate and assuage their grief. If they weigh, therefore, his *anger* and his *favor* in an equal balance, they will always find it verified, that while the former is but for a moment, the latter continues to the end of life; nay, it goes beyond it, for it were a grievous mistake to confine the favor of God within the boundaries of this transitory life. And it is unquestionably certain, that none but those whose minds have been raised above the world by taste of heavenly life really experience this perpetual and uninterrupted manifestation of the divine favor, which enables them to bear their chastisements with cheerfulness" (Calvin on Ps. 30:5, trans. Anderson [Grand Rapids: Eerdmans, 1949]).

undisputed and secure conviction, "Never will I waver!" (v. 6). This expression of an unworried trust in oneself is attributed to the godless in Ps. 10:6, and it is characteristic of the fool (Prov. 1:32). Warnings against self-satisfaction are expressed in Deut. 8:1ff. and 1 Cor. 10:12. But the psalmist confesses that through Yahweh's רצון he assumed this position of undisturbed assurance (v. 8). A graphic illustration describes the solid station: העמדתי להררי עז (cf. Ps. 18:34; 27:5; et al.). But what happened then was that Yahweh "hid his countenance" and transferred this unruffled person to a state of fright. In other words, sickness and suffering were sent by Yahweh. His wrath (v. 6) assailed him who had previously been so fortunate. From his affliction he cried out (קרא; שוע in v. 2) and brought his prayer before the Lord (v. 8). The psalmsinger reminds us of his prayer of complaint and pleading, from which only a few words are quoted in vv. 9-10. The question מה-בצע בדמי is at first sight most peculiar, but its meaning is established in the second half-verse. As in Ps. 6:5, the petitioner confronts Yahweh: If I die ("go down to the pit"), Yahweh, you lose a person who could otherwise praise you and declare your אמת. In שאול people no longer praise Yahweh (Ps. 6:5; 88:10ff.; 115:17). Accordingly, Yahweh would have to record a loss and not a gain if the person sick unto death were to enter שאול. This unique motive for intervening presented to God in the plea reveals the psalmist's understanding of his life. The purpose of his existence is the praise of God. The only reason advanced for Yahweh's rescue (cf. on Ps. 6:6) is that this praise should not be extinguished. In v. 10 the characteristic petitions of a lament (cf. H. Gunkel and J. Begrich, *EinlPs* §6) are mentioned. The petitioner prays to be heard (שמע) and for clemency (חנן). He summons Yahweh as his helper (עזר). But this reminder of the coming of calamity and of the lament is immediately eclipsed again by God's act of turning to the rescue (v. 11).

[**30:11**] By his intervention Yahweh has turned the whole thing around. הפך denotes a fundamental and total reversal of all existing conditions. In this sense the verb occasionally occurs in connection with the tradition of the destruction of Sodom and Gomorrah. As helper and rescuer, Yahweh has turned the lament of the sufferer into a round dance. The round dance is the highest expression of joy at a festival (Judg. 21:21; Jer. 31:13; Lam. 5:15). The penitential garment (שק) which the penitent wore has been exchanged for festal apparel. It is Yahweh himself who has brought about this reversal (cf. Ps. 23:5). The creedal statement in v. 5 has its experiential background in this happening.

[**30:12**] The song of thanksgiving of an individual began with a hymnic statement. With a statement of praise the psalm also concludes. The first phase of the report is developed from the hymnic beginning (vv. 1-3); the second phase runs up to the concluding praise (6-12). With למען reference is made in summary to the second statement. On כבוד with the meaning "heart," cf. on Ps. 3:3. Songs of thanksgiving without ceasing are to issue from the mouth of him who has been saved.

Purpose and Thrust

It is significant for Psalm 30 that from the perspective of thankful praise the affliction experienced appears in a special light. Suffering is fitted into the course of life in a comprehensive way. There was once a time of unchallenged self-assurance (vv. 6-7); Yahweh's grace provided this undisturbed good fortune. But then misfortune suddenly closed in. Yahweh went into hiding.

His wrath assailed the human being (for אף, cf. on Ps. 6:1). Life sank into the distress of sickness and into the "domain of death." What was the meaning of this angry act of Yahweh? In the light of the reversal (v. 11) and of the rescue that has taken place, this question is not dealt with in brooding contemplation, but is answered from a conviction based on the experience of a rescue: If Yahweh gives grace, the entire weight and burden of affliction collapses to a single "brief moment" (רגע). There is but a weak remembrance of the weeping of an evening! Now grace and jubilation, thankfulness and praise prevail. Ushered in is the truth: αὕτη ἡ ἀσθένεια οὐκ ἔστιν πρὸς θάνατον ἀλλ' ὑπὲρ τῆς δόξης τοῦ θεοῦ (John 11:4). The new reality of the nearness of God and the help of God fills life and determines the understanding of existence. The purpose of life is the praise of God (vv. 9, 12). The חסידים are called to join in the glorification of God which the individual proclaims (v. 4). For what the individual has experienced in the line of help from God is not really his own experience and property—something that points merely to the private sphere. As the formulary of the prayer of thanksgiving in the congregation was a given pattern, so one's own experience of weal and woe, but especially the experience of the help and rescue by Yahweh, is to be witnessed and transmitted to the congregation in the vessel of preformulated statements. It would be an incalculable failure if this witnessing and transmitting were not to take place, if the one who has been rescued were to remain silent (v. 12; cf. Ps. 32:8; 66:16; et al.). "What is involved here is certainly not a process of teaching in the usual sense of the word, a transmission of a proved philosophy of life, but a testimony in the strict sense of the word, that is, a word that has been empowered by an act of God that has preceded it: (G. von Rad, *God at Work in Israel* [1980]). Thus also the maxims that are coined in such circumstances (cf. v. 6) are intended not so much for conveying general information but much more as a disclosure supported by concrete experience.

357

Psalm 31

Prayer, Trust, and Thanks
of One Mortally Threatened

Literature

H. Schmidt, *Das Gebet der Angeklagten im Alten Testament*, BZAW 49 (1928). C. Winkler, " 'In deiner Hand ist meine Zeit.' Besinnung zu Ps 31,16," *Bibel und Leben* 10 (1969) 134-137. W. Beyerlin, *Die Rettung der Bedrängten in den Feindpsalmen der Einzelnen auf institutionelle Zusammenhänge untersucht*, FRLANT 99 (1970).

Text

To the choirmaster. A psalm of David.
31:1 In you, O Yahweh, have I taken shelter,
let me never be put to shame!
In your righteousness rescue me![a]
2 Incline your ear to me,
rescue me hastily![b]
Be a protecting[c] rock for me,
a firm fortress to help me!
3 For you are my rock and my fortress.
For the sake of your name, O Yahweh,[d]
be pleased to lead and guide[e] me;
4 be pleased to free me from the net
that has secretly been set for me!
For you are my refuge.[f]
5 Into your hands I commend my spirit,
you redeem me, O Yahweh, faithful God!
6 You[g] hate those who cling to vain nonentities;
but I trust in Yahweh.
7 I will rejoice and be glad in your goodness,
that you have looked at my distress,
that you have taken note of the adversities of my soul.[h]
8 that you have not delivered me into the hand of the enemy
but have set my feet on a wide field.

9 Be merciful to me, O Yahweh, for I am distressed,
my eye is blurred on account of grief. ‘ ’[i]
10 Indeed, my life is spent in lamentation,
and my years (flit by) in sighing.
My strength wastes away in ‘misery,’[j]
my bones are becoming weak.[k]
11 In the presence of all my enemies
I have become a disgrace
and a ‘feud’[l] to my neighbors,
an object of dread for my acquaintances.
Those who see me on the street
run away from me.
12 I am forgotten, out of mind like a dead man,
I am like a smashed vessel.
13 For I hear the whisperings of many
—horror round about—
how they confer with one another about me,
conspire to take my life.
14 But as for me, I trust in you, O Yahweh.
I say, You are my God.
15 My future lies in your hand; save me
from the hand of my enemies and persecutors!
16 Let your countenance shine over your servant,
help me in your goodness!
17 O Yahweh, let me not be put to shame, for I cry to you;
may the wicked be put to shame—fall silent to Sheol.
18 May the lips of lying fall silent,
they who in haughtiness ‘ ’[m] speak impudently against
the righteous!
19 How bountiful, ‘O Yahweh,’[n] is your goodness,
which you have intended for those who fear you
(and) prepared for those who take shelter with you before men!
20 You shelter them in the protection of your countenance[o]
against the calumnies[p] of the people.
You keep them safe in a shelter
against the strife of tongues.
21 Praised be Yahweh,
that he has wondrously shown his grace to me
in the ‘time of oppression’![q]
22 But I—I thought in my fright:
I am ‘cast away’[r] from your eyes.
But you heard
my loud cry to you.
23 Love Yahweh, all you who are pious!
Those who are faithful Yahweh protects.
But he repays in full measure
him who is haughty.
24 Be strong and confident in heart,
all you who wait for Yahweh!

1a Gk and Ps. 71:2 add וְהַצִּילֵנִי.
2b Perhaps we should read מַהֵרָה here.
c ε´ and Ps. 71:3 read מָעוֹן.
3d Following 1 Ms and S, we will very likely have to supply יהיה for the sake of the meter. For the problem of the meter, see below, “Form.”
e Instead of תנחני ותנהלני, S has only נַחֲמֵנִי.

4f Perhaps the pointing מָעוֹזִי is to be preferred.

6g Following 1 Ms Gk, Jerome, and S, we will here have to read שָׂנֵאתָ, for the apodosis introduced by ואני will otherwise not be intelligible in its tendency toward the opposite direction.

7h With the translation ἔσωσας ἐκ τῶν ἀναγκῶν τὴν ψυχήν μου, Gk indicates how יִדַע בְּ is to be understood in the context. It would be problematical to consider a Hebrew text הוֹשַׁעְתָּ מִצָּרוֹת on the basis of the translation in Gk.

9i נפשי ובטני (= "my soul and my body") is surely a supplementary addition that is to be eliminated as such.

10j Gk and S read בְּעָנְיִ instead of בעוני (= "in my debt"). Even better is σ´: בְּעָנְיִי (cf. v. 7). For בעוני in the MT there is no clue in Psalm 31.

k KBL connects עששו with the Akkadian word uššu (= "sorrow"). No correction seems necessary here.

11l מאד (= "very much") has a peculiar position in the text and fits poorly in the context. In the emendation it has been suggested to read מוֹרָא, מָנוֹד, or מָגוֹר. Best of all probably would be Briggs: מָדוֹן (= "feud"), cf. Ps. 80:6.

18m ובוז is not present in S and will have to be eliminated from the overloaded second half-verse. Other commentators eliminate עתק or even עתק עתק עַל־צַדִּיק.

19n Following 3 Mss and Gk, we are to insert the divine name יהוה for the sake of the meter (see below).

20o Following Ps. 61:4, it is easy to correct בְּנָפֶיךָ: בסתר כְּנָפֶיךָ: "in the protection of your wings." But פָנֶיךָ could also be possible.

p רְכֶסִי, from רֹכֶס, is a hapax legomenon. Following Bickell and Duhm, we might correct: מֵרְכִילֵי.

21q בעיר מצור (= "in the fortified city") does not make sense at this point. Following Wellhausen and Duhm, we ought to read בְּעֵת מָצוֹר.

22r נגרזתי is found only here in the OT. Very likely the consonants were interchanged. More fluent is נִגְזַרְתִּי (cf. Isa. 53:8; Ps. 88:5; Lam. 3:54).

Form

Psalm 31 consists of two parts that are clearly distinguished: vv. 1-8; 9-24. These two parts both express lament, trust, and thanksgiving. For that reason there would be support for the view that in Psalm 31 we would have to think of two different songs (thus H. Schmidt). It becomes apparent, however, that two concurrent parts within a single psalm are present also in Psalms 18; 30; and 102. Obviously the form-type in which two phases are noticeable was a well-known phenomenon. Here it is striking that in most cases the narrative of the individual song of thanksgiving that has recourse to profound lamentation contains this peculiar double report. On the individual elements of the structure of Psalm 31, the analysis of the type will contribute decisive points.

The metrical reconstruction of Psalm 31 brings with it great difficulties. H. Gunkel declares regarding the problem of the principle: "In such a text it is difficult to say how far one is entitled to smooth it out." The symmetry of the parallelism of members is often disturbed by three-part passages that provide considerable resistance to the attempt at a practical reconstruction of the meter. Therefore we will have to begin with the observation that in Psalm 31 we are dealing with a "mixed meter." Only with great caution can the individual parts be coordinated. Especially in vv. 2-4 are the difficulties considerable. Let us therefore only for these verses state how the accentuation would have to be managed: in v. 1: 3 + 2 + 2; in v. 2 very likely: 3 + 2 and 3 + 3; in v. 3: 3 and 3 + 2. In vv. 4 ff. we then encounter the following picture: double triple meters are present in vv. 5, 6, 7 (in addition, an isolated triple meter), 8, 9, 12, 15, 19, 22 (up to עֵינֶיךָ), 24. Vv. 10, 13, 16, 20 (up to אִישׁ), 23 are to be read in the 3 + 2 meter. The $2+2+2$ meter is present in vv. 4, 11 (twice), 21, 22 (in the second part of the verse); $2+2$ in v. 20 (second part); $4+3$ in v. 14; $4+4$ in v.17; and $3+4$ in v. 18.

The first survey (see above) already showed that a variety of forms and elements of expression are to be discovered. But before the analysis deals with the individual units of form, we must assign the totality of the psalm to the form group of prayer songs. See above, Intro. §6, 2. In individual instances, however, the interpretation of the outline of the organization is frustrated by the form-critical observation that in vv. 1-17 there are petitions, descriptions of distress, and statements of trust, while between vv. 17 and 18 a sudden change, a turning point, can be established. In v. 18 the person persecuted by enemies obviously has a reason and the power to confront his adversaries with the demand for silence. He has been heard! Therefore he can praise and thank Yahweh in hymnic style (vv. 18ff.). In v. 22 the turn of events that has taken place is clearly witnessed to: "But you heard my loud cry when I cried to you!" The psalm closes with a paraenesis to all who hope in Yahweh (vv. 23f.).

We will have to proceed from the thought that Psalm 31 was transmitted as a prayer formulary. We will have to show to which setting this formulary points.

Setting

The last verses of the psalm clearly show that the singer and petitioner of Psalm 31 addresses a group of human beings. Obviously, as was customary for a *todah*, he has assembled an audience of the cultic community about him for the purpose of presenting the prayer song in their midst and bearing witness to what has happened. Cf. above, Intro. §6, 2aγ. The situation is the one recognizable in Ps. 22:22, in which the song is intoned. We need not inquire about a personal life situation. The prayer formularies standardize the life situation and let it appear only in outlines in which the petitioner could find a place for and bear witness to his own suffering and experience. Whether and to what extent the prayer songs produced and perhaps also taught by rote by the priesthood were supplemented and made specific by means of the inclusion of individual experiences cannot be ascertained. And yet, the living nature of the process of the transmission, reception, and supplementation can hardly be exaggerated. Especially multilayered, extensive prayer songs show traces of a process of transmission which can hardly be traced in detail. From Psalm 31 we can deduce the following: Life was weak and disturbed (vv. 9, 10, 12), encompassed by abuse (v. 11). Friends turned away (v. 11). Enemies rose up with lies (v. 18) and slander (v. 20). Murder was planned (vv. 4, 13). There was danger of life and limb (v. 5). All of these statements make it seem likely that this formulary was fashioned for an innocent person who was persecuted, who had hid himself in the temple area and had pleaded for Yahweh's legal aid. Especially v. 1 reminds us of the institution of the divine jurisprudence (*Gottesgerichtsbarkeit*). Cf. H. Schmidt; W. Beyerlin. But we should explain that the contours of that which was institutional have become very blurred. Specific references to the sacral process of divine jurisprudence cannot be discerned. Therefore we will have to think of conventionalized forms of speech rather than of statements referring directly to a judicial act.

According to everything we have said so far, the date of composition can hardly be determined. A contact with the "confessions" of the prophet

Jeremiah—often noted—in no way provides occasion for maintaining that the psalm was a "patchwork of citations." Rather, we should think of standardized formulary speech in such connections.

Commentary

[Title] On למנצח, cf. above, Intro. §4, No. 17. On מזמור לדוד, cf. Intro. §4, No. 2.

[31:1-3] The lament and prayer song of the petitioner fleeing to Yahweh begins with the statement, בך יהוה חסיתי (Pss. 7:1; 11:1; 16:1). In the protective area of the sanctuary he prays for Yahweh's helpful intervention, for he who does not come to know God's gracious attention is "put to shame." His life is forfeited and lost. The preposition בְ in בצדקתך seems to suggest the conception that צדקה is a saving area of power in which Yahweh creates acceptance and rescue (K. Koch, "*Sdq* im Alten Testament," Diss. Heidelberg [1953], 35ff.). Yet, the "righteousness of God" is the perfection of the judging and rescuing presence of power to which the petitioner in his distress appeals. It is a fact worth noting that innocent people who are persecuted, who depend on the righteousness of God and are waiting for the *iustificatio iusti*, hope for rescue and acquittal from the צדקה. This recognition of the saving righteousness, which Luther acquired in the Psalms and in Rom. 1:16f., belongs to the foundations of Reformation theology. But already Augustine had seen the essentials.[1] In any case it would be important not to understand צדקה as celestial—note the suffix—but in the context to interpret it as personal. The cry הטה אלי אזנך (v. 2) prays for an answer. Urgency is indicated by the wish מהרה הצילני. The contingency of persecution and oppression becomes clear from the desire for protection on the part of the petitioner: May Yahweh be his "protective rock" and "firm fortress." For the sacral tradition of צור, cf. the comment on Ps. 18:2. Verse 4, introduced by כי, points to the trust of the petitioner. The certainty claimed personally could be an inducement for Yahweh's intervention. On סלעי ומצודתי, cf. Ps. 18:2. But may the protection asked for be effective also outside the sanctuary—that is the wish of the singer. In the petition תנחני ותנהלני the interest is in the permanence of the bestowal of salvation (in this sense already לעולם in v. 1 is to be understood). Cf. Ps. 23:3. On למען שמך, see O. Grether, *Name und Wort Gottes im Alten Testament*, BZAW 64 (1934) 53.

[31:4-5] The statements in v. 4 reveal that the petitioner is being persecuted by insidious enemies (on the theme "enemies of the individual," see above, Intro. §10, 4). As the hunter sets out a camouflaged net (G. Dalman, *AuS*, 6:335), so the oppressors try to catch their prey and lay them low (Pss. 9:15; 25:15; 140:5). But may Yahweh intervene and rescue! With the declaration in v. 5 the persecuted person delivers his life into the power of Yahweh; he surrenders it to him.[2] רוח is the breath of life and so the potential of life altogether (L. Köhler

---

1. "For it is the righteousness of God, which becomes ours too when it is given to us. But it is called the righteousness of God, lest a human being think he has righteousness in his own right" (Augustine, "Enarrationes in Psalmos," *Migne,* 36/37, 233).

2. "This is one of the principal places of Scripture which are most suitable for correcting distrust. It teaches us, first, that the faithful ought not to torment themselves above measure with unhappy cares and anxieties; and secondly, that they should not be so distracted with fear as to cease from performing their duty, nor decline and faint in such a manner as to grasp at vain hopes and deceitful

OT Theology 137f.). פקד בידך—this declaration entails a complete expropriation of existence. Life is delivered into another person's area of power and ownership. To what extent the conception is influenced also by the verb פדה cannot be ascertained. On פדה, cf. J. J. Stamm, *Erlösen und Vergeben im Alten Testament* (1940) 14. It is also not easy to decide whether the perfect form פדיתה is a perfect of certainty (thus H. Gunkel) or whether the answer to prayer should here be presupposed already. An interpretation in the sense of the second explanation would be very unlikely in the context. Yahweh is called אל אמת—the faithful, dependable God (cf. 2 Chron. 15:3). From the very beginning, Psalm 31 firmly insists on an enduring proof of the reality of salvation (לעולם, v. 1). In this context אל אמת is the appropriate designation of God.

[31:6] If v. 6 should now have to be read according to the MT, even though the ואני with its tendency toward the opposite direction would then make for difficulties, we could for a moment think about traces of an oath of cleansing that ended in a declaration of trust and loyalty over against Yahweh (cf. the comment on Ps. 7:3ff.). However, if we read שָׂנֵאתָ—and that is more likely—then v. 6 in its context would have to be understood as follows: As אל אמת, as the faithful God, Yahweh proves his reliability by letting the idolaters feel his effective wrath. Terms like הבלים (Deut. 32:21; 1 Kings 16:13, 26; Jer. 8:19; 14:22) or הבלי שוא (Jonah 2:9), as prophetic denunciations of the heathen numina, could have their "Sitz im Leben" in the cult of renunciation. But the psalmsinger does not belong among those who go for "idle nonentities" (on שמר, cf. Hos. 4:10; Jonah 2:9); he trusts in Yahweh.

[31:7-8] The words אגילה ואשמחה בחסדך at the beginning of v. 7 could be understood as a vow for a future song of thanksgiving or as a song of thanksgiving itself. Both interpretations are possible. On חסד, cf. the comment on Ps. 5:7. If Yahweh bestows his "goodness," he has taken note of the affliction and distress of him who laments, has not "let him be put to shame," and accordingly has not delivered him to the enemies. For the meaning of the root רחב in במרחב, cf. the comment on Ps. 4:1.

[31:9-18] While vv. 7 and 8 already contain the tones of the song of thanksgiving, the psalmsinger once more descends to the depths of affliction and oppression in the second phase of the psalm, which begins at v. 9. The plea for a merciful bestowal of salvation is again renewed—and that with reference to distress (צר) and fears that strangle life. The power of life is diminishing. That is what the phrase עששה בכעס עיני (cf. Ps. 6:7) means. In vv. 9 and 10 we could think of the lament of one who is mortally ill. But, very likely, standing formulas of expression from the lament of one who is ill have in this passage found their way into the song of one who has been persecuted. He is fenced in with abuse (v. 11). Even friends and acquaintances forsake and flee him as redolent of

---

helps, nor give way to fears and alarms; and, in fine, that they should not be afraid of death, which, though it destroys the body, cannot extinguish the soul. This, indeed, ought to be our principal argument for overcoming all temptations, that Christ, when commending his soul to his Father, undertook the guardianship of the souls of all his people. Stephan, therefore, calls upon him to be his keeper, saying: 'Lord Jesus, receive my spirit' (Acts 7:59). As the soul is the seat of life, it is on this account, as is well known, used to signify life" (Calvin, on Ps. 31:4, trans. Anderson [Grand Rapids: Eerdmans, 1949]).

calamity (cf. Pss. 38:11; 55:13; 88:8, 18). Forgotten like one who has died, smashed like a clay vessel—these are two juxtaposed statements that illustrate the misery.

For the second simile, cf. Jer. 22:28; 48:38. But the threatening danger is above all reported in v. 13. He who was persecuted heard the whispering of the enemies who were planning an attack on him. מגור מסביב could have been a conventional expression—an exclamation that described the inescapability of a danger (Jer. 6:25; 20:10; 46:5; 49:29). The purpose of this plot is לקחת נפשי. But in the midst of this deadly affliction the petitioner trusts in Yahweh (cf. v. 6). He quotes the declaration of trust אלהי אתה. On אלהי, cf. O. Eissfeldt, " 'Mein Gott' im Alten Testament,'' ZAW 61 (1945/48) 3-16. Then follow words of trusting resignation. On the relation of עתות and the Akkadian 'anatu-ettu, cf. the comment on Ps. 9:9. On the petition in v. 15, cf. vv. 4 and 8.

פנים in v. 16 is a "visualization'' of Yahweh (L. Köhler, OT Theology 123f.). The "shining countenance'' would be a sign of the gracious and friendly presence of God (Num. 6:25), while the "receding'' of the light of his countenance (Ps. 4:6) is an expression of his wrath. Is the petitioner in his prayer for Yahweh's shining countenance thinking of a theophany? Would an appearance of God manifest the goodness (חסד) of God? Cf. the comment on Ps. 7:6-9. On v. 17, cf. v. 1. Yahweh proves his bestowal of salvation and his power when he causes the רשעים to be silent and to go down to שאול. On שאול, cf. Ps. 6:5. In v. 18 it becomes clear that slanderous accusations have been raised against the psalmsinger. The petitioner pleads for Yahweh's intervention to silence the lies.

[31:19-22] In vv. 19-21 unmistakable hymnic elements come into prominence. מה at the beginning of v. 19 and ברוך at the beginning of v. 21 are clear signs of the language of the hymn that comes into its own in the song of thanksgiving. For those who fear him and shelter themselves with him, Yahweh has designed and prepared a bountiful goodness. Accordingly, salvation was there long ago. It was hidden, and it crops out in the act of the hearing of prayer. On נגד, cf. Ps. 23:5. בני אדם, like אנוש in Pss. 9:20; 10:18, denotes the enemies of the individual who are human beings, not God—no matter how arrogantly they may behave (v. 18). As in v. 19, so also in v. 20, generally obligatory and valid experiences are for the first expressed in hymnic form. Yahweh shelters all who seek refuge with him "in the protection of his countenance.'' סתר פניך is the sheltering area of nearness to God. On פנים, which is probably original here, cf. v. 16. The calumnies of the enemies lose their power in the realm of God's presence. In v. 21 the personal experience of salvation is now expressed. The petitioner has been wondrously blessed. On הפליא חסדו לי, cf. Ps. 17:7. Yahweh's bestowal of salvation has become a fact. It is a miracle. In v. 22 the petitioner once more looks back and points out how he stood on the brink of despairing hopelessness. But Yahweh heard his cry.

[31:23-24] The song of thanksgiving always shows a tendency to bear witness to events, to recount experiences, to teach, and to exhort. This didactic tendency turns up in the paraenetic word of exhortation of vv. 23 and 24 (cf. G. von Rad, OT Theol, 1:359, n.8). There is an invitation to enjoy the love of Yahweh. He preserves the faithful (cf. Ps. 12:1). Gk presents a different statement; it is closely related to Isa. 26:2 and Exod. 34:7. "He repays in full measure him who is haughty''; here the accusative case represents the direct object (BrSynt §90c). Verse 24 could be an addition (cf. Ps. 27:14).

Purpose and Thrust

We will have to begin with the observation already made, that in Psalm 31 individual passages are assembled and woven together to make a whole. This fact makes it difficult to recognize the scope or even just a continuous thread. The interpreter will be tempted to orient himself to general patterns: petitions, descriptions of distress, trust, and thanksgiving, and to let the nuances go by the board in favor of a generalizing total conception. Still, in regard to details, the features of the petition—which is particularly intimately interwoven with the expressions of trust—should be pointed out. In many respects Psalm 31 is the model of prayer that is confident of being heard. The petitioner never tires of trustingly attaching every sentence of the petition to expressions of confidence. Especially the act of self-surrender to Yahweh is expressed again and again. It arrives at its zenith in the statement, ''Into your hands I commend my spirit; you redeem me, O Yahweh, faithful God!'' (v. 5). According to Luke 23:46, it is the prayer of Jesus as he dies on the cross. But the trusting self-surrender is controlled by the certainty that Yahweh has not only looked upon and taken note of the entire distress-ridden, abused, and persecuted life, but has also accepted it (v. 7). Even in the face of enemies that rise up with lies and hatred and in a situation of utter forsakenness, we hear: ''You are my God, my future lies in your hand!'' (vv. 14f.). The psalm concludes with thanksgiving and praise. All petitions are fulfilled. The entire psalm, especially vv. 19f., certifies who the אל אמת (v. 5) is. In his faithfulness and dependability Yahweh grants goodness and sheltering, protection and freedom to the rescued person, who had imagined himself cast away (v. 22). From trouble and thanksgiving, from the experience of divine help, the paraenesis emerges with which the psalm closes. Let him whose hopes rest on Yahweh's help be confident and of good cheer (v. 24). The prayer is a witness to the אל אמת (v. 5). The truth of God is the confirmation of his grace and faithfulness.

The Blessedness
of the Forgiveness of Sins

Literature

E. Baumann, "Struktur-Untersuchungen im Psalter I," *ZAW* 61 (1945/48) 140f. R. G. Castellino, "Psalm XXXII, 9," *VT* (1952) 37-42. A. S. van der Woude, "Zwei alte *Cruces* im Psalter," *OTS* 13 (1963) 131-135.

Text

Of David. A *maskil*.

32:1 Blessed is he whose transgression is forgiven,[a]
whose sin is covered!

2 Blessed is the man to whom Yahweh
does not impute offenses,
in whose heart is no treachery!

3 When I kept silence, my bones wasted away[b]
from daily groaning.

4 For day and night there lay heavy
on me your hand.
Changed was 'my tongue'[c]
'as'[d] in the heat of summer. Selah.

5 Then I informed you of my transgression,
did not hide my guilt.
I said: I will confess
my evil deeds[e] to Yahweh.
Then you forgave
the guilt of my transgressions. Selah.

6 Therefore prayer should be made
to you by every pious person
at the time when he finds[f] (you).
"Then when mighty waters come flooding up,
they will not assail you."

7 You are my protection,
you guard me against distress.
With rescuing 'shields'ᵍ
you encircle me. *Selah*.
8 I will show and teach you the way you should go,
will advise you—on you is my eye!
9 'Be'ʰ not without understanding, like the horse and mule,
'whose strength'ⁱ only bit and bridle tame.
No one shall come near you!
10 Many are the pains of the wicked,ʲ
but he who trusts in Yahweh, him he will hedge in with goodness.
11 Be glad about Yahweh and rejoice, you who are righteous,
and shout for joy, all you who are upright!

1a שׂוּי

נ here represents נָשָׂא. The spelling can be thought of as an accommodation to the parallel כסוי.

3b A number of Mss have כָּלוּ.

4c The MT is unintelligible, for לְשִׁדִי, from לְשָׁד (= "oil cake," "baked goods," Num. 11:8) is absurd. The correction already suggested by Olshausen, לְשׁנִי, seems appropriate. **d** MT: "in the heat of summer." Better: כְּחַרְבֹנִי (Σ,Τ).

5e Mss Gk, α´, σ´, Jerome have כְּשֶׁעִי .

6f In the construction of this verse part, רַק is difficult and strange. A correction to רַע gives rise to problematical changes of the word מצא. G. Müller corrects to עֵצָם רַע ("at the time when mischief is predominant"). E. Baumann, however, has: רק לעת בהמצאו = "only then when you let yourself be found" (*ZAW* 61, 141).

7g רני would be plural, from the infinitive רן (רנן). Gk, α´, Jerome take רני ("my rejoicing") as a form of address for God (Baethgen). These explanations are very questionable. The emendation of Budde is appealing: מָגִנֵּי ("With shields of rescue you encircle me").

9h According to the context, we expect the singular תְּהִי (2 Mss).

i עֶדְיוֹ = "his ornament." Gk has τὰς σιαγόνας αὐτῶν = "his cheeks." S. Mowinckel thinks of עֲדִי as a term that not only has the meaning "ornament" but can also mean "strength" or "passion" (*PsStud*, 1:52f.). Very likely we will do better to read עֻזּוֹ.

10j For the position of the adjectival attribute, cf. BrSynt §58.

Form

In the meter of Psalm 32 it is worth noting that in vv. 3-5 two sections of similar versification and ending with *selah* follow each other (vv. 3-4 and 4-5) and that in each case they are characterized by the meters 3 + 2, 3 + 2, 2 + 2. This middle section of the first part of the psalm (vv. 1-7) is framed by two felicitations (at the beginning in vv. 1-2): 3 + 2, 3 + 2 (3) and didactic, or confessionlike, statements in vv. 6-7: 2 + 2 + 2, 3 + 2, 2 + 2, 2 + 2. The meter of the second part of the psalm (vv. 8-11) is of a different type. Here the sequence is: 4 + 3, 4 + 4, (2) 3 + 4, 4 + 3. This second part of the psalm therefore is definitely different from vv. 1-7.

Psalm 32 belongs to the form group: prayer songs (see above, Intro. § 6, 2). Significant is the address to Yahweh in vv. 4-7, to which v. 3 should also be added. These verses, which really make up the middle section of the psalm, contain descriptions of distress and—in v. 7—expressions of trust. When an imperative summons to praise comes into prominence in v. 11, we are to take notice that Psalm 32 wants to be understood as a *todah*, a song of thanksgiving by an individual. See above, Intro. §6, 2aγ. Such songs of thanksgiving—even when they appear only rudimentarily—are most often to be understood as a fulfillment of a vow. Thus the psalm has all the characteristics of a *todah:* description of the distress, prayer to God and help received, thanksgiving, or summons to praise. The turn of events is signalized by the passage in vv. 8f., which should probably be thought of as a statement by Yahweh. There is opposition to this view, most recently by F. Crüsemann, *Studien zur Formgeschichte von Hymnus und Danklied in Israel,* WMANT 22 (1969) 238f. The point is made that such a quotation of a word of Yahweh is unusual, that we should rather think of a "generalizing wisdom address to other human beings" (239). However, a question in return would be in place: Where do we find such a generalizing wisdom address in the singular directed to another human being? But, above all, which human being could presume to say to someone else, "I will show and teach you the way you should go, will advise you—on you is my eye!" (v. 8)? On the basis of the contents we can think only of a statement by Yahweh (see below, "Commentary").—Worth noting, further, are the wisdom elements in Psalm 32. The influence of didactic poetry is unmistakable. See above, Intro. §6, 5. Verses 1 and 2 present a felicitation that is characteristic of didactic poetry of wisdom literature. Cf. the comment on Psalm 1; but also H. Schmidt, "Grüsse and Glückwünsche im Psalter," *ThStKr* 103 (1931) 141-150; W. Janzen *"Ašrē in the Old Testament,"* HThR 58 (1965) 215-226 (with the suggestion to translate: "To be envied is he who . . ."). In Psalm 32 also v. 10 is a passage molded by prudential wisdom. Accordingly, the prayer song presented in v. 11 as a *todah* in intention and with a formal point is strongly permeated with the wisdom characteristics of didactic poetry. We should probably assume that the psalm was used as a liturgical formulary. In no case will we be able to think of the prayer song as a penitential psalm.

Setting

The song of thanksgiving of an individual revealed in v. 11 is based on the event of experiencing the salvation that was conveyed through the word of God in vv. 8-9. In the presence of a group of people the speaker tells about his distress and about his pardon (vv. 3-5). Such a *todah* had its "Sitz im Leben" in the sanctuary. The situation described in Ps. 22:22 could be taken for granted (cf. the summons in v. 11). More often, the songs of thanksgiving in the Psalter tend toward reporting experiences and toward teaching, toward confession and challenge. This is where elements of didactic wisdom poetry gain entrance. In the course of the history of transmission this takes place at an increasing pace. Psalm 32 is to be dated fairly late.

But how is the petitioner's distress recognizable in the prayer song to be defined and explained in detail? H. Schmidt thought of a person seriously ill. But we have to admit that no petition for healing is expressed. The distress from which the petitioner knows he has been rescued is the distress of sin. Not sickness and healing, but guilt and forgiveness are the determining themes of the psalm. Thus we might carefully ask whether Psalm 32 should be associated with sacrifices for sin and with rites of cleansing (S. Mowinckel, *Religion und Kultus* [1953], 89). One such possibility is that a poem originally belonging to such rites later came to be dissociated from the cultic connection.

Commentary

[**Title**] On לדוד, see above, Intro. §4, 2. On מַשְׂכִּיל, cf. Intro. §4, No. 5.

[32:1-2] The song of thanksgiving begins in a happy but at the same time weighty manner with two felicitations introduced by אַשְׁרֵי (cf. H. Schmidt, "Grüsse und Glückwünsche im Psalter," *ThStKr* 103 [1931], 141-150). These felicitations are exultant declarations of a human being who proclaims his own experience of salvation (v. 5b) to others as he recruits and informs: אַשְׁרֵי נְשׂוּי־ פֶּשַׁע. Three terms for "guilt" are mentioned in vv. 1-2, and they are to be grasped exactly in their semantic character. פֶּשַׁע is "breaking away from God" (F. Delitzsch), "the revolt of the human will against the divine will" (L. Köhler, *OT Theology* 170). חַטָּאָה denotes the "failure," "miss" (L. Köhler, 169). And עָוֹן has the meaning "perversion," "distortion" (F. Delitzsch); it expresses the "attitude that is not in harmony with God's will" (L. Köhler). On נָשָׂא פֶּשַׁע, cf. J. J. Stamm, *Erlösen und Vergeben im Alten Testament* (1940) 67f. It is "difficult to say whether the expression is simply based on the picture of sin which is taken away like any other object or whether this picture had a special form that goes back to some practice" (J. J. Stamm, 69f.). In any case, the individual locutions which describe the forgiveness of sin in vv. 1-2 have become standing formulations. That is especially true in the case of כסה חטאה = "to cover sin" (J. J. Stamm, 72f.). The phrase לֹא חָשַׁב עָוֹן is very likely based on a declaratory act (G. von Rad, *OT Theol*, 1:378f.). The person who experiences the profound, comprehensive healing effects of forgiveness is called blessed. That is the way the threefold statement wants to be understood. רוּחַ, translated as "heart," is to be understood in connection with the ethical-religious neutrality of this concept (cf. H. W. Wolff, *Anthropology of the OT* [1974], 38). "Heart" and "will" can be both inactive and energetic, upright or deceitful. When Yahweh forgives, the entire direction of thinking and willing is without deceit.

[32:3-5] The narration of the personal experience of the miracle of forgiveness has the nature of an illustrative demonstration which bears witness to the blessedness stated in vv. 1-2. But first of all the reference is to the torment and burden of existence plagued by guilt. The guilt that is retained in humans and passed over in silence has a deleterious effect on physical well-being. Life is consumed and corroded by the power opposed to God. The Psalms see the secret relation of guilt and illness on a more profound level than that of a rationally understood causality (G. von Rad, *OT Theol*, 1:274f.). If a person is silent, not open toward God, then "his bones waste away." Such distress is most often understood in the OT as the effect of the wrath of God (cf. the comment on Psalm 6). The petitioner of Psalm 32 speaks of the "hand" of Yahweh lying and pressing down heavily on his life (cf. Ps. 38:3). In the heat of the fever the tongue dries up (cf. Ps. 22:15). But the turn of events begins when he who is breaking apart makes known his transgression and no longer conceals his guilt in silence before Yahweh. This is not only the "relieving power of the word that communicates" in a generally phenomenological sense (G. van der Leeuw, *Phänomenologie der Religion* [1933], 419), but existence that opens up and confesses to Yahweh. The resolve אוֹדֶה עֲלֵי פְשָׁעַי לַיהוה broke the ban. On הוֹדָה in the sense of "confess," cf. Prov. 28:13. But to the confession of the guilt Yahweh immediately reacts with the consolation of forgiveness (Prov. 28:13; 1 John 1:9).[1] We should note that the liberation from his sin is more important for the psalmist than his physical recovery, which he does not mention with a single

---

1. But the words also teach, that as often as the sinner presents himself at the throne of mercy, with

word (cf. J. J. Stamm 132). The rescue of forgiveness is the source of healing (Matt. 9:2). The text provides an impetus to give attention to those psychic convulsions and devastations that are the result of the failure to confess guilt openly. It is obviously an archetypal psychological experience of man that hidden and encysted guilt disturbs all of life from deep within and possibly manifests itself in the processes of physical illness.

Concerning the theme "guilt and forgiveness" the comparison with a "late Babylonian poem" is instructive. Here a petitioner expresses a "lament to quiet the heart for every god." He confesses: "My lord, the sins are grievous, the omissions are heavy. My goddess, the sins are grievous, the omissions are heavy." Through the wrath of the gods, through a weird curse of sickness, the harm has come about: "The Lord in his wrath has given me an angry look. The god has turned against me in his wrath; the goddess, angry with me, has made me sick." But in the lament and prayer a moving uncertainty and lack of orientation concerning the world of the gods now reveals itself. The song begins with the words, "May the wrath of my lord subside against me; may the god whom I know not give me rest; may the goddess whom I know not give me rest!" Corresponding to this latter uncertainty about the gods, there is uncertainty and unclearness concerning the personal ego: "The sin that I have committed I know not; the omissions I am guilty of I do not know; the abomination that I have eaten I do not know; the abomination on which I have stepped I do not know." From this distress emerges the pathetic description of the situation: "Continuously I look (for help)—no one extends a hand to me; I weep— no one comes to my aid; I cry out in my lament—no one hears me; I am in torment, am covered (with a cloth), cannot see." The plea for rescue from the "swampy waters" and for "release" of the burden of the ban brings the lament to a close. For the text, cf. S. Langdon, *Babylonian Penitential Psalms*, 39-44; A. Falkenstein and W. von Soden, *Sumerische und akkadische Hymnen und Gebete* [1953], 225ff.

[**32:6**] The narration of the distress of sin and of the forgiveness personally experienced (vv. 3-5) switches to a "didactic conclusion" in v. 6 introduced by עַל־זֹאת. The experience of distress and rescue should prompt every pious person who lives in a convenant with Yahweh to pray to God—רק מצא לעת. This statement, very difficult to grasp in its construction, is surely to be associated with Isa. 49:8; 55:6 according to meaning. But what is this: the time in which a person finds (Yahweh)? Is it "the hour of the divine presence in the festival cultus" (A. Weiser)? Can the time be fixed sacrally in this manner? Wouldn't the point of time derive its definition rather from the event of Yahweh's merciful attention, which is not subject to foreign control (Isa. 49:8; 55:6)? But the meaning of the didactic tendency is no doubt the following: He who takes refuge with Yahweh at the proper time and opens up to him will remain untouched by the surging waves of ruin. For the metaphor מים רבים, cf. Ps. 18:4; Isa. 8:7; 17:12; 23:3. The thought is of the sudden burst of ruinous torrents. But the חסיד, who calls to Yahweh at the right time, is stationed on safe ground high above the valley (G. Dalman, *AuS* I 211).

[**32:7**] In v. 7 Yahweh's sheltering protective power is glorified in a trusting

ingenuous confession, he will find reconciliation with God awaiting him. In other words, the Psalmist means that God was not only willing to pardon him, but that his example afforded a general lesson that those in distress should not doubt of God's favor towards them, so soon as they should betake themselves to him with a sincere and willing mind" (Calvin, on Ps. 32:5, trans. Anderson [Eerdmans, 1949]).

confession. He protects against distress. With rescuing shields he encircles him who entrusts himself to him (cf. the comment on Ps. 3:3). In the course of the didactic communication this statement is also to be understood by way of example.

[32:8-9] Regarding vv. 8 and 9, H. Gunkel defends the conception that the psalmist is the speaker and, like a sage, addresses the inexperienced. He points to parallel statements in Ps. 34:11 and Job 15:17. In the course of his interpretation עיני is corrected to בְּנִי. F. Delitzsch too is of the opinion that the speaker in vv. 8-9 could not be Yahweh. His reason: "The person addressed would then have to be the author, who has, however, already attained to the knowledge that is here involved." We must oppose these explanations. (1) Already in the meter vv. 8ff. differ from the other didactic maxims of Psalm 32. (2) Upon closer investigation, the individual statements in vv. 8-9 clearly show themselves to be divine utterances, above all, the words: עליך עיני—איעצה— בל קרב אליך. Against the argument of Delitzsch, we should be reminded that an individual song of thanksgiving takes all of its perceptions from the conclusive divine oracle, which not infrequently is quoted in the Psalms (cf. J. Begrich, "Das priesterliche Heilsorakel," *ZAW* 52 [1934], 81-92). (3) In Ps. 16:11 and in Psalm 25 mention is made of Yahweh's showing the way which is hoped for and bestowed personally. Verses 8-9 therefore are to be understood as the words of a divine statement quoted in a song of thanksgiving. The promise עליך עיני ("on you is my eye") assured the petitioner of the healing presence of God (cf. Ps. 33:18). And the assurance בל קרב אליך, which is reflected in vv. 6-7, declared the unimpeachable status of him who has been granted a reprieve. Of course, we have to take into consideration that the language of "wisdom" seen in Psalm 32 has also had an effect on the reproduction of the speech of God— above all in v. 8a. Here, however, the suffix in the singular makes it appear impossible for us to think of the psalmist as the speaker (cf. over against this the address in v. 11). Also, v. 9a receives a specific meaning if we think of an exhortation of Yahweh's that was addressed to a foolish, unruly, and obstinate person who wanted to be responsible for his own fate without God (vv. 3-4). And this is where the statement of experience in v. 10 immediately comes into play. It does not involve a "naive theory of retribution" (R. Kittel) but a reality that someone experienced and suffered in his own body. The psalmist himself shared the manner of existence of the רשע. On him rested the guilt of turning away from Yahweh. He did not want to open up and surrender his life to God. Therefore he suffered מכאובים רבים (cf. vv. 3-4). The wasting away of the body was an effect of the life-style of the רשע. In any case, that is the way it is explained and affirmed by the psalmsinger, to whom all of the distress suffered appears in a new light on the basis of the blessedness of forgiveness (vv. 1-2) and of the experience of rescue through the divine חסד (v. 10b). Opposite the torpidity and the defiance of the רשע stands the existence of the בוטח, surrounded by goodness. It is important that also in this context nothing is said about a healing. In place of the רבים מכאובים we have the חסד.

[32:11] The psalm closes with an invitation to joy and jubilation about Yahweh that originated in the hymn type. And it is no surprise that the צדיקים and the ישרי-לב are encouraged with special emphasis to take part in grateful praise.

Purpose and Thrust

The interpretation of Psalm 32 in the commentaries has in part been clouded by serious misapprehensions. B. Duhm remarks—especially in view of v. 10: "It is convenient to imagine that religion is there for the purpose of guaranteeing our good fortune and of restoring it to us quickly after disturbances, and that those who are continuously afflicted are impenitent and ungodly; that is not Christianity." In these words the "theory of retribution" is so far removed from the basic reality of the song of thanksgiving that it appears only as a distorted, abstract dogmatic assertion. The secret of Psalm 32, however, lies in the fact that this song from the very beginning takes the hearer and reader into the cheering reality of forgiveness and the bestowal of salvation. The life-style of the רשע, who persists in a closed circuit of guilt and turning away from God, is avoided as simply impossible (vv. 3-4). "Forgiveness" and "goodness" are the gifts coming from Yahweh that are spontaneously given to him who opens up his life and confesses his guilt (v. 5). It is simply impractical to impute a crass eudaemonism to the psalmist. What "blessedness" is—true blessedness—is revealed in Psalm 32 in the first place, and that in a surprising way. Forgiveness of guilt (vv. 1-2) and חסד—that is true blessedness, and therefore not at all is it in the first place the "rapid restoration," the external healing. Thus also the opinion of H. Gunkel is very questionable when he says, among other things, "The inner experiences of which the psalmist speaks are always together with external ones, yes, actually only inspired by these." We could in the first place ask: What right have we to this distinction between "inner" and "outer" experience? Does this not involve a very problematical anthropology that is determined by idealistic-dualistic principles? Again, we could ask, Where does Gunkel find clues for his claim that the inner experiences of the psalmist are actually inspired only by the external ones? After all, there is only one theme in the entire song of thanksgiving: the relation of the human being to God broken and restored through forgiveness. And this human being is no entity in two parts but one unit in body and soul. All the modern speculations about the "ancient causality of guilt and illness" are, in spite of everything, questionable in their point of departure because they begin with a division of the human being, which then has to be restrained again by means of a secondary construction ("causality"). When Gunkel asserts concerning Psalm 32 (one of seven penitential psalms of the church) that "the penitence of the psalmist surely is only distantly related to the Christian variety," he projects a dualistic anthropology into the term "Christian." But wherever the church has prayed Psalm 32 as a penitential song—without the anthropological constraint of categories—it was introduced to a more profound level of the body-soul unity before God.

When the apostle Paul quotes Ps. 32:1-2 in Rom. 4:7-8 as a witness for the δικαιοσύνη χωρὶς ἔργων, this quotation is in the first place occasioned completely externally through the verb חשב (λογίζεται) in Gen. 15:6 and Ps. 32:2 (cf. Rom. 4:3, 8). But there are factual analogies involved. חשב is a verb that expresses the declaratory bestowal of righteousness, of forgiveness. Paul focuses the attention of the reader and interpreter on the free gift of which Psalm 32 speaks. And with this thought in mind, we will have to be careful that profession and confession (vv. 5-6) do not become a new ἔργον to which the bestowal of salvation is subordinated.[1]

---

1. On the theology of Psalm 32, cf. K. Barth, *CD* 4/1, 577f.

Psalm 33

Praise of the Creator
and Lord of the World

Literature

A. Deissler, ''Der anthropologische Charakter des Psalms 33 (32),'' *Mélanges Bibliques rédigés en l'honneur de A. Robert* (1957) 225-233. K. Koch, ''Wort und Einheit des Schöpfergottes in Memphis und Jerusalem: Zur Einzigartigkeit Israels,'' *ZThK* 62 (1965) 251-293. W. H. Schmidt, *Alttestamentlicher Glaube in seiner Geschichte* (1975), cf. Index.

Text

33:1 [a]Rejoice, O you who are righteous, concerning Yahweh,
   for the upright, praise is fitting.

2 Praise Yahweh with the lyre,
   play to him skillfully with the harp of ten strings!

3 Sing a new song to him,[b]
   pluck the strings beautifully with loud shouts!

4 For Yahweh's word is truthful,
   and reliable all his deeds.

5 He it is who loves righteousness and justice.
   The earth is full of Yahweh's goodness.

6 By Yahweh's word the heavens were made,
   and by the breath of his mouth their entire host.

7 He who collects the waters of the sea in a 'bag,'[c]
   he lays the primal seas up in storehouses.

8 All of the earth is afraid before Yahweh,
   before him all inhabitants of the world tremble.

9 For he, he spoke, and it took place;
   he, he commanded, and there it stood.

10 Yahweh breaks[d] the counsel of the nations,
   thwarts the plans of the peoples.

11 But Yahweh's counsel stands forever,
   the plans of his heart (are valid) on and on.

12 Blessed the people that (calls) Yahweh its God, —
 the nation that he chose as his inheritance!
13 Yahweh looks down from heaven,
 beholds all human beings.
14 From the place where he is enthroned he looks down
 on all earth dwellers.
15 He it is who has formed their hearts, all of them,[e]
 he observes all their deeds.
16 Of no avail is the size of his army to the king,
 the hero is not saved by the greatness of his strength.
17 Of no avail are horses for the victory,
 the greatness of their strength does not bring a rescue.[f]
18 But Yahweh's eye[g] (rests) on those who fear him,
 who wait for his goodness,
19 that he may save their lives from death
 and sustain them in time of famine.
20 Our soul waits for Yahweh.
 [h]He is our help and shield.
21 For our heart rejoices in him,
 for we trust his holy name.
22 Your kindness, O Yahweh, (rule) over us,
 even as we hope in you.

1a MT lacks the title. Gk has Τῷ Δαυιδ. Was this heading lost, or was this psalm adopted into the collection of the Davidic psalms only later?

3b A few Mss, c, T have ליהוה (in assimilation to the customary call, e.g., in Pss. 96:1; 98:1).

7c כנד = "as for a dam." But Gk, Jerome, T, σ´ read בַּנֹד = כַּנֹּאד ("as in a bag"); with this reading compare the parallel באצרות. For the meaning, see below ("Commentary"). MT is probably thinking of the miracle of the sea (Exod. 15:8; Ps. 78:13).

10d The perfect forms הפיר and הניא denote "repetitive actions," BrSynt §41a.

15e Gk: κατὰ μόνας ("apart," "alone") (יְחַד); but MT is to be preferred.

17f Gk and T have read: יְמַלֵּט; but MT is to be preferred.

18g 1 Ms, Gk, S read the plural עֵינֵי (cf. Ps. 34:15). But on עין cf. Ps. 32:8.

20h Gk simplifies the transition to the second half-verse with ὅτι (כִּי).

Form

In its 22 lines Psalm 33 lets us recognize an "acrostic song" (Bickell); it contains as many lines as the alphabet has letters (cf. Psalms 38; 146; Lamentations 5). The text is transmitted in good condition and in the main exhibits double triple meters: 1-4, 9, 13-22. A thoroughgoing reconstruction of double triple meters (e.g., by means of correction of the construct combination חסד יהוה to חסדו in vv. 5ff.), however, does not accomplish its aim. In the midsection of the song there are mixed meters: 3 + 4 in vv. 5 and 8; 4 + 3 in vv. 6, 7, 10, 11, 12.

Psalm 33 belongs to the form group of songs of praise. On the group תהלות, see above, Intro. §6, 1. For a more detailed grasp of the hymn, cf. F. Crüsemann, *Studien zur Formgeschichte von Hymnus und Danklied in Israel*, WMANT 32 (1969) 129ff. The psalm begins with an "imperative hymn" in vv. 1-4 (Crüsemann, 129). The real main section (vv. 5-19), which in "a very free and sovereign manner places next to each other elements of form and style that are arrived at entirely differently" (130), begins at vv. 5 and 7 with participial statements. Thematically the main section is clearly articulated: vv. 4-9 deal with the "word of Yahweh," vv. 10-12 with the "counsel of Yahweh," vv. 13-15 with the seeing "eye of Yahweh," and vv. 16-19, in the style of a confession, with the one who alone is the true helper and rescuer. As in Psalm 135, one can clearly discern the proximity of the form of an imperative hymn and an attached corpus in Psalm 32 (Crüsemann, 131).

Setting

Already Ewald had recognized that the song of praise Psalm 33 had been intoned in connection with a festival. All the attempts of former times to prove a historical situation must be considered off the mark. Also the eschatological interpretation, as attempted by W. Staerk, does not catch the essential statement of the psalm. We must rather assume that Psalm 33 belonged to the context of cultic obeisance before Yahweh, the king, creator of the world, and Lord of the world. Cf. Pss. 95:6; 99:9; 100:4; also see above, Intro. §10,1. However, we must begin with the assumption that Psalm 33 is to be dated relatively late (cf. the "alphabetizing form," but also the possible reflective reference to Genesis 1). But a precise historical assignment is not possible.

Commentary

[33:1-3] The imperatives of the hymnic introit summon us to take part in the praise of Yahweh. Addressed and stirred up are the צדיקים and the ישרים who according to ancient sacral tradition are allowed to enter the sacred area and appear before Yahweh (Ps.118:19f.; cf. especially Psalms 1; 15; 24; and Ps. 100:4). Before the *deus praesens* the song of praise is intoned. On נאוה in the hymn, cf. Pss. 93:5; 147:1. Musical instruments accompany the song of praise. כנור is the lyre with the attached resonance box, נבל originally the lyre with the slanting yoke (cf. K. Galling, *BRL* 390f.). For the importance of *musica sacra* for the festival worship, cf. Ps. 92:3 and Psalm 150. The music of the instruments sounds forth with joy to Yahweh. שיר חדש (v. 3) is not the "new" song in relation to time, but that last, all-encompassing hymn that breaks out of the category of space and time, which also makes its appearance in Psalms 96 and 98 (also cf. Isa. 42:10; Rev. 5:9). שיר חדש no doubt carries with it an "eschatological" accent, which is, however, mortised into the "supratemporal" statements of the hymn. היטיבו נגן really means: "do the playing well" (cf. Isa. 23:16). On תרועה ("festival shout"), cf. P. Humbert, *TEROU'A: Analyse d'un rite biblique* (1946). A booming shout of joy is to exalt Yahweh's might and majesty.

[33:4-9] With the characteristic כי, the main section of the hymn begins in v. 4. In solemn sequence the reasons are named why exultation and praise are due Yahweh. In vv. 4-9 the wondrous power of the דבר־יהוה first takes its place in the midpoint of the hymnic meditations. About the quality of the דבר v. 4 speaks in a basic statement. The "word of Yahweh" is ישר, and everything he creates proves to be באמונה (cf. Ps. 19:8; Deut. 32:4). But דבר is a hypostasis. The sovereign subject is Yahweh himself. He "loves righteousness and justice" (v. 5). Of this fact the צדיקים (v. 1) especially are here reminded. On the phrase צדקה ומשפט in the Psalms, cf. Pss. 11:7; 37:28; and often. Under חסד־יהוה we are probably to understand especially the benevolent deeds of creation as proof of the universal healing power of God. The covenant will of Yahweh is determinant for the universe. Here we have a remarkable variation of the older liturgical conception as we find it in Isa. 6:3 and Ps. 8:1. In accordance with the hymnic tradition, Psalm 33 too points out especially Yahweh's deeds of creation, and emphasizes that the heavens were called into being by the דבר־יהוה. Obviously reference is here made to creation through the word, which is also the tradition obtaining in Gen. 1:6, 14 (cf. Psalm 147). On the wondrous creation of the heavens, cf. Ps. 8:3. In the parallelism רוח פיו is the synonymous term for דבר־יהוה. The "breath of the mouth" (cf. Isa. 11:4), which is emitted when the word is spoken, has brought into being (cf. Ps. 147:4; Isa. 40:26) the "host of the heavens," the stars. But without question, רוח in this passage means more than "wind." Instead, it here stands as a synonym to דבר and therefore signifies the creating word. Yahweh's breath is creative vital force. The creative word of Yahweh has erected the powerful heavenly world. This foundational event is in v. 7 described with conceptual rudiments of myth. מי הים, or תהומות, here refers to the "waters above the firmament of the heavens" (המים אשר מעל לרקיע, Gen. 1:7). The "ocean of the heavens" Yahweh has gathered up (like stored supplies) in a bag (on כנס, cf. Neh. 12:44; Eccles. 2:8, 26) and laid it up in a storehouse. These "storehouses of the heavens" are spoken of also in Job 38:22; Jer. 10:13; Ps. 135:7. The pictures, interlaced with mythical concepts, illustrate the sovereign way in which Yahweh overcomes the archetypal powers (תהומות) of chaos (cf. H. Gunkel, *Schöpfung und Chaos in Urzeit und Endzeit* [1894], 95). In a similar way, Deutero-Isaiah describes the world-conquering power of Yahweh (Isa. 40:12ff.).

It is worth noting how Psalm 33 always emphasizes the fact that between Yahweh and the world of creation there exists not only an original relationship of creation but above all a historically contemporary life relationship (vv. 5, 8). The Creator is Lord of the world. The inhabitants of the earth "tremble" and "are afraid" in the sight of him who sustains all life and on whose word the universe plainly is dependent. On תבל, cf. the comment on Ps. 24:1. Again and again the hymn bursts forth in visionary descriptions of the world situation, in which all of creation is associated with Yahweh alone (cf. Psalms 96; 98). Finally and emphatically, v. 9 speaks of the wondrous power of the דבר־יהוה. The word of God is efficacious, dynamic. As the authoritative command of the sovereign Lord, it is able to execute (Ps. 148:5; Isa. 55:11). This is a reference to the tradition that prevailed in Gen. 1:3.

The mention of the divine word in Psalm 33 as a creative potentiality requires a history-of-religions overview. The creative power of the divine word is rather frequently referred to in Egyptian religious history (H. Kees, *Der Götterglaube im alten Ägypten* [1941], 180). According to a Memphis inscription, e.g., Ptah became the heart and tongue of Atum, the creator god. Thoth emerged from the heart, Horus from the tongue. The gods are formed and the universe is created by means of what is thought in the heart and what is ordered by the tongue. The narrative then reports concerning the origin of the world: "The lord of all says: Numerous are the origins (?) which came forth from my mouth." About Thoth we read: "Things are done according to his will, whatever issues from his mouth; his word turns into deed, and his command becomes reality" (cf. A. Erman, *Ein Denkmal memphitischer Theologie*, SAB [1911], 916ff., 936ff.). On the temple wall at Dendera (at the time of Emperor Nero) we can read: "Thoth, who rests on truth; what springs for my heart immediately becomes reality, and what he has spoken remains forever (cited in O. Grether, *Name und Wort Gottes im Alten Testament*, BZAW 64 [1934], 143).

Also in Mesopotamia the word of the divinity is praised as powerful in effect. In a "prayer for uplifted hands" for Nanna we read: "When your word roars by in the heavens like the wind, it brings abundant food and drink to the land; when your word goes out on earth, it causes lush grass to grow; your word makes sheepfold and cattle-pen fat, makes creatures numerous. Your word brings justice and righteousness, so that human beings speak the truth; your word is far away in heaven, is on earth hidden; no one can get to the bottom of it. Who knows your word? Who can match it?'' (A. Falkenstein and W. von Soden, *Sumerische und akkadische Hymnen und Gebete* [1953], 224). Additional texts from Mesopotamia are given in O. Grether, *Name und Wort Gottes im Alten Testament*, 140ff. On this problem, also cf. L. Dürr, *Die Wertung des göttlichen Wortes im Alten Testament und im antiken Orient*, MVAG 42, 1 (1938).

The difference between the biblical and the ancient Near Eastern understanding of the word of God O. Grether sees as follows (in *Name und Wort Gottes . . .* , 144): ''While in many points a similarity to biblical views emerges, still, on closer inspection, it becomes apparent that in the consideration of the word of God as the principle of creation and world preservation there is a profound difference between the Bible and the extrabiblical religions. In the former, the true perception and the unconditional recognition of his lordship forms the basis for the belief in creation that is founded on divine revelation and guarantees its purity. In the latter that presupposition is lacking, and the divinity is placed into a partly magic, partly naturalistic, partly pantheistic relation, or in some other distorted relation to the world. This difference also reacts back on the word. In the Bible it serves to glorify God in his superiority over the world and to guarantee his claim to lordship over nature. In the extrabiblical contexts the word is looked upon as a magical or natural magnitude or as an emanation of the divinity, so that the divinity is dependent on nature or is identified with it.'' Also cf. G. von Rad, *OT Theol*, 1:143.

The history-of-religions problem of the ''creative word'' from which the universe has emerged was treated by K. Koch in a completely new discussion (*ZThK* 62 [1965] 251-293). There particularly the ancient Egyptian ''Memphis theology'' is investigated. Koch thought that these documents were of such concern for the Christian theologian (1) because they speak of the creation of the world through the word of God— at least 1700 years before the composition of Genesis 1, and (2) because they speak of a god who is above a sexual distinctness (254). In spite of all that, the creator god in Egypt is thought of as entirely ''personal'' and not as an unspecified archetypal ground of all being (260). The text cited on p. 264 is commented on by Koch as follows: ''The word of creation is a part of the deity itself; it never fully separates from the speaker but transfers its 'substance' to the creature that is generated by the utterance'' (264). ''All of life comes into being through the creative word of the one God'' (265). According to Koch, the juxtaposition of the word and work in Ps. 33:4 reminds us of the doubling of speaking and doing in the monument of Memphis theology (273). Also other texts of the OT are viewed in the light of the ''Memphis theology'' and are critically discussed. In the process Koch concludes that in the OT the report concerning the creative word is ''anything but uniform'' (283). Instead, we are to observe:

1. In Memphis, as in Jerusalem, the idea of the creative word of God as the primary mode of divine activity was developed only gradually in the course of a complicated history of tradition.

2. In the latter place as well as the former this word is more than a mere intellectual construct; it is something independent, full of numinous power.

3. The word of the Creator is in both cases traced back to the mightiest and the only really divine figure; in Israel to Yahweh, worshiped exclusively from of old, in Egypt to Ptah (Amon), who encompasses all other deities.

The fact is, therefore, ''that both religions are similar in one respect, which is by no means the same in every religion'' (Nos. 1-3 above were also quoted, p. 284). Finally, Koch took up the question about the ''uniqueness of Israel'' (285ff.). He posed the question to which we shall later return: ''Which characteristics in the hymnic and didactic Israelite utterances of God are so clearly distinguished from the Egyptian parallels that they explain how it came about that Israel increasingly separated itself from the ancient Near Eastern community of religious thinking?'' (288). This question leads to the later, more detailed disclosure: The uniqueness of Israel is not a matter of principle or something obvious; rather, it emerges only ''in centuries-long movements in the history of tradition'' (291). Thus Koch saw the modern positivism of revelation refuted by

377

Israel's self-understanding gained from research in history. And it is certain that Koch has here a creditable achievement—in view of that mechanical differentiation between biblical revelation and extrabiblical religion of nature, which again and again still crops up in Christian theology. Just the same, under the heading "Purpose and Thrust" we will have to come back to Koch's main theses.

[33:10-12] The theme of the hymnic main section (vv. 4-19) in vv. 10-12 is עצת־יהוה (v.11). Since the area of creation is at the same time the area of Yahweh's lordship (v.10; cf. Ps. 24:1-2), the plans of the peoples that strive for historical power cannot be realized (cf. Isa. 8:10). The Creator of the world is in every moment of history the Lord of the world. Yahweh's plan alone has stability (v.11). The manner in which Yahweh's resolution that governs history is spoken of reminds us very much of Isaiah (Isa. 14:24; 46:10). If דבר־יהוה in Psalm 33 is the effective power of creation, then עצת־יהוה is the continuing power of directing history. And because Yahweh's "word" and "counsel" are becoming known in Israel (Ps. 76:1), for that reason the nation whom God has chosen is called blessed. On אשרי (v. 12), cf. H. Schmidt, *Grüsse und Glückwünsche im Psalter*, ThStKr 103 (1931) 141-150.

[33:13-15] The Creator and Lord of the world is the God enthroned in heaven (v. 13). The statements of the hymn move within the conceptions of the Jerusalem tradition (see above, Intro. §10, 1). From heaven Yahweh beholds the earth dwellers (Pss. 11:4; 14:2; 102:19). The Creator and Lord of the world is the judge of the world. Nothing escapes his omniscience. From his heavenly "dwelling place"(מכון־שבתו) he beholds all people. This universal office of judgment is according to v. 15 based on the fact that Yahweh has "formed" the hearts of all. There are similar statements in Pss. 94:9; 139:13ff.; Zech. 12:1. The macrocosmic relation "Creator and Lord of the world" is therefore in vv. 13-15 transferred to the realm of the central human expressions of life: the Creator of the heart is the Lord and judge of man.

[33:16-19] In v. 15, after the glorification of Yahweh's power of creation and his lordship has penetrated to the heart of the being, in vv. 16-19 all the power factors of this world are shown to be as nothing. Applicable maxims of the sacral tradition of the "holy war" are in vv.16-17 elevated to the status of universally binding mottos (on this, cf. G. von Rad, *Der Heilige Krieg im alten Israel*, ATANT 20 [1951], 82). Thus in v. 16 the thought is now certainly no longer exclusively of Israelite kings. In a very basic sense the point is that human power and greatness—even in their most powerful exaltation—is unreliable and void. Verse 17, beginning with שקר would have to be translated: "Lie, deception is . . . ." Horses as the epitome of "worldly" power (Isa. 30:15f.; 31:1f.) do not provide rescue. The only reliable protective power is "Yahweh's eye" (v. 18); this surrounds the one for whom God is a lively reality—i.e., the one who "fears him." חסד in this context is the divine goodness and covenant faithfulness that expresses itself in protection and preservation. He who is surrounded by "Yahweh's eye" is rescued from famine and death (Pss. 34:9; 37:19). Cf. Chr. Barth, *Die Errettung vom Tode in den individuellen Klage- und Dankliedern des Alten Testaments* (1947) 53ff.

[33:20-22] Verses 20-22 are the concluding stanza. The congregation at praise "waits"(חכה) for Yahweh—it looks for his coming. But in this expectation

Yahweh is the support and protection of those who are his (cf. v. 18). Joy and trust characterize the life of the people of God in the area of God's presence (בְּשֵׁם קָדְשׁוֹ). Finally, a petition for merciful attention ascends to Yahweh (v. 22).

Purpose and Thrust

The exultation of the צַדִּיקִים who live in the covenant of Yahweh and have experienced his saving work is expressed in Psalm 33 as the שִׁיר חָדָשׁ. In the process of revelation of the old covenant, Israel has come into contact with the power of the "word" and the "counsel" of Yahweh and has become sure of it. The people of God have learned that only under the effective watchfulness of the "eye of God" are protection and help to be found. And now hidden realities are disclosed through the hymn in the light of the power of revelation. An ultimate, fundamental state of affairs is illumined. Creation and history are plainly dependent on Yahweh. No power has a place beside him. Therefore the nations who carry on their existence according to their own laws of life and political plans tremble. All warlike power is void. In the brilliance of the universal lordship of Yahweh it is revealed who is in command. And even now the צַדִּיקִים, the members of the chosen people (v. 12), are shouting for joy and are happy in their God. Psalm 33 is not "eschatological" in the sense that it presents an end-time picture; its "eschatology" is intrahistorical; i.e., in the midst of moving, historical life it opens wide the vision of the secret and the miracle of reality in creation and history, a reality that is always valid and finally determinative. For the hymn, the unconditional, "final" lordship of God is a present event which changes the previous view of the world and brings new realities into view.

In a discussion with K. Koch, whose history-of-religions investigation raises questions for the conventional understanding of the "uniqueness of Israel," a basic consideration is first needed. Obviously, Koch means to question a theology of the word of God that skips over and fails to take note of historical relativities—a theology he calls "positivism of revelation." But now, of all people, precisely that theologian who is usually reproached for an "absolute" Word-of-God theology and the positivism of revelation, namely, Karl Barth, has on the relation of revelation and religion issued a number of basic statements which we shall do well to consider. In his *Church Dogmatics,* 1/2, 282, we read: "In his revelation God has actually entered a sphere in which His own reality and possibility are encompassed by a sea of more or less adequate, but at any rate fundamentally unmistakable, parallels and analogies in human realities and possibilities. The revelation of God is actually the presence of God and therefore the hiddenness of God in the world of human religion. By God's revealing of himself, the divine particular is hidden in a human universal, the divine content in a human form, and therefore that which is divinely unique in something which is humanly only singular." Accordingly, we will again and again have to begin with the realistic and limitless human and historic conditionality of the biblical word (M. Noth). All forms of positivism of revelation are to be denied and rejected. But this knowledge and insight does not release us from the obligation to distinguish the characteristic quality of biblical language not only in the history of tradition (thus Koch) but also in view of the biblical texts before us. In this process we have to begin by asserting that it is the word of Yahweh, the God of Israel, of which Psalm 33 speaks. This word as the "phenomenon of creative power" does not appear in isolation; it is to be viewed and interpreted from the context of Yahweh's speaking in the OT and in connection with biblical statements about this speaking. History-of-religions research always leans toward snipping out a phenomenon, isolating it, and juxtaposing it with a comparable phenomenon in a different religion. By this method there emerge suggestive conceptions of the closest relationships between the two phenomena that are held up to the light and compared, over against which the biblical context remains in the dark. But there should be food for thought in the fact that already in Psalm 33 itself the peculiarity, the truth, and the proof of Yahweh's word are expressed in the contest with the "counsel of the nations" and the "plans of the peoples" (v. 10). Yahweh's word is a word that has been confirmed in history and one that carries out its plan in a creative manner. Thereby the proof of Yahweh's creative power is given—not in some (mythical) primordial time, but in historical reality.

Thanks and Instruction
of One Who Has Been Rescued

Literature

H. Wiesmann, "Psalm 34 (Vulgate 33)," *Bibl* 16 (1935) 416-421. N. H. Snaith, *Five Psalms (1; 27; 51; 107; 34): A New Translation with Commentary and Questionary* (1938). L. J. Liebreich, "Psalms 34 and 145 in the Light of Their Key Words," *HUCA* 27 (1956) 181-192. W. Vischer, "Du texte au sermon—Psaume 34," *ETR* 44 (1969) 247-264. J. J. M. Roberts, "The Young Lions of Psalm 34,11," *Bibl* 54 (1973) 265-267.

Text

    Of David, when he feigned madness before Abimelech
    so that the latter drove him out and he went away.
34:1 I will praise Yahweh at all times,
    his praise shall always be in my mouth.
  2 My soul boasts of Yahweh;
    the poor shall hear it and be glad!
  3 Exalt Yahweh with me;
    let us together exalt his name!
  4 I sought Yahweh, then he answered me
    and freed me from all of my fears.
  5 'Look'[a] to him, and 'you'[b] will be radiant,
    and 'your'[c] countenance need not be ashamed.
  6 Here is a poor man who called, and Yahweh heard
    and helped him out of all his troubles.
  7 Yahweh's angel encamps
    round about those who fear him and saves them.
  8 Taste and see how good Yahweh is!
    Blessed the man who takes refuge with him!
  9 Oh, fear Yahweh, you his saints,
    for those who fear him, they lack nothing!
 10 'Rich people'[d] have want and go hungry,
    but those who seek Yahweh, they lack no good thing!

11 Come, O sons, listen to me!
The fear of Yahweh I want to teach you!
12 Who is the man who desires life
and loves good days in which he beholds^e good fortune?
13 Keep your tongue from what is evil,
your lips from wicked talk!
14 Stay far away from evil and do what is good,
look for peace and pursue it!
15 Yahweh's eyes (turn toward) the righteous,
and his ears toward their crying.
16 Yahweh's countenance (turns) against the sinner
to wipe out their remembrance in the land.
17 They cry,^f and Yahweh hears
and saves them from all their troubles.
18 Near is Yahweh to all broken hearts,
and he helps those who are of a broken spirit.
19 Many are the sufferings of the righteous man,
but from all of that Yahweh frees him.
20 He guards all his bones,
not one of them is broken.
21 The wicked is killed by disaster,—
he who hates the righteous must pay for it.
22 Yahweh redeems the soul of his servants;
no one who trusts in him is punished.

5a The MT would literally have to be translated: "They looked at him and became radiant, and their countenance should not be ashamed." Who is the subject? What sense does the statement convey? A correction is unavoidable. In 8 Mss, α´, S, and Jerome, הביטו is read as the imperative הַבִּיטוּ.
b Gk, α´, S, Jerome read וּנְהָרוּ.
c In keeping with the corrections in the first half-verse, the suffix is to be changed, as in Gk, S, Jerome, to: וּפְנֵיכֶם.
10d MT has: "Young lions have want." The word כפירים is probably not transmitted correctly. Gk: πλούσιοι = כְּבֵדִים or כַּבִּירִים ("the mighty"); B. Duhm: כֹּפְרִים ("deniers," "deserters"). Still J. J. M. Roberts (*Biblica* 54 [1973] 265ff., again tried to rescue the "young lions." He refers to Job 4:7-11 and to Babylonian maxims.
12e Gk: ἀγαπῶν ἡμέρας ἰδεῖν ἀγαθάς = לראת ימים טובים. This is a matter of simplified word order.
17f Gk, S, T add צַדִּיקִים. The addition has become necessary after vv. 16 and 17 have in the text tradition been exchanged in their sequence (see below, "Form"). But we ought to follow MT.

Form

In alphabetical sequence the lines of Psalm 34 follow each other (on the acrostic psalms, cf. the comment on Psalm 9/10 under "Form"). Missing is the ו-line. A transposition of the ע-line behind the פ-line is necessary (see the context in v. 17; on the sequence פ-ע, cf. Lamentations 2–4). The last line of the song (v. 22) is to be considered a later addition. The alphabetical form of a psalm naturally causes the thought sequence to be forced at times and not infrequently to be abrupt.

The double triple meter predominates. Exceptions are vv. 6, 8, 18 (4 + 3), and 10 (3+4). The added closing verse is to be read in the 4 + 4 meter.

Psalm 34 provides considerable difficulties for form-critical analysis. Most often the starting point is the purpose clearly indicated in vv. 4-6, which brings the psalm close to being a song of thanksgiving of an individual (cf. Gunkel and Begrich, *EinlPs* §7). Thus also D. Michel concludes: "The perfect forms of v. 4 report . . . the facts of distress and rescue. In v. 6 we find . . . the inversion typical for a song of thanksgiving" *(Tempora und Satzstellung in den Psalmen* [1960], 67). The hymnic anacrusis in vv. 1f. would correspond to this. But F. Crüsemann misses "the double direction of speech," "the constitutive feature of the form of this type." Also, the introduction does not come from the song of thanksgiving (F. Crüsemann, *Studien zur Formgeschichte von Hymnus und Danklied in Israel,* WMANT 32 [1969], 296). Crüsemann concludes: "This psalm is not a song of thanksgiving, but it is also not a hymn and not a wisdom song. It escapes entirely from classification in the normal types. None of the form elements noticeable in it characterizes its form overall. The acrostic form has in this case completely burst out of all the traditional types; something new and distinctive has arisen" (296f.). Just the same, one can hardly forgo pointing out the elements of the mixed type that according to Crüsemann too shows "something new and distinctive" and to ascertain the determinative trend of the whole from the dominant forms. The intentions (even if not the pure forms) of a song of thanksgiving are, as noted above, unmistakable. And yet they are caught up in a didactic poem which is conceived under the influence of wisdom traditions. See above, Intro. §6, 5. So far as the history of tradition is concerned, the example of a poem originating in a song of thanksgiving but now predominantly didactic in nature is easily explained. For the address to the community was among the characteristics of the old *todah* (Ps. 22:22)—an address in which the experiences of the singer were communicated in confession and teaching.

Setting

It is probably subject to question whether Psalm 34 had that "Sitz im Leben" which is otherwise to be taken for granted in individual laments. Is not a didactic poem designed to follow an alphabetical schema a typical "piece of desk work" (H. Schmidt)? Conceptions and opinions of this kind lean toward a negative and not infrequently caricaturing picture of "the scholar bent over his scroll" and the poet expressing himself in rigid maxims. We will have to consider the art form of the acrostic a peculiar, special entity that appeared in exilic and postexilic times and in which the beginning of every verse served as a prop for the memory. Just the same, it is worth noting that the psalmist proceeds and how he does it. His wisdom experiences refer to his own life experiences (vv. 4-6) and are based on them. Even if the "I" in the formularies of the songs of thanksgiving and even more in a didactic poem has a standardized function, still the life experiences of the "I" that is speaking are vital.

Commentary

[Title] On לדוד, see above, Intro. §4, No. 2. The rest of the heading makes an effort to provide a historical setting for this "psalm of David" and in doing so commits the error of confusing Achish of Gath with Abimelech (1 Sam. 21:12-15). No internal reference to the old story of David is given anywhere in Psalm 34.

[34:1-3] The psalmsinger wants to "praise" Yahweh at all times. ברך as a term for praising has the meaning: to acknowledge someone in his position of power and his claim to greatness with due formality" (F. Horst, "Segen und Segenshandlungen in der Bibel," *EvTh* 7 [1947], 31). For the one rescued (v. 4) the praise of Yahweh becomes a determining course of life. Verse 1 has the character of a vow. On נפשׁ in v. 2, cf. G von Rad, *OT Theol,* 1:153. The song of thanksgiving of the person rescued boasts of Yahweh, but this is at the same time a witness and a message to the ענוים (on ענו, see above, Intro. §10, 3). The oppressed and those in need of help are to take heart and rejoice at the experience of rescue on the part of the psalmist. In this way the entire psalm takes on a kerygmatic direction toward a goal which must be considered carefully in the didactic passages. But in all the lines of the psalm Yahweh's name is to be extolled and exalted. The ענוים are included in this praise. The surpassing working power of the saving and revealing presence (שׁם) of Yahweh is to be witnessed to.

[34:4] The retrospective narrative of the one giving thanks in v. 4 describes the horizon of the didactic statements then following in great brevity. The sufferer "sought" Yahweh. On דרשׁ as a technical term for the visit to the sanctuary, cf. Amos 5:5; 1 Chron. 21:30; 2 Chron. 1:5. In the holy place Yahweh then "answered" (ענה) through the mouth of the priest (cf. J. Begrich, "Das priesterliche Heilsorakel," *ZAW* 52 [1934] 81-92). His word proved to be effective and "freed from all fears." Yahweh's rescue brought about a real change of life. This fact, too, is important for understanding the didactic statements, which we have usually preferred to categorize as a "naive theory of retribution" (Kittel et al.).

[34:5-10] Corresponding to the kerygmatic-didactic aim (v. 2b), all those in need of help are encouraged to look up to Yahweh (v. 5). In this process the psalmsinger proceeds from revelation experienced and from his turning to the "countenance of God," which bestows its healing reflection on those who seek him. On נהר in the sense "be radiant with joy": Isa. 60:5. פניכם אל־יחפרו means אל־יבושׁו: "They will not be put to shame," i.e., they will be heard and helped.

In v. 6, beginning with זה, the fate experienced by the psalmist is pointed to by example and by special emphasis (cf. Lam. 3:1; also H. -J. Kraus, BK XX). Verse 6 thus interprets the statements of v. 5. As the instrument of Yahweh's effective help, which is bestowed on those praying and those who fear God, v. 7 names the מלאך־יהוה. Especially the verb חנה lets us see that the psalmsinger here refers to age-old tradition (cf. Gen. 32:1, 2; Exod. 14:19; Josh. 5:14; Zech. 9:8; Ps. 103:20f.). A "messenger" from the heavenly host pitches camp round about the recipient of salvation. In a picturesque way this statement brings to bear the protecting and helping presence of the salvation of God (cf. Ps. 91:11). The psalmist invites the hearer to "taste" and to "see" the goodness of Yahweh. טעם has the meaning "to sample," "to partake of a little" (1 Sam. 14:24, 29; 2 Sam. 3:35; Jonah 3:7). Thus the hearer is , as it were, to take a trial taste of the saving goodness of God that is at hand. We could ask whether the psalmsinger is conscious of the fact that his proclaiming report palpably offers and transmits the present help of God. Called "blessed" are all those who take refuge in Yahweh (cf. Ps. 2:12).

Time and again the psalmist approaches his hearers with exhortations. So also in v. 9. The "saints of Yahweh" are to "fear" God. קדשׁיו, according to M. Noth, refers to human beings only in this passage of the OT (*GesStudzAT*

277); on the problem, cf. also the comment on Ps. 16:3). The proclamation in v. 9a is applied to a basic experience formulated like a confession: Those who fear Yahweh lack nothing. The help personally experienced is expanded to an experience of salvation of all those who fear God. In v. 10 the didactic statement shows an even stronger development in the form of a contrast: ''the rich'' are in want and go hungry, but those who seek Yahweh (on דרשׁ, cf. v.4) suffer no lack of any good thing. In a sharply defined black-and-white drawing the manner of conduct and life of the human being is here portrayed. Is this not the ''retribution theory'' of nomistic-dualistic Judaism clear as day? At the conclusion (cf. ''Purpose and Thrust'') a further explanation of the ''doctrine of retribution'' of Psalm 34 will be in order.

[34:11-17] In v. 11 the psalmsinger makes makes his appearance as a teacher of wisdom (cf. Prov. 2:1; 3:1). He wants to ''indoctrinate'' (אלמדכם) his hearers and considers them his students (''sons''). The substance of the teaching is the ''fear of Yahweh.'' Many commentators interpret יראת יהוה in a general sense as the ''Yahweh religion,'' but this explanation does not do justice to the specific meaning of ירא in Psalm 34. He who fears Yahweh recognizes and acknowledges his reality. יראת יהוה is not a religious theory but a message concerning the proper, appropriate behavior and life of a human being in view of the reality of God. This communication takes place in the form of questions and answers (cf. G. von Rad, *OT Theol*, 1:359, n. 8). Simple, practical, and down to earth is the question about anyone's desire for a fortunate life (v. 12). For this question there is extant a literary parallel from Egypt (from the time of Tutankhamen): Couroyer, ''Idéal sapiental en Egypte et en Israël,'' *RevBibl* 57 (1950) 174ff. The archetypal human desire for a successful, pleasant life is addressed.[1] We could call the question ''eudaemonistic.'' But the answer (vv. 13-14 now teaches the ''fear of Yahweh'' and maintains that all desirable joys of life come to him who in his everyday life exhibits the יראת יהוה. Specifically, this means (v. 13): He is fortunate who keeps his speech under control (Ps. 141:3; Prov. 4:24; 13:3; 21:33; Sir. 28:13ff.; Matt. 12:36; 1 Peter 3:10-12). Even this attitude would prove whether a human being lives before the living God. A fortunate life in the יראת יהוה further means (v. 14): to stay away from evil (cf. the comment on Ps. 1:1), to do what is good (cf. Amos 5:15), to look for peace and pursue it.[2] On

---

1. ''The prophet does not inquire if there be any man so disposed, as if all men voluntarily brought upon themselves the miseries which befall them; for we know that all men without exception desire to live in the enjoyment of happiness. But he censures severely the blindness and folly which men exhibit in the frowardness of their desires, and the vanity of their endeavors to obtain happiness; for while all men are seeking, and eagerly intent upon acquiring, what is for their profit, there will be found scarcely one in a hundred who studies to purchase peace, and a quiet and desirable state of life, by just and equitable means. The prophet therefore admonishes his disciples, that nearly the whole world are deceived and led astray by their own folly, while they promise themselves a happy life from any other source than the divine blessing, which God bestows only upon the sincere and upright in heart. But there is in this exclamation still greater vehemence, the more effectually to waken dull and drowsy minds to the course of this world; as if he had said, Since all men earnestly desire happiness, how comes it to pass, that scarcely anyone sets himself to obtain it, and that every man, by his own fault, rather brings upon himself various troubles?'' (Calvin, on Ps. 34:12, trans. Anderson [Eerdmans, 1949]).

2. ''What does that mean, 'on our part'? That we agree here on earth, that we love our neighbor as ourselves. Love your brother as you do your own self, and be at peace with him'' (Augustine, ''Enarrationes in Psalmos,'' Migne, *PL*, 36/37: 318).

the directives in v. 14, cf. Ps. 37:27; Prov. 3:7; 13:19; 16:6, 7; Job 28:28; Heb. 12:14. Thus vv. 13 and 14 contain the characteristics of the צדיק (also cf. the comment on Psalms 1 and 15). The "righteous man" experiences a fortunate life, for Yahweh's eyes are turned toward him, and Yahweh's ears hear his crying in the hours of distress (cf. Pss. 1:6; 32:8; 33:18). Here it gets to be very clear: true good fortune in life is to stand before the living God in the יראת יהוה. The עשי רע (v. 16) and רשעים (v. 21) on the other hand experience the resistance and wrath of Yahweh. Their זכר ("remembrance") is blotted out (cf. the comment on Ps. 1:4, 6). The צדיקים experience the reality and the saving activity of Yahweh, especially in distress (v. 17).

[35:18-22] That Psalm 34 inculcates no "naive theory of retribution" is clear especially in vv. 18-20. The צדיקים are not simply the healthy people and those who overflow with vitality. The reaction of God to their "religious good behavior" does not produce in them an untroubled good life "according to plan." The "good fortune" (v. 12) of which the psalmist speaks lies at a deeper level. The צדיקים are those who suffer. They experience many pains. The נשברי־לב are people who are seized by a deep despair about themselves. Their natural trust in life is broken and ruined. Such a breakdown always points to the final depths of the relationship to God. But precisely he who despairs of himself stands under the promise of God's nearness. The נשברי־לב experience the blessing of their life-relation to Yahweh in that he is near them in the brokenness of their inner being (v. 18). This nearness of God is never anything static, anything metaphysically at rest above humans, but a movement emanating from God, who intervenes on earth and demonstrates his liberating, salutary presence (v. 19b). Thus it can be said of the צדיקים that all their bones are under Yahweh's protection (v. 20); no arbitrary act can assail them (John 19:36). To suffering righteous people Yahweh sends his saving power. No calamity can destroy them. The רשע on the other hand is "killed" by disaster (v. 21); he suffers the ruin of the "evil death" (cf. Chr. Barth, *Die Errettung vom Tode in den individuellen Klage- und Dankliedern des Alten Testaments* [1947], 53ff.). On the problem of this-worldly activity that determines one's destiny, cf. the comment on Ps. 7:13-16. The hatred which the "wicked" entertains over against the "righteous" (the צדיק therefore also bears the hatred of the רשע among his "many sufferings") finds a judge in Yahweh (cf. the comment on Ps. 14:6). The concluding verse (v. 22) points to the (final) redemption of the servants of God and diverts the judgment announced in v. 21 away from those who trust in Yahweh.

Purpose and Thrust

It is curious how depreciatory and unappreciative the estimates of Psalm 34 are in almost all commentaries. R. Kittel writes: "Throughout the poem the naive theory of retribution rings out as the basic tone, according to which God lets his own succeed unconditionally." And B. Duhm remarks in a depreciatory way: "It is remarkable that it is always the lesser spirits who make the biggest splash and advertise themselves as teachers of mankind; they probably do it not from arrogance but from innocence." These judgments force us to take careful notice of the essential statements of the psalm. In the process the following should be noted:

1. Psalm 34 is from its starting point and its intention a song of thanksgiving. Even if the traces of an actual experience of deliverance are only weak (vv. 4, 6), they are still unmistakably present. The didactic statements therefore are rooted in an event, in an actual experience: Yahweh has answered a person who sought him and feared him; from all his needs and fears he has freed him. The horizon and background of all didactic statements therefore is—and that is what must be established first of all—not an abstract theory ("theory of retribution") but something that has taken place.

2. The thanksgiving, narration, and teaching of the psalm have a purpose. The hearers, especially the ענוים, are to take to heart the message and teaching transmitted and be glad (v. 2). The psalmsinger wants to draw his hearers into his own experience of the reality of God's salvation (v. 3); he wants to let them behold and taste how good Yahweh is (v. 8). He wants to transmit to them the decisive attitude toward God, the conduct of the ירא and the דרש (vv. 9, 10). In the course of this urgency to proclaim and to share, the psalmist expands his personal experience of salvation to generally valid confessions and didactic directions that in part are derived from the ideas of חכמה.

3. If we should now ask how the psalmsinger really comes to speak so "naively" and "innocently" about the salvation of the righteous and the ruin of the ungodly, we should first of all note that "naive eudaemonism" is in a remarkable way breached in Psalm 34. The צדיקים are those who suffer (vv. 18-19). The "eudaemonism" (v. 12) is determined not from the side of human expectation of good fortune; the nearness and reality of Yahweh alone holds true good fortune; which of course includes everything that is desirable from a human standpoint (cf. G. Bornkamm, "Der Lohngedanke im Neuen Testament," *EvTh* 2/3 [1946], 143-166).

But there is another perspective. The doubts about the righteousness of God—those painful scruples that come up, e.g., in the book of Job and in Psalm 73—arise the moment God's bestowal of salvation is delayed (cf. the comment on Psalm 9/10, "Setting"). This painful and problematical situation is not given in Psalm 34. The exegete should therefore not inject "more profound reflections" as a measure of his judgment here where there is thanksgiving and teaching based on the immediate experience of salvation.

4. A special role is taken by יראת יהוה (v. 11). Again and again the invitation to "fear God" is heard. But ירא in Psalm 34 means to recognize Yahweh in his actuality, particularly in his reality for salvation, and to behave accordingly. It is simply undeniable that in the psalm which is dismissed with such judgments as "formalistic" and "theoretical" there is a burning fire that wants to be applied to the hearers. History-of-religions research has reached its limits where it changes realities into phenomena and theories; that is seen in its interpretation of Psalm 34.

5. Once we have recognized the specific presuppositions and associations in which the didactic statements of Psalm 34 are involved, we should also not overlook the degree to which traditional conception of wisdom sheds its rays on the didactic poetry. For חכמה is true what in Psalm 34 can be ascertained by traces: "In its 'teaching about the good things', this ethic is, in fact, astonishingly realistic. It never criticizes man's search for happiness and fulfillment, even its excesses. It simply presupposes this search as a fact. This desire for happiness—we ought, rather, to say in more restrained terms: this desire to survive without coming to grief and to know that life is secure within an order

that is beneficial—is planted deep within man and is accepted without question. Indeed, the wise men themselves advocate it in that they indicate the roads which lead to it.'' (G. von Rad, *Wisdom in Israel* [1972] 81). In the light of these comments especially Ps. 34:12ff. would have to be seen and understood.

Psalm 35

Plea for Yahweh's Assistance against False and Hostile Witnesses

Literature

H. Schmidt, *Das Gebet der Angeklagten im Alten Testament*, BZAW 49 (1928). G. Rinaldi, "Testimone di violenza (Ps 35:11)," *BibOr* 2 (1960) 62. J. A. Soggin, "*Škwl* nel Salmo 35,12," *BibOr* 9 (1967) 67f. W. Beyerlin, *Die Rettung der Bedrängten in den Feindpsalmen der Einzelnen auf institutionelle Zusammenhänge untersucht*, FRLANT 99 (1970).

Text

Of David.[a]

35:1 Fight, O Yahweh, against those who fight against me,
　　　wage war against those who war against me!

2 Take up shield and buckler,
　　rise up to help[b] me!

3 Wield spear and 'battle-ax'[c]
　　against those who persecute me!
　　Say to my soul,
　　"I am your help!"

4 Let them come to disgrace and shame
　　who seek my life;
　　in ignominy let them retreat
　　who have planned evil against me.

5 Like chaff before the wind let them become,
　　and may the angel of Yahweh make his attack 'on them'![d]

6 May their path be dark and slippery,
　　and may the angel of Yahweh pursue them!

7 For without cause they spread their net ' '[e] for me,
　　'a pit'[f] they dug for me.

8 May ruin come to him unaware!
　　And the net he laid for me, may it catch him himself;
　　May he be the one to fall into destruction![g]

389

9 But I will exult about Yahweh,
be joyful about his help.
10 All my members shall say,
Yahweh, who is like you?
You who rescue the weak
from the hands of the stronger
' '[h] and the poor man from him who would rob him!
11 Wicked witnesses appear,
ask me what I do not know.
12 They repay me with evil for good,
'seek'[i] my life.
13 But I, when they were sick, put on sackcloth,
chastised myself with fasting
—oh, that my prayer might return to my breast!—
14 as though it were for my friend and brother.
I went about[j] as in mourning[k] for my mother,
blackened and bowed down.
15 But at my fall they exulted and banded together,
rose up against me as one man.
'Strangers'[l] whom I do not know
'pinch their eyes shut'[m] without ceasing.
16 Like ruthless mockers of the refuge,[n]
'they gnash'[o] at me with their teeth.
17 Lord, how long will you look on?
Save my life from 'those that roar,'[p]
from the lions my only possession!
18 I will praise you in a large gathering,
exalt you before a crowd of people!
19 Do not let lying enemies exult over me,
do not let those who hate me without cause pinch their eyes shut!
20 For they do not speak of peace.
And against the quiet people in the land
they contrive cunning schemes;
21 they open wide their mouths against me
and call, Aha! Aha!
We saw it with our own eyes!
22 You have seen it, O Yahweh; please do not be silent,
Lord, be not far from me!
23 Arise, awake for my right,
My God and my Lord, for my cause!
24 Vindicate me according to your righteousness, O Yahweh,
My God, 'let them not exult'[q] over me!
25 Let them not say to themselves,
Aha! 'Aha!'[r]—our pleasure!
Let them not say, We have swallowed him up!
26 Let them be put to shame and disgrace, all of them,
who are happy about my misfortune!
Let them clothe themselves in dishonor and disgrace
who make a name for themselves against me!
27 Let those exult ' '[s] who have a desire for my righteousness,
let them always say,
Great is Yahweh, who desires
the salvation of his servant!
28 My tongue shall proclaim your righteousness,
your praise every day!

1a Gk suggests the addition מִזְמוֹר.

2b Many Mss of Gk translate as if their original text had read לְעֶזְרָתִי (εἰς βοήθειάν μου, "for my help"). But בְּ indicates motion toward a goal (BrSynt §106a).

3c MT literally: "and lock up." In the context this reading does not make sense. We should adopt the pointing וְסָגֹר. סָגֹר (Akkadian: *šikru*) is the "double battle-ax" (KBL 650).

5d In the verb (in agreement with Gk and רדפם in v. 6) the suffix of the third person plural should be inserted: דְּחָם.

7e MT: "for without cause they laid the pit of their net in my path." שחת רשתם is hardly possible. On the other hand, in v.7b the object of חפרו is lacking. The text is obviously corrupt on account of transpositions. We should remove שחת from v. 7a and insert it in v. 7b.

f חנם is a repetition from v. 7a that distorts the text. It has to be replaced by שחת ("pit"). See note **e** above.

8g S suggests that instead of בשואה we read the word בַּשּׁוּחָה ("into the pit"); but MT could also be possible (cf. v. 8aα).

10h עני turns up in unique doubling and should very likely be emended.

12i MT literally: "childlessness for my soul" is surely corrupt (R. Kittel to the contrary); Cheyne: הִכְשִׁילוּ נַפְשִׁי ("they let my soul stagger"). Best of all: שָׂכוּ ("they lie in wait for"); לְ would then be dittography. J. A. Soggin wants to introduce the root כלל; he assumes that an archaic causative verb, formed with שׁ has been retained. Translation: "My very essence is destroyed" (*BibOr* 9 [1967], 67f.).

14j *Atnah* under התהלכתי is in the wrong place.

k אבל as construct form of אָבֵל ("mourning") (Ges-K §93hh).

15l נֵכִים (from נכה, "strike"?) is unintelligible. The correction frequently suggested, נָכְרִים (ר dropped) would be appropriate.

m קרעו ("tear apart," "lacerate") is too strong and hardly correct in this context. It would be better to read קרצו (צ instead of ע, cf. v. 19) or קראו ("they cry").

16n The text in MT, which is most often said to make no sense, is fully acceptable if מעוג from the root עוג ("to be twisted") denotes the place to which one turns (the refuge). Cf. KBL 545 on 1 Kings 17:12.

o Perhaps it would be better to read חרקו.

17p MT: "Rescue my life from their devastations" (?). The meaning of this statement is not comprehensible. Suggestions for correction: מִשֹּׁאֲגִים (from those that roar"); מִשֹּׁאֲפִים ("from those that hanker"); מִשִּׁנֵּיהֶם ("from their teeth"). The first suggestion would agree with the parallel word מכפירים ("from the lions").

24q If אלהי is for the meter's sake taken with the second half-verse, ו would have to drop out.

25r האח is here a case of haplography. Cf. v. 21 aβ.

27s The doubling of the verb is metrically not comprehensible. Very likely וישמחו is to be omitted. Cf. BHK³.

Form

This rather extensive psalm is not easily comprehended as to form and structure. It may be that originally there was a very regular verse structure (H. Gunkel). But in its present condition the song is in any case very uneven, and in its metrical form it can hardly be reconstructed to approximate a well-balanced original form. Still, we can determine that the 3 + 2 meter must have been determinative at one time: vv. 1-3a; 4aγ/4b; 8aβ/8b; 9; 10aαβ; 13b; 14aα; 15; 17aβ; 17b; 26; 27. Double duple meters, which in the first half-verse probably have to be corrected to a triple meter (cf. BHK³), are present in vv. 3a and 4aαβ. The following are to be read as double triple meters: vv. 5-7; 11; 16; 18; 19; 22-24; 28. A 4 + 3 meter is found in v. 13a. Three-member verse forms should perhaps be thought of in vv. 10; 12; 20; 21; 25; perhaps also in v. 8.

Psalm 35 should be classified as belonging to the form group: prayer songs. See above, Intro. §6, 2. Petitions and appeals addressed to Yahweh are expressed particularly in vv. 1-8 and 22-26. In v. 7 the petitioner affirms his innocence in view of his enemies and accusers, and in vv. 11ff. the descriptions of the distress of the oppressed singer are in evidence. Worth noting is the fact that the psalmsinger is minded to hasten to perform a song of thanksgiving (*todah*, vv. 9f.) and in v. 18 presents a vow of praise. Also vv. 27f. confidently look forward to future praise. The form of the vow of praise is excluded, if we advocate the view that de facto the *Gattung* of a (disrupted) song of thanksgiving is present in rudimentary form (thus H. Schmidt). To the petitions and appeals in vv. 1ff and 22ff. we wish to add the note that the petitioner of the psalm adopts calls for help that originally belonged to the institution of holy war. Cf. G. von Rad, *Der Heilige Krieg im alten Israel,* ATANT 20 (1951). Yahweh is called on to carry on the war for the oppressed petitioner, to fight for him (1f.). We can clearly recognize the expectation of a "miracle of salvation" (J. Begrich) in v. 3. Thus the bestowal of salvation was formulated: "I am your help!"

Even though the condition of the text in Psalm 35 is severely damaged, it would still be an exaggeration to proceed with extensive and radical corrections such as B. Duhm undertakes.

Setting

What is the situation of the petitioner in Psalm 35? The first appeal in v. 1 already identifies the state of affairs. The petitioner is persecuted by enemies. More precisely, he is accused. False witnesses and determined persecutors arise against him (vv. 11, 3, 12). The righteousness and innocence of the oppressed psalmist lies in the balance. Thus we could with H. Schmidt assume that a person who is falsely charged and persecuted brings his complaint before Yahweh in the holy place and awaits a divine judgment (BZAW 49 [1928], 34). But the situation is more complicated. In the first place we should note that only weak clues for a reference to the institution of divine jurisprudence elaborated by W. Beyerlin can be documented (on the institution: FRLANT 99 [1970]). Also we would have to ask of what importance the sickness discernible in v. 15 may have been (cf. צלע in v. 15). Did this sickness provide an occasion for leveling accusations based on a posteriori conclusions regarding the cause (cf. John 9:2)? Who are the enemies? See above, Intro. §10, 4. In vv. 23f. the petition and demand that Yahweh grant an acquittal becomes very clear. But does this petition still have a realistic reference to the institution? Is this not rather a matter of a whole battery of formulations and formulas that were put together in later times? The many questions which the psalm imposes can hardly be adequately answered.

Commentary

[Title] On לדוד, see above; Intro. §4, No. 2.

[35:1-8] The petitioner of the psalm is involved in a legal case and a war with his "enemies" (see above, Intro. §10, 4). In his prayer he seeks refuge with Yahweh as the judge (cf. the comment of Psalm 7) and warrior (see above, Intro.

§10, 7). He commits his lost cause to Yahweh. The "war hero" Yahweh Sebaoth (Ps. 24:8, 10) is asked to arm himself (v.2), to take up the protective large shield to cover the one persecuted (cf. 1 Sam. 17:7) and the buckler as a weapon. On קומה, cf. the comment on Ps. 7:6-9. חנית וסגר are the footsoldier's weapons which Yahweh is to wield against the enemies as protection for the one who is being threatened (v. 3). But the most effective aid is the promise ofYahweh: ישעתך אני. Here we have the model of a "priestly oracle of salvation," which —as, e.g., also in Lam. 3:57—is conveyed as an authoritative divine verdict to one who is oppressed (J. Begrich, "Das priesterliche Heilso-rakel," *ZAW* 52 [1934], 81-92). Under such a proclamation the persecuted person would be sure of the protective power of Yahweh. Cf. Isa. 49:25 as a parallel to the oracle of salvation in v. 3: ־יריבך אנכי אריב ואת־בניך אנכי אושיע את. But the help of Yahweh is revealed when the enemies come to shame and disgrace (v. 4). In vv. 5-6 violent desire for judgment is expressed. Like chaff the persecutors are to be blown away (cf. Ps. 1:4; G. Dalman, *AuS* III 126-139). The מלאך יהוה as an invisible warrior of the heavenly host (cf. the comment on Ps. 34:7) and witness of the present power of God is to make his attack on the "enemies" and drive them away. A dark and slippery road is to lay them low (cf. Ps. 73:18). In the OT the power of Yahweh is operative in decisions affecting the secular area of reality. "All the curses of those psalms spring from the pure source of selfless zeal for God's honor"—thus Franz Delitzsch is bold to explain concerning the "psalms of revenge." In any case, we will have to hear the words of the psalm with great restraint, and we may not bring the NT ἀγάπη, understood in an emotional and ultimately psychic-humanizing sense, up against the OT plea for God's real demonstration of power.

As the motive for God's judgmental intervention, the malicious procedures of the "enemies" are mentioned (v. 7). Without cause they set out nets and dug pits (G. Dalman, *AuS* VI 334ff.). The ruin (שׁואה) is to come to the persecutors in an "immanent nemesis" (v. 8). The enemies' misdeed is to fall back on their own heads (cf. Pss. 7:15; 9:15; 57:6; 141:10; the comment on Ps. 7:13-16).

[35:9-10] These verses press forward to the song of thanksgiving. The petitioner of the psalm is sure of salvation and vows that he will sing an exulting song of thanksgiving to Yahweh. The help will come. In this vow pointing to the future we should not see the remnants of a song of thanksgiving once sung long ago but rather evidences of an unconditional certainty of being heard. "All members" of the body will recover and shall say: יהוה מי כמוך. The anticipated statements of thanks and praise show all the marks of a hymn. The question remains whether the song of praise and thanksgiving of the "members" contains a reference to the sickness of the psalmsinger (so H. Gunkel with reference to Pss. 6:2; 31:10; 51:8).

[35:11-16] The descriptions of the lament in vv. 11-16 present the entire weight of distress to Yahweh. עדי חמס (v. 11) allege accusations which the oppressed person "does not know"; fanciful evidence of misdemeanor turns up. And this hostile stance, in which the persecutors want to expose the עני (v. 10) and separate him from Yahweh, is in stark contrast to the conduct adopted by the psalmsinger himself when the present enemies were formerly sick in bed (v. 13). He was good to them (vv. 12f.). But now they repay the good with evil. Accordingly, we might conclude that the cause for the acute hostility in Psalm 35 should in fact be sought in a serious illness, from which the adversaries reason back to an "old offense." But the psalmsinger behaved altogether differently: when the present enemies were sick, he did not seek to ferret out theirmisdemeanors, did not fling an accusation, but prayerfully interceded for those in suffering (cf. F. Hesse, "Die Fürbitte im Alten Testament," diss. Erlangen [1951], 65ff.). As a sign of sympathetic penitence, he put on sackcloth and mortified himself with fasting (Lev. 16:29, 31; Isa. 58:3, 5) in order to stand with the afflicted and to avert their misery. ותפלתי על־חיקי תשוב is best understood (with F. Nötscher) as a parenthesis, in which the intercessory prayer is, as it were, taken back in view of the enmity now being revealed (cf. Matt. 10:12f.). Verse 14 continues in the description of the intimate sympathy which the psalmist expressed for the misfortune of his neighbor. He looked at them as friends and brothers, went into mourning as for his own mother, was "blackened" (with ashes of the penitential rite: Josh. 7:6; Ezek. 27:30; Lam. 2:10), and "bowed down" (cf. 1 Kings 18:42; Isa. 58:5). That is the way the man now persecuted behaved. The "enemies" on the other hand exulted about the "fall" (v. 15). צלע (cf. Ps. 38:17; Job 18:12) could refer to an injurious fall but also to a sudden change in life because of sickness. People "band together," and even strangers enter the scene with hostile, malicious gestures. The accusers and persecutors, who want to bring to light "secret offenses," despise the place where the person threatened could find refuge and aid (מעוג = "refuge"); like threatening beasts of prey, they gnash their teeth (v. 16).

[35:17-26] Verse 17 inaugurates a series of cries of supplication, which contain expressions of trust and lamentation. אדני כמה תראה—with this question Yahweh is moved to intervene (v. 17), for like "roaring lions" (cf. the comment on Ps. 7:2) the enemies threaten the life of the petitioner: יחידתי ("my only possession," cf. the comment on Ps. 22:20). A vow of thanks in v. 18 interrupts the cries of supplication and bears witness to the certainty of being heard (on v. 18, cf. Pss. 22:22; 40:9; 116:14). Verse 19 pleads that Yahweh might intervene against the lost and malicious enemies (cf. Ps. 69:4; John 15:25). The slanderers disturb the שלום (v. 20), the prosperous and well-ordered state of life; they think up cunning devices against him who quietly and peacefully (רגע) lived his life in the שלום-order of the land. האח האח—those are the cries of sinister, triumphant mockery (v. 21). The formulation ראתה עינינו could be a standing phrase of court procedures in which witnesses support an assertion. But against the false witness of his enemies, the psalmsinger takes refuge with the highest witness, Yahweh (v. 22). Yahweh is called on to intervene in the legal procedure (v. 1) and not to keep silence. On העירה והקיצה in v. 23, cf. the comment on Ps. 18:46, but also Pss. 7:6; 44:23; 59:4. Verse 24 prays for Yahweh's legal aid. On צדק, cf. Ps. 5:8. The triumph of the enemies Yahweh should bring to nought (vv. 24-26). נפשנו in v. 25a H. Gunkel beautifully translates "our delight" (literally, "our gullet"—in connection with בלע, "devour"). On v. 26, cf. v. 4.

[35:27-28] But the psalmsinger even now calls for exultation and praise from all those who "desire" his צדק (v. 27). חפצי צדקי here has the meaning: "who have a desire for my righteousness," or, "who wish the restoration of my undisturbed way of life in relation to Yahweh." The psalmist glorifies Yahweh, for he is certain that he wants the "salvation" of his servant. The meaning of שלום here is synonymous with צדק and designates the undisturbed way of life. Verse 28 then already goes over to the hymnic forms of the song of thanksgiving. צדק is Yahweh's salutary restorative function that heals torn and wounded ways of life.

Purpose and Thrust

Among the other songs of its type and group, the lament of one who is falsely accused shows a special nuance of its own, in that a bitter experience is unfolded before Yahweh. Whereas the petitioner was always careful to sympathize with the distress of his neighbor, to heal and to bind up by means of intercessions (an example of צדק!), there appear in the hour of his own need people and powers who want to ruin the psalmist and separate him from God (vv. 13ff.). As false witnesses and accusers they arise to deliver the death-blow of a final judgment of God to a life that is obviously being punished. In this plight the petitioner of Psalm 35 takes refuge with the witness (v. 22), judge (vv. 1ff.), and "war hero" Yahweh. He prays for an effective and visible demonstration of God's intervention (vv. 4ff., 24ff.) and wants to shelter himself in the protective might of the promise: ישעתי אני (v. 3b). It is worth noting with what bold certainty the lamenting and praying psalmist looks forward to the salvation event. Again and again—while still engulfed by dangers—he goes over to expressions of a song of thanksgiving (vv. 9-10, 18, 27-28). On the theological significance of the laments of one who is persecuted, though innocent, cf. the comment of Psalm 7 ("Purpose and Thrust").

The Way of Life of the Ungodly
and the Fortunate Life
of the Community of God

Literature

E. Baumann, "Struktur-Untersuchungen im Psalter," *ZAW* 61 (1945/48) 141-146. L. A. F. Le Mat, "Textual Criticism and Exegesis of Psalm 36," *Studia Theologica Rheno-Traiectina* (1957). L. Jacquet, "Abîme de malice et abîme de bonté, Ps. 36," *BiViChr* 81 (1968) 36-47. W. Beyerlin, *Die Rettung der Bedrängten in den Feindpsalmen der Einzelnen auf institutionelle Zusammenhänge untersucht*, FRLANT 99 (1970).

Text

To the choirmaster. Of Yahweh's servant, of David.

36:1 'Pleasing'[a] is transgression to the ungodly
deep within 'his heart.'[b]
There is no fear of God
before his eyes.

2 For he smooths (the way)[c] before him for himself
to find 'transgression'[d] and to hate.

3 The words of his mouth are lie and deception;
he gave up acting wisely and well.

4 He plans wickedness on his bed,
he walks the way that is not good,
evil he does not despise. —

5 O Yahweh, your goodness (reaches) to heaven,
your faithfulness up to the clouds!

6 Your righteousness is like the mountains of God,
your judgments like 'the great primal sea.'[e]
You help people and animals,

7 O Yahweh,[f] how precious is your goodness!
'To you come'[g] the children of human beings,
find protection in the shadow of your wings.

8 They feast on the fat of your house,
at the brook of your joys you give them to drink.

9 Indeed, with you is the fountain of life,
  in your light we see light.

10 Continue your goodness to those who know you,
  your righteousness to those who are of an upright heart!

11 Do not let the foot of the arrogant come upon me,
  nor the hand of the wicked drive me away! —

12 The wicked 'are bewildered,'ʰ they fall,
  they tumble and cannot get up again.

1a MT = "Guilt speaks to the ungodly. . . . " Accordingly, and oracle of the פשע would be involved. But such a conception is unusual and rare. All mystifications (cf. H. Gunkel) come to grief in the context. The oracle of the פשע is missing. Rather, in vv. 1ff. a description of the riotous ways of the רשע is given. If we, considering these facts, for the moment disregard the unusual נאם, v. 1 contains clear statements about the רשע, in the depths of whose heart פשע dwells. The first word would then have to be a verbal or adverbial modifier. An easy adjustment would be to read נָעִים, with Ehrlich, or to correct to נָאוָה, perhaps also as a verb, נָעֵם. In the context of the psalm this correction would be very meaningful, for it contrasts those things that are "pleasant" and "lovely" for the רשע with the "delights" of him who knows Yahweh's goodness (vv. 5ff.). On the text-critical problems, cf. L. A. F. Le Mat, 4ff.
b MT = "in my heart." In agreement with the context, we should correct to לִבּוֹ, following a few Mss Gk, ο, εβρ´, Jerome, S.
2c The verse does not present the difficulties commonly seen in it. If החליק על = "to make things smooth over against someone" ("to flatter someone," Prov. 29:5), then החליק אל must be translated: "to make smooth over against someone" (namely, "to oneself," cf. בעיניו). Literally: "for he smooths things out for himself before him." That is a description of the riotous ways of the רשע.
d MT = "to find his transgression, to hate." Better, following Gk: עון ולשנא.
6e Here we will very likely have to supplement כתהום (cf. the parallelism).
7f יהוה should here be added to v. 7aα for the sake of the meter.
g אלהים and the following ו cannot possible be correct. B. Duhm conjectures, in keeping with Ps. 65:2, אֵלֶיךָ יָבֹאוּ, "they come to you."
12h שם ("there") cannot be translated in a temporal sense and is remarkable in the context. The parallelism (two verbs in succession) suggests that we read שָׁמְמוּ instead of שָׁם.

Form

Is Psalm 36 a unity? The answer to this question is in doubt. B. Duhm and H. Schmidt presuppose two songs (A, vv. 1-4, 12; B, vv. 5-11). Thematic considerations are determinative in this division: Psalm 36A deals with the riotous ways of the ungodly; Psalm 36B with the delight of the community of God. Yet the psalm is undoubtedly a unity (see below).

The double triple meter is dominant (vv. 2-3, 5-12). In v. 1 two 3 + 2 verses are to be assumed. Verse 4 (at the conclusion of the first train of thought in Psalm 36) contains a three-member meter 3 + 3 + 2. Psalm 36 presents many difficulties for form-critical analysis. In view of vv. 6ff. we cannot doubt that this is a prayer song. Above all, in vv. 10ff. the characteristics of praying and pleading clearly appear. Verses 1ff. describe the riotous course of the enemies who are persecuting the petitioner and thus the distress in which he finds himself. The prayer song (see above, Intro. §6, 2) is interlaced with statements of confession (v. 9) and wisdom. Thus the psalm comes close to the classification: didactic poetry (see above, §6, 5).

Setting

Who is the petitioner in Psalm 36? The answer is given in v. 11: a person who is persecuted by insolent enemies (see above, Intro. §10, 4), but who has sought protection with Yahweh (v. 7). But this is the peculiar feature of the psalm: the petitioner does not depict his personal exigency and pray for God's intervention, as is customary in the prayer song. Instead, in a contemplative, descriptive manner of presentation on vv. 1-4, he speaks of the riotous course of the ungodly and in vv. 5-9 describes the good fortune of the security in the holy place. Only in vv. 10f. do the petitions appear. Obviously a reflective wisdom poetry has here had a strong influence on the prayer song. The contemplative method of contrasting is significant.

But that Psalm 36 displays a unity is evident above all in the fact that the sheltering and heartening protective area of the sanctuary stands in contrast to the threats of the enemies and persecutors (vv. 1ff.). Still, it will hardly be possible to recognize a definite reference to an institution in Psalm 36. The institution of God's jurisprudence elaborated by W. Beyerlin could be sensed only at a distance (cf. FRLANT 99, 1970). Otherwise the hymnically tuned confessions about the saving area of the sanctuary (v. 9) remind us of psalms that extol the good fortune and the salvation to be found on Zion.

It is difficult to say when the psalm is to be dated. The tendency is to assume a late date. That older traditions have found a place in a prayer song that is close to didactic poetry can hardly be doubted.

Commentary

[Title] On למנצח, cf. above, Intro. §4, No. 17. On לדוד, cf. Intro. §4, No. 2. עבד־יהוה (as in Ps. 18:1) is an honorary title of David.

[36:1-4] If the correction is undertaken in v. 1 and we read נעם instead of נאם, an appropriate understanding of the context is possible. For if נאם־פשע would not be corrected, an "oracle" of the פשע would have to become recognizable. To be able to assume that this "oracle" is found in v. 1b could hardly be possible. The reconstructions undertaken on the basis of Ps. 14:1 come up against difficulties in the context of Psalm 36 (v. 2). In other words, we would have to think of v. 1 already as a description of the רשע. His life is governed by פשע ("deep within his heart"). פשע is the rebellion, the insurrection against Yahweh (cf. L. Köhler, *OT Theology* 170). In the parallel half-verse we are told what it means to be governed by פשע: the רשע knows no "fear of God." Yahweh is not a living reality who questions his life and whom he has to fear. Cf. Pss. 10:4; 11:13; 14:1; 73:11; 94:7. The רשע asserts himself through cunning and intrigues ("he smooths the way before him for himself"), and he strives only to achieve "transgression" and "hatred." עון is "an intention not in accord with God's will" (L. Köhler, 170). Ominous statements (און) and defamations are his weapons (v. 3). The רשעים are פעלי און (v. 12; see above, Intro. §10, 4, and Le Mat, 57ff.). The רשע has ceased being wise and good. השכיל is a word taken from the terminology of wisdom teaching (Prov. 10:5, 19; 14:35; 15:24). The "fear of God" proves itself in wise and good conduct in keeping with the principles of חכמה. But every thought and act of the ungodly is directed only to און. און denotes the sinister and disastrous course of life and originally probably extended to magic practices (J. Pedersen, *Israel I-II* [1926], 431; S. Mowinckel, *PsStud* I 1-58). On v. 4aα, cf. Ps. 4:4; Mic. 2:1. The way of the רשע is לא־טוב

(Isa. 65:2; Prov. 16:29). On the description in vv. 1-4, cf. Psalm 14. The fact that vv. 1-4 describe the enemy of the petitioner is not revealed until v. 11. Statements intended to persuade Yahweh to intervene have, in the first part of the psalm, become descriptive observations. In aninstructive (not "moralizing" — thus B. Duhm) manner the way of life of the רשע is displayed. That is the "ungodly"! His disastrous, sinister deeds threaten the petitioner of the psalm.

[36:5-9] At v. 5 of Psalm 36 so great a change takes place that the opinion could be voiced that a new psalm begins here. But at this point the psalmsinger suddenly turns away from the behavior of the רשע and glorifies the temple's fullness of blessing (v. 8), where he has looked for asylum. Not the sinister activity of the רשע but Yahweh's goodness fills the universe. In Psalm 36 the און of the wicked and Yahweh's חסד are contrasted. In v. 5 חסד and אמונה form a synonymous pair in the parallelism. חסד is the benevolent affection of Yahweh for those who know him and live in his צדקה (v. 10); אמונה denotes the steadfastness and faithfulness in which this goodness is effective. On חסד, cf. the comment on Ps. 5:4-7. Also cf. H. J. Stoebe, *THAT* I 600f. (additional bibliography there). The "range" of חסד and אמונה corresponds to the reality of God (1 Kings 8:27): Pss. 57:10f.; 108:4f. The statements in vv. 5ff. clearly display hymnic accents. In his "goodness" and "faithfulness" Yahweh reigns in צדקה and משפט (v. 6). These synonymous terms point to the incorruptible order of justice and salvation that is at work in God's covenant and that asserts itself against slander and unrighteousness (vv. 3, 11).

The doxologies of the hymn then strive to adduce comparisons. The צדקה is like "the hills of God," i.e., mighty, high-towering mountain ranges. On these "superlatives," cf. Pss. 50:10; 80:10. Over against "the hills of God" there is the immeasurable, mighty depth of the תהום. On תהום, cf. Gen. 7:11; Ps. 24:2. The similes extend into mythical areas. The psalmsinger extols the power of God that provides justice and salvation, to which he has entrusted his life in view of the רשע (v. 11). Verses 7b/8aα see the help of Yahweh (ישע) stretched out to its full extent over the world of human beings and animals (cf. Pss. 104:14, 21, 27f.; 147:9; Job 38:39ff.). The effect of the "goodness" is universal. Here thoughts of the creation psalms echo through (Psalms 33 and 104). מה in the hymn is an exclamation of wondering insight (cf. Pss. 8:1, 4; 31:19; 104:24). The בני אדם (here thought of in the universal sense again) "come to you" (corrected according to Ps. 65:2) and find protection in the shadow of Yahweh's wings. בצל כנפיך יחסיון is an "avowal of asylum" (G. von Rad, *OT Theol*, 1:402; cf. Pss. 17:8; 57:1). The persecuted petitioner flees to the sanctuary and seeks refuge in Yahweh's protective area, which is indicated by means of the image of the outstretched wings of the cherubim. In the sanctuary, however, the one who seeks protection has access to the fullness of the blessings of God's presence (v. 8). דשן ביתך is a breviloquence which thinks of the fat pieces of flesh of the sacrifices (Isa. 43:24) that were offered there. דשן is a symbol for nourishing fullness (Jer. 31:14). נחל could hint at mythological conceptions of a stream, such as turned up, e.g., in Ps. 46:4 and in Ezek. 47:1ff. (see above, Intro. §10, 2). In any case, v. 8 sings about the wonder of the refreshing fullness of salvation that is enjoyed in the holy environs of the presence of God (cf. Ps. 65:4, 9).

With Yahweh is the "fountain of life" (v. 9). At the אל חי all life has its origin (Jer. 2:13). This could again be a reference to the tradition recognizable in Ezek. 47:1ff. Verse 9b should not be corrected, for the text in MT presents a suitable parallelism to v. 9a. The "light of Yahweh" is (as is clear from the construct connection in Pss. 4:6 and 89:15) the "light of his countenance," i.e., the brightness of the *deus revelatus*. Accordingly, v. 9b would be saying: In light of your revelation presence "do we see light." But ראה־אור means "life" (cf. Ps. 49:19; Job 3:16). Thus the psalmsinger confesses in the hymn: we receive the light of life from the light of the presence of God. Worth noting, by the way, is the transition from the third person plural to the first person plural in v. 9. This transition emphasizes the confessional character of v. 9.

[36:10-12] In vv. 10f. prayers are brought before Yahweh. Verse 10 still remains very general and prays for the continuance of the goodness of Yahweh for those who know him. On ידע cf. the comment on Ps. 9:10 (but also Pss. 79:6; 87:4). Verse 10 is an intercession. But the psalmsinger without question thinks of himself as being in the group of those who know Yahweh and are "of an upright heart." The only specific prayer statement occurs in v. 11. Here it becomes evident that an insolent enemy is threatening the psalmist. In the formulation בוא רגל the basic conception probably is that the victor places his foot on the neck of the one who is defeated (cf. Ps. 110:1). The petitioner prays that his enemy may not defeat him. May the hand of the רשע not chase him (out of the area of the sanctuary)! Verse 12 has the flavor of certainty of being heard and of being saved. The פעלי און, whose way of carrying on was described in vv. 1-4, will fall and never rise again.

Purpose and Thrust

To understand the essential statements of Psalm 36, we will have to begin with v. 11. The psalmist is threatened; the רשע oppresses and persecutes him. In this situation the psalmsinger now contrasts the life-style of the רשעים and the fullness of blessing of the presence of God, or the community of God. On one side there is און, on the other חסד. In descriptions that are based on motifs of lamentation the existence of the ungodly is depicted; in hymnic glorifications the fullness of salvation of the place where Yahweh is present is praised. Greater than all the sinister and disastrous excesses of the רשעים is Yahweh's worldwide gracious activity. Therefore Psalm 36 can also close with the perfect tense of certainty (v. 12). The power of blessed and righteous governance emanates from the place of God's presence. To this place those without rights and those who are helpless come. Here they find the fullness of salvation, the fountain of life, and the Lord of all of the world. The NT church will understand vv. 5-9 only with reference to Jesus Christ. In him God is present as the "fountain of life" (John 14:19) and the bulwark against all powers that rise up against "the elect" (Rom. 8:32ff.), accusing them and killing them.

Psalm 37

Instruction regarding
Yahweh's Righteous Governance

Literature

E. Otto, ''Der Vorwurf an Gott: Zur Entstehung der ägyptischen Auseinandersetzungs-literatur,'' *Vorträge der orientalischen Tagung in Marburg. Fachgruppe Ägyptologie 1950 (1951)*. G. von Rad, *Wisdom in Israel* (1972). S. Morag, ''ומתערה כאזרח רענן (Psalm XXXVII,35),'' *Tarbiz* 41 (1971/72) 1-23.

Text

Of David.
37:1 Do not fret about the wicked,
[a]do not be angry concerning evildoers,
2 for like grass they will dry up quickly
and wither like a green plant.
3 Trust in Yahweh and do good,
dwell in the land and keep faithfulness!
4 And have your joy in Yahweh,
for he will give you what your heart desires.
5 Commit your way to Yahweh
and trust in him; he will tend to it.
6 Like light he lets your righteousness rise,
and justice[b] for you like the noonday sun.
7 Be still before Yahweh and wait for him!
Do not fret about the success of the fortunate person—
about the man who plots cunning devices!
8 Cease from anger and depart from the grudge!
Fret not; it only leads to wickedness.
9 For the wicked are destroyed,
but those who hope in Yahweh ' '[c]
will possess the land.
10 Only a short time, and the ungodly will have disappeared;
and if you look at his place, he no longer is there.

11 But the poor will possess the land
   and will have their joy in the fullness of prosperity.
12 Mischief the wicked plots against the pious
   and gnashes his teeth against him;
13 but the Lord laughs at him,
   for he sees that his day is coming.[d]
14 The ungodly[e] draw the sword
   and bend their bows
   to fell the poor and the weak,
   to murder those who walk uprightly.
15 Their sword pierces their own heart,
   and their bows are broken.
16 Better is the little of the righteous
   than the 'great'[f] riches of the ungodly.
17 For the arms of the ungodly are broken,
   but Yahweh supports the righteous.
18 Yahweh knows the days of the blameless,
   their inheritance remains forever.
19 They are not put to shame[g] in times of adversity,
   and in the days of hunger they are filled.
20 For the ungodly perish,[h]
   and the enemies of Yahweh—like the glory of the pastures
   they vanish, vanish in[i] smoke.
21 The ungodly must borrow and cannot pay,
   but the righteous can spend and give.
22 For those whom he blesses possess the land,
   but those whom he curses are destroyed.
23 Yahweh guides the steps of the man,
   'he supports him whose way'[j] pleases him.
24 If he falls, he will not sprawl down,
   for Yahweh supports his hand.
25 I was young, grew old,
   but never did I see a righteous man forsaken
   or his children begging for bread.
26 All his days he can give and lend,
   and his descendants become a blessing.
27 Withdraw from evil, and do good,
   and you will remain living forever.
28 For Yahweh loves justice,
   forsakes not his godly people.
   'The wicked'[k] are 'destroyed'[l] forever,
   and the seed of the ungodly is exterminated.
29 The righteous will posssess the land
   and live in it forever.
30 The mouth of the righteous utters wisdom,
   and his tongue speaks justice.
31 His God's direction (he bears) in his heart,
   his steps[m] do not waver.
32 The ungodly lies in wait for the righteous
   and seeks to kill him.
33 But Yahweh does not give him up to his power,
   does not let him be condemned when he is judged.
34 Hope in Yahweh and preserve his way,
   and he will exalt you to possess the land;
   when the ungodly are exterminated, you will look on.
35 I saw the ungodly 'frolic,'[n]

'exalt'[o] himself like a green 'cedar.'
36 'I came by'[p]—and he was gone,
I looked for him—he no longer could be found.
37 Preserve 'innocence,'[q] and 'practice uprightness';[r]
the end of (such a) man is prosperity.
38 The reprobate are all destroyed,
the end of the ungodly is ruin.
39 ' '[s] The help of the righteous (emanates) from Yahweh,
he is their refuge in time of trouble.
40 Yahweh helps them and saves them,
he frees them from the ungodly and helps them,
for they seek refuge with him.

1a A number of Mss read וְאַל.
6b Many Mss S : וּמִשְׁפָּטֶיךָ.
9c In the meter המה presents difficulties and will probably have to be eliminated.
13d 6 Mss have the perfect בָא.
14e In the coordination of the half-verses in the course of the text transmission confusion has entered. The following coordination would be appropriate:

חרב פתחו רשעים   לטבוח ישרי־דרך
ודרכו קשתם   ולהפיל עני ואביון

Of course, there will be some question whether the two concluding clauses introduced by לְ should not be thought of as secondary additions. In that case the original text could have read:

חרב פתחו רשעים ודרכו קשתם

This correction is suggested by v. 15. Arbitrary are all attempts to "provide a place" for the two concluding clauses elsewhere in Psalm 37 to fill out fragmentary half-verses.
16f רבים is a wrong assimilation to רשעים. Following Gk, Jerome, S, we should here read רָב parallel to מעט.
19g In the parallelism the correction יִוָּרְשׁוּ is often recommended instead of יבשו; but the MT should probably be followed.
20h As in v. 14, so also in v. 20 there are difficulties in the appropriate coordination of the half-verses. The text is corrupt. Some words seem to be missing. The following correction would be imaginable:

כי רשעים יאבדו   כיקר כרים כלו
ואיבי יהוה......   בעשן כלו

20i A number of Mss, Gk, Jerome, have כְּעָשָׁן.
23j The grammatically exact translation would have to ignore the laws of parallelism ("on the part of Yahweh the steps of a man are steadied—and indeed, of that man, whose way pleases him." But with גבר the first half-verse ends. Therefore we have to read כּוֹנָנוּ and (following B. Duhm) בְּדַרְכּוֹ.
28k MT: "forever are they preserved." But in the alphabetical sequence the ע-verse is to be expected. Gk [ℵA] suggests the addition of the word עַוָּלִים (ἄνομοι); this word could have been lost through haplography, but it is demanded also by the parallelism.
l The introduction of the word עַוָּלִים and the parallelism demand the correction נִשְׁמְדוּ (cf. Gk).
31m Gk: וְלֹא.
35n MT: "I saw the wicked in violence." Gk recommends the correction appropriate for the parallelism, עַלִּיץ (ὑπερυψούμενον, "overbearing").
o MT: "and one who strips like a green native." The text is corrupt and without meaning. Gk reads: καὶ ἐπαιρόμενον ὡς τὰς κέδρους τοῦ Λιβάνου ("and lifted up like the cedars of Lebanon"). Also, cf. S^{Aphr}. A corresponding Hebrew text would be: וּמִתְעַלֶּה

‫כְּאַרְזֵי הַלְּבָנוֹן.

36p Corresponding to the parallel ‫ואבקשהו‬ we should, following Gk, Jerome, and S, here read:
‫וָאֶעֱבֹר.

37q MT has incorrectly changed the nouns in v. 37 to adjectives. Following Gk, Jerome, S, and T, we should read ‫תֹּם‬.

r Following Gk, S, T: ‫יָשָׁר‬.

39s ‫ו‬ should probably be eliminated, following a few Mss Jerome, S.

Form

The alphabetical sequence of the acrostic pattern determines the form of Psalm 37 (on the acrostic form, cf. the comment on Psalm 9/10). The arrangement of stanzas always has two complete verses come together and appear to be related to each other in thought. In the flow of the whole, of course, there is a lack of strict thought progression.

In the versification the double triple meter is dominant: vv. 1-3, 6, 11-13, 15-17, 19, 22-24, 28-30, 33, 35, 36, 38, 39; the 3 + 2 meter is to be assumed in vv. 14(?), 26, 27, 31, 32; 4 + 3 in vv. 8, 10, 18, 21, 37; 3 + 4 in v. 5. Three-member verses should be recognized in vv. 4, 7, 9, 25, 34, 40. The metrical explanation of vv. 14 and 20 must remain open.

Psalm 37 belongs to the form group, didactic poetry. See above, Intro. §6, 5. Experiences and perceptions are expressed and presented in the form of OT wisdom poetry. As an acrostic poem the psalm is more than a collection of maxims. Although without a strict progression, the presentation remains dedicated to its three themes: "Fret not over the successful wicked people" (vv. 1, 7b); "Trust and hope in Yahweh; the righteous will not be put to shame but will possess the land" (vv. 3, 7, 19, 22, 34); "The evildoers will come to an evil end. Only a short time, and the wicked will be no more" (vv. 2, 10, 20). Cf. G. von Rad, *Wisdom*, 203f. The type of didactic poetry which we have in Psalm 37 is comparable to the Egyptian "literature of partition" ("Auseinandersetzungsliteratur," E. Otto).

Setting

The didactic poetry of Psalm 37 is transmitted in the style of those instructional exhortations which are characteristic of the ‫הכמה‬. The teacher represents himself as an old, experienced man who aims to soften and call to their senses the youthful "fanatics of righteousness." Still, there could be no mistaking the "autobiographical stylization," which is a typical device of the teaching of wisdom (cf. Prov. 24:30-34; Sir. 51:13-16; 33:16-19; G. von Rad, *Wisdom*, 36). Also in vv. 35f. the report in the first person singular once more comes through. Psalm 37 should be dated relatively late. It is close to the Torah psalms (G. von Rad, *Wisdom*, 49). The leading themes and the connections to tradition are postexilic (cf. M. Noth, *The Laws in the Pentateuch* [1966] 101).

Commentary

[Title] On ‫לדוד‬, cf. above, Intro. §4, No. 2.

[37:1-11] The teacher of wisdom who brings the word in Psalm 37 is addressing a person whose inmost being is aflame against the "evildoers" (v. 1). For the understanding of the psalm it is essential that we isolate the terms ‫מרעים‬ ("the wicked") and ‫עשה עולה‬ ("evildoers") from general categories of moral value. In the OT we are dealing with a group of human beings whose life and activity is judged and understood from the viewpoint of Yahweh. The "wicked" withdraw from the rule of God and resist his will. The fretting of the pious is therefore not simply "moral indignation" but a passionate inquiry about the living reality of Yahweh, about the power of his rule in this world (cf. Prov. 24:19). From the very beginning, angry indignation concerning the unchallenged, successful life of the "evildoer" is represented as superfluous and senseless (v. 2). "Quickly" the judgment of death is carried out in their case. As green vegetation suddenly dries away in a hot, searing wind, so also the existence of the "wicked" unexpectedly falls away into ruin (Job 14:2; Isa. 40:6f.). Fretting and being angry (v. 1) would be a sign of mistrust vis-à-vis the judgmental reality of Yahweh. Therefore the teacher of wisdom in his exhortation recommends trust in Yahweh (v. 3), an upright walk, and a display of unwearied steadfastness (אמונה) in life on the land—which is thought of as the highest evidence of blessing and the epitome of the goodness of God that sustains life. In v. 4 the one being instructed is called on to desist from every type of quarrel with Yahweh (in respect to the ungodly) so that he may confidently receive and enjoy the full blessing that God presents to his servants. Bold indeed is the concept of "refreshing oneself," even that of "being pampered by Yahweh" (on ענג, cf. G. von Rad, *OT Theol*, 1:382; on *fruitio Dei*: K. Barth, *Church Dogmatics* 2/1, 653ff.). He who subordinates himself to the rule of Yahweh may with pleasure enjoy the good fortune of nearness to blessing (cf. v. 11; Isa. 58:14; Job 22:26; 27:10). He enjoys the great privileges of free prayer, which in ancient times were granted the king (cf. the comment Pss. 2:8; 20:4). But the threatening worries and temptations that present themselves at the thought of the ungodly are to be "turned over" (גול, cf. Ps. 22:8) to Yahweh (v. 5). He will prove to be the active (עשׂה), intervening God. He will not be indifferent, whether Yahweh is worshiped or not (Mal. 3:13ff.). Life will not roll along gray and indiscriminate. The "righteousness" (צדק) of the צדיק will "arise" like the sun (v. 6); conduct becoming the covenant (צדק) will come through with flying colors and become evident in his blessings. The "thought of reward" often assumed in Psalm 37 completely fades out of the picture here, for it is not true that a pious person would be rewarded for his good deeds, but the obedient manner of life as such beams forth as evident proof of belonging to God and of the blessing inherent in this belonging to God. We should ask whether all of these "thoughts of reward" and "ideas of retribution" that some would find in Psalm 37 should not be subordinated to this determinative viewpoint (cf. K. Koch, "Gibt es ein Vergeltungsdogma im Alten Testament?" *ZThK* 52 [1955], 1ff.). To trust in Yahweh (v. 3) and to "turn over" to him the burden of temptation (v. 5)—that would mean "being still" and "waiting" (v. 7; cf. Ps. 62:1, 5)—even when the ungodly machinations have success and good fortune. In all seriousness this exhortation recommends patient waiting (v. 8).[1] He who angrily takes to fretting enters the precincts of evil (Pss. 39:1; 73:2; Eph. 4:31).

---

1. "As if to say: You are annoyed that in spite of good behavior you suffer misfortune and things will not turn out as you would really like, and still you see how things go for the unrighteous person after all of his wantonness, so that it has become proverbial—the greater the rogue, the better the luck! But be wise, dear child, do not let this move you; wait for the Lord, your heart's desire will come in great abundance. But it isn't time yet. The rascal's good fortune must happen and have its day until it is over. Meanwhile you must entrust things to God, have your joy in him, be pleased with his will, so that you do not hinder his work in you and in your enemy, as those do who do not cease to rage until they have brought their plans through head first or have let them end in ruin. The psalmist uses a fine Hebrew word here: *sile domino et formare ei*, 'Be quiet and be compliant.' As a fetus in the womb is developed well, so you too are in this case conceived in God, and he wants to form you properly, if you will hold still" (Luther, German Commentary on Ps. 37:7, WA 8; 216, 30ff.).

In v. 9 the fundamental, two-sided statement is recorded: "The wicked (מרעים, v. 1) are destroyed, but those who hope in Yahweh will possess the land." On the "land," which Yahweh has given as the gift of blessing and as the foundation of life, the fate of those who have turned away from Yahweh and those who hope in him will be decided. Here too no reward is involved, for both—the ungodly and the righteous—have received the land as a pledge of Yahweh's bestowal of blessing and life-preserving goodness. From the "wicked" will be taken what they did not accept in grateful obedience. They have forfeited life in the realm of lordship and salvation. But those who are in close contact with Yahweh, who are "intent" (קוה) on him, inherit the land's range of life and blessing (cf. Ps. 25:13; in the eschatological sense: Isa. 57:13; 60:21; 65:9). It does not take long—"quickly" (v. 2) the ungodly disappears (v. 10; on the construction of the sentence, cf. BrSynt §13a). Over against the רשעים stand the ענוים (see above, Intro. §10, 3); on the life-sustaining land they enjoy the fullness of blessing (cf. the comment on v. 4).

On the theme "hope," cf. W. Zimmerli, *Der Mensch und seine Hoffnung im Alten Testament* (1968), "Die Hoffnungsaussagen der Psalmen," 33f.

[37:12-20] The צדיק reflects about the life-style of the רשע not from the remoteness of dogmatic contemplation; he is oppressed (v. 12) and threatened on account of his צדקה. Like a beast of prey the ungodly lies in wait for him (cf. Ps. 35:16). The צדיק is the suffering party, the weak one, who sees himself confronted by a greater power. But the teacher of wisdom points out the superior, triumphant laughter of Yahweh, the Lord of the world (Ps. 2:4), who already sees the day of ruin approach the wicked. The רשעים with their deadly weapons (v. 14) succumb to an "immanent nemesis" (v. 15; cf. the comment on Ps. 7:13-16). In view of this judgment and in the conviction that God intervenes in the fortunes of life in this world, the wisdom saying of the psalm comes to the conclusion that the slender subsistence of the צדיק is better than the great riches of the רשע. Thus it is clearly stated: it is determinative for a person to be צדיק. In this mode of existence, all good fortune is included (cf. Prov. 15:16; 16:18; Pss. 4:7; 84:10). The life and activity of the רשעים has an end (v. 17). But the צדיק inherits Yahweh's support (v. 17b), and his life's pathway lies under the watchful eye of God (v. 19; cf. Ps. 33:19). The "ungodly" on the other hand disappear like the green of the meadows (v. 20: cf. v. 2).

[37:21-29] The discoveries which prudential wisdom has acquired concerning the fate of the צדיק and the רשע are in vv. 21-29 strung together among other things. In times of distress (v. 19) the רשע is suddenly penniless (v. 21a), while the צדיק is in a position to give to others and to help (v. 21b). The צדיק receives the blessing of the endowment of the goodness which the land provides, but the רשע is struck by the curse of annihilation (v. 22; on the theme "blessing and curse," cf. J. Pedersen, *Der Eid bei den Semiten* [1914]; S. Mowinckel, *PsStud* V; J. Hempel, "Die israelitischen Anschauungen von Segen und Fluch im Lichte altorientalischer Parallelen," *ZDMG* 79 [1925], 20ff.). In all of his undertakings the "righteous" is accompanied by Yahweh and receives his help (vv. 23-26). "By Yahweh his steps are guided" (cf BrSynt §36b). The teacher of wisdom appears as the witness for this experience (v. 25). Here we have that "autobiographical stylization" referred to under "Form." "Here we definitely have, rather, a traditional stylistic form in which the teacher could, from time to time, clothe his instruction, and which also allowed of being extended into larger units. Our modern interest in the biographies of the biblical authors should not. therefore, be misled, for here we are scarcely dealing with genuine experiences; at any rate they appear in a highly conventionalized form'' (G. von Rad, *Wisdom* 38). The purpose is clear: every admonition is based on experience (v. 27). Life, not theory, is its source. But the mysterious principle of justice according to which Yahweh proceeds when he blesses the צדיק and rejects the רשע is in v. 28 called משפט. This משפט is above all legal aid, saving justice for the חסיד, who even in the worst distress is not forsaken. Verse 29 takes up the statement of v. 11 again.

[37:30-40] Verses 30 and 31 deal with the powers in the existence of the צדיק that show the way and determine life. He speaks חכמה to himself. On הגה, cf. the comment on Ps. 1:2. The complex concept חכמה denotes the wisdom of life that emanates from Yahweh (Prov. 2:6) and in all situations is able to find the right way. משפט here points to the conception of valid rules of life that emanate from Yahweh's expression of his will. תורה (v. 31) is the direction of God (cf. the comment on Psalm 19B). We are not to hear an echo of Jer. 31:31-34 in v. 31 (cf. also Pss. 40:9; 19:8). Here special attention will have to be due the Torah-understanding determined by the influence of the gift of salvation in postprophetic times. Cf. H.-J. Kraus, ''Zum Gesetzesverständnis der nachprophetischen Zeit,'' *Biblisch-theologische Aufsätze* (1972) 179-194. Verse 32 begins like v.12 and describes the attacks which the צדיק must suffer. The will to destroy of the רשע, which gives vent to its fury against the ''righteous man,'' is unfathomable. In vv. 32 and 33 we can recognize terms and conceptions from the prayer song of one who is persecuted innocently (cf. the comment on Psalm 7).

בהשפטו reminds us of the sacral trial in which the צדיק awaits the help of Yahweh against the false accusations of his enemies. The teacher of wisdom states: Yahweh will not permit the persecuted innocent person to be condemned. In v. 34 the exhortation and promise are again stated. The one who is obedient experiences the ''exaltation'' that he may possess the land, while the ungodly are destroyed. The fact that the ''righteous one witnesses'' this destruction (cf. BrSynt §106a) indicates that Yahweh's actual intercession does not remain secret to him. The תראה of v. 34 is then immediately in v. 35 documented by means of report from experience, which begins with ראיתי. First the picture of the happy and haughty רשע is drawn (v. 35). But ''quickly'' (cf. vv. 2, 20) everything changed: the ungodly one had vanished (v. 36); careful investigations determined that he could no longer be found. And again there is an exhortation: v. 37. It is a matter of considering the end (אחרית; vv. 37-38). ''The thoughts in the psalm are simple and are not developed in any complex way. Its conclusion is that it is the end that is important. The end (אחרית) of the wicked is destruction, the end of those who trust in Yahweh is salvation (vv. 37ff.). By 'end' the psalm obviously means the conclusion of a way of life in which God's salvation and judgment are then finally visible to men'' (G. von Rad). Decisive is the fact that also Israel's wisdom thinking opens up to the future. In the ''future'' it will become evident how the trial now in progress will come out. The outcome of a matter of which the content and the truth is now still hidden is what is meant.

Verses 39f. speak of Yahweh's readiness to help. Yahweh is the origin and fountain of all help that comes to the righteous. He is their refuge in times of trouble. The liberating power of the God of Israel is the subject. Finally therefore, the psalm does not solve a problem but promises liberation from the oppression of the ungodly. Thus the didactic poem, in spite of all the spiritual discussion brought in, in the final analysis actually provides no solution of the problem but rather a testimony to the deliverance.

Purpose and Thrust

The teaching of wisdom in Psalm 37 contains experiences, exhortations, and promises. But now the explanation would certainly err if the content of the report of experiences would be thought of as intending to declare: "There *is* righteousness!" In this sense H. Gunkel thinks Psalm 37 transmits "faith in retribution." This understanding is not appropriate. At the center of Psalm 37 stands not "righteousness" or "retribution," but the testimony to the actual intervention of Yahweh in the life of human beings. That is a vital difference. The "experience" of Psalm 37 is witness, testimony. And nowhere can a principle of righteousness or an idea of retribution—standing as it were above God or representing him—be recognized in the wisdom poem. So also, the exhortations do not call us to faith in righteous retribution but to trust in Yahweh.

These momentous revisions in basic assumptions make possible a new approach to the essential statement of the psalm. Here we will have to begin with the thought of the possession of land, which is peculiarly emphasized. Yahweh has given his people a land which is to be at one and the same time a basis for making a living and a pledge for salvation. On this land a great division takes place in the chosen people. There are people who gratefully enter the service of Yahweh, are beholden to him in all things, and live from the fullness of his goodness: the צדיקים. And on the other side there are people who turn away from Yahweh and his gifts, who proudly seek their fortune and want to kill the צדיק who reminded them of Yahweh—the רשעים. The situation which the wisdom teaching addresses is clear from the beginning: "righteous people" fret and become angry about the רשע, who, as an ungrateful evildoer and schemer in God's realm of lordship, dares to exist on the basis of his gift of life and salvation. The comfort of the OT psalm is the message that Yahweh will soon intervene. The צדיק will experience it. Indeed, that *is* comfort when we consider that the צדיק is in danger of death (vv. 14, 32). Is Yahweh a living God? Can he show his power in the midst of this world? These anguished questions never entered the field of vision of idealistic psalm interpretation; it transposed God and the world, but above all the relations between God and world, into the realm of ideas and took offense (under the influence of humanitarian ideas) about the "inferior morality" of the theory of retribution. The NT (again, under the sway of humanitarian ideas) was called on as a witness for a purer ethic of love. Overlooked was the fact that all this-worldly hope for God's intervention again made its appearance, e.g., in the macarisms of the Sermon on the Mount (Matt. 5:5; cf. Mark 10:30). Only when the connections are really seen and are recognized in their unfathomable depth should we speak of overcoming and breaking through OT statements in the NT. The spiritual distance of anyone who wants to analyze "ideas" in Psalm 37 is never able to get the essence of things into focus.

Psalm 38

Prayer from Sickness, Guilt, and Hostility

Literature

R. Arconada, ''Psalmus 37/38 retentus, emendatus, glossatus,'' *VD* 10 (1930) 48-56, 107-116. R. Martin-Achard, ''La prière d'un malade: Quelques remarques sur le Psaume 38,'' *Verbum Caro* 45 (1958) 77-82. C. Riggi, ''L' 'auxesis' de Salmo 38 nel 'De Officiis' di S. Ambrogio,'' *Salesianum* 29 (Torini 1967) 623-668.

Text

A psalm of David. For the incense offering (?).

38:1 O Yahweh, punish me not in your anger
and chastise me not[a] in your wrath,

2 for your arrows whir down on me,
and your hand 'rests heavily'[b] on me.

3 There is nothing healthy in my flesh because of your grudge,
nothing whole in my bones because of my transgression.[c]

4 For my transgressions grow over my head,
like a heavy burden they are too heavy for me.

5 My wounds smell rotten, fester
because of my folly.

6 I[d] am upset, bowed down low;
all the time I go about mourning.

7 My loins are all aflame,
nothing is healthy in my flesh.

8 I am exhausted and utterly shattered[e]
I cry from a groaning heart.

9 Lord, before you lies all my longing,
my sighing is not concealed from you.

10 My heartbeat flutters, strength has left me,
and the light of my eyes '   '[f] is extinguished for me.

11 My friends, '   '[g] 'they too'[h] 'have fled from me,'[i]
and my neighbors stay away.

12 Those who lie in wait for my life laid snares,
   and those who seek my distress are talking of wickedness,
   plan deceit all day long.ʲ
13 But I am deaf, do not hear,
   and like one dumb who opens not his mouth.
14 Yes, I became like a man who does not hear
   and in whose mouth no answer could be found.ᵏ
15 For I wait for you, O Yahweh,
   you will answer, Lord, my God.
16 For I think, they shall not exult over me;
   when my foot wavers, not boast about me!
17 For indeed, I am resigned to my fall,
   and my pain is always before my eyes.
18 Yes, I confess my transgression,
   am troubled about my lapse.
19 They who 'without cause'ˡ fight against me are strong,
   many they are who senselessly hate me.
20 They reward the good with evil for me,
   accuse me,ᵐ because I follow after the good.
21 Do not forsake me, O Yahweh,
   my God, be not far from me!
22 Hasten to my aid,
   O Lord, my salvation!

1a In v. 1b many Mss add the negative וְאַל, which is implicitly given (as a consequence of v. 1a).

2b ותנחת is probably not an original repetition of the same verb in the parallel member. Gk has read וַתִּנַּחַת, T וַתָּנַח. Consonant with the topicality of the language of the Psalms would be וַתִּכְבַּד, cf. Ps. 32:4.

3c Gk, σ´, and S present the plural חַטֹּאתִי.

6d On this meaning of עוה, cf. 1 Sam. 20:30; Isa. 21:3; Prov. 12:8 (KLB 686).

8e 8 Mss: וְנִדְכֵּאתִי.

10f גַּם־הֵם in 10b has a very disturbing effect and probably was not original there.

11g The text of 11a is disturbed. ורעי gives the impression of a secondary supplement.

h גַּם־הֵם from v. 10b could have had its original place in 11a (cf. Jer. 12:6).

i יעמדו (cf. also the parallelism in v. 11b) is hardly original, and נגעי ("my blow") will therefore probably have to be corrected. Gk offers the text ἐξ ἐναντίας μου ἤγγισαν, which corresponds to the Hebrew מִנֶּגְדִּי נָגָשׁוּ.

12j The three-member verse construction obviously presents difficulties. Very likely the words מבקשי נפשי ודרשי רעתי are to be thought of as a secondary supplement.

14k V. 14 is an echo of v. 13 and might be thought of as an expanding addition.

19l חיים ("living ones") does not fit well in the context. Consonant with the topicality of the language of the Psalms would be חִנָּם (Pss. 35:19; 69:4; 109:3; Lam. 3:52).

20m On שׂטן and its meaning, cf. Pss. 71:13; 109:4, 20, 29.

Form

Psalm 38 belongs among the "acrostic songs" (Bickell), which contain as many verses as the alphabet has letters (cf. Psalms 33; 146; Lamentations 5). The meter varies. The double triple meter dominates: vv. 1, 2, 6-9, 13, 15, 17, 19, 21. The 4 + 4 meter is present in vv. 3, 20; 4 + 3 in vv. 10, 11, 14; 3 + 4 in vv. 4, 14; 3 + 2 in v. 6; and 2 + 2 in vv. 18, 22.

The psalm belongs to the form group, prayer songs. See above, Intro. §6, 2. Significant is the address to Yahweh in the second person singular that runs through the entire psalm. The development is easily recognized. Cries for help in dire distress are found at the beginning and at the conclusion of the prayer song (vv. 1, 21-22). In vv. 2ff., i.e., in the extensive middle section, descriptions of the distress are emphasized. The three themes of this description are: sickness, guilt, and enmity. Accordingly, the psalm is to be assigned to the group of psalms that have to do with sickness and healing (cf. K. Seybold, *Das Gebet des Kranken im Alten Testament: Untersuchungen zur Bestimmung und Zuordnung der Krankheits- und Heilungspsalmen,* BWANT V, 19 [1973]). In v. 14 Yahweh is confronted with incentives for hearing the prayer and for intervening.

Setting

The direction of the cultic-liturgical heading (להזכיר) cannot be the starting point for determining the setting; the explanation of the term (cf. above, Intro. §4, No. 16) is problematical. The essential clues must be derived from the prayer as such. Here there is no doubt: the psalm has to do with a person who is very sick (vv. 2, 3, 5, 7, 10, 17), who recognizes his suffering as a judgment of his guilt (vv. 1, 3), and in penitential garb (v. 6) now appears before Yahweh for help and an answer to his prayer. We may be reminded of the situation described in Lev. 13:1-46. But this very sick person, who is very likely suffering from leprosy (v. 5), is at the same time under indictment (H. Schmidt, *Das Gebet der Angeklagten im Alten Testament,* BZAW 49 [1928], 30). His enemies have ferreted out transgressions of his in order to prove to the sufferer what the real cause of his sickness is (see above, Intro. § 10, 4); but he knows that he is innocent (v. 19). Still we cannot declare that the institution of divine jurisprudence clearly asserts itself. The statements of the prayer song contain a plethora of standing formulations, suggesting that a formulary is involved which was adopted particularly in cases of sickness and in situations where accusations accompanied the sickness (John 9:2). In any case, the petitioners are conscious of the fact that their sickness represents a major disturbance at the very root of their lives, and that the petition for healing must be accompanied by a confession of guilt. Psalm 38 displays the beginning of such reflection. It comes close to the problem of the book of Job and should be dated relatively late. More detailed clues for dating the psalm can of course not be discerned.

Commentary

[Title] On מזמור לדוד, see above, Intro. §4, No. 2. On להזכיר, see Intro. §4, No. 16.

[38:1] The petitioner knows that he is under the wrath of God. As in Ps. 6:1, this fact imparts a distinctive stamp to the suffering and lamenting, praying and pleading (cf. the comment on Ps. 6:1). Sickness and misfortune are thought of as the results of Yahweh's wrath. In the OT the association of guilt and sickness is inseparable (cf. G. von Rad, *OT Theol,* 1:274f). The wrath of God makes it obvious that human life is marked by guilt. Sickness, therefore, in the OT is not an anonymous fate but the reaction of God to the guilt of transgression. Yahweh ''reproves'' (יסר) the human being through physical distress.

[38:2-10] In lamentation the psalmsinger in vv. 2-10 reports concerning the sickness that has left its mark on his life. Yahweh approaches the sufferer like an enemy and shoots ruinous arrows at him from on high (cf. Ps. 91:5; Job 6:4). Ancient Near Eastern mythology also speaks in this way about demonic arrows that have struck the sick person and have poisoned him. The affliction burdens the sick like a heavy weight; it is Yahweh's hand that makes itself felt as it presses down (cf. Pss. 32:4; 39:10). The picture of the sickness of leprosy can rather clearly be recognized in vv. 3-5. The flesh is covered with wounds (on אֵין־מְתֹם, cf. Isa. 1:6), the bones are deformed (v. 3). And immediately there is the additional remark: מִפְּנֵי חַטָּאתִי. The sickness is the herald of guilt; it announces a transgression which, so to speak, has erupted to the outside and become manifest. In the lamenting description of his affliction the psalmsinger therefore immediately also lays bare his guilt. The body which is covered from head to toe with wounds is a witness to the overwhelming transgression (v. 4) that sweeps over the sick man like a flood (cf. Pss. 69:2, 15; 124:4). Helplessly, he who is struck by the wrath of God collapses under the weight of developing guilt that reaches full growth in punishment. When v. 5 speaks of evil-smelling, festering wounds, the first thought is of leprosy. The reference to "folly" (אִוַּלְתִּי) renews the thought of guilt. In v. 6 the psalmsinger presents himself like a penitent: confused, bowed down, and dressed in mourning clothes (cf. Ps. 42:9; Isa. 58:5). One can imagine the petitioner avoiding residential areas (Mark 5:3), and there cowering in putrefaction and depravity (v. 7). From depths of exhaustion and frustration come cries of a groaning heart (v. 8). But even in the midst of sickness and lamentation the psalmsinger is sure that Yahweh hears (v. 9) his praying and lamenting (v. 1). Verse 9 therefore witnesses to the confidence of being heard; the cry of him who is mortally sick is not hidden from Yahweh. Still v. 10 immediately continues the description of the lamentable situation. The heart of the sick man "wavers." The *pilp.* סְחַרְחַר would literally have to be translated: "flit to and fro." The reference is probably to the fear-inspiring, disjointed pounding of the heart at the moment of utter exhaustion. In distinction from Pss. 6:7; 13:3, v. 10b is then probably referring to an actual loss of the ability to see (and therefore not only a figurative allusion to the physical collapse).

The affliction of the sufferer is aggravated by the fact that even close friends and neighbors flee from the human being who is guilty and stricken by the wrath of God (v. 11). They avoid the man who is afflicted with misfortune (cf. Ps. 88:8, 18; Job 19:14, 15; Lam. 1:2; and often). The friends and neighbors have suddenly turned into enemies (v. 12), for their entire attention now turns to the question, Why must the sick man endure such suffering? What is he guilty of? For what transgression is this obvious wrath of God inflicted on him? (See above, Intro. §10, 4). The setting of snares (cf. Ps. 109:11) and plotting deception points to the zeal with which people look for the guilt. The "enemies" want to level an accusation against the sufferer. By means of the proof for the causal transgression they want to arrive at a sacral condemnation and ban the sufferer from their circles.

[38:13-20] Verse 13 now tells us how the psalmsinger acted in this whirlwind of sickness and enmity. He feigned deafness over against the accusations and never opened his mouth for any passionate protest (cf. also v. 14).[1] This patient way

---

1. "In the first place, he intimates that he was so overwhelmed with the false and wicked judgments of his enemies, that he was not even permitted to open his mouth in his own defense. In the second place, he alleges before God his own patience, as a plea to induce God the more readily to have pity upon him; for such meekness and gentleness not only, with good reason, secures favor to the afflicted and the innocent, but it is also a sign of true piety" (Calvin, on Psalm 38:13, trans. Anderson [Eerdmans, 1949]).

of committing to Yahweh everything that happened should in the prayer song probably be understood as the motive for God's intervening (H. Gunkel), but above all it bears witness to the faith of the servant of God, who even in the worst of suffering trusts in Yahweh alone (Psalm 22; Isa. 53:7; 1 Peter 2:23). The context in v. 16 shows that the psalmsinger turns to Yahweh alone and unerringlywaits for his answer (cf. Ps. 130:5). It is the "oracle of salvation," the completely authoritative consolation of the priest to which the petitioner looks forward (J. Begrich, "Das priesterliche Heilsorakel," *ZAW* 52 [1934], 81-92). The כ‍-sentences in vv. 15-18 probably should all be understood as dependent on vv. 13-14; i.e., here are communicated—as evidence—the reflections that the person who is silent vis-à-vis the accusations of his enemies carries within himself. And v. 20 then speaks again about the enemies. But first: What thoughts pass through the mind of the psalmsinger—while he ignores the attacks of the enemies? He speaks to himself (אמרתי): They shall not exult or triumph over me (v. 16)! The petitioner initially deals only with his pain and with his guilt (vv. 17-18). He openly confesses his transgression before Yahweh. But there is a difficulty here. If we assume that in vv. 15-18 the petitioner is departing from the challenges of his enemies and is speaking about his own reflections, about his turning to Yahweh, and about the confession of his guilt—how then are we to understand v. 19? How can the psalmsinger in v. 18 declare that he confesses his transgression, while he in v. 19 asserts that the enemies have no cause for any accusation at all? Are we dealing with two different conceptions of guilt here? Does the accusation of the enemies have to do with a presupposition of guilt which, in the form of serious slander, seeks to separate the sufferer from Yahweh? And does the confession of sins by the one who is here lamenting (cf. also vv. 1, 3, 5) contain the disclosure of transgressions which are not discernible by any enemy and which also cannot bring about separation from Yahweh (v. 9)? In any case, in v. 19 the calumnies of the enemies spoken of in v. 12 are rejected. In the lament the sufferer points to the power and great number of his persecutors. Friends and neighbors (v. 11) repay the psalmsinger's kindnesses with evil (cf. Pss. 35:12; 109:4). Here a motive of the oath of cleansing, or the declaration of innocence, comes through: the persecuted person has done good deeds for his neighbors, he has pursued that which is good (v. 20b).

[38:21-22] At the conclusion the plea of the sufferer again comes into prominence (vv. 21-22). He who is persecuted by his friends prays that Yahweh may not forsake him (Pss. 22:11, 19; 35:22; 71:12). On אלהי, cf. O. Eissfeldt, " 'Mein Gott' im Alten Testament," *ZAW* 61 (1945/48) 3-16. Mortally ill, the psalmist pleads for a quick intervention—certain that Yahweh is his salvation, his help.

Purpose and Thrust

The singer of Psalm 38 walks through the darkest abysses of suffering, of abandonment by God, of loneliness. Sickness, guilt, and enmities in the circle of his neighbors and friends—these are the afflictions. The sum total of the misfortune can be encompassed in the reference to the "wrath of God." In the second place, specific ailments are recognizable (leprosy?), but the one who is lamenting bears the characteristics of the suffering servant of God described in Psalm 22 and Isaiah 53. If we disregard the mysterious and enigmatic guilt→ affliction causality (cf. the comment on Psalm 6), then there appears the figure of the sufferer, who achieves his final expression in the "servant of God" of Isaiah 53.

In listing Psalm 38 among the "seven penitential psalms," the church has entered into the depth of suffering and the complexity of the statements of Psalm 38 for the purpose of bearing witness to human perverseness and frailty. In this connection it may be important that in the passion narrative of the Gospel according to St. Luke (23:49) there is an echo of Psalm 38:11. In his death on the cross Jesus suffers the distress of utter forsakenness, for even his relatives and friends stand apart from him. Jesus Christ stands in solidarity with outcasts (cf. the comment on Psalm 22, "Purpose and Thrust") and makes their fate his own. In this event God confronts all sufferers as their help and salvation (v. 22).

Psalm 39

Wrestling for Hope and Help in
Transitory Life

Literature

E. Baumann, "Struktur-Untersuchungen im Psalter I," *ZAW* 61 (1945/48) 146-155.
D. W. Thomas, "נצב in Psalm XXXIX 6," *Studies in the Bible (Festschrift M. H. Segal)*, Publications of the Israel Society for Biblical Research 17 (1964) 10-16.

Text

To the choirmaster. Of Jeduthun.[a] A psalm of David.
39:1 I decided: I want to be careful about my 'words,'[b]
    so that I may not transgress with my tongue;
    I want to 'fit'[c] my mouth with a bridle
    as long as the ungodly (stands)[d] before me.
2 Dumb and quiet was I,
    was silent—without effect.
    Then my pain was stirred up,
3 hot within me did my heart become;
    at my groaning a fire kindled—
    then my tongue had to speak,
4 Let me know my end, O Yahweh,
    what the measure of my days is,
    so that I may know[e] how transitory I am.
5 Behold, you have set my days only a span's length,
    my life is like nothing before you.
    Only 'like'[f] a breath does every person stand upright, (*Selah*)[g]
6 only like the specter of a dream does one walk along.
    Only for nothing does one heap up 'blows'[h]
    without knowing who harvests them.
7 But now, on what does 'my hope'[i] rest, O Lord?
    My waiting is for you alone.
8 Rescue me from all those 'who rise up against me,'[j]
    do not let me become a jest of the fool.

9 I (now) remain dumb, do not open my mouth,
   for you have done it.
10 Take away from me your torment,
    under the 'pressure'ᵏ of your hand I pass away.
11 If you chastise a man with punishments on account of guilt,
    you destroy his 'glory'ˡ like the moth,
    every man is but a breath! *Selah.*
12 Hear my prayer, O Yahweh,
    and listen to my crying, be not silent to my tears!
    For I am a stranger before you,
    a sojourner, like all my fathers!
13 'Look'ᵐ away from me, that I may rejoice
    before I go my way and no longer exist.

1a *Kethib:* לידיתון; *Qere:* לִידוּתוּן.
b MT: "I want to be careful about my ways"; but the parallelism suggests that we read דְּבָרַי.
c The repetition of אשמרה is hardly original. Gk (ἐθέμην) has read אָשִׂימָה (cf. 2 Kings 19:28).
d Gk guarantees this translation, although a correction (בְּעָמֹד) instead of בעד; so F. Wutz) is not necessary.
4e For the addition of the conclusion, cf. BrSynt §176c.
5f The translation "Everything is surely but a breath, and every human being is only a 'seedling' " (נִצָּב)—so F. Wutz in connection with MT—is problematical. It is easy to follow S and read כְּהֶבֶל.
g סלה here is situated in the wrong place and separates a combination of verses that belong together (vv. 5b/6aα).
6h MT: "They raise a fuss about nothing," but the suffix in אָסְפָּם demands an object for יצבר. Accordingly, הָמוֹן or הוֹנִים would have to be read instead of יהמיון.
7i The parallelism prompts us to read מִי תִּקְוָתִי, following Gk and S.
8j The pointing leads us astray. The parallelism and the topicality of the language of the Psalms suggest reading פְּשָׁעַי (Ges-K §116i) (Isa. 66:24; Ezek. 20:38).
10k MT points to the Aramaic word תִּגְרָה ("strife"), that has taken the place of the appropriate and probably original מִגְבוּרַת (Gk ἀπὸ τῆς ἰσχύος—"from the power").
11l חָמוּד ("desirable") should probably be read חֶמְדּוֹ, following Mss.
13m הָשַׁע in MT (from שעע, "paste over") is surely a slip of the pen for שְׁעֵה ("look"), cf. Job 7:19; 14:6.

Form

The meter of Psalm 39 is irregular and agitated. The following meters are to be noted: 3 + 3 in vv. 1aγ/1b, 5b/6aα, 6aβ/b, 8, 12aδ/b, 13; 3 + 2 in vv. 1aα/β, 3aβ/b, 7, 9; 2 + 2 in vv. 2a, 2b/3aα; 4 + 3 in v. 5a; and 3 + 4 in vv. 10, 12aαβγ. Three-member meters appear in v. 4 (3 + 3 + 3) and v. 11 (4 + 3 + 2). This reconstruction of the meters can only be an attempt to inventory the individual verses.

The psalm belongs to the form group, prayer songs (see above, Intro. §6, 2). In vv. 4ff., 7ff., and 12ff. the address and plea to Yahweh in the second person is clearly discernible. Moreover, time and again there are descriptions of the distress, as well as reflections carrying over into the form group, didactic poetry. On didactic poetry, see above, Intro. §6, 5. Characteristic is the fact that the specific descriptions of distress present an opportunity for axiomtic meditations about the frailty and transitoriness of life. This gains expression in the form of the whole psalm, which is highly individual. Already the introit with its tendency toward "biographical features" (vv. 1-3) is unusual. But there probably really is a "biographical stylization," such as should also be observed in Psalm 37 (cf. the comment on Psalm 37, "Setting"). Then the passage vv. 4-13 should probably be thought of as a uniform prayer of petitions. In keeping with the trend of thought, a division into three sections might be undertaken: vv. 4-6, 7-11, 12-13. H. Gunkel views the layout of the psalm from v. 7 on as disrupted; he attempts to provide a restoration of the logical sequence. But the transpositions are very questionable. We should try to take up the received text in its sequence of verses, to interpret it, and to understand the sense of the statements.

Setting

For the situation of the petitioner the following facts that can be gleaned initially from the psalm might be important: (1) A severe "blow" (v. 10) has been received by the psalm's petitioner; obviously, what is involved is a sickness that has come on suddenly and that threatens life itself (cf. especially the statements in v. 11). (2) The life of the petitioner is near death, the "end" (v. 4), and yet there is something lacking in the consistency and depth of insight into the unavoidable fate. (3) "Enemies" (see above, Intro. §10, 4) have arisen against the person beset by the disaster. They mock him and spy on him (vv. 1, 8). As often in the prayer songs of people who are oppressed, the enemies play the part of accusers. Their purpose is to trace the reason for the collapse back to a transgression and to bring this into the light of day. Yet, all these disclosures of situations should not be freighted too heavily. The reflection and meditation of the didactic poem lets us know that the specific reference has been only the cause and the eliciting motive for meditation and didactic statements that aim at basics. Wisdom traditions that can be traced back to early Egyptian literature have in relatively late times shaped Psalm 39. Of course, firm clues for dating the psalm are wanting.

Commentary

[Title] On למנצח, see above, Intro. §4, No. 17. On לידותון, see Intro. §4, No. 18. On מזמור לדוד, see Intro. §4, No. 2.

[39:1-3] The psalmsinger begins with a reference to a decision he reached earlier. He reports that he decided to watch his words very carefully and to bridle his mouth. This disciplined silence takes place in view of the רשע; the petitioner might become guilty of an error in his presence. What is meant here? What error might the petitioner be thinking of? When taken with other psalm passages, the assertion in v. 9 indicates what the danger is that threatens. When the psalm petitioner says to God concerning the disaster that has befallen him, אתה עשית (v. 9b), the possibility exists that he might be quarreling with Yahweh and become guilty of evil (Ps. 37:8; also cf. Ps. 73:15; Mal. 3:14f.). Thus, the honor of Yahweh, who comes to meet the petitioner in the unfathomable mystery of an activity that brings disaster, is thought of first and is held in higher esteem than all the obvious eruptions in lament and description of distress. Where other sufferers among the psalmists cry out, he is silent (Ps. 37:7), remains dumb and quiet (v. 2). But this self-imposed silence in honor of God has taken the petitioner far away from good fortune (מטוב). He had obviously assumed that Yahweh would "hear" his conscious silence. But that did not happen. The sufferer remained stuck fast in his distress. "Then my pain was stirred up"—

thus begins the account that reports the turn of events. From the midst of his silence lamentation breaks forth. It was not possible to remain quiet any longer (cf. Ps. 32:3; Jer. 20:9). The heart "became hot"; on חַם־לִבִּי, cf. Deut. 19:6. Like a fire did it blaze forth and break out. Then the tongue just had to speak. Thus the psalmsinger provides a look into the inner history of the origin of his prayer song that begins at v. 4.

[39:4-6] A preliminary train of thought should be recognized in vv. 4-6. If we follow the MT, we encounter a curious picture: in v. 4 the psalmist prays for instruction concerning the transience and mortality of his life, in vv. 5-6 he complains (הִנֵּה) to Yahweh about the vanity of his existence. This observation induced Gunkel to change the first word in v. 4 to אוֹדִיעֲךָ ("I let you know"). This correction, which is not documented in any text, he explains as follows: "The text is based on a deliberate alteration, because one was offended at the altogether too bold and humanizing word." But can and may one relieve the unique tension that should be observed in vv. 4-6 by means of this substitution? The petitioner prays to Yahweh for enlightenment concerning the fate of death that engulfs him, concerning the transitoriness of his life. Certainly this can only mean that Yahweh should show him that the quick way into death is an irresistible fate. Yahweh is to teach him that the end must come. In other words, the petitioner of the psalm demands final clarity; from the mouth of Yahweh he wants to hear the truth about mortal life. But at the same time (vv. 5f.), he remonstrates before Yahweh concerning this brief, futile life in order to move him to intervene. Man is a הֶבֶל ("a mere breath," "a nullity"; cf. Pss. 62:9; 94:11; 144:4; Eccles. 1:2). Even the solid, erect man is like a nullity. Like a vision in a dream he goes his way (v. 6). Similarly, an Egyptian text can read, "The time a person spends on earth is only a vision in a dream" (A. Erman, *Die Religion der Ägypter* [1934], 238f.). Heaping up riches is foolishness (Luke 12:18 ff.). This hollow vision and phantom of human existence (cf. Pss. 73:20; 102:11; 144:4) implicitly contains an appeal to Yahweh that he might have mercy and intervene.

[39:7-11] In these verses the agonies of the petitioner of the psalm emerge more clearly. Amid the emptiness and decrepitude of the shadowy existence (vv. 5f.) that has the sign of death on it, he asks about the hope of his life (v. 7). Where is it? Verse 7b contains an expression of trust: תוֹחַלְתִּי לְךָ הִיא. Amid the hollow, transitory life the petitioner prostrates himself toward Yahweh, waiting and expectant, hoping for help. A first grant of an intervention of the part of Yahweh would consist of this, that the adversaries are overcome. The psalmist is dealing with enemies who are bent on attempting to represent his misfortune as just punishment for an offense he committed (see above, Intro. §10, 4). They mock him who is heavily afflicted, and they behave like "fools" for whom God does not exist, practically speaking (cf. the comment on Ps. 14:1). Thinking about the enemies has obviously reminded the petitioner of the psalm of his resolve (v. 10). He therefore commits himself anew to total silence. For how can one lay anything to the charge of Yahweh? Contradiction and invariable evaporation of the cries and complaints are characteristic of Psalm 39. The knowledge that Yahweh will inevitably act (אַתָּה עָשִׂיתָ) and the plea for compassion are wrestling with each other. As in the transition from v. 4 to v. 5, so there is development from v. 9 to v. 10. The silenced withdrawal in the face of the unfathomable act of God again and again returns to the appeal to a compassionate intervention of Yahweh. The suffering is נגע (v. 10), torment of God. Under the mighty hand of Yahweh the sufferer passes away (cf. Ps. 32:4). We are here probably dealing with a mortal illness. And immediately (as always in the Psalms) the indissoluble correction between guilt and illness is seen: Yahweh chastises the human being for guilt (v. 11). Here cf. G. von Rad, *OT Theol,* 1:274. As moths consume garments (cf. G. Dalman, *AuS* V 15), so the beauty of the body is destroyed. May we in this picture think of a leper who brings the prayer song before Yahweh? In v. 11b the reference to the nullity of human life is taken up anew.

On סלה (erroneously also after v. 50), cf. Intro. §4, No. 13.

[39:12-13] In v. 12 petitions for being heard are expressed. The lamenting petitioner pleads for a divine answer to prayer and in this connection points out his existence as a גר and a תושב on Yahweh's land. Both terms remind us that Yahweh has granted the fugitive, alien life an abode. He is the Lord of the land. It belongs to him. The Israelites are guests and sojourners (Lev. 25:23; 1 Chron. 29:15; Ps. 119:19; Heb. 11:13) who are entrusted to his care. Of course, we could also ask whether the terms גר and תושב could not also refer to the asylum function of the sanctuary (cf. גור in Ps. 15:1). In that case the petitioner would be referring to his sojourn in the temple area and to the goodness of God present there, who has promised the bestowal of his salvation to those who are persecuted and helpless.

The petition of v. 13 is unusual. It contradicts what has been prayed for in v. 12. This tension is characteristic of the whole psalm. Usually the OT psalm petitioner prays, ''Consider me'' (Pss. 13:3; 25:19; 59:4; 74:20; 89:14; 119:159; and often). Now we hear, ''Look away from me'' (cf. Job 7:19; 10:20f.; 14:6). This petition is induced by the consciousness of being stricken by Yahweh and of being obliged to feel the heavy hand of God. Not Yahweh's nearness but his turning away would once more lift the darkness of life. That is the thought of deepest despair. It is necessary to observe that Psalm 39 is permeated by two sensations that are at war with each other. Therefore it is wrong to neutralize the tensions by means of corrections of the text and by transpositions. On v. 13b we should finally call attention to the fact that the petitioner is here speaking of his imminent death. ''The dead exist, but they are 'no longer at hand' as living human beings'' (Chr. Barth, *Die Errettung vom Tode in den individuellen Klage- und Dankliedern des Alten Testaments* [1947], 60).

Purpose and Thrust

The situation on the basis of which we are to understand Psalm 39 can be recognized clearly: A person who is mortally ill is praying to Yahweh. He sees his impending death before him as an inevitable fate (vv. 4-6, 13). He is waiting for God to certify unequivocally that his life has reached its goal (v. 4). And for him everything he has suffered in the line of physical distress and oppressing pain (v. 10) goes under the banner: כי אתה עשית (v. 9b). This excess of suffering causes a man to be tempted to rebel against God and to say something untoward. But to avoid this temptation, the psalmsinger had determined to remain silent and to bear his suffering patiently (vv. 1-3). But driven by despair and pleading cries, these self-imposed limits are broken (v. 3). The petitioner wrestles for hope and help in a life that seems transient, hollow, and senseless. He asks God for his intervention, for a final fulfillment that gives meaning—for an answer which may have a clearing and helping effect. But the psalm breaks off in despair; it is plunged into darkness without parallel. In the face of death all of life becomes dubious and stretches toward the one and only hope (v. 7). But where is this hope as death relentlessly approaches (vv. 4, 13)? The psalmist is in the depths of abandonment by God (Ps. 22:1). As the book of Job raises questions above itself and longs for a final act of God, so also Psalm 39 looks for an answer beyond the limits of certainty set in the Old Testament.

Psalm 40

Song of Thanksgiving
of One Who Has Been Rescued
and
Cry of Distress
of One Who Is Being Persecuted

Literature

E. Baumann, "Struktur-Untersuchungen im Psalter I," *ZAW* 61 (1945/48) 155-159. N. H. Ridderbos, "The Structure of Psalm XL," *OTS* 14 (1965) 296-304. E. Vogt, "Gratiarum actio Psalmi 40," *Verbum Domini* 43 (1965) 181-190. J. Becker, "Israel deutet seine Psalmen,"*Stuttgarter Bibel-Studien* 18 (1966) 70ff. J. H. Eaton, "The King's Self-Sacrifice. A Reinterpretation of Psalm 40," *Alta, The University of Birmingham Review* 3 (1967) 141-145. N. Airoldi, "Il Salmo 40B," *Rivista Biblica* 16 (1968) 247-258. L. Rost, "Ein Psalmenproblem," *ThLZ* 93 (1968) 241-246. F. Crüsemann, *Studien zur Formgeschichte von Hymnus und Danklied in Israel* WMANT 32 (1969) 258-263.

Text

To the choirmaster. Of David. A psalm.
40:1 Unerringly did I hope in[a] Yahweh;
    then he inclined to me
    and heard my crying.
  2 He drew me up from the horrible pit,
    from filth and mire,
    and set my feet on a foundation of rock,
    made my steps secure.
  3 He put a new song in my mouth—
    a song of praise to our God.
    Many are to see it and fear
    and trust in Yahweh.

4 Blessed is the one who sets[b]
his trust on Yahweh,
does not turn to the proud,
who are entangled in a lie.
5 Much have you [c] accomplished,
O Yahweh, ‘ ’[d] your wonders
and your plans for us!
Nothing is like you.
Should I want to report and speak (of them),
they are innumerable.
6 Sacrifices and gift offerings you did not want,[e]
but ears you did insert in me.
Burnt offerings and sin offerings you did not demand!
7 Then I said, Behold, I am coming!
In the scroll of the book it is written about me.—
8 I would like to do, my God, what pleases[f] you.
Your direction is in my heart!
9 I delight, ‘O Yahweh,’[g] in publishing righteousness
in the great congregation.
Indeed, my lips I do not close;
‘ ’[h] you know it.
10 Your[i] righteousness I did not hide
in the depths of my heart.
About your faithfulness and help I freely speak:
I do not conceal your grace and truth
from[j] the great congregation.
11 You, O Yahweh, will not withhold
your mercy from me;
your grace and truth
will always guard me.

12 For sufferings have encompassed me—
without number.
My (own) sins have caught up with me;
I can no longer look up.
More numerous are they than the hairs of my head,
my courage forsakes me.
13 Please, O Yahweh, save me;
‘ ’[k] hasten to come to help!
14 Let them together fall into shame and disgrace
who seek my life ‘ ’[l].
Let them retreat into ignominy
who desire my misfortune.
15 Let them be transfixed with shame
who call ‘ ’[m], Aha! Aha!
16 Let them exult and be glad in you,
all who seek you.
They shall say ‘ ’[n], Yahweh is great!
all who desire your help.
17 But I am miserable and poor
—the Lord thinks of me.[o]
My helper and deliverer you[p] are,
my God, do not delay!

1a A number of Mss simplify the construction by adding אֶל.
4b Gk and S have incorrectly read שָׁם. We should follow MT.

5c אתה is peculiarly exposed and is sometimes (though without sufficient reason) corrected to אָתָנוּ.

d אלהי should probably be eliminated for the sake of the meter.

6e No doubt, there are disturbances in vv. 6-8; the verses depart from the metrical order. But the text-critical corrections and conjectures, which in part arbitrarily turn statements into their very opposite, are not justified. Restraint is in order here. In the interpretation (''Commentary'') the present text form will be studied very carefully and elucidated on the basis of the context of vv. 1-11.

8f The tenses in v. 8 should be understood as *Perfecta declarationis*. Cf. D. Michel, *Tempora und Satzstellung in den Psalmen* (1960) 92f.

9g An arsis is missing in the meter. It is best supplied by adding יהוה from v. 9b.

h Cf. note **g**.

10i The reading צדקתי found in Gk[B] is noteworthy.

j A number of Mss of T read בְּקהל (as in v. 9a).

13k יהוה should here be eliminated for the sake of the meter.

14l לספותה (''to snatch them away'') is an epexegetical addition and should be eliminated.

15m V. 15b as an explanatory half-verse exceeds the meter. לי and very likely also the second האח are to be eliminated (cf. Ps. 70:3).

16n תמיד is metrically excessive and should very likely be eliminated.

17o Perhaps we should read חוּשָׁה (corresponding to Ps. 70:5) and adjust the understanding of the complementary half-verse to the context. (On vv. 13-17, cf. Psalm 70.)

p According to the conception of N. Airoldi, אתה is not a personal pronoun but a form of the verb *'atā*, which has the meaning ''come.'' The translation ''My helper and deliverer, come!'' would fit into the parallelism (*Rivista Biblica* 16, 1968, 247 ff.).

Form

Psalm 40 separates into two different songs that in form and theme clearly diverge. Psalm 40A (vv. 1-11) belongs to the form group of those prayer songs which stand out as ''songs of thanksgiving of an individual.'' See above, Intro. §6, 2aγ. On the other hand, the prayer song Psalm 40B (vv. 12-17), with its descriptions of distress and its laments, is clearly molded on the basic form of imploring and pleading. H. Gunkel and J. Begrich called this ''type'' an individual lament (*EinlPs* §6). But form criticism must surely go a step further. In the case of Psalm 40 it can show that the address of Yahweh in the second person, so characteristic of the song of thanksgiving of an individual, is noted only beginning at v. 5. Cf. F. Crüsemann, 259. Verses 1ff. are to be assumed to be a backward glance. Verses 3f. are to be thought of as an acknowledgment of inspiration from which the song of thanksgiving originated, accompanied by best wishes for all who trust in Yahweh (v. 4).

The question arises whether the two sections of Psalm 40, which have been characterized as two different psalms, can in some way—if not in a formal way, then at least by content—be related to each other. Basically, of course, nothing would prevent our understanding the phases of pleading and thanking as complementary. See above, Intro. §6, 2. But upon closer inspection we find that there is no inducement for joining the two entities. We have to begin with the assumption that two different psalms have been joined into one in Psalm 40—for what reason cannot be ascertained. If vv. 13-17 appear in Psalm 70 (which see!) as an independent song, we may assume that Psalm 40B was originally transmitted in isolation. At least, we ought to cite H. Gunkel's conjecture: ''The accretion probably stems from a person who in spite of all thanksgiving still had many things to complain about and who lived in a time in which the types were already very much mixed.'' Yet instead of this psychologizing conjecture we should more simply think of a seamless transition from one element to the other in copying. In the following, the interpretation is restricted to Psalm 40A in its preliminary investigations. For Psalm 40B, cf. the comment on Psalm 70. Accordingly, only a song of thanksgiving is to be dealt with.

The meter in vv. 1-11 (12) in the first place shows the "five-pulse meter" (3+2): vv. 2-5, 8-9, 10 (3+2 3+3+2). Verse 1 will have to be read in the 3+2+2 meter, and v. 11 in the 3+2 2+2 meter.

Setting

From Psalm 40A, the following can be deduced initially regarding the situation of the petitioner. From the retrospection in vv. 1f. we learn that the thanksgiving was preceded by an awful time of distress. Life had fallen into the area of death, into the realm of the dead (v. 2). Perhaps we may be permitted to assume that the petitioner was mortally ill but then experienced rescue and recovery (v. 2). But now the song of thanksgiving is being intoned "before the great congregation" (v. 10). If v. 7 is interpreted appropriately (see below), we may consider that the one who is giving thanks published his psalm in the scroll of a book in which there was a report about him. This publication could then be understood to be the actual thankoffering which took the place of the bloody offering. If we look at it this way, the criticism of offerings in v. 6 would also be explained. Also the emphatic reference to the inspiration of the song of thanksgiving and praise in v. 3 would be motivated. And at the same time comprehensive aspects would open up that would disclose an understanding of the process of psalm writing. Not only would we be able to assume that formularies with prayer songs, petitions, and thanksgivings (for every eventual situation and institution) were available in the sanctuary; also liturgical formularies that were composed by priests and recited after them by those who prayed in Israel—including activities such as are discernible in v. 7—would have to be taken for granted. Accordingly, a petitioner and singer would have presented (i.e., put on display in the sanctuary) the prayer song which he himself had composed (written out by himself or by a professional scribe) as an offering, or instead of an offering. This author—and Psalm 40A would nicely explain this—is not a priest (cf. L. Rost *ThLZ* 93 [1968], 241ff.). He is unmistakably influenced by prophecy—not only in his criticism of sacrifices (v. 6) but also in his consciousness of inspiration (v. 3), and not least of all in the way and manner in which he speaks of his absorption of the Torah in his heart (v. 8). For the last-named characteristic points to dependence on Jer. 31:31ff. and Ezek. 36:26ff. According to this, a corresponding postexilic origin would have to be assumed. Therefore we would be dealing with a prophetically inspired thanksgiving. Nothing indicates that in Psalm 40 we could be dealing with a "royal psalm" (to reject the thesis of J. H. Eaton).

The prayer song so exhibited in the sanctuary would probably have been preserved and transmitted to posterity in the temple archives—possibly together with Psalm 40B, so that the combination of the two psalms also could be indicative of a process of transmission.

Commentary

[Title] On למנצח, see above, Intro. §4, No. 17. On מזמור and לדוד, see Intro. §4, No. 2.

[40:1-2] In vv. 1-2 the psalmsinger looks back to a time of distress and temptation. In the midst of misfortune and suffering he confidently hoped in Yahweh. קוה קויתי describes unerring, expectant clinging to Yahweh, such as again and again is mentioned in the prayer songs that have grown out of distress (cf., e.g., Ps. 130:5). Then Yahweh inclined down to the depths. Verse 1b speaks of the miracle of being heard. Concerning the situation of his distress the psalmsinger in v. 2 speaks in metaphors. יון—טיט—בור שאון are concepts that describe the subterranean, chaotic abode of the dead (Ps. 69:2, 14; cf. Chr. Barth, *Die Errettung vom Tode in den individuellen Klage- und Dankliedern des Alten Testaments* [1947], §7). The symbolism is typically Near Eastern. Also in Akkadian prayers we read, "Take away your punishment, draw me up from the morass" (A. Falkenstein and W. von Soden, *Sumerische und akkadische Hymnen und Gebete* [1953], 271). Very likely these conceptions are derived from the archetypal model of the myths of a descent into hell (Ishtar's descent into hell). Accordingly, the psalmist fell into the realm of the dead, i.e., into the "sphere of death" (Chr. Barth). Life threatened to be extinguished, the domain of death embraced him who was suffering (from a serious illness?). Concerning Yahweh's "inclining" and "drawing someone up," also cf. Ps. 18:6ff. The rocky foundation (זלע) is the quintessence of all that is firm and unshakable.

[40:3] Worth noting in v. 3 is the understanding of the song of thanksgiving: thanksgiving is not a return gift of a human being to God, but a gift of God to human beings. Yahweh lays (נתן) the song into the mouth of the one who has been rescued. For an understanding of the Psalms, this reference to the "inspiration" of the petitioner is extremely important. It will be impossible to weaken the statement of v. 3 by, let us say, referring to the petitioner's taking over preexistent formularies of thanksgiving. Rather, here we actually have the understanding of a fully inspired expression (cf. also a corresponding expression in the psalms of thanksgiving of Qumran; M. Burrows, *The Dead Sea Scrolls* [1955], 414). And proceeding from this conception, light is also shed on the term שיר חדש (cf. Pss. 33:3; 144:9): it is the spirit-driven message developed by Yahweh. Again and again the individual song of thanksgiving tends to become a testimony, a message, and teaching for others. In this song Yahweh's bestowal of salvation is to be made "visible"—as the *verbum visibile* for the listening congregation. The message of thanksgiving is to produce certainty concerning the living reality of Yahweh (ירא) and confidence in him. On the combination ירא־ראה, cf. Ps. 52:6; Isa. 41:5. But also cf. Ps. 34:2ff.

[40:4] H. Schmidt understands v. 4 to be the speech of the officiating priest. That is hardly possible. The "felicitation" comes from the mouth of the one giving thanks, who with his testimony would like to lead many to a trust in Yahweh (cf. Ps. 34:8). There is danger that the sufferer, the oppressed person, is under the spell of the superior power of deceitful and slanderous enemies, who want to separate him from Yahweh (see above, Intro. §10, 4). The "proud" look for guilt in the life of the sufferer and with the power of their lie can win the day over him. The salvation lies in trust in Yahweh, in a full turn to him. Verse 4 therefore contains one of those didactic sentences which frequently occur in the Psalter (cf. G. von Rad, *OT Theol,* 1:359).

[40:5] This verse applies the miracle of the rescue of an individual's life (vv. 2-3) to the fullness of bestowels of salvation over against Israel. Without parallel and countless are the deeds of Yahweh: cf. Pss. 92:5; 104:24; 106:2; 139:18. The psalmist here sees the limits of his powers of expression and therefore merely indicates the wondrous acts of God in a hymnic style.

[40:6-8] In vv. 6f. the understanding of the text presents a number of difficulties. The text obviously has become disordered. The meters cannot be reconstructed. Emendations are of no help. Therefore we must carefully follow the individual statements. For the first, the psalmsinger states that Yahweh does not want sacrifices and gift offerings. זבח is the sacrifice that is eaten by a group at a meal (cf. L. Köhler, *OT Theology* 182). Associated with the festivals of thanksgiving in the holy place were sacrificial meals (cf. the comment on Ps. 22:26). מנחה denotes the gift offering which was presented as a gift of homage before Yahweh (L. Köhler, *OT Theol* 184). But these offerings Yahweh does not want—so the psalmist declares as he points to another fact, "Ears you did insert in me." What does that mean? Beyond question, this strange manner of expression contrasts obedience with offerings (1 Sam. 15:22). Before this new reality of relation to God also burnt offerings and sin offerings pale away (v. 6b could be a supplement). עולה is the burnt offering; the entire animal is burned up as a "gift of homage that rises in the fire"(L. Köhler). חטאה (probably better חטאת) is the type of offering that bears its meaning and purpose in its name (cf. L. Köhler, 188). The words הנה באתי in v. 7 could be a standing formulation from the liturgy of the festival of thanksgiving (cf. in Ps. 118:19: אבא־בם אודה יה). Ready for thanksgiving, the psalmist refers to his approaching steps. Though in the usual liturgy of offerings the burnt offerings and sin offerings were and are the things brought forward by him who approached to present a sacrifice, now an altogether different gift is presented. The sentence "In the scroll of the book it is written about me" probably contains a reference to the song of prayer and thanksgiving composed in prophetic inspiration (v. 3), which was exhibited in the sanctuary as a "sacrificial gift." Such an act of presentation is attested in the stele inscriptions of Asia Minor. Therefore we may conclude "that also in Israel a written report about the deeds of the petitioner and about Yahweh's acts in his behalf was displayed publicly in the temple. 'In the scroll of the book it is written of me' then means: In the written scroll is recorded what I have done, what I have suffered, and how Yahweh rescued me. But that is nothing but a written form of the song of praise that people were accustomed to present orally in the sanctuary—which in this case probably takes place additionally. Then the praise here formulated in writing and presented in a scroll takes the place of the offering" (H. J. Hermisson, *Sprache und Ritus im altisraelitischen Kult*, WMANT 19 [1965], 45; cf. 43ff.). In v. 8 the testimony of obedience already expressed in v. 6 is taken up—and now in a specific sense which can be explained and understood only with reference to prophetic promises of the OT. Joy in the will of God and the intimate appropriation of the Torah in the heart come about in the light of the prophetic promises in Jer. 31:31-34 and Ezek. 36:26ff. The petitioner knows that he belongs among those who are experiencing the mystery of fulfillment. Joy in the expression of God's will in his command-ments is an essential theme of postexilic Judaism (cf. especially Psalm 119). The תורה is the object of veneration and love. This fact cannot be interpreted as "nomism." Cf. H. -J. Kraus, "Zum Gesetzesverständnis der nachprophetischen Zeit," *Biblisch-theologische Aufsätze* (1972) 179-194. The prophetic spirit that permeates all the statements of Psalm 40A is unmistakable.

The question how we are to understand the rejection of the sacrifices in the Psalms will have to be investigated very carefully from case to case. Basically, two conceptions confront each other. At first it was supposed that in Pss. 40:6; 50:13; 51:6 the prophetic protest against sacrifices had its effect. But S. Mowinckel definitely contended that in the so-called anticultic psalms it is not that sacrifices are rejected but rather that the emphasis has shifted from sacrifice to the song (*PsStud* VI 51). On the problems, cf. J. J. Stamm, "Ein Vierteljahrhundert Psalmenforschung," *ThR* NF 23 (1955) 61f. After all that has hitherto been written on Psalm 40A, we must emphatically ask whether the alternative view of things is appropriate. Rather, we will surely have to begin with this, that two points coincide: (1) The petitioner is moved and motivated from the side of prophecy; accordingly, in v. 6 he reverts to prophetic judgments rejecting the cult of sacrifices, as found, e.g., in Amos 5:22; Isa. 1:11; and Jer. 6:20. (2) But the acute act in the area of the cultus is the substitution for the thankoffering by means of the gift of the "scroll of the book," which reports the misfortune and the rescue of the petitioner. Even if such a substitution for the thankoffering of the song of thanksgiving may have been an older custom, still the antithethical, prophetic pathos that accompanies the act discernible in v. 7 is unmistakable. In general, concerning the criticism of sacrifices we will have to consider the sensible declaration of G. von Rad: "The importance of these expressions is obvious: but as things still are today, we must beware of seeing in them the most valid criticism, and indeed the spiritual 'supersession,' of worship by blood-sacrifice as such. They did not supersede it, and were not meant to do so. They derive from the traditions of the Temple singers, who certainly had good reason for confronting the idea of the cult held by the higher-ranking priests with their own somewhat revolutionary one. These utterances were therefore very extreme watchwords, which their authors certainly also meant to be taken radically, and which were well suited to shake people out of the complacency which was a constant danger besetting the sacrificial cult. But it is wrong to see in them the breakthrough to a general self-evident truth. The truth of these utterances lies in their harmony with all the orders and 'truths' upon which Israel's worship rested, and from which it built itself up and received its complex character" (G. von Rad, *OT Theol,* 1:368f.). Now, for Psalms 40A it is characteristic that the obedience which contrasted (v. 6) to the sacrificial cult—corresponding to the message of the prophets—realizes its specificity in relation to the Torah (see above). This happened in the postexilic era of תורה-piety. And, very likely, the entire psalm should be dated to this time. H. Gunkel explains: "Even under the dominion of the Law, which takes an altogether different position regarding the sacrifices, in certain pious circles of laity the spirit of the prophets lived on, and these have been naive enough to combine the veneration of the Law and the thoughts of the prophets; they read the Torah in the prophetic sense, skipped over the multitude of stipulations in it about the sacrifices, and kept to the moral laws and probably also to 'ceremonial' laws pertaining to the individual." A special role in this prophetically influenced תורה-piety will have been played by Deuteronomy (Deut. 6:6; 30:11ff.) and Jeremiah (Jer. 31:31-34; cf. Ps. 19:7 and the corresponding explanations). Thus the one who is giving thanks brings before Yahweh a declaration of obedience vis-à-vis the תורה instead of the sacrifices. Worth noting is the typological interpretation of Ps. 40:6-8 in Heb. 10:5ff.

[40:9-11] The psalmist in his thanksgiving bears witness before the "great congregation" (v. 9). He appears as a messenger of joy (cf. בשׂר); it is possible that the influence of Deutero-Isaiah reveals itself in the use of this verb (cf. Isa. 40:9; 52:7). He who is giving thanks proclaims—under a banner of joy—צדק. Yahweh's "righteousness" was in Israel no norm, no principle of justice, but deed, bestowal of salvation, proof of his faithfulness of promise and partnership. Cf. *THAT* II 507ff. The individual in time of need experienced Yahweh's צדק. In the song of thanksgiving he had to witness to this "righteousness" and confess it. In various pictures vv. 9 and 10 state that thanksgiving is always an open, unreserved confession. The bestowal of Yahweh's faithfulness and help cannot remain hidden in a person's inner being; it must be confessed and witnessed to "before the great congregation" (Pss. 22:25; 35:18). In v. 11 the trust in the permanence of the salvation experienced is then expressed. And for the future the petitioner of the psalm knows that he is protected by Yahweh's "grace and truth." At this point the connection to the prayer song that follows is given. The thanking psalmist finds himself in new dangers. Verse 12 forms the transition to an independent psalm which has been added secondarily to vv. 1-11. For the interpretation of vv. 13-17, cf. Psalm 70.

Purpose and Thrust

Yahweh has snatched a human being out of the realm of death and has given life back to him. This is the origin of his thanksgiving. But this thanksgiving is not "a return," a human answer or "offering" (Mowinckel)—*Yahweh* has put the song of thanksgiving into the mouth of the singer. Only Yahweh's giving makes the witness of those who have experienced his help possible. Thus the song as a message turns to "the great congregation" and appeals to it to recognize God's reality and to trust in Yahweh. The help experienced is seen in the larger parameter of God's deeds of rescue among his people. Also the statements of v. 6 turn into a message. He who receives Yahweh's help is not placed in a relation to God that transcends the sacrifice; he stands in a relation of obedience indicated by the תורה, which indeed transcends all intermediates when the revelation of God's will lives in the human heart. In other words, thankfulness begets new obedience.

Psalm 41

Persecuted Treacherously by Friends

Literature

J. Coppens, "Les Psaumes 6 et 41 dépendent-ils du livre de Jérémie?" *HUCA* 32 (1961) 217-226. J. v. d. Ploeg, "Le Psaume XLI dans une recension de Qumrân," *RB* 72 (1965) 210-217. F. Crüsemann, *Studien zur Formgeschichte von Hymnus und Danklied in Israel*, WMANT 32 (1969) 242f.

Text

To the choirmaster. A psalm of David.

41:1 Blessed is the one who looks after the lowly 'and the poor';[a]
    in the day of misfortune Yahweh rescues him.

2 ' '[b] He keeps him alive; he is praised in the land.
    'He does not surrender him'[c] to the greed of his enemies.

3 Yahweh supports him on his sickbed,
    all of his bed you change in his sickness.[d]

4 I said, O Yahweh, be merciful to me!
    Heal me, for I have sinned against you!

5 My enemies speak ill 'against'[e] me:
    When will he finally die and his name die out?

6 And when somebody comes to visit, he speaks delusion,
    gathers mischief, ' '[f] tells about it on the street.

7 They join in whispering 'against me,'[g]
    all those who hate me ' '[h] think evil of me:

8 May a hopeless situation be his lot;
    he who lies sick shall never get up again.[i]

9 Even my closest friend, whom I trusted,
    who ate my bread, shows off against me ' '[j].

10 But you, O Yahweh, be merciful, raise me up again
    that I may pay them back!

11 By this I know that you love me,
    that my enemy does not exult over me.

12 But me you support because of my innocence,
    you let me stand before your countenance forever.

13 Praised be Yahweh, Israel's God,
from eternity to eternity!
Amen. Amen.

1a If we follow MT, we will probably have to follow Gk and T and for the sake of the meter supplement וְאֶבְיוֹן. Of course, the text in MT contains difficulties, and these are emphasized again and again in the commentaries. In v. 1, are good fortune and salvation really promised to him who is ready to help? The questions have to do with exegesis.

2b יהוה should be eliminated for the sake of the meter; there is dittography.

c MT: "May you not surrender me." Here the copyist mistakenly went over to the tone of a lament. Gk, σ´, S, and Jerome have וְלֹא יִתְּנֵהוּ.

3d The alterations of the text frequently undertaken have no foundation. Thus, e.g., H. Gunkel: כָּל־מַכְאֹבוֹ הָפַכְתָּ לְחָיִל ("all his suffering you turn to strength"). We will probably have to stay with the MT. For the meaning of the statement, see below.

5e For the sake of the meter we had probably better read רְעָה עָלָי.

6f יָצָא ("he goes away") was probably inserted in the second half-verse for simplification, and should perhaps be eliminated for the sake of the meter.

7g The text can probably be evened out by means of an easy transposition. עָלַי should be placed ahead of כָל־שֹׂנְאַי. *Atnah* is to be transposed accordingly.

h Cf. note **g**.

8i On v. 8, cf. G. R. Driver, *VT* 1 [1951], 248; T. H. Gaster, *VT* 4 [1954], 73-79.

9j The second half-verse is too full. עָקֵב is to be eliminated. Does עֵקֶב (or עָקְבָם) belong to v. 10?

Form

The text contains difficulties. But because the meter 4 + 4 (except in vv. 10 and 13: 4 + 3) determines the form of Psalm 41, corresponding text-critical measures are not only possible but mandatory.

In the form-critical analysis we must first observe that in v. 1 the beginning is made with an אַשְׁרֵי-sentence that speaks of Yahweh in the third person. Cf. H. Schmidt, "Grüsse und Glückwünsche im Psalter," *ThStKr* 103 (1931) 141-150; and the comment on Psalm 1. Such wishes of good fortune are preferably expressed in didactic poems. Cf. above, Intro. §6, 5. A general, instructive statement is made, in which the petitioner communicates his experiences. In v. 3 a sudden change of style occurs. Abruptly the psalmist leaves the congratulatory-didactic introduction and speaks of Yahweh in the second person. Beginning at v. 3 we can clearly recognize that Psalm 41 is to be thought of as a prayer song. See above, Intro. §6, 2. In vv. 4-10 the prayer for relief from distress, the petitions together with corresponding descriptions of distress, is recapitulated in restrospect. Verses 11f. indentify the new situation. The sufferer has been heard. He has experienced the miracle of being rescued. Therefore vv. 11f. have the form of the song of thanksgiving of an individual. See above, Intro. §6, 2a (also F. Crüsemann, 242f.). Accordingly, there are three elements that need to be considered: instruction, prayer, and thanksgiving. These forms and intentions are combined in a prayer song.

Setting

Songs of thanksgiving by an individual have their "Sitz im Leben" in the sanctuary. There they tell about the situation of the distress and about the petition to Yahweh. But they also bear witness to the miracle of being heard and to the rescue from the depths of suffering. The one who gives thanks then turns to the assembled congregation. He testifies concerning Yahweh's help. And in his testimony he teaches, he refers to the didactic statements of the wisdom poetry and the didactic poetry of Israel in which he communicates his experiences. The conventionalized, generally valid statements are, so to say, the reservoir of experience of the people of God in which the individual deposits his experience and comprehension, and from which he then also draws. The situation of the petitioner emerges from the prayer song in clearly observable contours. He lay mortally ill on his "bed." Cf. the comment on Psalm 6; likewise R. Martin-Achard, "Approche des Psaumes," *Cahiers Théologiques* 60 (1969) 49ff.; K. Seybold, *Das Gebet des Kranken im Alten Testament: Untersuchungen zur Bestimmung und Zuordnung der Krankheits- und Heilungspsalmen*, BWANT V, 19 (1973). The sick person was surrounded by enemies, by friends who had become enemies. See above, Intro. §10, 4. These enemies looked for clues for a slanderous accusation, and they maliciously exploited confidences.

In view of the entire psalm, one can come to the conclusion "that the diverse functions of the various speaking parts are no longer alive and therefore the original 'Sitz im Leben' had probably been forsaken" (F. Crüsemann, 243). It is possible that Psalm 41 has a long road of tradition behind it in which it was reconstructed and newly formed. This would explain the change of style in v. 3. What we have here is probably a prayer song that is to be dated as relatively late. A dependence on the book of Jeremiah (J. Coppens) cannot be determined. Also cf. the comment of Psalm 6.

Commentary

[Title] On למנצח, see above, Intro. §4, No. 17. On מזמור לדוד, see Intro. §4, No. 2.

[41:1-3] The didactic maxim begins with a felicitation (cf. Pss. 34:8; 40:4; 65:4). The one who is giving thanks transmits to his hearers very definite experiences that he has made in the great crisis of his life. In his felicitation he recommends his own perception. At the beginning of Psalm 41 the one who looks after the lowly (and the poor) is called blessed. The construction השכיל אל is documented in Neh. 8:13 and causes no difficulties. But the content of v. 1 is nevertheless unusual. All the parallel passages (Pss. 32:1f.; 34:8; 40:4; 65:4) speak of the blessedness of the right attitude to God. For this reason a number of commentators are inclined to recognize the noun אֵל in the preposition אֶל and to make corresponding changes in the text. But the statement in v. 1 is peculiar and unique. Blessedness is assigned to him who deals prudently and with discernment, or piously (השכיל) with the poor. Is this felicitation the result of the bitter experience that all the friends and acquaintances sinned against the psalmist when he was "poor" and "helpless"? Or did the psalmist himself in earlier times give proof of his "fear of God" by treating the "poor" with discernment? In any case, instead of the fear of God which is otherwise mentioned in the felicitations we have here goodness over against the helpless. To look after the lowly—that is a characteristic of the צדיק. He who conducts himself in this way will not be forsaken by Yahweh in the depth of misfortune. His life will be preserved (v. 2); his good name will remain on the lips of all people. In other words, the calumnies and accusations of the enemies (see above, Intro. §10, 4) do not reach their goal, his life is not surrendered helplessly to the "greed"(נֶפֶשׁ = "gullet," "greed") of his enemies. The promises of the felicitation continue in v. 3. If the affected person takes sick, Yahweh supports him on his sickbed. The parallel sentence כל־משכבו הפכת בחליו has the meaning: you alleviate his sickness, turn it to advantage. On מִשְׁכָּב, cf. G. Dalman, *AuS* VII 186. The felicitation in vv. 1-3 contains the promise (not the dogma!) that Yahweh will not forsake the צַדִּיק whose צְדָקָה proves itself in his relation to the "poor" (Ps. 34:9ff.).

[41:4-10] In a section introduced by אֲנִי־אָמַרְתִּי, the psalmist refers to his earlier complaint, to the outcry on the יוֹם רָעָה (v. 1). This lament reveals the situation the psalmist was in. In sickness and forsakenness he cried for help: יהוה חָנֵּנִי (v. 4). He prayed for healing. נֶפֶשׁ does not denote the "soul" but weak, frail life which is in need of healing and help and languishes for it. In the background of v. 4b lurks the conception of the inextricable connection of sickness and guilt (G.von Rad, *OT Theol*, 1:274f.). Also cf. Pss. 6:1ff.; 32:3f.; 38:3f. But the fact of the serious sickness immediately called the enemies to the scene. They quickly put in an appearance to level accusations against him who was visibly being punished and to see to an immediate expulsion of this bearer of mischief. The whisperings of the enemies are cited: "When will he finally die and his name die out?" The enemies wish for the death of the sufferer, they can hardly wait for his life to be erased, and they hope that beyond the grave the name of this person, punished by God as he obviously is, will be forgotten forever.

The suffering this man had endured in his sickness was incomprehensible. Then his neighbors and friends came to "look after him." For such sick calls, cf. Job 2:11ff. But these acquaintances who appear so solicitous "speak delusion"; they slander the sick man by citing transgressions as causes of the sickness. "Empty" and "vain" (שָׁוְא) things they bring up. At their sick visits they gather clues for disastrous results (אָוֶן), and then they set in motion dark rumors and baleful slander in the alleys. The suffering psalmist heard the hostile whisperings and sensed the evil thoughts of those who hated him (v. 7). The enemies harbored the wish, "May a hopeless situation be his lot!" דְּבַר־בְּלִיַּעַל probably cannot simply be understood rationally (in accordance with the obvious analysis בְּלִי־יַעַל = "without advantage"). That בְּלִיַּעַל must refer to a sinister power of death is apparent from Ps. 18:4. Something ghastly is to "assail" (צוּק) the sufferer. People whisper this wish from one to another and at the same time inflict it on the sick person like a conjuring curse: אֲשֶׁר שָׁכַב לֹא־יוֹסִיף לָקוּם. This sentence sounds like a sorcerer's incantation. And we could ask with S. Mowinckel whether the "enemies of this individual" are perhaps trying to achieve their goal by means of the sinister practices of witchcraft and conjuration (see above, Intro. §10, 4).

To this group of enemies even the most intimate friends were joined. אִישׁ שְׁלוֹמִי is the man with whom the psalmist has concluded an indestructible relation of trust and friendship: the most intimate friend. The sign of such an inviolable union of trust is the common meal, אוֹכֵל לַחְמִי. The communion meal begets *communio* (cf. J. Pedersen, *Der Eid bei den Semiten* [1914], 24f.). But all these sacrosanct ties have been fractured by the friends; they have left the common level of life, have elevated themselves and demeaned the sufferer. The prayer song closes with a cry of distress that Yahweh may raise the sick man up again, "that I may pay them back." This purpose clause at first estranges. But as soon as we inquire more closely how this "retribution" could be imagined, many questions arise. Without question, the thought cannot be that the recuperating sick man wants to revenge himself personally on these sinister rascals. Rather, the "retribution" must consist of the thought that the slanderers may through the saving intervention of Yahweh be revealed as רשעים and may in shame and disgrace suffer a judgment of God to come over them. Could anything more than this be meant? And is expectation of that sort not perfectly in line with many other statements in the Psalter?

[41:11-12] The present situation is addressed by vv. 11-12. They assume that the event of answering and bestowing of healing has taken place. The psalmsinger has recognized and still recognizes (ידעתי) the fact that Yahweh takes pleasure in him, and he recognizes this from the fact that the enemy cannot exult over him, which surely means that he cannot exult over his death. The certainty of healing in the OT is given to afflicted people in a this-worldly manner. No spiritualizing, Christian idealism can elevate itself above this fact. God is really Lord and Savior in the field of human distress and sickness. God can overcome the hostile powers that want to separate the pious from Yahweh. The biblical idea of knowledge has its own distinctive stamp. In v. 11 "the subject is not comprehension of the nature of Yahweh but the comprehension of the immediately merciful and helpful God" (W. Zimmerli, *Erkenntnis Gottes im Buche Ezechiel,* ATANT [1954], 44). By means of the act of recuperation God "justifies" the person against the enemies that accuse him: Pss. 18:20ff.; 66:18f. This observation immediately leads to v. 12. The psalmist is "innocent" (תם), his rescue proves that the accusations of the enemies were not valid. This proof of innocence does not preclude that the petitioner could point to his transgressions in v. 4 (for the double concept of guilt in the Psalms, cf. the comment on Ps. 38:13-20). The embodiment of received help and healing is "standing before the countenance of Yahweh" (cf. Ps. 16:11). In the song of thanksgiving the psalmsinger here refers to the place of God's presence.

[41:13] The doxology closes the collection of the Psalms of David (Psalms 3-41). Later hands affixed the double אמן from the liturgical responsories. This is a sign that the Psalter in all its parts was adopted and appropriated by the congregation.

Purpose and Thrust

The psalmist is appalled at the sinister breach of trust which he had to endure in times of the greatest distress. As a helpless and poor creature the psalmist was watched, slandered, and by disrespectful statements separated from God and man. The lament once more gives expression to this hideous event. But the sufferer was helped. Yahweh had compassion on him and did not let the enemies triumph. With this judgment rendered by God a heavy condemnation descends on all those who abusively disowned him who was suffering and helpless. And thus one can understand it that the didactic maxim of the song of thanksgiving (vv. 1-3) pronounces him blessed who does not despise the poor man but looks after him. Thus the psalm, on the background of the sinister activity (vv. 4-10), proclaims the promise, "Blessed are the merciful, for they shall obtain mercy" (Matt. 5:7; 25:31ff.).

Worth noting is the relation between sickness and guilt which may be recognized in Psalm 41. Of it one can state: "Rehabilitation is also the main concern of the psalms that deal with sickness: restoration of the right relation to God, restoration of health, and , following that, restoration of the state of justice vis-à-vis other humans" (L. Wächter, *Der Tod im Alten Testament* [1967], 32).

Psalm 41

The subject is justice: before God and before others. The motive of Yahweh's intervention, however, is indicated in v. 11 by means of the love for the one who is poor and suffering. In the OT this love stands under the banner of very definite and concrete bestowals; in v. 11 by overcoming the enemies. The recognition of salvation takes place in an effective event. And the quintessence of a renewed relation to God is to stand before Yahweh's countenance "forever" (v. 12). Priestly prerogatives are here received by the individual. This is the reason for thanksgiving and praise.

Longing for the Place
of Yahweh's Presence

Literature

H. H. Rowley, "The Structure of Psalm 42/43," *Biblica* 21 (1940) 45-55. N. H. Snaith, *Hymns of the Temple (Ps 42/43; 44; 46; 50; 73)*, 1951. A. Klawek, "Sehnsucht nach Jerusalem," *RBL* 8 (1955) 173-184. J. B. Bauer, "Ad Deum qui laetificat iuventutem meam," *Verbum Domini* 40 (1962) 184-189. E. Beaucamp, "Prière d'un fils d'Israël en exil, Ps. 42f. (41f.)," *BTS* 69 (1967) 2-5. J. Schreiner, "Verlangen nach Gottes Nähe und Hilfe. Auslegung von Psalm 42/43," *BiLe* 10 (1969).

Text

To the choirmaster. A *maskil* of the Korahites.

42:1 As a hind[a] pants
over the waterbrooks,
so my soul pants
for you, 'O Yahweh.'[b]

2 My soul thirsts for 'Yahweh,'[c]
the God of 'my'[d] life.
When will I come and 'behold'[e]
the countenance 'of Yahweh'?[f]

3 Tears have become my food
day and night,
while 'they'[g] all day say to me,
Where is your God now?

4 Of this I think and pour out
my soul within myself,
how I entered 'the tent of the glorious Lord,'[h]
'Yahweh's'[i] house,
amid exultation and thanksgiving—
in festival procession.[j]

5 Why are you so broken up, my soul,
and [k] groan within me?

Wait for 'Yahweh,'[l] for I will still thank him,
'the help of my countenance and my God.'[m]

6 My soul is broken up within me,
therefore I think of you
from the land of Jordan and the Hermon range, [n]
from Mount Mizar.

7 Flood calls to flood
as your torrents rage.
All your breakers and waves
have gone over me.

8 By day 'I keep an eye out'[o] for Yahweh,
'and' for ' ' his goodness at night.
'I sing'[p] a prayer by myself
to the God of my life.

9 I speak to God, my rock,
Why have you forgotten[q] me?
Why must I go in mourning,
under oppression from the enemy?

10 While my limbs are all broken up,
my adversaries revile me,
for they say to me all day long:
Where is your God now?

11 Why are you so broken up, my soul,
and groan within me?
Wait for 'Yahweh,'[r] for I will still thank him,
the 'help'[s] of my countenance and my God!

43:1 Judge me, 'O Yahweh,'[t]
Take charge of my lawsuit
before the unfriendly people!
From men of cunning
and wickedness deliver me!

2 For you are the God of my refuge!
Why have you cast me off?
Why must I go in mourning,
under oppression from the enemy?

3 Send your light and your faithfulness;
may they be my guides,
bring me to the holy hill
and your dwelling places!

4 Then will I come to 'your'[u] altar, ' '[v]
to the God of 'my' joy. ' '[w]
'I will exult'[x] and give thanks with a lyre,
'O Yahweh,'[y] my God!

5 Why are you so broken up, my soul,
and ' '[z] groan within me?
Wait for 'Yahweh,'[aa] for I will still thank him,
the help of my countenance and my God!

42:1a In order to gain the 3 + 2 meter (see below, "Form") also in v. 1a, an expansion of the first half-verse is sometimes advised: (כַּאֲשֶׁר) כְּמוֹ אַיֶּלֶת. But there is no justifiable reason for a correction in the MT.

b S has יהוה. Transpositions of אלהים to יהוה in the Elohistically revised part of the Psalter are mandatory.

2c Cf. note **b**.

d V. 8b suggests that we should read לְאֵל חַיָּי also in v. 2.

e MT: "and I will appear"; a few Mss, S, T have וְאֶרְאָה. Is the dogma that no human being can see God (Exod. 33:20) the basis for this pointing?
f Cf. note **b**.
3g 4 Mss, S, and v. 11 suggest reading בְּאָמְרָם.
4h Without a doubt בַּסָּךְ, corresponding to the parallel בית אלהים must be pointed בְּסֹךְ; סֹךְ = "arbor," "tabernacle" (KBL 656). Cf. Gk ἐν τόπῳ σκηνῆς. אֶדַּדֵּם (= "I let [them] proceed") is unintelligible in the context. With θαυμάστης Gk points to אדיר as an epithet for God, cf. Ps. 8:1.
i Cf. note **b**.
j Gk ἤχου ἑορταζόντων = הָמוֹן חוֹגְגִים; but we should probably follow MT.
5k A few Mss, Gk σ′, S, supply וּמַה־ (cf. v. 11; Ps. 43:5), corresponding to the first half-verse.
l Cf. note **b**.
m MT: "the aid of his countenance." Following Gk, S, T, we should read יְשׁוּעַת פָּנַי. אלהי is to be taken into v. 5 from v. 6: וֵאלֹהָי (cf. a few Mss Gk S, v. 11, and Ps. 43:5).
6n 1 Ms, S:וְחֶרְמוֹן; see under "Commentary."
8o MT: "In the daytime Yahweh announces his goodness, and at night his song is with me, a prayer to the God of my life." The text in MT not only departs from the meter, but it also forsakes the train of thought. An emendation is unavoidable. H. Gunkel suggests:
יומם אֲצַפֶּה ביהוה   וחסדו בלילה
For the first half-verse, cf Mic. 7:7; for the parallelism, Ps 92:2. The mistake therefore evidently came about by miscopying אצפה to צוה.
p The spelling שירה is striking. In consequence of the emendation suggested in note **o**, we should read אָשִׁירָה, "I will sing." T. H. Gaster, "Psalm 42,8," *JBL* 73 (1954) 237f. wants to derive שירה from the Ugaritic *šrt* = "dream vision" and reconstructs a different picture of the text.
9q An assimilation to Ps. 43:2 is hardly appropriate. 2 Mss read זְנַחְתָּנִי instead of שכחתני.
11r Cf. note **b**.
s Following 1 Ms Gk θ′, we ought to read יְשׁוּעַת (cf. note **m**).
Ps. 43:1 t Cf. note **b**.
4u Following 4 Mss, Jerome, we ought to read מִזְבַּחֲךָ, for the sake of the meter.
v אלהים should be taken up in the suffix; cf. note **u**.
w MT: "to the God of the joy of my exultation." The verse is overloaded. Following 1 Ms, we should read שִׂמְחָתִי. גילי is to be taken with the following verse line.
x Assimilating to וְאוֹדְךָ, we would have to read אָגִילָה instead of גילי.
y Cf. note **b**.
5z In accordance with Ps. 42:5, the supplementary ומה should be eliminated: וַתֶּהֱמִי.
aa Cf. note **b**.

Form

There can be no doubt that Psalm 42/43 forms a unit. The refrain of the three-strophe song turns up in Ps. 42:5, 11 and in Ps. 43:5. How closely Psalm 42 and 43 belong together is also shown by a comparison of Ps. 42:9 and Ps. 43:2, as well as by the entire context. Therefore the following structure results: Ps. 42:1-5, 6-11; Ps. 43:1-5.

The Qinah meter (3 + 2) dominates. Exceptions are to be noted in the refrain (3 + 2 and 4 + 3), as well as in Ps. 42:1 (2 + 2; 2 + 2) and in Ps. 43:1 (2 + 2 + 2; 2 + 2).

Psalms 42 and 43, closely associated through the refrain and to be considered a unit, are to be assigned to the form group, prayer songs. See above, Intro. §6, 2. Worth noting are the details of the situation and the descriptions of the distress. Not until Psalm 43 do the supplications clearly emerge, while in Psalm 42 the self-revelation of the soul pining for the living God stands in the foreground. Time and again the refrain's exhortation to quiet oneself, i.e., the consolation and the exhortation to be patient addressed to one's own spirit, emerges. At the same time the petitioner looks forward to the moment of thanksgiving for the rescue already accomplished ("I will still thank him, the help of my countenance and my God"). The introductions to the addresses to Yahweh and to the petitioner's own soul (vv. 4, 9f.) are striking. The Hebrew designation for the form group present in Psalms 42 and 43 appears distinctly in v. 8. The petitioner "sings" (שׁיר) a תפלה. Therefore the designation "prayer song" is the appropriate name for that form group which so far has been called "individual lament" (on the individual lament, see H. Gunkel and J. Begrich, *EinlPs* §6).

Setting

The place of origin of the prayer song is indicated precisely in Psalm 42/43. The precise description in Ps. 42:6 is unique in the Psalms, and beyond that in all of Hebrew poetry. The petitioner is at the sources of the Jordan (on the exact location, cf. Ps. 42:6, "Commentary"). Why the singer of the lament is in this region (outside the territory of Israel: Ps. 43:1) we are not told. The psalm does not indicate that he is in exile or that he fled the country. Also, there is no information about the person of the lamenting singer. Certainly we are here not dealing with a king (against A. Bentzen, *Messias—Moses redivivus—Menschensohn* [1948], 20). Finally also the question about the life situation of the lamenting poet cannot be answered conclusively. Destructive powers want to kill him (Ps. 42:7). He must go about in mourning (Pss. 42:9; 43:2). Yahweh had "forgotten" him (Ps. 42:9) and "cast him off" (Ps. 43:2). Reviling enemies surround him (Pss. 42:9f.; 43:1, 2). From this distress, forsakenness, and oppression the lamenting singer longs for the place of God's presence.

The date of origin of the prayer song can hardly be determined. Of course, if we assume that the petitioner of the psalm was exiled (E. Beaucamp), corresponding points of reference could be considered; but for such an explanation the definite clue is not available. It is not unlikely that Psalm 42/43 belongs to preexilic times. So far as the procedure of transmission is concerned, we can assume that the singer of the prayer song brought the text (cf. "scroll of the book" in Ps. 40:7) to the temple after his rescue; there it may well have been preserved in the temple archives.

Commentary

[Title] On למנצח, see above, Intro. §4, No. 17. On משׂכיל, see Intro. §4, No. 5.

A series of psalms in the Psalter are ascribed לבני־קרח: Psalms 42; 44–49; 84; 87; 88. Who are these Korahites? In the OT we encounter various items of information that can hardly be reconciled with one another. Originally the Korahites are supposed to have been a Horite-Edomite generation (Gen. 36:5ff.). Concerning this generation 1 Chron. 2:43 reports that it joined the Judeans. In postexilic times the Korahites appear as a separate group in the records of the temple personnel. At first they are doorkeepers of the temple (1 Chron. 9:19; 26:1, 19); later they appear as a guild of singers (2 Chron. 20:19). When the Psalter therefore transmits "songs of the Korahites," we have to assume that the בני־קרח were editors of a book of songs. Otherwise, the Korahites are numbered among the Levites (Exod. 6:21; Num. 25:58; 1 Chron. 6:7); but at times there must have been heavy controversy among the personnel of the temple (Numbers 16; cf.

M. Noth, *A History of Pentateuchal Traditions* [1981; orig., 1948] 125f. More recently, great emphasis is placed on the "Zion theology" of the Korahites in connection with a late dating of basic assertions regarding Zion (cf. the comment on Psalm 46). Cf. G.Wanke, *Die Zionstheologie der Korahiten in ihrem traditionsgeschichtlichen Zusammenhang*, BZAW 97 (1966). But concerning the thesis of G. Wanke, see H. M. Lutz, *Jahwe, Jerusalem und die Völker: Zur Vorgeschichte von Sach. 12:1-8 und 14, 1-5*, WMANT 27 (1968) 213ff.

[42:1-4] The first verse of the prayer song begins with an impressive comparison. As a hind (איל for אילה, cf. Ges-K §122f.) pants "over" (על) the waterbrooks, so the lamenting poet pants for Yahweh. אפיקי־מים here are obviously the dried-out brook gulleys (cf. Joel 1:20; Ps. 126:4), in which an animal dying of thirst looked in vain for water. For the simile in Ps. 42:1 there is a Ugaritic parallel: *'n kṣd aylt* (C. H. Gordon, *Ugaritic Handbook* II: *Text* 67 I 17); but H. Donner considers the Ugaritic parallel very unreliable. And Donner also suggests an emendation for v. 1 (cf. H. Donner, "Ugaritismen in der Psalmenforschung," ZAW 79 [1967], 333 and 335f.). The animal yearning and crying for water is an effective picture of the torment and the consuming desire with which the petitioner stretches out toward Yahweh. His נפש "thirsts" for God (v. 20; cf. Ps. 63:1). נפש here—and beyond that throughout the whole text of Psalm 42/43—denotes "the self of the needy life, thirsting with desire" (H. W. Wolff, *Anthropology of the OT* [1974] 25). The expiring נפש cries for the living God. אלחי is the God who is not subject to any change or limitation, who therefore has no part in the fate of the divinities that die and rise again. The אלחי has demonstrated his life in the history of the people. God is appealed to in the oath. In him people in prayer look for the fountain of life (Ps. 36:9). Life knows that it is dependent on him, and sustained and determined by him (Ps. 42:8). Cf. H.-J. Kraus, "Der lebendige Gott," *Biblisch-theologische Aufsätze* (1972) 1-36. This God is present in the sanctuary. Therefore the petitioner longingly asks about the moment when he can enter the holy precincts. On בוא as the technical term for solemnly entering the sanctuary, cf. Ps. 118:19. ראה פני יהוה means: entering the immediate proximity of the *deus praesens*, the temple (Isa. 1:12). Accordingly, the prayer song is not sung in the sacred precincts (cf. Ps. 42:6). In v. 3 the psalmsinger describes his torment: tears are his food (cf. Pss. 80:5; 102:9). Nothing is said about the ultimate reason for the tears. Is the psalmist suffering from a dreadful disease (thus H. Gunkel)? But in his suffering and sorrow, reviling enemies surround the petitioner (see above, Intro. §10, 4). In derision and challenge they ask, איה אלהיך (cf. Pss. 79:10; 115:2; Joel 2:17). It is worth noting that this question is often asked by the heathen. At a time of struggle for existence on the part of Israel or of a member of God's people, they question the existence and effectiveness of Yahweh. But the psalmsinger in v. 4 recalls (זכר) the happy security in the worshiping community in which he once strode in procession on festal days. For this recollection of the security of earlier days, cf. Pss. 22:9f.; 71:6; 77:5ff. The singer "pours out his נפש," i.e., he gives free reign to his remembrance and thoughts (Pss. 62:8; 102, title; 142:2). On עלי with the meaning "within me" cf. Pss. 142:3; 143:4. Once the psalmist proceeded into the sanctuary (עבר). The imperfect depicts incidents of the past with lively sympathy (BrSynt §42b). The temple sanctuary is called סך אדרים (cf. "Text") and בית יהוה. The denotation of the temple as "tabernacle" is archaizing and recalls the tent sanctuary (cf. Pss. 27:5; 76:2; Lam 2:6). With exultation and thanksgiving the congregation entered the sanctuary area (cf. Pss.

100:4; 118:19f.). המון חוגג denotes the swirl of the festival hymns that were intoned with a loud sound at the entrance to the sanctuary (cf. Amos 5:23; Ezek. 26:13). By remembering the festival days of joy the petitioner wants to restore himself. He does not want to forget what good things Yahweh has bestowed on him (Ps. 103:2).

[42:5] From the recollection of the happy security in the celebrating congregation springs the comfort which the psalmist addresses to his own נפש. Psalm 42/43 here shows some similarity to the "prayers for quieting the heart" from Mesopotamia that have become known, but the OT lacks all signs of quieting oneself that operates with magic incantations. The comfort addressed to the dissolving, disintegrating power of the נפש has its origin in the assurance: As I once praised and thanked Yahweh (v. 4), so I will give thanks to him again (עוד). Therefore there is really no reason that the נפש should dissolve and disintegrate amid groaning. Almost in wonder the psalmist asks himself, What are you doing? He encourages himself to wait patiently and focuses his thoughts on the song of thanksgiving and is certain: Yahweh is my help and my God (on אלהי, cf. O. Eissfeldt, " 'Mein Gott' im Alten Testament," ZAW 61 [1945], 48, 3-16).

[42:6-11] In v. 6 the prayer begins anew. The psalmsinger (as in v. 5) describes the disintegration (hithpael of שיח) of his נפש, i.e., the dissolution of his vital power. We could think of a serious sickness. In his distress the psalmist "thinks" of Yahweh. זכר has the meaning "to stretch out toward . . . in prayer," cf. Pss. 63:6; 77:3; 119:55; Ezek. 6:9; Zech. 10:9; Neh. 4:8. The supplication originates at a very specific place, which is now described in v. 6. ארץ ירדן, as is clear from the context, is very generally the area of the sources of the Jordan. The peculiar plural חרמונים could refer to the entire mountain range from the actual Hermon (Jabal ash-Shaykh) to Paneas. Accordingly, the geographical area specified would be the headwaters of the Jordan in the Hermon range. The last place name, הר מצער, then specifies a peak in the Hermon range, the "little hill," which G. Dalman looked for northeast of Paneas near the village Zaora (G. Dalman, PJB 5 [1909], 101-103).

Far from the sanctuary, i.e., far from Yahweh, the psalmsinger hears the incessant raging of the תהום, the chaotic, destructive flood. Here the scene of the well-known torrents of the area of the headwaters of the Jordan and conceptions of the chaotic, destructive archetypal flood (cf. Akkadian tiāmat) come together. Destructive forces emanating from Yahweh have stormed in on the petitioner (cf. Pss. 18:4; 69:2; 88:7). In his desperate state the sufferer now looks toward Yahweh and waits for his intervention. On צפה, cf. Ps. 5:3; Mic. 7:7. He asks for a sign of Yahweh's goodness. On חסד, cf. the comment on Ps. 5:4-7. The prayer song that comes forth from distress is called תפלה. On אל חיי, cf. v. 2. Full of trust are the appropriations of healing signalized by the suffix. Yahweh is the "rock" (v. 9) of the petitioner (cf. Pss. 18:2; 31:3; and often); he is the rescuing firm ground in the swirl of destruction. Yet, frightened and perplexed are the questions that are uttered in two sentences introduced by למה. The sufferer is sure he is forgotten by God; he must go about in the dust-covered garment of the penitent (Pss. 35:14; 38:6; Job 5:10; 30:28), while the enemy oppresses him. רצח in v. 10 (from רצח) probably would mean "break-up," "dissolution of death." The psalmsinger feels death in his bones. Here too we could think of a mortal sickness. And in the midst of this dissolution of physical strength there is heard the incessant taunt of the enemies: אֵיּה אֱלֹהֶיךָ (cf. v. 3). For the refrain in v. 11, cf. v. 5.

[43:1-5] Suffering from a mortal sickness, the afflicted person is also accused by the "enemies." No matter how we may describe the distress of the psalmsinger, in Ps. 43:1 it becomes evident that he is also persecuted with charges and accusations. There must be a reason for the dissolution of physical strength—that is the logic of the hostile accuser. In this plight the persecuted psalmist appeals to Yahweh the judge and pleads for his intervention (cf. the comment on Pss. 7:8f.; 9:4; 26:1). Away from home (cf. Ps. 42:6), the psalmist is surrounded by a גוי לֹא־חָסִיד—by those who do not know the tie to Yahweh that promotes loving relations. "Cunning" (מִרְמָה, cf. Pss. 5:6; 17:1; 34:13; 36:3; and often) and "wickedness" (עַוְלָה, cf. Pss. 37:1; 107:42; 119:3; and often) are the weapons of the "enemy" (see above, Intro. §10, 4); they are liars and slanderers. In v. 2 (as in Ps. 42:9) a double Why?-question is directed to Yahweh, together with an expression of trust. In the choice of words Ps. 43:2 varies the statements of Ps. 42:9. The psalmsinger is sure that he is "cast off" (זנח). Now in v. 3 he pleads for Yahweh's intervention. And yet, while, e.g., in Ps. 18:7ff. Yahweh himself appears to rescue the petitioner, the psalmist in Ps. 43:3 prays that Yahweh would send forth אוֹר and אֱמֶת (as it were, as helpful intermediaries and servants). Yahweh's "light" is a protective and guiding force that accompanies the righteous (cf. Job 29:2ff.); Yahweh's "faithfulness" is the proof of the constancy of his healing. אוֹר and אֱמֶת, these two forces for protection and healing, sent by Yahweh as "guides," are to lead the petitioner and bring him to Yahweh's sanctuary. By variation from Ps. 42:4, the reference to the sacred area now is made with the designations הַר־קׇדְשְׁךָ (Pss. 2:6; 15:1; 43:3) and מִשְׁכְּנוֹתֶיךָ (Pss. 46:4; 84:1; 132:5, 7). No doubt, Jerusalem is meant. But the psalmsinger has a clear conception of the entrance to the sacred area, based on what he experienced earlier (Ps. 42:4): he wants to approach the altar of Yahweh and in this place of thankofferings joyfully exult and sing his song of thanksgiving. With an accompaniment on the lyre (cf. K. Galling, BRL 390f.), the תּוֹדָה is intoned. On the refrain in v. 5, cf. Ps. 42:5.

Purpose and Thrust

In his commentary on the Psalms, H. Gunkel declares that we recognize "from the heartfelt notes struck by the psalm that what the psalmist desires from the bottom of his heart is the very same thing for which true religion at all times thirsts, the sure experience of the living God, and we understand"—so Gunkel then continues—"the psalmist, who from the dark valley of his sufferings looks up to those heights of life." This explanation raises the question whether it is appropriate to generalize the statements of Psalm 42/43 according to religious phenomenology in this manner. The prayer song is permeated—as has been clear from the beginning—by motives of the songs of Zion. All the longing of the thirsty and languishing petitioner is directed to Zion, to the place Yahweh has chosen to bear witness to his presence there. It is this height, and therefore not any of the "heights of life," for which the heart of the petitioner longs. The election of Zion as the place of God's presence has in the NT been transferred to Jesus Christ and his community. In the light of fulfillment we recognize anew that only in the place of God's presence and the assembled congregation are life and salvation to be found. Apart from this reality a consuming sadness operates.

441

Psalm 42/43

And only the word of comfort addressed to one's own being is able to convert the experiences of deliverance of the past to an exhortation for waiting that is at once patient and happy in hope. God himself must intervene, and by means of his emissaries (''light'' and ''faithfulness'') bridge a dark chasm.

Psalm 44

Prayer Song of the People
Conscious of Innocence

Literature

N. H. Snaith, *Hymns of the Temple (Ps 42/43; 44; 46; 50; 73)*, 1951. E. Lákatos, "Psalm 44," *RB* 76 (1955) 40-42. E. Vogt, "Psalmus 44 et Tragoedia Ezechiae regis," *Verbum Domini* 45 (1967) 193-200. W. Beyerlin, "Innerbiblische Aktualisierungsversuche—Schichten im 44. Psalm," *ZThK* 73 (1976) 446-460.

Text

To the choirmaster. Of the Korahites. A *maskil.*

44:1 'O Yahweh,'[a] with our own ears we have heard,
    our fathers have told us,
    the work that you finished in their times
    in remote antiquity—'you, with your own hand'![b]

  2 Peoples you drove out,[c] but them you planted;
    nations you broke to pieces, but to them you gave free reign.[d]

  3 For they did not win the land by their own sword,
    and their own arm did not gain the victory for them,
    but your right hand and arm
    and the light of your countenance,
    for you were favorable to them.

  4 You are my king 'and God,'[e]
    who 'ordains' Jacob's rescue.

  5 With you we beat down our opponents,
    in your name we tread our adversaries underfoot.

  6 For I do not trust in my bow,
    my sword does not bring me victory,

  7 but you grant us victory over our enemies
    and bring to shame those who hate us.

  8 'We boast in God'[f] every day
    and thank your name[g] at all times. *Selah.*

9 And yet you have cast us off and covered us with shame
   and did not go out with our armies.
10 You let us flee before the enemy,
   so that those who hate us could[h] snatch up booty.
11 You delivered us like animals for slaughter
   and scattered us among the peoples.
12 You sold your people for a trifle
   and took in no profit at its sale.
13 A disgrace you made[i] us for our neighbors,
   a scorn and derision for all our surroundings.
14 You made a proverb of us among the peoples,
   a shaking of the head among the nations.
15 Every day my shame is before my eyes,
   and my disgrace 'covers'[j] my countenance
16 against the noise of the taunters and revilers,
   in view of the enemy and the avenger.
17 All this came over us, yet we had not forgotten you
   and had not betrayed your covenant.
18 Our heart did not withdraw,
   nor did 'our steps'[k] leave your path,
19 that you have thrown us down in the home of jackals[l]
   and covered us with darkness.
20 If we forgot the name of our God
   and stretched out our hands to strange gods,
21 would not 'Yahweh'[m] notice that?
   For he knows the depths of the heart!
22 Indeed, for your sake we are being killed all the time,
   are considered sheep for the slaughter.
23 Awake! Why are you sleeping, Lord?
   Wake up, do not cast us away forever!
24 Why do you hide your countenance,
   forget our distress and oppression?
25 Indeed, we are bowed down to the dust,
   the earth sticks to our body.
26 Arise to help us!
   Deliver us for your goodness' sake!

1a In the Elohistically revised part of the Psalter, יהוה is to be substituted as the original reading.

b MT: "you, your hand" (in the context of v. 2a). Even under the assumption that both words belong to v. 2a, we should have to read בְיָדְךָ (not so, Joüon, Gr. §151c). Still אתה בידך is to be taken with v. 1b; only through this arrangement is the parallelism rounded off properly.

2c In the commentaries הורשת is often substituted for by means of גֵּרַשְׁתָ or שֵׁרַשְׁתָ. But for הורשת in the MT, cf. KBL, 407 (Exod. 15:9; 34:24; Num. 14:12).

d For the meaning of שלח, cf. KBL 975.

4e MT: "you are my king—O God, ordain . . ."; the imperative is impossible in this position. Gk, α´, S suggest that we read וַאלֹהַי מְצַוֶּה (cf. Ps. 74:12). For the sentence introduced by אתה־הוא, cf. S. R. Driver, *A Treatise on the Use of the Tenses in Hebrew* (1892), App. V §200; BrSynt §30a.

8f הלל is otherwise construed with the accusative. Therefore, following Gk, we would have to read הִלַּלְנוּ (or הִתְהַלַלְנוּ).

g 1 Ms, Gk: וּבְשִׁמְךָ

10h 4 Mss, Jerome, S, T have לָנוּ, but the MT is preferable.

13i תשימנו (also cf. v. 14) in its double use gives the impression of being quaint. Perhaps we should substitute הָיִינוּ (corresponding to Ps. 79:4).

15j The suffix construction is bothersome; fitting for the text situation would be כְּסָתָה.
18k Many Mss have אֲשֻׁרֵנוּ.
19l For the change in the text to תַּנִּין, suggested by H. Gunkel, "dragon" (so already Calvin), and the conception of בִּמְקוֹם in the sense "instead of," "as"—cf. H. Schmidt.
21m Cf. note **a**. The fragments of Psalm 44 found in Cave I at Qumran do not provide solutions in text-critical matters (D. Barthélemy and J. T. Milik, *Qumran Cave I* [1955], 71).

Form

The text of Psalm 44 is very well preserved. Therefore the meter is easily recognizable too. The double triple meter stands out as dominant. Only the following exceptions to this determinant meter are to be noted: v. 3 surely closes with 2 + 2 + 2; vv. 17 and 23 begin with 4 + 3, and v. 18 will probably have to be read in the 3 + 4 meter.

In the form-critical analysis and in the determination of the form group, we will have to begin with a study of vv. 9-26. In this main section, which is determinative for the whole psalm, we have a prayer song that was intoned by the community. See above, Intro. §6, 2a, and H. Gunkel and J. Begrich, *EinlPs* §4. The actual prayer song with its petitions and descriptions of distress is preceded by a larger introit. It refers to Yahweh's saving deeds at the beginning of Israel's history, especially at the time of the occupation of the land (vv. 1-3). The recollection of Yahweh's activity in the early days contains an appeal to a confirmation of the divine faithfulness; but it is also the presupposition and the reason for the trust stated in vv. 4-8. The main section of the prayer song of the community in vv. 9-26 could be divided into three parts: vv. 9-16, description of distress; vv. 17-22, reflections and questions that refer to the cause of the present misfortune; vv. 23-26, petitions and pleas to Yahweh.

Setting

The people are hard pressed by enemies—that is the situation from which Psalm 44 has to be understood. The armies of Israel have been defeated (v. 9); terrible pillage has resulted (v. 10); many have been killed (vv. 11-12); and the neighbors look down on the defeated people with derision (vv. 13-16). At moments of such distress Israel gathered in the sanctuary (2 Chron. 20:4ff.). A fast was proclaimed. Led by a precentor, the congregation then sang the song of lamentation (2 Chron. 20:5ff.). The voice of a single precentor is clearly recognizable in vv. 4, 6, and 15. That this individual is a military leader or even a king (H. Schmidt) is not stated unconditionally. The individual singer could also be a representative of the community so that his statements should be applied directly to actualities of the people's life (cf. the laments in the book of Lamentations). For details about the occasions of community lamentation, their rites and liturgy, cf. H. E. von Waldow, "Anlass und Hintergrund der Verkündigung Deuterojesajas," diss. Bonn (1953); see also above, Intro. §6, 2a.

Of course, great difficulties immediately arise when we investigate the historical situation from which Psalm 44 could have emerged. E. Vogt begins with the assumption that Psalm 44 presupposes the miseries of a lost war; he thinks he sees clues that remind us of the catastrophe of the year 701 B.C. (*Verbum Domini* 45 [1967], 193ff.). A different view seems to open up if a note in b. Sota 48a is considered. There it is said that Ps. 44:23a was in the time of the Maccabees sung daily by the Levites. Also the church fathers of the Antioch school maintained that Psalm 44 is to be dated in the time of the Maccabees.

Calvin too takes up this synagogal and early church tradition and writes in his Commentary on the Psalms: "It is uncertain who the author of the psalm is, except that it is clearly established that it was composed by someone else than David. But the laments it contains especially fit that wretched and calamitous time at which the wild tyranny of Antiochus raged, unless one would like to extend it further, because after the return from the exile practically no time was free from painful troubles."

The conception that Psalm 44 is to be dated in the time of the Maccabees was understandably received as very welcome by B. Duhm. He points to the events described in 1 Maccabees 9. But there is no shortage of voices either that vote for an earlier dating. H. Schmidt thinks of the Persian era—shortly after the return from the exile. E. Janssen accepts an origin in the 6th century (*Juda in der Exilzeit* [1956], 19). And, finally, A. Weiser, pointing to 2 Chron. 20:6ff., thinks that a preexilic dating may not be completely excluded. No doubt Psalm 44 contains age-old traditions (see under "Commentary")—in this respect Weiser is right. But very likely the historical question as such is not at all important. Beside most ancient traditional characteristics, the communal laments show evidences of very recent adaptation. Therefore it is easy to think of cultic formularies which in the course of their history in the holy place have experienced corrections and updating. We must therefore exercise restraint in respect to precise dating and keep the perspective of the history of tradition open.

Commentary

[Title] On למנצח, see above, Intro. §4, No. 17. On לבני־קרח, cf. Psalm 42, title. On משכיל, see above, Intro. §4, No. 5.

[44:1-3] In these verses the assembled community calls to mind the great deeds of God. It reminds itself first of all (v. 1a) of the process of transmission by which the "work of Yahweh" done in ancient times has become familiar to the present generation. On the term פעל, cf. G. von Rad, "Das Werk Jahwes," *Studia Biblica et Semitica, Th. C. Vriezen dedicata* (1966) 290-298. Under the characteristic historical term פעל v. 1 has taken up Israel's traditions of election (so H. Wildberger, *Jahwes Eigentumsvolk*, ATANT 37 [1960], 25). It is these traditions that are spoken of. Fathers have reported to their children (cf. Ps. 78:34; Exod. 10:1f.; 12:26f.; Deut 6:20ff.). Obviously the reference here is not to the main cultic tradition but to the family and clan tradition. The content of the tradition is the work (פעל) of Yahweh (cf. Pss. 64:9; 77:12; 90:16; 92:4; 95:9; 111:3; 143:5). In a hymnically accented reminder the community rehearses before Yahweh his foundational saving deeds (v. 2). At the time of the acquisition of the land, Yahweh drove out nations and "planted" Israel (on נטע, cf. Ps. 80:8; 2 Sam 7:10; Jer 11:17; 12:2; and often). Because this foundational saving deed is at present put in question (v. 9ff.), because the enemies are driving out Israel and are ransacking the land, therefore the original works of God are recalled. An appeal is made to Yahweh's saving faithfulness, a plea for a constant realization of the original deeds. And in this appeal the assembled community declares in a confessional statement that all the saving deeds of the past exclusively came about through Yahweh's acts, without assistance on Israel's part (v. 3). The basic traditions about the acquisition of the land are in this passage simplified without question and subordinated to a confessional theme—the credo of the holy war (cf. G. von Rad, *Der Heilige Krieg im alten Israel*, ATANT 29 [1951], 82). According to the conceptions of holy war, Yahweh carries on the wars of Israel without any assistance on the part of his people. Through his intervention ("his right hand and his arm ") he wins the victory. The only motive for all these merciful, powerful deeds is כי רציתם. The recollection of all these gracious deeds naturally (in view of the later lament and prayer song) entails a hidden appeal: that Yahweh may graciously again intervene so powerfully and support his helpless people who trust in him alone.

[44:4-8] The statements of vv. 4-8 are an expression of trust. This trust has its roots in the work of God described in vv. 1-3. The individual verses are hymnically acclamatory. In vv. 4 and 6 a precentor speaks for the community (cf. Pss. 60:9; 68:24; 74:12; 83:14; 89:47, 50; 135:5). He praises Yahweh as king and God. On מלך, see above, Intro. §10, 1. On אלהי: O. Eissfeldt, " 'Mein Gott' im Alten Testament," *ZAW* 61 (1945/48) 3-16. The trust appeals to the fact that Yahweh puts forth ישועות ("rescues," "deeds of salvation") for his people in keeping with a standing foundational order. With Yahweh (ב of accompaniment: BrSynt §106b), i.e., in the strength of his power of revelation (בשמך), the people are sure that they are able, like a steer (Deut. 33:17), to knock down their adversaries and tread them underfoot (cf. Ps. 60:12). For the meaning of שם in v. 5, cf. O. Grether, *Name und Wort Gottes im Alten Testament,* BZAW 64 (1934) 50. Verse 6 could once have been spoken by a king, but it applies equally well to one who speaks on behalf of the community. As in v. 3, so also in vv. 6 and 7 reference is made to the confessional statements of the holy war. Only Yahweh grants the victory. Concluding the statements of trust, v. 8 points out that the cultic community is always indebted to Yahweh for praise and thanksgiving. This reference is important, for in vv. 17ff. the attention is directed to the faithfulness and constancy of worship life.

[44:9-16] The prayer song actually begins in v. 9. In sharp contrast to vv. 1-3, it describes the shame and disgrace being suffered by the people of God in the present time. On זנח, cf. v. 23; Pss. 60:1, 10; 74:1; 77:7; 88:14; Lam. 3:31. The reference to the fact that Yahweh has not taken the field with the armies (v. 9b) is an echo of the archaic conception that יהוה צבאות accompanied Israel's conscripted army into battle (1 Sam. 4:3-11; Num. 10:35). Here too, then, very ancient traditions are expressed.

The present picture of distress is then described in very broad and general strokes. The army of the people of God had to flee before the enemy (cf. the contrast to v. 2), was plundered and mowed down like cattle for slaughter. On the picture of "sheep for slaughter," cf. G. Dalman, *AuS* VI 194f.; Zech. 11:4ff.; Jer. 12:3. In connection with the reference to the scattering of the people, we would think of the exile (Ezek. 5:10, 12; 12:14f.; 20:23; 22:15; 29:12). Yahweh "sold" his people (cf. Judg. 2:14; 3:8; 4:2, 9; 10:7; 1 Sam. 12:9; and often). But he did not have profit in mind (v. 12). In other words, the lamenting community is not able to grasp the sense of the misfortune.

In vv. 13-16 Yahweh is confronted with the distress of being exposed to the scorn and derision of the neighbors. Compare Pss. 79:4; 80:6; Deut. 28:37; 1 Kings 9:7; Jer. 18:16; 24:9; Lam. 2:15f. שים משל in v. 14 means: "to render a song of derision" (K. Budde, *Geschichte der althebräischen Literatur* [1909], 10). The sign of scornful derision was the "shaking of the head" (Ps. 22:7; Jer. 18:16).

[44:17-22] Worth noting are the reflections that are now made in vv. 17-22 about the causes for the catastrophes of war. According to the original conception, schematically elaborated in the Deuteronomistic history, the victory of the enemy was an angry reaction to the breach of the covenant and the defection from Yahweh. But such a lapse the praying community contests most vehemently. It is expressly emphasized: We have not forgotten Yahweh and have not renounced his covenant (v. 17); we have not deserted the path pointed out by the expression of Yahweh's will (v. 18); we did not turn to strange gods (v. 20). With these declarations the people cleanse themselves and affirm their innocence. Already in v. 8 it was expressly pointed out that their worship life distiguished itself by faithfulness and constancy in praise and thanksgiving. How are we therefore to understand the protestations of innocence? Are these the "beginnings of Pharisaic piety" (R. Kittel)? The relation between the statements of innocence and oath of cleansing of the prayer songs of those who have been accused cannot be overlooked (cf., e.g., Ps. 7:3ff.). The thought of "self-righteousness" therefore is not far removed. A people that lives within the covenant and its stipulations is צדיק. It is sure that it is just as free of actual guilt as he who is persecuted unjustly, and therefore it is unable to recognize the immediate application to the present time of causality of guilt and punishment. Incidentally, the plaintive songs of the book of Lamentations have an altogether different tone. Thus the prayer song of Psalm 44 tends toward a new understanding: "for your sake we are being killed all the time" (v. 22). The suffering comes to the community because it belongs to Yahweh. It is experiencing martyrdom—that is the new understanding of the psalm, which really is anything but "Pharisaic." Here too experiences of the individual laments have been adopted: the צדיק must suffer much (Ps. 34:19)—it is an essential mark of his existence that (without mention of guilt) enmities and torments assail him (cf. Psalm 22). This interpretation ties the uniqueness of election to the mystery of the suffering of the righteous. An unfathomable facet of the existence of Israel here reveals itself, and it would be most inappropriate to short-circuit the uniqueness of election into a "Pharisaic arrogance."[1]

Details in vv. 17-22: Worth noting in v. 17b is the expression שקר ברית (cf. שקר אמונה in Ps. 89:34); it means to break the covenant relation by fraudulent actions. מקום תנים in v. 19a is the location which jackals frequent, in other words, either the desert (Jer. 4:29) or the empty field of ruins (Isa. 13:22; 34:13; Lam 5:18). The fact that Yahweh sees through the hidden depths of the human heart is in the history of tradition a hymnic assertion in connection with the oath of cleansing (cf. the comment on Ps. 7:9; 139:23f.; 1 Sam. 16:7; Jer. 17:10).

[44:23-26] Stormy petitions form the conclusion of the prayer song of the community in vv. 23-26. On the signal to arise, עורה, cf. the comment on Ps. 7:6 (also Pss. 35:23; 59:4f.; 78:65). The community prays for Yahweh's intervention (v. 24) and refers to the self-abasement as it is practiced in the ceremonies of prostration in the sacral penitence. On קומה, cf. Ps. 7:6.

---

1. Calvin in his Commentary on the Psalms has a different understanding of v. 22. He sees there a statement by which God should be motivated to intervene: "Yet it is neither vain nor out of place that the faithful here plead with God that they suffer wrongfully for his sake, in order that he may the more vigorously set himself for their defense. It is right that he should have respect for the maintenance of his glory, which the wicked endeavor to overthrow, when they insolently persecute those who serve him" (Calvin on Ps. 44:22, trans. Anderson [Eerdmans, 1949]).

Purpose and Thrust

Reflections on the essential content of the statements of Psalm 44 understandably concentrate on the question whether finally the oppressed, suffering people of God could ever be in a position consistently to reject the thought of its own guilt. Alongside the judgment that Psalm 44 speaks of a "Pharisaic self-righteousness" there is also the conception that the community refuses to see the reason for its suffering in its own sin (H. Gunkel). Thus Psalm 44 would have to be viewed as under the label of hardening. But all these explanations divert us from what is decisive. The community praying in Psalm 44 knows that it is founded on the gracious act of salvation of the distribution of the land (vv. 1-3), that it stands faithful and constant, praising and giving thanks in trust before Yahweh (vv. 4-8). It lives in an intact covenant (ברית, v. 17b). Therefore enmity and disgrace assail the people of God only because of its commitment to Yahweh (v. 22). It is not stated—unfortunately, v. 22 has been misunderstood—that the community is being killed because of its obedient observance of the commandments of God. The text records only the enigmatical עליך—"for your sake." Here the "signs of the cross" already rest on the OT people of God (cf. Rom. 8:36). Israel is chosen for suffering.

Psalm 45

A Song for the Marriage of the King

Literature

S. Mowinckel, *Psalmen-Studien III: Kultprophetie und kultprophetische Psalmen* (1923) 96ff. G. von Rad, "Erwägungen zu den Königpsalmen," *ZAW* 58 (1940/41) 216-222. A. Bentzen, *Messias—Moses redivivus—Menschensohn,* 1948. J. H. Darby, "Psalm 44 (45): The King and His Bride," *Irish Eccl. Record* 91 (1959) 249-255. P. J. King, "Study of Psalm 45 (44)," *Romae* (1959). E. Beaucamp, "L'Oint de Yahweh et la princesse étrangère," *BiViChr* 28 (1959) 34-45. J. Schildenberger, "Zur Textkritik von Psalm 45 (44)," *BZ* 3 (1959) 31-44. R. Tournay, *Les affinités du Psaume XLV avec le Cantique des Cantiques et leur interprétation messianique,* VTSuppl 9 (1963) 168-212. C. Schedl, "Neue Vorschläge zu Text und Deutung des Psalms XLV," *VT* 14 (1964) 310-318. E. Beaucamp, "Des justices plein ta main, de redoutables exploits plein ta droite (Ps 45,5c)," *Bibl* 47 (1966) 110-112. A. Macintosh, "The Meaning of אלהים in Ps. 45,7," *Trivium* 1 (1966) 183f. B. McGrath, "Reflections on Ps 45,"*Bible Today* 26 (1966) 1837-1842. J. A. Emerton, "The Syntactical Problem of Psalm XLV, 7," *JSS* 13 (1968) 58-63. J. S. M. Mulder, *Studies on Psalm 45* (1972).

Text

To the choirmaster. According to "Lilies" (?).
Of the Korahites. A *maskil.* A love song.

45:1 My heart overflows about good news;
I want to sing 'my song'[a] for the king!
May my tongue be (like) the pencil of a nimble scribe!

2 'You are the most beautiful'[b] among human beings,
grace has been poured over your lips,
therefore 'Yahweh,'[c] has blessed you forever.

3 Gird your sword to your thighs,[d] O hero,
may your highness and splendor

4 'grace your hips';[e]
go forth for the cause of truth, poverty, 'and'[f] justice!
May your right hand show your fearful deeds!

5 'May'[g] your pointed arrows frighten nations,
May the enemies of the king 'lose heart.'[h]

450

6 Your throne, O divine one,[i] (stands) forever and ever,
   may the staff of your reign be an arbitrating scepter!
7 You love justice and hate wickedness,
   therefore 'Yahweh,'[j] your God, anointed you
   with the oil of gladness among your companions.
8 Of myrrh and aloes ' '[k] are all your garments fragrant.
   From palaces of ivory 'the music of strings'[l] delights you.
9 A king's daughter[m] is coming 'to meet you'[n]—
   as the spouse at your right hand in gold of Ophir!
10 O daughter, hear, look, and incline your ear!
   Forget your people and your father's house!
11 And may he desire ' '[o] your beauty, for he is your Lord!
   'May she fall down before you,'[p]
12 ' ' the daughter of Tyre with gifts!
   May the rich 'of the nations'[q] pay homage to you.
13 All her splendor ' '[r] is 'corals, mounted'[s] in gold.
14 'Clad'[t] in colorful garments, she is led to the king.
   Maidens follow her, her young friends 'escort her.'[u]
15 'She is led'[v] with joy and exultation ' '[w] to the palace ' '[x].
16 May the place of your fathers be taken by your sons;
   may you appoint them governors throughout the world!
17 Your name I will publish from generation to generation,
   therefore the nations shall praise ' '[y] you forever!

1a מעשׂה in the meaning "song," "poem" is found only in this passage in the OT, and its suffix construction should probably be thought of as singular: מַעֲשִׂי.
2b יפיפית is a malformation. Following Gk, γ΄, σ΄, Jerome, we should read either יָפִי יָפוּ יָפִיתָ or יָפִיתָ.
c In the Elohistically revised section of the Psalter יהוה should be inserted as the original reading.
3d Gk, σ΄, T, S transmit the suffix of the second person (ירכך).
4e Corresponding to the verse arrangement of the entire psalm, the first two words of v. 4a should be drawn in so as to be read with v. 3b. This combination, or the questionable verse division undertaken in the MT is also indicated by the mistaken dittography והדרך and by different word order in 2 Mss, Jerome, S^mss. For the second והדרך, Gk has read וְהָדְרֵךְ. The text is disfigured. In the parallel passage the correction הֲדֹר חֲלָצֶיךָ, which is being suggested tentatively, lies closest; only a transposition of consonants would have to be undertaken. The confusion was probably caused by the dittography.
f If we disregard a correction of the word עֲנָוָה, the copula ו must be introduced before צדק (Gk, T, Jerome).
5g MT: "Your arrows sharpened, nations fall under you, into the heart of the enemies of the king." It is hardly possible that, leaping over the parenthetical עמים תחתיך יפלו, there can be reference to the victims of the arrows without a verbal modification. R. Kittel correctly refers יפלו to the sentence in v. 5b, but of course then we have to read, with Gunkel, יִפֹּל לֵב, "may the heart sink." V. 5a would then (with Gunkel) best be corrected to:

חציך שנונים עמים יָחַתּוּ

h Cf. under note **g**.
6i MT: "Your throne, O divine one, (stands) forever and ever." The king accordingly would be addressed as אלהים. In the ancient Near Eastern cult of kings that is certainly a common phenomenon, but without parallel in the OT. In thinking about a correction the thought might arise that the Elohistic redactor misread יְהְיֶה for יהוה and replaced it with אלהים. The idea that Yahweh is addressed in v. 6 could of course be suggested here if one disregards the context. For the text-critical problem, cf. C. R. North, *ZAW* 50 (1932) 27ff.; M. Noth, *GesStudzAT* 225. With North we should ask whether an abbreviated way of speaking could not also be present in v. 6. Then the verse would have to be understood

as follows: "Your throne is (like) the (throne) of God, namely, lasting forever and ever."
And finally, one could consider whether כִּסְאֲךָ אֱלֹהִים could not be understood like רוּחַ
אֱלֹהִים in Gen. 1:2: "your divine throne," or "your powerful throne." In this way G. R.
Driver understood the text. J. A. Emerton defends Driver's interpretation "Thy throne is
God for ever and ever" in the sense of: "Thy throne is like God's throne for ever and
ever." But we should still follow the MT (Heb. 1:8).

7j Cf. note **c**.

8k MT: "Myrrh, aloes, and cassia." According to the meter that is otherwise
determinant, קְצִיעוֹת has to be considered a later addition. "The writer probably wants to
substitute for אֲהָלוֹת, which was in his time rather obsolete, by means of the then better
known and more expensive קְצִיעוֹת" (H. Gunkel). For the construction of the sentence,
cf. BrSynt §14bα.

l According to Ges-K §87f., מִנִּי is a shortened form of מִנִּים.

9m MT: "Kings' daughters are among your dear friends." According to the meter,
however, נצבה certainly belongs to v. 9a. In that case we would have to correct to בַּת־
מְלָכִים (cf. v. 13a). In the contextual sense this reading is to be preferred.

n בִּיקְרוֹתֶיךָ (in Gk, σ´, Jerome, S considered singular) would, according to K. Budde,
have to be corrected to לִקְרָאתֶךָ.

11o Like בַּת־מֶלֶךְ in v. 13, also הַמֶּלֶךְ in v. 11 is obviously an explanatory expansion,
which is to be eliminated for the sake of the meter.

p MT in vv. 11b-13: "and fall down before him; and the daughter of Tyre with gifts; the
rich in the nation pay homage to you; all splendor inside is the king's daughter, of worked
gold (is her garment)." According to form and context the given text is not acceptable.
V. 11bβ belongs to v. 12 in the order of verses (cf. Gk). Thus the following text would
emerge:

וְהִשְׁתַּחֲוֶה לָךְ בַּת־צֹר בְּמִנְחָה

12q Gk: עַם הָאָרֶץ; but in the contexual connection, following T, we should probably read
עַמִּים.

13r בַּת־מֶלֶךְ is at this point an explanatory expansion that breaks the verse organization.

s For the rare פְּנִימָה most of the more recent commentaries have rightly substituted פְּנִינִים
(corresponding to the context). מְשֻׁבָּצוֹת would nicely accompany this. Accordingly, the
following suggested correction for the distorted text would result:

כָּל־כְּבוּדָּה פְּנִינִים מְשֻׁבְּצוֹת זָהָב

t לבושה surely refers to לרקמות and is to be joined to the correction לְבוּשָׁה in v. 14 (Gk,
σ´, Jerome).

14u MT: "her maiden friends are brought to her." In assimilation to אַחֲרֶיהָ, we should
probably read מְבִיאוֹת לָהּ (2 Mss, cf. S).

15v MT: "they are brought." Obviously, however, the contextual sense of the text deals
with the introduction of the queen. Therefore we should very likely read תּוֹבֵלֶנָה.

w תבאינה, an addition, should probably be eliminated for the sake of the meter.

x מלך, likewise an addition, should be eliminated for the sake of the meter.

17y The verse is overfull. וְעֶד (or עַל־כֵּן) must be eliminated for the sake of the meter.

Form

The condition of the text entails many problems for the effort to reconstruct the
hypothetical original text. Sometimes only conjectures provide progress. A
literal translation that unhesitatingly attaches itself to the MT has little prospect
for an intelligent comprehension of the song. An important clue for the sequence
of verses may be found in the meter. The fact that Psalm 45 (with the exception
of v. 3b) shows mostly 4-pulse meter is indicative for textual criticism. Beyond
that, the entire psalm (with the exception of the double 4-pulse meter in vv. 16
and 17) may be divided into 3-member verse structures (cf. H. Gunkel), so that
the verse structure 4 + 4 + 4 would be the device that prescribes the form. For the

text-critical development of Psalm 45 and the emphasis on tristichs, cf. J. Schildenberger (*BZ* NF 3 [1959], 31ff.).

   The psalm belongs to the thematic form group, royal psalms. See above, Intro., §6, 3. The Hebrew name of the form group is given in v. 1: מעשׂי למלך. The song of praise for the king comes from a heart that is excited with joy (v. 1a). We could even speak of the inspiration of a cultic prophet (S. Mowinckel, *PsStud* III, 101; doubted by J. Jeremias, *Kultprophetie und Gerichtsverkündigung in der späten Königszeit Israels,* WMANT 35 [1970], 110). There is no parallel to Psalm 45 in the OT—not even anything approaching it. The king is addressed, honored, and praised. This song of praise is only occasionally interrupted by descriptions of situation (see under ''Setting''), as they turn up in vv. 8f. and 15. In v. 10 a ''king's daughter'' is addressed. Best wishes for the ruler are expressed in vv. 5 and 16. The entire royal psalm approximates the tone and tenor of the ancient Near Eastern ''court style'' (H. Gressmann), which indulges in extravagant praise of the ruler and in the effort applies divine appellations and predications to the prince (cf. v. 6). On the type, cf. also H. Gunkel and J. Begrich, *EinlPs* §5.

Setting

The occasion at which the ''royal psalm'' was intoned with prophetic power is not hard to come by in the psalm itself. Psalm 45 is a song for the marriage of the king. This observation has in recent times precipitated many problems. How should the marriage of the king be interpreted? Is it a matter of a sacral celebration which, detached from an actual wedding, belongs among the sacral and ritual ceremonies of the annual cult of royalty? (cf. A. Bentzen, *Messias— Moses redivivus—Menschensohn,* 27; G. Widengren, *Sakrales Königtum im Alten Testament und im Judentum,* 78). Or must we think of a historical event?

   The *krt* legend in the Ras Shamra texts has given rise to the conjecture that the marriage of the king was a sacral act of the annual cultic-mystic celebration of the enthronement (J. Pedersen, ''Die *Krt*-Legende,'' *Berytus* VI, 2 [1941]; I. Engnell, *Studies in Divine Kingship in the Ancient Near East* [1943]).

   On the other hand, however, some thought there were clues for a historical referent of the psalm. A wedding of Solomon's or Joram's (2 Kings 8:16) came to mind. But even events at the court of the Northern Kingdom were considered (H. Gunkel). F. Hitzig related Psalm 45 to the marriage of King Ahab to the Tyrian princess Jezebel; H. Ewald pointed to Jeroboam II. In more recent times H. Schmidt suggested that he was able to advance three arguments in favor of the hypothesis proposed by F. Hitzig: (1) in connection with the בת־צר mentioned in v. 12, a person immediately thinks of Jezebel; (2) according to 1 Kings 22:39; Amos 3:15, and the excavations, there were ivory palaces (היכלי שׁן [v. 8]) in Samaria; (3) אהבת in v. 7 could be an allusion to the name Ahab. In connection with all of these attempts at interpretation we should state: (1) The assumption of a sacral ceremony of the mythical cult of the king is very remote for Psalm 45; all the expressions make us think of a special, one-time wedding celebration. (2) The historical interpretation assigns the psalm to a specific occurrence too quickly. For one thing, we should ask whether the psalm with its prophetically formulated expressions of perfection does not overreach any historical portrait of a king. Also we should have to consider that songs like Psalm 45 were transferable as formularies. At any rate—considering these circumstances—it is peculiar that a בת־צר is mentioned. But who would be able to determine which of the "daughters of Tyre" mentioned or not mentioned by name in the OT is here meant? Very likely more than one king of Israel or Judah married a בת־צר. What could be more obvious? But that the "ivory palaces" have to refer to buildings in Samaria is by no means proved. Also in Jerusalem we would have to reckon with rooms decorated with ivory. In any case, Solomon's throne, for example, was of ivory (1 Kings 10:18). The statements in vv. 2b and 6a, as well as the hereditary succession assumed in v. 16, would, in connection with the prophecy of Nathan (2 Samuel 7), argue for the Kingdom of Judah (cf. A. Alt, "Das Königtum in den Reichen Israel und Juda," KlSchr II 116-134).

Commentary

[Title] On למנצח, see above, Intro. §4, No. 17. On על־ששנים, see Intro. §4, No. 21. On לבני־קרח cf. the comment on Ps. 42, Title. On משכיל, see Intro. §4, No. 5.

[45:1] The singer of the royal psalm begins the song with a reference to his inspiration. Obviously, in the poet's way of thinking, this is a matter of a cultic prophet (cf. Psalm 2; S. Mowinckel, *PsStud* III). דבר טוב is meant not only aesthetically; the word of the cultic prophet is the "message of salvation" (cf. Isa. 52:7). His opus (מעשה) applies to the king and serves for his elevation and glorification. When in v. 16 the tongue is likened to the pencil of a scribe which registers the letters on wooden tablets, potsherds, papyrus, or leather, we may assume that it was customary to put in writing songs of praise addressed to the king. On מהיר, cf. Isa. 16:5; Prov. 22:29; Ezra 7:6. Very likely this is a foreign word imported from Egypt.

[45:2] The king is celebrated as the most beautiful person among human beings. The reference is to his beaming appearance, the extraordinary majestic bearing (Ps. 50:2). Such praises are found in many reports of ancient Near Eastern glorifications of kings (cf. K. Grzegorzewski, "Elemente vorderorientalischen Hofstils auf kanaanäischem Boden," Diss., Königsberg [1937], 34ff.). Also in the Petersburg Papyrus No. 1116 B recto, we read about the Egyptian king that he is *nfr-rhw* = "the most beautiful of human beings" (?). Cf. L. Dürr, *Ursprung und Ausbau der israelitisch-jüdischen Heilandserwartung* (1925) 7. הוצק is then to be thought of as a prophetic perfect (Ges-K §106n). The prophet sees the king in a vision as of incomparable perfection. He joins future attitudes to the picture of his nature. His words are charming (cf. Eccles. 10:12).

Worth noting is the use of על־כן both in v. 2b and also in v. 7. From a future picture of perfection indicated by the prophetic perfect a deduction is made. What does that mean? Does the singer have a visionary archetypal picture in mind to which Yahweh's eternal blessing applies? In that case, the prophecy of Nathan (2 Samuel 7), mixed with idealized conceptions of the ancient Near Eastern cult of kings, would form a background for Psalm 45. On ברך in the sense "to acknowledge someone in his position of power and his claim to greatness with all due form," cf. F. Horst, "Segen und Segenshandlungen in der Bibel," *EvTh* 7 (1947) 31. For the "blessing" of the king, cf. the comment on Psalm 21.

[45:3-5] In vv. 3-5 the king is described as a brilliant warrior. The vision and wishful thinking present the picture of a victorious combatant who all alone, without an army, engages the enemy. With sword at his side, encased in greatness and splendor (cf. Ps. 21:5), may the ruler fight for צדק—אמת—ענוה. Here the king appears as the helper of all the disfranchised and as the protector of the mode of existence that is faithful to the community (cf. Isa. 11:2ff.; Ps. 72:4). The "right hand" of the ruler is addressed in v. 4b as an independent force that should prompt the king not to shrink back from things "fearful" (נוראות). In the battle against the enemies (v. 5) the nations should be frightened and despair under the missiles of the majestic warrior. The singer here sees the ruler in the midst of the tumult of battle (cf. Pss. 2:9; 21:8f., 12). All the adversaries should lose heart at his appearance.

Assuming that the translation "Your throne, O divine one, (stands) forever and ever" is correct, how must we evaluate the fact that the human king is here addressed as אלהים? The deification of the king in the ancient Near East can be documented in the greatest variety of examples. Cf. Chr. Jeremias, *"Die Vergöttlichung der babylonisch-assyrischen Könige*, AO XIX Nos. 3-4 (1919); B. Meissner, *Babylonien und Syrien*, I (1920) 46ff.; H. Jacobsohn, *Die dogmatische Stellung des Königs in der Theologie der alten Ägypter* (1955); H. Gressmann, *Der Messias* (1929) 42ff. The historical and mythological backgrounds of these apotheoses of a human king have to be investigated carefully from case to case (cf. H. Frankfort, *Kingship and the Gods* [1948]; D. J. Gadd, *Ideas of Divine Rule in the Ancient East* [1948]). In Israel—and, as far as we know, especially in Jerusalem—the ancient Near Eastern royal traditions regarding the divinity or godlikeness of the ruler have been reflected in two ways: (1) a modified "statement of adoption" has been taken into the royal psalms, according to which the enthroned king is credited with the position of a "son of God" (cf. Ps. 2:7); (2) some OT statements move the earthly king very close to Yahweh: David is כמלאך האלהים (2 Sam. 14:17, 20; Zech. 12:8) or even כאלהים (Zech. 12:8). But that the king is called אלהים without reservation is nowhere documented (unless in Ps. 45:6; possibly one could also refer to Isa. 9:6). Thus we would have to assume that the ancient Near Eastern deification of the earthly king, which is also well documented in Canaan through the Amarna texts, prevailed in a singular way that contradicted faith. This could be possible in the exceptional psalm in which the ruler is addressed and glorified, but that is to be taken with great restraint, for the basis for a comprehensive ideology of the divine kingship could in no case be gained from Psalm 45. The basis is too narrow for that. "The fact that in the Old Testament we in all probability in regard to the Jerusalem kingship meet with changes and alterations of the conceptions of a God-king ideology rather indicates that this ideology was of course not adopted on Israel's soil—and from the presuppositions of the Old Testament faith could not be adopted" (M. Noth, "Gott, König, Volk im Alten Testament," *GesStudAT* 226).

In Heb. 1:8 the θεός-address in Ps. 45:6 is taken up and transferred to Christ.

On Israel's kingship in the light of ancient Near Eastern royal ideology, cf. K. H. Bernhardt, *Das Problem der altorientalischen Königsideologie im Alten Testament* (1961); J. A. Soggin, *Das Königtum in Israel* (1967); J. Gray, "Sacral Kingship in Ugarit," *Ugaritica* VI (1964) 289-302; S. H. Schmidt, *Alttestamentlicher Glaube in seiner Geschichte* (1975²).

[45:6-8] In the prophecy of Nathan (2 Sam. 7:16) in the OT the eternal duration of the throne for the dynasty of David is pronounced in a foundational manner. To this fact the singer could be alluding in v. 6a. שבט (also cf. Ps. 110:2) is an (originally magical) symbol of power which the incumbent ruler holds in his hands. מישר denotes the arbitrating power of the scepter. In v. 7, in the prophetic-hortatory form already noted in v. 2a, love of צדק is attributed to the ruler. We could explain that fixed verbs like prophetic perfects have a contemporizing, promising, and fulfilling character. For the clause introduced by עַל־כֵּן, cf. the comment on v. 2. The anointing is a bestowal of power like the blessing mentioned in v. 2. Israel's kings are anointed (1 Sam. 10:1; 15:17; 2 Sam. 12:7). Oddly enough, this custom of anointing kings is familiar only in pre-Israelite Syria-Palestine as well as among the Hittites, but neither in Mesopotamia nor in Egypt (cf. M. Noth, "Amt und Berufung im Alten Testament," *Bonner Akademische Reden* 19 [1958], 15; J. A. Knudtzon, *Die El-Amarna-Tafeln* [1915], No. 51, 4ff.; A. Goetze, *Kulturgeschichte des alten Orients* III, 1 [1933], 84 A.2). The anointing of a person with oil takes place in a festive act; it is an expression of joy (Isa. 61:3; G. Dalman, *AuS* VI 143). As the queen is accompanied by her companions and friends (v. 14), so the king's companions form an honor guard for the king at the festivities. The oil is mixed with expensive essences so that all the garments of the anointed one are fragrant with myrrh and aloes (v. 8; Ps. 133:2). The singer describes the splendor of the kingship that streams forth with joy and pleasant aroma. He hears the music of strings issuing from the ivory palaces—from the halls decorated with carved ivory (on the archaeological questions, cf. G. E. Wright, *Biblical Archeology,* [1957] 129-142). String players make an appearance before the king (1 Sam. 16:17).

In a review of vv. 1-8, we might inquire about the significance, e.g., of the prominence given to the anointing. Is this a reminder of the enthronement of the ruler, looking back to an event long since past, or is the entire installation ceremony being repeated cultically (cf. the comment on Psalm 132)? Could the king's marriage (vv. 9-17) perhaps have been taken up in the act of a cultic event of the Jerusalem monarchy (in connection with the archetypal data of 2 Samuel 7)? In view of vv. 1-8, questions arise that are similar to those connected to Psalm 2 (see "Setting"). It is altogether possible that the king's marriage was preceded by a festive repetition of the installation of the heirs of David in a "royal Zion festival." In any case, the statements prompt us to think of a cultic act rather than of abstract reminiscences.

[45:9-15] In v. 9 the description of the marriage ceremony begins. The spouse of the king is a בַּת מְלָכִים. She takes her place of honor to the right of the king, adorned with gold of Ophir. Immediately the singer turns to the queen with a word of exhortation (v. 10). With this marriage she leaves her people and her father's house and becomes a member of a new community. In this situation the call is suitable: "Forget your people and your father's house!" The king is now אֲדֹנִי, master, of the foreign daughter of a king. By means of obeisant prostration (הִשְׁתַּחֲוָה) this incorporation and subordination is strikingly expressed. With gifts of homage (מִנְחָה) the בַּת־צֹר steps before her spouse—while emissaries of the nations present their gifts (cf. Ps. 72:10f.). In vv. 13-15 the splendid procession of the foreign king's daughter is described: corals mounted in gold and colorful dresses—that is her adornment. She is accompanied by female servants and friends. When v. 15 reports that the queen is led into the palace, obviously the entire festive ceremony is reenacted in the courts. Therefore also מִן־הֵיכְלֵי שֵׁן (v. 8b) is not (as many exegetes wish) to be corrected to מִן־כְּלֵי שֵׁן.

[45:16] A wish for the king is expressed in v. 16. May the dynasty be guaranteed through progeny and undisturbed succession. Here a stable dynasty, such as is present in Jerusalem, is taken for granted. Thoughts of a grand empire are evidently involved when the singer expresses the wish that the sons of the king will be installed as שָׂרִים, i.e., as officials in high places all over the world (cf. the comment on Psalm 2). Or should בְּכָל־הָאָרֶץ apply only to hereditary territorial possessions of the kingdom? In that case, conditions of government could be meant such as were introduced in Judah by Rehoboam, according to 2 Chron. 11:23.

The psalm closes with the wish that the song of praise may outshine time and space.

Purpose and Thrust

Psalm 45 is a song for the marriage of the king. The question immediately arises for what reason and with what thinking such a psalm was taken into the canon. No doubt, it cannot be labeled "profane," for all its statements refer to the Jerusalem cult of the king. A marriage of the ruler closely belongs to the worship life of the "royal sanctuary." But what is the significance of such a psalm? How was the psalm understood at the time it was taken into the canon? The monarchy had certainly fallen into ruin. Even if one could at that time possibly impute a messianic understanding to those psalms in which the king alone was the center of attention, how should the wedding event be adopted "spiritually"? At this point allegories take drastic measures and interpret the bride as the community of God. These directions of interpretation have found their way into the church's exegesis. They are hardly correct.

If we begin with the laudations of the king in our quest to ascertain the essence of the content of the statements of the psalm, we will have to demonstrate that the attributes of perfection point above and beyond the empirical reality to an "ideal" figure (H. Gunkel) or to an archetypal picture visionarily conceived. "The royal psalms show the kingdom and office of the anointed one according to his—still hidden—divine *doxa*, which he has for them even now and which can become manifest at any moment (G. von Rad, *ZAW* 58 [1940/41], 219f.). In Psalm 45 this entire glory of radiant, aromatic beauty, of joyfully resounding string music, and of military power is painted with every imaginable Near Eastern color and projected into the existence of the ruler (on the theological problem, cf. the comment on Psalm 2, "Purpose and Thrust"). This king represents the royal presence of God on earth. In this sense Heb. 1:8 transfers the statement of Ps. 45:6f. into the great Christ hymn: Jesus is God; in him, "at the end of days" there appears "the reflection of the glory and the image" of the Father (Heb. 1:1ff.).

If we now turn to the wedding sounds of Psalm 45, it strikes us how strongly the theme of paying homage before the king comes to the fore. The incorporation, the powerful integration and subordination, of the radiant splendor of foreign nations is illustrated by the entrance of the Tyrian king's daughter into the palace. Here the emphasis of the second part of the psalm lies. The theme that stands out in Isa. 60:3ff., for example, also dominates Ps. 45:11ff.

However, the splendor that lies over Psalm 45 proceeds from the prophetically viewed beauty of the eternal kingdom (2 Sam. 7:16) that has sloughed off all traces of transcience, hiddenness, and disfigurement (cf. Isa. 53:2) and brings with it only joy and celebration, stringed music, and perfect happiness.

Psalm 46

Yahweh Is a Mighty Fortress

Literature

A. F. Puuko, "Zur Exegese von Psalm 46," *Studia Theologica* I (1935) 29-33. N. H. Snaith, *Hymns of the Temple: Ps 42/43; 44; 46; 50; 73* (1951). H. Schmid, "Jahwe und die Kulttraditionen von Jerusalem," *ZAW* 67 (1955)168ff. E. Rohland, "Die Bedeutung der Erwählungstraditionen Israels für die Eschatologie der alttestamentlichen Propheten," diss., Heidelberg (1956) 123ff. L. Krinetzki, "Der anthologische Stil des 46. Psalms und seine Bedeutung für die Datierungsfrage," *MThz* 12 (1961) 52-71. M. Weiss, "Wege der neuen Dichtungswissenschaft in ihrer Anwendung auf die Psalmenforschung," *Bibl* 42 (1961) 255-302. L. Krinetzki, "Jahwe ist unsere Zuflucht und Wehr: Eine stilistisch-theologische Auslegung von Ps 46 (45)," *BiLe* 3 (1962) 26-42. J. H. Hayes, "The Tradition of Zion's Inviolability," *JBL* 82 (1963) 419-426. S. L. Kelly, "The Zion-Victory Songs: Psalm 46, 48 and 76," diss., Vanderbilt (1968). J. Jeremias, "Lade und Zion: Probleme biblischer Theologie," *G. von Rad zum 70. Geburtstag* (1971) 183-198.

Text

To the choirmaster. Of the Korahites. According
to *alămot*. A song.

46:1 'Yahweh'[a] is for us refuge and protection,
   well proved as a help in troubles.

2 Therefore we are not afraid, even if the earth 'shakes'[b]
   and the hills topple into the middle of the sea.

3 Though its waters toss and surge,
   though hills quake before its presumption:
   'Yahweh Sebaoth is with us,
   the God of Jacob is a fortress for us.'[c] *Selah.*

4 The branches of the stream delight the city of God;
   The Most High has 'sanctified his dwelling.'[d]

5 'Yahweh'[e] is in the midst of her, therefore she will not be shaken,
   'Yahweh'[f] helps her at the break of day.

6 Nations rage, kingdoms totter.[g]
   Thunder rolls—the earth dissolves!

7 Yahweh Sebaoth is with us,
   the God of Jacob is a fortress for us. *Selah.*

458

8 Come and behold the works of Yahweh,
  who spreads dismay on earth!
9 Who controls wars to the end of the world,
  who breaks bows and shatters lances,[h]
  who burns chariots[i] in fire.
10 Stop and realize that I am 'Yahweh,'[j]
  exalted among the nations, exalted on earth!
11 Yahweh Sebaoth is with us,
  the God of Jacob is a fortress for us! *Selah.*

1a In the Elohistically edited part of the Psalter יהוה is to be inserted as the original reading.
2b המיר has the meaning "exchange," and in this passage it can in no way be retained in any different literal sense. Gk: ἐν τῷ ταράσσεσθαι. It is best to read בְּהָמוֹג (Ps. 75:3). Other suggestions: בְּהָמֹר, בְּהָמִישׁ, בְּהָמוֹת.
3c סלה at the end of v. 3 as well as the arrangement of the psalm in three uniform strophes suggest that we insert the refrain (vv. 7 and 11) also after v. 3.
4d MT: "the most holy one among the dwellings of the Most High." But according to Pss. 43:3; 84:1; 132:5 the plural of מִשְׁכָּן would have to be מִשְׁכְּנוֹת. Gk: ἡγίασεν τὸ σκήνωμα αὐτοῦ ὁ ὕψιστος ("the Most High has sanctified his tabernacle"). The corresponding Hebrew text would be: קִדֵּשׁ מִשְׁכָּנוֹ עֶלְיוֹן.
5e Cf. note **a**.
f Cf. note **a**.
6g Perhaps it would be better to read מָגֹו here; but we could stay with the MT too.
9h יְקַצֵּץ is probably better.
i Gk: Θυρεούς (עֲגָלוֹת).
10j Cf. note **a**.

Form

By means of the dominant refrain in vv. 7 and 11, which is also to be inserted after v. 3 (see above), the psalm is divided into three parts (strophes): vv. 1-3; 4-7; 8-11. In the meter the weighty long verses give expression to the power and loftiness of the song. The meter in detail is to be construed as follows: 4 + 4 in vv. 1, 6, 10; 4 + 3 in vv. 2, 4, 8; 3 + 4 in the refrain (vv. 3, 7, 11), as well as in v. 5; and 3 + 3 in v. 3. A three-member verse occurs in v. 9 (4 + 4 + 3).

Various attempts have been made to explain the peculiar form and *Gattung* of Psalm 46. Even H. Gunkel is responsible for much confusion in connection with the psalm before us. He moved the song close to the hymns, pointed to its "prophetic manner of speech," and, emphasizing the central theme "Zion," declared that this is an "eschatological song of Zion." One insight emerges from this confusion as instructive: Psalm 46 is to be assigned to the form group, songs of Zion. See above, Intro. §6, 4; H. Gunkel and J. Begrich, *EinlPs* §8 II.

The type "songs of Zion" has been investigated in detail by Jörg Jeremias (*Probleme biblischer Theologie*, 189f.). The psalms that belong to this group, Psalms 46; 48; 76; (and 87) are not only similarly arranged; they also reveal the same syntactical constructions in their chief statements:

(1) Emphatic and almost like headings at the beginning, there are in each case confessionlike, fixed statements, almost throughout in the form of predicate nominatives, which describe God as the inhabitant and protector of Zion, or Zion as a fortress splendidly furnished and fortified by God.

(2) These fixed statements are factually documented with sentences the verbs of

which are in the perfect tense: Yahweh is Lord and protector of Zion because he has warded off the attack of the nations.

(3) At the conclusion, particular consequences for the hearer are regularly mentioned in the form of imperative sentences which in Psalms 48 and 76 are preceded by jussives and which invite the hearer to acknowledge Yahweh (Ps. 46:8a, 10), to take part in a festival procession (Ps. 48:11ff.), to perform a *todah*, and to pay his vows (76:10f.). (Nos. 1-3 are quoted verbatim from Jörg Jeremias, 190.)

Not only as to form—in the middle members in variable degrees of conformity—but also as to content are the songs of Zion allied in like themes and conceptions.

In Psalm 46 the characteristics of confession and trust cannot be overlooked. They provide the inducement for recognizing the psalm as a "community song of confidence" (L. Krinetzki). Still it would be appropriate to persist in the explanation that Psalm 46 is a song of Zion. For that J. Jeremias has provided the necessary presuppositions.

We cannot detect how the "methods of the new science of poetry" represented and promoted by M. Weiss are able to inaugurate a method of interpretation that fits the psalm. The negations "neither eschatological, nor cultic, nor historical" settle just as little as the positive descriptions of the "unitary character" of the psalm and the "fixing of being in words" (*worthafte Setzung des Seins*).

Setting

Where, at which occasion, and when was Psalm 46 sung? Before we enter upon such questions, we should first call to our attention the fact that a community sang this song. The subject and the place of the song is the city of God—no doubt, Jerusalem. But at which occasion was such a psalm that radiates certainty and trust intoned? While in earlier times the thought was of a definite historical situation (e.g., of the approach of Sennacherib in the year 701 B.C., or of the threat to Jerusalem by Alexander the Great, or of events in the time of the Maccabees), the tendency in our own day is to turn more and more to the question of the cultic situation of Psalm 46. Gunkel's prophetic-eschatological understanding has already definitely steered toward this cultic manner of interpretation; however, it still unmistakably orients itself historically insofar as it is on the lookout for the elements of an "eschatology" given in OT prophecy and now taken up in worship. On the other hand, S. Mowinckel and H. Schmidt defend the view that the "ideas and conceptions" of Psalm 46 are traditions specifically rooted in worship from which the prophets borrowed their statements and perceptions. Psalm 46 is coordinated with the controversial "festival of Yahweh's enthronement" (on this festival, see above, Intro. §10, 1). Thus H. Schmidt, for instance, declares that in the cultic explanation of Psalm 46 we have to presuppose that "the entry of Yahweh into his dwelling and therewith the annual renewal of his rule as king was celebrated with resounding exultation." The song of confidence accordingly is based on the fact that the enthronement of Yahweh had just been celebrated (H. Schmidt, *Die Thronfahrt Jahves am Fest der Jahreswende im alten Israel* [1927], 24). This explanation is correct in suggesting that Psalm 46 embraces Zion traditions that are intimately associated with a cult which (as we will still want to show) very likely points back to a pre-Israelite time (H. Schmid, "Jahwe und die Kulttraditionen von Jerusalem," *ZAW* 68 [1955] 168ff.). But the "festival of the enthronement of Yahweh" is controversial and very problematic.

In his dissertation, "Die Bedeutung der Erwählungstraditionen Israels für die Eschatologie der alttestamentlichen Propheten," E. Rohland develops a new understanding of the cultic situation of Psalm 46. Beginning with an analysis of the type, he detects an "oracle of being heard" in v. 10 of the "community song of confidence." From these observations Rohland concludes that Psalm 46 has its "Sitz im Leben" in a cultic festival of community lament which came to a salutary conclusion and was then refashioned into a "song of confidence of the community." Is this explanation appropriate? We may certainly consider v. 10 an "oracle of salvation and of being heard" (cf. J. Begrich, "Das priesterliche Heilsorakel," *ZAW* 53 [1934], 81-92). The suggested cultic situation is also well worth considering. And yet we will have to ask whether S. Mowinckel and H. Schmidt were not on the right track. The Zion traditions so clearly outlined suggest that we think of an (annually recurring) Zion festival which at its climax performed pre-Israelite cultic traditions (cf. the comment on Psalm 132). After conveying the ark up to Zion in a procession dating back to the time of David, a great prostration before "King Yahweh" took place in the sanctuary (cf. Pss. 95:6; 99:5; 100:4; see above, Intro. §10, 1). At this occasion the age-old cultic traditions of Jerusalem break forth and let the city of God appear with its God-king in the splendor of universal glorification. The conceptions in most instances come from the pre-Israelite, ancient Canaanite area. In connection with the prostration before King Yahweh, Psalm 46 can be understood as consisting of: the glorification of Zion, the oracle of salvation (v. 10), and the expression of confidence. Psalm 46 belongs to the preexilic worship on Zion and is probably very old.

Commentary

[Title] On למנצח, see above, Intro. §4, No, 17. On לבני־קרח, cf. the comment on Ps. 42, title. On על־עלמות, see above, Intro. §4, No. 24.

[46:1-3] If in our analysis of form above we have referred to the fact that the subject and central theme of Psalm 46 is the city of God, Zion, we must now immediately correct that statement as referring merely to form. It is not Jerusalem that is the "refuge and protection" in troubles and catastrophes, but Yahweh. He himself as the *deus praesens* is the "mighty fortress," as especially the refrain emphatically points out. But מחסה is especially the "safe, inaccessible place" (Ps. 104:18)—in the Psalms mostly a metaphor for the asylum function of the sanctuary (Pss. 14:6; 61:3; 62:7f.; 71:7; and often). The peculiar phrase נמצא מאד points to the splendid proof of help that Yahweh represented for his people in times of need. The community therefore in v. 1—confessing and trusting—calls to mind the protective power of its God so far experienced (cf. Ps. 48:9). And in v. 2 a conclusion for the future is drawn: "We are not afraid," even when the worst threats confront us—when the earth shakes and the hills (the symbol of all that is firm and enduring) "topple into the middle of the sea." The author here visualizes an earthquake, a mighty catastrophe of nature that goes beyond all experience. We immediately think of the innumerable earthquakes that have afflicted Syria and Palestine up to our own times; cf. Isa. 24:19f.; 54:10; Hag. 2:6. For the meaning of בלב in v. 2b, cf. BrSynt §117e.

Verse 3 deals with the enmity of chaotic powers against that which is established and firm. Mixed into the picture of a tidal wave caused by the earthquake are primeval, mythical metaphors: the archetypal flood lifts its head in "presumption" and causes the hills to quake. On המה, cf. Ps. 65:7; Isa.

17:12; 51:15. "Israel seems to have expected a final insurrection of these uncreated powers against Jahweh" (G. von Rad, *OT Theol*, 1:152).

A few comments on the refrain (surely to be inserted already after v. 3): יהוה צבאות is the cultic name of God enthroned on Zion (see above, Intro. §10, 1). אלהי יעקב as an Israelite name of God recalls the central sanctuary, Bethel— the place where the tradition of the patriarchs concerning the "God of Jacob" had its anchor (cf. A. Alt, "Der Gott der Väter," *KlSchr* I, 1ff.). But if יהוה צבאות too is originally a cultic name of an Israelite sanctuary (Shiloh—see above, Intro. §10, 1), the tradition of Israel in the names of God in the refrain should be especially emphasized. משגב is the citadel situated on an inaccessible height (Isa. 33:16; Jer. 48:1; Pss. 9:9; 18:2; 48:3; 59:9; and often). On the formulation of confession and confidence "Yahweh Sebaoth is with us," H. D. Preuss states, "The community of the city of God makes the confession, 'Yahweh Sebaoth is with us' (עמנו). Yahweh is at the same time also given the title God of Jacob. His city is one of refuge in battles. For 'with us,' cf. also Zech 8:23; and 2 Sam. 5:10" (H. D. Preuss, " . . . Ich will mit dir sein," *ZAW* 80 [1968], 151). Thus the formulation of confession and confidence is moved into a larger context.

In vv. 4ff. ancient Jerusalemite cultic and place traditions prevail in the paslm, traditions which require special analysis and review. Cf. above, Intro. §10, 2. From the discussion in Intro. §10, 2 let us here bring together at least the chief points.

The psalms of Zion contain a series of characteristic statements about the city of God that can be explained neither from the topography of Jerusalem nor from any mythical-eschatological conceptions (thus H. Gunkel). Rather, Canaanite-Ugaritic parallels have opened up a new understanding of the statements and pictures which together have the function of glorifying and therefore of the poetic-mythical exalting of the details of place. On the Canaanite-Ugaritic parallels, see above, Intro. §10, 2. Here we list only the main themes:

(1) Zion is called the hill in the north. The name צפון, disregarding all geographical descriptions of locations (pointing to northern Syria), has the significance of pointing to the mountain of the gods, the "Olympus" that reaches up to the heavenly world. Cf. Isa. 14:13f.

(2) As "mountain of the north," and that means, as seat of the gods and throne of the "Most High God" (see above, Intro. §10, 1), Zion is the center of the world (Ps. 48:2), a paradisaically beautiful location of joy and bliss (Lam. 2:15).

(3) In Jerusalem there are streams flowing that "delight" the holy city (Ps. 46:4). Here too it is not a matter of a particular location but of traditions such as also appear in Genesis 2 and Ezekiel 47. The paradisaical Garden of Eden is watered by streams. In this statement of glorification, Zion is the place where the subterranean archetypal waters emerge and in controlled form moisten the land and make it fruitful.

(4) Against the city of God there arises the raging of the nations. In Ps. 46:3 it is chaotic waters that, loosed by an earthquake, rush up against the hills. In Ps. 46:6 the chaotic and destructive forces appear in the "historicized form" of "nations." This revolt of the nations as the godless and chaotic forces which attack "like floods" is mentioned repeatedly in the OT (e.g., Pss. 2:2; 48:4ff.; Isa. 17:12f.; 6:23).

(5) And still the city of God is invincible (Ps. 46:6ff.). It cannot be taken by storm (2 Sam. 5:6; Pss. 87:5; 125:1f.; Isa. 26:1; and often). The attack of the nations is repulsed. Yahweh shatters the enemy with his thunder (Ps. 46:6), with his rebuking (Ps. 76:6; Isa. 17:13), with the fear of God (Ps. 46:8; Isa. 17:14). Cf. J. H. Hayes, "The Tradition of Zion's Inviolability," *JBL* 82 (1963) 419-426.

The antiquity of all these traditions of glorification emerging in the songs of Zion can hardly be doubted. And yet a contrary thesis has been brought forward: G. Wanke, *Die Zionstheologie der Korahiten,* BZAW 97 (1966). According to it, psalms such as Psalm 46 are to be considered "products of the postexilic literary activity" of the Korahites. "This especially for the reason that the theology reflected in Psalms 46; 48; and 76 can no longer be claimed as an old tradition . . . '' (115). For a critique of the thesis of G. Wanke, cf. H. M. Lutz, *Jahwe, Jerusalem und die Völker,* WMANT 27 (1968) 213ff., and above, Intro. §10, 2.

[46:4-7] "Delighted" by streams, like a paradisaical place, the "city of God" appears in v. 4. Pictures of an archetypal cult tradition illumine the sanctuary (see above). This eliminates the view of H. Gunkel that the enraptured eye of the poet is here seeing an eschatological vision. But the waters of the stream have a "delighting" effect because they bring about fruitfulness and fullness of life (Ps. 65:9). There is no mention of a "watery firmament."

The city of God contains the "dwelling of the Most High" (v. 4b). The עליון (see above, Intro. §10, 1) lives on Zion; the thought is of the temple (cf. Pss. 43:3; 84:1; 132:5). The עליון has "sanctified" (קִדֵּשׁ) his dwelling, i.e., he has secluded it and made it unapproachable (Exod. 19:23). Yet no immanent power of the city of God makes Jerusalem an immovable rampart, but only the presence of Yahweh (v. 5) and his helpful intervention "at the break of day." It is worth noting that in Psalm 46 all statements glorifying the city of God are strictly applied to the majestic person of Yahweh. His presence, he himself makes Jerusalem the "mighty fortress." Incidentally, early morning is the time of God's answer and God's help (cf. Pss. 90:14; 143:8; J. Siegler, "Die Hilfe Gottes 'am Morgen,' " *Nötscher-Festschrift* [1950], 281ff.). The chaotic revolt of the nations (see above) is struck down by means of Yahweh's voice of thunder (cf. Psalm 29)—the earth dissolves at this sound. Thunder is the sign of divine intervention (1 Sam. 2:10; 7:10; 12:16ff.; Isa. 30:30f.; and often). We should add: "At the revolt of the nations . . . as in Amos 1:2, Yahweh's voice of thunder sounds forth. There is no mention here of a point from which Yahweh departs. As in Amos 1:2, Yahweh's coming in the sounding forth of his voice is characterized as a coming in the thunderstorm, an interpretation that goes beyond that of Judg. 5:4 and Mic. 1:3. The reaction of nature in Ps. 46:6, as in Judg. 5:5 and Mic. 1:4, is that the earth shakes" (Jörg Jeremias, *Theophanie: Die Geschichte einer alttestamentlichen Gattung,* WMANT 10 [1965], 14). But the question remains whether conceptions of the holy war were combined with this view; cf. G. von Rad, *Der Heilige Krieg im alten Israel,* ATANT 20 (1951) 12ff.

[46:8-11] At the beginning of the third part of the psalm there is an invitation to behold the works of Yahweh (cf. Isa. 33:13). The reference is to the destructive works of God which put a stop to rebellious powers. With his annihilating "dismay" Yahweh can intervene everywhere on earth. On שִׂים שׁמּות, cf. Ezek. 10:2; Ps. 78:43. From the city of God Yahweh is able to give evidence of his power "to the ends of the earth." The area of influence of the עליון is universal; the center of the world is the hill of God (cf. Isa. 2:2). The weapons and implements of war are broken by Yahweh. For the war chariots equipped with iron plating, cf. M. Noth *GI* (1956³) 133. According to ancient custom, chariots and weapons taken as booty are burned (Josh. 11:6, 9; Isa. 9:4; Hos. 2:20; Exod. 39:9f.). We should inquire to what extent the tradition of holy war (G. von Rad, *Der Heilige Krieg im alten Israel,* ATANT 20 [1951]) and the conceptions of an eternal kingdom of peace (Isa. 2:4; 11:6ff.; W. Eichrodt, *Die Hoffnung des ewigen Friedens im alten Israel,* 1920; J. J. Stamm and H. Bietenhard, *Der Weltfriede im Lichte der Bibel* [1959], 47ff.) entered into the statements of v. 9.

Verse 10 could be declared an "oracle of salvation." Yahweh himself speaks and calls on the hostile forces to stop their revolt and recognize Yahweh. It is peculiar that only in this passage in the OT is a "strict formula of recognition" with אנכי used (W. Zimmerli, *Erkenntnis Gottes nach dem Buche Ezechiel,* ATANT [1954], 24 A. 35). On the meaning of the "formula of recognition" and on the homogeneity of recognition and deeds of Yahweh, cf. W. Zimmerli, 40.

As the עליון (v. 4), Yahweh is the "exalted One" over nations and lands (cf. Isa. 57:15).

Purpose and Thrust

The certainty of the community singing in Psalm 46 is based on Yahweh, on the God of Israel who has proved himself in troubles. Emphatically the refrain again and again stresses the fact that the helpful presence of Yahweh forms that fortress which is untouchable and invincible even in the great catastrophes of nature and history. In a world under incalculable threats this protective and healing power of Yahweh becomes manifest in the city of God, Jerusalem. But only to the degree that Yahweh is in the midst of this city (v. 15) does it prove to be an indestructible refuge. The *certitudo* of the trusting congregation is therefore based on the majestic person of God. If the look slips away from Yahweh, immediately a dangerous *securitas* (Luther) that boasts of this-worldly spheres of power creeps in. The *certitudo* says, "Yahweh Sebaoth is with us, the God of Jacob is a fortress for us"; the *securitas* on the other hand calls out, as if with a magic word: "The temple of Yahweh! The temple of Yahweh! The temple of Yahweh!" (Jer. 7:4).

The frequently expressed opinion that Psalm 46 harbors the danger of providing a haven for hardened security is not true. Also in its central part, which glorifies the city of God, we read expressly, "Yahweh is in the midst of her; therefore she will not be shaken." One gets the impression that the psalmsinger is actually passionately concerned about speaking only of Yahweh in reference to the glory and invincibility of the city of God and about exalting his power. Here the community will be able to learn that not "the church" is the indestructible fortress on earth but only the church in which God himself is present. And through this presence of God and rule of God a new understanding of life in the world of nations and of wars will be opened up.

Psalm 47

Exultation over Yahweh's
Triumphant Ascension

Literature

O. Eissfeldt, "Jahwe als König," *ZAW* 46 (1928). K. H. Ratschow, "Epikrise zum Psalm 47," *ZAW* 53 (1935) 171-180. M. Burrows, "כי in Ps 47,3.8a.10c," *ZAW* 55 (1937) 176. J. Muilenburg, "Psalm 47," *JBL* 63 (1944) 235-256. H.-J. Kraus, *Die Königsherrschaft Gottes im Alten Testament*, BHT 13 (1951). A Caquot, "Le Psaume 47 et la royauté de Yahwé, *RHPR* 39 (1959) 311-337. H.-J. Kraus, *Worship in Israel* (1966) 205ff. J. Morgenstern, "The Cultic Setting of the 'Inthronement Psalms,' " *HUCA* 35 (1964) 1-42. Y. Kil, "כל העמים תקעו כף (Ps 47)," *Ma'yānōt* 9 (Jerusalem 1968) 223-237.

Text

To the choirmaster. Of the Korahites. A psalm.
47:1 All you peoples, clap your hands,
shout to 'Yahweh'[a] with exultation!
2 For Yahweh, the Most High, is terrible,
a great king over the whole earth.
3 Peoples he subdued[b] under us,
and nations (he laid) under our feet.
4 He chose[c] our inheritance for us—
the pride of Jacob, whom he loves. —*Selah.*
5 'Yahweh'[d] went up with a shout of exultation,
Yahweh at the sound of the trumpet.
6 Sing to 'our God,'[e] sing!
Sing to our king, sing!
7 For the king of the whole earth is 'Yahweh,'[f]
—sing an art song!
8 'Yahweh'[g] has become king over the peoples,
'Yahweh'[h] sits on his holy throne.
9 The nobles of the nations are assembled
'with'[i] the people of the God of Abraham.
For 'to Yahweh'[j] belong the shields of the earth;
highly exalted is he.

1a In the Elohistically edited part of the Psalter יהוה is to be inserted as the original reading.

3b For the form ידבר, cf. Ps. 18:47 (KBL 199).

4c Most commentators prefer to avoid the curious phrase יבחר־לנו את־נחלתנו by means of the correction יַרְחֵב instead of יִבְחַר. But we could stay with the MT (see below).

5d Cf. note **a**.

6e Following Gk and parallel to למלכנו, we should read לֵאלֹהֵינוּ.

7f Cf. note **a**.

8g The insertion of יהוה instead of אלהים seems likely for the reasons presented in note **a**. However, we do need to take note of Isa. 52:7.

h Cf. note **a**.

9i Gk: μετὰ τοῦ θεοῦ (also cf. S). Thus we could assume haplography and correct to עִם עַם.

j Cf. note **a**.

Form

In Psalm 47 the double triple meter appears in vv. 3-6, 9. In the meter 3 + 4 we are to read vv. 1, 2, 8. And two verses are found to be in the meter 3 + 2: vv. 7, 9 (second full verse).

Psalm 47 belongs to the form group, songs of praise. See above, Intro. §6, 1. In its basic structure the psalm is to be assigned to the imperative hymns. Cf. F. Crüsemann, *Studien zur Formgeschichte von Hymnus und Danklied in Israel,* WMANT 32 (1969) 79 A. 3. The peculiarity of this song of praise, or hymn, lies in the fact that a central theme is determinative and provides occasion for a tighter arrangement. The psalm glorifies Yahweh's rule as king. But since a group of such hymns can be found in the Psalter, an obvious suggestion is to designate these songs that praise the kingship of God as "hymns to Yahweh the king." Psalms belonging to such a thematic group among the songs of praise are Psalms 93; 96; 97; 98; 99. See above, Intro. §6, 1b.

The structure of Psalm 47 is easily noted: The hymnic beginning in v. 1 imperatively calls for exultation. There follows—introduced by the כי characteristic of songs of praise—the main event, in which the reasons for the glorification of Yahweh as God and king are mentioned (vv. 2-5). A renewed—imperative—call for praise then turns up in v. 6. And again, introduced by כי, a second corpus of reasons (vv. 7-9) follows. Cf. H. Gunkel and J. Begrich, *EinlPs* 33ff.

Setting

The much discussed principal question is, At what occasion were the "hymns to Yahweh the king" intoned? Already Calvin in his commentary on the Psalms recognized that it is evident "from the whole context" that Psalm 47 was "intended for the solemn assemblies." There can be no doubt that a cultic situation is at the root of the song of praise. But which situation is meant? This question should first be answered in the context of the other "hymns to Yahweh the king," especially in reference to Pss. 95:6; 96:9; 99:5; 100:4. After the cultic community made its entry (Pss. 95:6; 100:40) into the sanctuary (of Jerusalem), a great prostration before the ark, the throne of Yahweh (Ps. 99:1, 5) took place. At this point the hymns in praise of Yahweh were sung. The God of Israel is celebrated as the king of the world (see above, Intro. §10, 1). But in this connection the question arises, What cultic act preceded the prostration in the sanctuary? Ever since the studies of P. Volz (*Das Neujahrsfest Jahwes* [1912]) and S. Mowinckel (*PsStud* II), there is in the explanation of the "hymns to Yahweh the king" a reference to the ceremony of an enthronement of Yahweh. But on the problem whether there was an enthronement festival in Israel, see above, Intro. §10, 1. On the cultic event of the entrance of the ark, cf. the comment on Psalm 132. If in these cited passages the acceptance of an enthronement festival of Yahweh is questioned, we should point out that in Psalm 47 individual statements permit us to think of the course of a cultic enthronement: vv. 5, 8. The hymn looks back to the event of Yahweh's going up (עלה in v. 5), proclaims the enthronement as completed (מלך in v. 8a), and sees the God-king now sitting on the throne (ישב in v. 8b). In view of explanations of the cultic act of the bringing up of the ark as a cultic repetition and contemporizing of events of the time of David (election of Zion, election of the dynasty of David) as presented in connection with Psalm 132, we must now in connection with Psalm 47 consider the following: (1) It could be that in pre-Israelite Jerusalem an enthronement festival of the royal divinity was celebrated. This festival and its sacral traditions and conceptual forms would then later have had some effect on the worship of Israel. (2) It could be that, in the course of the cultic history of Jerusalem, Assyrian or Babylonian influences brought the idea and use of an enthronement of the divinity to Jerusalem. (3) In Psalm 47 we could have a pictorial illustration that was taken from the model of an enthronement of an earthly king. (4) A possible dependence of Psalm 47 on Deutero-Isaiah (cf. Isa. 52:7) should also be considered (W. Baudissin, *KYRIOS* III [1929], 235f.; H.-J. Kraus, *Die Königsherrschaft Gottes im Alten Testament,* 106ff.; idem, *Worship in Israel* [1966], 204f; also see above, Intro.§10, 1).

In the interpretation of Psalm 47, however, we must in any case begin with the fact that the hymnic glorification was presented before the God-king Yahweh, who was invisibly enthroned above the ark. It would be a mistake to deduce a cultic ritual from Psalm 47 that presumably at one time accompanied a dramatic enthronement procedure. Thus, e.g., K. H. Ratschow calls Psalm 47 a "ritual sampler" (*ZAW* 53, 180), and M. Burrows wants to recognize the triple occurrence of the כי, which surely is a standing element of style in the hymn, as a sign of a kind of producer's direction for the ritual: "Perhaps the כי of these verses was not originally the conjunction but an abbreviature: either כ for כְּהֵנִים or כי for כֹהֲנֵי יהוה" (*ZA W* 55, 176). Over against that, however, we must begin with the fact that Psalm 47 is a complete unit in itself—a hymn to King Yahweh enthroned in the sanctuary.

Commentary

[Title] On למנצח, see above, Intro. §4, No. 17. On לבני־קרח, cf. the comment on Psalm 42, title. On מזמור, see above, Intro. §4, No. 2.

[47:1] The hymnic introit in v. 1 calls on the nations to give homage to King Yahweh with enthusiasm and joy. The conceptions that are connected with the kingship of Yahweh are universal (see above, Intro. §10, 1). Over all the world (v. 2), over all nations is Yahweh Lord and king. Clapping of hands is an expression of enthusiastic joy (Ps. 98:8; 2 Kings 11:12). On הריע, cf. Ps. 98:4, 6; Zeph. 3:14; Zech. 9:9; and תרועה in Ps. 47:5. All nations are to join in Israel's laudatory glorification of Yahweh (cf. the comment on v. 9).

[47:2-5] In the principal section introduced by כי the great deeds of Yahweh are praised. They provide reasons for worldwide praise of God. Yahweh is the עליון

(v. 2). The title מלך implies the conception of a monarchical culmination of the pantheon of the gods in which the God-king appears as the "Most High" (see above, Intro. §10, 1). נורא = "frightful," "fear-inspiring" is Yahweh in his powerful majesty (Deut. 7:21; Dan. 9:4; Neh. 1:5; and often). Resistance to him is impossible. As the great king (מלך גדול) Yahweh rules the whole earth (Pss. 24:1; 95:4f.; 97:5). As the Creator, the עליון is ruler of the world: אדון כל־הארץ (Ps. 97:5). All lands are filled with the כבוד of the God-king (Ps. 8:1; Isa. 6:3).

A first proof of Yahweh's power over against foreign nations is seen by the hymn in the event that laid the foundation of Israel, the victory over those population groups which were resident in Canaan before the immigration of the people of God. Beyond that, the thought probably included the subjugation of foreign nations by David. In any case, the singer knows how to show from the history of Israel that Yahweh demonstrated his rule over the עמים in great victories. The nations were subdued under the feet of Israel. In the ancient Near East it was customary for the victor to place his foot on the neck of him who was subdued (Josh. 10:24; Ps. 110:2; also cf. Egyptian and Babylonian depictions).

נחלה in v. 4 (in the parallelism: גאון יעקב) is very likely the land of Israel (cf. Isa. 58:14), the transfer of which to the people of God was an act of Yahweh's rule over all the powers that possessed this area (Deut. 4:38). The עליון assigns to the nations the areas of their homes and their migrations (Deut. 32:8ff.). For Israel he has chosen the "inherited land," the "pride of Jacob."

By means of סלה (cf. Intro. §4, No. 13), v. 5 in the main section of the psalm is separated from the "reason" for the praise, introduced by כי. For while vv. 2-4 point out the world rule of Yahweh based on powerful historical deeds, v. 5 refers to the cultic act which took place immediately before the homage now being celebrated. In other words, vv. 2-4 are universally historical, whereas v. 5 is cultically oriented. In עלה the procession of the ark must surely be described (cf. the comment on Psalm 132). This cultic act takes place to the accompaniment of "shouts of exultation" (on תרועה, cf. P. Humbert, *TEROU'A, Analyse d'un rite biblique* [1946]). The sound of trumpets accompanies the ascent: cf. H. Seidel, "Horn und Trompete im alten Israel unter Berücksichtigung der 'Kriegsrolle' von Qumran," *Wissenschaftliche Zeitschrift der Karl-Marx-Universität Leipzig* (1956/57) 589-599.

Concerning v. 5 we should consider two questions that have to do with (1) the ascent of Yahweh, (2) the blowing of the שופר.

(1) If we consider the bringing up of the ark of Yahweh as described in Psalm 132 and 1 Samuel 6 with reference to its meaning and its purpose, we see that what is involved is a cultic repetition of an occurrence from the time of David that has to do with the election of Zion. The ancient Israelite shrine of the ark of Yahweh Sebaoth takes up its dwelling in the sanctuary of Jerusalem. The dark Holy of Holies of the temple is the goal of the cultic act. Here the God-king Yahweh "dwells" (1 Kings 8:12, 13) and "is enthroned" over the cherubim throne (Ps. 99:1ff.). The temple is therefore the goal of the procession. But we could legitimately ask whether this proposed method of approach is appropriate. The temple is the earthly counterpart of the heavenly sanctuary. Where the temple is, heaven and earth come together (see above, Intro. §10, 2). Therefore we would have to consider that the procession to Zion is at the same time an ascent to the heights of heaven. The divine מלך and עליון is "king of heaven" (cf. the comment on Ps. 29:9f.); before him not only the portals of the sanctuary but also the "gates of heaven" open (cf. the comment on Ps. 24:7ff.). On עלה in the sense "to ascend (to heaven)": Gen. 17:22; 35:13; Judg. 13:20.

(2) The sound of the trumpet (שופר) and the תרועה accompanied not only the

ascent of the God-king but also the enthronement of the human king (2 Sam. 15:10; 2 Kings 9:13). This parallel is worth noting. Even more important have the connections between blowing the שׁופר in Psalm 47 and the trumpet or shouts of New Year's Day been considered (cf. Num. 29:1; Ps. 81:4). This festival practice continued all the way to the Mishnah. In it the so-called *Shofaroth* and *Malkiyoth* (cf. S. Mowinckel, *PsStud* II 42f.) are valid as traditional lections for the Jewish New Year festival. And so the conclusion is drawn that Psalm 47 belongs to the "Israelite New Year festival." This explanation could be right if the first festival day of the Feast of Tabernacles was considered New Year's Day also in preexilic times. That the ascent of the ark of Yahweh was celebrated on the first day of the Feast of Tabernacles in Jerusalem is easy to prove (cf. the comment on Psalm 132). On the problems of the calendar of festivals, cf. E. Kutsch, "Das Herbstfest in Israel," diss., Mainz (1955).

[47:6-8] In v. 6 a new hymnic introduction is encountered. There is a summons to sing and play before the God-king. This appeal is very likely addressed to the temple choirs and musicians. With the suffix of the first person plural there is emphatic indication that the God of Israel is the king of the world. He is מלך כל הארץ (cf. v. 2 and also Ps. 97:5). For that reason he deserves to have a משׂכיל sung (see above, Intro. §4, No. 5).

While the section vv. 2-5 brings out especially the praiseworthy universally historic facts of the kingship of Yahweh and only in v. 5 refers to the cultic act, the second part of the psalm (vv. 6-9) only in v. 7 indicates the universal importance of Yahweh's kingship (but also cf. v. 9b) and more pronouncedly refers to the cultic events (vv. 8f.). Through Yahweh's ascent into the temple he has become the king of the nations. מלך יהוה (in the word order of the verbal sentence) must be translated, "Yahweh has become king!" A proclamation of the enthronement that is close to the event is here present (cf. the comment on Psalm 24). On the syntactical problems, cf. L. Köhler, "*Jahwä mālāk*," *VT* 3(1953) 188f.; J. Ridderbos, "JAHWÄH MALAK," *VT* 4 (1954) 87-89; D. Michel, "Studien zu den sogenannten Thronbesteigungspsalmen," *VT* 5 (1956) 40-68. The subject standing first in the parallel formulation יהוה ישׁב על־כסא קדשׁו indicates a sentence describing a state or condition. Yahweh now sits on his holy throne. The "seat of the throne of Yahweh" is the ark (cf. Jer. 3:16f.; Ps. 99:1; M. Dibelius, *Die Lade Jahwes* [1906]). The song of praise is addressed to יהוה צבאות, the God who is present above the ancient Israelite ark-shrine (see above, Intro. §10, 1, and the discussions on Ps. 24:7ff.).

The ancient Near Eastern cultic traditions for the entrance and the glorification of the God-king will have to be considered as a parallel document. Already very early texts discovered in Mesopotamia were exploited for the enthronement of the royal divinity and enlisted for the interpretation of the OT (P. Volz, *Das Neujahrsfest Jahwes* [1912]; H. Zimmern, *Das babylonische Neujahrsfest*, AO 25 [1926]; S. Mowinckel, *PsStud* II). Especially the Marduk hymns received much attention. The divinity enters the temple in procession, is solemnly enthroned, and receives the homage of the festival congregation. In a song of Nabonidus addressed to Shamash we read: "Shamash, great and mighty Lord, when you make your entrance in Ebab-bara, the dwelling in which you find rest, may the gates, the entrances, the shrines, and the pedestals be glad before you, like 'flowers' exult in your presence! When you take your place in your lordly room on the throne of your judgment seat, may the gods of your city and your temple appease your disposition, and may the great gods bring joy to your heart!" (A. Falkenstein and W. von Soden, *Sumerische und akkadische Hymnen und Gebete* [1953], 288). For the Egyptian cultic acts, cf. K. Sethe, *Amun und die acht Urgötter von Hermopolis*, Abh. d. preuss. Akad. d. Wiss., phil.-hist. Kl. (1929); H. Kees, *Der Götterglaube im alten Ägypten*

(1941). It is inappropriate to subject these cultic events to a uniform ancient Near Eastern pattern (cf. H. Frankfort, *Kingship and the Gods* [1948]; C. J. Gadd, *Ideas of Divine Rule in the Ancient East* [1948]). On account of the Ras Shamra discoveries, the Babylonian parallels have receded somewhat into the background—in favor of the Syrian-Canaanite expression of the God-king cults that has become known from ancient Ugaritic sources.

[47:9] Also v. 9 especially (in the first part of the verse) calls attention to realities of the cultus: together with the "people of the God of Abraham," the נדיבי עמים are assembled to pay homage to Yahweh. נדיב is the powerful, influential prince (Pss. 83:12; 107:40; 118:9; 146:3). One may certainly imagine that at the great annual festivals in Jerusalem there were emissaries of foreign nations present. The psalmsinger sees this as a sign for a realization of the universal rule of God (cf. vv.2ff.). We could ask whether with the mention of the אלהי אברהם the universalism of Jerusalem's מלך-tradition has reference to the Abrahamic promise in Gen. 12:1ff.; 22:18.

While a separating סלה stands between the universal-historical statements in vv. 2-4 and the cultic reference in v. 5, a universally directed statement begins in v. 9b after an expressly cultic reference (vv. 8f.) with a freshly inserted כי (cf. כי in vv. 2 and 7). In a valid statement we are told that "the shields of the earth" belong to the high and uplifted God. מגני־ארץ is in the OT a term in the singular number, one that obviously is to be understood as synonymous with נדיבי עמים. This relation is clear from Pss. 89:18 and 84:9, for in Ps. 89:18 מגן is parallel to מלך, and in Ps. 84:9 the parallelism משיח—מגן is to be noted. The "shields of the earth" are therefore the kings of the nations. And so a description in v. 9 at first taken from the cultus (v. 9a) is enclosed in a foundational statement in v. 9b.

Purpose and Thrust

The hymn to Yahweh the king, Psalm 47, wants to enlist all nations for the event and fact of Yahweh's elevation to be the universal world-king and Most High God (עליון). All foreign powers are to join in singing the song of praise of the assembled congregation of Israel. The motive for this universal obeisance and glorification is given in the fact that in the course of history Yahweh has already proved to be the sovereign Lord in the world of nations. By overcoming nations and by giving to Israel room for existence among the nations Yahweh has given proof of his historical power. Also the fact that emissaries in high places among foreign nations are present in the worship of Israel interprets the wide-ranging power of the hymn as a realization of the world dominion of God.

In the NT the conceptions of Psalm 47 are taken over by the Revelation of John for the purpose of illustrating the exaltation and world dominion of God and his Christ (Rev. 4:2, 9; 5:1f.; 6:16; 7:10, 17; 19:4; 21:5). The kerygma of the hymn to Yahweh the king can rightfully be transferred typologically by the church to the ascension of Christ into heaven. For as the subject in the OT is that the אלהי אברהם (v. 9), coming from the hiddenness of the beginning of election, is praised as the King of the world and Lord of the nations, so the homage of the risen and exalted one applies to Jesus of Nazareth who has come in lowliness; to him is given all power in heaven and on earth (Matt. 28:18).

Psalm 48

The Glory of the City of God

Literature

J. Morgenstern, "Psalm 48," *HUCA* 16 (1941) 1-95. J. A. Bewer, "Note on Psalm 48,8." H. Schmid, "Jahwe und die Kulttraditionen von Jerusalem," *ZAW* 68 (1955) 168ff. E. Rohland, "Die Bedeutung der Erwählungstraditionen Israels für die Eschatologie der alttestamentlichen Propheten," diss., Heidelberg (1956) 131ff. A. Deissler, "Der anthologische Charakter des Ps 48 (47)," *Sacra Pagina 1 = BEThL* 12 (1959). P. Häring, "Gross ist der Herr in unserer Gottesstadt," *Beuron* 36 (1960) 94-104. L. Krinetzki, "Zur Poetik und Exegese von Ps 48," *BZ* 4 (1960) 70-97. M. Palmer, "The Cardinal Points in Psalm 48," *Bibl* 46 (1965) 357-358. S. L. Kelly, "The Zion-Victory Songs: Ps 46; 48 and 76," diss., Vanderbilt (1968). O. H. Steck, *Friedensvorstellungen im alten Jerusalem*, TheolStud 111 (1972). A Robinson, "Zion and *Ṣāphōn* in Psalm XLVIII, 3," *VT* 24 (1974) 118-123.

Text

A song. A psalm of the Korahites.
48:1 Great is Yahweh
and greatly to be praised
in the city of our God.[a]
His holy mountain,[b]
2 splendidly rising,
is the delight of the whole world;
Mount Zion, far to the north,
the city of the great king.
3 'Yahweh'[c] in its towers
shows himself as a protection.
4 For behold, kings[d] came together,
kept approaching[e] together.
5 They looked up—immediately they became numb,
frightened, confused.[f]
6 Trembling seized them there,[g]
fear like that of a woman about to give birth;

471

7 'as'[h] when the east wind shatters
   the ships of Tarshish.
8 As we have heard it,
   so we have seen it
   ' '[i] in the city of our God:
   'Yahweh'[j] has firmly founded it forever.—*Selah*.
9 We think about your mercy, 'O Yahweh,'[j]
   in your temple.
10 Like your name, 'O Yahweh,'[j]
   so your glory (extends)
   'to'[k] the ends of the earth:
   with help is your right hand filled!
11 Mount Zion rejoices,
   the daughters of Judah shout for joy
.   about your judgments.
12 Walk around Zion, go about her!
   Count her towers!
13 Turn your thoughts to 'her'[l] rampart,
   examine [?] her citadels,
   so that you may tell
   the coming generation
14 that 'Yahweh'[m] is this:
   Our God forever and eternally.
   He will lead us.
   (*'al mūt*)[n]

1a Is the MT original? Or would we have to read גְּדוֹלָה וּמְהֻלָּלָה and עִיר (without בְּ) (BHK³)? Contextual considerations suggest that we follow the MT.

2b The conclusion of the verse in the MT is formal and in terms of content, not appropriate. הַר־קָדְשׁוֹ is to be taken with v. 2aαβ.

3c In the Elohistically revised part of the Psalter יהוה is to be inserted as the original reading.

4d Gk^Mss read מַלְכֵי הָאָרֶץ and interpret the MT in the sense of Ps. 2:2. The MT is to be preferred.

e With a reference to Gen. 14:3, the correction חָבְרוּ is often recommended, but the MT reading is certainly possible (Judg. 11:29; 2 Kings 8:21).

5f Although the verb is missing in S, 4 Mss read נִפְחֲזוּ.

6g שָׁם is missing in σ′, S.

7h It is in keeping with the context and correct to read כְּרוּחַ with a number of manuscripts.

8i בְּעִיר־יְהוָה צְבָאוֹת is probably to be taken as an explanatory gloss or variant reading for בְּעִיר אֱלֹהֵינוּ and is to be eliminated on formal and contextual grounds.

j Cf. note **c**.

10k In keeping with the context, we ought to read עַד (S) or אֶל instead of עַל.

13l With a few Mss and Gk we should probably read לְחֵילָהּ.

14m Cf. note **c**.

n עַל־מוּת at the end of v. 14 can hardly be explained. Is this a cultic-liturgical note? Or is it a fragment of the title of Psalm 49? Are we to follow a few Mss and read עֲלָמוֹת as in Ps. 49, title? Gk^A has εἰς τοὺς αἰῶνας (עוֹלָמוֹת); T has עֲלָמוּת; F. Nötscher literally: "about dying." See other conceptions under "Commentary."

Form

The metrical circumstances of Psalm 48 cannot be clarified according to the usual measures in vv. 1-2 and 8ff. But initially we should establish the fact that the meter 3 + 2 is determinative in vv. 2aγ/2b, 3-7, 9, 12, 13, 14aβ/14b. A three-member verse organization in the meter 2 + 2 + 2 is to be noted in vv.

1, 2, 8, 10, 13/14; 2 + 3 + 2 in v. 11. In vv. 8 and 10 it looks as if a conscious effort was made to achieve an effect, in that the 2 + 2 + 2 meter is followed by a triple meter:

8:	10:
כאשר שמענו	כשמך יהוה
כן ראינו	כן תהלתך
בעיר אלהינו	על־קצוי־ארץ
יהוה יכוננה עד־עולם	צדק מלאה ימינך

The structure of the song is easily analyzed. The laudatory glorification of the city of God (vv. 1-3) is followed by a description of an attack of the nations and their defeat. Verses 8-11 deal with the astonished acknowledgment of the power of Yahweh on Zion and in the world, while vv. 12-14 are to be understood as an invitation to join a procession.

Increasing prominence is being given to the question whether Psalm 48 should be understood as a song organized by strophes. Here M. Palmer supports the conception of L. Krinetzki that Psalm 48 is a 4-strophe poem in which each strophe refers to one of the four points of the compass: north, v. 2; east, v. 7; south, v. 10; west, v. 13. With this conjecture of "theological geography," Jerusalem is indicated as the "navel of the world" (M. Palmer, *Bibl* 46 [1965], 357ff.). Still the reconstruction of a "theological geography" will have to be thought of as speculative and the assumption of strophic organization as less than likely. For the north turns up in connection with a very definite statement about Zion (cf. A. Robinson, *VT* 24 [1974], 118ff.), the east as the "east wind" (v. 7), the south and the west not at all in so many words. On strophic organization, see above, Intro. §5, 3.

In the form-critical analysis of Psalm 48 we encounter difficulties similar to those in Psalm 46. H. Gunkel considered Psalm 48 a hymn. And yet, after all that was said about Psalm 46 under "Form," we have to say that the psalm belongs to the thematic form group, songs of Zion. See above, Intro. §6, 4. For elaboration on the literary form, cf. Jörg Jeremias, "Lade und Zion: Probleme biblischer Theologie," *G. von Rad zum 70. Geburtstag* (1971) 183ff. Cf. the comments on Psalm 46.

Setting

Since vv. 4-7 deal with an attack against the city of God and with the repelling of this attack, therefore the question about the situation of the psalm presupposed in these verses arises again and again. While older commentaries thought of the wondrous rescues of Jerusalem, thus, among others, of the events of the year 701 B.C., H. Gunkel tried to understand Psalm 48 as "eschatological." In his estimation, the descriptions of the final attack of the nations were prophetic and visionary. Subsequently, however, the cultic traditions in Psalm 48 have been recognized more distinctly (cf. the excursus on Psalm 46, and above, Intro. §10, 2). Not visions of the future but traditional glorifications of the city of God, its impregnability and its heavenly splendor are reflected in the conceptions of the hymnically expressed song of Zion. Age-old traditions have been applied to Jerusalem (very likely already in pre-Israelite times). There can be no doubt that mythical elements are involved.

But how were these old cultic traditions adopted and visualized by Israel? S. Mowinckel and H. Schmidt think of dramatic presentations which were staged in connection with the "festival of the enthronement of Yahweh."

In the words הנה (v. 4) and ראיני (v. 8) H. Schmidt thinks he sees definite references to a play. A parallel is pointed out in the symbolic shooting of an arrow in the cultus of Egypt. The supposition of a mythical and dramatic course of the festival of the enthronement of Yahweh, however, is very problematical (see above, Intro. §10, 1). Psalm 48 should probably be associated with the festival act of prostration before the world-king Yahweh (cf. Pss. 95:6; 99:5; 100:4; cf. the comment on Psalm 24). From v. 9 this "Sitz im Leben" emerges clearly: בקרב היכלך = "inside the temple" Yahweh is honored as a mighty king, and his "royal city" (v. 2) is glorified. Instructive too in this connection is the verb דמינו in v. 9. The cultic community in the "inner temple" recalls the "grace of Yahweh" in comparisons, in parabolic images. The important statements are made about the function of the old (mythical) cultic transmissions: they illuminate the "grace of Yahweh." The traditional glorifications and descriptions serve the purpose of demonstrating that זה יהוה = "this is Yahweh" or "so is Yahweh" (v. 14). Thus the cultic traditions enter the service of the hymn and its kerygma.

From vv. 12ff., the invitation to walk about the city of God, we learn that a procession has joined in the prostration before the God present on Zion. In view of this invitation, we might even conclude that the song of Zion, Psalm 48, had its "Sitz im Leben" immediately before this procession. This introduced the solemn "instruction in viewing" which was to be received in the walk around the city of God.

Psalm 48 probably is to be dated in preexilic times. For the opposing view, see G. Wanke, *Die Zionstheologie der Korachiten in ihrem traditionsge-schichtlichen Zusammenhang*, BZAW 97 (1966); see above, Intro. §10, 2; and H. M. Lutz, *Jahwe, Jerusalem und die Völker*, WMANT 27 (1968) 213ff.

Commentary

[Title] On שיר, see above, Intro. §4, No. 1. On מזמור, Intro. §4, No. 2. On לבני־קרח, cf. the comment on Ps. 42, title.

[48:1-3] These verses deal with the beauty and praiseworthiness of the city of God on Mount Zion. Here Yahweh reveals himself as גדול (cf. Pss. 96:4; 99:2; 145:3; or מלך גדול in Ps. 47:2). With מהלל מאד the hymnic tendency of the song is begun. עיר אלהינו (cf. also v. 8) seems to be an inherited ancient designation of the "city of God." The city of Yahweh is situated on Zion, the "holy hill" (cf. Ps. 2:6). In v. 2, four assertions are made concerning the holy mountain and the city of God located there: (1) The hill is יפה נוף = "rising beautifully"; on יפה, cf. Ps. 50:2 (מכלל־יפי) and Lam. 2:15 (כלילת יפי); the hill of God is praised as a place of perfect beauty. (2) The "holy hill" has a location that blesses the whole world and is central; it is משוש כל־הארץ (cf. Lam. 2:15), and its brightness makes the earth rejoice; paradisaical conceptions are evoked here. (3) Zion is described as a hill ירכתי צפון (cf. the excursus on Psalm 46). (4) Zion is the city of מלך רב; Yahweh is the "great king," the "world ruler" (cf. מלך גדול in Pss. 47:2; 95:3 and the corresponding title of the great kings in Akkadian: *šarru rabû*).

All the assertions place Zion in the light of universal glorification. In the city of God the king of the entire world rules (see above, Intro. §10,1). But it is not the city of God as such, with its this-worldly might, that possesses the radiance of transcendent inaccessibility. Yahweh is the one that here proves to be the protection. He is the one who gives to the city of God its invincibility (cf. Ps. 46:5, 7). ארמון is the citadel (KBL 88). On נודע as a term for God's self-revelation, cf. Pss. 9:16; 76:1; Exod. 6:3; Ezek. 20:5, 9; Isa. 19:21. On משגב, cf. Ps. 46:7, 11. With assertion No. 4, preparation for the section in vv. 4-7, which reports the attack on the city of God, is now prepared for.

[48:4-7] כי־הנה in v. 4 now introduces a parabolic illustration. Ancient cultic traditions (cf. the excursus on Psalm 46) are taken up and promoted to the level of a visionary demonstration. Here kings conspire and march up to the city of God. Manuscripts of the LXX correctly interpret מלכים in remembrance of the parallel passage in Ps. 2:2: βασιλεῖς τῆς γῆς = "kings of the earth." The attack of the nations led by "the kings of the earth" is the historical way in which chaos surges up against the central bulwark, the seat of the Creator and world ruler. What is involved here is a historicizing variant to the primordial battle of chaos in creation myths (cf. H. Gunkel, *Schöpfung und Chaos in Urzeit und Endzeit* [1895]). But the attacking forces of the enemy "look up"—and immediately they become numb with fright and confusion (v. 5). But what do they look up at? Why do they become numb with fright? In Ps. 77:16 it is the waters of chaos that tremble because they get to see Yahweh. That will probably also be the reason for the paralyzing fright of the nations and their kings: they behold the מלך רב who appears in his כבוד before the enemies (Isa. 66:18) and as "the lofty one" (Ps. 46:10) is about to break up (Ps. 46:9) the levy of the forces of chaos. With this unusually sudden turn of events compare Isa. 29:8. The fear created by "God's fright" paralyzes and confuses the enemy (Ps. 46:6, 8; 1 Sam. 14:15; Isa. 8:9; 17:13; 29:5; 33:3). For a comparison of this trembling fear with birthpains (v. 6), cf. Isa. 13:8; 21:3; Jer. 4:31; 6:24.

The picture in v. 7 of the ships of Tarshish smashed by the "east wind" is unusual. The parable belongs to the Phoenician-Syrian area and would be suitable for Mount צפון there (*Jebel el 'Aqra*), for the "ships of Tarshish" are the splendidly equipped (Phoenician) transmarine ships that sailed all the way to Tartessus in Spain (Jonah 1:3). In addition, it seems "as if the 'east wind' is nothing short of the technical term for every heavy wind that packs destructive force," for actually the heaviest storms in the Syrian-Canaanite area come from the west (G. Dalman, *AuS* I 109). Very likely רוח קדים is an element of the myth (Isa. 27:8; Jer. 18:17; Ezek. 27:26; Job 27:21).

[48:8-11] We could assume that the description in vv. 4-7, taken over from cultic tradition, was graphically presented to the assembled congregation by a single speaker. In that case vv. 8-11 would be a hymnic response, a confirming statement by the cultic community. The assertion in v. 8 has the force of emphatically corroborating the reliability of God's deed illustrated in the mythical archetypal pictures: the description in vv. 4-7 (כאשר שמענו) is confirmed by experience (כן ראינו). Yahweh has proved in the city of God that he is the invincible king (on this, cf. נמצא מאד in Ps. 46:1). The thought here is, even if not of specific events, then in any case certainly of historical events which confirm the effects of a "primordial occurrence." The effectively accented sentence יהוה יכוננה עד־עולם is a hymnic confession (similar to the refrain in Ps. 46:5). Again we should note: Yahweh himself provides the city of God with its invincible might. Verse 9 speaks of the completion of the cultic act which is to be presupposed as the "Sitz im Leben" for the glorification of

Yahweh and his city. The community "compares," it illustrates Yahweh's חסד. The verb דמה provides valuable information about the manner in which old cultic traditions of a mythical character were adopted in Israel. We could speak of paradigmatical demonstrations in which the glorification of Yahweh and his holy city was undertaken. The concentration there is entirely on the שם of Yahweh (v. 10). Yahweh, the God of Israel, is God Most High (עליון in Ps. 46:4) and מלך רב (v. 2) over all the world. His name and fame extend to the ends of the earth. On the synonymous use of שם and תהלה, cf. O. Grether, *Name und Wort Gottes im Alten Testament*, BZAW 64 (1934) 52. And so Yahweh appears before the world: his right hand is filled with צדק. And צדק here has the meaning "bestowal of salvation" (cf. G. von Rad, *OT Theol*, 1 373). But, according to Psalm 48, Yahweh bestows his power of salvation in beating down the chaos of the attacks of nations (vv. 3-7) and thereby creating a universal kingdom of peace (Isa. 2:2ff.). Mount Zion rejoices, and the "daughters of Judah" (the cities of the country, Num. 21:25; Josh. 17:16) shout for joy למען משפטיך (v. 11). משפטים are the annihilating deeds with which Yahweh defeats the hostile forces (cf. Psalm 97; above all, Ps. 97:8).

[48:12] This verse calls for a procession. Thus in connection with the glorification of the temple (v. 9) a solemn procession around the city of God must have taken place.

What was the significance of this solemn procession around the city of God? From Egypt we know that the walls of Memphis were circumnavigated with the *Sokar* boat. This was a matter of a procedure of the fertility cult (H. Kees, *Der Götterglaube im alten Ägypten* [1941], 95). But closer apparently is another parallel in the Egyptian cultus: at the *Sed* festival a procession round about the walls took place. By this procedure the temple area of the deity was consecrated (H. Kees, 168, 192, 296). An OT parallel to this ceremony of consecration could perhaps be found in Neh. 12:27ff. But such a cultic ceremony does not issue from Psalm 48. Rather, one gets the impression that the glory and invincibility of Zion are being celebrated when the towers and citadels "are examined." It could be that already in v. 8 with the verb ראינו reference is made to the procession and the act of becoming acquainted with the fortifications. We could also ask whether here an original magical procedure was reinterpreted by Israel. This act of magic might have had the purpose of fortifying the city, just as the march around the walls of Jericho (Joshua 6) was intended for the destruction of a fortified place (and was then also given a new interpretation in Israel). We can hardly think of a "procession of thanksgiving" (H. Gunkel).

[48:13-14] Counting the towers (v. 12), carefully studying the glacis (חיל, v. 13), and examining (?) the citadels (ארמון, cf. v. 3)—all this is to provide an indelible impression of the strength and protective power of the city of God. Succeeding generations are to hear about this (cf. Ps. 102:18). Yet all the glories of Zion point to Yahweh (cf. v. 3): זה יהוה (v. 14). The concluding verse then looks into the future and expresses the confidence that Yahweh will always remain the same. In his invincible power he will "lead" his people. With the verb נהג the local tradition of Jerusalem is transferred to the historical dimension of Israel. Yahweh will (like a shepherd) precede his people (Ps. 78:52; Deut. 4:27; Isa. 49:10; 63:14).

על־מות is best explained (if an explanation is possible at all) as a cropping of על־עלמות. And this cropped fragment would fit nicely to שיר in the heading: על־עלמות שיר

(cf. Ps. 46, title). Rather highly imaginative is the conception of A. R. Johnson, who construes a contrast between Yahweh, the "God of life," and *Mot,* the divinity of death which emerged especially in the nature mythology of Ras Shamra. Johnson translates:

> . . . Our God is forever and ever.
> May he lead us against "death"!

(A. R. Johnson, "The Role of the King in the Jerusalem Cultus," *The Labyrinth,* ed. Hooke, 92).

Purpose and Thrust

Inside the temple the OT community, by prostration and the glorification of Yahweh, emphasizes for itself the world power of its "great king" (v. 9). The place where Yahweh is present is called the "delight of the world." Yahweh's renown spreads from here to the ends of the earth. The forces of chaos in the arena of history that rise up against the "great king" are in numbing fright cut down at his appearance. The invincibility of the city of God rests alone on the fact that Yahweh is in her midst (v. 3; cf. the comment on Psalm 46, "Purpose and Thrust"). The protective power of God is proved and unchallenged. The NT community will try to understand Psalm 48 in view of Matt. 16:18. It will, however, have to keep strict watch that the sovereign majesty of Yahweh is not overshadowed by the immanent splendor of any "churchliness" that is present. Also consideration will have to be given to the fact that all bestowals of God's protection and salvation have universal significance. The "great king," who is present in the community of Israel and protects the city of God, at the central site of the earth guards creation against the incursion of chaos which is released in the form of the uprising of nations. His judgments are a guarantee for the salvation of the world. The joy over this universal protective and saving power is in Psalm 48 not eschatological but cultically present. The ultimate reality of the world is, as in a parable, visible to worshiping faith in a fully this-worldly way.

Concerning the Vanity
of Human Wealth

Literature

P. Volz, "Psalm 49," *ZAW* 55 (1937) 235-264. J. Lindblom, "Die 'Eschatologie' des 49. Psalms," *Horae Soederblomianae* I, 1 (1944) 21-27. Chr. Barth, *Die Errettung vom Tode in den individuellen Klage- und Dankliedern des Alten Testaments* (1947) 158-161. J. van der Ploeg, "Notes sur Psaume 49," *OTS* 13 (1963) 137-172. R. Pautrel, "La Mort est leur pasteur (sur le texte du Ps 49,14)," *RSR* 54 (1966) 531-536. E. Tromp, "Psalm 49: Armoede en rijkdom, leven en dood," *Ons Geestelijk Leven* 45 (1968/69) 239-251. G. von Rad, *Wisdom in Israel* (1972) 203ff. L. G. Perdue, "The Riddles of Psalm 49," *JBL* 93 (1974) 533-542.

Text

To the choirmaster. Of the Korahites. A psalm.
49:1 Hear this, all you nations,
    take it to heart, all inhabitants of the world,
  2 you simple people as well as you lords' sons,
    rich and poor alike!
  3 My mouth shall announce wisdom,
    the thinking of my heart is prudence.
  4 I incline[a] my ear to the word of wisdom,
    to the lyre I entrust my secret.
  5 Why must I be afraid in evil days,[b]
    when the wickedness of swindlers[c] surrounds me,
  6 who trust in their own riches
    and boast about their great wealth?
  7 'Yet'[d] no one can ever 'redeem himself'[e]
    or pay to God[f] a ransom, . . .
  8 [Too costly is the price of redemption of 'his'[g] soul;
    he must give it up forever!][h]
  9 . . . that he may live on forever,
    not see the pit.

10 Indeed, we see it: the wise die.
Together do fool and imbecile perish.
And they leave their riches[i] to others.

11 'Graves'[j] are their homes forever,
their dwelling place for all time.
They have called[k] lands their own.

12 But man in his splendor 'does not consider'[l]
that he is like cattle that is destroyed.[m]

13 This[n] is the lot of those who are full of confidence,
the 'fate'[o] of those who are pleased with their own speech (*Selah*).

14 Like a herd death shepherds them,
to the underworld 'they sink down'[p]
. . . . . .[q]

15 But 'Yahweh'[r] redeems my soul,
he rescues me from the power of the underworld![s]

16 Do not be afraid when a man becomes rich,
when he 'increases'[t] the splendor of his house.

17 For in death he takes none of that along,
his treasure does not go down with him.

18 Even though he may bless his soul while living
and 'praise it'[u] that 'it is well'[v]—

19 'he'[w] must still go to the generation of his fathers,
who do not see the light forever.

20 Man in his splendor does not consider
that he is like cattle that is destroyed.

4a MT begins with the conception that the teacher of wisdom receives the מָשָׁל in an act of inspiration. A correction (הַטּוּ אָזְנְכֶם, following Ps. 78:1) is hardly in place.

5b Corrections of the verse begin with presuppositions that alter the sense. אִירָא in v. 5a is confirmed by אַל־תִּירָא in v. 16a. For the meaning of the assertions, see below ("Commentary").

c Gk read עָקְבִי (probably in view of אִישׁ in v. 7 and אָדָם in vv. 12, 20). But we should follow the MT. For the meaning of עָקֵב, cf. Jer. 17:9.

7d MT: "A brother a man does not redeem" or "A brother does not redeem a man." Following 8 Mss, we should probably read אַךְ.

e By analogy we would have to read *niphhal* יִפָּדֶה (on the inf. abs. *qal* in connection with a *niphhal* form, cf. Ges-K §113w).

f Perhaps, considering the Elohistic redaction, we should read יהוה.

8g Following Gk, we should correctly read נַפְשׁוֹ here. MT applies the suffix to עָקְבִי.

h V. 8 is to be thought of as a parenthesis secondarily added. The assertion made in v. 7 is here emphatically supported. V. 9 is joined to v. 8 syntactically and logically.

10i We could ask whether it would not be better to place v. 10b after v. 11; that would provide a meaningful verse there, logically (and also metrically).

11j MT: "their inner being" does not fit here. Following Gk, θ´, T, we should read קְבָרִים.

k Following Gk, θ´, S, we should eliminate ב in בְשָׁמוֹתָם. An old legal custom consisted of calling out the name of the new owner over an object during the transfer of property (see below, under "Commentary"). MT was led astray by the phrase קָרָא בְשֵׁם.

12l MT: "Man in his splendor does not (stay) overnight." In v. 20 we have יָלִין instead of the more comprehensible verb יָבִין. Vv. 12 and 20 may be checked against each other as "refrain."

m נִדְמוּ as the relative clause to כַּבְּהֵמוֹת.

13n זֶה does not refer to the previous statement but to the statement following in v. 14. סֶלָה after v. 13 splits this connection.

o Parallel to דַרְכָּם in v. 13a, it is better (corresponding to Job 8:13) to read אָרְחוֹתָם = "their ways."

14p The text in v. 14 is irreparably corrupt. Only the first words can tentatively be reconstructed. In doing so the following new word order (together with corresponding corrections) is to be preferred: שַׁתּוּ כצאן מות ירעם לשׁאול שַׁחוּ וַיִּרְדוּ = "they shifted" would therefore best be corrected to שַׁחוּ = "they sink," and וַיִּרְדוּ = "and they dominated (trod on)" should in connection with לשׁאול be corrected to a form of ירד = "go down" (cf. v. 17b).

q A logically based reconstruction of the second part of v. 14 is impossible. MT: "And there ruled over them upright people in the morning, and their form (?) for consuming the underworld, without dwelling for him." Perhaps, guided by the context, one can consider as "firm points" לְבַלּוֹת ("for consuming") and מִזְּבֻל ("without dwelling"). Accordingly, the fate of those is depicted who have gone down to the underworld. That much can still be discerned from the disfigured text.

15r יהוה instead of אלהים in the Elohistically revised part of the Psalter.

s מִיַּד־שְׁאוֹל belongs to the second half-verse and is obviously wrongly set off by *atnah* because the meaning of the peculiar but not abnormal position of כי (Ps. 128:2) was not recognized.

16t Perhaps better with the pointing יַרְבֶּה = "he increases."

18u MT from v. 18 on has wrongly presupposed the second person. That this is a mistake becomes evident as late as v. 19b. Vv. 18-19 deal with the rich man's fate of death. Thus we should probably read וְיוֹדֶה instead of וְיוֹדֻךָ (the suffix refers to נפשׁ).

v Also כי־תיטיב לך is to be corrected accordingly: יֵיטַב לָהּ, "it is well."

19w Instead of תבוא, logically: יָבוֹא.

Form

Psalm 49 is transmitted in very bad condition textually. This fact in part has effects on metrical relations. The 3 + 3 meter is determinative, and that in vv. 1-7 and 12-20 (the second part of v. 14 is not comprehensible; see above, "Text"). In vv. 8-11 a careful analysis should establish the following: v. 8: 3 + 2; v. 9: 2 + 2 (?); v. 10: 3 + 4 (3); v. 11: 3 + 3 (3); if we should place v. 10b behind v. 11b, the meter 3 + 3 would be formed in the verse structure that results. Before we enter upon the question of the analysis of the type, we should ask whether individual verses or parts of verses were possibly inserted into the psalm secondarily. H. Gunkel was of the opinion that vv. 10 and 15 should be thought of as additions. These additions, he thought, have unsettled and distorted the text. Without doubt, this is a weighty opinion. But we will have to note that Gunkel at this point operated exclusively with (very idiosyncratic) considerations that had to do with the content. We must emphasize that a removal of vv. 10 and 15 on formal grounds is out of the question. In contrast, v. 8 will surely have to be considered a gloss. After this clarification, as far as the *Gattung* of Psalm 49 is concerned, we should first point to the fact that the elements of language and thought belonging to "wisdom poetry" turn up in most of the verses of this psalm (H. Gunkel and J. Begrich, *EinlPs* §10, 2). This was the traditional classification. More appropriate from the viewpoint of thought and material would be an approach from the classification, didactic poetry. See above, Intro. §6, 5. Already the introit of the psalm puts its stamp on the whole. In vv. 1f. we have a didactic opening call (cf. Deut. 32:1; Isa. 28:23). For an explanation of the "didactic opening call," cf. H. W. Wolff, BK XIV/1, 122. The teaching as such we should be able to assign to the group of poems dealing with problems and reflection, such as Psalms 73 and 139 (G. von Rad, *Wisdom*, 48ff.). In the process we must note the fact and the degree that elements of the prayer songs of individuals—both their petitions and descriptions of distress and also their thanksgiving—have influenced didactic poetry. In vv. 16f. the form of the oracle of salvation is imitated. Cf. J. Begrich, "Das priesterliche Heilsorakel,"

ZAW 52 (1932) 81-92. Even if the echoes of the named "types" seem to be a matter of stylization, we have no right to eliminate the foundational events. H. Gunkel has proceeded cleverly in his commentary along these lines. To achieve purity of "type," he has made corrections. But it is in agreement with the will to bear witness in the didactic poems of the Psalter to point to an event—be it ever so indistinct. The confession in v. 15 is the clearest expression of connections that are not surrendered, which remind us of a song of thanksgiving, but are now incorporated in didactic poetry as an expression of confession and absolution (or, better, redemption).

Setting

If we follow the MT, we cannot fail to notice that the author of Psalm 49 was surrounded by enemies (v. 5); he suffered under the oppressive superiority of rich people (v. 6). As an inspired singer (v. 4), the psalmist in vv. 7-14 unveils the background of the dreadful fate of death already decreed over the imprudent, self-secure potentates. Like the author of Psalm 73, so also the singer of Psalm 49 knows the "final mystery": אבינה לאחריתם (Ps. 73:17b). This charismatically grasped "revelation" is then summarized in a sentence of thanksgiving in v. 15. In vv. 16ff. the psalmist then passes on his experience to comfort all those who have to suffer from the pressure of influential people of power. The crucial experience gained by the singer in his own evil days (v. 12) he shares with the one who suffers a similar situation (v. 20). But the didactic poem rises above all specific relations and addresses itself to "rich and poor alike" (v. 2). The rich man is to be warned, the poor man to be comforted. The wisdom of Psalm 49, however, has its roots not in a theoretical act of contemplation but in the reality of an encounter with God (v. 15)—in the event of a disclosure that brings salvation. Psalm 49 is the result of a response of petition and thanksgiving as determined by "wisdom teaching." The occurrence of distress and deliverance is disclosed instructively and in a universalizing way (v. 4). The song belongs among the late OT psalms and applies to the circle of "the poor." For these "poor ones," see above, Intro. §10, 3. Obviously the situation was such that in a specific tradition or period of Israel's history the nefarious activity of rich and evil-minded people represented a tormenting hardship for the poor (cf. Psalm 73).

Commentary

[Title] On למנצח, see above, Intro. §4, No. 17. On לבני־קרח, cf. the comment on Ps. 42, title. On מזמור, see above, Intro. §4, No. 2.

[49:1-4] Psalm 49 begins with a relatively broad introduction (vv. 1-4). Like a prophet, the singer calls out to an immense audience: "all nations," "all inhabitants of the world." חלד, in Ps. 17:14 problematical in the text, is a term for "world" occurring only in this passage in the OT. Gk translates חלד with ἡ γῆ in Ps. 17:14 and with ἡ οἰκουμένη in Ps. 49:1. The messenger of God (v. 4) knows that he has responsibilities vis-à-vis the whole world. And yet the song is specifically addressed to "the rich and the poor." The parallelism with its chiastic effect shows that the construct combination בני אדם can have the meaning "simple people," while בני־איש designates "lords' sons," the "distinguished people" (cf. the comment on Ps. 4:2). The burden of the message is חכמות = "wisdom" (v. 3). Thus the basic character of the whole psalm is determined also by its terminology. "Wisdom" is, to be sure, thinking, considering, and communicating on the part of the human heart, but its content is inspired. Verse 4 deals with the mystery of inspiration. The author inclines his ear to the other world in order to receive the determinative statement with which he can alarm the rich and comfort the poor. Here משל is the "wisdom saying" (Gk παραβολή); cf. O. Eissfeldt, *Der māschāl im Alten Testament* (1913); J. Pirot, "Le *'māschāl'* dans l'Ancien Testament," *RScR* 37 (1950) 565-580; A. R. Johnson, "משל," VT Suppl 3 (1955) 162-169. On this announcement in v. 4, cf. Ps. 78:2. It is worth noting that "wisdom sayings" are considered inspired by God. In this we should not let ourselves see a "manipulation of late prophecy"; rather, it is a part of the essence of the OT חכמה that it is in principle rooted in the reality of God, in the יראת יהוה (Prov. 1:7). It is further worth noting that wisdom poems were sung to the accompaniment of the lyre. On כנור, cf. K. Galling, *BRL* 390f. The mystery (Gk translates חידה with πρόβλημα) is "revealed" in the inspired song.

[49:5-6] First the singer in vv. 5-6 considers the distress of "evil days" (cf. Pss. 27:5; 41:1; and often), days in which he was hemmed in by the "wickedness" of the "rich" (and therefore influential) people. On עון in the basic meaning "an intention that is not in accord with God's will," cf. L. Köhler, *OT Theology,* 170. Involved are people of power who trust in their riches (v. 6) and who deceive those without influence—the poor—and take advantage of them. The question introduced by למה communicates a real situation of distress; it introduces us to the fearful perplexity of those who are helplessly at the mercy of the rich and powerful. The singer himself has experienced this situation.

[49:7-14] In the lament of one who is surrounded by enemies Yahweh is usually implored to rise against the adversaries and to annihilate them (cf. the comment on Ps. 7:6f.). In the later psalms—especially those influenced by the wisdom poetry—the verdict of God against the enemies prayed for and expected is presented as a reasonable and even now discernible judgment. The dark fate of death already exerts its influence on the life of the rich person and imposes a situation of despair on it. The powerful and secure person is not in a position to ransom himself from this fate of death, not even with an offer of all his riches (v. 7). On the meaning of פדה, cf. J. J. Stamm, *Erlösen und Vergeben im Alten Testament* (1940), 16. For פדה in the meaning "to ransom oneself from the death penalty by means of a payment," cf. Exod. 21:29f.; Prov. 6:35; 13:8. God himself pronounces by means of death a judgment on the rich man (v. 7b), and from God's hand the powerful individual cannot ransom himself. The rich man's influence here is subject to insurmountable limits. In v. 8 the final and always recognizable powerlessness of the rich man is emphasized with special force: the ransom of the נפש is "unattainable." Here the rich man must forfeit his self-glorifying aims and purposes. He cannot "live forever" (v. 9) and escape the "grave," the underworld.

There are difficulties with v. 10. First, we could of course place v. 10b after v. 11b. There this part of the verse easily fits. But then we will have to ask about v. 10a, How is this statement to be understood? Obviously the singer wants to call attention to a situation that is observable everywhere; thus, in any case, the introduction כי יראה must be understood. But does v. 10a now want to say that death is the great "equalizer" (Gunkel), that it is simply an established fact that both the wise and the foolish die? Where then is the significant accent in the context of the psalm? Is v. 10a after all (as Gunkel supposes) a maxim that found its way into the song secondarily? Or could we hazard the interpretation: "the wise die" (i.e., those who think about their end and stay close to God must die); how much more is it true that the imprudent, foolish rich people (cf. v. 12) perish!? Still the meaning of v. 10a remains difficult in the context. G. von Rad states: "No one has provided a satisfactory solution for v. 10" (*Wisdom*, 204, n.16). On Psalm 49 also cf. G. Fohrer, *KuD* 14 (1968) 256ff. In any case (in the context of the whole psalm), the intention of v. 10 is to state that perturbed faith should firm itself up again through the realization that there is a basic order of life that governs all people" (G. von Rad, 263f.).

Verse 11, however, is easily understood in the context. The rich cannot purchase for themselves "eternal life," an everlasting communion with Yahweh, who is life. Graves are their homes (cf. Eccles. 12:5) "forever." By death they are separated from all riches. In 11b the powerful activity of the rich is described, who like kings have their names broadcast over countries (2 Sam. 12:26 ff.). קרא שם designates a court action by means of which a conveyance takes place (cf. K. Galling, "Die Ausrufung des Namens als Rechtsakt in Israel," *ThLZ* [1956], 65-70). On v. 11b, cf. Isa. 5:8; Luke 12:16-21. But in death all possessions must be surrendered to others by the rich (v. 10b; Ps. 39:6; Sir. 14:15). In the midst of his splendor the rich man (in v. 12 consciously designated אדם) does not realize how transitory he is. Like cattle he passes from existence (cf. Eccles. 3:19). Verse 13 then introduces a description of rich people which is of great visionary power. While the affluent self-reliantly and self-importantly prattle away (cf. Ps. 73:6ff.), they are already like a large herd being driven into the underworld by death. We could ask whether the "personification" of מות includes reminders of the divinity *mōt*, which has become familiar through the Ras Shamra texts. It is important that the rich even now, in the midst of life, are being driven down into שאול by מות. For the meaning of שאול, cf. the comment on Ps. 6:5. But מות is in the employ of God (v. 7b) and executes his judgment over the wicked potentates.

[49:15] In this verse the psalmsinger comes back to his own lot. As v. 5 shows, he was surrounded by deceitful power brokers. Verses 7-14 disclose (by inspiration) the fate of death of these rich and influential men. But how are we now to understand v. 15, that difficult, much-discussed verse? As the excursus here following will show, the understanding of לקח is decisive. The verb reminds us of the Enoch and Elijah traditions (Gen. 5:24; 2 Kings 2:3, 5). Its basic meaning here is "remove." "The most likely solution, then, is to understand the sentence as the expression of a hope for a life of communion with God which will outlast death. In any case, we have no sufficient knowledge of the ideas of post-exilic Israel about what happens after death to say that this interpretation of the confession in Ps. 49 is *a priori* impossible" (G. von Rad, *Wisdom*, 204). So also H. W. Wolff writes: "The overcoming of death's agony is not manifested in any elaborate hope of the beyond, but in the calm certainty that the communion with Yahweh cannot be ended by death, because of his faithfulness" (*Anthropology of the OT* [1974], 109).

In the interpretation of v. 15 two relations should be observed. (1) Verse 15 could be understood as the thankful counterpart of vv. 5-6. In that case v. 15 would have the meaning of triumphant certainty: Yahweh rescues my נפש from the power of the enemies, which in the Psalms is usually thought of as the "sphere of שְׁאוֹל." This certainty would be very meaningful after the opening in vv. 7-14. If this relation is acknowledged, then we cannot speak of a hope for a life after death in view of v. 15, but we can indeed speak of the certainty that Yahweh rescues from the sphere of death. This is the sense in which Chr. Barth interprets Ps. 49:15 (Chr. Barth, *Die Errettung vom Tode in den individuellen Klage- und Dankliedern des Alten Testaments* [1947], 158ff.). This understanding is supported also by the statement, among others, in v. 10a: חֲכָמִים יָמוּתוּ. In v. 10a the חָכָם, the singer of our psalm (v. 3), acknowledges that he himself is under this general fate of death.

(2) An altogether different relation of thought would be possible. We could think of v. 15 as the counterpart to v. 7—especially when both verses were introduced by אַךְ. פדה in v. 15 would then have to be understood in the sense of the application of words as they are determinative in v. 7. In other words, in v. 15 the rescue from the fate of death is meant. While the rich man can bring no price to ransom his נפש from God in the hour of death (v. 7), Yahweh himself intervenes for the poor, rescues them from שְׁאוֹל, and "removes" them. לקח would then of course have to be understood in the sense of Gen. 5:24 and 2 Kings 2:3ff.: by means of an extraordinary intervention Yahweh at death rescues from שְׁאוֹל the poor (vv. 5-6) who were oppressed in their lifetime. This meaning of לקח could also be assumed in Ps. 73:24. For this interpretation of Ps. 49:15, cf. J. J. Stamm, *Erlösen und Vergeben im Alten Testament* (1940), 16. Stamm even supports the view that in v. 15 the mystery announced in v. 4 is revealed: "The removal to God is its own comfort in view of the injustice of this world" (v. 17). Similarly also G. von Rad, *OT Theol* 1: 406. If we follow this interpretation, then Ps. 49:15 would express a real certainty of resurrection that would establish a conception such as is given in the NT, e.g., in the parable of the rich man and poor Lazarus (cf. H. Gressmann, *Vom reichen Mann und armen Lazarus,* Abh. d. kön.-preuss. Akad. d. Wiss. [1918]). This interpretation as it was last given is contested by L. Wächter, *Der Tod im Alten Testament* (1967), 196. With a strict emphasis on the parallel passage present in v. 15, he declares: "The assertion now no longer lets us divine anything like a removal, but rather takes its place among similar psalm verses that speak of preservation from an evil and early death. Therefore we had better dispense with Psalm 49 as proof for hope beyond death" (196). But is this disclaimer really appropriate? Does Psalm 49 belong to the context of those didactic and problematic poems that lie before us also in Psalm 73? And would not this context be determinative in interpretation? On Ps. 73:24, L. Wächter explains, "This would therefore give expression to the hope that the communion with God thought of as good fortune might also endure beyond death" (197). Finally, we should still note that there is no urgent need, formal or in terms of content, to eliminate v. 15.

[49:15-20] By means of the disclosures introduced by אַךְ in vv. 7ff. and 15, certain facts were expressed by the psalmsinger. Now he turns with comfort and solace to all who (like him) groan under the pressure of influential men of power (cf. vv. 5-6). In vv. 16-20 the communication (vv. 7-15) is clothed in the form of an exhortation and repeated. It is worth noting that the wisdom poet sees a threatening danger even in becoming rich (v. 16), a danger that is approaching the poor person and represents a tensile test to his faith in the righteous God (cf. Ps. 73:2ff.). In thought content v. 17 corresponds to vv. 11b/10b. Verse 18 describes the self-satisfied human being who "blesses" himself, i.e., provides himself with the wholesome vital powers and luxuriates in prosperity (cf. Luke 12:19). Verse 19 corresponds to the assertions in v. 11, and v. 20 takes up v. 12 again.

Purpose and Thrust

We have to begin with the fact that the rich in their luxurious way of living not only radiate temptation and doubt concerning the righteousness of God (cf. vv.

16ff. and Psalm 73) but that they even as deceitful enemies hem in the poor (v. 5). The decision concerning the final reasons for this confused life situation belongs to God. The mystery is announced through the inspired singer of wisdom (v. 4). And since the intricacies in the contrast between poor and rich are general among human beings, therefore the author moves from his own experiences (vv. 5-6) to a worldwide message (vv. 1-4). The essential content of the charismatic announcement is the visionary reference to the fact that the self-reliant and self-satisfied rich in the midst of their radiant life are but beasts fattened for the slaughter of death. They are already being driven down to שְׁאוֹל by their shepherd מוּת and have neither the means nor the possibilities to ransom (vv. 7f.) themselves from this fate of death, which already is darkening their life. The one who is poor, on the other hand, who sets his hope entirely on God (the singer of our song stands in suspense between "petition" and "thanksgiving"), is rescued from שְׁאוֹל by Yahweh himself and in an incomparable manner is removed from the shadowy existence of the underworld. Luke 16:19ff. provides the great illumination of the essential content of Psalm 49. Determinative is Luke 16:25. There the rich man is told, "Remember that you in your lifetime received your good things, and Lazarus in like manner evil things; but now he is comforted here, and you are in anguish." This great "reversal" appears already in Psalm 49. However, as in Luke 16:19ff., we should reflect that the poor man and the rich man in their present life receive specific messages concerning the end. This "end" is the actual destination of all ways, the true telos of complicated and opaque processes. We may well have to declare with G. von Rad that assailed and disturbed faith is again confirmed "through the realization that there is a basic order of life that governs all people." But Psalm 49 deals not only with the charismatic messages of reality in which "the end" of all things is revealed: in the light of the experiences which, for instance, are expressed in the songs of thanksgiving of individuals in Israel (cf. the confession in v. 15). But there are also prophetic impulses perceptible where the message of reality in didactic poetry stands in judgment and disarms the imposing world of wealth and success.

Psalm 50

The Appearance of Yahweh for Judgment

Literature

W. Caspari, "Kultpsalm 50," *ZAW* 45 (1927) 254-266. G. von Rad, *The Problem of the Hexateuch and Other Essays* (1966) 22-25. P. Auvray, "Le Psaume L. Notes de grammaire et d'exégèse," *RB* 53 (1946) 365-371. E. Baumann, "Struktur-Untersuchungen im Psalter I," *ZAW* 61 (1945/48) 159-169. A. Weiser, "Zur Frage nach den Beziehungen der Psalmen zum Kult: Die Darstellung der Theophanie in den Psalmen und im Festkult," *Bertholet-Festschrift* (1950) 513-531. N. H. Snaith, *Hymns of the Temple* (1951). E. Würthwein, "Der Ursprung der prophetischen Gerichtsrede," *ZThK* (1952) 1-16. E. Beaucamp, La Theophanie du Psaume 50 (49)," *Nouvelle Revue Théol.* 91 (1959) 897-915. W. Beyerlin, *Herkunft und Geschichte der ältesten Sinaitraditionen.* (1961). H. P. Müller, "Die kultische Darstellung der Theophanie," *VT* 14 (1964) 183-191. F. Schnutenhaus, "Das Kommen und Erscheinen Gottes im Alten Testament," *ZAW* 76 (1964) 1-21. A. M. Dubarle, "La manifestation théophanique de Dieu dans la liturgie d'Israël," *Lex Orandi* 40 (1967) 9-23. A. Maillot, "Une liturgie d'alliance? Psaume 50," *BiViChr* 80 (1968) 14-20. N. H. Ridderbos, "Die Theophanie in Psalm 50,1-6," *OTS* 15 (1969) 213-226. Jörg Jeremias, *Kultprophetie und Gerichtsverkündigung in der späten Königszeit,* WMANT 35 (1970) 125-127. E. Kutsch, " 'Bund' und Fest: Zu Gegenstand und Terminologie einer Forschungsrichtung," *Theol. Quartalschrift* 150 (1970) 299-320. M. Mannati, "Le Psaume 50 est-il un *rîb?*" *Semitica* 23 (1973) 27-50. H. Gese, "Psalm 50 und das alttestamentliche Gesetzesvertändnis," *Festschr. f. E. Käsemann* (1976) 57-78.

Text

A psalm of Asaph.

50:1 God, God,[a] Yahweh
speaks and calls the earth
from the rising of the sun to its setting.

2 From Zion, the crown of beauty, he radiates forth ' ';[b]

3 our God comes and does not keep silence.
Fire devours things before him,
round about him mighty storms arise.

4 He calls to the heaven above[c]
and to the earth. His people he wants to judge.

5 "Gather together my faithful ones[d] for me,
those who in sacrifices made a covenant with me!"

6 And the heavens are to proclaim his righteousness,
that he is a 'God of justice.'[e]—*Selah*.

7 Hear, my people, I want to speak,
Israel, I want to bear witness against you!
'Yahweh,'[f] your God, am I.

8 Not because of your sacrifices do I reprove you,
your burnt offerings are always before my eyes.

9 I do not accept the bull from your house
nor the goats from your sheepfolds!

10 For mine are the beasts of the forest,
the animals on the 'hills of God.'[g]

11 I know all the birds of 'the heights';[h]
whatever moves about on the fields is mine.

12 If I were hungry, I would not tell you,
for mine are the earth and its fullness.

13 Do I perchance eat the flesh of bulls
and drink the blood of goats?

14 Offer to 'Yahweh'[i] thanksgiving
and pay your vows to the Most High!

15 Call to me in the day of trouble,
and I will rescue you, and you will honor[j] me!

16 But to the wicked Yahweh says,
Why do you count up my commandments
and take my covenant into your mouth

17 while you actually hate discipline
and cast my words behind you?

18 When you see a thief, with him you make common cause,
and with adulterers you keep company.

19 Your mouth expresses itself in evil,
and your tongue aids and abets wickedness.

20 'Shameful things'[k] you say about your brother,
calumny you cast on the son of your mother.

21 That is what you have done; were I to keep silence,
you would (then) think that I am just like you.[l]
I hold it up to you and put it squarely before your eyes.

22 Consider this well, you who forget God,
lest I tear to pieces and no one rescues!

23 He who offers thanks honors me.
He who walks 'uprightly,'[m] to him I will show 'my'[n] salvation.

1a אל אלהים cannot be translated "God of gods." But the powerful introit with its heaping up of the names of God should not be corrected (cf. Josh. 22:22).

2b אלהים is to be eliminated for the sake of the meter. Together with the half-verse יבא אלהינו ואל־יחרש we would have a double four-pulse meter.

4c For מעל in an adverbial sense, cf. Gen. 27:39; 49:25.

5d While MT transmits direct discourse of God, Gk and S have לו חֲסִידָיו.

6e MT has "that God is judge." But in view of the sentence structure it will probably be better to undertake a different way of separating the consonants: אֱלֹהֵי מִשְׁפָּט.

7f In the Elohistically revised Psalter we should in this passage assume יהוה to have been the original reading.

10g בהררי אלף would have to be translated "cattle hills." But it would be best to read (corresponding to Ps. 36:6): בהררי־אֵל.

11h הרים is impossible in view of הררי in v. 10. Gk, S, T read שָׁמַים or מָרוֹם.

14i Cf. note **f.**

15j A deliberate correction of an original וָאֲכַבְּדֶךָ (cf. Ps. 91:15) is often taken for granted here; but we should probably follow the MT (cf. v. 23).

20k MT: "you sit"; but both in view of the parallel passage and in view of the construction of the half-verse, we ought to read בֹּשֶׁת (interchange of consonants).

21l The infinitive construct היות is syntactically impossible at this point. We should probably read היו (K. Budde).

23m MT: "and he who prepares the way, the road." Such an interpretation of the text is impossible. It is best to read (with Graetz and Gunkel) וְתָם דֶּרֶךְ (cf. Job 4:6; Prov. 13:6). **n** בישע אלהים cannot be fitted into the metrical scheme; we should probably read בִּישְׁעִי.

Form

The shape of the text of Psalm 50 is transparent; the meter is uniform throughout. After v. 1 has been introduced with a three-member meter $(3+3+3)$ and vv. 2/3a with a double four-pulse meter, the chain of double triple meters is virtually never broken. Exceptions occur only in the following verses: v. 7: $3+3+3$; v. 18: $4+3$; vv. 21 and 23: $3+4$; and in v. 21b a four-pulse meter occurs which could perhaps act as a parallel construction to the introductory formula in v. 7aα. The words ולרשע אמר אלהים (v. 16) will probably have to be considered a gloss.

The structure of the psalm presents itself as follows: description of the appearance of God and call for the gathering of the חסדים, vv. 1-6; treatment of the offering in the first section of the body, vv. 7-15; concerning the proper obedience over against Yahweh's expression of his will, vv. 16-23. Worth noting is the fact that there are words of Yahweh in the first person present in all three parts: in v. 5 Yahweh himself speaks; in v. 7 the formula שמעה עמי ואדברה introduces a rather long speech of God which is interrupted only in v. 16aα by means of the (secondary) new introduction ולרשע אמר אלהים. The basic character of the psalm therefore is prophetic. But this observation brings with it a difficult problem, the magnitude of which has not been recognized until recent times. Are the statements of Psalm 50 "imitations of a prophetic manner of speech and thought" (H. Gunkel) in a later (perhaps late exilic) time, or do we here find evidence of prophecy emerging in the cultus? S. Mowinckel, G. von Rad, A. Weiser, and E. Würthwein have declared themselves in favor of the second suggestion. Weiser considers the psalm a "liturgy." Thus the question arises whether Psalm 50 is poetry that imitates the prophetic art form, or whether we must presuppose a current cultic situation. Added to the indicated problem we at the same time have the form-critical question about the *Gattung* before us. Here too an overview should initially be useful. H. Gunkel adds Psalm 50 to the group of the "prophetic psalms" (H. Gunkel and J. Begrich, *EinlPs* §9). A Weiser calls it a "liturgy." Here a festival cult is presupposed in which the two parts of Psalm 50 are thought to have their "Sitz im Leben": the theophany and the words of judgment. But this is exactly the point at which the problems become acute. For there is no doubt that the question concerning the form group to which Psalm 50 is to be assigned must be asked and answered in direct connection with the determination of the "Sitz im Leben," that is, of the festival cult. Immediately, however, the difficulty arises, which festival cult is to be thought of? Which "Sitz im Leben" is our starting point? It is worth noting that already Calvin in his commentary on the Psalms advanced the thought of a cultic situation in which in a festival (*sollemni ritu*) the remembrance of the covenant of God was renewed (*ac si Deus foederis sui memoriam renovaret*). In this connection we should report on studies that interpreted Psalm 50 on the basis of a "covenant renewal festival."

While S. Mowinckel in his *PsStud* II integrated the process of a covenant renewal ceremonial completely with the larger cultic complex of the dramatic-mythical enthronement festival of Yahweh (and so, too, still in the book *Le décalogue* appearing in 1927), it was A. Alt who in his research on apodictic law first addressed the cultic act of the regularly repeated covenant renewal as the predominant worship event of the early history of Israel. His theses can be summarized thus: (a) The apodictic law of God had its "Sitz im Leben" not in a secular act but in a cultic one. (b) The solemn ceremonial at the foot of Mounts Ebal and Gerizim (Deuteronomy 27) indicates such a worship act of the cultic transmission of apodictic law. (c) In Deut. 31:10ff. an ordinance regulates the worship act that is to take place "every seven years." (d) The celebration of the renewal of the covenant and the transmission of the law that is to take place "every seven years" is to be viewed in conjunction with the sacral fallow that became mandatory at regular intervals and with a cancellation of all special responsibilities of law and debt. Accordingly, the covenant festival would be an institution of ancient Israel. A. Alt's presentation gives rise to the thought that this institution of the early times was not able to have its way for long but had to fail already in ancient times. But the "enthronement festival of Yahweh," so important for S. Mowinckel, vanishes completely from view as far as Alt is concerned (also for G. von Rad). While Alt in the course of form-critical research on apodictic law arrived at the thesis that Israel had a covenant renewal festival, G. von Rad came upon it via a form-critical investigation of the whole Sinai pericope. Great importance was attached to this festival in the cultic history of Israel. Every year (very likely also in the time of the kings) the great ceremonial is supposed to have taken place. Von Rad therefore separates the festival of the renewal of the covenant from the connection with sacral fallow and the jubilee year which were so important in Alt's investigations, and thus he expands the sphere of application of this festival. Finally, A. Weiser in his commentary on the Psalms assigned a vast rank and significance to the covenant festival. For S. Mowinckel it was the festival of the enthronement of Yahweh that, like a great magnet, pulled together and unified the most disparate fragments of the OT; for A. Weiser the "covenant festival" is the key to most of the Psalms.

In the first four editions of the present commentary, the conception adopted was that a cult-historical differentiation had to be introduced. A brief summary follows: (1) The thesis of A. Alt would have to be adopted, in the sense that a cultic act of covenant renewal is posited for ancient Israel—a cultic act that was associated with the sacral fallow that occurred "every seven years"; this festival would have to be dated in the early days of Israel. (2) All incorporations of a "covenant renewal festival" into an enthronement festival of Yahweh are to be rejected, since the existence of a divine enthronement festival is to be questioned (see above, Intro. §10, 1). (3) The ceremony of the covenant renewal had a history in the cultus of Israel that is very difficult to grasp; after it apparently had fallen into disuse very early, certain texts of the OT indicate that the cultic institution, to be sure, had also found a place in Jerusalem, but that in the time of the kings a restitution of the relationship of God and people played a role in a festival act of worship only in epochs of comprehensive reformation (e.g., at the time of Hezekiah and of Josiah; cf. H.-J. Kraus, *Worship in Israel* [1966] 35ff.). This would explain the fact that the Psalter contains only a very small number of evidences of a covenant renewal ceremonial. Actually one could mention only Psalms 50 and 81. Associated with all these hypotheses and concerns are questions that have to do with the speaker of the word of judgment in Ps. 50:7ff. Does this really have to do with a prophet (a cultic prophet)? Or even with a figure of a "mediator of the covenant" (H.-J. Kraus, BK XV, editions 1-4)?

In recent investigations the whole institution of a "covenant renewal festival" has become questionable. We can only briefly indicate the essential arguments here:

(1) As early as 1955 E. Kutsch in his Mainz dissertation declared: "An annual covenant renewal festival to be celebrated at the Feast of Tabernacles, or even a Feast of

Tabernacles that would have been understood to be a covenant renewal festival, most likely . . . never existed (E. Kutsch, *Das Herbstfest in Israel* [1955], 158). This thesis, together with a challenge to the traditional understanding of ברית, has been repeated in E. Kutsch, " 'Bund' und Fest," *Theol. Quartalschrift* 150 (1970) 299ff.

(2) The attempt to relate the covenant-cult hypothesis to Deut. 31:9-13 is rendered impossible by the research of L. Perlitt, *Bundestheologie im Alten Testament,* WMANT 36 (1969) 115-128. Also, every claim of a dominant meaning of the "covenant" in the early times of Israel is opposed by the fact of "covenant silence" by the prophets of the eighth century (L. Perlitt, 128ff.).

(3) A more exact investigation of Psalm 50 will have to work out the peculiarity and context of this psalm. There new aspects will reveal themselves.

We will accordingly have to make a new start. Psalm 50 cannot be divorced from a relation to a festival cult—no matter how constituted. Jörg Jeremias has opened up a new understanding by grouping Psalms 50; 81; and 95 together in the form-group, "great festival psalms" and by introducing a contextual interpretation that has advanced the exegesis (J. Jeremias, *Kultprophetie und Gerichtsverkündigung in der späten Königszeit,* 125ff.). On this form-group, see above, Intro. §6, 6. The three psalms named are an entity by themselves within the Psalter. At the center of things there is always a speech by Yahweh which represents the seriousness and force of a judicial pronouncement. Who were the speakers of this Yahweh speech when it was performed at a cultic occasion? And which cultic occasion is involved? J. Jeremias refers to the language peculiarities observed in Psalms 81 and 95 and concludes that "in these psalms circles similar to those standing behind Deuteronomy gain a hearing. In that case, we would . . . have to reckon with Levitical authorship of the Psalms" (126). This explanation refers to conclusions made earlier by A. Bentzen and G. von Rad (A. Bentzen, *Die Josianische Reform und ihre Voraussetzungen* [1926]; G. von Rad, *Das Gottesvolk im Deuteronomium* [1929]; id., *Deuteronomium-Studien* [1948²], 41ff.). But who is the speaker in Ps. 50:7ff.? In reference to the "formula for self-presentation" occurring in v. 7, Jeremias calls attention to the investigation of W. Zimmerli, "Ich bin Jahwe," [1953], *GesAufs* 11ff. Zimmerli had shown that the formula for self-presentation "has no real 'Sitz im Leben' in prophetic speech . . . It clearly . . . does not belong to the type of prophetic speech" (34f.). Thus the conjecture is that in Psalms 50 and 81 a priest spoke those words (40). This gives rise to a clear picture: In the "great festival psalms" priestly (Levitical) speakers take the floor. They actualize the commandments of God in a speech of judgment. Such "Levitical sermons" should be dated relatively late; they have their counterpart in the Chronicler's historical writing. Here we would have to start with the thought that the Levites of later times occasionally presupposed spiritual and prophetic charismata for their service, or "that in postexilic times prophets arose in Levitical circles" (J. Jeremias, 127). Thus the prophetic character of Psalm 50 is largely explained. There remains the question of the particular festival in which Psalm 50 has its "Sitz-im-Leben." The two main parts of Psalm 50 (but also the corresponding contents of Psalm 81) precipitate the question anew: Where, in which festival cult did the proclamation of the theophany and the contemporizing of the commandments have their setting? Can the theophany of Psalm 50 be seen only in the perspective of Trito-Isaiah (E. Beaucamp)? Does it suffice to declare with A. Jepsen that Psalms 50 and 81 prove only that the psalmists knew the Decalog, but not that it was transmitted in the cultic festivals (A. Jepsen, *ZAW* 79 [1967], 303)? In the final analysis, wouldn't the hypothesis of a "covenant renewal festival" (differentiated as to cultic history) have to be considered (see above; cf. H.-J. Kraus, *Worship in Israel* [1966] 134ff., 189ff.)? Did not a cultic festival such as we can deduce from Psalm 50 have a previous history? And, indeed, in a festival that reached back to the most ancient (Shechemite) traditions, one that originated in Northern Israel and which only seldom came into use in Jerusalem in preexilic times? In the works both of E. Kutsch and also L. Perlitt one misses a detailed reference to so important a passage as Deut. 26:16ff., in which, after all, the point is that the ברית-declarations and the ברית-obligations of the partners of the covenant have been set down—*expressis verbis*. Also, it is remarkable that L. Perlitt in his rejection of the covenant festival cult did not refer to Psalms 50 and 81 at all— psalms which in the investigations of G. von Rad played so important a role. Questions remain.

Commentary

[Title] On מזמור, see above, Intro. §4, No. 2. Psalms of Asaph, in addition to Psalm 50, are found in the collection of psalms at Psalms 73-83.

[50:1-6] In these verses the occurrence of a theophany is described. The reference to Yahweh's appearance begins in solemn form. Three divine names announce the mystery of the epiphany in which Yahweh now fills all things and is the primary reality. On the heaping up of divine names, cf. Josh. 22:22. אל is the archaic, ancient Canaanite term which has become known particularly through the texts of ancient Ugaritic (cf. O. Eissfeldt, *El im ugaritischen Pantheon,* Berichte über die Abhandlungen d. Sächs. Akad. der Wiss., phil.- hist. Kl. 98, 4[1951]). אל אלהים is to be translated variously. The "Most High God" or the "God of gods" would be אל אלים or אלהי אלהים. Yahweh makes his appearance speaking and calling. Originally accompanied by the roar of thunder (Psalm 29), the appearance of God is here accomplished entirely by a message in words (vv. 7ff.). "From the rising of the sun to its setting," all the world is permeated by Yahweh's call. H. Gunkel sees the significance of this assertion in that the Jews dispersed to all lands in postexilic times are to be reached by a far-reaching address. But this explanation is not adequate. The universal radiance of the divine appearance is traditionally rooted in the cultic traditions of Jerusalem. On theophany, cf. above all J. Jeremias, *Theophanie,* WMANT 10 (1965) 62f. Jeremias has shown that Yahweh's coming in brilliant light, as it is announced in vv. 2f., is really associated with the other theophanic conceptions, i.e., those of God's coming in storm and fire (Ps. 18:12; Hab. 3:4). מציון = "from Zion" Yahweh radiates forth. This place-tradition shows that the Sinai theophany has been transferred to Jerusalem (on "theophany," cf. the comment on Ps. 18:7-15). And obviously we have here a cultic representation of the divine appearance and the proclamation of judgment (vv. 7ff.) that was realized on Zion. For a description of a theophany, cf. Judg. 5:4ff.; Deut. 33:2; Isa. 30:27; Hab. 3:3ff.; and often. When Zion is called "crown of beauty" (cf. also Lam. 2:15), this specification belongs to the context of the glorifying of Jerusalem (cf. the comment on Psalm 46). הופיע refers to Yahweh's appearance in the brilliance of light (cf. Deut. 33:2; Pss. 80:1; 94:1). In v. 3 (as in v. 1) there is further emphasis on the fact that Yahweh appears in order to speak. The proclamation of the word of God is the content and purpose of the theophany. But the "coming" of Yahweh is accompanied by the numinous effects of a thunderstorm. Lightning (אֵשׁ) and storm (נִשְׂעֲרָה מְאֹד) are ancient and traditional symbolical conceptions of theophany (cf. the comment on Psalm 29, ''Setting''). Also cf. Pss. 18:8; 97:3; Isa. 30:27. The inaccessibility and holiness of him who is appearing is thus announced.

In v. 4 heaven and earth are called on as witnesses (cf. Deut. 31:28; 32:1; Isa. 1:2). This is probably a matter of an ancient cultic appeal which was made before Yahweh at an assembly of the tribes (cf. Deut. 31:28). The God who is appearing wants to ''judge'' (דִּין) his people. This is the decisive accent: Yahweh appears for an act of judgment; the speech in vv. 7ff. is one of judgment. We would still have to investigate what role this act of judgment might have played in the judgment speech in the covenant renewal cult. It is worth noting that in the book of Micah (Mic. 1:2ff.) a similar theophany of judgment is reported (secondarily also in Mic. 6:1ff.). For the act of Yahweh's judging, the cultic community is called to assemble (v. 5; cf. Deut. 31:28). Yahweh himself brings about the assembly of the חֲסִדִים, those who have graciously been taken into covenant relation. The indication of the situation in v. 5b is significant: the חֲסִדִים who are being invited and called to appear before Yahweh the judge have concluded the covenant with Yahweh at the sacrifice. Such a covenant sacrifice is mentioned in the OT in Exod. 24:6ff. On the covenant sacrifice, cf. R. Schmid, *Das Bundesopfer im Alten Testament,* Studien zum Alten und Neuen Testament, 9 (1964) 97ff. The people addressed in v. 5 have at the sacrifice concluded Yahweh's covenant, i.e., the covenant that originates with Yahweh and always goes back to his initiative. Do we not at this point have to assume that (at the sacrifice) an act of cultic covenant renewal took place?

If we may presuppose that Psalm 50 reflects a cultic course, then we should have to ask how this course is to be explained. Surely we would have to assume that first (at the sacrifice) the covenant with Yahweh was newly concluded, that then a theophany occurred (perhaps in connection with the sacrifice—cf. Zeph. 1:7), and that finally a speech of judgment exhorted the people. But now G. von Rad in his form-critical investigations of the Sinai pericope sees the course of the covenant renewal festival (e.g., after Deuteronomy) in the following way: (1) historical presentation of the Sinai events, paraenesis; (2) presentation of the law; (3) covenant obligation; (4) blessing and curse. How would the cultic course recognizable in Psalm 50 relate to this scheme? In Ps. 50:5 the covenant obligation is presupposed as having just been completed. Consequently we would have to consider whether ''Yahweh's judging (דִּין), which now emerges through the prophetic speech of judgment, perhaps represents a cultic further development and concretization of that cultic phase in which ''blessing and curse'' were once expressed. We shall see that the speech of judgment in vv. 7ff. in a very remarkable way excludes a particular religious attitude (curse) but comes out with another one as full of promise (blessing). May we assume that ''curse and blessing'' were in this way actualized in a Levitical speech of judgment?

[50:6] As the אֱלֹהִי מִשְׁפָּט Yahweh wants to appear before the assembled community (v. 6). In the process the heavens (cf. v. 4) are to proclaim and certify ''his righteousness.'' צֶדֶק here leans toward the meaning ''actual sense of justice.'' On סֶלָה, which concludes a division, see above, Intro. §4, No. 13.

[50:7-15] The Levitical speech of judgment which begins in v. 7 is a first person speech by Yahweh. A prophetical fullness of power reveals itself in a priestly sermon. שִׁמְעָה עַמִּי, like שְׁמַע יִשְׂרָאֵל (Deut. 6:4), seems to have been a traditional "call to attention" which had its setting in the cultus and which introduced the commandments and the contemporizing of these commandments in a speech of judgment. The address is to "all of Israel," which was thought of as a unit and was spoken to as such—even after the times of division and dispersion. Yahweh appears as the judge. He "bears witness" against his people. On העיד ב, cf. Amos 3:13; Ps. 81:8; Jer. 42:19; and other passages. With his word God at his appearance closes in on the people assembled. יהוה אלהיך אנכי is especially the immediately present and fully empowered self-image of Yahweh, the covenant God. Here (as in Exod. 20:2) the speech of law and justice is introduced with a fundamental revelation of Yahweh. Cf. W. Zimmerli, "Ich bin Jahwe," *Geschichte und Altes Testament* (A. Alt zum 70. Geburtstag) 179-209.

On Ps. 50:7 W. Zimmerli makes an important observation: "The transposition of predicate and subject in a nominative sentence here, which wants to place special emphasis on the name Yahweh (replaced by אלהים in the context of the Elohistic Psalter), makes it possible to identify clearly the subject and the predicate. יהוה אלהיך אנכי can only be translated, 'Yahweh, your God, am I.' The foundation of the arrangement of the sentence is thus guaranteed not only for the Holiness Code but also for the Decalog. The fluctuation in the translation of the introduction [of the speech] may rightly disappear from scholarly literature" (loc. cit., 204f.). Reference has already been made to Zimmerli's explanation that the self-presentation formula belongs not to prophetic but to priestly speech (see above).

The theme of the judgment speech now beginning is the proper worship of the people of God. Obviously, the Levitical priests knew that they were empowered to be in charge of the proper cultic realization of the relation between God and people. Prophetic proofs of the bestowal of power exercise an influence. The speech of law and justice strives to exclude false attitudes and to establish true worship of Yahweh. Psalm 50:8ff. deals with the role played by sacrifices in the worship of the covenant people. Here we will have to follow very carefully the assertions with their own gradations. In v. 8 it is first expressly emphasized that sacrifices and burnt offerings as represented in the cultic practice of Israel are not simply to be rejected and condemned totally (as many exegetes want to prove from Psalm 50). Yahweh does not accuse his people *because* these sacrifices are brought before him, but he strictly rejects the effects which those who bring them expect of them. He rejects the expectations harbored by the community vis-à-vis their sacrifices and burnt offerings. Obviously a pagan and magical conception that governs the whole cultic life has stolen its way into the existing sacrificial system adopted and regulated in Israel. While it is altogether proper to celebrate a fellowship meal with Yahweh in the sacrifice (זבח) and to make a covenant (v. 5b), and while there is no doubt that the gift of homage in the עולה is always before the eyes of God as a sign of veneration and adoration on the part of the people (v. 8b), the community still serves altogether different purposes and goals with its sacrificial cultus. This becomes clear in vv. 9-13. Yahweh is expected to accept (לקח, v. 9) the animal, recognize the value of the sacrifice, satisfy his hunger (v. 12), and enjoy it. In other words, the idea is to purvey strength to Yahweh, make an impression on him, allay his wrath, and achieve a favorable disposition. It is these purposes and goals which—dominating the whole cultus—are associated with the offering that the prophetic speech opposes. Yahweh does not accept these animal sacrifices (v. 9). For details, cf. G. Dalman, *AuS* VI 90, 172, 283, 375. The magic conception of a necessary importation of power to divinity is strictly rejected, for "the earth and its fullness" belongs to Yahweh. He is the Creator and Lord of the world. This is a reference to ancient cultic conceptions of the Jerusalem tradition (see above, Intro. §10, 1). To the Creator and Lord of the world all animals belong. No one can give anything to God that he would not already have owned long ago. Thus the guilt of Israel consists of this, that the people have forgotten (v. 22) the majestic reality of their God. But in the theophany and self-presentation Yahweh approaches his people anew. Naively anthropomorphic pictures of God, as if he ate the flesh of the animals and drank the blood of goats are cleared away (v. 13). Rejected are all expectations which human beings harbor respecting the possibility of being able to make an impression on Yahweh. This is where the emphasis lies. And as the false cultic procedures that are distant from God are eradicated and condemned beneath the weight of the sovereign self-assertions of Yahweh, the proper worship of Yahweh is simultaneously brought into prominence (vv. 14-15). Here there is no mention of sacrifices and burnt offerings in the comprehensive sense. The assembled community is called on to offer (זבח) the תודה and to pay its vows to the עליון (v. 14). Yahweh is that עליון, the "Most High God," the Creator and Lord of the world. In this designation of God from the Jerusalem cultic tradition (see above, Intro. §10, 1) the statements of vv. 9-13 are practically summarized. No one can influence the עליון by means of gifts, but certainly Israel ought finally to recognize the gifts of the עליון and to thank him. That would be proper worship.

Special recognition is due the arrangement in vv. 14f. regarding the תודה. The explanation can follow the investigations of H. J. Hermisson, *Sprache und Ritus im altisraelitischen Kult*, WMANT 19 (1965) 35f. Verse 15 clearly indicates how the worshiper goes about presenting a תודה to Yahweh: In his petitionary prayer he has made a vow of praise in a situation of greatest distress, and thereby has promised to proclaim publicly the rescue and aid experienced through Yahweh. For the תודה, see above, Intro. §6, 2aγ. The vow of thanksgiving could also hold out the prospect of a sacrifice. But "while the thanksgiving can certainly get along without the sacrifice, the sacrifice cannot do without the thanksgiving" (H. J. Hermisson, 35). Now the question arises of the significance of the accent on the תודה over against the other sacrifices. "The opinion that 'material' sacrifices are here rejected and 'spiritual' praise is demanded does not do justice to the text. This is clearly a polemic not against the sacrificial cultus as such but against a definite, doubtlessly very primitive understanding which thinks of sacrifices as the food of the divinity" (H. J. Hermisson, 36). Is there adherence then to the actual presentation of a תודה-sacrifice? The formulation זבח תודה could lead us to answer this question in the affirmative. Still, one easily refers this formulation to the presentation of the song of thanksgiving. This song of praise "must of necessity be presented before the assembled community, and to indicate this it is not necessary to use the verb זבח. The verb rather indicates that the song of praise is presented as an offering. If we keep this in mind, then in addition, of course, the sacrifices of animals are not excluded. The speech does not require any revolutionary changes in the cultus, but it switches the emphases—or perhaps one should prefer to say, it arranges them properly" (H. J. Hermisson, 36). Also v. 15 comes under the light of these corrections. In the day of distress the human being should not try to influence Yahweh, but should call (קרא) and confidently look forward to Yahweh's action.

[50:16-21] At v. 16 a new section of the speech begins. Again the subject in this authoritative speech of law and judgment is the proper worship before Yahweh. In vv. 7-15 the subject was the proper service of sacrifice, but here we are to deal with life under the expression of Yahweh's will and his covenant ordinances. Theophany and judgment speech in Psalm 50 penetrate the entire cultic foreground and take hold of the innermost recesses of the person (cf. Isa. 29:13ff.; Deut. 6:4ff.). Is Yahweh actually being served? Do the community and every single individual of the people of God live in the sphere of influence of the reality of God? Or have religious, magical, hypocritical manipulations crept in, by means of which the majestic lordship of Yahweh has been side-stepped? The introductory formula ולרשע אמר אלהים, a secondary interpolation in v. 16, leads to an understanding of the second phase of the speech (vv. 16ff.). Still, we should at least consider the possible interpretation that the speaker sailed into an individual person in the circle of the assembled cultic community (H. Schmidt), or perhaps addressed a specific type. In any case, the speech becomes very specific. The person to whom the prophetic word is applied is called רשע. From the contents of what follows we are to ascertain whether this characterization is correct. As in vv. 7-15, so also in vv. 16ff. we are dealing with a speech by Yahweh.

The address in v. 16, zeroing in on an individual, is more caustic than that in vv. 8ff. The inquiry is as severe as the guilt-revealing "reproach" of the prophets. The thought is of a person who continuously takes into his mouth and "enumerates" Yahweh's assertions of his will and his covenant arrangements. One could ask whether ספר perhaps refers to a specific custom of regularly recalling God's commandments (as, e.g., in Deut. 6:7ff.). For since חקי certainly—as the context indicates—refers to the Decalog, we could perhaps think of counting the Ten Commandments on the ten fingers. It is not unusual for חקי and בריתי to be in parallel construction, but it corresponds to the Deuteronomic way of thinking, which is discernible in vv. 16ff.

In v. 17 the person who always has the commandments of God in his mouth is accused of having rejected מוסר. מוסר denotes the "existential" combination of obedience and discipline into which Yahweh's covenant and covenant law place human beings (cf. Jer. 2:20; 5:3; 7:28; Prov. 15:10). Yet this immediate life relation in obedience and discipline is hated by the person addressed through the prophetic word. He throws the words of God (like peels of a fruit) back over his shoulders and does not let them determine or lead him. He is open game for all wickedness that comes his way (vv. 18ff.). From the Decalog only three commandments are selected (as examples): not to steal, not to commit adultery, not to bear false witness. In reference to these commandments it is demonstrated—in spite of all outward interest in confession—that the will of God is despised and violated. For the citation of individual apodictic legal statements of the Decalog in prophetic speech, cf. Hos. 4:2; Jer. 7:9. On the prophetic condemnation of lip-confession, cf. Isa. 29:13ff. Piercing the religious formalism and ritualism, the word penetrates to the heart of the person and unmasks him actually as a רשע (v. 16). The reference to the apodictic commandments (vv. 18-20) surely is to be explained on the basis of the cultic content of the covenant festival. At the ceremony of covenant renewal the apodictic commandments were proclaimed anew (A. Alt, *KlSchr* I 327ff.). The judgment speech in vv. 16-21, in a word of law and judgment (that obviously concludes the ceremonial), rules out all external piety, every formal lip-confession, as ungodly and godless "religiosity." Yahweh is not silent over against the hypocritical measures of his covenant partners (v. 21). Yahweh comes forth (v. 3) to destroy among his people the erroneous thought that one can communicate with God in human relations and categories. God is God and not a human being (Num. 23:19; Hos. 11:9). Theophany and prophecy cause the world of human falsehood to collapse—and especially where religion and cultus practice this falsehood in the most subtle way. The concluding verse segment אוכיחך ואערכה לעיניך underlines the fact of the confrontation with the reality of God that gives new orientation, which in the Levitical sermon expresses itself in prophetic authority.

[50:22] This verse probably belongs to the speech section vv. 16-21 and is to be understood as a call of warning and a threat. The human beings described in vv. 16-21 are portrayed as those who "forget God," i.e., those who no longer recognize God's reality, which is peculiar to God and completely different from all human conceptions and expectations. The verb טרף hints at the "tearing" of a lion. He who is struck by Yahweh's judgment, which is only alluded to in v. 22b, is hopelessly lost (אין מציל). It is worth noting that the second section of the speech (vv. 16-22) concludes differently from the first. In vv. 14-15, instead of the false, usurped offering cult, the proper offering service pleasing to Yahweh was substituted. In v. 22, on the other hand, the disobedient are warned and threatened. More precisely, we would have to speak of an "ultimate admonition" (J. Jeremias, 125). And here it is striking that the speech of judgment does not announce an attendant punishment—as is customary in prophecy.

[50:23] This verse is to be taken as a summary of the two sections of the speech. Here the two proper ways of behavior before Yahweh are emphasized and held up to the light of a comprehensive promise. He who offers thanksgiving honors Yahweh; this is the first part of the sentence. Accordingly, sacrificial service does not yet come under the light of promise but only under the statement: יכבדנני. The "upright walk" (תם דרך) is determined in the covenant arrangements of Yahweh. He who lives in the discipline of Yahweh and does not cast his word aside (v. 17) will "see the salvation of Yahweh" (cf. Ps. 91:16).

Purpose and Thrust

Theophany and the judgment speech are the two intimately connected events that impinge on the assembled community in the worship act of covenant renewal (v. 5b). The theophany confronts the cultic community with the transcendent, otherworldly reality of God, which puts an end to the religious delusion that God might be a partner in a deal or a silent numen on the same plane with human beings (v. 21aβ). In the judgment speech Yahweh himself speaks through the mouth of an authorized spokesperson who is responsible for the proper worship of God. The guilt of Israel, the people of the covenant, is revealed in two judgment speeches (vv. 7-15; 16-22). The sacrificial system is set in the context of a new relation to Yahweh in vv. 7-15. The erroneous conception that one could make an impression on Yahweh with gifts falls prey to derision and scornful rejection in the face of the shining majesty of the עליון, the Creator and Lord of the world. Only those sacrifices that bear witness to the thanksgiving and veneration of the people (vv. 8, 14-15, 23a) are pleasing to God.

The attitude of the individual human being under the covenant laws of Yahweh is the burden of the second section of the speech (vv. 16-22). Here the innate life questions of the covenant people Israel are the subject. On Sinai Yahweh made a covenant with Israel and revealed his will, his covenant arrangements, especially in the form of the apodictic commandments of the Decalog. What is the position of God's people over against these commandments? From Deut. 6:4ff. we are to learn that all conceivable efforts were undertaken to keep God's will before one's eyes everywhere and at all times. But the danger of a religious and ritualistic formalism threatened. The covenant arrangements were mechanically recited, but the obedient and disciplined life under the commandments (v. 17) was despised, i.e., God himself was forgotten (v. 22). Against this contempt of Yahweh the threatening and warning word was raised (v. 22). The entire psalm therefore is doubtlessly in the tradition of a cultically rooted renewal of the relation of God and people. Also in the late times of Levitical preaching, which are characterized by an amazing prophetic consciousness of full power and mission, intentions come to a head and into validity which could have their roots in older cultic transmissions.

Psalm 50 displays classically what the appropriate human attitude is to the God who intervenes in this life. Whether God comes or whether he stays away is beyond human control. But as soon as God comes, his becoming present can bring salvation—or downfall—for human beings. In each case the person's responsibility is revealed, and he is found to be guilty. That divine activity does not become savingly effective by means of pious efforts such as overabundant sacrifices; such things make no impression on God (vv. 8ff.). Such an endeavor may even lead to hypocrisy and thus achieve the very opposite (v. 16). No, God's salvation comes exclusively to those who become conscious of their forgetfulness of God and at the same time with praise and thanksgiving—because they have in spite of that not perished—flee to the area of God's salvation (vv. 22f.). At the same time, in every distress and without thinking of their own respectability and worthiness they dare to turn to the mighty God (v. 15) and thereby to demand the continuity of divine saving activity (K. Koch, "Meditation über Ps 50:14-23," *Herr, tue meine Lippen auf* Bd V, ed. G. Eichholz [1961], 479f.).

Psalm 51

Prayer for Forgiveness of Guilt and Renewal of the Heart

Literature

C. Steuernagel, "Psalm 51," *Sellin-Festschrift* (1927) 151ff. R. Galdos, "Psalm 50 'Misere mei, Deus'; exegetica explicatio," *VD* 10 (1930) 67-79. R. Arconada, "Psalmus 50/51 (Misere) retentus, emendatus, glossatus," *VD* 11 (1931) 197-206. N. H. Snaith, *Five Psalms: Ps 1; 27; 51; 107; 34; A New Translation with Commentary and Questionary* (1938). R. Press, "Die eschatologische Ausrichtung des 51. Psalms," *ThZ* 11 (1955) 241-249. H. J. Stoebe, " 'Gott sei mir Sünder gnädig': Eine Auslegung des 51. Psalms," *BiblStud* 20 (1958). G. J. Botterweck "Sei mir gnädig, Jahwe, nach deiner Güte: Eine Meditation über Ps 51(50), 3-14,"*BiLe* 2 (1961) 136-142. E. Beaucamp, "Justice divine et pardon . . . (Ps LI,6b)," *A la rencontre de Dieu: Mémorial A. Gelin* (1961) 129-144. P. E. Bonnard, "Le vocabulaire du Miserere," *A la rencontre de Dieu: Mémorial A. Gelin* (1961) 145-156. E. R. Dalglish, *Psalm Fifty-One in the Light of Ancient Near East Patternism* (1962). G. Giavini, "Salmo 51 (50): Miserere," *Ambrosius* 42 (1966) 280-288. N. H. Ridderbos, "Ps 51,5-6," *Studia Biblica et Semitica, ThC Vriezen dedicata* (1966) 299-312. H. Gross, "Theologische Eigenart der Psalmen und ihre Bedeutung für die Offenbarung des Alten Testaments—dargestellt an Ps 51," *BiLe* 8 (1967) 248-256. A. Caquot, "Purification et expiation selon le psaume LI," *RHR* 169 (1966) 133-154. J. K. Zink, "Uncleanness and Sin: A Study of Job 14,4 and Psalm 51,7," *VT* 17 (1967) 354-361. K. Condon, "The Biblical Doctrine of Original Sin," *ITQ* 34 (1967) 20-36. L. Neve, "Realized Eschatology in Psalm 51," *ET* 80 (1968/69) 264-266.

Text

To the choirmaster. A psalm of David. When the prophet Nathan came to him after he had gone in to Bathsheba.

51:1 Be merciful to me, O 'Yahweh,'[a] according to your goodness,[b]
according to your compassion blot out my wicked deeds!

2 Completely[c] wash away my guilt from me
and cleanse me of my sins!

3 For my wicked deeds I[d] acknowledge,
and my sins I have always before my eyes.

498

4 Against you alone have I sinned
  and done what is wicked in your eyes;
  so that you may be correct in your sentence
  and may be blameless in your judgment.
5 Behold, I was born in guilt,
  in sins did my mother conceive me.
6 Behold, you have pleasure[e] in truth in what is hidden,
  and in what is secret you teach me wisdom.
7 Purge me with hyssop, that I may be clean,
  wash me, that I may be whiter than snow!
8 Let me enjoy[f] exultation and happiness,
  that the bones which you have broken may rejoice!
9 Hide your countenance from my sins
  and blot out all my guilt!
10 Create a clean heart within me, 'O Yahweh,'[g]
  and bring a steadfast, new spirit into my breast!
11 Cast me not away from your countenance
  and do not take your holy Spirit from me!
12 Let me again feel the joy in your help
  and support me with the spirit of obedience!
13 Then I will teach your ways[h] to the wicked,
  that the sinners may turn to you.
14 Rescue me from blood, O Yahweh, '   '[i]
  that my tongue may shout for joy about your righteousness!
15 Lord, open my lips,
  that my mouth may proclaim your praise!
16 For in sacrifices you have no pleasure,[j]
  and 'if I were to bring'[k] a burnt offering, you would not want (it).
17 'My sacrifice,'[l] 'O Yahweh,'[m] is a broken spirit;
  a bruised and broken heart, O God, you do not despise.
18 In your mercy show goodness to Zion,
  build the walls of Jerusalem!
19 Then right sacrifices will delight you, '   '[n]
  then bulls will be brought to your altar.

1a In the Elohistically revised part of the Psalter we are to read יהוה instead of אלהים.
b Gk: τὸ μέγα ἔλεός σου. A corresponding complementation of הַגָּדוֹל would make us presuppose a 4 + 4 meter; but the MT is probably to be preferred.
2c *Ketib:* הַרְבֵּה; *Qere* and a number of Mss: הֶרֶב.
3d Frequently אֹדֶעַ = "I confess" (with a change in pointing) is read instead of עֲדֵעַ; but the MT is probably to be preferred (cf. the parallelism).
6e The MT reading of this text is difficult to understand. What is meant by v. 6a, "You have pleasure in truth in what is hidden"? On this, cf. "Commentary" (below). A correction, however, is hardly necessary. Worth noting is H. Gunkel's suggestion, to read חִפַּשְׂתִּי (= "I have traced down") instead of חָפַצְתָּ. But an appropriate understanding of the text offered by the MT is possible.
8f S has תַּשְׂבִּיעֵנִי ("satisfy me"); but we should probably follow the MT.
10g Cf. note **a**.
13h A number of Mss, S have דרכך (singular); but we should follow the MT.
14i אלהי תשועתי is to be eliminated from the verse for the sake of the meter; there is an interpolation.
16j Gk makes the assertions positive and provides the following text:
ὅτι εἰ ἠθέλησας θυσίαν, ἔδωκα ἄν·
ὁλοκαυτώματα οὐκ εὐδοκήσεις.
But this understanding of the text is not appropriate; the context refutes it (cf. vv. 17, 19); there a contrast is set up to the previous negative position regarding sacrifices.

k *Atnaḥ* is in the wrong place. Following T and for the sake of the meter, וְאֶתְנָה is to be taken with v. 16b.
17l MT: ''sacrifice of God''; syntactically, difficulties arise, for the plural זבחי does not fit well with רוח. Originally the reading here was probably זְבְחִי.
m Cf. note **a.**
19n עולה וכליל should probably be considered an explanatory interpolation.

Form

The psalm text is transmitted reliably and also provides clear metrical arrangements. The 3 + 3 meter is determinant. Only three verses are exceptions: vv. 1 and 11 are to be read in the 3 + 4 meter, and v. 17 in the 4 + 4 meter. An analysis of the structure yields the following picture: title; vv. 1-2, petition; vv. 3-6, acknowledgment of guilt; vv. 7-9, plea for deliverance from sin; vv. 10-12, prayer for a clean heart and a willing spirit; v. 13, vow to praise and teach; v. 14, petition; v. 15, prayer to make praise possible; vv. 16-17, thoughts about the right offering; vv. 18-19, intercession for Jerusalem. It has been recognized a long time that the last-named section, vv. 18-19, is a later accretion which corrects the thoughts about offerings in v. 15 in a striking way and inserts a time-conditioned plea: to build the walls of Jerusalem. H. Gunkel remarks concerning vv. 18-19: ''A later, timidly legalistic pious person who was not able to grasp the lofty sense of the psalmist quietly took offense at the fact that the psalmist spoke so freely of sacrifices, which after all are prescribed by God's law.'' We see that the problems raised in Romans 14 are already acute in the Old Testament.

Psalm 51 belongs to the form-group, prayer songs, in which descriptions of distress and petition dominate, but in which the prospect of the hour of thanksgiving (*todah*) is then also entertained (vv. 13, 15f.). On the prayer songs, see above, Intro. §6, 2.

Setting

The petitionary prayer is customarily presented before Yahweh in the area of the sanctuary. When the singer in v. 7 prays for purgation ''with hyssop,'' rituals of cleansing of the cultic site are being referred to. But what is the petitioner's situation? What distress does he have to suffer? In the more recent explanations of the psalm the conception dominates that the confession of guilt always is connected with the petition for healing from a serious illness. The opinion is that physical suffering always precipitates the question about guilt as the cause and thus is the first inducement for a confession of guilt. Thus H. Gunkel sees the psalmsinger as a person who is seriously ill, and he points to v. 8, where mention is made of the ''broken bones'' of the one who is praying. F. Nötscher, however, considers v. 8 an expressive illustration of inner suffering and refers the thought to a sickness. In any case, we will have to be careful not to carry over into all the psalms the dogma of a causal connection between sickness and guilt. That it was completely customary—even in more ancient times—to intone songs of prayer and petition in a situation of guilt (even without any symptoms of sickness) is shown by the narrative in 2 Samuel 12, to which the title of Psalm 51 refers. But even if we may detect a reference to sickness in v. 8, we should take note that according to the wording of the individual verses ''being freed from his sins was more important for the psalmist than a restoration of health, which is never mentioned'' (J. J. Stamm, *Erlösen und Vergeben im Alten Testament* [1940], 132).

When is Psalm 51 to be dated? It has long been recognized that the title gives no clue about the author and the historical occasion. The psalm is unthinkable for the time of David. On the question about the significance of the title, see below, "Commentary." Clues for a time setting of Psalm 51 have to be found in the contents of the prayer song itself. Here two observations are to be emphasized: (1) The prayer for a clean heart and a "spirit of obedience" (vv. 10-12) reminds one of Jer. 24:7; 31:33; 32:39; Ezek. 36:25ff. (2) The thoughts about the value of sacrifices in vv. 16f. point to the prophetic protest against the sacrificial system (Amos 5:22; Isa. 1:11; Jer. 6:20; and often). Thus important points of view about the dating are given. Of course, whether the reference of Psalm 51 to Jer. 31:31-34 and Ezek. 36:25-27 can be thought of in this way, that in it a kind of "realized eschatology" is proved, seems rather doubtful in any case. On "realized eschatology" in Psalm 51, cf. L. Neve, *Expository Times* 80 (1968/69) 264ff. Nevertheless, it is certain that Psalm 51 is to be dated later than Ezekiel 36. If vv. 18-19 are to be thought of as an accretion which most probably can be dated to the time of Nehemiah (building of the walls!), then the time of Nehemiah should be given as the terminus ad quem. Thus a relatively clear picture results. Such a determination of time in the explanation of the prayer songs is not always possible. Also after looking at Psalm 51 we should still ask whether a prior form of the prayer does not point back to an earlier time. After all, with its supplementation in vv. 18-19 the psalm clearly shows that prayer formulations in the course of time were subject to expansion and modifications. Therefore we will always have to think of the formulary character of the prayer songs as our point of departure.

Commentary

[Title] On למנצח, see above, Intro. §4, No. 17. מזמור לדוד, Intro. §4, No. 2.

The situation to which the reader and petitioner of Psalm 51 is to go back is reported in 2 Samuel 12. Such a reference, even if it does not coincide with "historical facts," should not simply be disregarded as a secondary accretion and therefore as immaterial. H. J. Stoebe correctly emphasizes: "It would now be completely wrong to simply discard such titles as fictional inventions and later accretions to the text. On the contrary, they carry considerable weight with us, for they are living proof of how the community heard and understood; they are, so to say, illustrations and, as such, evidence both of faith and of first interpretation" (H. J. Stoebe, *BiblStud* 20, 17).

[51:1-2] In his distress the petitioner and singer of Psalm 51 appeals to the goodness and mercy of Yahweh. On חסד, cf. the comment on Ps. 5:4-7. The real wrong with which Psalm 51 has to do is פשע, "breaking away from God" (F. Delitzsch, the "revolt of the human will against the divine will" (L. Köhler, *OT Theology* 170). This guilt stands between God and man—heavy and burdensome (cf. Psalm 32). In v. 1b the underlying conception obviously is that the sin is registered. מחה denotes the act of blotting out (Num. 5:23; Isa. 43:25; Ps. 109:14). Are we to presuppose specific rites here? Num. 5:23 reminds us of the judgment of God. But we should not be allowed to introduce this conception in Psalm 51 (against H. Schmidt). The Babylonians speak of tablets on which sins are registered, and they ask that these tablets be broken (H. Zimmern, *KAT*[3] 402). Exodus 32:32 and Ps. 69:28 speak of "books" which Yahweh keeps in Israel. In v. 2 the concepts for guilt are varied. עון has the meaning "perversion," "distortion" (F. Delitzsch). The word expresses "an intention not in accord with God's will" (L. Köhler, *OT Theol* 170). And חטאת denotes "failure," "miss" (L. Köhler, 169). כבס is a very strong verb which can have the meaning "to full." The petitioner is pleading for a thorough cleansing of his guilt, which is basically represented as defilement, as filth and defect. In the background here, without question, there are procedures of cultic cleansing—acts of cultic illustration, "in which the penitent let himself be bathed or he himself washed himself and his clothes, while at the same time forgiveness of sins was pronounced over him" (H. Gunkel and J. Begrich, *EinlPs* 179). On the terms in v. 1, cf. J. J. Stamm, *Erlösen und Vergeben im Alten Testament* (1940) 74ff. The guilt is intolerable; it must not only be softened and diminished but must be eliminated completely: blotted out, washed away, made to disappear from the sight of God. The petitioner knows "that the removal of this intolerable thing cannot be his own work but only God's: a divine blotting out, cleansing, and washing away . . . " (K. Barth, *CD* 4/1, 579).

[51:3-6] These verses deal with the recognition of guilt. The petitioner confesses that he clearly sees his offense. "The subject is emphatic" (A. Cohen). The offense is always before the guilty one's eyes. As in Psalm 32, the pressure and threat of the tormenting sin is expressed (also cf. Ps. 38:4 ff.)[1]

> We might here mention a remarkable parallel from the Akkadian psalm literature:
>> "Who is he who for all time has not fallen into sin against his God,
>> who for all time observed the command?
>> Human beings, as many as they are, know about sin!
>> I, your servant, have sinned again and again in all things,
>> stood before you, but again and again sought unrighteousness.
>> Lies I spoke again and again, dismissed my sin lightheartedly,
>> said harmful things again and again; all this you should know!"
>> (A. Falkenstein and W. von Soden, *Sumerische und akkadische Hymnen und Gebete* [1953], 272).

[51:4] The interpretation of the words לך לבדך חטאתי in v. 4 has resulted in heated debate.[2] How is this confession to be understood? Has the petitioner of the psalm sinned against Yahweh himself through idolatry (Baethgen), or is guilt over against human beings viewed as sin against God? H. Gunkel rejects both conceptions and judges, among other things, "The interpretation of the word often attempted, that all sin, also that against human beings, is in the last analysis only an insult to God, is a distortion of the text." This judgment is not appropriate. Already very early in the OT offenses against other human beings are viewed as sin against God (Gen. 39:9). And in 2 Sam. 12:13 David confesses

---

1. "True penitence is no dead knowledge concerning sin committed but a living, sensitive consciousness of it (Isa. 59:12), for which as the object and cause for unrest and pain it is always present, and this sadness of penitence which takes in the whole personality of the person is of course not a matter of merit that brings about grace, but it is nevertheless the condition without which no bestowal of grace is possible" (F. Delitzsch).

2. "Against you only have I sinned and done what is evil in your sight. For only you are without sin. I am justly punished as one who does not have anything to punish in another. I am rightly blamed as one who does not have anything to blame another for" (Augustine, *Enarrationes in Psalmos* [Migne, *P.L.* 36/37, 590]).

חטאתי ליהוה after he had violated Bathsheba. In this passage there is doubtlessly a remarkably similar confession. He who transgresses God's commandments sins against God himself—that is no doubt the idea underlying v. 4. In addition, it is unmistakable in the text that there is an allusion to the First Commandment and how this allusion is made. The whole thing has to do with Yahweh himself. Cf. W. H. Schmidt, *Das erste Gebot,* TheolEx 165 (1970) 41. Sin is transgression of the First Commandment. Besides, vv. 4f. are to be viewed as an element of the so-called "court doxology" *Gattung.* He who has committed sin is called on to "give honor to" Yahweh (cf. Josh. 7:19; F. Horst, "Die Doxologien im Amosbuch," *ZAW* 47 [1929], 45ff.; G. von Rad, *OT Theol,* 1:375). In the confession of guilt the honor and majesty of God are at stake; therefore v. 4 has the goal of *Deum justificare* (Luther). In a confession of guilt over against God himself, the petitioner submits to the righteous judgment of Yahweh. דבר is (as the parallel passage shows) God's sentence of judgment. The psalmist acknowledges this under all circumstances, and to it he submits "for good or evil." To give God the honor, to yield to him—that, according to Luther, is the prerequisite of faith (H. J. Iwand, *Glaubensgerechtigkeit nach Luthers Lehre* [1941], 11f.).

[51:5] The basic declaration of the judgment doxology in v. 4 is further expanded by means of profound insight into man's fateful deterioration into guilt as it is expressed in vv. 5-6. עוון and חטא have from the hour of birth been the determining forces under whose signature life began. The petitioner wants to say that the primordial cause, the root cause of my existence, is interwoven with corruption.

> Statements of this kind in the OT are to be understood neither as genetically caused nor one-sidedly moral and sexist, nor as having a didactic tendency. Rather, in the final analysis this is a matter of shedding light in the presence of Yahweh on the final depths and basic foundations of human existence. The total depravity that is determinative for humans from the beginning is here acknowledged (Gen. 8:21; Job 14:4; 15:14f.; 25:4; Ps. 143:2; John 3:6). These biblical passages have been taken up in the church's doctrine of original sin but have frequently lost much in weight and effectiveness because the force of existential insight was considerably undone by erudition and was volatilized by genetic or moral-sexual viewpoints.

> Misleading are the statements of H. Gunkel that the OT does not recognize the total depravity of human nature but only affirms weakness vis-á-vis what is good, and that thus the OT statements are "a preparation for the church's doctrine of original sin." On the contrary, the OT emphasizes the total depravity, the degeneracy of guilt of human existence with an altogether different force than the church's doctrine of original sin. On the problem, cf. K. Condon, "The Biblical Doctrine of Original Sin," *IThQ* 34 (1967) 20-36.

[51:6] The statement of v. 6 has been called very enigmatic. It is obvious, however, that v. 6 should be related immediately to the context of v. 5. This connection is suggested by the fact that both verses are introduced by the word הן. The petitioner calls attention to special insights and perceptions in vv. 5 and 6. He has looked into abysses that are opened only to penetrating sight. אמת in peculiar parallelism to חכמה could denote the reliable knowledge of wisdom that forges ahead to discover the causes of things, a knowledge that Yahweh grants (תודיעני) in the area of what is hidden and concealed. Such knowledge (v. 5) that makes progress in discovering the most remote causes pleases Yahweh. We honor God in unreserved, total knowledge of ourselves, in that insight which is also able to see and express the hidden connections of depravity. Here clear relations to OT wisdom teaching are discernible. A passage like Jer. 17:9 should not be overlooked. Beyond that, it is peculiar that most of the OT assertions that speak of a total, basic depravity of human existence belong to the wisdom poetry of the book of Job (Job 14:4; 15:14f.; 25:4ff.). And yet the insight into the hidden depths of the degeneracy of guilt is not the result of human contemplation, but a gift of divine communication and revelation (תודיעני, v. 6). Cf. Job 11:6.

[51:7-9] The psalmist prays for absolution and pardon in vv. 7-9. The petition תחטאני באזוב ואטהר (v. 7a) alludes to an ancient ceremonial of cleansing. אזוב is probably not identical to the Greek ὅσωπος, as people have always thought and have correspondingly referred to the *Hyssopus officinalis L.* It is much more likely that marjoram (*Origanum Maru*) is involved. Cf. G. Dalman, *AuS* I 543-545. Very likely a whisk of hyssop shrubs was made with which water or blood was sprinkled on the penitent to indicate absolution. Cleansing power was attributed to the shrub as such. In a Babylonian prayer to Marduk the sinner prays: "May the tamarisks cleanse me, the . . . -growth release me, the palm pulp blot out my sins; may the basin of holy water of Ea and Asariluchi bring me good luck!" (A, Falkenstein and W. von Soden, *Sumerische und akkadische Hymnen und Gebete*, 306). Obviously, widespread cultic rites of cleansing are involved (Num. 19:18). A thorough washing (כבס, cf. v. 2) should let the sinner appear "whiter than snow" (cf. Isa. 1:18). If a number of exegetes want to identify a healing from leprosy with the cleansing with hyssop (cf. Lev. 14:4f., 49ff.), we should point out that the rites of cleansing of the OT are mentioned also in other connections (e.g., Exod. 12:22; Num. 19:6, 18). Incidentally, we could hardly assume that the rites of cleansing mentioned in Psalm 51 are all still practiced. It certainly is obvious that we are to think of ancient cultic practices which still survive only in conventional formulas of the petitionary prayers. In v. 8 the psalmist thinks of the תרועה of the festival of thanksgiving, the תודה (cf. the comment on Ps. 27:6). The petitioner would like to hear the exultation and the shouts of joy of the one who has experienced Yahweh's salvation. But pardon would mean that Yahweh has "let his countenance shine" and has "lifted it up." Yet, for a time God hides his countenance in view of the sins (v. 9). Dark and threatening, the guilt (and in Psalm 51 it is always only the guilt) stands between Yahweh and the petitioner. מחה (cf. 1b)—may God "blot out" that which is intolerable, that which separates.

[51:10-12] Only an act of God, only his intervention can turn all things around. In vv. 10-12 the psalmsinger prays for new creation in his depraved inner self (cf. v. 5). Incomparably bold is the use of the verb ברא in v. 10. This word in the OT is absolutely strictly reserved for the creative work of God only (cf. P. Humbert, "Emploi et portée du verbe *bārā* dans l'Ancien Testament," *ThZ* 3 [1947]); it is never used in reference to a human undertaking. God alone is always the subject of this verb. God's creation (cf. Gen. 1:1) is fundamentally different from all human endeavor; unique is his creative activity—free of all presuppositions and contacts, uplifted above all chaotic impossibilities. The "clean heart" one cannot provide for oneself; no rite can bring it to life. Only God's independent, creative act can renew a person's heart. That is the knowledge of the petitions of Psalm 51, which tower so steeply in the OT. But not only for cleansing of his heart does the psalmist pray; at the same time he desires a "steadfast spirit" which also in the future is redeemed from all inconstancy and fickleness (on נכון, cf. Pss. 78:37; 112:7). While לב in the OT simply denotes the center of human existence as the seat of all feeling, thinking, and willing, רוח refers to the effective power emanating from Yahweh that pervades all feeling, thinking, and will (cf. Ezek. 36:26ff.). If Yahweh removes (לקח) this hallowing רוח that leads man to God's center of power, then that is a sign that this person has been banned and "cast away" (השליך; v. 11) from his presence. רוח קדשׁ in Psalm 51 is the power of God that selects, cleanses, and in the innermost being motivates a person obediently to fulfill the will of Yahweh (Ezek. 36:27). רוח קדשׁך is nothing short of the guarantee of belonging to Yahweh and being in communion with Yahweh. The psalmist has only one worry: that Yahweh could cast him away and remove the Holy Spirit from him. On אל־תשׁליכני, cf. Pss. 27:9; 41:12; 71:9; 140:13. But pardon would mean that the "joy of salvation" (שׂשׂון ישׁעך) returns again (cf. v. 8a). And again the psalmist prays for Yahweh's support in view of the future (v. 12). רוח נכון (v. 10b) is explained in v. 12b as the "supporting spirit of willing obedience." The nearness of these words to the prophets' words in Jer. 24:7; 31:33; 32:39; Ezek. 36:25ff. is unmistakable. Jeremiah and Ezekiel proclaim that Yahweh himself will put his תורה into the heart of man and thus create joyous, willing obedience through his רוח. For the future the petitioner awaits such a "support" and consolidation of his life through the רוח נדיבה (cf. Ps. 143:10). With his petitions he therefore appeals to the great prophetic promises which in Jeremiah and Ezekiel go beyond the "old covenant." There lies the unique significance of the psalm.

[51:13-17] This section contains a vow (v. 13), petitions (vv. 14-15), and thoughts about the right, God-pleasing sacrifice (vv. 16-17). In his vow the psalmsinger declares that he wants to teach the פשׁעים the ways of Yahweh, so that they may turn to God. Cf. Ps. 22:22 in connection with this vow. The one who has experienced Yahweh's salvation becomes a witness to Yahweh's reality and goodness. דרך is a term for the expression of Yahweh's will and instructions documented especially in the Deuteronomic literature (cf. Psalm 25). In v. 13 the basic conception is that only through an acquaintance with the ways of Yahweh is the wrong way of the sinner recognized. Only so is a return possible. The authority of him who teaches has its foundation in the living experience of the ישׁועה of Yahweh.

About the meaning of the petition in v. 14 the commentaries contain divergent conceptions. Is the petitioner under threat of blood vengeance (so H. Schmidt)? Or are we to read מדומם ("before the quiet" of the underworld) instead of מדמים? The interpretation of B. Duhm is probably correct: "דמים can only mean the same thing here as in Ps. 30:9—death through sickness Yahweh has sent, not presumably a violent death at the hands of enemies, which are after all not mentioned anywhere." The psalmist prays for deliverance from death. צדקה in v. 14b does not have only the meaning "bestowal of salvation" (G. von Rad, *OT Theol*, 1:373). "We would rather have to paraphrase this way: The petitioner wants to praise God's righteousness which shows itself in new help for him, a guilty human being'' (H. J. Hermisson, *Sprache und Ritus im alt-israelitischen Kult,* WMANT 19 [1965], 49).

In v. 15 the petitioner of the psalm (thinking of the instruction and thanksgiving vowed in v. 13) prays that Yahweh may open his lips, i.e., that he may empower him to proclaim the glory of the rescuer. As in Ps. 40:3 (which see), the psalmist awaits an inspiration. He knows that he is completely dependent on God. Also the testimony to Yahweh's great deeds can succeed only if Yahweh ''opens'' the mouth of the speaker.

Thoughts about sacrifices in vv. 16-17 are intimately connected with the vow spoken in v. 13. It was customary for the one who prayed and presented petitions to bring sacrifices after his rescue (cf. Ps. 54:6). But the psalmsinger of Psalm 51 knows that Yahweh wants neither sacrifices nor burnt offerings. The rejection of the sacrificial system spoken of by the prophets (Amos 5:22; Isa. 1:11; Jer. 6:20) is taken up here and followed obediently. But what now in Psalm 51 takes the place of sacrifices? In v. 17 the psalmist declares, ''My sacrifice is a broken spirit.'' The petitioner therefore brings no substitute sacrifice, but he offers himself as the sacrifice. Human beings with a לב־נשבר ונדכה are seized with a deep despair about themselves. The brokenness of their natural confidence in life and self points to a condition of frightful anguish and despair vis-à-vis God. But such bottomless despair mysteriously conceals within itself the miracle of nearness to God. The psalmsinger presents to God the heart of a contrite penitent and pleading petitioner—in the certainty that this offering does not fall under a declarative judgment of rejection, but that it is pleasing to Yahweh: cf. Ps. 34:18; Isa. 57:15; 61:1.[3]

[51:18-19] The later accretion in vv. 18-19 expresses a petition which might easily be associated with the building of the walls carried out at the time of Nehemiah. On this petition, cf. Pss. 102:13, 16; 147:2; Jer. 31:38; Isa. 26:1; 33:20; 62:6. When in v. 19 then by means of an emphatic (double) אז the attention is directed to a legitimate new sacrificial system in newly rebuilt Jerusalem, obviously the statement of v. 16 is to be seen in a new light. The author of v. 19 apparently is thinking of an inner reformation of the sacrificial system that no longer falls under the prophets' protest. He looks over the tremendous confession of v. 17, which already points the way to Rom. 12:1, and clings to the OT cultic laws and to the worship regulated by these laws. This faithfulness over against the order of worship and this love over against the weak (1 Cor. 8:7ff.) should not be measured according to an enthusiastically usurped ''prophetic ideal,'' but one should try to understand it in its context. On זבחי־ צדק, cf. Ps. 4:5. There also a discussion of R. Schmidt, *Das Bundesopfer inIsrael,* Studien zum Alten und Neuen Testament 9 (1964) 40.

Purpose and Thrust

At the time of the Reformation Psalm 51 was among the influential Bible texts to which Luther appealed in his doctrine of justification. Even if details in this

---

3. ''This is the sweetest, most beautiful promise. If a person could only believe it, that our afflictions are for God the most acceptable sacrifices. (1) To preach, (2) to suffer and to be disquieted—these please our God and are his finest sacrifices. He is here not speaking of the sacrifice of praise. Humiliation is the greatest sacrifice, because it happens to the old man . . . So do our afflictions please God that one is equal to a thousand sacrifices before God. A disquieted spirit is a greater sacrifice than all the sacrifices of Leviticus. Yes, indeed, if a person could only believe it'' (Luther, Erlangen Ed., 17, 225f.).

Reformation interpretation were overstated and the text occasionally was "overinterpreted," nevertheless there can be no doubt that the essential statement of the psalm was correctly and appropriately grasped by Luther and Calvin. The petitioner knows that he is entirely dependent on the merciful activity of God. From God's mercy alone he expects the blotting out of the guilt which is looked on as the corruption (v. 5) that totally permeates the human being. Only God can eliminate the threatening, dark wall of separation, sin, that separates God and human beings and blot out what is intolerable. Only by God's creative, renewing power can the heart be cleansed and led to a new obedience. Also the future is in the hands of God alone. If God sends the spirit of willingness and constancy, then the psalmist is saved from fickleness and unfaithfulness. Even the witness of thanksgiving (v. 15) is exclusively left in the hands of powers furnished by Yahweh. Everything is God's act. The *sola gratia* shines forth from every verse. No gift, no condition comes between God and man. No sacrifice has an effect on Yahweh. Only the pleading and trusting human being is the sacrifice, he who with body and life surrenders himself to God, who has nothing else to offer but a heart that is bruised and broken (v. 17). The human being presents himself to God as what he is. For him nothing remains except to plead for forgiveness and to confess his guilt.[4] In its extreme of knowledge and wisdom (v. 6) which has been won from the prophetic word of the OT, Psalm 51 stands out in the Psalter. Its peak statements are unique. And its fullness of insight is incomprehensible.

On the beloved statement that Psalm 51 rises to "New Testament heights," H. Gese declares: "Actually, in this psalm of lament no 'outside' distress is lamented, but the only distress is sin, and the petitioner is worried about nothing else but his personal relation to God. A more precise analysis of structure with form criticism as its starting point would show that the ontology here present distinguishes very sharply between an outward world of appearances and an inner, true existence that is hidden. This true existence is the relation of God and soul. Corresponding to this, there is the highest spiritualization of the concept of sin (sin against God alone; having sinned 'personally'), the *sola gratia* conception of the forgiveness of sins, in an intellectual spiritual new creation in active, 'mystic' self-surrender, the reinterpretation of sacrifice as the recognition of the separation from God, etc. . . . Here one should not judge on the basis of the 'history of piety,' . . . but note how a sudden advance of an Old Testament tradition is executed in new forms of reality . . . " (H. Gese, *Von Sinai zum Zion: Alttestamentliche Beiträge zur biblischen Theologie*, *EvTh*Beih 64 [1974], 23f.).

---

4. "This is proof that remission of sins does not take place through works but through grace alone, or that works do not justify but only faith. Therefore there is no other satisfaction for sins than free remission of sins. Other satisfactions are fictions. In sum, all the words of this psalm point to the fact that we cannot by any work still the wrath of God and earn grace" (Luther, Erlangen Ed., 17, 249).

The Punishment of the Rich Man
of Violence

Literature

J. Jeremias, *Kultprophetie und Gerichtsverkündigung in der späten Königszeit Israels*, WMANT 35 (1970) 120.

Text

To the choirmaster. A *maskil* of David. When Doeg, the Edomite, came and told Saul, "David has come to Ahimelech's house."

52:1 Why do you boast of wickedness, 'O man of might,'[a]
'against the pious man'[b] at all times?

2 Harm you are plotting, your tongue is
like a sharp knife,
[you schemer]![c]

3 You love evil instead of what is good,
the lie instead of right speech.[d]—*Selah.*

4 You love all words of ruin,[e]
you cunning tongue!

5 But God will ruin you forever,
he will 'annihilate'[f] you and sweep you out of the tent;
uproot you from the land of life!—*Selah.*

6 The righteous may behold and tremble
and laugh about him,[g]

7 Behold, there is the man who did not take
'Yahweh'[h] as his 'refuge'![i]
He relied on his great wealth,
looked for refuge in his wickedness.

8 But I am like a greening olive tree
in the house of 'Yahweh.'[j]
I trust in 'Yahweh's'[j] grace
always and eternally.

508

9 I praise you, ʿO Yahweh,ʾᵏ eternally,
for you have done it.
I hope in your name, that it is good,
in the presence of your pious people.

1a הַגִּבּוֹר is hardly meaningful in the context unless one thinks of a derisive address. We might read הַגֶּבֶר (cf. v. 7a; Isa. 22:17).

b The entire v. 1 in its present form is distorted. V. 1b would literally have to be translated, "the grace of God all the time." In the parallelism, however, the reading suggested by S, אֶל־חָסֵד, or even עַל־חָסִיד, would be suitable.

2c עשה רמיה should very likely be removed from the verse structure (3 + 2) on account of the meter and should be thought of as an addition.

3d In a consistent reconstruction of the 3 + 2 meter, דבר is most often eliminated and we read מִצֶּדֶק.

4e Does דברי have to be eliminated here too? In that case, בְּלִיַּעַל could have been the reading. But we should follow Mt.

5f Following α´, Jerome, and T, we should point יַחְתְּךָ.

g S here offers a different text: ‎ויראו צדיקים וישמחו ויבטחו ביהוה.

7h In the Elohistically revised part of the Psalter יהוה is to be read instead of אלהים.

i A better pointing is מָעֻזּוֹ (cf. Ps. 27:1).

8j Cf. note **h.**

9k For the sake of the meter, יהוה should probably be added at this point.

Form

In Psalm 52 the 3 + 2 meter dominates. The attempt can be made to restore this meter to all verses by means of corrections (cf. H. Gunkel). But a few questions remain. For while, e.g., in v. 3 we could read (by shortening) מצדק instead of מדמר צדק and thus gain a 3 + 2 meter, the text before us in the MT of v. 5 still resists radical recastings. Here a 3 + 3 + 3 meter should probably be assumed. Verse 5 in any case comes much into prominence in the whole verse (see below).

Great difficulties beset a form-critical analysis of Psalm 52. Only with difficulty can the reference of the individual statements be recognized. This is where we will have to find clarity. Verses 1-8 present a speech that is characterized by strong emotions. It is addressed by a "pious man" (v. 1) to a "schemer" (v. 2). The person addressed is obviously a rich man (v. 7) who wants to have nothing to do with trust in Yahweh (v. 7a). Him the speaker of Psalm 52 opposes in a self-presentation in steadfast faith (v. 8).

Verse 9 contains a very expressive *todah* formula and accordingly points to an act of thanksgiving before Yahweh which a person delivered from distress experienced. Cf. F. Crüsemann, *Studien zur Formgeschichte von Hymnus und Danklied in Israel*, WMANT 32 (1969) 275; see above, Intro. §6, 2aγ. Can the psalm be understood on the basis of v. 9? That is the deciding question. H. Schmidt begins with the song of thanksgiving in v. 9, presupposes a "liturgy for a thankoffering for a vow," and considers vv. 1-8 a retrospective narrative that recalls the distress of being oppressed before Yahweh's intervention. But can there be any such thing as a retrospective narrative"? H. Gunkel even thinks he can discern an "individual lament" in vv. 1-8. But clearly against that is the character of these verses as address, established above. Of course, addresses to the wicked are not infrequent in the psalms designated by Gunkel as "individual laments" (cf. Pss. 4:2; 6:8; 58:1; 62:3; 119:115). But it is unusual that a longer address to the רשע precedes a short verse of thanksgiving and nothing more, not even a retrospective narrative in which the state of distress and the prayer are called to mind. Upon closer inspection, vv. 1-8 unmistakably show the influences of prophetic forms of speech—the basic outlines both of a guilt-disclosing philippic and of a juridical announcement (v. 5). Above all, Isa. 22:15ff. could be adduced as a formal pattern for the speech in Ps. 52:1-8. In v. 7 the traces of a satirical song are discernible (so R. Kittel with reference to Isa. 14:10ff.). Can a connection between the lament elements pointed out by Gunkel and Schmidt and the prophetic features of the psalm be made? Jörg Jeremias, looking at Psalm 52, thinks of an imitation of a liturgy of lament: "In the place of prophetic lament and juridical announcement we have in it indictment and malediction against an individual in the form of an address (vv. 1-5); as in real liturgies of lament, the effect is then described which the fall of the wicked person exercises on the guiltless, and confession of confidence as well as praise, which presupposes the answer to prayer, concludes the psalm" (WMANT 35 [1970], 120). But does the speech in vv. 1-8, borne by prophetic authority, thereby become assimilated, not so much to the lament, as also to a liturgical course, and in this assimilation become absorbed? Would we not have to be consistent and begin at v. 9, i.e., at the situation of the *todah*? Then the speech in vv. 1-8 could reflect the discussion with an influential accuser which has been settled in the sacred place and in which the oppressed person made use of prophetic forms of speech that were given to him in a formulary. Cf. W. Beyerlin, *Die Rettung der Bedrängten in den Feindpsalmen der Einzelnen auf institutionelle Zusammenhänge untersucht*, FRLANT 99 (1970).

Setting

The person addressed (vv. 1ff.) is a rich (v. 7), cunning man of power (vv. 2, 4) whose power and influence have become a trial for a pious man (חסיד). This חסיד can probably be found in the circles of the "poor" and the "helpless," who place their hope entirely in Yahweh. A theme of חכמה is touched (cf. Psalm 73) in Psalm 52—the motif of the "righteousness of God." However, it is worth noting that Psalm 52, removed from all reflecting and tormenting deliberations, steps up to the influential man of power with a prophetic-dynamic address. The problem therefore is not analyzed and thought through but approved prophetically. Verse 9, with the song of thanksgiving, points to the temple area. The conjecture of A. Bentzen is unlikely, viz., that Psalm 52 was the philippic of a king as it was spoken before the attack against mythical powers of destruction.

Even an approximate determination of the time of origin is hardly possible. The reference to the dependence of the psalm on prophetic forms of speech and style must suffice here.

Commentary

[Title] On למנצח, see above, Intro. §4, No. 17. On משכיל, Intro. §4, No. 5. On לדוד, Intro. §4, No. 2.

The statement of the situation refers to 1 Sam. 22:9-19 and is no doubt secondary (cf. only v. 8: the mention of the temple).

[52:1-4] Here the speech of the psalmist in the style of a prophetic philippic closes in on the cunning man of power, the עשׂה רמיה (v. 2); cf. Isa. 22:15ff. For the beginning of a speech with מה, cf. Ps. 50:16; Isa. 31:5. The style form of a question beginning suddenly is also found in Ps. 2:1. As a parallel we could mention an Akkadian call of adjuration in which we read: "Why are you furious, possessed, your eyes bloodshot, your mouth frothing gall, the hairs of your chest raised?" (E. Ebeling, *ZDMG* 69 [1915] 94). The rich man of power (v. 7), who is irreverently called גבר, glories and brags about his wickedness. His misdeeds are directed against the חסיד. Thus the one addressed in v. 1 is numbered among the "enemies of the individual" (see above, Intro. §10, 4). He thinks up הוות (cf. 5:9). He makes his appearances as the cunning calumniator. Like a sharpened razor (cf. K. Galling, *BRL* 378f.) is his tongue (cf. Pss. 55:21; 57:4; 64:3; 140:3; Jer. 9:2, 7). He is a עשה רמיה, an "inventor of schemes" (Ps. 101:7). In v. 3 the complete perversion of this man's attitude is described. Over against רע and שקר he has the relation of "loving" (אהב). Cf. Isa. 5:20. צדק as a contrast to שקר in v. 3b has the meaning "truth" (cf. also Prov. 12:17; 16:13). The address in v. 4 is harsh and sarcastic (cf. Ps. 120:3).

[52:5] In the prophetic speech the guilt-revealing and verdict-substantiating philippic is followed by the court announcement of the "threatening word" capable of a verdict. Verse 5 too is to be understood in this sense. The judgment on this slanderous evildoer is here being announced (F. Nötscher). The introductory גם now gives the reaction of Yahweh. The man of violence will be annihilated and swept out of the tent like dirt (cf. Ezek. 26:4; Sir. 10:17). Up to this point he was solidly rooted "in the land of life" (cf. Ps. 27:3), but now he will be uprooted. The "threatening word" therefore speaks of a "death by judgment" that will assail the עשה רמיה.

[52:6-8] The effect of this judgment on the צדיקים, on the persecuted חסיד (v. 1), is described or announced in vv. 6-8. The צדיקים will "behold and tremble" (H. Gunkel). This consonance of יראו and ייראו is found also in Ps. 40:3. In "fear" the צדיק recognizes God's real intervention in the world of men. At the same time he can "laugh" about the change that has taken place—in "joy over the final breakthrough of the long hidden and misjudged righteousness" (F. Delitzsch). Cf. Pss. 58:10; 69:32. Even though in Prov. 25:17 malicious joy over misfortunes is strictly forbidden, we still must observe that in v. 7 sounds of a "satirical song" (cf. Isa. 14:10ff.) are heard. The fallen one lies flat on the ground—bereft and stripped of all hybris and self-secure powers of influence. He becomes an example of unbelief. Thus he becomes a mockery who trusts in great riches and a crafty ability to make his own way! The חסיד on the other hand, the singer of the psalm, describes himself as one who has been preserved by Yahweh. He is like a green olive tree in the temple area (G. Dalman, *AuS* VI 58). To this very day cypresses and olive trees stand in the sacred area of the Dome of the Rock in Jerusalem. For the picture, cf. Ps. 92:12f.; Jer. 11:16; but also Ps. 1:3. The picture represents constant sojourn in the area of nearness to God (cf. Ps. 23:6). Such a way of life is a fruit of "trust" (בטח).

[52:9] This verse takes us into the situation of the liturgy of a festival of thanksgiving. The petitioner gives thanks (אודך) for all that Yahweh has done, for his bestowal of salvation. On כי עשית, a hymnic reference to the helpful intervention of Yahweh, cf. Ps. 22:31; Isa. 38:15. Also כי טוב is a hymnic short formula that is peculiar to the song of thanksgiving (cf. Pss. 54:6; 100:5; 106:1; 135:3). The doxology for Yahweh's great deeds is intoned נגד חסידיך (cf. the comment on Ps. 22:22).

Purpose and Thrust

The certainty that God rules and judges rightly is in the OT won in the midst of everyday life. This is where the decision is made whether God is God, whether God really intervenes and looks after human beings. For the חסיד and צדיק, who lives in a manner in keeping with the covenant, the figure of the rich man of power, who in sovereign manner asserts himself and with cunning makes his way, represents a profound, unbridgeable trial. This influential calumniator enjoys a good life, lives a long time—he has all the signs of a man blessed by God, while the poor חסיד suffers from the sly schemes of this rich man. And yet, the חסיד knows that God rules and judges. Bold and prodigious is his assurance. Like a prophet he, in the midst of oppression, attacks the great man, brings his guilt into the light of day, and in philippic addresses presents the reasons for a verdict (vv. 1ff.). Like a prophet the oppressed man announces the end to the man of power and thinks of him as cast out and hurled from life as an example of the righteous judgment of God. He stands there as a warning for unbelief, for lack of trust in Yahweh. The חסיד, however, experiences the constant bliss of nearness to God. His trust prevails to let him express thanks for the bestowal of the help and salvation of Yahweh. The this-worldliness of this demonstration of God's power is not done away with by the NT, but judgment and grace are nevertheless hidden and preserved in the mystery of the crucified Christ.

Psalm 53 (See the comments on Psalm 14)

Psalm 54

Supplication amid Hostile Oppression

Literature

J. Becker, "Israel deutet seine Psalmen," *Stuttgarter Bibel-Studien* 18 (1966) 64f. W. Beyerlin, *Die Rettung der Bedrängten in den Feindpsalmen der Einzelnen auf institutionelle Zusammenhänge untersucht,* FRLANT 99 (1970).

Text

> To the choirmaster. A *maskil* of David. When the Ziphites
> came and told Saul, David is in hiding among us.
> 54:1 'O Yahweh,'[a] in your name, help me,
>   vindicate me through your might!
>   2 'O Yahweh,'[b] hear my prayer,
>   listen to the words of my mouth!
>   3 For 'presumptive people'[c] have risen against me,
>   and violent men seek my life.
>   They do not have God before them.—*Selah.*
>   4 Behold, 'Yahweh'[d] is my helper,
>   the Lord is the support of my life.
>   5 May the evil turn back[e] upon my adversaries!
>   Destroy them, 'O Yahweh,'[f] in your faithfulness![g]
>   6 Thus I will gladly bring you offerings,
>   will thank your name ' ',[h] because it is so good;
>   7 that it may save me from all trouble
>   and my eye may gloat over my enemies.

1a In the Elohistically revised part of the Psalter we are to read יהוה here instead of אלהים.
2b See note **a.**
3c MT = "foreigners" (foreign enemies?). Following Mss, T, and Ps. 86:14, it is better to read זֵדִים.
4d See note **a.**
5e *Ketîb,* T: יָשׁוּב or יָשׁוֹב; *Qere* and many Mss, Gk, σ´: יָשִׁיב; S, Jerome: הָשִׁיבָה. *Ketîb*

is to be preferred; the jussive suits the context better than the imperfect.

f Cf. note **a.**

g The rare form באמתך should not be changed to בְּחַמָתְךְ. There is no cogent reason for the change.

6h For the sake of the meter יהוה should at this point be eliminated.

Form

This short, compact psalm is transparent and clear in its text. The 3 + 3 meter dominates and should also in v. 6b be reconstructed by the elimination of יהוה. In v. 3 the versification has three sections, which of course has given rise to a question that is hardly appropriate, namely, whether v. 3b could be a later addition.

We should start with an analysis of the structure; title; vv. 1-2, petition and wish; v. 3, description of the distress; v. 4, expression of trust; v. 5, wish, vow of praise with a view toward the moment of the thanksgiving.

Psalm 54 is to be assigned to the group, prayer songs (תפלה). See above, Intro. §6, 2. Petition, wish, and description of distress predominate. Together with the vow of praise, the prospect of a *todah* is kept in mind. See above, Intro. §6, 2aγ.

Setting

The petitioner of the psalm is surrounded by enemies and hard pressed (v. 3). He has suffered injustice (v. 1). Therefore he prays for Yahweh's intervention and for a visible defeat of his adversaries (v. 5). Petitions of this kind were in the OT most frequently spoken in the area of the temple. The psalmist probably belongs to uninfluential, poor members of the OT people of God, who seek refuge with Yahweh. There is nothing that points to the suggestion that there is a king involved (against A. Bentzen). Rather, everything indicates that we should think of connecting the psalm with God's jurisdiction in the sanctuary. An innocently accused person takes refuge in the temple area. He asks for Yahweh's judicial decision (v. 1) and for defeat of the enemies. Cf. W. Beyerlin, FRLANT 99 (1970).

Concerning the date of origin we can hardly suggest anything precise. That the psalmist belongs to the party of the Sadducees (B. Duhm) is not proved by the psalm. Perhaps one could deduce from the profiled שֵׁם-theology of the song that Psalm 54 is post-Deuteronomic, which would leave the question open whether Deuteronomy with its considerably older cultic traditions could in this connection be a historical criterion (cf. G. von Rad, *Deuteronomium-Studien* [1948²]).

Commentary

[Title] On למנצח, see above, Intro. §4, No. 17. On בנגינת, Intro. §4, No. 9. On משכיל, Intro. §4, No. 5. On לדוד, Intro. §4, No. 2.

The statement in the title regarding the situation secondarily associates Psalm 54 with the history of David, specifically with the story of 1 Sam. 23:19. On the significance of these subsequent connections, cf. the comment on Psalm 51, title.

In reference to the secondary connection of a number of psalms of David to the history of David, the question arises about the internal or external motive. What impelled the transmitters and editors to make the connection, e.g., between Psalm 51 and 2 Samuel

12 and between Psalm 54 and 1 Sam. 23:19? This question will have to be asked over and over. In the two psalms referred to as examples certain peculiar and noteworthy associations of words and expressions can be noted. In Ps. 51:4 the petitioner confesses in view of his guilt: לך לבדך חטאתי; this singular confession of the OT has its echo in David's admission in 2 Sam. 12:13: חטאתי ליהוה. In Ps. 54:3 the phrase בקשו נפשי is prominent; in David's story we read in 1 Sam. 23:15, לבקש את־נפשו. We cannot lightly dismiss these suggestions and associations. They reveal a scribe's enthusiasm that tries to establish the historical settings of the Psalms and wants to anchor the individual songs in associations with events.

[54:1-2] Psalm 54 begins with a petitionary call, with the vocative יהוה, so characteristic of the prayer songs but altered to אלהים in the Elohistic part of the Psalter. בשמך follows adverbially. In his affliction, the petitioner expects help and rescue from Yahweh's שם. The "name" is the bearer of the power of revelation, of the גבורה ("heroic might") of God active on earth. It is in full independence the sign of Yahweh's relationship to the world and presence in it in his chosen people. Cf. O. Grether, *Name und Wort Gottes im Alten Testament,* BZAW 64 (1934), 44ff. The preposition ב in בשמך depicts the שם as the tool or medium by which Yahweh proves his גבורה (cf. Pss. 66:7; 71:18; 89:13; and often) to be effective in the world. Yahweh is called on as a judge; he is to "vindicate" (דין, cf. Gen. 30:6; Deut. 32:36). Thus the petitioner suffers injustice, and he is persecuted by slanderous enemies. Verse 2 pleads for a hearing of this petitionary call and prayer.

[54:3] Introduced by כי, v. 3 gives reasons for the petitionary call in vv. 1-2 by referring to "presumptuous" (זדים cf. Ps. 86:14) and "violent" (עריצים, cf. Ps. 86:14; Jer. 15:21; Job 6:23; 27:13) people who seek the life of the petitioner. The "enemies of the individual" here arise (see above, Intro. §10, 4). They have an accusation to bring against the psalmist. The inner connections of this slanderous accusation and persecution are not mentioned. In any case, the petitioner is in peril of death. Only a single judgment is pronounced on the persecutors, but a very significant one: "They do not have God before them." The רשע does not live in the יראת יהוה; he flees and alienates the reality of God. On סלה, see above, Intro. §4, No. 13.

[54:4-5] In this verse an expression of trust is heard. The petitioner—in contrast to his enemies—has Yahweh "before his eyes" and trusts in him. On this contrast, cf. Ps. 52:7-8. On בסמכי נפשי, cf. Ps. 118:7. Immediately after the expression of trust, there is a wish—that Yahweh may "turn back" on the persecutors themselves the evil they have planned for the psalmist. With this wish the effect of an "immanent nemesis" in the "sphere of action which creates fate" is prayed for (on this, cf. K. Koch, "Gibt es ein Vergeltungsdogma im Alten Testament?" *ZThK* 52 [1955], 1ff.; G. von Rad, *OT Theol,* 1:385). The evil generated by wicked motives should strike back at the evildoer. On the theological problems of this "immanent nemesis," cf. Ps. 7:13-16. In v. 5b it becomes evident that Yahweh himself has his hand in "the area of fateful deeds." Yahweh's שם and his גבורה were appealed to in v. 1. His אמת is to show itself effective in the defeat of the enemies. אמת is here "faithfulness," "constancy," which Yahweh shows to those who trust in him.

[54:6-7] These verses look forward to the hour of the festival of thanksgiving.

The petitioner makes the vow: בנדבה אזבחה־לך. The reference to the "freewill" offering is to be understood in connection with a fixed offering terminology (cf. Ezek. 46:12; Ezra 3:5; 2 Chron. 31:14), which obviously involves a renunciation of magical, mechanistic conceptions of offerings and provides opportunity for the spontaneity of human feelings. For the vow of an offering of thanksgiving, cf. Pss. 40:6ff.; 50:14; 61:8. The petitioner wants to thank the שם, that is, the power of Yahweh present and active on earth and especially at the cultic center. This vow of thanksgiving corresponds to the address to the שם in v. 1. כי־טוב is a short hymnic formula from the liturgy of the festival of thanksgiving (cf. Pss. 52:9; 100:5; 106:1; 135:3). The psalmsinger is full of hope and confident as he looks forward to the event of rescue (v. 7). The defeat and annihilation of the persecutors is for him "a sight for sore eyes" because Yahweh's אמת (v. 5) manifests itself in the exercise of power (cf. the comment on Ps. 52:6). Also cf. Pss. 58:10; 59:10; 92:11.

Purpose and Thrust

A remarkable emphasis in Psalm 54 is placed on the world-immanent bearer of Yahweh's power of revelation, the שם. It embraces God's גבורה (v. 1b) and his אמת (v. 5b). God's juridical power is called on in the שם to provide proof of righteousness and help. The wish that the evil set in motion by the enemies may backfire on themselves is appealed to Yahweh the judge, who in his שם is present in this world. Is God the ruler? In the OT that is to be decided in the midst of life. The proof lies in the enemy not triumphing.

Worth noting also is the contrast that is expressed in the assertions about the enemies and in the self-assertion of the petitioner (cf. vv. 3 and 4). While the violent slanderers are ungodly and godless people, Yahweh at every moment is the support and mainstay of the existence of the psalmist. Trusting and confident, the petitioner keeps his thoughts focused on the moment when his complaint will be altered and the offering of thanksgiving will be brought.

Psalm 55

Prayer of One Hopelessly Surrounded and Betrayed by His Friend

Literature

H. Birkeland, *The Evildoers in the Book of Psalms*, Avhandlinger utgitt av Det Norske Videnskaps-Akademi i Oslo 2, Hist.-Filos. Klasse (1955). G. W. Anderson, "Enemies and Evildoers in the Book of Psalms," *BJRL* 48/1 (1965) 16-29.

Text

To the choirmaster. With stringed music. A *maskil* of David.

55:1 Hear my prayer, 'O Yahweh,'[a]
and do not withdraw from my pleading!

2 Give attention to me and answer me;
I 'perish'[b] for trouble.

3 'I am dismayed'[c] about the blustering of the enemy,
about the afflictions[d] because of the evildoer.
For they 'direct'[e] trouble to come my way
and attack me fiercely.

4 My heart quakes in my chest;
death's terrors have fallen on me.

5 Fear and trembling come over me,
horror hems me in.

6 (I thought:) If only I had wings like a dove,
I would fly away and find a resting place.

7 Behold: I would like to flee far away,
take up lodging in the wilderness.—*Selah.*

8 I would like to hasten to a safe place
before the 'raging of the storm,'[f]

9 before the 'ruinous storm'[g] 'of her throat,'[h]
'the torrent'[i] of her lips.
For I must see violence
and brawling in the city.

517

10 They sneak around her by day and by night
on her walls.
Trouble and toil is in her midst,
11 ruin in her inner being.[j]
In her market there is no end
of oppression and deceit.
12 For 'had'[k] only 'my'[l] enemy reviled me,
I would bear it . . . [m]
'Had'[n] he who hates me boasted against me,
I could conceal myself from him.
13 But you are a person of the same kind as I,
my acquaintance and a close friend,
14 for together we experienced the bliss of fellowship
in 'Yahweh's'[o] temple.—
'May they quake and go their way![p]
15 'May death descend'[q] on them!
May they go to the underworld alive,
for in their chambers there is only wickedness ' '[r]!
16 But I cry to God,
and may Yahweh help[s] me.
17 In the evening, in the morning, and at noon
I sigh and groan.—
And he heard my voice,
18 rescued my life for salvation. . . .
'For archers are approaching to me,'[t]
there have come to me
19 'Ishmael and Jalam'[u] and the inhabitants
of the east 'all together,'[v]
who do not exchange
and do not fear God.
20 He has lifted up his hand against 'his friend,'[w]
has violated his covenant.
21 Smoother 'than butter'[x] was his talk,
but war was on his mind.
His words were more gentle than oil,
but they were daggers!
22 Cast your care [?] on Yahweh;
he holds you upright!
He will never let
the righteous waver.
23 But you, 'O Yahweh,'[y] will hurl them
into the deepest pit;
the men of blood and deception,
may they not live out half their days!
But I trust in you.

1a In the Elohistically revised part of the Psalter we should read יהוה instead of אלהים.
2b אריד, from רוד = "freely rove about." In the context this expression is very unlikely. N. Schlögl suggests אֹבֵד, "I perish" (F. Delitzsch: אוּרַד, from רדד, "I am trodden underfoot").
3c According to meter and sense, ואהימה belongs to v. 3. F. Delitzsch reads וְאֵהוֹמָה (from הום), "I am dismayed." Gk: ἐταράχθην; σ´: συνεσχύθην; Jerome: *conturbatus sum*.
d עקה occurs only here. Is this an Aramaism for צָרָה ("affliction")? For the translation, cf. KBL 730.
e יָמִיטוּ = "they cause to waver." In the sentence structure this verb is impossible.

According to Gk (ἐξέκλιναν) we would have to read יִטּוּ (cf. Ps. 21:11). There is noexplanation for מ.

8f סעה occurs only here ("to be impetuous"?). Hupfeld suggests סְעָרָה (cf. Ps. 107:25). Very likely we should read מֵרוּחַ סֹעָרָה in v. 8b. מִסַּעַר ("before the storm") belongs to v. 9 metrically.

9g MT: "Bewilder, Lord, split [?] her tongue." The text is surely corrupt here. If מסער from v. 8b is, for the sake of the meter, added to v. 9a, and if instead of בַּלַּע we point בֶּלַע (Ps. 52:6), the term "ruinous storm" results.

h In place of אדני, which is impossible here, we must have a term parallel to לשונם. Best of all: גְּרוֹנָם, "her throat." For this parallelism, cf. Ps. 5:9.

i Following S, we should here point פֶּלֶג. "In his flight from evil tongues (Sir. 51:2, 4ff.), the author compares himself to a person who seeks refuge from a destructive storm, from the brook that has gone out of its banks" (H. Gunkel).

11j The terms will presumably have to be varied here. Very likely we are to read בְּתוֹכָהּ.

12k According to Gk, we should read לוֹ (Ges-K §159x) instead of לֹא. MT: "for it is not an enemy who reviles me."

l Following F. Buhl, we should prefer the reading אוֹיְבִי חֵרְפַנִי.

m וָאֶשָּׂא is metrically too short; probably a second word has dropped out.

n Cf. note **k**.

14o Cf. note **a**.

p MT is unintelligible and corrupt ("we wandered among the mass of people"? Ps. 42:4?). But according to the meter נהלך ברגש belongs to v. 15. Certainly at this point in the psalm a curse is to be expected (cf. v. 15)—thus H. Gunkel. Instead of ברגש it is better to read בְּרַעַשׁ ("with quaking," Ezek. 12:18). In the curse, יַהֲלֹכוּ should then be read instead of נהלך.

15q Following *Qere*, Mss. Gk, α´, σ´, Jerome, and S, we are to separate יַשִּׁיא [א]מָוֶת: "may death overtake them" (cf. Ps. 89:22).

r בְּקִרְבָּם seems to be an epexegetical accretion to במגורם and is to be eliminated for the sake of the meter.

16s It would be better to write יהוה instead of אלהים, and והוא instead of ויהוה.

18t MT: "that they cannot come close to me, for in great numbers they are with me." The text is unintelligible and corrupt. It is best to read (with transposition of a few letters): כִּי קְרֵבִים לִי רַבִּים (H. Gunkel, H. Schmidt).

19u MT: "God will hear it and answer them." The text is without sense and disfigured. Ehrlich suggests the emendation יִשְׁמָעֵאל וְיַעֲלָם. This correction is substantiated by the sense of the content רבים in v. 18 and וְיֹשֵׁב קֶרֶם.

v Following Ehrlich, we should read כָּלֹה instead of סלה; that would insure the meter.

20w MT: "against his conditions of peace" (plural of שׁלוֹם). We should read שְׁלֹמוֹ (cf. Ps. 7:4).

21x מַחְמָאֹת occurs only here. Two Mss σ´, Jerome, T read מֵחֲמָאֹת or מֶחְמָאָה.

23y Cf. note **a**.

Form

If we look at Psalm 55 from the viewpoint of the meter and for the present postpone the literary-critical problems, we can state that the $3+2$ meter predominates. The following exceptions are to be noted: $3+3$ in vv. 1, 4, 17, 19 (second verse structure); $2+2$ in vv. 9b, 22 (second verse structure); metrically too short is the verse concluding with וָאֶשָּׂא.

Psalm 55, however, is clearly not a unified composition. A watershed that divides the song into two parts, divergent as to contents, is to be established in v. 18. The first part concludes with the words פדה בשלום נפשי. Then the reader is transported to an entirely different situation. Verses 18aβ-23 are "the remainder of a poem that was inserted here by mistake" (H. Gunkel). In this second part a new prayer is intoned in which new persons turn up. Also, Arabic tribes are mentioned (v. 19) that have no relation to the city mentioned in vv. 9f. We must therefore begin with the thought that vv. 1-18aα and vv. 18aβ-23 are two different songs. H. Gunkel wants to add also v. 22 to the first song; but the pertinent proof is lacking.

An analysis of the structure results in the following picture: vv. 1-2, introduction (call to Yahweh); vv. 3-5, description of the distress; vv. 6-9, thoughts of flight; vv. 9-14, renewed description of the distress (particularly in view of the faithless friend); vv. 14bβ-15, curse; vv. 16-18aα, exclamations of lament and proclamation of the help received. In the second part of the psalm the situation is as follows: vv. 18aβ-21, description of the distress; v. 22, promise of encouragement and help (oracle of salvation?); v. 23, statements of trust and certainty.

Both parts of Psalm 55 belong to the form group, prayer songs. The group name is expressed in v. 1: תפלה. In the basic section, descriptions of distress and petition predominate. Yahweh is addressed (in the second person). The change in meaning of the transition is weakly discernible in vv. 18 and 22. On the "prayer songs," see above, Intro. §6, 2.

Setting

While the petitioner of the first part of the psalm is the prey of ruinous machinations in a city (vv. 9ff.), the singer of the second part of the psalm thinks of himself as persecuted by Arabic tribes (vv. 18aβff.). Both prayer songs have in common the painful realization that a friend has entered the ranks of the cruel persecutors (vv. 12ff.; 20f.). Very likely this motif was the deciding factor for the fusion of two songs that were originally completely different. Both parts point to the cultus in their chief assertions. Verses 1-18aα conclude with a proclamation of the help experienced, which is peculiar to the song of thanksgiving; the petitioner therefore has been heard (in the holy place). In v. 22 the section vv. 18aβ-23 contains a priestly oracle of salvation, by which the petitioner is encouraged to present his distress before Yahweh. And to him (as a צדיק) the help of God is promised. In the first part of the psalm we cannot tell in which "city" (v. 9b) the petitioner suffers persecution, slander, and insult; the second part of the psalm, however, takes us to the southeast (v. 19). Finally, the question about the date of origin of the two parts of Psalm 55 causes great difficulties. In this matter we can agree with W. O. E. Oesterley, "Style and language suggest the postexilic rather than the preexilic period."

Commentary

[Title] On למנצח, see above, Intro. §4, No. 17. On בנגינת, Intro. §4, No. 9. On משכיל, Intro. §4, No. 5. On לדוד, Intro. §4, No. 2.

[55:1-2] These verses contain the call to Yahweh customary in the prayer of lament and petition. The psalmist prays for merciful attention and an answer to his pleading.

[55:3-5] The distress from which the psalmsinger calls is first described in agitated lamentation in vv. 3-5. The enemy (רשע—אויב) is persecuting him. See above, Intro. §10, 4. As we learn from vv. 9ff., general disorder "in the city" is the reason for the excesses against the חסיד, who holds to Yahweh. From v.

3b one could conclude that the persecutors resorted to the magic power of the curse as their weapon with which to "steer" אָוֶן toward the oppressed person. Verse 4 describes the dread and fear of death that has befallen the psalmist. He sees himself surrounded by powers of corruption (v. 5).

[55:6-9] In the situation of such persecution promoted by all possible means, two ways were opened for the person threatened: either he fled to distant areas—to the hills (cf. Ps. 11:1), to the wilderness (v. 7), or he took refuge in the sanctuary. The psalmsinger now reports in vv. 6-9a that he seriously contemplated moving out into the wilderness, there to sojourn, at least to be out of reach by his enemies. For the comparison to the dove, cf. G. Dalman, *AuS* VII, 264. (וָאמַר, by the way, is to be thought of as a facilitating transition which, as a so-called anacrusis, is not counted metrically.) נדד in Isa. 16:2; Jer. 4:25; 9:9 denotes "scaring up" birds. In the wilderness the hunted would like to "settle down in peace" (for this meaning of שכן, cf. Deut. 33:20; Ezek. 31:13). In the long run, the fugitive is naturally "fair game" in the area of the wilderness, for he lacks the connections that protect him.

A different picture in vv. 7f. describes how he who was pursued by a storm of slander and by a torrent of curses wanted to find a place of safety. As a traveler, surprised by a thunderstorm, in the midst of a gale and the sudden rising of torrents, hastily looks for a place of safety, so he who was threatened by enemies at first had only one goal in mind: immediately to take cover in any protected place. As the psalmist reveals these considerations (vv. 6-9), he naturally refers to the fact that these obvious ways of escape were not taken by him, but that he looked for refuge alone with Yahweh. In other words, vv. 6-9 are a veiled expression of trust.

[55:9-14] The thoughts of flight considered in vv. 6-9 came about during the excessive persecutions. Verses 9b-14 now describe the oppression anew in the style of a lament. The entire city in which the psalmist is at home was marked by הַמֹּס, רִיב, עָמָל, הַוּוֹת, תֹּךְ, and מִרְמָה. A plethora of terms describes the total depravity of the place. Obviously the city has fallen into the hands of criminal elements that have instituted a rule of violence. Day and night watchmen walk about the houses on wall walks. In the marketplace, the center of the courts, justice is twisted. What is involved therefore is a far-reaching perversion of all good order that has happened in the hometown of the psalmist. And he himself, the petitioner of the psalm, experiences particularly heavy persecution from the tyrannical wielders of power. But his inner shock is especially intensified by the fact that among the enemies there is a very close friend. With him the psalmist formerly shared the delight of the cultic community in the sanctuary of Yahweh. Now the communion is broken. The heaped-up titles of friendship (v. 13), after the betrayal of trust, are just so many accusations. Indeed, the loss of communion in the OT is tantamount to being thrust into the "sphere of death" (Chr. Barth, *Die Errettung vom Tode in de individuellen Klage- und Dankliedern des Alten Testaments* [1947] 26).

[55:14-15] In vv. 14bβ-15 he who has been persecuted now steps up to his enemies with a curse. We may be permitted to assume that the oppressed man did not choose the flight contemplated earlier (vv. 6-9a), but in his acute distress first spoke the profane oath. In his distress this oppressed person thus appealed to a judgment of God which reminds us of Num. 16:33 and very likely also has in mind the story there told. Perhaps it is the pretention of office on the part of the violent rulers that induced the psalmist to inflict also on his enemies the judgment that fell on the company of Korah.

[55:16-18] In vv. 16 and 17a the petitioner describes himself. At the customary times for prayer (cf. Dan. 6:10) he cries to Yahweh. One would like to assume that this self-description refers to the situation in the sanctuary. The psalmsinger is now in the sacred area and is waiting for the fulfillment of his curse and the annihilation of the enemies who are lying in wait for him.

In vv. 17b and 18aα the first part of the psalm comes to a close in the proclamation of the salvation event. The *Gattung* of the concluding verse is a fragment of a song of thanksgiving. He who was persecuted has been heard and saved. He has been transferred to a prosperous condition (שׁלוֹם), to a situation in which he is unassailable.

[55:18-21] The interpreter of Psalm 55 is transferred to a new situation at v. 18aβ. The lament in this part of the psalm arises from warlike oppression. Archers (Ishmael and Jaalam) are pursuing the psalmist. On the combination of רבים and יִשְׁמָעֵאל, cf. Gen. 21:20. According to Gen. 25:12-18, the Ishmaelites were a group of tribes that had its raiding territory in northwestern Arabia (Gen. 25:18) and in the Sinai desert. Gen. 37:25f.; 39:1 reports an incursion of the rapacious camel caravans (the Elohist in the same connection speaks of Midianites). In v. 19 Ishmael and Jaalam (very likely another group of nomads) are called יֹשֵׁב קֶדֶם. It now seems self-evident that we should think of a warlike incursion by the two nomadic groups also in vv. 18aβff. The enemies are described as cruel; they do not recognize an "exchange" (חליפות), i.e., they do not turn over a prisoner of war by way of exchange. In the raid of this robbery action a ברית (v. 20) has been violated. That is, the group to which the petitioner is to be thought of as belonging had an "agreement" with the group of nomads. The ברית is inviolable (cf. J. Pedersen, *Der Eid bei den Semiten* [1914], 32). Whoever violates it is guilty of a wicked deed of unimaginable consequence. A bond of friendship has been broken in a dastardly manner (v. 21). Behind the mark of friendly words the face of a murderer hid. That is the situation.

Now we can of course ask the question whether the situation described in vv. 18aβff. corresponds to actual occurrences or whether this is a parabolic reference to some other enemies. But it does seem unlikely that an image would be held on to for so long. There probably are actual specific events involved. But where are we to look for the situation? Where should we localize the events? It seems apparent that we should think of the southeastern or southern border territory. But then the question arises again, Could the second part of the psalm be very old or originate in the diaspora (H. Gunkel)? For such indications of place outside the holy land, cf. Pss. 42:6; 61:2; 120:5. All questions of this type can hardly be answered. It would be very difficult to uncover and recognize more specific events in Psalm 55.

[55:22-23] Verse 23 is an oracle of encouragement and salvation which is offered to the oppressed person (cf. J. Begrich, "Das priesterliche Heilsorakel," *ZAW* 52 [1934], 81-92). He is called on to submit his care [?] to Yahweh, and he at the same time receives the assurance that the צדיק is never left in the lurch by

Yahweh. To this assurance, v. 23 is added as an expression of trust. The petitioner is sure that Yahweh will hurl his enemies into destruction; his trust is unwaveringly in Yahweh.

Purpose and Thrust

Three themes are common to the two (originally different) parts of the psalm: (1) the deadly persecution by a cruel enemy, (2) the breach of fellowship and the betrayal of a friendly relationship, (3) the help of Yahweh experienced by the persecuted person. In the OT, Yahweh shows his power on earth, in the midst of everyday life. His power of salvation beats back even the great band of criminal despots who have conquered a city. The armies of sinister groups of nomads are rebuffed by him. There has been a theory that the petitioner of Psalm 55 may perhaps have been a king. In that case two songs of royal provenance would have come together to form a single psalm. As a parallel to such a royal prayer song, for instance, one would have to adduce sections of Psalm 18. But it would seem more plausible that individual members of the dispersed (postexilic) community are here presenting their affliction in the sanctuary. They are living in a world of insidious enemies, and they flee to Yahweh. Worth noting in this connection would be the thought of the first part of the psalm, vv. 6-9. Security cannot be found in remote, inaccessible places, but only with Yahweh.

Fearless Trust amid Persecution

Literature

E. Baumann, "Struktur-Untersuchungen im Psalter I," *ZAW* 61 (1945/48) 169-173. J. Becker, "Israel deutet seine Psalmen," *Stuttgarter Bibel-Studien* 18 (1966) 64. G. Giavini, "Salmo 56 (55)," *Ambrosius* 63 (1967) 157-160.

Text

To the choirmaster. According to "A Dove on Far-off Terebinths."[aa] Of David. A *miktam*. When the Philistines seized him in Gath.

56:1 Be merciful to me, 'O Yahweh,'[a] for men desire to catch me!
All day long they press in on me in hostility.[b]

2 My oppressors are consumed with desire all day long.
Indeed, they are many who war against me. ' '[c]

3 ' '[d] But I hope in you—

4 I hope in 'Yahweh'[e] without fear.
What can a mortal do to me?

5 All day long 'they confer and plan together.'[f]
Against me they direct all their plans.
For harm [6] they lie in wait, 'they are on the lookout;'[g]
they watch my every step in detail,
for they are out to take my life.

7 'Take note'[h] of their wickedness!
In wrath upset the peoples, 'O Yahweh'![i]

8 My misery you have taken note of,
my tears have been gathered in your bottle.
[Are they not in your book?]

9 Then they will give way,
my enemies retreat—
on the day when I call.—
Thus I know that 'Yahweh'[i] is on my side.

10 In God, 'whose'ʲ word I praise,
  in Yahweh, 'whose'ᵏ word I praise,

11 in 'Yahweh'ˡ I trust without fear;
  what can men do to me?

12 On me, 'O Yahweh,'ᵐ are your vows;
  I will want to bring thankofferings to you.

13 For you have saved my life from death,
  [and—is it not so?—my feet from ruin]ⁿ
  that I may walk before 'Yahweh'ᵒ
  in the light of life.

Title aa To suit the sense, it is probably better to read אֵלִים (cf. F. Baethgen and H. Schmidt).

1a In the Elohistically edited part of the Psalter we are to read יהוה instead of אלהים.

b Literally: "a warrior presses in on me."

2c מרום ("height," "pride," "above"?) is in this passage unintelligible and does not belong to the verse structure. It is possible that the words מרום יום אירא once formed a special part of a verse, which now—completely disfigured—at the end of v. 2 and the beginning of v. 3 disturbs the sequence of parallelism.

3d Cf. note **c**.

4e Cf. note **a**.

5f MT: "All day long they offend my words." The text is not transmitted correctly here. Gk: ἐβδελύσσοντο ("defiled") (יתעבו? N. Schlögl). σ´, S suggest that we think of the root יעץ ("plan"). Thus it is best to read: יְדָבְרוּ יְוָעֵצוּ (for the *niphal* of דבר, cf. Ps. 119:23). Also possible is the correction דִּבְּרוּ עֶצֶם (Kautzsch and Bertholet): "they speak insults."

6g *Ketîb*: יַצְפִּינוּ: *Qere* and Mss: יִצְפּוֹנוּ ("they hid themselves," "they lie in wait).

7h MT: "on account of the wickedness—rescue for them." The text is meaningless. Gk, Jerome, S read אין instead of און. The corresponding reconstruction עַל־אוֹן אין (F. Baethgen) does not help. Best of all: פלס = "take note" (Prov. 4:26; 5:6, 21)? Akkadian *naplusu*.

i Cf. note **a**.

10j As in v. 4, we should probably read דְּבָרוֹ here.

k Cf. note **j**.

11l Cf. note **a**.

12m Cf. note **a**.

13n The words הלא רגלי מדחי (like v. 8b) should probably be understood to be a secondary accretion.

o Cf. note **a**.

Form

Psalm 56 provides a peculiar text situation. A number of conspicuous repetitions (vv. 1/2; 4aα/11) disturb the flow of thought. It is not a matter of a refrain in vv. 4aα and 11. The double triple meter predominates. Exceptions: v. 1 (4 + 3); 5bβ/6 (3 + 3 + 3); 7 (3 + 4); 9a (2 + 2 + 2); 9b (4); 13 (3 + 3 + 2, with removal of the secondary accretion הלא רגלי מדחי).

Psalm 56 belongs to the form group, prayer songs (תפלה). See above, Intro. §6, 2. Yahweh is addressed in the second person. The change from prayer to thanksgiving is discernible in vv. 12f. The vow to provide praise, which the petitioner was accustomed to take on himself when in distress, is performed. The תודה (v. 12) is presented. See above, Intro. §6, 2aγ. Delivered from death, the petitioner walks in the light of Yahweh (v. 13). The structure of the prayer song is easily seen: vv. 1-2, petition and description of distress; vv. 3-4, expression of trust; vv. 5-6, description of distress; v. 7, prayer for Yahweh's intervention; vv. 8-11, assertion of confidence; vv. 12-13, impulses for thanksgiving.

Setting

Who is the petitioner of Psalm 56? In view of the fact that the enemies are described as warriors, one could be inclined to think of a general or a king. But this conception is refuted by the statements of vv. 5f. and 8. An unknown petitioner of Israel is pursued by enemies (see above, Intro. §10, 4) and in the description of his distress grasps at metaphors from the area of kingship (cf. the comment on Psalm 3). Concerning the place and time of the prayer song no details can be ascertained. H. Gunkel's thought of a pious person who is sojourning among heathen in the diaspora is based on a misapprehension of עמים in v. 7 (see below).

Commentary

[Title] On למנצח, see above, Intro. §4, No. 17. על־יונת אלים רחקים is very likely a familiar tune according to which the song is to be intoned. On לדוד, Intro. §4, No. 2. On מכתם, Intro. §4, No. 4. The situation given in the title refers to the story of 1 Sam. 21:11ff. and secondarily shifts the psalm to events in David's time.

[56:1-4] The singer of the psalm calls to Yahweh (חנני יהוה) and immediately supports his call in distress with a lamenting reference to enemies who greedily hunt down (שאף I) the oppressed singer and attack him in warlike fashion. The description of the persecutors shows a certain tension; on the one hand, the source of power of the opponents is compared to an army while, on the other hand, the enemies are referred to (cf. Pss. 10:18; 66:12) as אנוש ("frail human beings"). Verse 2 gives the impression of a repetition (not a variant) of v. 1. In v. 3 expressions of trust arise from the midst of the description of the distress. The petitioner fearlessly professes faith in Yahweh's power to protect. At the same time he recognizes the complete impotence of his enemies (v. 4). Even more than the word אנוש (v. 2a), the word בשר expresses the frailty and mortality of the adversary that invades the scene so powerfully (cf. Isa. 2:22; 31:3; 40:6). "In the Old Testament flesh is always what distinguishes man qualitatively from God, not in the sense of a matter-spirit dualism, but of a contrast between strength and weakness" (E. Jacob, *Theology of the OT* [1958] 158).

[56:5-7] In v. 5 the lament over the wicked schemes of the enemies begins anew. The counsels and plans of the persecutors probably are marked by malevolent calumnies. They aim at a frame-up (לרע). As hunters chase their quarry and carefully follow their tracks (Lam. 4:19), so the enemies lie in wait for every step their prey takes. They want to kill him. Worth noting is the use of the term קוה, which has the meaning "to aim at." In view of these threats, the petitioner calls to Yahweh as the judge (v. 7). Since the wicked deeds of the enemies in this connection are called און, we may perhaps think of magic manipulations (see above, Intro. §10, 4); with curses and imprecations the enemies pursue their prey. But the God who is enthroned on Zion is the judge of the nations (see above, Intro. §10, 1). The appeal to the divine judge of the nations is an element

10 In God, 'whose'ʲ word I praise,
   in Yahweh, 'whose'ᵏ word I praise,
11 in 'Yahweh'ˡ I trust without fear;
   what can men do to me?
12 On me, 'O Yahweh,'ᵐ are your vows;
   I will want to bring thankofferings to you.
13 For you have saved my life from death,
   [and—is it not so?—my feet from ruin]ⁿ
   that I may walk before 'Yahweh'ᵒ
   in the light of life.

Title aa To suit the sense, it is probably better to read אֵלִים (cf. F. Baethgen and H. Schmidt).

1a In the Elohistically edited part of the Psalter we are to read יהוה instead of אלהים.

b Literally: "a warrior presses in on me."

2c מרום ("height," "pride," "above"?) is in this passage unintelligible and does not belong to the verse structure. It is possible that the words מרום יום אירא once formed a special part of a verse, which now—completely disfigured—at the end of v. 2 and the beginning of v. 3 disturbs the sequence of parallelism.

3d Cf. note **c.**

4e Cf. note **a.**

5f MT: "All day long they offend my words." The text is not transmitted correctly here. Gk: ἐβδελύσσοντο ("defiled") (יתעבו)? N. Schlögl). σ´, S suggest that we think of the root יעץ ("plan"). Thus it is best to read: יְדָבְרוּ יְנַעֵצוּ (for the *niphal* of דבר, cf. Ps. 119:23). Also possible is the correction דְּבְרוּ עֶצֶם (Kautzsch and Bertholet): "they speak insults."

6g *Ketib*: יִצְפִּינוּ: *Qere* and Mss: יִצְפּוֹנוּ ("they hid themselves," "they lie in wait").

7h MT: "on account of the wickedness—rescue for them." The text is meaningless. Gk, Jerome, S read אין instead of און. The corresponding reconstruction עַל־אָון אֵין (F. Baethgen) does not help. Best of all: פלס = "take note" (Prov. 4:26; 5:6, 21)? Akkadian *naplusu*.

i Cf. note **a.**

10j As in v. 4, we should probably read דְּבָרוֹ here.

k Cf. note **j.**

11l Cf. note **a.**

12m Cf. note **a.**

13n The words הלא רגלי מדחי (like v. 8b) should probably be understood to be a secondary accretion.

o Cf. note **a.**

Form

Psalm 56 provides a peculiar text situation. A number of conspicuous repetitions (vv. 1/2; 4aα/11) disturb the flow of thought. It is not a matter of a refrain in vv. 4aα and 11. The double triple meter predominates. Exceptions: v. 1 (4+3); 5bβ/6 (3+3+3); 7 (3+4); 9a (2+2+2); 9b (4); 13 (3+3+2, with removal of the secondary accretion הלא רגלי מדחי).

Psalm 56 belongs to the form group, prayer songs (תפלה). See above, Intro. §6, 2. Yahweh is addressed in the second person. The change from prayer to thanksgiving is discernible in vv. 12f. The vow to provide praise, which the petitioner was accustomed to take on himself when in distress, is performed. The תודה (v. 12) is presented. See above, Intro. §6, 2aγ. Delivered from death, the petitioner walks in the light of Yahweh (v. 13). The structure of the prayer song is easily seen: vv. 1-2, petition and description of distress; vv. 3-4, expression of trust; vv. 5-6, description of distress; v. 7, prayer for Yahweh's intervention; vv. 8-11, assertion of confidence; vv. 12-13, impulses for thanksgiving.

Setting

Who is the petitioner of Psalm 56? In view of the fact that the enemies are described as warriors, one could be inclined to think of a general or a king. But this conception is refuted by the statements of vv. 5f. and 8. An unknown petitioner of Israel is pursued by enemies (see above, Intro. §10, 4) and in the description of his distress grasps at metaphors from the area of kingship (cf. the comment on Psalm 3). Concerning the place and time of the prayer song no details can be ascertained. H. Gunkel's thought of a pious person who is sojourning among heathen in the diaspora is based on a misapprehension of עמים in v. 7 (see below).

Commentary

[Title] On למנצח, see above, Intro. §4, No. 17. על־יונת אלים רחקים is very likely a familiar tune according to which the song is to be intoned. On לדוד, Intro. §4, No. 2. On מכתם, Intro. §4, No. 4. The situation given in the title refers to the story of 1 Sam. 21:11ff. and secondarily shifts the psalm to events in David's time.

[56:1-4] The singer of the psalm calls to Yahweh (חנני יהוה) and immediately supports his call in distress with a lamenting reference to enemies who greedily hunt down (שאף I) the oppressed singer and attack him in warlike fashion. The description of the persecutors shows a certain tension; on the one hand, the source of power of the opponents is compared to an army while, on the other hand, the enemies are referred to (cf. Pss. 10:18; 66:12) as אנוש ("frail human beings"). Verse 2 gives the impression of a repetition (not a variant) of v. 1. In v. 3 expressions of trust arise from the midst of the description of the distress. The petitioner fearlessly professes faith in Yahweh's power to protect. At the same time he recognizes the complete impotence of his enemies (v. 4). Even more than the word אנוש (v. 2a), the word בשר expresses the frailty and mortality of the adversary that invades the scene so powerfully (cf. Isa. 2:22; 31:3; 40:6). "In the Old Testament flesh is always what distinguishes man qualitatively from God, not in the sense of a matter-spirit dualism, but of a contrast between strength and weakness" (E. Jacob, *Theology of the OT* [1958] 158).

[56:5-7] In v. 5 the lament over the wicked schemes of the enemies begins anew. The counsels and plans of the persecutors probably are marked by malevolent calumnies. They aim at a frame-up (לרע). As hunters chase their quarry and carefully follow their tracks (Lam. 4:19), so the enemies lie in wait for every step their prey takes. They want to kill him. Worth noting is the use of the term קוה, which has the meaning "to aim at." In view of these threats, the petitioner calls to Yahweh as the judge (v. 7). Since the wicked deeds of the enemies in this connection are called און, we may perhaps think of magic manipulations (see above, Intro. §10, 4); with curses and imprecations the enemies pursue their prey. But the God who is enthroned on Zion is the judge of the nations (see above, Intro. §10, 1). The appeal to the divine judge of the nations is an element of the cultic tradition of Jerusalem (cf. the comment on Psalm 7). Thus it is a mistake to want to see in עמים a reference to the "heathen" to whom the petitioner is delivered "in the diaspora" (H. Gunkel).

[56:8-11] Words of assurance are spoken by the psalmist in these verses. The petitioner knows that Yahweh has not only seen his tears but that he has carefully taken note of all his misery. Like precious water, the tears are carefully preserved by him in a bottle (for this picture in another connection, cf. Job 14:17; Hos. 13:12). The explanatory inquiry הלא בספרתך refers to the conception that Yahweh keeps a "notebook" (cf. Mal. 3:16; Job 19:23). Upon the recognition that Yahweh has taken note of all misery follows the assurance: The enemies will give way when I call to him (v. 9). The witness becomes the judge. Worth noting is the sentence: זה־ידעתי כי יהוה לי. That Yahweh sides with the psalmist, that he is "for him" (cf. Rom. 8:31), is learned from the victory over the enemies. The helping power of Yahweh shows itself visibly in an intervention that beats back the persecutors. Knowledge of God and "assurance of salvation" are gained from an act of God, from an event. Verse 11 is a curious repetition of v. 4aα, which can hardly be thought of as a "variant"; neither should we think of a refrain. Does the psalmist want to point out that in the near future he will praise the divine "oracle of salvation" (דבר, cf. Ps. 130:5) as proof of the actual intervention of Yahweh? On the oracle of salvation, cf. J. Begrich, "Das priesterliche Heilsorakel," *ZAW* 52 (1934) 81-92. As in v. 4aβ, trust in Yahweh is revealed (here too, this is a repetition). To the terms אנוש (v. 1) and בשר (v. 4b), the word אדם is now added as a further characterization of the frailty of the enemy.

[56:12-13] Verse 12 points to the situation of the song of thanksgiving. The petitioner declares that he wants to pay the vows he has made in the form of sacrifices of thanksgiving. On v. 12a, cf. 2 Sam. 18:11; Prov. 7:14. כי at the beginning of v. 13 indicates that vv. 12 and 13 are connected. The reason for giving thanks is proclaimed and confessed in v. 13. The persecuted person has been "rescued from death" by Yahweh (cf. Chr. Barth, *Die Errettung vom Tode in den individuellen Klage- und Dankliedern des Alten Testaments* [1947]). און is "the embodiment and symbol of life" (Chr. Barth, 34). Cf. Pss. 27:13; 116:8, 9; Job 33:30; John 8:12. From the sphere of death the psalmist has been transferred to the realm of life—through Yahweh's intervention.

Purpose and Thrust

In the OT a persecuted and mortally threatened human being recognizes from the divine utterance of an "oracle of salvation" (דבר) and from the defeat of his enemies that God is for him (v. 9b). In the midst of all distress and oppression the petitioner of Psalm 56 reaches out to this proof of salvation and help in trust and assurance. The song of thanksgiving in vv. 12-13 shows that his cries in distress and his prayers have been answered.

Psalm 57

The Glory of God's Protection
Fills the World

Literature

H. Schmidt, *Das Gebet der Angeklagten im Alten Testament*, BZAW 49 (1928) 21. E. Baumann, "Struktur-Untersuchungen im Psalter I," *ZAW* 61 (1945/48) 173-176. E. Beaucamp and J. P. de Relles, "Psaume 57 (56), 8-12," *Feu Nouveau* 9, 17 (1966) 20-26. W. Beyerlin, *Die Rettung der Bedrängten in den Feindpsalmen der Einzelnen auf institutionelle Zusammenhänge untersucht*, FRLANT 99 (1970) 129-135.

Text

To the choirmaster. (According to) *'al-tašhet.'* [a] Of David.
A *miktam.* When he fled from Saul into the cave.

57:1 Be merciful to me, 'O Yahweh,'[b] be merciful to me,
for with you my life seeks refuge!
In the shadow of your wings 'I will hide'[c]
until the misfortune is past.

2 I cry to 'Yahweh,'[d] the Most High,
to God, who intercedes for me.

3 May he send from heaven and help me!
'Let them be ashamed'[e] 'who seek' '   '[f] my life.—*Selah.*

4 Amid lions I must lie
who greedily seek men.
Their teeth are spear and arrow;
and their tongue is a sharp sword.

5 Be uplifted above heaven, 'O Yahweh'![g]
Above all the world (may) your glory (appear)!

6 A net they have laid for my steps
and 'discouraged me.'[h]
They have dug a pit for me,
but they fell into it themselves. —*Selah.*

528

7 Content is my heart, 'O Yahweh,'[i]
 content is my heart![j]
 I will sing and make music.
8 Awake, my glory!
 Awake, lyre and harp!
 I will waken the dawn!
9 I will give thanks to you, O Lord, among the peoples,
 I will make music to you among the nations.
10 For great is your goodness up to heaven;
 your faithfulness (reaches) up to the clouds!
11 Be uplifted above heaven, 'O Yahweh'![k]
 Above all the world (may) your glory (appear)!

Title a The translation of אל־תשחת has not been cleared up. (According to) ''Let It Not Spoil''? Or (according to) ''Do Not Destroy''? Or (emended) ''According to the טחשתי''? In any case, this is probably the name of the tune according to which Psalm 57 is to be intoned.

1b In the Elohistically revised part of the Psalter we ought to insert יהוה here instead of אלהים.

c Gk (ἐλπίζω) could suggest that we should here read אֵיחַל. We would have to assume that a change of terms has taken place. Following Isa. 26:20, we would best read אֶחָבֶה = ''I will conceal myself.''

2d Cf. note **b**.

3e MT: ''He defames me who snatches at me [or 'crushes me']. *Selah*. God sends his grace and truth.'' The text has been disordered in the arrangement of form and content. סלה has been relegated to a wrong position. נפשי in v. 4a should doubtlessly be joined to v. 3. If we consider ישלח אלהים חסדו ואמתו an explanatory accretion to the objectless word ישלח, and if we now remove this part of the verse from the original connection, the remaining words read: חרף שאפי נפשי. In this context we must have an optative sentence. Therefore an improvement would read: יַחְפְּרוּ שֹׁאֲפֵי נַפְשִׁי.

f The section of the verse ישלח אלהים חסדו ואמתו is to be eliminated as a secondary interpolation (cf. Note **e**).

5g Cf. note **b**.

6h MT: ''My life is afflicted.'' Following Gk, we should read כָּפְפוּ.

7i Cf. note **b**.

j נכון לבי is lacking in Psalm 108:2. But we should follow the MT in Psalm 57.

11k Cf. note **b**.

Form

In the meter of Psalm 57 we have to recognize two phases. The double triple meter is used in vv. 1-5 and 10-11, while the 3 + 2 meter is determinative in vv. 6-9. The analysis of the structure, which should purposely be made to precede the question about the history of form, provides the following picture: v. 1 begins with the cry for help and the appeal to Yahweh in the second person; in vv. 2-5 we have a description of the praying, the prayers, and the situation; v. 6 expresses the certainty of being heard; and vv. 7-11 provide assertions that express trust and thanks. We will have to classify Psalm 57 in the form group, prayer songs. See above, Intro. §6, 2. And yet the psalm is ''complex as to type'' (W. Beyerlin, 134), because—obviously in the situation of the prayer—there is a constant crossover to the language of the *todah*. Because the psalmist is already in the sanctuary (v. 1), he participates in the expressions of thanksgiving that are presented here—even while he is still in the position of the petitioner (see above). But in no case may we emend v. 5 as if it were a duplicate of v. 11 that mistakenly was entered after v. 4. Verses 5 and 11 are separate pleas that determine the actual profile of the psalm.

Setting

Who is the petitioner of the psalm? What is his situation? A. Bentzen thinks of a king as the petitioner but overlooks the fact that motives of royal psalms are more frequently taken up by unknown petitioners, or by the prayer formularies fashioned by the priests. Worth noting is the suggestion first made by H. Schmidt and more recently again by W. Beyerlin. Psalm 57 is placed into the context of those prayers in which falsely accused and persecuted individuals had to stay in the sanctuary overnight with their accusers (v. 41), there to await the divine judgment. This institutional connection is easily recognized—in comparison with the other "psalms of enemies of individuals." He who has been persecuted with accusations has been admitted to the sanctuary area; the bestowal of Yahweh's protection has been applied to him—but only with a stipulation: "until the misfortune is past" (v. 1). But the misfortune is past when the decisive judicial act has been completed and the acquittal of God has been received. "The expectation of rescue in Psalm 57 therefore revolves entirely about the conceptions which have already turned up in Psalms 11; 17; 26; and 27" (W. Beyerlin, 132). In this matter, v. 5 (11) is to be compared with Ps. 7:6-7 (which see!).

Worth noting in Psalm 57 are the traditions of the sanctuary of Jerusalem. When the "shadow of Yahweh's wings" is mentioned (v. 1), we are by this formulation reminded of the throne of the cherubim. On עליון, the customary name for Yahweh in Jerusalem, see above, Intro. §10, 1. Above all, the phrase about the כבוד of God as filling the whole world points to traditions of the temple of Jerusalem (cf. Isa. 6:3). A determination of the psalm's time of origin is hardly possible, and yet there is nothing that contradicts the assumption of a preexilic origin. Here, of course, we have to remember that the psalm could have served as a formulary and probably was in service over extended periods of time; it thus would have been adapted, and its nuances also newly fashioned.

Commentary

[Title] On למנצח, see above, Intro. §4, No. 17. On לדוד, Intro. §4, No. 2. On מכתם, Intro. §4, No. 4. The (secondary) reference to the setting transfers Psalm 57 to the context of the events described in 1 Samuel 22ff.

[57:1-5] Psalm 57 begins with a cry for help, made especially emphatic by the repetition of the word חנני. And here the petitioner immediately points to the right of asylum to which he lays claim as one who is being persecuted. Nothing indicates that the assertion בך חסיה נפשי is to be understood in the "spiritualized sense" (thus G. von Rad, *OT Theol,* 1:402). The symbols of the protective power of Yahweh active in the holy place are the wings of the cherubim outstretched above the ark (cf. Pss. 17:8; 36:7; 61:4; 63:7). Here the petitioner hides from misfortune. The call is interwoven with expressions of trust.

The situation of calling is described in v. 2. The oppressed person turns ʾhe עליון (see above, Intro. §10, 1). He is sure that the עליון Yahweh is an אל ʾtercedes for him (on the meaning of גמר, cf. Ps. 138:8). Petition and wish ʾnunicated in v. 3. Yahweh is the "Most High God" in heaven who can intervene and help powerfully.[1] There is continuous allusion to cultic traditions of Jerusalem. But the help of Yahweh would show itself visibly and actively in putting to shame the enemies of the petitioner (see above, Intro. §10, 4, and cf. the comment on Ps. 56:9). It could be that v. 4—as H. Schmidt thinks—describes the situation in the sanctuary. Slanderous accusers threaten the life of the psalmist. Together with them he has to endure the incubation in the sanctuary (cf. Ps. 17:3). Like rapacious lions the adversaries (cf. Ps. 10:9f.; and often) appear before the persecuted and falsely accused person. The slanderous talk of the adversaries penetrates like a sword to the soul of the one attacked (cf. Pss. 52:2; 59:7; 140:3). In this distress the petitioner appeals to the heavenly judge and prays to him for the implementation of his appearance in glory. Verse 5 therefore has its rightful place here. On the appeal to the judge of the world, cf. Psalm 7. The psalmist basically prays for a theophany and attaches his prayer to the cultic-visionary traditions of Jerusalem, according to which Yahweh's כבוד blazes over heaven and earth and fills them (cf. Pss. 8:1; 113:4; 148:13; Isa. 6:3; Num. 14:21; Isa. 40:5). Yahweh as king and judge should now step forward and implement his wonderful power.

[57:6] This verse describes the dangers that have been precipitated for the one persecuted and accused by the enemies. They have maliciously laid a net and dug a pit for him. On these pictures drawn from the area of hunting, cf. G. Dalman, *AuS* VI 334f. But this malicious action hits back at the persecutors themselves in the manner of the "fatefully effective sphere of activity" (on this, cf. Pss. 7:15; 9:15; 35:7, 8; and explanations given there). About the "self-judgment" of the enemy the psalmsinger speaks with great conviction. The tense in נפלו corresponds to the prophetic perfect ("The prophetic perfect. That, he is sure, is what will happen." A. Cohen). Verse 7a we could still attach to v. 6 and so recognize in this segment a full statement of trust and assurance. On נכון in the meaning "confidently," "firmly," cf. Pss. 78:37; 112:7. But v. 7a also belongs to the song of thanksgiving. The transition is here in flux, although סלה in v. 6 points to the beginning of the anticipated song of thanksgiving in v. 7.

[57:7-11] Hymnic elements are mixed into the song of thanksgiving. On vv. 7-11, cf. Ps. 108:1-5. In v. 8 the song of praise and thanksgiving begins with a morning song. The morning hour in the Psalter is the hour of the bestowal of salvation and help (cf. the comment on Pss. 46:5; 90:14; 143:8); J. Ziegler, "Die Hilfe Gottes 'am Morgen,' " Nötscher-Festschrift [1950], 281ff.). After the night of incubation and trial (Pss. 17:3; 57:4), the saving decision of God arrives in the morning (cf. Ps. 130:5-6). In this hour he who was just now hard pressed exults over the help of God and over the passing (עבר, v. 1b) of the misfortune. כבודי should not be corrected (for the description of the נפש with the term כבוד, cf. Ps. 4:2). For the musical instruments, cf. K. Galling, *BRL* 389ff. "Waking the dawn" should be understood not so much "lyrically" (so H. Gunkel) but rather originally mythically. And when in v. 9 thanksgiving and the song of

---

1. "In the words before us, he glories in the divine help with as much assurance as if he had already seen the hand of God interposed in his behalf. When it is said, *he shall send from heaven*, some consider the expression as elliptical, meaning that he would send *his angels;* but it seems rather to be an indefinite form of speech, signifying that the deliverance which David expected was one not of a common, but a signal and miraculous description. The expression denotes the greatness of the interposition which he looked for, and *heaven* is opposed to earthly or natural means of deliverance" (Calvin, on Ps, 57:3, trans. Anderson [Eerdmans, 1949]).

praise "before the nations" are mentioned, here too the viewpoint of the "poetical-solemn" (H. Gunkel) should not come into play. The praise of the God of the nations is related to the cultic traditions of Jerusalem (see above, Intro. §10, 1). כי in v. 10 introduces the "chief element" of the hymn. The glorious power of Yahweh, the highest God in heaven, to whom the petitioner appealed (v. 5), has appeared as חסד and אמת. In v. 11 the call of appeal (cf. v. 5) in the hymnic part of the psalm is once more taken up and submitted to a universally directed accent of doxological and confessional character. And yet, we should assume that all that was said about the song of thanksgiving is to be understood in the sense of anticipation.

Purpose and Thrust

Recollection and reference show how Psalm 57 can be interpreted and understood: David fled before Saul and temporarily found protection in a cave (v. 1). Similar in the institution of divine jurisprudence (cf. "Setting") is the experience of the man who is persecuted by hostile accusers and who finds protection in the temple area—in expectance of acquittal by his God. Not the area of protection represented by the temple, however, but the presence of God is the essence of refuge, trust, and confidence. The invocation of Yahweh shows that God bestows grace (v. 1) when he intervenes for the oppressed (v. 2). The persecuted person waits for help from the highest heights. In agreement with the hymnic traditions of Jerusalem, he may know that Yahweh's כבוד fills the whole world and that the appearance of glory accordingly can also come to the oppressed person as a bestowal of rescue and as a change of his fate. The descriptions of the distress show how serious the situation is. Yet he is content (v. 7). He is sure of being heard. He trusts that Yahweh graciously intercedes for him. For that reason the sounds of thanksgiving already arise; the *todah* in the area of God's protection and in the assurance of being heard is anticipated (vv. 7ff.). The praise of God resounds, although the deciding turn of events has not yet taken place. The universal claim which the giving of thanks in v. 9 reveals is rooted in the Jerusalem predicates of God: Yahweh is the Most High, the Creator of the world, and the judge of the nations (see above, Intro. §10, 1).

Psalm 58

"There Is a God Who Judges on Earth"

Literature

N. Nikolsky, *Spuren magischer Formeln in den Psalmen*, BZAW 49 (1927). H. H. Schmid, *Gerechtigkeit als Weltordnung*, BHT 40 (1968). Jörg Jeremias, *Kultprophetie und Gerichtsverkündigung in der späten Königszeit Israels*, WMANT 35 (1970) 120f.

Text

To the choirmaster. *"al tašhet."* [a] Of David. A *miktam.*

58:1 Do you reliably administer justice, 'you gods,'[b]
  do you judge the children of men uprightly?

2 No, you decide with 'wicked'[c] hearts on earth,
  injustice your hands weigh out.

3 Degenerate are the wicked, gone astray from the womb,
  from their mother's lap 'they speak'[d] lies!

4 They (carry) poison ' '[e] like the serpent,
  like a deaf serpent that closes its ear,

5 that does not want to hear the voice of the conjurers,
  of the skillful incantation.

6 O God, break their teeth in their mouth!
  Smash the bite of the lions, O Yahweh!

7 May they dissolve like running water,
  'wither like grass along the pathway'![f]

8 Like the snail, dissolving as it goes along!
  'a woman's'[g] miscarriage that does not see the sun!

9 Before 'their'[h] thorns 'grow'[i] for the shrub,
  like 'thorny brush,'[j] like 'weeds'[k] he blows them away.

10 The righteous man rejoices when he sees the vengeance,
  (when) he bathes his feet in the blood of the wicked.

11 And men shall say, Indeed, there is a reward[l] for the righteous!
  Yes, there is a God who judges on earth!

533

Title a Cf. Ps. 57, note **a**.

1b אֵלֶם is difficult to interpret ("struck dumb"? "company" [A. Cohen following Kimchi] ?). Gk and Jerome are thinking of אֵלָם. But obviously the shocking (mythological) address אֵלִים (cf. Ps. 82:1) has suffered a change.

2c Instead of עוֹלֹת, which does not fit into the context, we should follow S, T and read עֶוֶל (double copying of the ת).

3d The participial construction precipitates syntactical difficulties. Following Gk, we should prefer דִּבְּרוּ.

4e חמת is a simplifying repetition that must be eliminated for the sake of the meter.

7f MT: "Let him step on his arrows—as though they were cut off." The text is corrupt. It would be reasonable to undertake a transposition and improvement like: כְּמוֹ חָצִיר בַּדֶּרֶךְ. In that case the verb would have to be derived form מלל I = "wither."

8g The construct form is impossible here and probably represents a copyist's error for אִשָּׁה.

9h The suffix form סִירֹתֵיהֶם documented by one Ms, S is in keeping with the context.
i One Ms has suggested the reading יְנוּבוּ, which is suitable to the context.
j and **k** MT: "As lively as the blaze; it blows them away." The text is disordered and meaningless. For חי we could read חוֹחַ ("thorn," "snag"; H. Schmidt); for חרון we could read חָרוּל ("spurge," "weed").
11l פרי = "fruit," "reward" (Isa. 3:10; Prov. 11:30).

Form

The expansive verses of this psalm present a plethora of drastic pictures in a very original, robust language. "In no other psalm are there so many exuberant pictures in so narrow a compass" (F. Delitzsch). The meter is characterized by long verses: 4+4 and 4+3. These two meters are distributed as follows: 4+4 in vv. 1, 4, 6-11; 4+3 in vv. 2-5.

In the matter of form criticism Psalm 58 presents a considerable number of difficulties that have an effect on the understanding of details. We begin with a careful attempt to grasp the structure and the thought sequence of the psalm overall. In vv. 1f. אלים are addressed (as in Ps. 82:1, a psalm which in many respects is comparable to Psalm 58); vv. 3-5 are to be understood as a description of the distress that depicts the monstrous way of the אלים; v. 6 is a prayer address to God which is followed by corresponding wishes (vv. 7-9); vv. 10f. speak of joyous effects of divine justice for the righteous. By the petition in v. 6 Psalm 58 is characterized as a prayer song; but this is true also on account of the descriptions of the distress that are characteristic of the תפלה. See above, Intro. §6, 2. The address to the אלים in v. 1 has about it a prophetic severity. Thus we can understand J. Jeremias' speaking of a "cultic prophet's lament" (120). But the liturgy would have to be based on a recognizable cultic procedure. In this respect the psalm confronts us with questions that can hardly be answered, especially since the situation to be presupposed is not clearly discernible.

Setting

Who is the speaker? What is the situation in which his words, or his prayer (v. 6), are spoken? There is no possible way of looking behind the scenes of this prayer song. A king as the speaker (A. Bentzen) cannot be documented in any of the verses. Whether a (cultic) prophet as the speaker may be assumed, or whether this is an imitation of a prophetic manner of speech, remains unclear.

And also the situation is finally not discernible. Is the scene to be located in the heavenly realm (address to the אלים)? Or are other powers addressed? For the possibilities of interpretation, see below (''Commentary''). H. Gunkel is of the opinion that the psalm was written ''rather late.'' But here too all criteria fail. But we should not fail to note that there are archaic touches discernible in vv. 1f.

Commentary

[Title] On למנצח, see above, Intro. §4, No. 17. On לדוד, Intro. §4, No. 2. On מכתם, Intro. §4, No. 4.

[58:1-2] Psalm 58 begins with an abrupt introductory question addressed to the אלים. In an investigation of their activities that comes close to a prophetic message, the אלים are called to account. Is the administration of justice of the אלים reliable (אמן) and upright (מישרים)? Before we pursue the answer to this question in v. 2, we should first ask what the meaning of the term אלים is and what conceptions are associated with it. The mythological background of the idea of אלים that sit in judgment is discernible in Ps. 82:1. Heavenly authorities administer justice, and judgmental activity on earth is to be traced back to them. These אלים are בני עליון—divine beings that are subordinate to the Most High God, and accountable to him (cf. Ps. 82:1). The עליון (see above, Intro. §10, 1) as the one who summons to an accounting is also in the background of Ps. 58:1. On this fact the prophetic authority of the question in v. 1 is based. Now of course there is the (mythological) conception that these beings subordinated to עליון have brought the righteous administration of justice of the ''Most High God'' Yahweh into confusion. As demonic authorities they have interjected themselves and have disturbed the righteous order of the עליון (cf. Gen. 6:2; 1 Kings 22:20ff.; Job 1:6ff.). The disintegration of ''justice and righteousness'' on earth is accordingly projected into the superworld of the אלים, or בני האלהים, or also בני עליון. Here we get to see the demonic intermediate cause that ruins the dependable and right administration of justice of the עליון Yahweh. Insofar as these demonic ἐξουσίαι (''authorities'') directly determine and govern the representatives of the earthly order of justice, we could follow H. Gunkel in understanding the address אלים as a ''sarcastic expression for authorities.'' Could it be then that worldly ''authorities'' are addressed after all? The foundational circumstances of the case can hardly be cleared up (cf. the comments on Psalm 82). Still—no matter how we interpret—the juridical office of the אלים is important for life. ''If this administration of justice is not practiced in the proper manner, then 'the foundations of the earth are shaken' (Ps. 82:5), then the cosmic order is destroyed'' (H. H. Schmid, 91f.). The question in v. 1 is asked on the authority of the עליון. It is immediately answered in v. 2 (as in a guilt-revealing reproach of the prophets). Introduced by אף, the verse represents an emphatic contrast to the preceding (cf. Ps. 44:9). לב עול is the central, determining power from which the verdict of the demonic אלים emerges. חמס is the result of the process of considering a matter in court. For the idea of the court procedure as weighing, which is at home particularly in Egyptian mythology, cf. Job 31:6; Dan. 5:27. In any case, therefore, there is persistence in the primal religious fact that it is the divinity itself that administers justice. Curious, therefore, and worth noting is the attempt in the theodicy to trace the false administration of justice back to the subordinated demonic powers (אלים).

[58:3-5] The voices and tools of the demonic forces (אלים) on earth are the רשעים. In vv. 3-5 their abysmal nature is described. Their existence from the moment of birth is under the banner of degeneracy and deviation. They constantly speak lies. On כזב, cf. M. A. Klopfenstein, "Die Lüge nach dem Alten Testament," diss., Bern [1964], 226ff. They carry poison (v. 4) and threaten the life like dangerous serpents. פתן (Ugaritic bṯn; Akkadian bašmu) is very likely a horned viper or a cobra. In any case, the רשעים resemble the serpents that cannot be charmed (v. 5). No one has power over them, no one can repel them. Snake charming is mentioned in Egyptian and Babylonian literature, and in the OT in Jer. 8:17; Eccles. 10:11; Sir. 12:13. Even the experienced sorcerer (cf. Deut. 18:11) cannot overcome the dangerous power of evil. The question might be asked whether the image in v. 5 reflects effective curses with which people in ancient times opposed a dangerous adversary. This view suggests itself because certain magical acts are variously recognizable in the individual laments (see above, Intro. §10, 4).

[58:6-9] The curses in vv. 6-9 have their peculiarity in that the psalmist does not want to have a direct effect—presumably as a "sorcerer"—on the evildoer, but he appeals to Yahweh's intervention. The psalmsinger knows that he is completely ineffective against demonic powers; therefore he applies his wish of annihilation and curse against the evil forces in a petition by way of Yahweh. Thus we should note that this is not a case of an individual petitioner—as otherwise in the prayer songs—praying for victory over his personal enemy, but rather one in which the destruction of all demonic powers is fervently wished for. May Yahweh break the poisonous teeth of the death-dealing liars and smash the rapacious bite of the lions! The רשעים are compared to lions (cf. Ps. 10:9; and often). Lions were crushed with iron clubs (2 Sam. 23:20). Then every one of the "maledictions" that follow in vv. 7-9 has a strong power of implementation as a curse. The pictures are drastic and impressive. As water runs off and oozes away, so the evildoers should disappear (v. 7a). Like grass along the pathway they should wither away (cf. Matt. 13:4). Verse 8a is problematical. The hapax legomenon שבלול is usually translated "snail"; G. R. Driver (in agreement with the parallelism) thinks of "miscarriage" (*JTS* 34, 41ff.). But in v. 8a we ought to expect a picture different from that in v. 8b—variation in the closest areas is a characteristic of the psalm. Like a miscarriage the entire existence of the רשעים should be "annulled" (for the picture, cf. Job 3:16; Eccles. 6:3). Verse 10 is very corrupt and can be reconstructed only tentatively. Here, too, images of total disappearance and being blown away are chosen.

[58:10-11] The צדיק, who suffers both under the unfair and ruined order of justice and the slanderous and violent development of the רשעים, is allowed to enjoy himself when Yahweh intervenes and in a great bloodbath destroys the demonic world of power and injustice. The footbath of the "righteous man" in v. 10b is a picture that is exaggerated to the highest degree, one that corresponds to the totality of the demand for righteousness. Under the visible show of power by God, human beings, indeed everyone, should call out in confession, "Yes, for the righteous there is a reward"; his life is not senselessly and uselessly surrendered to the demonic excesses of evildoers. Over all אלים there is an אלהים, namely, Yahweh, who judges on earth.

Purpose and Thrust

The psalm leaves aside all the personal quarrels which most of the time form the background of lament and petition. The psalmsinger suffers under a corruptworld order. His view embraces the whole of it: the heavenly world, from which the verdicts of justice emanate, and the whole breadth of the human sphere of life. The בני אדם (v. 1) and אדם (v. 11) are the subject. And under this horizon of universal breadth, the agents of the wickedness that emanates from demonic areas above the world, the רשעים, and the צדיקים, who live within the order of Yahweh's covenant and justice, meet. Dark and abysmal is the picture of the רשעים in vv. 3-5. The petition for annihilation in vv. 6-9 wants to remove from the created world—which after all was called into being by the God of justice and righteousness—all that has been found to be intolerable (cf. the comment on Ps. 8:2). There can be no thought here of a wish for revenge and retribution. The psalmsinger is one of the πεινῶντες καὶ διψῶντες τὴν δικαιοσύνην (Matt. 5:6). The voice of these men of God is also not silent in the NT (Rev. 6:10). It is when injustice has become intolerable that the plea for God's intervention resounds. With vague demands for "love" and "humanity" there is no getting at the prophetic power of these petitions. And also the joy of the צדיק in v. 10 cannot be understood, if one holds the superficial judgment that this is a matter of "joy at another's misfortune" (*Schadenfreude*) or "satisfaction about the revenge." Revelation 18:20 also invites to the joy over the redeeming, all-embracing judgment of God that comes into view in vv. 10-11. The ultimate is at stake. Is God the Lord and ruler of the world? Or do demons and demoniacal rulers hold sway? With prophetic power v. 11 wins its way through to the confession which overcomes all misinterpretations and denials of God and which will be spoken by all people: "There is a God who judges on earth!" In this last, comprehensive judgment it is revealed that the life of the oppressed צדיק has a reward (cf. G. Bornkamm, "Der Lohngedanke im Neuen Testament," *EvTh* 6 [1946], 143-166).

Psalm 59

"Deliver Me from My Enemies, O My God!"

Literature

H. Schmidt, *Das Gebet der Angeklagten im Alten Testament*, BZAW 49 (1928). J. Becker, "Israel deutet seine Psalmen," *Stuttgarter Bibel-Studien* 18 (1966) 59f.

Text

To the choirmaster. ' *àl tašhet.'* [a] of David. A *miktam*. When Saul sent men to watch the house in order to kill him.

1 Deliver me from my enemies, O my God,[b]
   from my adversaries protect me!

2 Deliver me from evildoers,
   and from the men of blood rescue me!

3 For, behold, people are lying in wait for me,
   mighty men are after me.—
   Wickedness and error I did not ' '[c] (perpetrate)!

4 Without my being guilty of wickedness—they charge and take their positions.
   Awake for me and look!

5 And you, O Yahweh ' '[d] Sebaoth, ' '[e]
   awake, to visit all nations!
   Do not pardon all the faithless evildoers!—*Selah*.

6 They return every evening,
   howl like dogs,
   and prowl around the city.

7 Behold, they foam at the mouth,
   swords are ' '[f] their lips. ' '[g]

8 But you, O Yahweh, laugh about them,
   you mock at all the peoples!

9 'My refuge,'[h] for you will I hope,

538

for 'you,'[i] 'O Yahweh,'[j] are my fortress!

10 'My gracious God'[k] comes to meet me,
   'Yahweh'[l] lets me look down on my adversaries.

11 Do not kill them, that my people may not forget it,
   scatter them with power and throw them down!
   'Deny them,'[m] O Lord, [12] the sin of their mouth,
   the word of their lips, that they may be struck in their pride!—
   On account of the curse and the lie which they speak,

13 in wrath annihilate 'them all,'[n] that none may remain!
   Then it will be recognized that Yahweh
   rules in Jacob
   to the ends of the earth.—*Selah.*

14 [They return every evening,
   howl like dogs,
   and prowl around in the city.

15 They run around[o] after grub;
   if they are not filled, they stay overnight.]

16 But I will sing to your power,
   will exult over your goodness in the morning;
   for you have become my fortress,—
   a refuge in the day of trouble!

17 [My refuge, to you will I sing,
   for 'you,'[p] 'O Yahweh,'[q] are my fortress!
   My gracious God. . . .]

Title a Cf. the comment on Pss. 57, title; 58, title.

1b One Ms, Gk, S read אלהים, which—as a number of manuscripts also indicate—would in the Elohistic psalter have to yield to an original יהוה; yet the MT is to be preferred.

3c The address יהוה here exceeds the meter (3 + 3) and is to be considered an accretion.

5d V. 5a is metrically stretched too far by fillers. אלהים will have to be eliminated in favor of the ancient divine name יהוה צבאות.

e אלהי ישראל is to be eliminated as an interpolation.

7f חרבות may not be changed to חֲרָפוֹת (''invectives''). Cf. also Pss. 55:21; 57:4; 64:3. But then the preposition ב in בשפתותיהם is to be eliminated.

g As a rhetorical question (Ges-K §151a) כי־מי שמע (''For who hears it?'') exceeds the meter.

9h The variant in v. 17a suggests that we read עֻזְּי; this correction of the suffix would correspond to the context.

i On account of the meter we could be allowed to supply אתה in this address to Yahweh (cf. v. 8a).

j In the Elohistic Psalter יהוה is probably the original reading in this passage.

10k The reading אֱלֹהֵי חַסְדִּי is suggested by the variant reading in v. 17bβ. The genitive modifies the word immediately preceding in the construct state in the adjectival sense; cf. J. Weingreen, ''The Construct-Genitive Relation in Hebrew Syntax,'' *VT* 4 (1954) 50-59.

l Cf. note **j**.

11m According to the meter and the development of the verse, מגננו אדני belongs to v. 12. But then a correction is inescapable. It is best to read מְנָעְמוֹ מֵחַיל (H. Gunkel, with reference to Num. 24:11; Job 31:16; Eccles. 2:10).

13n If the MT is retained (and there is nothing against that), then we have to read כֻּלָּם in this passage.

15o *Ketīb:* יְנוּעוּן; *Qere:* יְנִיעוּן.

17p Cf. note **i**.

q Cf. note **j**.

Form

"The structure of the psalm is curious" (W. O. E. Oesterley). Verse 14 could at first sight be understood to be a return of v. 6, and v. 17 as a refrain of v. 9. Beyond that, rudiments of v. 10 at the end of v. 17 (אלהי חסדי) indicate that also a repetition of v. 10 is present in traces. For reasons of form and type, however, it is out of the question to call the repetitions "refrains." It is a matter of variants within the text. Verse 14 (introduced by ו) provides the same text as v. 6, but with v. 15 it brings in an amplification; v. 17 departs from v. 9 in two places: the reading is עֻזִּי instead of עֻזּוֹ, and (in connection with the vow of thanksgiving in v. 16) v. 18 reads אזמרה instead of אשמרה (v. 9a). An appropriate explanation is still wanting as to how these variants (cf. also Psalms 56 and 57) are to be understood.

The double triple meter dominates: vv. 1-6; it is true, in vv. 4b-5 transpositions are probably required: (5aα/β-4b/6b), 9, 10, 12b/14aα, 15-17 (except אלהי חסדי). Verse 8 is in the 4 + 3 meter; vv. 11-12a in the 4 + 4 meter. Verse forms in the 2 + 2 + 2 pattern are to be found in vv. 6 and 13.

In its decisive expressions Psalm 59 is characterized as a prayer song (תפלה). The address to Yahweh in the second person, the call for help, and the petitions determine the picture of the psalm; but so do also the descriptions of the storming and blustering of the enemies. The petition and wish that Yahweh judge and overcome the evildoers are determinant, especially for the section vv. 11-13. See above, Intro. §6, 2. In detail the following structure can be observed: vv. 1-2, call to Yahweh; vv. 3-4a, description of the distress and profession of innocence; vv. 4b-5, appeal for a judgmental intervention of God; vv. 6-7, lament about the blustering of the enemies; vv. 8-10, assertions of trust; vv. 11-13, the petitioner's desire for a verdict; vv. 14-15, variant reading of v. 6 and expansion of the description of the distress; v. 16, vow of thanksgiving, which in v. 17 is referred to v. 10 with an assertion of trust.

Setting

The petitioner of Psalm 59 is persecuted by enemies. The dangerous weapon of these adversaries is the sword of the word. Obviously, the persecuted psalmist, who affirms his innocence in vv. 3 and 4, is slandered and falsely accused of a crime. From the vow of thanksgiving in v. 16 we learn that the psalmist intends to thank Yahweh and make music to him "in the morning" for the redemption experienced. He has therefore sought refuge in the sanctuary (v. 16) and through a long, critical night waits for the intervention of God "in the morning" (cf. the comment on Ps. 57:8). There is nothing that points to the psalmist's having been a king (against A. Bentzen). The conception of H. Gunkel that the psalmist "is living among heathen" and that he issues his lament and petition from a typical "pogrom frame of mind" is based on a misinterpretation of גוים (v. 8). Psalm 59 could have originated in preexilic times. It is closely related to the "prayers of the accused" (cf. H. Schmidt, *Das Gebet der Angeklagten im Alten Testament,* BZAW 49 [1928]). Still we should explain that every possibility of rediscovering or of reconstruing traces of the institution of divine jurisprudence is cut off by the exuberance of the assertions about the enemies. Here without question lie the psalm's uncertainties that touch the very content; but faced with the problem of their valuation, we should exercise restraint (see below).

Commentary

[Title] On למנצח, see above, Intro. §4, No. 17. On לדוד, Intro. §4, No. 2. On מכתם, Intro. §4, No. 4. The (secondary) reference to the situation transfers Psalm 59 to the context of the events described in 1 Sam. 19:11.

[59:1-2] The petition for rescue and protection expressed in these verses points to the function of the sanctuary as asylum. Here the oppressed and persecuted sufferer expects that Yahweh will become his משגב (vv. 9, 16). The enemies are plural in number (on the enemies of the individual, see above, Intro. §10, 4). In the terms referring to the enemies a definite order of climax is observable: איבי—מתקוממי—פעלי און—אנשי דמים. The persecutors want the death of the psalmist; therefore they are the אנשי דמים (cf. Pss. 5:6; 26:9; 55:23).

[59:3-4a] In a series of complaints, the psalmsinger describes the activity of his enemies. They watch for him and lie in wait for him. They are עזים (cf. Ps. 18:17)—men "of might," whose purpose is to accuse the persecuted person. For that reason an affirmation of innocence is heard (v. 3b) amid the lamenting description. On this affirmation of innocence, cf. the comment on Ps. 7:3ff. פשע is "a breaking away from God" (F. Delitzsch), the "revolt of the human will against the divine will" (L. Köhler, *OT Theology* 170). חטא denotes "to fail, miss" and "violation of a given command" (L. Köhler, 169). עון in v. 4a has the meaning "wrong intention," it expresses "an intention not in accord with God's will" (L. Köhler, 170). But the psalmist rejects all suspicions and calumnies (on this meaning of רוץ, cf. Job 15:26; 16:14; Pss. 18:29; 62:3).

[59:4b-5] In these verses the persecuted petitioner appeals to the judge Yahweh Sebaoth. On the meaning of the divine name יהוה צבאות, which recalls the cultic tradition of Jerusalem, see above, Intro. §10, 1. This יהוה צבאות is the judge of the nations (cf. the comment on Ps. 7:7 and above, Intro. §10, 1). This conception (occurring also in v. 8b) is not specifically postexilic. It does not apply to "the heathen," but it rather corresponds to the universally applied sacral traditions of the sanctuary in Jerusalem. In עורה (v. 4b) and הקיצה (v. 5), the appeal uses cultic "reveille calls" of the Canaanite nature myth, by which a dying divinity is urged to reawaken and live (cf. G. Widengren, *Sakrales Königtum im Alten Testament und im Judentum*, F. Delitzsch-Vorlesungen [1952, 1955], 67f.). To be sure, the mythological background of these calls is entirely absorbed in the OT Psalms. But the formulas summon Yahweh to an effective intervention in the appeal of a persecuted innocent. This intervention of Yahweh would be proved by the fact that the בגדי און (cf. Ps. 25:3) are not pardoned.

[59:6-7] In the lament of these verses the enemies of the psalmist are compared to wild dogs which howl and prowl around the city in the evening—"a picture of disgusting, self-seeking, and hateful activity" (F. Nötscher). The variant in v. 14 adds a further extension in v. 15: The wild dogs greedily hunt for grub, and if they find none, they remain in the residential area of the city overnight, In v. 7 the psalmsinger passes over from the picture to the subject: the greedy persecutors "foam" (יביעון) at the mouth. הביע denotes the inflated, egregious talk of the slanderers (for הביע as an expression for vehement talk, cf. Pss. 19:2; 78:2; 119:171; 145:7). As deadly as swords are the words of the adversaries (for the picture, cf. Pss. 55:21; 57:4; 64:3).

[59:8-10] In the expressions of trust of these verses, the psalmist, in a visionary picture inherited from the Jerusalem cultic tradition (cf. Ps. 2:4), sees how Yahweh laughs at and mocks at the attacks of all the peoples that rise up against him. The strong anthropomorphism that appears in this picture illustrates the world domination of Yahweh and the sovereign reaction of the God who does not yet emerge from his hiddenness but already repels all resistance. The petitioner trusts Yahweh. Against the עזים (v. 3), Yahweh is עזי and משׂגבי (v. 9) for the psalmist; he is אלהי חסדי—the God who has compassion in goodness. By him the petitioner is brought to the point where he, justified and victorious, can look down on his enemies. In v. 11 all these expressions of trust are translated to a very specific desire for a verdict.

[59:11-13] The fact that Yahweh meets human beings benevolently (v. 10a) is in the OT always demonstrated by victory over the enemies. The petitions and demands expressed in vv. 11-13 are peculiar. The enemy is not to be killed suddenly. A swift end of the adversaries could be overlooked and forgotten as the signal justification of the prosecuted and slandered individual. Verse 11 therefore does not contain an inhumane impulse, but the urgent desire that the demonstration of God's intervention may be visible everywhere and of enduring effectiveness. If the enemy is "scattered" and then thrown down and in wrath annihilated, the worldwide intervention of the righteousness of God will be able to be recognized (v. 13). The petition already presented in v. 5b, that Yahweh would not pardon the enemies of the petitioner, receives its pointed development in vv. 11 and 12. Yahweh is not to regard their (sinful) accusations and is to strike the proud people with a deadly fate. Here we will have to presuppose that together with the persecuted individual also the hostile accusers are present in the area of the sanctuary and are waiting for God's juridical decision. They have pursued the psalmist with curse and slander. Now it must be revealed who was in the right. Coupled with the priestly word of an answer to prayer, which delivers the verdict, is the external sign of the destruction of the guilty one. Worth noting is the appearance of ידע in v. 13. "This too is a place where a statement of knowledge associated with a symbolic proof event can establish itself" (W. Zimmerli, *Erkenntnis Gottes nach dem Buch Ezechiel*, ATANT [1954], 56). Also significant is the petitioner's recourse in v. 13 to the traditional cultic conceptions of Jerusalem. That Yahweh "rules" (cf. Judg. 8:23) in Jacob and becomes recognizable in judicial activity—this fact is to become known "to the ends of the earth," for the God of Israel is the ruler of the world, or ruler of the nations (see above. Intro. §10, 1).

The petitioner's desire in vv. 11-13 for a verdict, which used to be charged to the impulses of the desire for revenge, has been the subject of the most varied reflections and evaluations. Thus Kant in his treatise *Religion within the Limits of Reason Alone* repeatedly asked the question: "Does morality have to be interpreted according to the Bible, or the Bible according to morality?" Such a question finds itself confronted by extreme statements of biblical exegesis which appeal to inspiration. Thus J. D. Michaelis was able to declare: "The psalms are inspired. If in them punishment is prayed for, it cannot be unjust, and we do not want to have a morality that is holier than the Bible. . . . It seems odd to me that we should criticize these psalms because of an obscure passage in the Sermon on the Mount, sometimes saying that the morality of the Old Testament was imperfect, and sometimes saddling the Psalms with I know not what interpretations. The people who do this often themselves think like the Psalms whose morality they so easily censure'' (J. D. Michaelis, *Moral,* ed. C. F. Stäudlin, [1872], 2:202f.). Cf. O. Kaiser, ''Kants Anweisung zur Auslegung der Bibel,'' *NZST* 11, 2 (1969) 125-128. We shall do well completely to exempt the hard and shocking, pointed statements of the ''enemy psalms'' from the tension between ''inspiration'' and ''morality.'' We will have to explain that an appropriate understanding of these statements can be introduced only in the light of v. 13. The knowledge ''that Yahweh rules in Jacob to the ends of the earth'' could not be understood in the OT in any other way than through the proof of the acts of God. This insight should be our starting point (cf. ''Purpose and Thrust'').

[59:16] If we disregard the variants in vv. 14-15 and 17, v. 16 already leads the way to the situation of the song of thanksgiving. The psalmsinger expresses a vow of thanksgiving. Exultation and song are to resound when Yahweh ''has become the refuge,'' when he has proved himself as the protective and intervening judge. On לבקר, cf. the comment on Ps. 57:8.

Purpose and Thrust

From the depths of slander and persecution a falsely accused individual calls to Yahweh for help. The enemies want to kill the psalmist and separate him from Yahweh. The appeal in vv. 4b-5 prays that God may come forward as the one who is alive and ''arisen.'' Dark and disgusting is the picture of the greedy enemies as the abysmal powers. But in the depth of the inescapable persecution there awakes (so to say, as an answer to and reflection of the reveille called out in vv. 4b-5) trust in Yahweh's power, which rules over the whole earth and mocks at all enemies. The judge of the peoples is the *Deus praesens,* מִשְׂגָּב—the refuge and protective fortress for him who is surrounded by hostile forces.

In the OT the salvation of God is effective in history; in symbolic manifestations it makes its entrance in the midst of this world and carries out the justifying verdict. It is under this presupposition that vv. 11-13 are to be understood (cf. the comment on Psalm 58, ''Purpose and Thrust''). It is not the cruel demand for revenge that dictates the petitions and demands, but the plea that the rule of God in Israel which is breaking out in judgment may not be overlooked or forgotten (v. 11a) but may become known in all the world (v. 13).

Manuscript Sigla

A		Codex Alexandrinus, LXX
α´		Aquila's Greek version of the OT
Arm		The Armenian version
B		Codex Vaticanus, LXX
Bo		The Bohairic version
Gk (or LXX)		The Septuagint (Greek version of the OT)
Gk^L (or L)		Lucian's recension of LXX
Gk^R		Codex Veronensis, LXX
MT		The Masoretic text of the Hebrew Bible
σ´ (or Symm)		Symmachus's Greek version of the OT
Syr (or S)		The Syriac version
T (or Targ)		Targum or Targums
θ´		Theodotion's Greek version of the OT
Vg		The Vulgate

A more complete list of sigla may be found in *Biblia Hebraica Stuttgartensia,* ed. K. Elliger and W. Rudolph (Stuttgart: Deutsche Bibelgesellschaft, 1977), pp. xliv-xlviii.

Hebrew Grammars Cited

Bauer-Leander	H. Bauer and P. Leander, *Historische Grammatik der Hebräischen Sprache des alten Testaments* I, Halle 1922.
BrSynt	C. Brockelmann, *Hebräische Syntax,* Neukirchen 1956
Joüon	Paul Joüon, *Grammaire de l'Hébreu Biblique,* Rome: Institut Biblique Pontifical, 1947².
Ges.-K	*[F. H. W.] Gesenius' Hebrew, Grammar, 2nd English edition revised in accordance with the 28th German ed. (1909) by A. E. Cowley,* Oxford 1910, reissued 1946.

Abbreviations

(See also "Manuscript Sigla")

ÄA	*Äegyptologische Abhandlungen*
AAOJ	*American Antiquarian and Oriental Journal*
AASOR	*Annual of the American Schools of Oriental Research*
AAWW.PH	Anzeiger der (k.) Akademie der Wissenschaften in Wien
ABR	*Australian Biblical Review*
AcOr	*Acta Orientalia*
AFLNW	(Veröffentlichungen der) Arbeitsgemeinschaft für Forschung des Landes Nordrhein-Westfalen
AfO	*Archiv für Orientforschung*
AJSL	*American Journal of Semitic Languages and Literatures*
AKM	Abhandlungen für die Kunde des Morgenlandes
ALBO	Analecta Lovaniensia Biblica et Orientalia
AnBib	Analecta Biblica
AncB	Anchor Bible
ANET	*Ancient Near Eastern Texts Relating to the OT*, ed. J. Pritchard
AnOr	Analecta Orientalia
ANVAO	Avhandlinger i Norske Videnskaps-Akademi i Oslo
AO	Der alte Orient
AOAT	Alter Orient und Altes Testament
AOB	*Altorientalische Bilder zum Alten Testament*
AOT	*Altorientalische Texte zum Alten Testament*
ARW	*Archiv für Religionswissenschaft*
ASTI	*Annual of the Swedish Theological Institute* (in Jerusalem)
ATA	Alttestamentliche Abhandlungen
ATANT	Abhandlungen zur Theologie des Alten und Neuen Testament

Abbreviations

ATD	Das Alte Testament Deutsch
BA	*Biblical Archaeologist*
BASOR	*Bulletin of the American Schools of Oriental Research*
BBB	Bonner biblische Beiträge
BeO	*Bibbia e Oriente*
BetM	*Bet(h) Mikra*
BEThL	*Bibliotheca Ephemeridum Theologicarum Loveniensium*
BHH	*Biblisch-Historisches Handwörterbuch*
BHT	Beiträge zur historischen Theologie
Bibl	*Biblica*
BibB	Biblische Beiträge
BiblOr	*Bibliotheca Orientalis*
BibOr	*Biblica et Orientalia*
BiblS	*Bibliotheca Sacra and Theological Review*
BiKi	*Bibel und Kirche*
BiLe	*Bibel und Leben*
BiLi	*Bibel und Liturgie*
BJRL	*Bulletin of the John Rylands Library*
BRL	*Biblisches Reallexikon*
BrSynt	C. Brockelmann, *Hebräische Syntax* (1956)
BSt	Biblische Studien
BVC	*Bible et Vie Chrétienne*
BWANT	Beiträge zur Wissenschaft vom Alten und Neuen Testament
BZ	*Biblische Zeitschrift*
BZAW	Beiheft zur *ZAW*
CBQ	*Catholic Biblical Quarterly*
CD	Karl Barth, *Church Dogmatics*
CJT	*Canadian Journal of Theology*
CR	Corpus Reformatorum
CRB	Cahiers de la Revue Biblique
CThM	Calwer Theologische Monographien
DBS	*Dictionnaire de la Bible, Supplément*
DLZ	*Deutsche Literaturzeitung*
DThC	*Dictionnaire de Théologie Catholique*
DTT	*Dansk Teologisk Tidsskrift*
ÉHPhR	*Études d'Histoire et de Philosophie Religieuses*
Er	*Eranos*
EstB	*Estudios Biblicos*
ET	English translation
EThL	*Ephemerides Theologicae Lovanienses*
ÉTR	*Études Théologiques et Religieuses*
EvTh	*Evangelische Theologie*
FRLANT	Forschungen zur Religion und Literatur des Alten und Neuen Testaments
Ges-K	*Gesenius' Hebrew Grammar*, ed. E. Kautzsch
GThT	*Gereformeerd Theologisch Tijdschrift*
HibJ	*Hibbert Journal*
HK	Handkommentar zum Alten Testament
HSM	Harvard Semitic Monographs
HTR	*Harvard Theological Review*
HUCA	*Hebrew Union College Annual*
IB	Interpreter's Bible
IDB	*Interpreter's Dictionary of the Bible*
Interp	*Interpretation*
ITQ	*Irish Theological Quarterly*

JAAR	*Journal of the American Academy of Religion*
JAC	*Jahrbuch für Antike und Christentum*
JAOS	*Journal of the American Oriental Society*
JBL	*Journal of Biblical Literature*
JBR	*Journal of Bible and Religion*
JJS	*Journal of Jewish Studies*
JNES	*Journal of Near Eastern Studies*
JPOS	*Journal of the Palestine Oriental Society*
JRAS	*Journal of the Royal Asiatic Society of Great Britain and Ireland*
JSOR	*Journal of the Society of Oriental Research*
JSS	*Journal of Semitic Studies*
JTS	*Journal of Theological Studies*
Kairos	*Kairos: Zeitschrift für Religionswissenschaft und Theologie*
KBL	Ludwig Köhler and Walter Baumgartner, *Lexicon in Veteris Testamenti Libros*
KJV	King James Version
KuD	*Kerygma und Dogma*
LThK	*Lexikon für Theologie und Kirche*
LV(B)	*Lumiere et Vie.* Bruges
MGWJ	*Monatsschrift für Geschichte und Wissenschaft des Judentums*
NKZ	*Neue kirkliche Zeitschrift*
NT.S	*Novum Testamentum.* Supplements
NTT	*Norsk Teologisk Tidsskrift*
NZSTh	*Neue Zeitschrift für systematische Theologie*
OLZ	*Orientalische Literaturzeitung*
Or	*Orientalia*
OTS	Oudtestamentische Studien
Paid	*Paideuma*
PEQ	*Palestine Exploration Quarterly*
PRE	*Paulys Real-Encyclopädie der classischen Altertumswissenschaft*
RAC	*Reallexikon für Antike und Christentum*
RB	*Revue Biblique*
RE	*Realencyklopädie für protestantische Theologie und Kirche*
RechBib	*Recherches Bibliques*
RSR	*Recherches de Science Religieuse*
RGG	*Religion in Geschichte und Gegenwart*
RoB	*Religion och Bibel*
RevBib	*Revista Biblica*
RQ	*Revue de Qumrân*
RÉJ	*Revue des Études Juives*
RÉS	*Revue des Études Sémitiques*
RSPhTh	*Revue des Sciences Philosophiques et Théologiques*
RHPhR	*Revue d'Histoire et de Philosophie Religieuses*
RThPh	*Revue de Theologie et de Philosophie*
SAT	Schriften des Alten Testament in Auswahl
SBM	Stuttgarter biblische Monographien
SBS	Stuttgarter Bibelstudien
SBU	Svenskt Bibliskt Uppslagsverk
ScrHie	*Scripta Hierosolymitana*
SEÅ	*Svensk Exegetisk Årsbok*
SJT	*Scottish Journal of Theology*

SNVAO	Skrifter Utgitt av det Norske Videnskaps-Akademi i Oslo
SO	Symbolae Osloenses
StOr	*Studia Orientalia*
StTh	*Studia Theologica*
SvTK	*Svensk Teologisk Kvartalskrift*
ThBl	*Theologische Blätter*. Leipzig
ThB	Theologische Bücherei
ThLZ	*Theologische Literaturzeitung*
ThQ	*Theologische Quartalschrift*
TRE	*Theologische Realenzyklopädie*
ThR NF	*Theologische Rundschau*, Neue Folge
ThLBl	*Theologisches Literaturblatt*
ThSt(B)	*Theologische Studien*, ed. K. Barth
TSK	*Theologische Studien und Kritiken*
THAT	*Theologisches Handwörterbuch zum Alten Testament*, ed. E. Jenni and C. Westermann
TWAT	*Theologisches Wörterbuch zum Alten Testament* (ET: *Theological Dictionary of the OT*, 1974ff.)
TWNT	*Theologisches Wörterbuch zum Neuen Testament* (ET: *Theological Dictionary of the NT*, 10 vols., 1964-1976)
ThZ	*Theologische Zeitschrift*
TT	*Theologisch Tijdschrift*
ThTo	*Theology Today*
TTK	*Tidsskrift for Teologi og Kirke*
TThZ	*Trier theologische Zeitschrift*
UF	*Ugarit-Forschungen*
UUÅ	*Uppsala Universitets Årsskrift*
VD	*Verbum Domini*
VF	*Verkündigung und Forschung*
VigChr	*Vigilae Christianae*
VT	*Vetus Testamentum*
VT.S	*Vetus Testamentum*, Supplements
WA	Weimar edition of Luther's works
WMANT	Wissenschaftliche Monographien zum Alten und Neuen Testament
WO	*Welt des Orients*
WUNT	Wissenschaftliche Untersuchungen zum Neuen Testament
ZAW	*Zeitschrift für die alttestamentliche Wissenschaft*
ZDMG	*Zeitschrift der deutschen morgenländischen Gesellschaft*
ZDPV	*Zeitschrift des deutschen Palästina-Vereins*
ZEE	*Zeitschrift für evangelische Ethik*
ZNW	*Zeitschrift für die neutestamentliche Wissenschaft*
ZThK	*Zeitschrift für Theologie und Kirche*

Index of Biblical References
(except the Psalms)

552

555

Index of Names and Subjects

557